The Big Book of Home Learning

Volume 3: Junior High to College

Also by Mary Pride

The Way Home
All the Way Home
Schoolproof

With Bill Pride

Prides' Guide to Educational Software

The Big Book of Home Learning

FOURTH EDITION

Volume 3: Junior High to College

Edited by Mary Pride

A PRACTICAL HOMESCHOOLING® BOOK

The Big Book of Home Learning Fourth Edition
Volume 3: Junior High to College
©1999 by Home Life, Inc.

Clip art images on pages 1, 3, 17, 381, and 422 provided by ©1990 Dynamic Graphics, Inc. Clip art image on page 509 based on image provided by ©1990 Dynamic Graphics, Inc. Clip art images on pages 120, 129, and 191 provided by ©1996 Corel Corporation. Clip art image on page 373 provided by ©1999 Gordon School of Art. Clip art images on pages 281 and 314 provided by ©1996 T/Maker Company. Clip art image on page 201 based on image provided by ©1996 T/Maker Company. Stock photo images on cover provided by ©1998 Corbus Corp Digital Stock, ©1999 Eyewire, and ©1997–1998 PhotoDisc.

Chart on page 474 from *How to Prepare for the CLEP,* 7th edition, by Doster, Ward, Hockett, Poitras, Bjork and Capozzoli Ingui. Copyright ©1995 by Barron's Educational Series, Inc. Prior editions copyright ©1990, 1985, 1983, 1979, 1975 by Barron's Educational Series, Inc. Reprinted by arrangement with Barron's Educational Series, Inc., Hauppauge, NY.

Library of Congress Cataloging-in-Publication Data:
Pride, Mary
    The big book of home learning / Mary Pride—4th ed.
       p. cm.
    Include bibliographical references and index
    Contents: v. 1. Getting Started — v. 2. Preschool & Elementary — v. 3. Teen & adult.
    1. Home schooling—United States. 2. Home schooling—United States—Curricula. 3. Education—Parent participation—United States. 4. Child rearing—United States. I. Title.
LC40.P75 1999
ISBN 0-7403-0008-3

Printed and bound in the United States of America

Liability Disclaimer

Trademarks

Table of Contents

How to Use This Book 7

Introduction 9

Part 1: Teaching Teens

1. Why High School at Home? . . . 13
2. It's a Wonderful Teen 17

Part 2: Building Future Leaders

3. Bible Curriculum 23
4. Bible Teaching Aids 31
5. Character Education 39

Part 3: Language Arts

6. Junior/Senior High English . . . 49
7. Phonics for Teens & Adults . . . 53
8. Creative Writing 57
9. Grammar for Teens & Adults . . 71
10. Literature 79
11. Speak, Debate, & Perform . . . 95
12. Spelling & Vocabulary 101
13. Classical Languages 111
14. Foreign Languages 121

Part 4: Math

15. Basic & Remedial Math 137
16. Algebra 149
17. Geometry 163
18. Trigonometry 169
19. Calculus 173

Part 5: Science

20. Junior High Science 181

21. Biology 191
22. Creation Science 201
23. Ecology 207
24. Chemistry 213
25. Physics 227
26. Engineering 239
27. Science Kits & Equipment . . 245

Part 6: Social Studies

28. Civics & Government 253
29. Economics 273
30. Geography 281
31. U.S. History 291
32. World History 319
33. Logic & Philosophy 339
34. Worldview 349

Part 7: Fine Arts

35. Art Skills 367
36. Art Appreciation 375
37. Musicianship 381
38. Music Appreciation 389

Part 8: Getting Ready for the Real World

39. Driver's Education 399
40. Independent Living Skills . . . 405
41. Physical Education 415
42. Volunteering 423

Part 9: The Test Years of Our Lives

43. How & Why to Take the PSAT/NMSQT 431

44. How to Take the SAT I 435
45. How to Take the ACT 447
46. How to Take the SAT II 453
47. To GED or Not to GED 459
48. College Credit for High School via AP or CLEP 467

Part 10: College & Career Preparation

49. Choosing a College & Major 477
50. What You Need to Know About College, But Probably Don't . 489
51. How to Apply to College . . . 497
52. Paying for College 503
53. College at Home 509
54. Learning the Ropes 519
55. Careers Without College . . . 523

APPENDICES

I.   The Myth of the Teenager . . . 535
II. Suggested Course of Study for Junior and Senior High School 541
III. Suggested Classical Reading List 551
IV. GED Requirements by State . 555
V.   Graduation Requirements . . 557
VI. High School Guidance Overview 561

Index 567

How to Use This Book

If you're looking for complete packaged curriculum for all the junior-high and high-school subjects, including correspondence programs and online academies, you're in the wrong volume. That's all covered in Volume 1 of the Big Book series.

If you're looking for product reviews for individual school subjects at the preschool through grade 6 level, you need Volume 2 of the Big Book series.

- But if you want to find the **best academic resources** for individual school subjects and you are or have a junior high or high school student, or an advanced preteen who has already whizzed through basic math, language arts, social studies, or science, and is ready for *more*
- Or you want to **supplement your existing packaged curriculum** with some carefully-chosen quality resources
- Or if your junior-high or high-school child is in school and you are **"afterschooling"**
- Or if you want to find out how to get your high-schooler **ready for college or a career**
- **You've come to the right place!**

If your teen's educational background needs strengthening, you probably should start by going over the resources in Volume 2. With a few exceptions, remedial courses for teens are usually less helpful than courses designed to teach the subject well the first time around. Otherwise, this volume is the place to be for junior high school and up.

The new format of this edition should make it even easier to use than past editions. All the information you need to contact the supplier of a product is in the margin right next to each review. Product photos are included too, where available, as well as "fun facts" and important sidelights on the chapter's subject. Feel free to use the rest of the margin space to jot down your own thoughts, or to "star" the products you are most interested in.

You will note that the reviews also include product price information. As always the information in *The Big Book of Home Learning* is as current and up-to-date as we could possibly make it. After the reviews were written, we contacted the suppliers for verification of prices, addresses, and other such information. Even so, *it is always wise to write or call the supplier to check on prices before ordering.* The prices in this book are included to help you com-

New Features of This Edition

- Hundreds of all-new reviews. These are marked with the notation "NEW!" next to the review in the margin.
- Complete updates of all reviews from previous editions. In almost every case, the price and ordering information has had to be updated. Only those products that have significantly changed since the last edition have the notation "UPDATED!" in the margin.
- Supplier addresses, phone numbers, and fax numbers are right alongside each review now, instead of in a separate index. (You asked for it, you got it!)
- Plus many reviews include email addresses and World Wide Web addresses for the supplier. Technology marches on!
- For the first time ever in a home-schooling book, we have taken photos of most of the products reviewed. See them for yourself!
- Brand-new chapter introductions bring you up-to-date on the latest homeschooling methods for each subject.
- Sidebars and other highlights provide commentary and additional points of view on chapter subjects.
- Finally, we felt it would be appropriate to celebrate the achieve-

ments of our wonderful home-schooled children by featuring some of the children themselves! So every section begins with a picture and brief description of a homeschooled student and his or her special achievement. These students were all originally featured in the "Show & Tell" section in *Practical Homeschooling*, and we are very proud of them!

pare different products for value and are not permanently guaranteed. Prices go up and down. Too, you will sometimes have to add state tax (depending on whether you and the supplier are in the same state or not, or whether the supplier has additional offices in your state). Both you and the supplier will feel better if the supplier does not have to return your order because the check you enclosed was not for the right amount.

Thanks to the way products are separated into chapters, and then presented in alphabetical order in each section inside a chapter, it shouldn't be hard to find any product you're looking for. If you have any trouble, the handy index in the back of the book will help you out.

Thank you for choosing *The Big Book of Home Learning*. The only resource with even *more* information is the CD-ROM edition—and as a *Big Book* purchaser, you're entitled to a discount on the CD-ROM. See the bind-in-card at the back of the book to check out your special offers!

Technical Terms

NEW! means this review did not appear in previous editions of *Big Book*

UPDATED! means this product has changed significantly since its review in the previous edition of *Big Book*. **"UPDATED"** does *not* refer to updated price and address information—*all* prices and address/phone/fax etc. have been updated.

Oversized means 8½ x 11".

Handy-sized means anywhere from 5 x 8" to 6 x 9".

Wide Format means the book is wider than it is high.

Double-page spread format means each two facing pages cover a single topic, usually with lots of visuals included.

Textbook includes information student is supposed to study, plus

exercises, and is not meant to be written in.

Worktext includes information student is supposed to study, plus exercises with space for student to write the answers.

Workbook does not include study information (or not much); it has exercises with space for students to write the answers.

Introduction

Hi! I'm Mary Pride, editor of this series, publisher of *Practical Homeschooling* magazine, and mother of nine homeschooled children, including four teenagers.

I'm here to tell you that if you are thinking about homeschooling a junior high or high school student today, or attending college at home, you are in luck. The resources available for these grade levels have multiplied tremendously in the last few years.

So, What's In *This* Volume?

Bible and Character Education. In the teen years we have thankfully moved beyond fluffy hand puppets. The Bible resources in this volume are more in-depth, challenging, and analytical. At this age level, character education also focuses on traits and social skills necessary for integrity in adult life.

Language Arts. Writing assignments and resources in this volume take on a more professional flavor. Grammar resources are *analytical* (sentence diagramming) and *condensed* (reviews of basic grammar). Literature becomes a formal subject, as does rhetoric (speech, drama, and performing skills). You will also find a chapter on remedial phonics for teens and adults. This is the only remedial area where special courses for older learners might really be helpful. Older students have wider life experience and can learn faster and more independently than the little kids for whom elementary and preschool phonics courses are developed. Also, kiddie phonics courses can be humiliating (and stultifying) to older students, who don't particularly enjoy being reminded that they were supposed to learn to read when they were six years old.

Classical and Foreign Languages. The wealth of resources available in these areas is truly staggering. Thanks to the Classical Education movement among homeschoolers, many are learning Latin, Greek, and Hebrew. Foreign languages are also popular, with many courses now designed specially for homeschoolers.

Math. We have chosen in this volume to concentrate on the math that truly belongs in junior high, high school, and beginning college courses: consumer math, pre-algebra and algebra, geometry, trigonometry, and calculus. We do cover basic math courses especially well suited to teens and adults.

Science. Biology, chemistry, and physics are what colleges want to see, and here they are. Junior high/middle school science is divided into General Science, Life Science, Earth Science, and Physical Science. Other science topics covered include creation versus evolution, ecology and conservation, and engineering.

Social Studies. These subjects are ideally suited for the teen and adult years, when the student has a richer background of reading and life experi-

Mary Pride, publisher of Practical Homeschooling and editor of The Big Book of Home Learning

ences. Thus you'll find in this volume courses and resources that explain in depth how the economy works, and how government works (and is *supposed* to work), as opposed to the necessarily more superficial resources in the Preschool & Elementary volume. Geography at this level is mostly World Geography—if your student is weak in this area, you should find these courses and resources particularly helpful. Since at the high-school level, history is typically divided into U.S. History and World History, we have separated it into these chapters for your convenience, apologizing in advance to our Canadian and overseas readers for the lack of homeschool resources covering *their* history! And instead of waiting until the college years, when students typically have their thought patterns challenged and changed, we propose you parents begin worldview education at home, giving you a chance to impart *your* wisdom and point of view. This includes training in *logic* (so the student can distinguish between propaganda and truth), *philosophy* (sending a young man or woman to college without any knowledge of philosophy is just asking to have them intellectually seduced, in our opinion), *theology* (almost no useful material is available at this time for this age level, unfortunately), and *church history* (so they know what's been going on in the War of Ideas for the past several thousand years).

Fine Arts. From learning to draw to appreciating the paintings of Renoir, from piano lessons to making your own instruments, you can do it all at home. This section tells you how.

Real Life Skills. Babysitting. Making your own clothes. Cleaning the house. Even learning to drive. Parents always *used* to teach their children these things. Homeschoolers are also doing a lot more with physical education and sports than you might realize. And instead of the schools' "Family Life" courses, which seem designed to track kids into dating, single-parenthood or abortion, and their kids into daycare, we have lots of lovely material that teaches boys and girls how to have a *successful* family life.

Those Dreaded Tests. College-bound homeschoolers depend even more heavily than schooled children on standardized tests. That's because admissions officials like to see evidence of how our children stack up against schooled children. Until now, little has been published in homeschool circles about how to get ready for these tests, which ones to take, when they are offered, and all that other "guidance counselor" information. I am particularly proud of this section, as I personally reviewed just about every book in it, and spent several months digging out the "inside information" that you'd otherwise have to read tens of thousands of pages (no exaggeration) to find on your own.

Preparing for College or Career. Homeschooled children can and do go to college. But we should not automatically press the "College" button. Modern American higher education has many problems, and we tell you about them. Campus-based education also is expensive, so college education at home is attracting larger numbers of students (not all from the homeschool community, either!)—and we have resources for finding the best distance education options. If you decide college is for you, we point you to the resources you need to get your college application together, find the right college for you, and pay for it. You deserve to be aware of college alternatives as well, so we share some alternatives with you. Finally, some students prefer to skip college and go directly to a career. Where to find training? How to start you own business? What are the skills you need to rocket upwards in the business world? You'll find it all right here in this section.

One of the best things about homeschooling is that you get to pick the educational resources *you* want to use. We have tried to help you find the products you need to do the best job possible. Education isn't just the teacher's job, either; we hope many teens will read this book and get excited about helping to direct their own education. God bless you, and *carpe diem!*

PART 1

Teaching Teens

Homeschooler Howard Sweeney won First Place in the Detroit
Area Pre-College Engineering Program (DAPCEP). Howard was
selected for the five-week Paper Vehicle Program at the University
of Detroit. With the help of Auto CAD and a team of participants,
they designed and built a full-size paper automobile. The same year,
Howard was a National Finalist in McCall's Sew 'N Show contest.
From vests to vehicles, design is where it's at for Howard Sweeney!
His ambition is to become a robotics engineer.

Justin Luecke (15) of Ohio won his church's Bible Bowl scripture memory tournament, which took him to a number of exotic locations such as Texas, and awarded him with the two ribbons in this picture. The trophy in his other hand is for scoring first-place in a bowling competition. Furthermore, Justin is Technical Engineer and Head Carpenter for Christian Outreach Evangelism Ministries in Cincinatti. He runs sound and pyrotechnics for the gospel magic show they produce. He runs the sound board for the Youth Band at the Vineyard East, and will soon be playing keyboard. He has been home-schooled his entire life.

CHAPTER 1

Why High School at Home?

The teen years are tremendously important educationally. That's when a boy or girl turns into a young man or woman. These are the years when beliefs are formed, character is strengthened (or destroyed), and we set our life pattern. College then finishes the process, sometimes setting the student on a whole new life path.

1. *So, who do you want to form your teen's character and choices?*
   ☐ You ☐ The schools

2. *Who do you trust to ensure your teen is drug-free, sexually pure, and physically safe from assault and intimidation?*
   ☐ You ☐ The schools

3. *Who is planning to teach your teen your spiritual beliefs?*
   ☐ You ☐ The schools

4. *Who has the ability to devote the entire school day to academics and other important skills?*
   ☐ You ☐ The schools

5. *Who is willing to allow each student to get deeply "into" a subject, without ringing a bell to make him quit and move to another classroom?*
   ☐ You ☐ The schools

6. *Who is delighted to provide students the opportunity and resources to pursue grown-up interests . . . everything from helping Dad build an airplane (I know someone who did this) to becoming a professional goat breeder (I know someone else who did that)?*
   ☐ You ☐ The schools

7. *Who will instantly drop an educational method or product that isn't working, as opposed to using it for years even after it's been proven not to work?*
   ☐ You ☐ The schools

8. *Who respects and protects family life, and is deeply motivated to help your family become closer?*
   ☐ You ☐ The schools

Sunnydale High is based on every high school in America. What makes the show popular is the central myth of high school as horrific. The humiliation, the alienation, the confusion of high school . . . People out of high school respond to what's going on in the show, because I don't think you ever get over high school.

—*Joss Whelan, creator of Buffy the Vampire Slayer*

9. *Who loves your child more?*
   ☐ You   ☐ The schools

Now, let's turn it around the other way.

1. *Who is notorious for graduating students from high school who can't read or write competently, can't find Florida on a U.S. map, and can't tell you when Columbus sailed the ocean blue?*
   ☐ The schools   ☐ Homeschools

2. *Who introduced curriculum that teaches that sex with anyone or anything is OK, so long as you are "protected"?*
   ☐ The schools   ☐ Homeschools

3. *Whose graduates are packing out jail cells everywhere?*
   ☐ The schools   ☐ Homeschools

4. *Who makes a big noise about "Banned Books Week" at the same time that they ban the Bible and religious books from their libraries?*
   ☐ The schools   ☐ Homeschools

5. *Who forces children to associate solely with people of their own age group—including some who carry weapons to school and others who may have been convicted of robbery, rape, or even murder?*
   ☐ The schools   ☐ Homeschools

6. *Who has a major drug problem?*
   ☐ The schools   ☐ Homeschools

7. *Who refuses to teach impressionable teens the difference between right and wrong . . . or even state with conviction that there is such a thing as right and wrong . . . to the point that its graduates are, almost without exception, moral relativists who are unable to state or stand by any unchanging principles in their lives?*
   ☐ Homeschools   ☐ The schools

8. *Who tore down the Ten Commandments from their classroom walls, and disciplines teachers if they so much as carry a Bible to school or invite a student after class to attend a church function?*
   ☐ Homeschools   ☐ The schools

Given all the above, what is the best choice to make for your teen's education?
‗ ‗ ‗ ‗ ‗ ‗ ‗ ‗ ‗ ‗ (fill in the blanks)

But Isn't Homeschooling a Teen Difficult?

Teaching teenagers at home is easy. I can outline it for you in one step:

Let them teach themselves.

Maybe I should add one more step:

Get out of the way!

Oh, sure, you'll be involved in choosing curriculum (after all, you're paying for it!). You'll lend moral support, check on how much work is getting done, and provide necessary motivation when Johnny or Suzy slack off. You'll also answer any questions to which you know the answers, and (maybe) grade some papers and tests.

But honestly, once a young person has made it past his or her first decade, he or she is perfectly capable of working alone. In fact, they *ought* to work alone now and then. (When I say "alone" I mean "without constant adult supervision." Studying in groups is fine.) Studying without adults holding your hand is good for the soul. Good for the intellect. Builds strong minds 12 ways.

When teaching people of this age, your first and most important task is to teach them how to act on their own. This means saying, "I don't know . . . why don't you look that up?" may actually be better than running and finding them the answer. Even when you do know the answer, resist the temptation to just give it outright. Try asking, "How would *you* go about solving this problem?" first. This makes you appear wise and Socratic. If you really don't know the answers to *any* of the questions, consider getting a video course, hiring a tutor, signing them up for an online course, or purchasing the answer key!

But What About Socialization

I know, it would be a tragedy if 13-year-olds didn't have a large pool of people around to date and hang out with. After all, kids who attend school are never social outcasts, right?

We'd better discuss right now what we mean by "socialization." If you mean "instruction in etiquette and graciousness," the home is the ideal place to learn these skills. If you mean "making friends," school is certainly not the only place this can happen. Here's a short list of places your home-schooled young adults can meet and make friends:

- Church
- YMCA
- Health club
- Community college (many admit students as young as 16 years old)
- Library (many homeschoolers volunteer as library aides)
- Homeschool support group
- 4-H Club
- Community theatre
- Hobby clubs (e.g., model railroading, juggling, chess . . .)
- Computer users group
- Museum (volunteer as a docent!)
- Community service organization
- Job
- Hospital (no kidding—if your child has a chronic illness or needs regular therapy, often this is a great place to meet other kids in similar situations)
- Online (again, no kidding—I know from experience you can form some great friendships this way!)
- Even the public school—some more enlightened school districts allow homeschooled children to participate in extracurricular activities, including clubs and sports (it's only fair—we *do* pay our taxes)

Most of these environments allow you to meet a variety of people, not just those of exactly your own age. Furthermore, in most of these places you are working with others to accomplish a worthy goal. Finding others who share your goals is a great way to form friendships that last.

But I Could Never Teach Algebra (or Biology, or French . . .)

You don't have to. Use this book to look up the resources available for subjects you feel totally incompetent to teach. You'll be amazed!

Many parents have found a new joy in learning right along with their children. The subjects that eluded us in school often make much more sense the second time around. Plus, we have resources nowadays developed specifically for use at home without an expert teacher.

Classroom teachers are trained in classroom management skills. They are not usually experts in the subjects they are credentialed to teach. Few rocket scientists teach high-school physics. Few French teachers have an accent that would deceive a native of Paris. And with 20 or more unruly high-school students to teach, all of whom would rather be anywhere than the classroom, it's really amazing that they can teach anything at all.

What Other Ways Can My Teen Learn at Home?

I thought you'd never ask. Besides self-study and parental instruction, consider these options:

- **Co-op classes with other homeschool families.** You share your skills and do big projects together. A math whiz can teach math and science classes, while an artist can give art classes another day. This co-op can meet only one afternoon, or several days of the week.
- **Take a few classes** at a friendly private school or community college
- Get together with friends and **form a school** just for homeschoolers. No, this is not a contradiction in terms. The school is really a more formal co-op with a building and supplies of its own. Kids only attend the classes of their and their parents' choice.
- **Hire a tutor** for that difficult subject. Be imaginative. Sometimes another child is a great tutor—even an older brother or sister. Sometimes a *younger* brother or sister is such a whiz that they can do the tutoring.
- **Persuade a relative or friend to help out.** It helps if your friends are all Mensa members.
- **Hire an online tutor or sign up for an online class.** Many online services now offer "Homework Help" of some sort. You can log on, pour out your problems, and some sympathetic and knowledgeable person will help you get past the snag. If Homework Help isn't enough, actual online classes are now available, coincidentally often in the most parent-unfriendly subjects, such as math and science.

But Does This Count as Homeschooling?

You bet it does! The "home" in "homeschooling" means that *the family is in control*. No school board, no teacher, no bureaucrat, no textbook committee in the state or national capital, is dictating what and how your child will learn. Not anymore. You as the parent have the authority and the responsibility. If you're wise, you'll let your students earn more and more of that authority and responsibility for themselves, until finally they are totally in control of their own educations. Together, you make the choices. Together, you figure out what works best. Not what some "expert" theorizes "ought" to work best, but what truly meets your goals as a family. If all goes well, your whole family will learn to *love* learning. And that's what it's all about!

CHAPTER 2

It's a Wonderful Teen

I don't believe in Santa Claus, the Easter Bunny, or the Pillsbury Doughboy.

Neither do you.

That is, we don't believe that they actually exist in the sense that you and I exist. You won't see Mr. Claus and his reindeer flying by overhead, or the Easter Bunny peeking out from under your boxwood hedge. You also won't see any fat little men popping out of your pastry tube—and if you do, I would check what they're putting in your drinking water!

In another sense, though, these fictional creations are real. *They sell a lot of product.* That is what they were designed, or have been adapted, to do.

I now present, for your consideration, the thought that "teenagers" are just another such fictional creation. The entire Consumer Youth Culture was invented earlier this century. It owes its ongoing existence not to young men and women, but to a group of adult Madison Avenue merchants with a shipload of overpriced and often useless products to sell. By encouraging a "culture" of conformist rebellion ("Let's all wear the same clothes to show how individualistic we are!") and mindless consumerism ("Let's mug that kid for his sneakers!"), plus a dash of Peter Pan ("I won't grow up and you can't make me!"), it is possible to create a class of customers with significant money to spend and very little discretion as to how they spend it.

Teenagers did not use to exist. This is a fact. The most popular article ever printed in my magazine, *Practical Homeschooling,* documented this beyond doubt. That article, which can be found in Appendix I, pointed out that the very word "teenager" didn't appear in any dictionary until the 1930s. Although some of the upper-class Gilded Youth of the 1920s exhibited a few teenage-esque characteristics, they thought of themselves as young men and women. Girls aspired to dress like women, and boys dressed like men. There were no special teenage hairstyles, music, clothes, or anything else. (Check out old books, magazines, and movies if you doubt this.) As for previous generations, the contrast with our day was even more pronounced. Childhood tended to blur straight into manhood and womanhood, and we're talking *responsible manhood* and womanhood.

He's cute, but he doesn't exist. Neither do teenagers.

When Great-Grandpa and Great-Grandma got married at age 15, or 16, or 19, they *stayed* married for the next 60 years. They raised their families, ran their stores and farms, made their own cloth, took care of the livestock, and did all this with competence.

Ever watch an old black-and-white movie with newsboys crying "Extra! Extra!" on the corner? Those were *boys*. Not even teens, some of them. They weren't doing it so they could buy a Walkman at Walmart, either. Usually their families needed the income they brought in. The same applied to the shoeshine boys, soda jerks, and little girl seamstresses in Bronx tenements.

Ever watch the movie *It's a Wonderful Life*? Did you notice the hero, George Bailey, serving as counter attendant and messenger boy in the corner pharmacy? He couldn't have been over 10 or 11, but he was expected to run the shop by himself while the pharmacist mixed up prescriptions in the back.

I'm not saying that it would be wonderful if all our 10-year-olds had part-time jobs . . . although having had my first job at age 11, I don't think it would hurt most of them! I'm just saying that the concept of extended childhood, now reaching to age 30, for pity's sake, where Generation X-ers are still trying to "find" themselves, is a modern invention.

And not a good one.

What Do You Get Instead of Teenagers?

One of the great benefits of homeschooling is that your children don't have to turn into sullen monsters when they hit the big One Three. Instead, they become increasingly responsible young men and women who are your best friends.

Let me try to describe what this means for your family, from my own experience with our current crop of teens and pre-teens.

At age 10, my daughter, Magda, volunteered to take over the family meal preparation. For the past four years, she has done a wonderful job with everything from lasagna to birthday cakes.

Sarah started her own newsletter at age 11, getting up early in the morning to use my computer for layout work. She takes care of all the little ones by herself while I'm stuck in front of the computer (like right now!). At age 11, she also could cook, sew, and draw better Japanese-style manga art than anyone her age I've ever seen. Now, at age 15, she is perfectly capable of running the entire mail-order side of our business by herself when we are short-handed.

When the editor of our magazine, *Practical Homeschooling*, left for another job and the person we'd selected to replace him wasn't available for another two months, Joseph, age 17, stepped in and did the entire job—cheerfully, I might add!

Ted, our 19-year-old, has had an especially difficult time of it these past three years. After a bout with pneumonia that almost killed him, and an extended hospital stay, he came home on a respirator. Two major spinal operations also took their toll. But through all this, he never once complained—and what's more, he kept up with his schoolwork, with the help of a laptop computer. He works part-time for our business as a bookkeeper, and has started his own web design and maintenance company, Websitters (*www.websitters.com*).

All my young men and women are adored by their little brothers and sisters. They are all friendly, affectionate with the family, and easy to talk to. They feel no special need for weird, expensive clothes. They do not fall down and worship media stars. This independence from the Consumer Youth Culture is normal for homeschooled teens.

Return to Normalcy

Those of you with homeschooled teens are reading this and thinking, "Hey, *my* kids can do all sorts of great things, too!" My point exactly. My children aren't endowed with super powers and abilities far beyond those of mortal men. If they seem exceptionally responsible and emotionally mature, that's not because I'm so wonderful in these areas, either. They're just normal homeschooled kids.

Now, I will be the first to admit there are many wonderful kids in public and private schools. But in an age-segregated, peer-dominant setting, kids come under lots of pressure to be not so wonderful. You know what I mean. Drugs. Sex. Gangs. Cliques. Pressure to pretend you aren't really that smart (so the other kids won't think you're a nerd). Racial hostility (which engenders *more* hostility a lot more often than it produces forgiveness). Pressure to be absolutely gorgeous and perfectly in tune with the latest fashions (and if you're not, you should hate yourself and everyone has a license to mock you).

Not to mention the curriculum, over which you as a parent typically exercise little or no control. You've read the newspaper and magazine accounts of parents battling teachers and school boards over texts they found profoundly offensive. How often do the parents win?

Homeschooling removes those negative pressures, and lets young men and women concentrate on academics and normal social development.

It's normal for kids to like babies and little kids, and for brothers and sisters to play together and enjoy each other's company. It's normal for kids to want to grow up, and to be anxious to gain skills that will cause adults to respect them. All over the world, throughout all time, young men and women have shared in these normal traits.

Other writers will tell you how homeschooling can help your children manifest exceptional qualities and succeed beyond your wildest dreams. They're not lying—if you put in the time and love, you get amazing results.

But for me, the emotional and spiritual benefits of having a loving family free from generation gaps, drugs, and other disasters sounds pretty good all by itself!

If you're not homeschooling already, let me encourage you to trade in your teenagers for young men and women who look exactly the same in the mirror, but who now have the chance to find themselves before they ever get lost in the first place.

PART 2

Building Future Leaders

Homeschooler Caleb Trent, Murfreesboro, TN, won first place in the American Legion High School Oratorical Contest held in Clarksville, TN. Caleb earned a $5,000 scholarship to a state-approved college/university and a $1,000 scholarship for representing Tennessee at the regional contest held in Raleigh, NC.

Homeschoolers Sean and Virginia Macha of Goldsboro, NC, were presented recently with Congressional awards for volunteer work. Sean qualified for a bronze award by helping out at the Edgewood School for the Developmentally Challenged. Virginia qualified for a silver by working at a wildlife refuge called Emily's Ark. Eric Dail, another homeschooler from the same area, also won a bronze Congressional award, for helping out the Council on Aging lawn mowing program. Eric takes classes both at home and at Wayne Community College. Sean and Virginia have been homeschooled all their lives; both are AWANA members. Sean is also involved in Civil Air Patrol; on December 18, he was presented his General Billy Mitchell Award and promoted to CAP Flight Officer. Congratulations to all three!

CHAPTER 3

Bible Curriculum

Play a little thought experiment with me.

Here come two young men. We'll call them *Charlie* and *Bob*. Charlie is versed in all of popular culture. He has seen every movie that stars Arnold Schwarzenegger, Denzel Washington, Sylvester Stallone, and Jim Carrey, not to mention Sharon Stone, Sandra Bullock, and Julia Roberts. He has watched every *Seinfeld* episode. He reads the newspaper and listens to the radio. But he has never read the Bible.

Bob is a culture hermit. He has no TV, VCR, or radio. He picks up news from talking to the neighbors. But he knows the Bible forwards and backwards.

Give Charlie and Bob a book. Ask them each to report on what the book meant and whether the author was right or wrong.

> If the book was written in the 18th century, who will understand it better?
> ☐ Culture Charlie   ☐ Bible Bob
>
> If it was written in the 19th century, who will understand it better?
> ☐ Culture Charlie   ☐ Bible Bob
>
> Now, the kicker—if it was written in our century, who will understand it better? (This is a trick question.)
> ☐ Culture Charlie   ☐ Bible Bob

Most *Big Book* readers probably expect that knowing the Bible will help you understand older literature. But *modern* literature? Actually, yes. Even today, writers continually draw upon the Bible and biblical symbolism when they want to deliver a powerful message. From the inane (a haircolor commercial declaiming, "Let there be light!"), to the classics (Shakespeare, Dickens, etc.), to titles on the bestseller list (for example, *Thy Neighbor's Wife*), only those who know the Bible pick up on what is really being said all around them.

In fact, you can't even understand many *comic books* today without knowing something about the Bible. I'll just list one recent example. Alex Ross and Mark Waid's *Kingdom Come* mini-series is wholly constructed around verses from the Bible book of Revelation. *Kingdom Come* is not from

NIV = New International Version, a popular translation among evangelicals

KJV = King James Version, the traditional Elizabethan English translation produced in the 17th century at the order of King James of England, and used in most Protestant churches until recently

NKJV = New King James Version, slightly updated modern edition with current words substituted for archaic words

In an interview in *Wizard*, the comic-book fan magazine, *Kingdom Come* creator Alex Ross called Superman, "The Ultimate Failed Christ Symbol." Superman tries to save everyone, but not being the Son of God, he fails. *Kingdom Come* depends for its impact on such biblical allusions and symbols.

some underground publisher, either. It was the publishing event of the season for DC Comics, the people who bring you Superman and Batman.

Kingdom Come is not a Christian comic. It's about an apocalyptic world jam-packed with superheros. Which is my point exactly. When comics try to be literate and powerful, what do you get? Bible verses!

But the Bible is much more than just literature. It's influential not only for its style, which in the King James Version shaped all of Western literature, but for its content—for what it says. It is a book of rules, relationships, and redemption. It tells you how to live, how to die, and what comes after. It talks about the beginning of time and predicts the end of the world. Whether you choose to believe the Bible or not, the fact remains that until very recently Western culture was created by those who did believe it, or at least pretended to believe it. You can't understand Western culture or history unless you study this Book.

I say "study," because there's a lot to learn when you read the Bible. Ancient Middle Eastern culture. Greek and Roman culture. Archaeology. Geography (the travels of St. Paul are a course in themselves). The histories of Israel, Egypt, Phoenicia, the Hittites, Assyria, Babylon, Persia, Greece, and Rome, to name a few. Monarchy. Military science. Comparison of the law of Moses to other law codes (including ours). Slavery in Israel (and the effect hearing about the escape of the Jews from slavery in Egypt had on Southern slaves before the Civil War). What Christian teaching on forgiveness really means, and what a difference it would make if the Serbs and Croats would apply it to themselves. As you can see, not only are a host of homeschool topics directly related to the Bible, but it makes an excellent starting point for discussing and understanding contemporary issues.

Bible Study

A Beka Books, a prominent Christian textbook publisher, has a complete **Bible curriculum lineup** for nursery school through twelfth grade.

Some noteworthy items: The Junior-High Map Journeys include flannel maps accompanied by removable symbols, labels, and figures, and packed with a lesson guide. Each has a different flannel map. The teacher's kits for the flannel map programs include flannel map, review questions, and teacher's guide.

Intended for grades 11 and 12, A Beka's Bible Survey curriculum covers the whole New Testament in one course. The teacher's kit include a student worktext and teacher's guide. *Mary Pride*

BJUP's secondary **Bible Education** program comes in six levels (A–F), corresponding to grade levels 7–12. Coordinated with each level is a 21 x 35" two-color wall chart.

Level A (grade 7) is "Learning from the Life of Christ." The wall chart is an amplified time line of the life of Christ. **Level B** (grade 8), "Portraits from the Old Testament," concentrates on role models from this time period. The wall chart for level B is a parallel timetable covering developments in Bible lands during Old Testament times. **Level C** (grade 9), "Lessons from the Early Church," covers Acts and the early Pauline epistles, with (what else?) a map of the journeys of Paul as the wall chart for this level. **Level D** (grade 10), "Themes from the Old Testament," introduces principles of Bible interpretation. The wall chart for level D summarizes the Old Testament books. **Level E** (grade 11), "Directions for Early Christians" covers the remaining New Testament books verse by verse or thematically, depending on which book is being discussed. For this level the wall chart is a table summarizing the New Testament books. Finally, "Patterns for

A Beka Bible Studies

Grades 6–12. Exodus, Life of Christ, Paul's Missionary Journeys flannel map studies, $21.95 each. Teacher's kits, $53.65 each, including the flannel map studies.
A Beka Book, Box 19100, Pensacola, FL 32523-9100. (800) 874-2352. Fax: (800) 874-3590. Web: www.abeka.com.

BJUP Bible Curriculum

Grades 7–12. Teacher's editions, $45.50 each (includes a student worktext). Student worktexts, $11 each. Wall chart for each level, $7 each. Shipping extra.
Bob Jones University Press Customer Service, Greenville, South Carolina 29614-0062. (800) 845-5731. Fax: (800) 525-8398. Web: www.bju.edu/press/

Christian Living," is the **level F** (grade 12) book. It takes a topical look at major Bible teachings under the two themes of "Loving God Completely" and "Loving My Neighbor As Myself." The level F wall chart is a summary of "fundamental doctrines." *Mary Pride*

If you are looking for an insightful, inexpensive Bible study course, the **Emmaus Correspondence Course Series** is definitely it! They have several series of books, including: *The Gospel of John, The Epistle of James, Old Testament Law and History, Old Testament Poetry and Prophecy, I'll Take the High Road, Basic Bible Doctrines, The Epistles of Peter and Jude,* and *New Testament Survey.*

These eight short books actually come from four different study programs that Emmaus offers. Emmaus Correspondence School offers a total of nine study series, consisting of two to eighteen books in each series. The study series include: *Salvation, Children, Christian Life, New Testament Book, Doctrinal, Bible Prophecy, Teacher Training,* and *Intermediate and College Credit Study.*

There is a study guide for several of the books if a group study is to be done outside of the correspondence school.

Emmaus offers the first book in any series free of charge. You then have the opportunity to read the book, study as you desire, and then order the next in the series, if you enjoy it. The way these books are designed, you can't help but enjoy them. They speak to the average person. You do not have to be a theology major or have a Ph.D. in languages to understand the texts. After reading a chapter, you are instructed to take the exam that is included. These exams can easily be used for a classroom situation, or, if you desire, Emmaus will grade the exams for you (an additional $2 is required, but that is for all the exams in one book).

With the wide variety of books offered and the inexpensive price, this series would make a excellent addition to any Bible curriculum. *Barbara Buchanan*

NEW!
Emmaus Correspondence Course Series

Grade 7–adult. Book prices range from $1.35 to $4.50. Shipping extra. *Emmaus Correspondence School, Dubuque, IA 52001-3099. (888) 338-7809. (319) 588-8000. Fax: (319) 588-1216. Email: acheek@emmaus1.edu. Web: www.emmaus.ch.*

Bible Beginnings for preschool children ages 2–4. Bible Foundations "Read Along" edition for grades K–1, and "Read Alone" edition for grades 2 and 3. Bible Discovery for grades 3–6. Bible Quest for grades 7–12. These make up **Explorer's Bible Study Curriculum for the Young Scholar**. In Volume 2 we reviewed the first three curriculum series. Now we're reviewing the teen curriculum. When complete, they will combine to form a comprehensive Bible-study solution for the school years.

NEW!
Explorer's Bible Study Curriculum for the Young Scholar

Entire curriculum, grades preK–12. Bible Quest (Grades 7–12): Genesis; Exodus through Joshua (God's People, God's Land); and Luke & Acts (Promises Fulfilled): Student Workbooks, $18.95 each; Home School Teacher's Manuals, $19.95 each; Answer Keys, $6.95 each; Music Curriculum, $7.95. *Explorer's Bible Study, PO Box 425, Dickson, TN 37056-0425. Orders: (800) 657-2874. Inquiries: (615) 446-7316. Fax: (615) 446-7951. Email: tom.ebs@mcione.com. Web: www.explorerbiblestudy.org.*

An example of how spiral learning works: In Bible Foundations, a first-through third-grader will be asked to describe the world before the Creation. In Bible Discovery, a third-through sixth-grader will be asked, "In what words did God command light to appear?" Finally, in Bible Quest, a teenager will be asked, "How do the first verses of Genesis deny atheism?" As you can see, while older children will be studying the same Bible passages as the younger ones, they will be analyzing them in the light of developing a Christian world-view rather than merely parroting back the Bible facts, as is more appropriate for younger children.

Words of Wisdom: Job, Psalms, and Proverbs will soon be available in both the Bible Discovery and Bible Quest levels. Eventually, these will be joined by *Judges, Prophets and Kings: Judges–Malachi* and *New Testament Epistles and Revelation*. This will result in five years at each level, plus one elective (*Words of Wisdom*).

Explorer's Bible Study Curriculum has some similarities and differences to other Bible curricula. Like most other programs available today, it is "spiral." That is, children study the same material repeatedly at different levels. In Explorer's case, they will go through many Bible portions four times during their school years: once in preschool, once in the early elementary grades, once in the later elementary grades, and once in the middle-school/high-school years. But Explorer's takes the spiral concept a bit farther. Every child in a family from grade 3 and up can be studying the same passages in the same week. That's because the Bible Discovery and Bible Quest workbooks run in "parallel." Similarly, once the Bible Beginnings workbooks are out, all preschool through grade 2 or 3 children in a family will be able to study the same Bible portions together, because Bible Beginnings and Bible Foundations will be designed with parallel Bible lessons.

The curriculum as a whole concentrates on teaching Bible facts in chronological order and in context. The workbooks are designed to be self-directed, and the lessons require practically no teacher preparation. In keeping with the factual emphasis, the courses are non-denominational, not seeking to present any particular emphasis or agenda.

Bible Quest, intended for grades 7–12, is the capstone of this curriculum. It continues to teach the inductive method, while introducing "worldview" topics as appropriate. Expect a lot of questions designed to make the student think about *why* the Bible uses a particular word and *why* a Bible personage acted as he did. Study notes at the end of each lesson provide additional background information, answer questions that the lesson may have raised, and provide additional worldview applications. It would be good to have an hour per weekday to allow enough time for discussing all the important questions Bible Quest raises.

A Home School Teacher's Manual is now available to accompany each workbook. This includes everything found in the Answer Key, plus additional home teaching helps, without adding all the extraneous (to home-school) info in the classroom teacher's manuals. If you also want the song cassette and song book for each curriculum level, you can buy them separately. The sections of the Home School Teacher's Edition include an introduction, a curriculum overview (in which we learn that this curriculum is geared to "develop mental thinking and comprehension" and follows the "spiral" theory of presenting the same material repeatedly at different grade levels), guidelines and rules for effective teaching, a weekly schedule for Bible memory work, and finally a complete copy of the student workbook with answers to all the questions in boldface.

This is not the curriculum for hands-on, funsy-wunsy activities. It's designed to efficiently make your kids into Bible experts and Bible thinkers, with as little fuss and wasted time as possible. If that's what you're looking for, then Explorer's Bible Study delivers. *Mary Pride*

Genesis: Finding Our Roots is a textbook you'll want to display. A companion to the more familiar *Adam and His Kin*, this gorgeous 112-page hardback features glossy photos of famous art works illustrating the themes of Genesis. The Doré engravings, medieval stained glass, and other works, with their captions, could form a mini art appreciation course.

But art is just a portion of Ruth Beechick's plan for this self-contained six-unit study exploring the humanities side of creation. Beginning with the main Scripture text (KJV) and cross-referencing other passages, a solo teen or an adult leading family study then launches into a choice of topics like these in Unit 1: Dragons, Day, World Views, and Myths of Creation. For further study, the text offers discussions of science textbooks, additional reading, and writing and project guidance leading to presentations and reports.

The author maintains a literal six-day creationism based on the work of Henry Morris, and she argues for the patriarchal authorship of specific sections of Genesis. Thus the units are divided into "God's Book of Creation" and the books of Adam, Noah, Noah's Sons, Shem, and Terah. Even if your theological approach to Genesis differs, you'll find intellectual challenge here.

Ever the educator, Beechick offers many sidebar helps, a glossary, and maps and charts to illustrate her points. "Teaching Helps" suggest answers to topic questions and ways to tailor the unit studies to particular needs of classrooms, homeschools, and Sunday Schools. Leave it on the coffee table and perhaps the family will teach themselves! *Cindy Marsch*

How does revelation set Christianity apart from all other religions? What does God reveal about Himself? What do all people know about God? In what various ways did God speak to people? What does the Bible teach concerning false revelations? What twelve tests can I use to judge purported "revelations"? Are special revelations occurring today? These are the crucial and timely questions that this combination text and workbook answers.

God's Revelation is rather unique in that it teaches systematic theology through personal Bible study. The questions, answers, and quizzes involve more than simply repeating back what the text says. The author's purpose is to lead the student in personal discovery through direct interaction with the Scripture. (No answers are provided for the workbook questions or quizzes; however, this is not a major flaw.)

The *God's Revelation* study is written from a conservative, evangelical perspective that the author also describes as "generally Reformed." The author believes that the charismatic gifts are still operational today, but offers other viewpoints—and necessary cautions—on this issue as well.

I was impressed with the tremendous amount of research that went into the writing of this workbook. Also included in this workbook are several appendices, including one about existentialism and neo-orthodoxy; a list of abbreviations; a glossary; a bibliography; subject, person, and Scripture indexes; and over 30 pages of endnotes.

I would consider this excellent resource a must for any high-school senior headed for college, and I would highly recommend it to all homeschooling parents. This type of teaching and study is sorely needed in our churches today. The author, Robert E. Fugate—a homeschooling father and pastor—is continuing his series of Essential Doctrines of the Christian Faith. The second volume is *The Bible: God's Words to You* and should be available by the end of the year 2000. *Rebecca Prewett*

If you have a junior-high or high-school student, and have never taught a formal Bible course at home, or your Bible studies have jumped this way and that without ever systematically going through the Old Testament and New Testament, **Ken Levy's** courses are the ones I recommend you start with.

For the Layman: A Survey of the Old Testament is a masterfully uncomplicated historical survey that leads you gently—and quickly—through all the books of the Old Testament in their chronological order. What's more, it does it in such a way that you will remember each book's major points. The whole course has in fact been condensed into two pages. A special laminated chart shows on one side exactly how each book fits into history, and on the other side the history of Israel book by book.

But you get a lot more than two pages. You get an attractive three-ring binder, with four cassettes and almost 100 pages of material built in, plus the laminated chart and some additional visual helps, e.g., an outline of important Bible dates, line-art drawings and descriptions of major taberna-

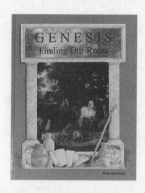

NEW!
God's Revelation
Grade 9–adult. $16.95 plus $3.50 shipping.
Thy Word is Truth Publishers, PO Box 34704, Omaha, NE 68134-0704.
Fax/Phone: (402) 491-0057.
Email: ThyWordTru@aol.com.
Web: members.aol.com/ThyWordTru/ index.html.

NEW!
Ken Levy's Bible Survey Courses
Grade 7–adult. Each complete course, $35. Additional binder with all course materials except for audiocassettes, $12. Shipping $5 for first binder plus $3 for each additional. Quantity discounts available.
For the Layman, 128 S. Fairmont Ave., Lodi, CA 95240. (209) 368-2955.
Email: ftlayman@aol.com.

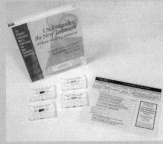

Also by Ken Levy, **Understanding the New Testament Without Attending Seminary** has a similar format. This brand-new course takes only six hours to finish and covers the *entire* New Testament, including each and every epistle, with the same cogent summaries of each book's major points as found in the Old Testament course. Intertestamental history and background information for each book leave you with the same amount of knowledge as a seminary survey course, in far less time. No particular prophetic view is advocated, although all are presented fairly, making this an ideal course for any individual or group Bible study.

Proverbs: Lessons for the Growing Years

Grades 7–12. $11.95 plus shipping. *Leadership Resources, 12575 South Ridgeland, Paylos Heights, IL 60463. (888) 572-6657. Fax: (708) 489-9771.*

NEW!
Reading and Understanding the Bible

Grade 4–adult. $6 plus $2 shipping. *Vic Lockman, 233 Rogue River Highway #360, Grants Pass, OR 97527. Fax: (541) 479-3814.*

cle furniture. Throughout the course, events are dated according to the best conservative scholarship, and the Bible is presented as the Word of God.

The course itself is just eight lessons long, each lesson taking about an hour. You listen to the lesson on cassette for 45 minutes, simultaneously following along and filling in the blanks on the provided course outline. There is room in the margin for your own personal notes and applications. I say "personal notes and applications" because the course doesn't bog you down in its author's spiritual insights, as so many do. The point here is to quickly gain the knowledge that will help you, in the author's words, "establish a foundation for future studies."

The foundation you'll be establishing is impressive. For the Layman may be efficient, but it is also detailed. All the minor prophets your other Bible curriculum has been skipping for years are covered here. And I bet you'll discover facts you never knew before about even the Bible books you've studied most. Instead of wallowing for weeks in Creation and the Flood, for example, you quickly discover that God literally "cut" a covenant with Abraham, and that the Egyptians practiced segregation (them here, the Jews there). You'll delve into details, from the Names of God to the order in which the tribes of Israel camped around the tabernacle, that you'd normally expect to find only in year-long courses. But you never bog down in these details, and the course keeps moving quickly enough to interest even the most reluctant Bible student.

The best way to use For the Layman is as once-a-week lessons, perhaps on Sunday. Each student should have his or her own binder, for note-taking. Happily, additional binders (with course sheets, tests, charts, etc.) are available at reasonable cost. If one hour each week is too much, you can further divide the course into half-hour segments. And if you truly can't afford to buy additional binders, the author allows you to photocopy additional sets of the course pages for your home use.

How much Bible can you learn in eight hours? You'll be surprised. Can it really be this easy? You'll be amazed. Highly recommended. *Mary Pride*

Proverbs: Lessons for the Growing Years is a 36-week inductive Bible study workbook targeted for junior and senior high students. Lessons are intended to be done at the rate of one per week throughout a standard school year. The course itself is well adapted to home or church use. Eleven lessons tackle the first nine chapters of Proverbs. Interspersed with these are 25 topical lessons on subtopics such as "Friends" and "Money and the Poor." Standard evangelical viewpoint throughout. (The author is a professor at Trinity Bible College). A 20-page teacher guide is included at the end of the student workbook that includes an explanation of the inductive study method and lesson helps and hints. Lessons frequently ask the student to "tattle" on himself in print, describing his weaknesses and sins, but the bulk of the questions focus on understanding what the Proverbs say. *Mary Pride*

"Hermeneutics is fun!" says Vic Lockman. That may not be the impression of most seminary students—probably because their textbooks are nothing like this jam-packed booklet.

Once again, Vic Lockman manages to teach some serious stuff in a fun, interesting way. The information presented in **Reading and Understanding the Bible** is vital in this day of vastly differing and often bizarre interpretations of Scripture. How did we get our Bible? What is the purpose of the Bible? How do we know if something is to be taken literally or figuratively? What on earth is meant by "synecdoche," "metonymy," and "litotes"—and why should I even bother learning such things? How can we interpret the parables, allegories, symbols, and typology in Scripture? How can we recognize and avoid false interpretations? How can we make sense out of prophecy? What are the general rules of interpreting Scripture?

The graphics and illustrations really aid in understanding and remembering what is being taught. Many examples are given from Scripture; for example, under the section dealing with allegories, you will study I Corinthians 3, Ecclesiastes 12:1-8, Ephesians 6:10-18, John 15:1, etc. The booklet also includes quizzes and a final exam.

Vic Lockman writes from a Reformed perspective; however, he does not cram this theological viewpoint down the reader's throat. This book is valuable for anyone who holds a high view of Scripture as the inspired and infallible Word of God. *Rebecca Prewett*

Remembering God's Awesome Acts combines Bible study and history with many subjects to create a notebook that will help your child understand the lives of the people that lived during Bible times. The approach is somewhat classical, and includes drawing, creative writing, geography, anthropology, archaeology, linguistics, speech and drama. The overall point of the notebook approach is to give a better understanding of the Bible. It is a combination unit study/workbook approach. The time frame covered goes through the life of Moses.

The set includes the student's notebook and a teacher's manual. The student's notebook is actually an extensive workbook that includes all the subjects and activities included in the curriculum.

The Bible—in this case, the New International Version—is the backbone of this text, but you can substitute another version. Discernment is taught by exposing speculative falsehoods often taught as factual history in comparison to what is written in the Bible. Your student gets a chance to draw maps of the location of historical events, and learns real hieroglyphics. He studies the pharaohs and the Egyptian gods, and how God defeated them. The linguistics of every continent will be studied, and techniques to help enable your child's development of language appreciation and study skills are covered. There are many drawing and creative writing assignments that allow for a diverse experience. The opportunity to give speeches and perform dramas adds even more depth to *Remembering God's Awesome Acts*.

There is a lot of material covered and the intensity might be somewhat overwhelming unless you make *Remembering God's Awesome Acts* the bulk of your curriculum during the time you are using it. It's designed in a way that will make you and your child want to dig deeper, and spend more time studying as you go. So plan on taking your time and getting the most out of the book. *Maryann Turner*

Rod & Staff's Truth for Life Bible studies course for grades 7 or 8 includes 35 topical lessons covering basic doctrines from a Mennonite perspective, each with discussion questions and activities.

Their latest catalog announces that a new program is being developed to cover the whole Bible chronologically in grades 5–7, plus another whole new Bible curriculum for grades 8–10, so you might want to write for information about these new programs. *Mary Pride*

What is a **Scripture Search**? A small 3-ring binder with a plan for reading through the Bible in a year, plus several forms you can use to organize your prayer life. There is a section for listing prayer requests and a sections

NEW!
Remembering God's Awesome Acts
Grades 5–12. $35 per set, $20 per additional student notebook. *Susan Mortimer, 731 W. Camp Wisdom, Duncanville, TX 75116. (972) 780-1683.*

Rod & Staff Truth for Life Bible Courses
Grades 7 or 8. Student book, $3.30. Teacher's book, $3.40. Shipping extra. *Rod and Staff Publishers, Box 3, Hwy 172, Crockett, KY 41413. (606) 522-4348. Fax: (800) 643-1244.*

NEW!
Scripture Search and Scripture Search Junior

Adults and children. $13.95 each plus $2.50 shipping.
Pritt Ministry Services, 358 Rockhill Rd., Quakertown, PA 18951. (215) 536-1650. Email: spritt@juno.com.

NEW!
Searching for Treasure: A Guide to Wisdom and Character Development

All ages. $17.95 plus $3 shipping.
Noble Publishing Associates, PO Box 2250, Gresham, OR 97030. Orders: (800) 225-5259. Inquiries: (503) 667-3942. Fax: (503) 665-6637.

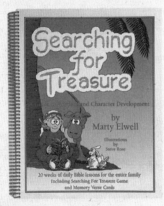

NEW!
Turning on The Light

Grades 10–adult. $7.99 plus shipping.
Presbyterian and Reformed Publishing Company, P.O. Box 817, Phillipsburg, NJ 08865. (800) 631-0094. (908) 454-0505. Fax: (908) 859-2390.

The appendices are not the typical "read this for further background." Appendix A includes the readings from Ephesians and Colossians which she uses in the study. Appendix B includes supplemental exercises for those with more spare time than most of us can seem to find. Appendix C lays out the steps for salvation. Finally, Appendix D explains the Reformed Faith.

for sermon notes. The main section contains forms for recording memory verses, what passage you read, what truths you found in the reading, whether it contained a promise, a precept, or a principle, and how you applied the truth that day. This is a well-organized way to record your devotional Bible reading with notes for future reference, and would make a great companion to your Bible.

Scripture Search Jr., the notebook for children, is much the same, minus the forms for sermon notes. The forms for recording the daily readings are more child-friendly. Your child will indicate whether he found a promise, a teaching, or a command. He will briefly note what he read about, any words he didn't know, and what the Lord wants him to do, based on what he read. This could be a simple, yet powerful, year-long Bible curriculum and the beginning of a lifelong habit.

Refills for both notebooks are available. *Rebecca Prewett*

The **Searching for Treasure** curriculum, written by a homeschooling mother, consists of 20 weeks of daily Bible lessons to be used with the entire family. The goal is to involve your family in Bible reading and memorization. (The Bible version used is the NIV.) The topics studied come out of the book of Proverbs and are divided into the following sections: Understanding Wisdom, Developing Right Relationships, Controlling Yourself, Controlling What You Say, Avoiding the Way of the Wicked, and Following the Way of the Righteous.

Younger children will learn a verse or a section of a verse per week, while older children will memorize more. Activities are simple and don't require a lot of preparation time or a lot of materials. You will need to cut out the Bible Memory cards and the game cards, which are printed on heavy stock. Also, you may want to copy the illustration for each lesson for younger children to color. Any additional materials depend on whether or not you choose to do the crafts, but most are items easily found in homes with children.

The lessons are easy to teach, as they are organized well and include everything you need to know. They include an explanation of the reading passage, discussion questions, prayer emphasis, and craft and game ideas. This is one of the best family-oriented studies I have seen and is completely non-intimidating, yet solid.

This curriculum can also be used in a family class. There is even a section on how to organize a "Family Night" program. *Rebecca Prewett*

Turning on the Light: Discovering the Riches of God's Word by Carol J. Ruvolo is unlike any introductory Bible study book you will encounter. Yes, it is broken down into lessons with the obligatory note section; exercises of review, application and digging deeper; and appendices at the end of the book. But, this is where the differences begin.

This is a study guide. Ruvolo says it best: "Serious Bible study encompasses specific prerequisites, techniques, and objectives. The prerequisites are (1) having an accurate view of the Letter (the Bible) and (2) having an accurate view of yourself. The techniques are (1) accurately observing what the Letter says, (2) responsibly interpreting what the Letter means, and (3) meaningfully applying the Letter's teachings to your life. The goals are (1) becoming conformed to the image of your Lord Jesus Christ, (2) glorifying your heavenly Father, and (3) learning to do the work your Father prepared for you to do." This is just what these seven little lessons do! This book definitely lives up to its title: it helps us to discover the wonderful riches that await us in God's Word.

Ruvolo's book is an excellent choice for a novice at Bible study or for the old pro—everyone can learn a new way of looking at the age-old Gospel of Truth. She doesn't spoon-feed you or expect you to know everything before reading the lesson; she guides you in just the right manner. *Barbara Buchanan*

CHAPTER 4

Bible Teaching Aids

Any Christian bookstore has a host of Bible study tools. There you can get your study Bibles, your concordances, your Bible atlases, your Bible dictionaries. What we have in this chapter are resources especially designed for or favored by homeschoolers, including videos, charts, maps, and more. But the Bible itself remains the best Bible study tool. Read it and write down the questions that pop up as you do so. Search for answers. You'll be surprised at the results!

Extra Help for Bible Study

Quick! Where can we read about the destruction of Sodom? Genesis, of course—but which chapter? What is the book of Habakkuk about? Can you give a summary of Revelation? Don't you wish you had a relatively painless way to remember what is found where in the Bible, and what themes are found in different chapters and books?

I would love to tell you the exciting story behind this book—how it was written by a blind veteran studying at a Bible College, how a tattered old copy was discovered in a family attic, and how the book came to be reprinted—but if I told all the details, this review could turn into a lengthy article!

This book is just what its title states: **The Bible in Verse**. Each chapter in the Bible is summarized by a four-line stanza.

How to use this book? The author first summarized Daniel in verse form in order to prepare for a test. He found this so helpful, and so did his fellow students, that he wrote verses for the entire Bible. I plan on reading each stanza after we read the corresponding chapter in Scripture, and reading other stanzas as introduction and review. I anticipate that, over the years, we will commit many of these stanzas to memory, and that this will serve to make the Bible more an integral part of our hearts, minds, and very lives.

The poetry in this volume is not hokey or trite. The language used has the same flavor as the KJV. Much of it is beautiful and stirring and is very much in keeping with the tone of the Biblical chapters themselves. This book is truly a valuable treasure for every homeschool bookshelf. *Rebecca Prewett*

NEW!
The Bible in Verse
All ages. $12.95 plus $3 shipping. *Pillar Publications, 3843 Winslow Drive, Fort Worth, TX 76109. (817) 922-8450. Fax: (817) 922-8449.*

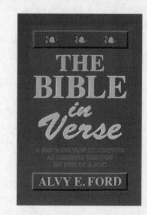

NEW!
BibleQuizmania

Grade 5–adult. Gospel Library: Easter Story, Christmas Story, Teachings of the Master (6 cassettes), $14.95 per title, $39.95 for all 3. Genesis series (3 cassettes), $14.95. Shipping extra.
Embassy Media, 3111 W. Alpine Ave., Santa Ana, CA 92704. (800) 593-5757. Fax: (714) 850-1614. Email: embassy@aol.com. Web: www.embassy-media.com.

At last—a Bible product designed for the way homeschoolers teach! On each **BibleQuizmania** cassette are dramatically read Bible questions and answers, including the verse reference, presented in the order in which the information appears in the biblical text, along with background music and sound effects.

The questions range from the easy—"What did God do on the seventh day of Creation?"—to the moderately difficult— "Where was Abraham living when God called him?" You have a 15-second pause to answer each question before the tape answers it for you. Use the scorepad to keep track of how well you did. Since answers and verse references are provided, you can use the tapes both as a great Sunday game and as an interest-sparker, providing motivation for your children to look up the references and learn the answers so they will score better next time. Stop the tape any time to discuss what you've learned.

The Gospel Library package includes six cassettes for a total of 300 questions and answers. The Genesis package has three cassettes for a total of 150 questions and answers. This product couldn't be easier to use. *Mary Pride*

NEW!
Faith Lessons

Grades 7 or 9 to adult. Each 2-video set, $34.99.
Zondervan Publishing House, Attn: Order Processing, 5300 Patterson Ave. SE, Grand Rapids, MI 49530. (800) 727-3480. Web: www.zondervan.com.

Volume 2, *Faith Lessons on the Prophets & Kings of Israel,* requires parental discretion. The first lesson, Innocent Blood, goes in some detail into the sexually oriented "worship" of the Baal cult, and its attendant infant sacrifices. Colored illustrations depict the priest and priestess, unclothed and seen from the side, about to have sex in front of the "worshippers." Sounds of a baby crying in distress accompany the illustration of a baby being placed in the red-hot hands of Moloch. This presentation brought tears to the eyes of many in the tour group, and is definitely too much for tender young teens. To his credit, Mr. Vander Laan does get around to explaining how evil the Baal cult was. However, the earlier part of his presentation almost makes it sound like the Israelites and Canaanites had good rea-

The **Faith Lessons** video series, formerly entitled "That the World May Know," was originally a project of Focus on the Family. During a Holy Land tour, Dr. James Dobson of Focus was so impressed by the presentations of historian Ray Vander Laan that he arranged for a two-camera video team to film these videos. After that, like other Focus projects, this was taken over by a Christian publisher—in this case, Zondervan.

Filmed on location in Israel, these videos help you understand the theological and cultural significance of a number of important Bible concepts, and apply them to our lives today, in a way you have never seen before. The cameras follow a tour group led by Mr. Vander Laan. He takes them to important sites, including archaeological digs generally off-limits to the public, and in these historically rich locations points out physical features that lead to spiritual lessons. For example, did you know that "Armageddon" literally means "the mountain of Megiddo," and that the city of Megiddo's location helped it control the main trade route of the ancient world? Sitting at the site of Megiddo and looking out over the plain of Armageddon, the tour group hears Mr. Vander Laan explain that this one location was probably the site of more battles than any other in the ancient world. Whoever controlled Megiddo, controlled the world, and a battle in Armageddon would naturally mean to Jewish hearers "a battle for the control of the world." That's why it was one of the three main cities (all along the trade route from eastern countries to Egypt) fortified by Solomon. Mr. Vander Laan then challenges his hearers to recognize the "Megiddos" that Christians ought to strategically seek to control (e.g., Hollywood, Washington, their own families).

Each volume of Faith Lessons includes two videos, each ranging from 50 minutes to 118 minutes, and a "Study Guide," a small, folded booklet with Bible reading suggestions and discussion questions (but no answers to those questions).

- Volume 1, *Faith Lessons on the Promised Land,* has presentations on Standing at the Crossroads (the significance of standing stones and city gates), Wet Feet (Jordan River, specifically the Israelite crossing and Jesus' baptism), Firstfruits (Rahab and Jericho), Confronting Evil (the Shephelah region and the Nazarites), and the Iron of Culture (more on the Shephelah, and the Israelites v. the Philistines).
- Volume 2, *Faith Lessons on the Prophets & Kings of Israel,* tackles the topics of Innocent Blood (Baal worship), Who is God? (Elijah v. the priests of Baal at Mount Carmel), Wages of Sin (Hezekiah v. the Assyrian army), The Lord is My Shepherd (shepherding in Israel), God With Us (the temple at Arad, what was in the temple at Jerusalem).
- Volume 3, *Faith Lessons on the Life & Ministry of the Messiah,* looks at Herod, Masada (where a handful of Jewish defenders held off the Romans for years before killing themselves and their families in a Jim Jones-like suicide spree—however, the video presentation is more in line with the modern Israeli interpretation of this as a monument to heroism), the Essenes, Jewish weddings, Rabbis and zealots, the Hellenistic culture and Sapphoris, a lesson on the Crusades entitled "Misguided Faith," and Living Water.
- Volume 4, *Faith Lessons on the Death & Resurrection of the Messiah,* delves into these topics and settings: When Storms Come (the Sea of Galilee), Piercing the Darkness (Jesus' encounter with demons at the Decapolis), the Gates of Hell (Decapolis again), the City of the Great King (Jerusalem), The Lamb of God (Bethany and the Mount of Olives), The Weight of the World (Garden of Gethsemane, olive press), Roll Away the Stone (crucifixion, tombs in the rock), Power to the People (Pentecost), and Total Commitment (the city of Caesarea).

Best if used along with a reliable Bible encyclopedia, such as Baker's, that is more solid in its applications. *Mary Pride*

sons for following Baal (e.g., God took care of them in the desert, but Baal was a god of the valleys and brought fertility, and he apparently had done a good job because the land was very fertile), when clearly the whole thing was a marketing job, as God Himself pointed out in the Bible. What evidence was there that Baal even existed? The X-rated sex antics of the priest and priestess, the XXX-rated "snuff film" violence done to babies, and the blessing of authority figures on sexual partying were what drew the crowds (it set my teeth on edge to hear them called "worshippers"), not any deep pious beliefs. The application Mr. Vander Laan draws here is our abortion holocaust, but he missed a real opportunity to point out that "free sex" encouraged by state and religious authorities and unencumbered by any feeling of responsibility to the resulting offspring is the marketing hook Satan uses to persuade formerly faithful people to abandon God. Such apostasies have *nothing* to do with any serious theological issues, and *everything* to do with selfish human lust. The theology and political philosophy *follows,* to justify what evil men already have decided to do. If the church can't or won't teach its unmarried people to be chaste, and its married people to be faithful (including *not* engaging in lustful thoughts, porn, or serial marriage), then it's only a matter of time until that church becomes a temple of Baal.

The role and meaning of the Ten Commandments today . . . antinomianism . . . the Noahic covenant . . . the Regulative Principle . . . legalism versus grace . . . separation of Church and State . . . how many massive volumes would you have to dig through to learn what all this stuff really means and why it matters?

With God's Law for Modern Man, Vic Lockman has made it easy, thought-provoking, concise, and even fun. You may ask, "How can cartoons and the Bible mix?" Well, these cartoons are neither silly, irreverent, nor out of place. I nev-

er thought it was possible for serious theology to be presented so simply and in such a visually-appealing manner.

This booklet, greatly influenced by the lectures of R.J. Rushdoony, distills and illuminates the contents of numerous volumes on my shelf. If you want to comprehend the essence of covenant theology, or make sure you are obeying the spirit of God's law, or understand where our government is going wrong—get this booklet! *Rebecca Prewett*

Raise your hand if you know all there is to know about the Temple at Jerusalem. Right . . . mine's not up either. While I have studied the Temple, and understand its importance, I've had limited resources. This 25-minute video from The Temple Institute taught me much more than I expected, and kept this non-television person rooted to her seat.

In Search of the Holy Temple begins by presenting the history of the Temple and brings you forward through time, sharing the great significance of this most holy place. Excellent computer-generated graphics give you a three-dimensional tour of the Temple as it would have been before its second destruction, and on-site footage gives a picture of the way things are today. Arriving in the present, you learn of the steps the Jews are taking toward rebuilding this important structure. You explore excavated portions of the Temple and visit buildings that house the implements that are being restored and recreated. You see these beautiful articles of worship, and demonstrations of their proper use as well.

Whether a homeschooler seeking resources, or merely one interested in the history of God's Temple, you should find this video fascinating. *Tammy Cardwell*

Christian drama can be a powerful tool. Done well, it can chisel open character and offer the audience a mirror to their own souls. Done poorly, it works as nothing more than someone's silly, overproduced ego trip. If you're going to do it, you want to do it well.

Whether you're looking for a resource for a support group activity, a way to help your teens share creatively at church, or for a possible family outreach, Carolyn Wing Greenlee's two slim comb-bound volumes are a wonderful encouragement that will help you do it well.

Into Their Skin, Both Now & Then is a 40-page "workshop" that looks at the hows and whys of writing biblical monologues. She shares both examples of actual monologues ("Joseph of Arimathea" and "A Daughter of Asaph") as well as thinking used in creating them. Lots of questions provide meaty food for thought.

But What If? walks you through the flipside of this process:

> What if Saul had gone to fight Goliath? . . . What if Ananias and Sapphira had repented before the Lord? The truth of God is fathomless, yet we can become superficial in our reading of his Word. We can be bereft of greater, richer depths of understanding simply because of the familiarity of the "stories" we know so well. Reversal Scripts can help us see these familiar stories in a new light.

Thirty-three pages of examples and lots of questions and ideas can help you to create surprising drama by turning the familiar inside-out. Both books express an attitude of worship, and stress simplicity, which are the keys for doing drama well at any age. *Michelle Van Loon*

NEW!
In Search of the Holy Temple
All ages. $19.95 plus $3.95 shipping.
American Portrait Films, PO Box 19266, Cleveland, OH 44119.
Orders: (800) 736-4567.
Inquiries: (216) 531-8600.
Fax: (216) 531-8355.
Email: amport@ix.netcom.com.
Web: www.amport.com.

NEW!
Into Their Skin, Both Now & Then
But What If?
Teen and adult. $8.50 per book plus shipping.
Earthen Vessel Productions, 9781 Point Lakeview Rd., Suite 3, Kelseyville, CA 95451.
Orders: (800) 233-6367.
inquiries: (707) 277-7087.
Fax: (707) 277-7088.

Launch to Discovery: In Search of Authentic Christianity features Dean Jones and explores the historic accuracy of the Bible, the true identity of Jesus Christ, how archeology supports the Scripture, the scientific accuracy of the Old Testament, the origin of the Bible, and why it is logical to accept the claims of Christ.

It struck me while viewing this tape that if your high schooler would find it beneficial, that would mean only one thing: you and your church have been asleep on the job. However, you might want to consider adding this to your video collection to use as a witnessing tool or to share with new believers. *Rebecca Prewett*

Standard's own **Standard Bible Atlas** is excellent for an adult reference and for teaching teens. Its 35 full-color maps, while not simplified enough to be used with young children, vividly present a lot of information. You get extras, such as Bible chronologies and cross-sections of Solomon's Temple, that make understanding the Bible much easier. *Mary Pride*

Standard Publishing has a nice series of **Bible maps and charts**. They come in huge illustrated paper packets and unfold to an impressive size. You will not want to permanently affix these to a wall, as they are printed on both sides. They fit great on even the smallest size bulletin board available from your local teacher's store. **Old Testament Maps and Charts** includes eight maps, from the Old Testament world and the Exodus to the Persian Empire, and four charts. The latter includes a view of the Tabernacle and its furniture, a simple Kings-and-Prophets timeline, a chronology of the Judges, and "The Bible Library," a view of the Bible books arranged by division. **New Testament Maps and Charts** has eight maps covering The World in Jesus' Day, with a map showing how Christianity spread in the first century and a map showing modern Palestine with Bible place names next to the modern names. Paul's journeys are covered in separate maps for the First/Second Journey and Third Journey. It also includes a historical chart, a view of Herod's Temple, a chart with proofs of the Resurrection, and "The Bible Library." **Acts Map and Chart** includes one map of all Paul's journeys and a chronology of Acts. All the maps in this series are colorful and contain just the important places and boundaries that everyone should know. *Mary Pride*

When you think of archaeology, do you think of: (a) imaginatively constructed dinosaurs collecting dust in a museum? (b) a bunch of sweaty graduate students brushing off shards of pottery in the hot sun? or (c) Indiana Jones?

Randall Price, with doctorates from both Dallas Theological Seminary and the University of Texas at Austin, does not fit any of the above definitions. Instead, he is committed to demonstrating in his book **The Stones Cry Out** that the archaeological record confirms the truths of the Bible.

Price is passionate about his subject matter. He writes, "Archaeology brings forth the tangible remnants of history so that faith can have a reasonable context in which to develop. It also allows faith to be supported with facts, confirming the reality of the people and events of the Bible so that skeptics and saints might clearly perceive its spiritual message within a historical context."

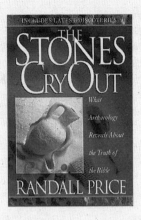

The book begins with a short introduction to biblical archaeology from a maximalist (literal interpretation/high view of Scripture) position.

The meat of the book is found in Price's 11 chapters. You'll visit some of the biggest controversies in biblical archaeology, including Sodom and Gomorrah, King David, the Dead Sea Scrolls, and the Exodus. For example, Price notes the exodus of the Jews from Egypt has left virtually no trace in the desert sands. Many people over the years have wondered, in light of vast number of people involved, why there was not any sort of archaeological proof that this journey actually took place. Price tackles the subject both analytically (the Egyptians *never* left records of any of their military defeats, plus people on a 40-year journey were going to use and re-use every item they had with them) and scientifically (satellite findings, volcanic records, and grain seeds).

Each chapter of this 437-page softcover ends with an application to our faith today. A wonderful study section rounds out the text. Along with a glossary, study notes, maps, and charts, you'll find a listing of museums around the world with biblical archaeology exhibits.

This book is aimed at a popular, not scholarly, audience. Even so, this is not light recreational reading. It is, however, an excellent introduction to biblical archaeology for your older high school student, or for you, written by a man who can see the shape of his faith in the pieces of the past. *Michelle Van Loon*

Hey guys, it's the Tower of "BAY buhl". . . not "BA buhl"!

It is true that not everyone cares about correct pronunciation, but I can still see many reasons for investing in this 167-page hardcover reference book written by W. Murray Severance. Consider how you encourage your children to aspire to accuracy in all things. Think of the confidence you would have, when speaking of Esther, if you knew that you were pronouncing Ahasuerus correctly. Look to the future when your son is a pastor and . . . Okay, I'll stop.

That's Easy for You to Say provides correct pronunciations for Old and New Testament names, archeological terms, names found on contemporary maps of the Middle East, weights, measures, kings, and the Hebrew calendar. The author forgoes the use of diacritical marks, which few people understand, in favor of spelling the word the way you should pronounce it and capitalizing the accented syllable (i.e., Elohim = EL oh heem)

While this book is by no means a necessity, it would be a tremendous addition to your reference library. *Tammy Cardwell*

This Bible memory plan, developed by evangelist Jerry Sivnksty (yes, that's how he spells his name), comes in four topical booklets, each with 130 Bible verses.

The booklets in **Two-Edged Sword Memory Program** are completely independent of each other. Booklet 1 has verses for daily living, booklet 2 has verses about character traits, booklet 3 is for Bible doctrine, and booklet 4 has verses about Christian family life. Each booklet has 26 subjects, with five verses in each subject.

If you are using the plan at home, the author suggests that you memorize verses during 26 weeks of the year and review or meditate upon them for the remaining 26. Naturally, he means that you would learn verses one week and review them the next, not that you would take half a year off from Bible memory!

Verses are well chosen, and the booklets include little boxes where you can check off your reviewing. Verses are supposed to be reviewed daily for five days, then monthly thereafter. All verses are from the King James Version. *Mary Pride*

If you have ever squirmed through a hideous Hollywood production of the life of Christ, with the man Jesus either a wimp or almost a statue chanting sound bites that twist the Scriptures, you'll find these interpretations refreshing. Bruce Marchiano joyfully acts the part of Jesus in this **Gospel According to Matthew**, with cameos in **Acts**. If film portrayals of Jesus do not violate your convictions, these videos will richly enhance your understanding of two books of the Bible.

The **Visual Bible series** has begun with these films the awesome task of presenting the entire Bible (NIV) in a word-for-word format that seeks to capture the truth of Scripture as faithfully as possible. Because the Word is beyond total comprehension by man and no actor can reproduce all that is meant in a particular passage, these videos will necessarily miss the mark time and again, but moments like Bruce Marchiano's take on the Sermon on the Mount are worth contemplation.

Have you ever considered the sight gags in Matthew 5–7, like a man pulling a log out of his own eye to see a speck in his brother's? Or the sober drama of Jesus telling a live crowd what it means to turn a cheek or give up a cloak? With simple outdoor and antique sets and with very few special effects, Richard Kiley's Matthew narrates as he dictates to scribes from his own home years after the Resurrection. We see onscreen chapter and verse captions as Jesus speaks with familiarity among the disciples and with heartfelt sorrow when he addresses the lost sheep of Israel. Marchiano's Jesus grins and hugs a bit too much for my family's taste, but he reminds us, too, of times when Jesus must have grinned!

The Acts video series is, like Matthew, presented in four cassettes of about an hour apiece but has a different flavor. There are no chapter/verse captions, the editing is a bit off, and it just doesn't have quite the polish of Matthew. The spareness, though, and large cast of characters help keep our minds on God's words and not on the actors onscreen. James Brolin's Peter must make bigger speeches and thus is an improvement over the quirky Peter in Matthew, but something smacks of "hokey" in Acts' blond angels in bedsheet robes who in Matthew remained off screen as voices. The production weaknesses in Acts make it a good choice for the audiocassette dramatization at a quarter the price of the videos.

I do not normally pay much attention to soundtracks, but the half-hour CD from Matthew is restful and stirring at the same time, reminding me almost subliminally of important scenes from the gospel narrative. *Cindy Marsch*

NEW!
The Visual Bible
All ages. Videos, $99.95 each set. Matthew soundtrack: CD, $15.95, audiocassette, $10.95. Acts audio dramatization, $24.95.
Visual Entertainment Incorporated, 9818 Bluebonnet Blvd., Suite B, Baton Rouge, LA 70810. (888) 387-2200. Fax: (888) 822-0329. Web: www.visualbible.com.

The **Westminster Shorter Catechism** has been a classic description of Christian belief for over 370 years now. Far richer in its theological detail than the Westminster Catechism for Young Children, it covers God, man, civil government, worship, sacraments, the 10 Commandments, the Lord's Prayer, and other essential issues.

In this book, professional cartoonist Vic Lockman has illustrated the meaning of each question and answer in the Shorter Catechism, along with explanations of the Bible background behind each question and application of what it means to us today. For example, in regard to Question 4, "What is God?" the answer is, "God is a spirit, infinite, eternal and unchangeable in his being, wisdom, power, holiness, justice, goodness, and truth." Each of these godly traits is then explained in text and cartoons. Looking for the moment at "holiness," Mr.

NEW!
The Westminster Shorter Catechism with Cartoons
Grade 5–adult. $19.95 plus $2 shipping.
Vic Lockman, 233 Rogue River Highway #360, Grants Pass, OR 97527. Fax: (541) 479-3814.

Lockman chooses to contrast false holiness (which he depicts as escapism, in the form of a cartoon of a man with a wire halo trying to flap his way up into heaven, while saying, "The world is the devil's. Away with me!") with true holiness (a cartoon of a young man reading the Bible, captioned "Set apart from sin to serve a holy God").

Throughout the book's 140 oversized pages, this technique of cartoon caricatures and other visuals are mixed with captions and explanations to make the catechism clear to good readers of all ages. Although children as young as nine or ten might be able to read the words—and can enjoy the cartoons—for best results, I suggest you use it with junior-high and older students. *Mary Pride*

NEW!
Where's That Found?
All ages. $8 plus shipping.
Daniel S. Dow, 4912 60th Street, Lubbock, TX 70414. (806) 788-0862. Email: ddow@odsy.net.

Where's That Found? The New Testament Memory Cards are small booklets designed to help people of all ages learn Bible facts. Basic drawings make the facts more visual. For example:

- The Bible book of Matthew covers the life of Jesus from his birth to his resurrection. The illustration: a baby with an arrow pointing towards a tomb.
- The book of Matthew was written to the Jews. The illustration: a Star of David with the number two in the middle.
- The book of Matthew emphasizes the fulfillment of prophecy. Illustration: a basket filled with the word "prophecy."
- Through the fulfillment of prophecy, the book of Matthew emphasizes Jesus' kingship and His spiritual kingdom. Illustration: a crown.
- Matthew was a tax collector. Illustration: A bag with the word "tax."
- Matthew has 28 chapters. Illustration: the number 28.

For children who need visual aids to remember, *Where's That Found* makes the facts easier to learn. The graphics are very basic, but the author suggests making copies and coloring them to enhance the pictures. I really appreciate anyone who willingly encourages users to copy the material instead of being interested in making money for extra copies. *Kathy Goebel*

World's Greatest Stories
All ages $6.95 each plus $1.50 shipping. Entire set (5 tapes) $29.75 plus $5 shipping.
World's Greatest Stories, PO Box 711, Monroe, CT 06468. (888) STORIES. (203) 459-4554. Fax: (203) 459-0807. Email: georgesarris@juno.com. Web: www.greateststories.com.

Give a listen to the great series of **The World's Greatest Stories** from the World's Greatest Book! The five volumes available in this audiocassette series are *The Prophets*, *The Life of Christ*, *Beginnings*, *Joshua and Esther*, and *Joseph and His Brothers*. On the *Beginnings* tape, for example, professional actor George Sarris brings the Bible stories of "In the Beginning," "A Lame Man at Lystra," "A Jailer in Philippi," "The Story of Ruth," and "The Raising of Lazarus" to life, using only his voice, background music, and sound effects. Every word on these tapes, except for an extremely brief intro and closing, is taken straight from the Bible (your choice of KJV or NIV). *Mary Pride*

CHAPTER 5

Character Education

The point of character education is to raise nonconformists. If we want our children to give in to peer pressure, all we have to do is leave them alone.

Character education teaches the difference between right and wrong. How should we act under various forms of pressure? That's also what character education is all about.

Today, three codes of conduct are warring for the hearts and minds of young people everywhere:

- **Code of Righteousness.** The goal here is to please God. One who follows the code can be called a *saint.*
- **Code of Honor.** The goal here is to earn the respect of yourself and others. If the others are unworthy, then the goal is simple self-respect. One who follows the code can be called a *hero.*
- **Code of Psychology.** The goal here is to fight off guilt feelings and feelings of inadequacy by forcing others to endorse and assist you. One who follows the code can be called a *victim/bully* (he considers himself a victim, but acts like a bully).

Libertarian Ayn Rand complained in her various books that the Christian church had exalted weakness to a virtue, enabling the undeserving and deliberately helpless to bully the productive and strong. Rand had a point, but actually biblical Christianity was not the culprit here. Liberal Christianity, the parent of today's political correctness, around the turn of the century abandoned biblical standards of right and wrong for the new psychological goal of personal happiness and freedom from guilt feelings. According to the liberal Social Gospel, the church was to blame for any unhappiness in the world. Under these conditions, those who used to be

Murder Made Attractive . . . In Children's Books

All those movies and TV shows made it look hard, risky. TV murderers always had such remorse

No one ever said how easy it is to kill someone.

Or how exciting.

—*from* Beach House *by R. L. Stine (New York, Scholastic Inc., 1992)*

The Value of Fake Praise

"You! I've just awarded you the prize for the hundred-meter dash. Does it make you happy?"

"Uh, I suppose it would."

"No dodging, please. you have the prize—here, I'll write it out: 'Grand prize for the championship, one hundred-meter sprint.'" He had actually come back to my seat and pinned it on my chest. "There! Are you happy? You value it—or don't you?"

I ripped it off and chucked it at him.

Mr. Dubois had looked surprised. "It doesn't make you happy?"

"You know darn well I placed fourth!"

"Exactly! The prize for first place is worthless to you . . . because you haven't earned it. But you enjoy a modest satisfaction in placing fourth; you earned it."

—*Robert A. Heinlein,*
Starship Troopers

called "sinners" now were poor unhappy wretches who deserved whatever help was necessary to lift them out of their pit of suffering. Personal responsibility vanished from view under this doctrine. So did any meaningful kind of character education, because who needs character if you can get further ahead by misbehaving and then whining about it?

Assuming I have convinced you that there is no benefit in persuading your children that their behavior is all someone else's fault (probably yours since you are the parent), that leaves the Code of Righteousness and the Code of Honor.

Star Trek fans will understand when I say that the Code of Honor is basically a Klingon code. Since it is based on the drive for respect, those who operate by this code can't ignore a personal insult. They must perpetually maintain their honor by fighting for it. The Code of Honor, while superficially attractive, perpetuates needless violence. Gang members today operate by some twisted variety of a code of honor. So did the South before the Civil War. I am convinced this is one of the main reasons the South lost the Civil War. Fighting for honor is directly at odds with the doctrine of forgiveness, and he who does not forgive those who trespass against him will not have his trespasses forgiven by God Almighty.

The Code of Righteousness only works if you properly understand what pleases God. In the case of Christians, this takes us right back to studying the Bible. Regardless of how the media today like to demonize Bible believers, even a superficial reading of the Bible tells us that loving your neighbor as much as you love yourself is Bible's main point when it comes to human relationships. According to the Bible's code of righteousness, "It is to a man's glory to overlook an offense." You don't have to fight someone just because he insulted you. Feuding and gossiping are not recommended by the Bible. Kindness, honestly, loyalty, faithfulness, care for the young and the deserving poor, and respect for the elderly are stressed. I think it's fair to say that most people still agree that this is a desirable list of virtues.

Why Can't Today's School and Church Teach Character?

William Kilpatrick's **Why Johnny Can't Tell Right from Wrong** is an excellent study on morality and education. In addition to exposing current problems and giving a history of morality in Western thought, Dr. Kilpatrick contrasts the modern values clarification and moral reasoning philosophies with the older character education models. The new methods depend on either feelings or abstract reasoning, both based on faith in the basic goodness of man. Since the premise is wrong, neither system works.

The bottom line of the book is that man is not basically good—men generally do not have the will to do what they know is right. And children are no exception. Kilpatrick contends correctly that a child must be trained in good moral character as a habit.

He asserts that stories and music are necessary for this training; stories give life meaning and provide good examples. An annotated book list is included. In the chapter "Music and Morality," he quotes Alan Bloom and Plato on the effects of music on the passions and argues that the problem with rock and rap is the beat itself. Parents and teens should read this chapter to clarify their thinking on the nature and uses of music, especially Christian rock. (Some chapters, due to existing conditions in the schools which are described, are not recommended teen reading.)

Homeschoolers can benefit from knowing the historical background of and arguments for character education. In addition, the chapters on stories are of both theoretical and practical use. *Charles & Betty Burger*

Until the mid-'60s or '70s there may have been disagreement about precisely *what* is right and wrong, but there seemed to be general agreement that there is such a thing as right and wrong. Today a quick look at TV or the newspaper shows many people are confused about what is right and wrong, and are reluctant to admit that there even is *any* objective standard of right and wrong.

Regrettably church youth are greatly confused as well. **Right from Wrong**, by Josh McDowell, presents the results of a survey of church youth (for more detail, see the note on the survey in the sidebar). Disturbing findings of this study include:

- 57 percent of the church youth surveyed either disagree, or are not sure, that there is such a thing as "absolute truth"
- 48 percent either agree, or are not sure, that "when it comes to matters of morals and ethics, truth means different things to different people"

So why should a homeschool parent be concerned? Our children have the Ten Commandments posted on the walls of their rooms. Our children memorize scripture. Our children know the difference between right and wrong, don't they?

Well, that is a big assumption. This book will provide a helpful context for homeschool parents to use in assessing how their kids are doing. Read it with your children, and use it as a way to open discussion.

Although McDowell hyperventilates slightly while making his points ("in the past three months . . . 66 percent of our kids . . . lied to a parent, teacher, or other adult"— this reviewer would have guessed the true figure to be more like 99 percent, and at least two-thirds of the kids admitted it), the findings are sobering, the recommendations for instructing our children are useful, and when you're finished with the book you can pass it along to the family at church whose kids are always telling yours what's on MTV.

The complete text of the survey, responses to each question, and a detailed analysis are presented in the final four chapters of the book, after the main text of the book concludes. This alone is worth the price of the book. *John Nixdorf*

Character Curriculum

Should character traits be "caught" or "taught"? Why not both? See what's available in character training at the young adult level below.

The spiral-bound **Christian Leadership** volume contains advanced character education, or preparation for adulthood. For example, rather than a more typical approach to self-discipline, the young person will work through student exercises, personal evaluations, Bible study, and goal-setting activities that will help him or her not only grow in self-discipline but also in leadership qualities. There are chapters titled "Leading in Being Unselfish," "Leading in Being a Godly Friend," "Leading in Outward Appearance," etc.—22 chapters in all.

I like the premise behind this approach: that young people should learn to lead others by their own godly examples. This is a refreshing and thoroughly Biblical approach that could be of great value to homeschools and youth groups. It could even be adapted for use with adults, although many of the examples pertain to more youthful situations. (I hope that, in the future, Plain Path Publishers will modify these materials or create others to

NEW!
Right from Wrong
Grade 8–adult. Paperback, $14.99. Hardcover, $19.99. Shipping extra. *Word Publishing. Generally available at Christian bookstores, ISBN 0-8499-36047 (paper), ISBN 0-8499-1079X (hardcover). PO Box 141000, Nashville, TN 37214. (800) 933-9673 ext. 92039. Fax: (615) 902-2450. Web: www.nelsonword.com.*

A NOTE ON THE SURVEY: The research was a statistically valid 1994 survey of church youth conducted by the Barna Research Group. This survey contained responses from 3,795 youth from thirteen denominations. These are what could be called "typical, good, church kids:"

- 73 percent are A or B students
- 73 percent live with their natural father and mother
- 86 percent have "made a personal commitment to Jesus Christ that is still important in your life today"
- 64 percent agree that the Christian faith is very important in their lives today

NEW!
Christian Leadership
Grades 7–12. Student Guide, $14. Teacher's Guide, $8. Add $3 shipping.
Plain Path Publishers, PO Box 830, Columbus, NC 28722. (828) 863-2736. Email: plain@juno.com

be used in discipleship programs and training for church leadership positions.)

I appreciated the reverent tone and the complete lack of condescension. I also appreciated suggested goals, for both the future and the present, such as, "I am determined that I will speak often about God's word to my own children" and "I will learn all that I can about the Lord so that I can easily speak about Him from the 'abundance of my heart.'" Also, I liked the thought-provoking questions: "How can I prepare now to become a parent who is obedient to Deuteronomy 6: 6–7?" "What are some spiritual things that Christian young people could talk about together?"

If you are discipling young adults, these materials are worth considering. *Rebecca Prewett*

The innovative and appealing **Conscience** game is meant to help young people and teens see the consequences of right and wrong actions. Unlike "decision-making" games, you don't get to choose which action you take. Rather, a roll of the dice (one positive die and one negative die) determines whether you follow the wrong path or the right one. Follow the wrong path long enough and you end up in the principal's office, the detention center, jail, or the morgue. Your goal is to be the first player to collect six gold stars (for good behavior) and one complete set of Right cards before collecting three black marks.

The gameboard is divided into six zones: Character, Charity, Crime, Drugs, Education, and Violence. An optional Sex zone (for teaching the benefits of abstinence) can be placed on the board on top of your choice of the Crime, Drugs, Charity, or Violence zones, when playing the game with older children.

Here's an example of how this works. Say you're in the Drug zone. The squares on the "Drug-Free" path are titled Respect Yourself, Don't Experiment, Avoid Druggies, Keep a Healthy Body, and Collect a Gold Star. There are two wrong paths. Contemplate Suicide, Opportunity Knocks, and Become Addicted are one path. The other path takes you through Deal Drugs, Opportunity Knocks, Experiment with Drugs, Associate with Druggies, Abuse Alcohol, and Start Smoking. The Opportunity Knocks card you draw when you land on that spot *may* give you a "second chance" to turn around your misbehaving ways. Regardless, you pick up a black mark and go to the penalty area if you follow the wrong path to its conclusion.

Conscience Check cards help you pick your direction. The Right cards, each of which correspond to one of the "good" squares on the board, are dealt out at the beginning. You have to get a set of four of the same color to win.

The Education zone is not homeschool-oriented. Wrong choices include Late for School, Skip School, Act Up in Class, and Don't Graduate. If you'd like to make your own Homeschool Zone overlay, try changing these to Hide Your Books, Pretend You Don't Understand, Lose Your Pencils, and Play Computer Games When You're Supposed to be Using the Expensive Educational Software We Bought You. OK, that last one was a bit long to fit on a square. But you get the idea!

Keep in mind that *Conscience* is a secular game. Pray, Trust in the Lord, and Obey the Bible are not options in this game. However, you can easily point out that it's not enough just to know right from wrong; you have to know *why* right is right and *how* to get the strength to do it. Here's where *Conscience* leaves off and the Bible comes in!

While you're playing the game, you'll learn to just hate following the wrong path. Whether this will translate into better behavior depends on how well you use this game—and all your other daily time with your children—to teach about these topics. *Mary Pride*

Only a few generations ago, Americans had vastly different hopes and expectations for their children. Take **Gaining Favor with God and Man**, for instance. Written in 1893, the book instructs children in such character traits as perseverance, self-reliance, industry, and self-control by means of true stories from the lives of successful men and women of that time and earlier. The young reader is exhorted in the best New England Yankee style to become successful by diligently making himself useful in his calling, forsaking evil companions and the society of buffoons, and improving himself by self-education. Christian piety is strongly urged in many places as the self-evident foundation of both public and eternal success.

The book is written in a lively, earnest style. Here's a snippet:

> *A young man became a clerk in a large warehouse of a New England city. After having served several months acceptably he hinted to his employer that he ought to be paid as much as a certain other clerk received.*
>
> *"If you will do what he does, you shall be paid as much," replied his employer.*
>
> *"And what is that?" the young man inquired.*
>
> *"He takes customers to the theatre, and gives them a drink occasionally, that he may sell them a bill of goods."*
>
> *Straightening himself up to his full height, and with the fire of indignation flashing in his eyes, our young hero answered, "I thank God that there is a poor-house in my native town, and I will go there and die before I shall do such dirty work," and he left the store. That was principle.*

Can't you just see the young Jimmy Stewart in the role, eyes flashing, denouncing the scalawags who want him to fleece a customer?

Principle can get you a job as well as lose you one, too, as the next excerpt shows:

> *Nicholas Biddle, president of the first United States Bank, found so much work on hand, at one time, that he asked a portion of his employees to work a few hours on the Sabbath. All but one consented; this one said, "I cannot conscientiously labor on the Sabbath."*
>
> *"Then you must give up your place to some one who will," answered Biddle.*
>
> *"Very well, I resign," said the young man, and withdrew. That was principle.*
>
> *The following day a gentleman waited upon Biddle, saying, "I want a perfectly reliable private secretary, to whom I am obliged to commit great trusts. Can you tell me of one?"*
>
> *"Yes," Biddle promptly answered. "I dismissed a young man yesterday because he would not work on the Sabbath. He has principle enough for you."*

Not only Nicholas Biddle, but also historic luminaries such as George Washington, Abraham Lincoln, John Bunyan, and Edward Burke are represented within the 400-plus gilt-edged pages of this hardbound book.

Gaining Favor with God and Man

Grade 7–adult. $18 plus $4 shipping. *Mantle Ministries, 228 Still Ridge, Bulverde, TX 78163. (877) 548-2327. (830) 438-3777. Fax: (830) 438-3370. Email: mantle3377@aol.com. Web: www.mantlemin.com.*

NEW!
Leaders in Action series

Grades 9-adult. Each book, $14.95. Shipping extra.
Cumberland House Publishing, 431 Harding Industrial Dr., Nashville, TN 37211. (888)439-2665. Fax: (800)254-6716. Email: Cumbhouse@aol.com.

Forgotten heroes like Elihu Burritt, the blacksmith who taught himself classical languages and philosophy while working the forge, and the humble manufacturer of Rising Sun stove polish, who began his industrial empire by selling the product door to door out of a carpet bag, parade through the pages of this book side by side with the Andrew Carnegies and Sir Walter Raleighs. Rich but selfish John Jacob Astor, idle Samuel Coleridge, and foolish Marie Antoinette are held up, along with scores of others, as warnings of how wealth, talent, and beauty alone are not enough to secure the esteem of our fellow man and the benediction of God in heaven.

For a mind-blowing experiment, try reading *People* magazine and *Gaining Favor with God and Man* on the same day. Everything in one contradicts the other. *Inc.* comes a little closer to it, with its exaltation of hard work, perseverance, and upward mobility, but loses out in the personal piety and humility department. Even *Moody Magazine* doesn't come close to the confident I-know-what's-right-and-wrong outlook of *Gaining Favor with God and Man.* (Dwight L. Moody himself gets favorable mention in the book, by the way).

The book does include a fair number of examples of Yankee do-goodism and anti-clannishness masquerading as disinterested philanthropy, as is inevitable. From Emerson and Louisa May Alcott on down, Yankees have been very fond of busybodies. (I was raised in Yankee New England, just outside of Boston, by the way!) The difference is that today the Yankee soul is dedicated to Save the Whales and Feed the Hungry, not Feed the Souls and Save the Hungry, as in times past. *Mary Pride*

"What is it exactly that makes a man a great leader? What constitutes genuine leadership? What character traits are necessary to steer men and nations in the way they should go?...These are particularly relevant questions in this difficult day of profound leaderlessness. There can be little doubt that we are the most over-managed yet under-led generation in recent memory—thus, our great imperious task is to somehow buck the trend and wrestle with such questions." So reads the forward to *Not A Tame Lion: The Spiritual Legacy of C.S. Lewis.* This is just one in Cumberland House's series of biographies about great leaders. Edited by George Grant, each biography in the **Leaders in Action series** is authored by a Christian writer both knowledgeable and passionate about his subject matter.

The five books published in the series so far cover Patrick Henry, Theodore Roosevelt, Robert E. Lee, Winston Churchill, and C.S. Lewis. Each book follows the same format. Part 1 is a chronological biography, with emphasis on both the spiritual development and leadership challenges that each man faced. Part 2 are short essays on different facets of the man's life, specifically relating to character. For instance, *Call of Duty,* the biography of Robert E. Lee, has thirty-one 3–5 page essays in this section combining direct quotes from him, along with analysis on each topic by author J. Steven Wilkins. Topics include Duty, Courage, Morale, Politics, Race Relations, Humor and more. You could easily use the short chapters from this section for reading, study, or inspiration separate from the rest of the book. Each one stands on its own. Part 3 is a look at the legacy of each man. This brief section includes a look at each man's accomplishments, some closing thoughts on their lives, a bibliography, endnotes, and the ribbon that ties each package together, plus a short listing called The Lessons of Leadership. This distills the leadership lessons that you can take away from your study of each man's life.

The format of these books make them perfect for both adults without a lot of free time to devote to reading, and for teens who are looking for a different slant on the basic biography, one that lets them crawl into the heads and hearts of the subject matter. The message of the series (faith creates character, character develops leaders worth following) is one that can't be repeated often enough today. The leadership/character lens is a wonderful one through which to examine the lives of these great men. George Grant has done an admirable job shaping this diverse material into a superb series. *Michelle Van Loon*

Sharon Scott, author of the books below, spent seven years with the Dallas Police Department as director of the First Offender Program. Working with "thousands of young people between the ages of 10 and 16 who had made such poor decisions that they had actually broken a law and been taken into custody (arrested)" she "began seeing that the number-one reason why kids were making bad decisions, including breaking laws, was because they did not know what to say to their friends when begged, bribed, dared, or challenged." It's easy to "Just Say No!" to some creepy guy hanging around the schoolyard, but not so easy to say no to your boyfriend, girlfriend, best friend, or the popular kids in school.

Sharon took this as a challenge to train teens in *positive* peer group techniques and peer pressure *reversal* techniques. So far she has trained over one million kids and adults in these techniques, and written several books, which have garnered endorsements from such sources as the Boy Scouts of America, the U.S. Department of Education, and the National Federation of Parents.

Mrs. Scott's **Positive Peer Groups** book gives instructions in how to set up a positive peer group program in your school. This book doesn't really apply to the home situation, but may be of interest to those of you with school connections. **When to Say Yes and Make More Friends** likewise is advice for kids on how to reach out and make good friends in school. The kids who most need this advice tend to be from broken or otherwise messed-up homes, as is evident by the case histories given.

The second edition of **Peer Pressure Reversal: An Adult Guide to Developing a Responsible Child**, a larger book, explains the Peer Pressure Reversal philosophy to parents and explains how to teach it to the kids, again by role-playing a number of situations. This takes 90-odd pages of the book. Section Four of the book has reinforcement suggestions ranging from the usual behavior modification techniques (positive reinforcement for encouragement and, for discipline, deprivation of privileges) to organized family activities and influencing the child's circle of friends.

Of interest to just about everyone is **How to Say No and Keep Your Friends** (now in its second edition) a book with the same message, but directed to teen and preteen readers. Mrs. Scott's philosophy is, "You can say no to trouble *and* be liked." The book's introduction provides statistics of how many teens get in trouble today and true examples of kids who messed up and then were introduced to her Peer Pressure Reversal system. The system includes these steps: Check Out the Scene (look and listen, ask yourself "Is this trouble?"), Make a Good Decision (think of the consequences on both sides and take action), and Act to Avoid Trouble (what to say and how to say it). This gets really specific. I'll list her 10 peer pressure reversal responses:

1. Simply say no
2. Leave
3. Ignore the peer(s)
4. Make an excuse
5. Change the subject
6. Make a joke
7. Act shocked
8. Use flattery
9. Suggest a better idea
10. Return the challenge

Sharon Scott's Peer Pressure Reversal Books
Grades 4–12.. Peer Pressure Reversal and Positive Peer Groups, $14.95 each. How to Say No and Keep Your Friends / How to Say Yes and Make Friends, $11.95 each. Package price for all four books (the "Teen Empowerment Collection"), $39.95. Shipping extra.
Human Resource Development Press, 22 Amherst Rd., Amherst, MA 01002.
Orders: (800) 822-2801.
Inquiries: (413) 253-3488.
Fax: (413) 253-3490.
Email: orders@hrdpress.com.
Web: www.hrdpress.com.

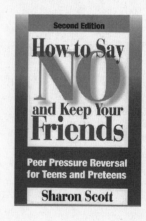

Each one of these responses is presented in detail, with cartoon illustrations, examples, and suggestions. Example (under Return the Challenge):

> *When a friend says, "I thought you were my friend. If you were, you'd do this with me," you can use one of several comebacks:*
>
> *"I am your friend; and that's why I'm not going to do this with you."*
>
> *"If you were my friend, then you'd get off my back when I say no."*
>
> *"With friends like you, who needs enemies? Stop trying to get me in trouble!"*
>
> *"Best friends don't try to boss each other around. Please let me do my own thinking."*
>
> *If your friend is being really unkind and pushy, a stinger zinger is: "Who said you were my friend?" (You can soften it, if desired, by laughing.)*

Learn other valuable techniques, such as the Thirty Second Rule (start trying to get out of the situation within thirty seconds or less) and the Two No Rule (never say no more than twice before leaving or changing the subject). This all takes practice, so the book provides numerous role-playing situations for kids to exercise their new skills.

Aside from the assumption that your child will be dating, the only area I really disagree with the author is her belief that *all* jealousy is wrong. Since God Himself is a jealous God, this can't be right. However, she's talking about overcontrolling girlfriends and boyfriends, who have made no marital commitment. With this in mind, her cautions are correct.

Your child *will* face peer pressure sooner or later—even while living at home, if he has friends from outside the family. *How to Say No* provides the tools needed to resist peer pressure with style. Kids are unlikely to discover such tools on their own. Since the consequences of giving into peer pressure today range from date rape to car accidents to drug addiction to an arrest record, this is nothing to fool around with. I heartily recommend this book to every parent. *Mary Pride*

PART 3

Language Arts

Homeschoolers Tyler (12) and Chad (10) Hollenbach of Newark, Delaware, published a weekly newsletter named CANAL WEEKLY for their summer baseball league. Each edition included a write-up on each of the ten games played that week, special features, and advertisements the boys sold and designed themselves. For all their hard work, the boys got a tremendous amount of praise and made $400 after paying their expenses.

Like most other homeschoolers, Misty Henson from Wichita, KA, loves to read. She also loves to write. What began with journal entries culminated in a published book, Secret Jealousy, when Misty was 15. It is the first in a planned series of detective stories for young readers.

CHAPTER 6

Junior & Senior High English

English courses in junior high are mostly concerned with grammar, spelling and vocabulary, note-taking, and reading from a variety of literary genres. High school English courses tend to have more writing assignments. They usually include a full year of American Literature and (choose one) British, European, or World Literature.

Many homeschoolers prefer to study these subjects separately. That's why you'll find separate chapters in this section devoted to grammar, literature, speech, and spelling and vocabulary. The advantage is that, once your student has mastered grammar and spelling to your satisfaction, he doesn't have to keep swimming the same weary laps year after year.

Still, some prefer the all-in-one-place handiness of an integrated English course. These are available from most major homeschool curriculum publishers. You'll find one such popular program below, as well as a unique "total language arts" program that is also quite popular.

Most colleges require four full years of high-school English as an entrance requirement. A year of Literature usually is considered a year of English, but only if the Lit course includes some writing assignments.

English Courses

Alpha Omega's Language-Arts LIFEPACs feature a worktext approach to composition. All forms of writing are covered, including some secular tales, and analyzed from a Christian perspective. The series emphasizes creative thinking, and (unlike some others) actually gets the student writing a goodly number of compositions.

Alpha Omega Language-Arts LIFEPACs

Grades 1–12. 10 LIFEPACs per grade. LIFEPACs: $3.50 each (Grades 1–10), $2.95 each (grades 11–12). Set of 10, $28.50 and up. Teacher's guides and answer keys extra. Books available for literature component of courses: The Hiding Place, $6.50 (grade 7); The Miracle Worker, $5.50; 20,000 Leagues Under the Sea, $4.95 (grade 9); In His Steps, $6.95 (grade 10); Our Town, $8.95; The Old Man and the Sea, $8.95 (grade 11); Hamlet, $3.99 (grade 12). Shipping extra.
Alpha Omega Publications, 300 N. McKemy, Chandler, AZ 85226.
Orders and inquiries: (800) 622-3070.
Fax: (480) 785-8034.
Web: www.home-schooling.com.

The organization of the courses is a mishmash, with grammar, usage, speaking, and writing mixed in with literature studies in no apparent order. I can understand why courses for schoolchildren keep repeating grammar and usage lessons grade after grade, since you can never be sure what the child was taught in his previous school. However, at home it's much more effective to study grammar separately and get it over with. Therefore, home schoolers might prefer to pick through these courses on a LIFEPAC by LIFEPAC basis, skipping the grammar and usage units and subunits (which merely interrupt the courses) and concentrating on the excellent literature, composition, and research units.

If you want to do this, it's best to get a copy of the Alpha Omega scope and sequence, which tells you exactly which LIFEPAC covers which subject. I have tried to highlight some of the more successful LIFEPACs below, as well as give you an idea of the basic structure of each grade's language-arts course.

In **grade 7**, students start off with a review of nouns, pronouns, and other basics. Speaking and listening skills come next, followed by a unit on biographies and one on sentence structure. Then come units on the "nature, structure, and usage of English" and some rinky-dink review, including simple stuff like punctuation and capitalization. The next unit is a study of Corrie ten Boom's book, *The Hiding Place*, about her experiences growing up in Holland, hiding Jews during the Nazi occupation, living in a concentration camp, and rebuilding her life around a new ministry afterwards. Then it's back to non-fiction literature, "learning to listen," and "speaking with gestures," all in the same unit. Finally, you work on writing sentences and paragraphs and pronouncing words correctly.

Grade 8 starts more usefully, with instructions in how to get more out of your reading and how to take notes, among other things. Grammar and usage are woven throughout this entire course, mixed into units on other topics, so I won't bother listing all the numerous places where they appear. Briefly, what you get is an introduction to word-study tools (dictionary and thesaurus), biblical standards for your speech, and critical reading skills. New literary genres studied are essays and autobiography. Composition skills include writing short essays and making an oral report. It's not organized this plainly, unfortunately: a typical unit includes the history of the English language, sentence construction, spelling exercises, and elements of an autobiography!

Grade 9 starts, as usual, with a grammar and usage review, and progresses to reviewing much of the new matter taught in grade 8 (dictionary use, history of languages, etc.). Students also learn about using visual aids in both writing and speaking, how to give a speech, and various types of letters. They learn to use the library (we hope this information is not really new to them by now!). You get the idea.

In **grade 10**, once again we are looking at the history of English. This time it's real history, starting with Anglo-Saxon and the Norman invasion of 1066. More info on how to give a speech follows, ditto on how to listen to a speech. More on writing sentences, grammar (gerunds, participial phrases, etc.), and ways to use words effectively. More on how to write "expository compositions," more on grammar and reading skills.

The first four units of **grade 11** are all skippable, being yet more grammar and usage review, and even review of how to use a dictionary (normally taught in grades 3–6), for goodness sake! LIFEPAC 9 is the most useful of all, being on the topic of research—how to do it, formulating your thesis statement, using the library, preparing a bibliography, taking notes, stating your thesis, outlining the paper, writing the paper and the footnotes, and putting it all together. I see no particular reason why you shouldn't purchase this LIFEPAC separately, for use with younger (seventh-grade and up) students.

The research unit in **grade 12** is LIFEPAC 3, which after a skippable subunit on reading for comprehension has useful information on searching for information in various media (indexes, dictionaries, readers' guides, magazines, directories, and card catalogs) and how to take college-style notes. Grades 9–12 also include quite a bit of literature study. See review in the literature chapter. *Mary Pride*

NEW!
Total Language Plus
Grades 5–12. Student study guides, $16.95 each or 4 for $65 (one year's worth, if you do a book each quarter). Teacher's manual, $3.75. It comes with the study guides. *Blakey Publications, P.O. Box 12622, Olympia, WA 98508. (360) 754-3660. Fax: (360) 754-3505. Email: tlp@integrityol.com. Web: www.integrityol.com/tlp.*

Wouldn't it be nice if teaching language arts were simple? Wouldn't it be nice if someone would figure out a way to keep all the subject areas in one place, centered around one book? Someone has. **Total Language Plus** is a streamlined, efficient curriculum that manages to hit all the language bases and still maintain a literature focus. Spelling, vocabulary, critical thinking, writing, grammar, dictation, reading comprehension, and even some fun projects are all a part of this novel-centered program.

Author Barbara Blakey has written study guides for age levels from fifth grade all the way up to honors high school English. You can plan on finishing one book per quarter, and the guides are conveniently priced in sets of four (you choose the titles, novels not included). Definitely plan on purchasing the teacher's manual. For under $5 you get a thorough overview of the program as well as teaching hints for each of the subject areas. It's well worth it!

First things first: TLP gets an A+ for their well organized and super-informative catalog. Each study guide description includes the overall themes of the novel as well as a heads-up for any possible controversial subject matter. While all the books may not be written from a Christian perspective, all the study guides most certainly are. Each novel has been chosen for its ability to withstand several weeks of study, its literary merit, and its interest to both boys and girls.

Teacher prep time is kept to a minimum. A planning grid in the front of each consumable guide tells you exactly what to cover each day in all the subject areas. An answer key is provided in the back of the book (just tear it out if you'd rather not tempt your student). Although it isn't mandatory that you read the novel being studied, I can't imagine not being able to interact over the subject matter. Moms, read the books!

The advanced high school guides, suitable for college prep courses, are meant to accompany a detailed study of American or British Literature. Each study guide may take up to a semester to complete, but they aren't intended as a full course. In addition to the novels, make sure your child has a good English handbook, dictionary, and thesaurus on hand. The spelling, grammar, and vocabulary portions are still there, but are of course more

How do these compare to other products on the market for home-schoolers? Probably most similar to the Progeny Press study guides (which I also like). However, TLP offers a more cohesively packaged product. If you are strictly looking for literature study, then Progeny Press is always a great choice. But for an all-in-one language package, Total Language is tops.

complex, spending more time on etymologies and word usage. Instead of the "Enrichment" critical thinking portion, there is now a "Communication" worksheet that focuses on the author's writing style, characterization, and literary techniques. Writing assignments are more specific and are of the well-crafted essay type. These studies are challenging and thought-provoking. Moms, you have got to read the books!

The study guides are workbook in format and are well laid out and easy on the eyes. No pictures or color, but an enthusiastic teacher can compensate for that.

About the only thing lacking are instructions for the teacher on how to grade the writing assignments. If you are not comfortable in this area, you won't find a lot of help here. If possible, try to enlist the aid of another homeschool teacher who is proficient in this area, or even find an off-duty English teacher. You also may want to check out Cindy Marsch's Writing Assessment Services for help. It's at *members.aol.com/cmarsch786/index.htm*
Renee Mathis

CHAPTER 7

Phonics for Teens & Adults

I hope you don't need this chapter, but if you do, it's not a big surprise. Lots of kids don't learn to read well, or at all, in public school. The reason, simply stated, is twofold:

(1) For a generation or more, **young schoolteachers-in-training have been taught** in their education classes **that phonics is a bad way to teach reading.** Instead, reading "experts" have convinced them to try a whole flock of untested theories, each a more dismal failure than the last. What these fads have in common is that they do not teach students how to sound out words in any systematic fashion. Deprived of the necessary tools for successful reading, it's hard to learn to read.

(2) **Kids learn in spurts,** and only when they're ready. But public schools are set up to process kids in groups rigidly segregated by age. Boys, who mature on average a year later than girls, are dumped into the same grade with girls who are a year more advanced emotionally. Result: many boys aren't ready to learn to read when the teacher's manual says they should be. Many girls aren't ready at age 5 or 6 either, and they too get labeled "hyperactive" or "ADD" or "dyslexic" when the real problem is the pace of the material.

The solution to both problems above: **phonics!** You *could* use any of the elementary phonics programs reviewed in Volume 2 to jump-start a teem or adult's neglected phonics education. But these programs were designed for young children, and many older students find them embarrassingly childish. That's why you'll find a respectable number of phonics programs designed for teens and adults in this chapter.

These are all good programs that have worked with many students. All you have to do is pick the one that best suits your teen's personality, the

If your preteen or teen can't read well or at all, does he have a *physical* brain-related problem (ADD and its cousins don't count)? If not, don't worry; he *can* learn to read!

ability level of the person who will be teaching (all these programs require a teacher or coach at first), and your budget.

Your teen *will* be able to read well someday soon. All it takes is diligent practice, and one of these fine programs.

Phonics Curriculum

Lockhart Reading Systems (formerly CHAR-L, Inc.) has an excellent intensive phonics program for children that was written up in Volume 2 of the *Big Book of Home Learning*. Her **Adult Phonics Program** is designed for older students with limited reading skills but follows a similar format. You get a 286-page manual (including writing forms, skills tests, and a dictionary of extended skills), along with two 90-minute cassettes, 96 reverse listening cards, test and answer sheets, and a mini-poster. This is a complete reading, spelling, and writing program that provides you with detailed instructions on every step of teaching, even telling you what to say as you write things on the board. First, the student will learn the 42 sounds of the alphabet, as well as how to write each letter, if they do not already know how to do so. Then they will learn blends, digraphs, phonics rules, common sight words, parts of speech, types of sentences, etc. Once this program has been completed, students will be reading and writing—and doing both well.

Who could benefit from this program? Parents who are removing a poor reader from the public schools may want to consider this, as there is absolutely nothing baby-ish or condescending about the program. I personally would like to see churches adopting a ministry of teaching reading to immigrants, public school "failures," and illiterate or marginally literate adults. The wonderful thing about this program is that it can be easily used in either a classroom or tutoring situation. It would be a valuable resource for anyone who wants to help older students become truly literate. *Mary Pride*

"Forty-two million Americans can't read!" the advertisement proclaims, and with that startling figure **The Phonics Game** proceeds to offer a revolutionary multimedia solution, attractively packaged in a customized plastic case.

A warning to first-time users: put aside the game play book, or you may become overwhelmed! Forty-seven pages explain the steps of phonics reading in a methodical, if not complicated, manner. You're better off to first pop the accompanying video in the nearest VCR. This energetic video tape demonstrates game play as well as correct phonics pronunciation. The narrator outlines each game on the video, relegating the playbook the role of reference manual. Don't have a VCR? Then use one of five audio cassettes also included.

Players learn the sound codes—provided on two 8 x 11" cards—and then have the choice of five possible phonics games. Suitable to the single student learning alone, 1–6 players may play each game in the course. The whole-family approach may prove effective, as some parent participation will enforce the success of the lessons.

The Phonics Game succeeds in teaching without boring exercises or repetitive drills. Unmotivated teens may actually learn faster with this multimedia game concept.

The kit includes a money-back guarantee with the credit card purchase of this product, but requires a few stipulations. A disclaimer hastens to point out that younger children will receive the most benefit of this teaching tool, while adults with poor reading skills may require more playing

Lockhart Level IV Adult Intensive Phonics Program

Grade 5 to adult. Parent's/Homeschooler Kit, $178 plus shipping. *Lockhart Reading Systems, Inc., 1370 Big Shanty Rd., Kennesaw, GA 30144. Orders: (800) 501-6767. Inquiries: (770) 428-6796. Fax: (770) 428-2247. Email: info@lockhart-reading.com. Web: www.lockhart-reading.com.*

NEW!
The Phonics Game

Ages 4–adult. $199.95 plus $14.95 shipping. 60-day guarantee. *The Phonics Game, 150 Paularino, Suite 120, Costa Mesa, CA 92626. (888) 792-7323. Fax: (714) 546-1204. Web: www.phonicsgame.com.*

time to reach proficiency. Considering the high cost of the product, the guarantee is admirable. You may return the course within 30 days for a full refund. *Lisa Mitchell*

Monica Foltzer, the author of the *Professor Phonics* phonics program (see the review in Volume 2), has also produced something that every reading instructor should be aware of: an incredibly inexpensive advanced phonics program for the older student. It goes by the name **A Sound Track to Reading** and is deliberately adult in its approach. Quickly reviewing (or, in the case of foreign students, introducing) the basic sounds, Sound Track quickly moves to words and sentences. By the simple device of adding a few common endings like *ing* and *ed* to root words, which older readers can easily learn to do, babyish vocabulary is eliminated from the start. It's inexpensive, too. *Mary Pride*

Starting Over is "a Combined Teaching Manual and Student Textbook for Reading, Writing, Spelling, Vocabulary, and Handwriting." The large (over 300 pages) spiral-bound manual is designed for use with older students and adults who read poorly or are nonreaders, suffer from dyslexia whatever their reading level, or are learning English as a second language.

Joan Knight, the author, has many years of experience in adult basic education and presently serves on the New York board of directors of the Orton Dyslexia Society. The Introduction and Foreword both repeatedly refer to *Starting Over*'s "humanistic approach."

Starting Over begins with a comprehensive battery of pre-tests. The course itself is "programmed"—that is, everything the teacher does or says is spelled out. Student and teacher can use the same book. Each page is labeled as either a teacher's page, a student's page, or a teacher and student's page.

Spelling rules, blending, and digraphs are mixed in between the introduction of some consonants. The consonants themselves continue to be introduced one at a time throughout the course, ending with consonant *Y* on page 274. Exceptions are included throughout the course, rather than segregated at the end. Vocabulary-building is emphasized within each Consonant Unit. This can be confusing for the novice teacher.

In keeping with the Orton philosophy, *Starting Over* uses a variety of techniques for a variety of learning styles. *Mary Pride*

From the people who brought you *Sing, Spell, Read & Write,* here's a literacy program for teens and adults. Over 150,000 people have already used this program to learn to read.

The heart of the **Winning** program is the sing-along song  cassettes. These are essentially the same songs as in *Sing, Spell, Read & Write,* adapted to fit what the publisher perceives are contemporary secular teen and adult tastes. The *SSR&W* ABC Song, for example, is now a rap instead of a bouncy kiddie tune. Other song tunes feature country and rock styles. The lyrics haven't changed much. The only difference in lyrics between the *SSR&W* version and the Winning revision is that Winning lyrics occasionally try to make learning to read sound hip.

A Sound Track to Reading

Ages 10–adult. Student's book, $12. Manual which includes student's book, $15. Shipping extra.
Professor Phonics, 4700 Hubble Rd., Cincinnati, OH 45247-3618. (513) 385-1717. Fax: (513)385-7920. Email: sue@professorphonics.com. Web: www.professorphonics.com.

Starting Over

Ages 16 and up. $24 plus shipping.
Educators Publishing Service, Inc., 31 Smith Pl., Cambridge, MA 02138. (800) 225-5750. Fax: (617) 547-0412. Email: epsbooks@epsbooks.com. Web: www.epsbooks.com.

Winning: The Race to Independent Reading Ability Home Kit

Grades 4 to adult, remedial. $175 plus $10 shipping.
International Learning Systems, 1000 - 112th Circle N., Suite 100, St. Petersburg, FL 33716. (800) 321-8322. Fax: (813) 576-8832. Web: www.singspell.com.

In all, the Winning Literacy Program has 1,755 spelling words, 70 learn-to-read stories written for older beginners (beginning with cartoon stories and ending with regular-sized newsprint), word recognition tests, word comprehension tests, story comprehension tests, and that optional life skills section I already mentioned. The stories are written to appeal mainly to minority, ESL, and blue-collar teens and adults. No Christian content whatsoever—presumably to get it into public schools, jails, and other government programs.

Songs included on the six cassettes are:

- "Phonics Song A–Z" (funky rap and comparatively listless jazz versions)
- "ABC Echoes" (repeating the alphabet sounds)
- "Short Vowel Song" ("A-a-a-a apple, e-e-e-e-egg . . .")
- "Ferris Wheel Blends Song" (practicing "ladder letters," e.g., "Ba-be-bi-bo-bu; bu-bo-bi-be-ba")
- "Letter Cluster Phonics Song" and "Letter Cluster Echoes"
- "All ABC Echoes" (a repeat of the ABC Echoes exercise on the first cassette)
- "Long Vowel Song" ("*Ay* for apron . . . *ee* for eagle . . .")
- "Two Vowel Song"
- "Silent E Song"
- "Mr. GH Song" (sounds of GH)

Comparing the cassettes from each version, the *SSR&W* kiddie singers have clearer diction and perform their songs more snappily.

Obviously, just listening to song cassettes isn't going to teach anyone to read, especially someone who's already failed to learn once. That's where the two bingo-like phonics games and the workbooks come in. The Winning Home Kit includes four workbooks, with covers resembling those of sports magazines, each with an accompanying (and equally thick) instructor's manual. The workbooks follow the *SSR&W* 36-step approach, teaching all the letters and their "first" sounds, then short vowels, "letter clusters," long vowels, and assorted bothersome mop-up sounds like silent *w* and *k*. By the end of this process, the student will have tackled every important phonics rule there is.

Along with all this come three sets of bingo-like flash cards and a set of green circular chips for playing phonics games, plus two phonics card games that drill letter sounds and clusters.

Book 1 simply introduces the letters—how to read them and write them in pre-cursive manuscript and cursive. Book 2 provides phonics exercises and activities—e.g., writing down the correct starting sounds of words or holding up the right short-vowel card—along with simple short-vowel stories in cartoon form. Each book includes pages for handwriting practice. In Book 3, stories break away from the cartoon format and regular reading comprehension tests are first introduced. (In Book 2, the student was only asked to recognize individual words from the story.) Book 4 continues to teach the rest of the letter clusters, and winds up with instructions on how to read and understand a calendar, table of contents, index, menu, signs and labels, parts of a newspaper. It also tells you how to fill out the following forms: social security application, driver's license, and job application.

The instructor's manual calls Winning a "virtually teacher-proof" program, and it is absolutely right. If you can read, you can teach this program. The student mainly teaches himself, only needing occasional help with directions, plus the expected feedback on his work. The instructor's manuals explain how the program works, give a complete programmed "script" for each lesson, and include a copy (on yellow paper) of the student book in the back with correct answers marked for each quiz. In fact, this program is *better* organized that *SSR&W,* and easier to use. All you have to do is pop in a cassette tape and read the instructor's manual. The student follows along doing the work in his book, and there you are! It all adds up to the best teen-and-adult literacy program I've seen. *Mary Pride*

CHAPTER 8

Creative Writing

Every American adult wants to write a book, or at least a letter to the editor that gets published in the local paper. If we can believe Albert Shanker, the president of the second-largest teacher's union in the country, though, most of us are doomed to frustration if we settle for just the writing instruction the local public school offers. In a speech given before a conference of teachers and school administrators in Denver in late September, 1989, he said,

> How many of our 17- to 18-year-old youngsters—the kids who are still there after about 29–30 percent have dropped out—our "successful" kids (not the at-risk kids, not the dropouts)— . . . what percentage of them can write a letter or an essay of one, two, three, four, [or] five pages and do a good job? . . .
>
> Well, the answer is, depending upon whether you take reading, writing, math, or science, the percentage of those still in school at age 17 and about to graduate who are able to function at that top level is: three, four, five, or six percent.
>
> Three, four, five, or six percent.
>
> The percentage of those able to write [a] one or two-paragraph letter with lots of errors in it is only 20 percent. In other words, 80 percent of those who have not dropped out cannot even write two paragraphs loaded with mistakes [that express] a single idea. . . .

That was 1989. This is now. And the percentages are just as bad, or worse, today. That's our mandate in this book—to beat the percentages! And I'm just the person to help you improve your creative writing. My personal writing style upon graduating college was, to put it charitably, vague and boring. (Not that it's that great now, but at least you can *understand* it!) So I know exactly what you're up against, and believe me, I sympathize.

Getting a cherished idea out of your head and onto paper is considerably similar to childbirth. The struggle . . . the suspense . . . the burdened feeling that finally, miraculously eases as the words come out. Face it, writing well is *tough*. But, with the proper instruction and lots of practice, it will get easier.

> **This chapter also includes handwriting improvement and keyboarding instruction just for teens. If you're going to write, why not make it *look* good as well?**

Free Sources of Excellent Writing Instruction

Before we get into actual school programs, consider what your local library has to offer. A good book is William Zinsser's *On Writing Well*. Zinsser is amusing, instructive, inspiring, approachable, and leftward leaning (just so you know). Still another widely-regarded text is E. B. White's *The Elements of Style*.

Most other books on the subject are, quite honestly, twaddle. Try to avoid those whose titles announce the big bucks you will shortly be earning with your writing. Generally these are hack pieces, written by and for hack writers. Anyway, you won't (let's be honest now) want to work through half-a-dozen books on writing; so just pick one good one, and start there!

Reading is still the best preparation for writing. If you want to be funny, read everything by P. G. Wodehouse. If drama is your calling, try starting with Dickens and Shakespeare. Soak up the best writing in your field and style, whether it be short story, play, or television scriptwriting. Then try to improve on it.

The children's book market operates by different rules, since children are supposed to be little alien lifeforms with peculiar tastes and needs. Thus the never-ending torrent of books convincing children that their parents were doing them a favor by divorcing; the torrid pre-teen sex novelettes; the smarmy stories of bunnies and kittens who discover the joys of unconditional self-love. Let me suggest a different path, the road taken by the writers of what we now consider children's classics. If you want to write for children, write a good clean book for adults and . . . then cut its size by 75 percent.

Writing Resources

A Beka's Handbook of Grammar and Composition for grades 11 and 12 is available in paperback. A Beka says, "This handbook provides a thorough treatment of all of those elements of grammar, mechanics, and usage that are necessary for correct, clear, and effective writing." Topics include The Writing Process, Specific Compositions, The Research Paper, Composing the Sentence, Choosing the Right Word. *Mary Pride*

A Beka's Handbook of Grammar and Composition
Grades 11–12. $13.20 plus shipping. *A Beka Book, Box 19100, Pensacola, FL 32523-9100. (800) 874-2352. Fax: (800) 874-3590. Web: www.abeka.com.*

NEW!
Building Believable Characters
Grade 9–adult. $17.99 plus shipping. *Writer's Digest Books, an imprint of F&W Publications, Inc., 1507 Dana Ave., Cincinnati, OH 45207. (800) 289-0963. Fax: (513) 531-4082. Web: www.writersdigest.com.*

I feel a little dubious about writing this review. On the one hand, there's a lot of useful information in **Building Believable Characters** that I have not seen crystallized as well elsewhere. On the other hand, the book is littered with street language and assumes you might want to write steamy sex scenes.

Here's what you get. Five successful authors share their expertise in a round-table discussion, for the first 24 pages of the book. They field questions such as, "What sort of planning goes into the creation of your characters?" and "Are you content to follow a passage of dialogue with 'he said/she said' or do you favor descriptive speech tags, e.g., *gasped, muttered, exclaimed, moaned, barked, roared, hissed, purred*, etc.?" This is easily the best part of the book, although even here you are assaulted with salty language and praise for adulterous characters. The rest of the book is devoted to the "Character Questionnaire," a series of questions to help you flesh out your main characters, and a "Character Thesaurus," with thousands of descriptive terms for each character trait, gesture, physical feature, etc. For example, you'll find 23 different mustaches, 31 noses, 41 beards, 102 facial types, 181 hairstyles, 360 facial expressions, and 5,000 given names and surnames. There's also a section on dialects and accents, with translations of American terms into their foreign equivalents. Again, earthy speech and sexual terms are included.

Of particular interest is that the pros' advice is the exact opposite of what you learned in your grade-school writing class. You are *not* supposed to embellish sentences with dozens of adjectives. You are *not* supposed to ceaselessly substitute action verbs for the word "said." You are *not* supposed to write dialog in complete sentences, or adorn it with numerous references to the characters' facial expressions, or use it as a substitute for narration. I just wish the pros had kept on talking—and that they'd kept it cleaner. *Mary Pride*

Some insiders tease with their knowledge, hoping to sell you another book or earn consulting fees. Sally Stuart, a prolific writer and researcher in Christian publishing, opens her treasures for your full inspection.

The 530-page **Christian Writers' Market Guide** does much more than list Christian publishers and periodicals (over 1,000 in all). Stuart includes on-line magazine publishers, greeting card publishers, ethnic, foreign, and other specialty markets. And information is cross-listed in lots of helpful ways, ranking the number of books of each type published by the major houses in a particular year, for instance.

Let's say you have a short humor "filler" you'd like to publish. More than sixty general periodicals accept them, plus almost forty in seven other categories. If *Purpose* sounds promising, you will find in its fuller entry (with fax, phone, and email info) that this Mennonite weekly take-home paper allows you to submit simultaneously elsewhere. *Purpose* buys fifteen fillers per year and pays four cents per word. You learn, too, that *Purpose* prefers first person and a strong story line, responds in nine weeks, and was in the Top 50 Christian Publishers list the last several years.

Just a beginner? Stuart details writers' conferences and groups, explains subsidy publishers, and even provides a helpful glossary.

This book is a must for Christian adults and teens ready to break into print. Stuart's wealth of tips may provide just the help you need. *Cindy Marsch*

Clear and Lively Writing is a *wonderful* book. Packed with activities designed to get the young writer going, it is all the creative writing curriculum you'll need. Practical classroom activities are combined with the technical information you need to teach writing as a logical process. By giving a child plenty of practice writing about topics that he chooses, the child will learn new writing techniques and effective writing habits with each genre he tackles.

The book is organized around "the writing process," meaning these three common-sense steps:

- Prewriting: Getting a clear idea of what you are going to write about.
- Drafting: Getting the words on paper.
- Editing: Modifying the composition.

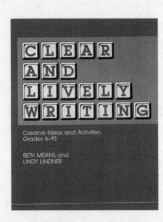

Interspersed throughout the book are sections titled "Teacher's Notebook"— ideas and advice to assist the teacher. "Tips from the Pros" are another help you'll find scattered throughout the book.

NEW!
Creative Writing and the Essay for the Beginner

Grades 7–12. $12 postpaid.
Dorothy Robbins, 11037 Erickson Way #79, Redding, CA 96003.
(530) 241-1149.
Email: der76@juno.com.

NEW!
Editor In Chief

Book A-1 (grades 4–6), $14.95. Book B-1 (grades 6–8), $15.95. Book C-1 (grade 8–adult), $16.95. All 3 books, $42.95. Shipping extra.
Critical Thinking Books & Software, PO Box 448, Pacific Grove, CA 93950-0448. (800) 458-4849. Fax: (831) 323-3277. Email: ct@criticalthinking.com. Web: www.criticalthinking.com.

Putting pencil to paper is one of the writer's most difficult tasks. Where to start? Numerous activities are given to facilitate this. In "Stop, Look, and Listen," the child stops, looks around, and lists all the things he sees. Then, he stops, listens, and lists the things that he hears. These are starting points. The authors stress that when the child first begins writing from the starting points, he shouldn't make judgments about whether these are good or bad ideas. Just get any and everything down on paper. This concept is carried through into the rough draft stage. "Creativity," the authors declare, "is not killed by judging if something is brilliant or mundane, serious or silly, good or bad; all creations are subject to judgments eventually. Creativity is killed by judging too soon."

Other activities in the book range from "Prewriting Choices Checklists," which help the student identify his ideal reader, the purpose or mood of his piece, to creating a "verbiary" which helps the student to build a list of verbs he can use. The book even shows the student how to pick the optimum verb while he is writing.

Filled with apt quotes, titles of other books helpful to the budding writer, and general "tricks of the trade," *Clear And Lively Writing* will definitely enhance your homeschool curriculum. *Cynthia Madsen*

Author Dorothy E. Robbins takes Rosalie Slater's Principle Approach as the basis for her curriculum. God has principles impregnated in everything He created—even the essay. That is the viewpoint of this gentle, if somewhat long-winded, creative writing curriculum. Dorothy Robbins focuses on the essay, setting out and explaining its three parts: introduction, body, and conclusion. She explains the topic sentence and paragraph, and discusses outlining and organizing material, and forms of discourse—exposition, description, narration, and argumentation. Most illustrations of the stated principles are either from the Bible or classical literature. She also emphasizes the importance of the young writer learning to express himself by being inspired by God so that he can, in turn, inspire others.

Creative Writing and the Essay for the Beginner assumes you already have a working knowledge of grammar and is strongly influenced by *The Plain English Handbook* by J. Martin and Anna Kathleen Walsh, now out of print. It uses extensive quotations from that work. *Cynthia Madsen*

This series of three books lets students put their language-arts training to use. This is great for really "cementing" what was previously only theoretical knowledge of spelling, grammar, and usage.

Each **Editor In Chief** workbook includes 33 editing exercises. These are in the form of essays or letters, each accompanied by a visual with additional information. For example, along with an article about "finding fingerprints" there is an illustration of fingerprint powder being dusted on a jewelry box, captioned, "A grey or black powder is used to dust hard surfaces for fingerprints. Chemicals are used on soft surfaces."

Your student, as the "editor in chief," has the job of finding and correcting all the errors in the written material. Each exercise includes at least one *content* error (described as "a discrepancy between the illustration/caption and the writing sample") and five to eight errors in spelling, mechanics, and grammar. Following the editing checklist at the beginning of the book, your child tracks down and corrects the errors. Answers are in the back of the book, along with explanations of what type each error was. A Guide to Grammar, Usage and Punctuation is also built into each of these workbooks, so students have detailed information about these rules, along with examples to demonstrate the rules.

The written material your student will be editing is itself educational, and the program is easy to use. I just wish there were more exercises! *Mary Pride*

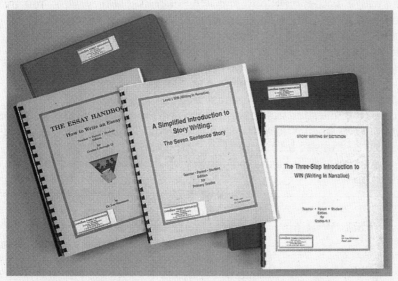

The Essay Handbook is designed to lead the student through the process of essay writing. The basic essay as it is taught in this program consists of four sections—setting, problem, reflection/solution, and conclusion—and is built in four steps:

- Essay Outline Note Forms: The writer uses a key word or short phrases to respond to questions that create the building blocks for each section.
- Essay Planning Sheets: The student transforms the words and phrases from Step 1 into key sentences and simple paragraphs.
- Rough Draft Writing Forms: Sentences and paragraphs are filled out, giving attention to capitalization, punctuation, and grammar.
- Final Draft Writing Forms: The budding essayist completes the final draft.

The book includes a basic essay model, which can be used for elementary and remedial junior and high school students, and an advanced essay model which can be used by regular junior high and high school students. You also get a list of suggested essay themes. Very little preparation or background is required, besides a good grammar handbook.

Two other books from the same author are also available: *The Term Paper Book* ($10) and *The Expository Writing Handbook* ($7). *Cynthia Madsen*

Levels A-1 and B-1 include lines below each exercise for the student to rewrite it properly, or to catalog the errors. By the time you get to level C-1, it helps for the student to know common editing symbols, as there is no space to completely rewrite the lengthier essays in this book (as if anyone would want to!).

NEW!
The Essay Handbook
Grades 5–12. $15 plus shipping. *Christian Family Resources, PO Box 405, Kit Carson, CO 80825. (719) 962-3228. Fax: (719) 962-3232. Call only between 1:00 PM–5:00 PM MST.*

The Exciting World of Creative Writing

Grades 7–12. $8. Test packet, $1. Shipping extra.
Christian Liberty Press, 502 West Euclid Ave., Arlington Heights, IL 60004. (847) 259-4444. Fax: (847) 259-2941. Email: enquire@homeschools.org. Web: www.homeschools.org. They take credit card orders, but not over the phone. Any other contact method will work.

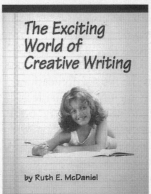

Ruth E. McDaniel takes an apprenticeship approach in introducing your junior-high or high-school writer to the nuts and bolts of creative writing in **The Exciting World of Creative Writing**. She writes in the first person, and loads of exercises and examples (mostly from her own writing, though there are a few excerpts from classic works) give you a chance to walk through the writing process right alongside of her.

Each of the 22 chapters in this consumable worktext focuses on one aspect of writing. For instance, in the chapter that discusses story openings and style, McDaniel presents examples (taken from her own work) of different story openings, along with a discussion of how and why she feels that they work. You are then asked to try your hand at a couple of different writing exercises, developing your own opening sentences for some story ideas. The chapter ends with a brief discussion on how you can begin to find your own unique writing "voice" (basically write, write, and write some more).

The text is a hybrid: part grammar and literature review and part Christian writing workshop. You may not share McDaniel's passion for writing for publication in Christian periodicals, and the text itself can be clumsy to use when it comes to filling in the blanks, but if you're looking for a low-cost way to learn a bit of the writer's craft, *The Exciting World of Creative Writing* might be the tool for the job. *Michelle Van Loon*

Format Writing

Grades 7–12. $11 plus shipping.
Wordsmiths, 1355 Ferry Road, Grants Pass, OR 97526. (541) 476-3080. Email: frodej@jsgrammar.com. Web: www.jsgrammar.com.

Format Writing, the latest by the author *of Jensen's Grammar and A Journey Through Grammar Land,* teaches expository writing: paragraphs, essays and research papers. It is designed for high school students and can be covered in 1–2 years. The types of formats covered in this 94-page softcover book are example, definition, classification, process, analogy, cause and effect, and comparison. You'll find sections on the following:

- Single Paragraphs
- Five Paragraph Essays
- Condensation and Precis
- Major, Research, and Position Papers

Each format is explained in terms of its structure, basic requirements, and items to consider. Examples are always given. The exercises include writing paragraphs and papers, expanding provided outlines into essays and reducing wordy sentences or paragraphs. Answer keys are provided for the reduction exercises and some rather lengthy instructions are provided for grading the other exercises.

Format Writing reflects a Christian lifestyle, and covers a wide range of topics. There is even a pro-homeschool comparison essay exercise in the *Format Writing* book!

My only complaint is that the book lacks page numbers. It would also have been nice to have a table of contents, so that you could use it as a quick look-up guide. We've been told that the next version of *Format Writing* will have an index, table of contents, and page numbers. *Teresa Schultz-Jones*

Every day, a new set of mistakes to correct and a couple of new rules to learn. That's the premise behind **Great Explorations in Editing**. For each day, the spiral-bound student book includes an error-laden sentence, in a "blackboard" style box on the page. Underneath, the student is expected to write a corrected version of the sentence. The teacher's guide includes the corrected sentences, and spells out why each correction is needed.

Another feature of this series (of which I only have seen Volume 1): vocabulary words are built into some of the sentences. The vocabulary words are sometimes used strangely, as in this sentence:

> *With advertent eyes, he followed his hand up to his forearm.*

I've read thousands of books in my life, and never encountered *advertent* used in that fashion!

You will search in vain for a logical sequence to the rules "taught" here. One typical five-lesson sequence jumps from "wordiness" to "choppy sentences" to "flowery language" to "transitions" to "run-ons." No readily apparent review is built in, either.

Volume 1 is divided into two sections: "A Lesson in History," in which the sentences follow each other day by day to tell a story, and "Amazing Facts," in which each day's sentences stand alone. "A Lesson in History" follows the adventures of a boy who starts daydreaming in history class. He dreams he's in the body of a bodyguard of King Philip of Macedonia, and that Queen Olympia is ordering him to assassinate the king. Accosted by one of the bodyguard's friends, our "hero" then utters this inexplicable line:

> *"I cannot kill a man! Will you kill him for me? You may keep all the reward promised me!"*

This is *very* weird and not at all what we'd expect. The standard textbook hero *will* refuse to commit murder, but *will not* try to enlist someone else to carry out the "contract"!

In my opinion, this and other lapses show that *Great Explorations in Editing* needs more editing itself. *Mary Pride*

I'm generally suspicious of books that have quotes of praise emblazoned on their cover, but was pleasantly surprised by **How to Write**. This 110-page paperback can easily be read in one sitting and will give you a clear understanding in what it takes to become a good writer.

The authors focus on the writing process rather than the mechanics of writing. They've broken the process down into three parts:

- Organizing: Selecting your points and collecting the details.
- Turning Out a Draft: Figuring out the theme, making an outline, and getting it on paper.
- Polishing the Product: Enhancing, sharpening, and focusing the final product.

You are guided through the steps and thought processes involved in writing a paper about online research (on the Information Superhighway). The authors explain through the use of examples and analogies how to approach writing the paper. They suggest and provide examples of imagined

NEW!
Great Explorations in Editing
Grades 7–9. Student book, $10. Teacher's guide, $15. Shipping extra. *Common Sense Press, P.O. Box 1365, Melrose FL 32666. Call (352) 475-5757 for a retail store near you; they do not sell retail themselves. Email: service@cspress.com. Web: www.cspress.com.*

NEW!
How to Write
Grades 7–12. $6.95 plus $4 shipping. *Storm King Press, PO Box 2089, Friday Harbor, WA 98250. (360) 378-3910. Fax: (360) 378-3912. Email: hmeyer@lookoutpoint.com. They do not take credit cards and are not equipped to handle billing, but you should be able to obtain their books through Amazon.com if you prefer not to use prepaid mail-order.*

conversations between you and your readers as a way of focusing your topic. There are some good examples of how slight changes in tone or precision can affect the entire flavor of a piece of writing.

The book is well-written, concise, and very readable. I'd recommend it to anyone serious about writing, particularly journalism. *Teresa Schultz-Jones*

Carole Thaxton, co-author of the popular KONOS unit-study curriculum (see its review in Volume 1), has provided a step-by-step guide through the writing process from her own class where she inspired and challenged each of her students to write a whole novel.

This is so exciting! I am going through **Learn to Write the Novel Way** in my teen co-op modern history class, and it is so well laid out that despite the distraction of my own newborn attending the class, I am able to keep an active class going. Once the students begin to write, their enthusiasm and trust in the process grows.

The complete course includes a student worktext and a teacher's manual with all the answer keys to the exercises.

In 13 steps carried out over a semester or entire year, students come up with good story ideas through examining the books they themselves love. They then take the process of story development apart and develop each part into their own work. Later they work on developing tense and mood, writing vividly and strongly, and then spend two whole months checking and developing skills in spelling, mechanics, and usage.

It is extremely important to move grammar *out* of the grammar workbooks and *into* the student's writing. Carole has done a fantastic job of sifting down these complex rules to those that are the most useful. She illustrates each rule with easily understood definitions and fun examples. Carole is never dry; your students will enjoy correcting their novels nearly as much as writing them! She also includes Biblical principles throughout her teaching so that students gain a moral vision for writing as well as good technique.

Finally, *Learn to Write The Novel Way* teaches the main points in layout, fonts, and bindings. The students present their "published" books at a book-signing reception. The only thing my students are adding are some added emphasis on illustrations, since I have several artists in my class. *Katherine von Duyke*

CONCURRING OPINION: Fiction, a demanding genre when done right, is popular in writing curricula designed to keep children happy. But these curricula can quash creativity with "failsafe" formulas, or they can encourage random wanderings in the field of prose. *Learn to Write the Novel Way* steers clear of both problems in the best approach I've seen to the homeschool fiction course.

Like Jill Bond's *Writing to God's Glory*, Carole Thaxton's worktext emphasizes the Christian's call to write with real excellence and keeps the student encouraged and motivated, even when tackling the tough stuff. But *Learn to Write the Novel Way* streamlines the process to a step-by-step, one-year (or one-semester) course, while Bond's book loses some usability and coherence in her attempt to provide too many things to too many people.

One major quibble here: Thaxton's book is nonreproducible, making it a pricey choice for large families, perfect candidates for the exciting group work encouraged in the curriculum.

In the KONOS tradition of "learning in context," students of *The Novel Way* immerse themselves in the project, addressing problems of character, plot, setting, point of view, and mechanics as they arise.

Each week's lesson on the yearlong plan includes a few hours of teacher-student interaction and several hours of independent work, first practicing

NEW!
Learn to Write the Novel Way

Grades 5–12. Complete course, $50. Additional student worktext, $39.95. KONOS Connection, 111 Bethea Rd., Fayetteville, GA 30214.(800) 780-6827. Inquiries: (770) 719-9549. Fax: (770) 460-1559. Email: 101352.3163@compuserve.com.

I am well experienced in teaching the process of writing, and have never had the luxury of being able to use a curriculum that contained all the elements I wanted. Carole has given homeschoolers a true gift in this work, which can be used within any unit of study the student might be following in another course. *Katherine Von Duyke*

Thaxton developed the program while teaching at the KONOS Academy of Prague, and the 218-page glossy paperback shows the fruit of much experience with homeschoolers and others. The teacher's manual, essential for its answers to the workbook exercises, also provides special notations for adapting the program to home and group scenarios.

the concepts learned that week, then applying them to the novel. The text is clearly laid out with instructions for each step, and even the grammar "checkups" are not too painful. A small sample of the excellent, thought-provoking content is found in the early challenge to choose characteristics of a "great book."

Students are encouraged to read Joshua 1 when they think they can't succeed, to ponder Psalm 139 when they feel they're not good enough. The Christian content is vigorous, not syrupy.

The most successful writing curricula face squarely the reality that writing is a hard journey. *Learn to Write the Novel Way* shows a clear path through the forest. *Cindy Marsch*

Words that Sell is one of my favorite books. It's a thickish oversized paperback crammed with advertising terms and slogans. I'll never forget the time we were reading this book, filling in the blanks left for a product name with our family name, and laughing our heads off:

Switch to . . . *Pride.*	They don't call us *Pride* for
Success starts with . . . *Pride.*	nothing!
Pride spoken here!	A major breakthrough in . . .
Pride means business.	*Pride.*
A little *Pride* can go a long way.	*Pride* is our middle name!
The *Pride* advantage.	Nothing's built like a *Pride.*
	Pride is our business.

I was smothering my giggles on Bill's shoulder in an attempt to avoid waking up our little Prides who do, indeed, go a long way every time my back is turned on them.

But *Words that Sell* also comes in handy for its primary function. Say you need a word that means "classic"—one that has a proven track record of consumer acceptance. How about *legendary . . . historic . . . antique . . . from the storied past . . . in the rich tradition of . . . redolent of another age . . . limited edition . . . quaint . . . hallmark of . . . timeless . . .* or *immortal?*

These words are more than mere synonyms. They *sell.* People like to see them. They have good vibes. And that's the point of *Words that Sell.* For every topic you'll find words and phrases culled from thousands of successful ads. You'll even find chapters on how to elegantly knock the competition or how to introduce your product pitch.

Words that Sell is invaluable to anyone who has a business. It could even come in handy for writing book reports and persuasive essays. Anyone who likes or needs to load his words needs this book. *Mary Pride*

Wordsmith is a one-book creative writing course designed by a professional writer for homeschooled kids in junior high and up. Part 1 teaches the student how to effectively use concrete nouns, vivid action verbs, and other parts of speech. Part 2 shows how to construct and vary your sentences. Part 3 explores sensory experiences, figures of speech, scene-setting, characterization, dialog, and other essential topics. Excellent instructions directed to the student (so Mom can take it easy), plenty of room to write your answers right in the workbook. Systematic, easy to use.

The follow-up book, **Wordsmith Craftsman,** can't be praised too highly. Picking up where *Wordsmith* left off, this truly excellent program for grades 10 and up teaches non-fiction writing systematically, efficiently, and amusingly. Beginning with essential pre-writing skills—which in author Janie B. Cheaney's view include outlining, summarizing, and note-taking—you learn how to write five types of personal letters (including stumpers

Words that Sell

Teen and adult. $15.50 plus shipping. *Timewise Systems, Inc., 510 Fillmore Ave., Tonawanda, NY 14151. (800) 523-8060. (800) 222-1934.*

NEW!
Wordsmith and Wordsmith Craftsman

Grades 7–12. Wordsmith: student workbook, $14, teacher's guide, $5. Wordsmith Craftsman, $14. Shipping extra. *Common Sense Press, P.O. Box 1365, Melrose FL 32666. Call (352) 475-5757 for a retail store near you; they do not sell retail themselves. Web: www.cspress.com.*

For younger kids, there's Wordsmith Apprentice. See its review in Volume 2.

Writer's Digest How-To Books

Grade 9–adult. Free catalog. *Writer's Digest Books, an imprint of F&W Publications, Inc., 1507 Dana Ave., Cincinnati, OH 45207. (800) 289-0963. Fax: (513) 531-4082. Web: www.writersdigest.com.*

NEW!
Writer's Digest Market Guides

Grade 3–adult. Market Guide for Young Writers (5th edition), $16.99. Teen–adult. 1999 Guide to Literary Agents, 1999 Children's Writers & Illustrations Market, $19.99 each. 1999 Novel & Short Story Writer's Market, $22.99. 1999 Writer's Market, $27.99. Writer's Market with CD-ROM, $49.99. Poet's Market, $22.99. Songwriter's Market, $22.99. Photographer's Market, $23.99. Artist's and Graphic Designer's Market, $24.99. Shipping extra. *Writer's Digest Books, an imprint of F&W Publications, Inc., 1507 Dana Ave., Cincinnati, OH 45207. (800) 289-0963. Fax: (513) 531-4082. Web: www.writersdigest.com.*

such as "letters of support" for friends in distress) and two types of business letters (letters of complaint and requests for employment). After this come excellent instructions in how to write paragraphs, how to pep up your writing, and how to develop a personal "voice." The last section, "The Essay," tackles this noble written form, and step by step teaches you how to succeed with four types of essays.

Plenty of examples are included, so you can see what you're aiming for. A study plan is also included, with weekly exercises, so you know just what to do when. All you need beside the book is a notebook for writing your assignments.

Wordsmith Craftsman does everything you can possibly expect of a one-book high-school writing course, and more. I heartily recommend this book. *Mary Pride*

The **Writer's Digest Books** catalog is stuffed with how-to books for budding writers: how to write for magazines, for newspapers, for anyone and everyone. The how-tos of humorous writing . . . short stories . . . poetry . . . novels . . . fillers . . . TV scripts . . . even how to write software user manuals! Plus lots of books on how to find an agent, how to submit proposals, how to collect maximum royalties, and so on.

Each and every one of the Writer's Digest books I have seen (and I have seen a lot) has a bottom-line, dollars-and-cents attitude. Generally this smacks more of the breathless, "I got $50 for my short story and you can, too!" than of the well-paid professional. These books also tend towards a chatty, and even risqué, cuteness familiar to readers of women's magazines. In all, these books are most helpful in their marketing advice and in alerting you to the guidelines for saleable hack writing (e.g., "This is how standard magazine articles look—go and do ye likewise"). *Mary Pride*

So you want to write for publication. So you write to me asking for advice. No! No! *Please,* no! All I would have told you anyway is to get one of these books.

The Market Guide for Young Writers is 320 indexed pages of

- profiles of successful young writers and editors
- how to prepare your manuscript
- answers to frequently-asked questions about copyright, author's rights, fees, etc.
- how to submit your writing online
- advice about markets and contests to avoid
- places to sell or place your writing
- writing contests for kids

The Guide to Literary Agents is 500 listings of agents who handle "nonfiction books, novels, juvenile books, textbooks, scripts, plays, and more!" This book is for those of you who are long, strong writers and really serious about getting published.

Children's Writer's & Illustrator's Market is dedicated to those who want to write for kids, as opposed to kids who want to write. Its 389 information-packed pages include what you need to know to get into this market (business basics, how to submit your work, the lowdown about working with agents, contract basics, etc.), and detailed listings for book and magazine publishers of all kinds—more than 850 buyers of freelance material in all.

Novel & Short Story Writer's Market is your guide to nearly 2,200 publishing houses, contests, conferences, and more. It also includes business basics to help you put on a professional face; articles and features de-

signed to help you break into this market; interviews with published writers; insider tales from book editors; the "Commercial Fiction Trends Report"; and articles detailing how some new writers made it into print. Over 675 densely-filled pages in all.

Also available in this series: **Photographer's Market**, **Artist's and Graphic Designer's Market**, **Poet's Market**, **Songwriter's Market**, **Mystery Writer's Sourcebook**, **Science Fiction Writer's Marketplace**, as well as the original **Writer's Market**. Each of these large, hardbound, annually-updated tomes includes well-organized listings of markets for your work, with plenty of information in each listing to help you find your best opportunities, as well as supplemental listings of clubs, associations, and contests, and advice for how to best prepare and present your work. Each of the latest editions of the *Market* series now include a dozen or so close-up interviews with people in the industry.

Finally, the venerable **Writer's Market**, the book most of you are looking for, recently celebrated its 75th anniversary. This monster book (over 1,100 pages) tells you in very small print what the publishers and editors of each magazine or book house are looking for. By squishing the over 8,000 contact listings so small, the book manages to save some space for a variety of other helpful features. These include basic information on getting published, preparing your manuscript, business basics, the basic markets (including specialty markets such as syndicates and greeting cards), "Current Trends in Publishing," a magazine editors' roundtable (find out what the editors want!), and interviews and features galore. Even though your library undoubtedly has a copy, it's worth getting your own if you're at all serious about getting—and staying—in print. *Mary Pride*

Those who will find **Writing Smart: Your Guide to Great Writing** most useful are students who need to move past the realm of creative writing into the forum of essays, research papers, professional letters, and lab reports.

This 176-page guidebook gives only a brief review of basic grammar, but does discuss how to compose good sentences and paragraphs. Editing is thoroughly covered, and a chart of proofreading marks may be helpful to the college-bound. With the use of such inviting topics as "Candy Bars and the Psychology of Taste," the author draws the student into learning about research techniques, outlining, and writing. Each chapter contains not only the necessary instructions but has the added benefit of test drills for learning comprehension. The chapters on Project Proposals and Professional Letter Writing would be beneficial for both the young entrepreneur and interested parents. Added benefit: a list of common letter-writing pitfalls.

Caution: *Writing Smart* does contain at least one offensive word, in the area addressing the common practice of students attempting to dupe a teacher with an essay. Parents could easily white-out the word, with no loss of understanding. *Lisa Mitchell*

Creating Fiction, written by Dave Marks, is designed for the older student who wants to learn how to write short fiction and submit his pieces for publication. This book is written to the student and does not require adult supervision. If your child is a real self-starter this is the book for you.

The philosophy of *Creating Fiction* is summed up at the beginning of the book in a letter to the prospective student. "Writers are artists. Their job is to reflect what they see in their culture to others." This does not go quite far enough, as many

NEW!
Writing Smart

Grades 7–12. $12 plus shipping.
ISBN: 0379-753-605.
Order Entry Dept., Random House, Inc., 400 Hahn Rd., Westminster, MD 21157. (800) 726-0600 ext. 3700.
Web: www.randomhouse.com.

NEW!
Writing Strands: Creating Fiction

High school and above. $22.95 plus $2 shipping.
National Writing Institute, 810 Daemon Ct., Houston, TX 77006. (800) 688-5375. (906) 658-3410. Fax: (906) 658-3411. Email: info@writingstrands.com. Web: www.writingstrands.com.

fiction writers, such as Charles Dickens and Jules Verne, have succeeded at changing or challenging their culture through their writing.

Each lesson succinctly and satisfactorily explains different elements of creative writing, such as dialogue, point of view, or symbolism. Exercises are suggested intermittently throughout the lesson. However, sometimes the exercises are presented in such an off-hand manner that it is not completely clear that they are an assignment to be done. Unless a student is extremely motivated, he may decide that doing the exercises is optional. Also, although an example may be given to illustrate a specific feature of creative writing, when the student is asked to incorporate that aspect of creative writing into a composition, there are no starting points, jumping off places, suggestions, or ideas for the student with writer's block.

The appendix contains several helpful features. Examples of student writing illustrate a completed assignment. You get concise explanations of the story elements and how they are created. And finally you'll find a section on formatting manuscripts, submitting manuscripts for publication, and magazines which accept work by young writers. *Cynthia Madsen*

Handwriting

This is the best source I have yet found for instruction in the popular, flowing, 19th-century style of handwriting known as "Spencerian" after its founder, Platt Rogers Spencer. As the booklet **Learning to Write Spencerian Script** says, it is "perhaps the most elaborate penmanship ever written by the human hand." This beautiful ornamental script, with its flourishes and varied stroke width, was the everyday writing "hand" of millions of people. It was designed for writing with reasonable speed, and can either be exceptionally clear (if you leave off the letter "shades" and flourishes) or impressively beautiful.

I discovered Michael Sull through the good offices of his pupil, Joan Donaldson, who in turn wrote an article for *Practical Homeschooling* about her style of homeschooling based on the philosophies of famed illustrator Tasha Tudor. Impressed by Joan's handwritten notes, I asked her where she learned to write like that, and here is the answer!

You have your choice here of a wide range of instructional methods and supplies. Probably the best choice for most of us is the **Penmanship Instruction Kit.** This includes the book *Learning to Write Spencerian Script*, one Peerless Oblique Penholder, six pen-points (you wear out pen-points often with this method), Higgins Eternal Ink, Guide sheets, and a cushion sheet. If that sounds like a lot of supplies, you're right—the Spencerian method requires special pens, points, and ink for success. The Guide sheets are placed under your writing paper to help you keep on a straight line and slant, and the cushion sheet under both to keep your pen from skipping or splattering.

About the *Learning to Write* booklet: it starts with basic letter forms, goes on to letters that use the same basic form, then to joins, capitals, and a brief discussion of "off-hand flourishing" (the topic is not fully covered in this book, but will be in Sull's newest book *Techniques for Off-Hand Flourishing*, to be published soon). This book is easy to follow and understand, and the best introduction to Spencerian writing I have seen.

For those for whom the Kit isn't enough, a 55-minute VHS instructional **video** will fill in the gaps. Here you can actually see exactly how letters are formed by watching writing expert Michael Sull. European and Australian readers will be delighted to know that this video is also available in PAL format, for a slightly higher price.

And if *that* isn't enough, you can sign up for a **correspondence course** of 17 lessons with 48 assignments. Every two weeks you send Michael your completed assignment, which he will evaluate, correct as necessary,

NEW!
Learning to Write Spencerian Script

Grade 9–adult. Learning to Write Spencerian Script, $15. Spencerian Script copybook set, $18. Spencerian Script Penmanship Instruction Kit, $30. Learning to Write Spencerian Script video (VHS), $40. Home Study Course, $50. Penholders, $10–$25. Supplies also available. Shipping extra.
Michael R. Sull, c/o The Lettering Design Group, 5830 Nall Ave., Suite 2, Mission, KS 66202. (913) 362-7864. Fax: (913) 362-2236. Email: ldg@qni.com. Web: www.spencerian.com

If John Henry was born with a hammer in his hand, young Spencer was born with a pen. As a child he first drew letters on birch bark, and soon he was scribbling everywhere. A born calligrapher, Spencer greatly admired John Hancock's elegant signature on the Declaration of Independence and desired to design a handwriting system that would produce that kind of grace, yet be easy to learn. The result, carried on by his disciples, was Spencerian writing, a complete system based on a few simple arm movements and seven basic strokes. Every letter is broken down into those strokes. The result is a gorgeous "copperplate" system of writing, quaint and elegant.

The Lord is my Shepard I shall not want.
Psalm 23:1

Spencerian

and mail back to you. The course costs cover Michael's time and the instructional material, and do not include the booklet or supplies. For quite a bit less you can get the course lessons *sans* mailed evaluations.

If you want even *more,* you can attend one of the **workshops** Michael Sull periodically offers. That is how Joan Donaldson got her start in Spencerian scripting.

Finally, let's not forget the **Spencerian Script Copybook Set.** Published in 1874 and usable at home or school, this set of five copybooks and one "theory" book has a line of idealized writing on each copybook page, which the pupil is supposed to copy below in the space provided. My own feeling is that you would be wise to at least pick up *Learning to Write Spencerian Script* if you plan to use the copybooks, since more than half the battle is being able to "see" whether you formed the letters correctly in the first place. *Mary Pride*

From the authors of the popular Portland State University italic handwriting program, here are two new books. Both are completely handwritten in italic, include space right on the pages for the handwriting exercises, and come with a special binding that allows the books to lay flat for easy practice. Both take a step-by-step approach, with handy teaching tips and illustrations right next to the examples.

Write Now: A Complete Self-Teaching Program for Better Handwriting (96 oversized pages, perfect bound) is, as the title suggests, a self-study program. This is the book you want if you or your student are functioning at the self-study level and are mainly interested in improving your handwriting skills. It actually summarizes everything in Books A–G of the Portland State University program. You start with basic (non-joined) italic and numerals: first lower-case families, then upper-case, finally the numerals, followed by writing practice and tips. Next you systematically make the transition to cursive italic, learning to make fancier capitals and to join lower-case letters swiftly and beautifully. No special writing equipment is required, although a section on "edged pen italic" is also included for those who want to put their new italic skills to use making beautiful greeting cards, envelopes, and so forth. For extra practice paper, you are allowed to photocopy the lined paper samples in the back of the book.

Italic Letters: Calligraphy & Handwriting (128 pages, perfect bound) concentrates on teaching calligraphy as an art form. This self-study text also begins with basic italic, but then goes on to teach Formal and Chancery italics. Cursive italic is also taught, but in much more condensed fashion than in *Write Now*. The book closes with tips on designs you can

NEW!
Portland State University Self-Study Italic Materials
Grades 7–12. Write Now! Book, $12.95. Video, $29.95. Italic Letters, $15.95. Shipping extra.
Portland State University, Continuing Education Press School of Extended Studies, PO Box 1394, Portland, OR 97207. (800) 547-8887 x4891. Fax: (503) 725-4840. Web: extended.pdx.edu/press/.

The Lord is my Shepherd; I shall not want. Psalm 23:1

Portland State University/Getty-Dubay Cursive Italic

create with your new calligraphy skills. You will need a pen with a calligraphy nib to do the exercises in this book.

The books are good value for money. I only wish they provided a bit more space to practice your new handwriting skills, and that they included some ongoing review of already-taught skills. As it is, you'll be practicing a lot on scratch paper and often turning back to previous lessons to remind yourself exactly how it is done. *Mary Pride*

Spencerian Handwriting set

Grades 1–12. Complete set (including theory book and all five copy books), $15.99. Individual copy books, $2.99. Theory book, $4.99. Shipping extra.
Mott Media/Homeschooling Book Club, 1000 E. Huron St., Milford, MI 48381-2422. (800) 421-6645. Fax: (248) 685-8776.

Mott Media has resurrected ye olde **Spencerian handwriting books** from ye tombe of oblivion. These books were used for over 100 years, and are based on the method of Platt Rogers Spencer.

Spencer's theory book reads like a catechism, with its questions and answers. "Will you measure and analyze small *r*? . . . How should the small *r* be formed?" The five accompanying consumable copy books take the student from writing the "short" letters on graphed paper to penning such sentences as "Angels are guardian spirits," (this was before the ACLU, remember) and "Modesty always charms." Like all Mott's Classic Curriculum, the books can be used at all age levels and at any pace that fits the student. *Mary Pride*

Usborne Calligraphy

Grade 7–college. Paperback, $7.95. Library-bound, $15.95. Shipping extra.
EDC Publishing, Division of Educational Development Corporation, 10302 East 55th Place, Tulsa, OK 74146. (800) 475-4522. Web: www.edcpub.com.

Calligraphy: From Beginner to Expert is an Usborne book. That means it's highly visual and crammed to the hilt with full-color illustrations. Text serves the illustrations, explaining how the effects are achieved, what the parts of the pen are, and so on. Topics covered are:

• the history of calligraphy	• ways to use calligraphy
• basic equipment	• unusual equipment (balsa pens, quills . . .)
• types of letters (capitals, miniscules . . .)	• Chinese calligraphy
• layout tips	• stenciling, rubbing, embossing, incising
• Gothic and Italic styles	• careers in calligraphy
• decoration and illumination	

The book closes with several pages of sample alphabets, numbers, and borders, and a complete index.

Calligraphy is an excellent introduction to the "pen arts," and actually provides enough information in its 48 pages for the beginner to get started in the style of his choice. Recommended. *Mary Pride*

Audio Forum Master Your Keyboard (Parts I and II)

Grades 7–12. Touch Typing, $34.50. Improve Your Typing, $34.50. Both courses, $64. Shipping extra.
Audio-Forum, division of Jeffrey Norton Publishers, Inc. 96 Broadstreet, Guilford, CT 06437. (800) 243-1234. Web: www.audioforum.com.

Keyboarding

Master Your Keyboard is designed to teach you to touch type in only four hours. This beginning-level program consists of three cassettes, a comb-bound "exercise book," and round red stickers to temporarily conceal the keys while you're taking the course. **Improve Your Typing**, with two cassettes and an exercise book, provides warm-up, accuracy, speed, and speed-accuracy drills, plus score sheets for recording your progress. The accuracy drills use the 500 most misspelled words. *Mary Pride*

CHAPTER 9

Grammar for Teens & Adults

Here is a quick self-test to see if you could use a little help in brushing up your grammar.

Find all the mistakes in the following passage, and correct them on separate paper.

Find the Mistakes

"Its a lovely day outside", Tanasha said. "Lets go out and play!"

"I dont know", Julie replied. "I would of brought my tennis racket if I'da known it was gonna be a nice day."

The two girls walked together to the park. As they neared it, a dog came up to them wagging it's tail.

The dog appeared to not belong to anyone. He laid down in front of Tanasha and refused to budge.

"Well what've we got here"? she wondered.

"I'll give you three guesses", Julie chirped. "First; its sick and can't move. Second: it want's a warm place to lay down. Three; it love's you and wants to be your's".

If that was painful to read, congratulations! You might not need this chapter after all. Did you count 24 mistakes? If not, read it carefully and try again. (The mistakes are all listed at the end of the chapter.)

If you thought that was too easy, here's another chance to show off your grammar knowledge. Identify which part of speech corresponds to the italicized word in each of the following sentences.

Name Those Parts

1. *Singing* on the mountaintop, she startled the birds.
2. I'm *singing* in the rain!
3. Her *singing* is quite good.
4. He is a *singing* fool.

Again, answers are at the end of the chapter.

Finally, here's a real tester. You'll hate me for this, because I'm going to ask you to *diagram* the following sentences. Again, you can check your work with the answers at the end of the chapter.

Sentences to Diagram
1. John and Fred went fishing together last Tuesday.
2. They caught a fine fat trout and three small minnows.
3. Upon returning home, the men boned and cleaned the fish.
4. John, that lucky fellow, got more fish to eat than Fred did.

What use is any of this in real life?" you ask. Good grammar won't make you a good writer or speaker. However, bad grammar adds a sour note to writing or speaking tainted by it.

By the time junior high rolls around, the typical student has already had six years of grammar instruction. Most curricula introduce a wee bit more grammar each year, after reviewing all the grammar from the years before.

This is an unnecessarily painful way to teach grammar. Ideally, it should all be taught at once, preferably somewhere between fourth and seventh grade, and then only reviewed as necessary. But we do not live in an ideal world, and lots of us make it through high school and even college innocent of the difference between a gerund and an appositive. Judging by advertisements and magazine columns, huge numbers do not know the difference between *it's* (a contraction meaning "it is") and the possessive *its* (meaning "that which belongs to it").

It behooves us to correct this sad situation, and that right speedily. Hence the admirable grammar resources available in this chapter for your discerning consideration. (Collect two brownie points if you noticed that last sentence wasn't really a sentence at all.)

Grammar Resources

The **Winston Grammar** series teaches grammatical constructions to students of all ages by pattern-building with colored flash cards, rather than by diagramming.

Each Winston Grammar program includes a set of worksheets bound with a pre- and post-test; a teacher's manual; quiz keys; and the color-coded noun function cards and parts-of-speech cards.

Volume 1, Winston Grammar, is designed for grades 3–8 and reviewed in Volume 2 of *The Big Book*. **Volume 2, Advanced Winston Grammar**, is for grades 9–12.

The Advanced Winston Grammar has 55 worksheets, as opposed to the 30 worksheets in the basic course, and is supposed to cover up through the high school level. After a review of the previous course, it goes on to such things as possessive adjectives and ellipses relative pronouns. The additional cards used in this course are: possessive adjective, possessive pronoun, pronoun/adjective, verbals, Tricky Words, and Tricky Word Clues.

Since this program uses a nonstandard notation to mark sentences, and does not teach diagramming, those pursuing a classic liberal-arts program should not make it their first pick. As you've noticed, the courses only cover parts of speech and sentence analysis. You will have to add instruction in capitalization and punctuation, grammar rules such as subject-verb agreement, and usage rules such as the difference between *lie* and *lay*. *Mary Pride*

UPDATED!
Advanced Winston Grammar
Grades 9–12. $30 plus $4 shipping.
Hewitt Homeschooling Resources, PO Box 9, Washougal, WA 98671.
Orders: (800) 348-1750.
Inquiries: (360) 835-8708.
Fax: (360) 835-8697.
Email: hewitths@aol.com.

Did you know that Sunday school was invented to help poor children learn to read, and that their text was the Bible? For centuries the Bible was used as a text for reading, literature, grammar, and composition, and Sunday school is just one of the educational enterprises in this tradition.

Alpha Omega Publications has a series based on this old concept. Designed to be used by individuals or groups who possess at least sixth grade skills, **Learning English with the Bible** is for anyone who wants to "learn grammar through studying God's Word." Alpha Omega suggests that the text can be used by individual students for review or enrichment, or by the whole family. *Learning English with the Bible: English Grammar Diagrams*, a companion book, revives the honored custom of learning grammar and parts of speech through diagramming sentences from the Bible book of Joshua. *Mary Pride*

The **ATIA Sentence Analysis** curriculum weighs several pounds, due to the many thick books it comes with. The parent set includes a hefty 202-page parent guide and an equally hefty 183-page answer key. Student materials include a textbook, consumable workbook, and a consumable Quizzes and Tests booklet. You need *all* these materials to complete the course; don't try to save money by skipping any of them.

In all, you get 18 lessons (each of which might last several weeks) grouped into three units: basic sentence elements, verbals and verbal phrases, and subordinate clauses. Under these topics, all of basic grammar is studied. Easy stuff, like subjects and main verbs. Hard-hitting stuff, like gerunds and participial phrases. In-between stuff, like learning that a sentence *must* contain a subject and a verb (unlike the last two of mine).

In keeping with ATIA's traditional and logical flavor, students get to diagram lots of sentences, starting in lesson 2. They are also expected to memorize definitions of grammatical terms, just like schoolkids did 100 years ago, back when they could both effortlessly create and understand complex sentences, no matter how long the distance between clauses, be the language as ornate as Addison could make it or as energetic as Dickens, even if the sentence went on for what seemed like miles, like this one.

Like other ATIA materials, the Sentence Analysis course is beautifully illustrated and replete with charts and lists. Scripture is the subject matter for both examples and practice sentences. Imaginative illustrations from nature are also frequently invoked to explain grammatical features. For example, the butterfly is likened to an action verb, while the chrysalis or pupa stage is likened to a "state of being," in which the pupa's goals are "both to 'exist' against the threat of its enemies and to 'link' one phase to the next."

The textbook for Sentence Analysis reads more like a reference book than a regular textbook. It does not really *teach* the material. Teaching requires introducing new information, isolating it from other information for emphasis, and repeating it for retention. Rather, the textbook is so densely packed with information and terminology that each new point is immediately succeeded by the next—sometimes within the same paragraph, or even the same sentence. Example:

> *Pronouns are generally classified as* personal, demonstrative, relative, interrogative, indefinite, reflexive, *or* intensive. *Not every category of pronouns can perform all nine noun functions. Neither* relative pronouns *nor* reflexive/intensive pronouns, *for instance, can fulfill the role of a sentence subject . . .*

This sort of prose gives the average reader a headache, unless he is a grammarian to begin with. The extensive glossary section is more useful,

Alpha Omega Learning English with the Bible

Grades 8–12. Student book, $7.99. Answer key, $4.99. Diagramming, $6.99. Complete set of three books, $17.95. Shipping extra. *Alpha Omega Publications, 300 N. McKemy, Chandler, AZ 85226. Orders and inquiries: (800) 622-3070. Fax: (480) 785-8034. Web: www.home-schooling.com.*

ATIA Sentence Analysis course

Grades 7–12. Parent set, $20. Student set, $26. Extra workbooks, $10 each. Extra sets of Quizzes and Tests booklet, $4 each. Shipping extra. *Institute in Basic Life Principles, Box One, Oak Brook, IL 60522-3001. (630) 323-9800. Email: cpallock@iblp.org. Web: www.iblp.org.*

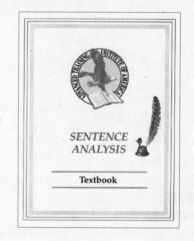

especially if you've spent the last 10 years fretting over what on earth an appositive is. However, it seems that the real textbook is the parent guide. That book includes instructions on how to teach each concept, activities to make the concepts clear, and indications of when each practice exercise ought to be completed in the workbook. By contrast with the textbook, the parent guide is clearly written, easy to follow, and the activities are fun. The one thing it does not do is explain where, when, or how you and the student are supposed to use the textbook!

Sentence Analysis covers all the grammar your child is ever likely to need, and does it all in one course. Much more efficient than dragging it out over 12 years, in my opinion. This course is not something to spring on your fourth-grader, but if you have the time to devote to a systematic study of grammar, you and your older children can walk away from Sentence Analysis really knowing something. *Mary Pride*

I love books that help you cut through the clutter and *quickly* learn or review the stuff you need to know. **Basics of Systematic Grammar** does just that. It's a programmed text designed to catch high-schoolers up on the basics of grammar. "Programmed" is eduspeak for "self-teaching." Here's how it works: You read the text on the left side of the page, while holding a piece of paper beneath it. Each text box teaches you a little bit, then asks a question about what you were just taught. You try to answer the question, then move your piece of paper down to read the answer. Then on to the next text box, and so on. Very simple, very straightforward.

Like any good programmed text, *Basics of Systematic Grammar* starts by teaching you how to use a programmed text! You then move on to nouns, verbs, and auxiliaries (helping verbs) . . . subjects, pronouns, and noun phrases . . . sentence patterns and adverbs . . . the parts of the noun phrase . . . and other parts of speech, such as conjunctions. At the end of this slim workbook are two checkup sheets for each of the five units. An excellent, quick grammar review for older students, and not a bad way to introduce the subject to anyone who missed it or muffed it in school. *Mary Pride*

BJUP Basics of Systematic Grammar

Grades 9–12. $9. Teacher's manual, $6.50. Shipping extra.
Bob Jones University Press Customer Services, Greenville, SC 29614. Orders: (800) 845-5731. Fax: (800) 525-8398. Web: www.bjup.com.

NEW!
Commas Are Our Friends

Grade 6–adult. $11.95 plus shipping. *Green Stone Publications, P.O. Box 15623, Seattle, WA 98115-0623. (206) 524-4744.*

Yes, you read that title right, and no, all 263 pages of this trade paperback are not a defense of the comma. In fact, **Commas Are Our Friends** is three novellas in one. Work with commas is sandwiched between a parts-of-speech adventure and the tale of "Mudhill's Monument," the legacy of a gazillionaire with a passion for grammar.

Young teens with a silly streak will lap up the fantastic adventures of Aloysius Muldoon, some-time-archaeologist, and the other comic characters in these stories. In each, crazed language partisans scheme to popularize their peculiar passion, and veteran English teacher Joe Devine snookers us into hearing them out while still maintaining our own dignity.

These shaggy-dog stories will provide a fun supplement to your grammar curriculum, or a good refresher, though the material could have been condensed into a tight three or four textbook pages. The comprehensive index shows just how much content hides within the silliness—there are nine entries under "clause" alone, and twelve for "phrase"—and you thought they were the same thing! *Cindy Marsch*

Enough About Grammar is not really a grammar book. It's about learning what you need to know about grammar to improve your *writing*. With this in mind, the first thing author Joe Floren does is expose the Grammar Emperor's New Clothes. "Grammar is imperfect," Mr. Floren announces, and he proceeds to prove this by giving a set of five sentences to a set of grammar experts and asking them some embarrassing questions. For example, "What part of speech is *camping* and what does it really modify in the sentence, 'We went camping every summer'?" He then shares the wildly different answers the experts came up with, all to make the point that perfect grammar (by which he means perfect grammatical *definitions*) is an unattainable goal.

That doesn't mean that boners in grammar *usage* are necessary. So after a bit more fun debunking such rules as "A preposition is something you should never end a sentence with," we move on to his real interest, teaching what he calls "Straightforward Writing." His two main points: straightforward writing is

- driven by clauses
- powered by active verbs

The remainder of the book is devoted to teaching you how to use parts of speech in Straightforward Writing, and how to recognize and conquer common grammar usage errors. Examples of good, bad, and ugly writing abound, with the bad and ugly compared to the good so you can see the difference between right and wrong.

A spiral-bound workbook with answer key is also available. I was unable to discern any obvious connection between the workbook and the book. Although the workbook refers to various pages of the book, the workbook exercises do not at all resemble the book exercises. This is not just because they are based on Bible sentences wherever possible. Compared to the book exercises, the workbook exercises cover relatively little territory, each page drilling the same exact skill the same exact way dozens of times. You can only stand to "underline the subject once and the verb twice" so many times, and what do you learn by "underlin[ing] both subjects when 'and' is used. With 'or,' just underline the last subject"? These exercises don't improve your writing skills or deal with any of the advanced usage topics that *Enough About Grammar* handles so well. *Mary Pride*

It's been said that what Saxon does for math, Frode Jensen does for grammar: no frills, incremental delivery of new material, and lots of practice. If **General Punctuation** represents the Jensen approach, you'll probably agree. The 102-page manual contains some brief instruction on the basics of punctuation and capitalization, a numbered index of all the rules that will be drilled (you're encouraged to copy this, put it in a plastic sleeve, and use it for reference), and a total of 66 exercises. There are 45 general lessons, to be done three times a week, and review exercises to use as necessary. The high-interest content of each reading is based on U.S. history.

To use *General Punctuation*, you read through the exercise, and on a separate sheet of paper, note all errors. Each sentence in an exercise is numbered, and the answer key not only shows the correct response, but references you back to the index number so you can easily review the rule. One gripe: though this is designed as a non-consumable, the paper is very flimsy. If you have a houseful, you may want to have a printer punch holes in the text and put it in a hard-cover binder. This text is worth the extra effort ... exclamation point! *Michelle Van Loon*

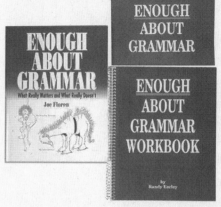
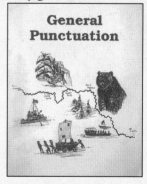

NEW!
Grammar Free Fall

Grades 6–12. $25 postpaid.
Terry Robertson, 1012 Camino Vista Aurora, Santa Fe, NM 87505-7812.
(505) 424-0627.
Email: Wldwmn7@aol.com.

Don't peek into the middle pages of **Grammar Free Fall** before you're ready—you'll get vertigo! That old nemesis of junior-high English, the sentence diagram, bristles there in all its skeletal glory. But in her encouragement to students completing the year, Terry Robertson assures, "You have found the reward in persistence, [in] patience, and in achieving what many believed was just 'too hard' for you."

Sentence diagramming teaches grammar mastery, and Robertson outlines step-by-step how she works with her own public high-school classes. Her method is particularly well-suited for homeschoolers trying to catch up on many lost years of grammar instruction. In fact, older students might have the advantage in grasping complex diagramming schemes.

The author begins a school year by having groups of students make posters to display particular parts of speech. Then slowly, day by day, she coaches students in first marking prepositional phrases, subjects, and predicates in sentences, then stitching them together into simple line diagram schemes. By the fourth quarter of the school year, they are ready to tackle gerund, participial, and infinitive phrases. In retrospect, students realize that diagramming has become for them a parachute of security when they're thrown out on their own to use "who" or "whom," to make subjects and verbs agree, and to modify, punctuate, and capitalize with competence.

This comb-bound text includes just 30 pages of instruction on the method, along with some pluralistic religious references and "gritty" cartoon characters. Much of the diagram material is hand-written, but this very hominess inspires confidence. Robertson provides another 70 or more pages of pre- and post-tests, sample sentences to diagram, and model charts and posters to assist your teaching. Take it one step at a time, check all that equipment, and enjoy the view on the way down! *Cindy Marsch*

Harvey's Elementary Grammar and Composition Harvey's Revised English Grammar

Elementary Grammar, grades 4–6, $11.99. Answer key, $3.99. Revised English Grammar, grades 6–12, $16.99. Answer key, $5.99. Complete set, $30.99. Shipping extra.
Mott Media/Homeschooling Book Club, 1000 E. Huron St., Milford, MI 48381-2422. (800) 421-6645.
Fax: (248) 685-8776.

This duo of classic grammars widely used in the McGuffey era requires (and produces) far more intellectual vigor than any workbooks available today. The teacher is urged to question the student and guide him to discovering the correct answer, rather than either giving him the answer or leaving him to "creatively" thrash it out on his own. As the introduction to the **Harvey's Elementary Grammar and Composition** says:

> *Great care has been taken never to define a term or to enunciate a principle without first preparing the mind of the pupil to grasp and comprehend the meaning and use of the term defined or the principle enumerated.*

That will give you an idea of what you're in for.

Students begin in the *Elementary Grammar* with the study of words, parts of speech, and sentences (figuring out principles concerning each along the way), and move on in **Harvey's Revised English Grammar** to complete sentence analysis and parsing (you may remember this as diagramming). Punctuation, orthography, etymology, syntax, and prosody are thoroughly covered in the latter; some composition is included.

The *Elementary Grammar* is not really "elementary" in the sense of "ridiculously easy." It is intended for grades 4–6, while the Revised Grammar goes through junior high and high school.

These are "programmed" texts; that is, everything the teacher is supposed to say and everything the student is supposed to answer is spelled out, albeit in somewhat outdated language. Example:

> *In the sentence, "Ellen and Mary study botany," what two words are used as the subject? "Ellen" and "Mary." Why? Because something is affirmed of them: both Ellen and Mary study botany.*

Both volumes are notably short on review. Subjects are introduced one after another, and it is assumed that the student has sufficient strength of mind to hang on to each new rule or term while not forgetting the old. *Mary Pride*

Jensen's Grammar presents material "incrementally." That means you don't learn a new skill or concept and then never come back to it. Instead, the just-learned skill is exercised again and again in future lessons until it hopefully becomes second nature.

The three volumes of Jensen's Grammar sequentially cover all grammatical concepts, with an emphasis on writing. Each workbook is completely self-contained; you don't need to buy any extra exercises, tests, answer keys, or a teacher's edition.

In all, the entire series includes 75 lessons, with exercises and tests for each lesson. Each lesson begins with a page of instructions explaining the new grammar concepts, followed by an exercise page. Tests are in the back.

Author Frode Jensen gives you permission to reproduce the tests and charts for personal use. If you have your children write their answers on a separate sheet of paper instead of writing in the workbook—which actually makes the exercises easier to grade—this means each workbook can teach an entire family.

Frode has tried to liven things up by having the exercises include vignettes. I can't call them "stories," since they merely set a scene and never tell you what happened! A surprising number of these vignettes involve weapons, either used in hunting or in battle scenes. Scenes range from ancient times through science-fiction scenarios.

Volume 1 of Jensen's Grammar covers basic parts of speech. **Volume 2** introduces the relative clause and sentence construction. **Volume 3** handles verbals. Where possible, rules and mnemonics are used to make grammar simpler and more memorable.

Teaching and grading time with this series is minimal. As it is being marketed in some quarters as a Christian series, I would have given it more points had I been able to find any actual Christian content. I also think it would have been far more interesting had the vignettes been tied together into a story from lesson to lesson, and had they been less violence-prone. I don't want my children thinking about battles and death almost every time they do their grammar lesson! *Mary Pride*

For those who themselves have a reasonable command of grammar and wish to help others, whether children or adults, who are not so fortunately endowed, this is a wonderful tool. "The central idea of **Learning Grammar through Writing** is to teach grammar to students by having them write compositions regularly and then correct their own work, by applying numbered grammar and punctuation rules." The book is divided into 13 sections—e.g., Verbs, The Sentence, Punctuation. Within each section you will find all the necessary rules and examples in nice large print. This helps, since your student has to either look up or memorize the rules and examples in order to use them to correct his work. The book is inexpensive and reusable. *Mary Pride*

Major Punctuation is the latest by the author of *Jensen's Grammar* and *A Journey Through Grammar Land*. **Major Punctuation** covers the five rules that govern how complete ideas are linked together into sentences. The author found that violation of these rules account for 75–90 percent of student writers' punctuation mistakes. The 78-page workbook requires minimal teacher input and provides seven weeks' worth of lessons (one per rule and two for combinations), a final test, and 10 weeks' worth of reviews.

· The lessons are quick and painless, about 5–10 minutes each, and you will
· find these exercises more interesting than what's usually found in grammar
· texts since they are examples from real books, such as *The Tale of Two*
· *Cities*, *Moby Dick*, *Pilgrim's Progress*, and *The Odyssey*.
·   At the beginning of each lesson week, you will read a short section ex-
· plaining the rule of the week. Each lesson has 20 sentences to be punctuat-
· ed and the appropriate rule cited. Lessons build upon what was previously
· learned, so the sequence of the book should be followed. Answers and
· teacher's notes are at the end of the book, along with a 3 x 5 help card that
· summarizes the five rules.
·   The book reflects a Christian lifestyle, and covers a wide range of topics,
· most of which would be more interesting to high school (or older) stu-
· dents. *Teresa Schultz-Jones*

Answers to Grammar Self-Test

Find the Mistakes

"It's a lovely day outside," Tanasha said. "Let's go out and play!"

"I don't know," Julie replied. "I would have brought my tennis racquet if I'd known it was going to be a nice day."

The two girls walked together to the park. As they neared it, a dog came up to them wagging its tail.

The dog appeared not to belong to anyone. He lay down in front of Tanasha and refused to budge.

"Well, what've we got here?" she wondered.

"I'll give you three guesses," Julie chirped. "First, it's sick and can't move. Second, it wants a warm place to lie down. Third, it loves you and wants to be yours."

It Should Say:

"It's a lovely day outside," Tanasha said. "Let's go out and play!"

"I don't know," Julie replied. "I would have brought my tennis racquet if I'd known it was going to be a nice day."

The two girls walked together to the park. As they neared it, a dog came up to them wagging its tail.

The dog appeared not to belong to anyone. He lay down in front of Tanasha and refused to budge.

"Well, what've we got here?" she wondered.

(*Alt.*) "Well, what have we here?" she wondered.

"I'll give you three guesses," Julie chirped. "First, it's sick and can't move. Second, it wants a warm place to lie down. Third, it loves you and wants to be yours."

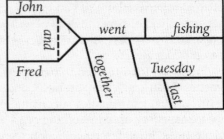

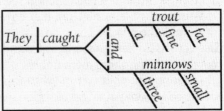

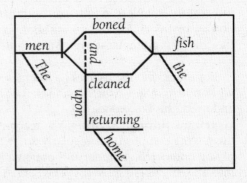

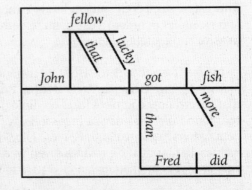

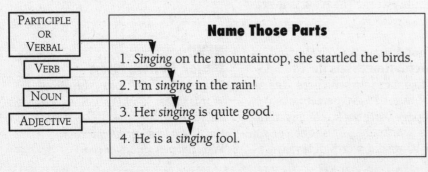

Name Those Parts

1. *Singing* on the mountaintop, she startled the birds.

2. I'm *singing* in the rain!

3. Her *singing* is quite good.

4. He is a *singing* fool.

PARTICIPLE OR VERBAL

VERB

NOUN

ADJECTIVE

CHAPTER 10

Literature

The average college graduate reads only one book a year. If you have a college degree and read one book a week, in other words 52 books a year, that would mean 51 of your fellow college graduates read no books at all, which is pretty pathetic. Could it be they don't like to read because they never learned to read really well (see the Phonics chapter)? Or do they simply lack the education needed to truly understand and enjoy anything more substantial than a magazine article?

I like to blame TV for a lot of things, but I don't blame TV for the decline in reading. Neither TV nor videos can hold a candle to a really good book, with you supplying the action and special effects in your own mind. Remember how disappointed you were when you saw Clark Gable in *Gone with the Wind* after reading the book first? The Rhett Butler in your mind was so much more dashing than even Hollywood's top male lead could ever be. (If you're too young to know what I'm talking about, think of any occasion when you read the book before seeing the movie. Case closed, unless the movie starred Harrison Ford.)

There is some evidence that TV breeds a short attention span, which would tend to discourage the reading habit, but then reading breeds longer attention spans, which would ultimately spell the death of MTV and similar frenetic entertainment if reading were a more popular habit.

Developing a Lifelong Reading Habit

The way to develop a lifelong reading habit, which is to say a lifelong *education* habit, is to read a lot when you are younger, and to be trained to get the most out of what you read. I am not talking about speed reading and skimming, but *understanding*.

You get out of reading what you put into it. The more you know about the people and places the author is writing about, and the more you are able to recognize the literary and cultural allusions the author makes, the more you will feel like the book is a friend, not a cold and inscrutable stranger.

Certain works of literature, such as the plays and poems of Shakespeare, are so much a part of English literature that to know them is to take a huge step forward in understanding the better class of books. That is why a good

How Fiction Teaches

It is my hope that *Mindbend* [a novel about the implications of medicine becoming a business rather than a charitable vocation] will help focus public attention on the gradual but quickening pace of the intrusion of business into medicine. By couching the problem in an emotional framework, it brings the process into personal perspective and allows the reader to understand the implications of the situation through identification with the main character, which I believe is one of the key values of fiction.

—*Best-selling author Robin Cook, author's note to* Mindbend

literature education should not only include instruction on how to get the most out of a book, but reading selections from the great works of the Western world.

Firing the Canon

Lately there has been a lot of pressure to change the literary canon to include brand-new works by minority and women writers. You can read these books, which are mainly chosen to reward the writer's political affiliations, if you wish, but they won't help you understand any works but themselves, whereas the books heretofore considered classics are mentioned again and again in everything from books written later, to movies, to magazines.

Even Disney Studios has made a practice of producing animated features based on classic children's literature (*Cinderella, Sleeping Beauty, The Little Mermaid, The Rescuers,* etc.).

This doesn't mean that the new versions faithfully reflect the originals, just that true classics have staying power and keep cropping up in unexpected new forms.

Maybe the same will be true, in time, for the new politically correct books added to the canon. Maybe. I tend to mistrust the staying power of works chosen for politically expedient reasons. The most famous political works of all—Karl Marx's *Das Kapital* and Adolph Hitler's *Mein Kampf*—are mercifully among the least-read books of our generation. "Often assigned, but never read if the student can help it"—that is the epitaph of works that don't deserve to be in the canon.

Appendix 3 of this volume includes a list of the standard "classics" teachers used to assign, with notes about each work. If you're serious about improving your literary knowledge, this list will be quite enough to start with. It includes a wide range of text types, from fiction to biography to treatise to philosophy to poem.

It's true, the list is rather saturated with Dead European Males. I don't hold this against them, although I am alive and female, and although there isn't a Hungarian on the list (Hungarian being the largest part of my personal ancestry). In their favor, none of these writers assumed his readers throughout all time would be European or dead. (Some of the more ancient writers probably did assume their readers would be male, but since males never developed a separate language from females, it doesn't matter.) These classic authors dealt with matters that touch all human beings, of whatever background. That's part of what makes them classics. The other reason they are classics is that they are superbly written and make memorable points. In other words, they are well worth reading, and we hope you will!

Meanwhile, the resources in this chapter may be useful in helping you "see" more in *all* the books you read, even if you never pick up a classic. Whatever effort you put into this is sure to be repaid in both wisdom and enjoyment for the rest of your life.

Curriculum for Future Literati

"Literati" means "people who are conversant with much famous literature." Thus, one such person should be a *literatus* or *literata*. However, you won't ever see either of these singular nouns, since by definition those who are *conversant* with literature like to *converse*. As in talk. As in flock. Together. Like birds of a feather. If you'd like to join this flock, here's what you need!

Fiction Is Medicine for the Soul

Vera had been Paige's dearest friend and the first person who ever cared about her. The week Vera was hospitalized—first disoriented and suffering, then comatose—had been the worst week of Paige's life. . .

The long hours of that week were engraved indelibly in Paige's memory . . . She . . . could still recall the faces of many of the strangers who, for a time, shared that room with her and Marty.

He said, "You and I were passing the time with novels, so were some other people, not just to escape but because . . . because, at its best, fiction is medicine."

"Medicine?"

"Life is so . . . disorderly, things just happen, and there doesn't seem any point to so much of what we go through. Sometimes it seems the world's a madhouse. Storytelling condenses life, gives it order. Stories have beginnings, middles, ends. And when a story's over, it *meant* something . . . maybe not something complex, maybe what it had to say was simple, even naive, but there was meaning. And that gives us hope, it's a medicine." . . .

She smiled and gently squeezed his hand.

"I don't know," he said, "but I think if some university did a long-term study, they'd discover that people who read fiction don't suffer from depression as much, don't commit suicide as often, are just happier with their lives. Not all fiction, for sure. Not the human-beings-are-garbage-life-stinks-there-is-no-God novels filled with fashionable despair."

—*Dean Koontz,* Mr. Murder
(G. P. Putnam's Sons, 1993)

A Beka's literature texts for grades 7–9 are mainly reading anthologies. Each book includes short stories, poems, and essays. Discussion questions are included for each reading selection, as are pronunciation guides where necessary. "Check Your Speed" sections tell you how many words per minute you were reading if you know how long you took at it. Author biographies and a complete glossary in each volume round out these offerings.

The emphasis in these grades is twofold: becoming aware of literary devices authors use in their work (characterization, scene-setting, plot, and theme), and developing a taste for fine literature. In the words of the introduction to the seventh-grade book, "Each book features a rich variety of important short stories, poems, essays, and plays and a good balance of serious and humorous pieces from the finest writers of America, England, and Europe."

Of People, the 576-page seventh-grade book, includes selections chosen for their emphasis on characterization. The selections are grouped under these topic headings: families and friends, people and animals, pilgrims, patriots, time out for Christmas, explorers, pioneers, men and women of genius, sportsmen, and legendary heroes. Some selections are excerpts from longer works such as *Don Quixote, A Christmas Carol, Robinson Crusoe,* and *Pilgrim's Progress.* Many other selections will be familiar to parents, such as the immortal poem "Casey at the Bat," while many others, though well-known in their own way, are likely to be unfamiliar to most readers, like Honoré Willsie Morrow's fascinating true tale of the boy pioneer who led his six younger siblings, including a baby, over 500 miles of the Oregon Trail when the adults in his party gave up because they thought the trip would be too hard! Many of the stories in this book are about Christians (e.g., Isaac Watts, the original martyred missionaries to the Auca Indians, William the Silent, and George Washington Carver). As advertised, each story and poem unfailingly presents us with a strong character. Some of the discussion questions lead the student to observe the literary techniques that spotlight these characters, though I'd like to see them brought out more explicitly. (Perhaps they are in the teacher's guides, which I haven't seen.)

Of Places, for eighth-graders, is supposed to draw students' attention to how each author sets a scene. Its 529 pages include excerpts from *Caddie Woodlawn, The Yearling, The Incredible Journey,* and *The Song of Hiawatha.* ("By the shores of Gitchee Gumee/By the shining Big-Sea-Water/Stood the wigwam of Nokomis . . ."), among dozens of other readings. The selections in this book are grouped by place, it's true—neighborhood, school, home, America, around the world, over all the earth, about the sea, upon the mountains, and in the realm of the imagination—but the questions and selections still focus mainly in on character, whatever the book title might say.

Ninth-graders move on to studying literary themes in a book appropriately titled **Themes in Literature**. This book more successfully carries out its mission, grouping selections in units with titles like "Truth and Wisdom," "Courage," "Humility," "Justice," "Temperance," "Beauty," "Faith and Hope," "Love," and "Time and Eternity" (an entire section on death and dying). Among famous authors anthologized in this volume are Count Tolstoy, Nathaniel Hawthorne (author of *Tanglewood Tales*), Mark Twain, Geoffrey Chaucer, the melancholy William Cowper, the frivolous and sensuous Giovanni Boccaccio, and Guy de Maupassant—to name just a few. In fact, you'll see a lot more famous names here than you did in the first two books in the series. Here also, for the first time, a large number of the selections dwell on death, dying, loss, and other painful themes.

A Beka's literature course for grades 10–12, called the Classics for Christians series, takes more of a "survey" approach. Grade 10 surveys world literature, grade 11 American literature, and grade 12 English literature. Again, many classics are included or excerpted. Each course has two books. In grade 10, for example, the first book, **Backgrounds to World Literature**, repeats

A Beka Literature Curriculum
Grades 7–12. Of People, Of Places, Themes in Literature, $16.20 each. Backgrounds to World Literature, Masterpieces from World Literature, Beginnings of American Literature, The Literature of the American People, Introduction to English Literature, The Literature of England, $14.35 each. All texts are paperbound. Student test booklets, teacher keys available for grades 10–12 courses. Shipping extra.
A Beka Book, Pensacola Christian College, Box 18000, Pensacola, FL 32523-9160. (800) 874-2352. Fax: (800) 874-3590. Web: www.abeka.com.

In the Classics for Christians series there are, as in the ninth-grade book, a large number of selections in which major characters die or anticipate the approach of death. This becomes almost ludicrous in places, as in *Masterpieces from World Literature,* where the entire section on classical Greece is so saturated with death that—well, let me just share some of the selection titles in this one section: "The Death of Hector," "Death to the Pagan and to the Christian," "Brevity of Life," "On Early Death," "The Dying Christian to His Soul," "Death Be Not Proud" (a poem by the 17th century Englishman John Donne which only seems to be included here because its subject matter fits the gloomy setting), "The Funeral Oration of Pericles," "The Death of Socrates," and "On Tragedy." Also included in this section is Sophocles' *Antigone,* a play about a sister who attempts to bury her dead brothers and in consequence is given the death penalty herself, the poem "Unhappy Dionysius," and "Elegy for Heraclitus."

This is not an isolated example: depressing tales and poems are found throughout the series. To pick some at random, how about Ambrose Bierce's *An Occurrence at Owl Creek Bridge,* which gave me nightmares after I saw the film in public-school ninth grade, or Poe's *The Pit and the Pendulum,* a classic horror tale, both found (among others) in volume 3 of this series?

In all, I would say that A Beka's upper-grades literature program is somewhat unbalanced. Kids don't need this much tragedy, especially in the suicide-prone teen years. My advice would be to lighten up on the death and misery. Bring on some Ogden Nash and P. G. Wodehouse!

Alpha Omega Language-Arts LIFEPACs

Grades 1–12. 10 LIFEPACs per grade. LIFEPACs: $3.50 each (Grades 1–10), $2.95 each (grades 11–12). Set of 10, $28.50 and up. Teacher's guides and answer keys extra. Books available for literature component of courses: The Hiding Place, $6.50 (grade 7); The Miracle Worker, $5.50; 20,000 Leagues Under the Sea, $4.95 (grade 9); In His Steps, $6.95 (grade 10); Our Town, $8; The Old Man and the Sea, $8.95 (grade 11); Hamlet, $3.99 (grade 12). Shipping extra.
Alpha Omega Publications, 300 N. McKemy, Chandler, AZ 85226. Orders and inquiries: (800) 622-3070. Fax: (480) 785-8034. Web: www.home-schooling.com.

As compared to, say, Bob Jones University Press, whose upper-grades American and British literature courses are so thorough as to be college level, the Alpha Omega courses are quite within the reach of average high-school kids. This is partly because they are not as extensive; you're looking at several literature LIFEPACs per grade instead of two-textbook sequences for both American and British literature. If you are mostly concerned about basic college skills and just want to introduce yourself or your students to literary history and its genres, Alpha Omega is a good choice.

the lessons of grades 7–9 by emphasizing literary devices, while the second book, **Masterpieces from World Literature**, presents reading selections in historical sequence. We then proceed, not to English literature (as one would expect, since it came next chronologically), but to American literature. The two volumes in this course cover American literature in chronological order, with the second one taking up at the later 19th and 20th centuries. Unusual features of this course include a lengthy study of the novel *The Scarlet Letter,* a post-Puritan story of two adulterers (one a minister) and how they deal with their guilt (not entirely in a satisfactory manner). English literature, in the 12th grade, is again presented in chronological order. The first book, **Introduction to English Literature**, includes the entire text of *Macbeth* and *Pilgrim's Progress,* as well as a good chunk of literary history and plenty from the works of early English writers from Venerable Bede through John Milton. **The Literature of England**, the last book of the series, studies English literature "as a reflection of the spiritual state of the British people through the ages," from the Restoration through the modern day. This whole series is *packed* with poetry—far more than I've seen in any other publisher's upper-grades books.

A notable feature of the grades 10–12 books is the integration of art with literature. Each book in this series is illustrated with dozens of full-color reproductions of famous art works. Also worth mentioning is that A Beka prefers to put its main emphasis on the literature itself, rather than the history of literature. *Mary Pride*

Literature study for **Alpha Omega** starts with *The Hiding Place* and non-fiction in grade 7, then proceeds to essays and autobiography in Grade 8. Grade 9 starts with grammar, but is mostly literature studies. New literary genres introduced are the short story (including "The Slip-Over Sweater" and the very moving science-fiction classic, "Flowers for Algernon"), poetry, drama (*The Miracle Worker*, the story of the woman who taught the blind, deaf, and willful Helen Keller to speak, read, and write), and the novel (*Twenty Thousand Leagues under the Sea* by Jules Verne, starring the infamous Captain Nemo). Students learn to look behind the scenes at conflict, characterization, plot, theme, language, setting, and symbolism, all of which is great.

Things perk up with the seventh LIFEPAC in grade 10, "Oral Reading and Drama," which is followed by "The Short Story" and "Studies in the Novel." Each of these LIFEPACs studies a famous example of its genre: the drama *Everyman*, short stories by Twain and de Maupassant, and the turn-of-the-century Christian novel *In His Steps*. Although we've looked at these literary forms before, we do pick up on a few new ideas, and it's a relief to have three units in a row on the same general topic.

The best units in grade 11 are LIFEPACs 5–9. LIFEPAC 5 is about poetry—its metre, appeal, imagery, and connotations. LIFEPAC 6 looks at non-fiction—its elements, types, topics for reading, and tips for composing it. LIFEPAC 7 looks at American drama—its history, how drama is put together and how it works, and a study of Thornton Wilder's *Our Town*. LIFEPAC 8, "Studies in the American Novel," again summarizes the history of the genre, then looks at a specific novel (Hemingway's *The Old Man and the Sea*). As a bonus this LIFEPAC includes information on how to write a critical essay.

LIFEPAC 5 of grade 12 has an in-depth introduction to medieval British literature, followed quite sensibly by LIFEPACs on Elizabethan literature and 17th- and 18th-century British literature. For some reason a unit on creative writing is interposed, then we're back to a LIFEPAC on Romantic and Victorian poetry. This is the best grade for literature studies, especially if you leave out the grammar and usage LIFEPACs. *Mary Pride*

Bob Jones University Press
takes a slightly different approach
to literature than A Beka, with a
four-grade series introducing students to literary themes, styles, and
devices, followed by a two-grade survey of American and British literature. Reading selections are included in each book, but they are not as
anthological in format as the A
Beka books, containing more literary history and textual analysis, and
are not as heavily loaded with poetry selections. Like the A Beka series, the BJUP series does include
many different authors and types of
literature. All student texts are
hardbound, very nicely laid out,
and copiously illustrated.

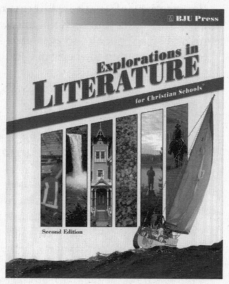

Explorations in Literature, the seventh-grade book, is organized into
six three-week units on the themes of courage, nature and man, generosity,
patriotism, humility, and the family. This book is intended to introduce the
rudiments of literary discernment, as students move from reading mainly
for pleasure to thinking more deeply about what they read. Themes in the
eighth-grade book, **Excursions in Literature**, are choices, friendships,
viewpoints, adventurers, discoveries, and heroes and villains. Again, the
book has a character-building emphasis, as the student is asked to identify his
own journey through life in terms of these themes. **Fundamentals of
Literature**, for grade 9, introduces the student to literary analysis. This
text introduces conflict, characterization, theme, structure, point of view,
and moral tone, with one unit devoted to each. Finally, **Elements of
Literature**, the 10th-grade book, waxes more philosophical by "focusing
on those literary details that define and distinguish interpretive literature."

If you want a formal course, be sure to get the teacher's manual or
teacher's edition. The teacher's *manuals* (grades 7 and 8) provide all the daily lessons, activities, and assignments. The teacher's *editions* (grades 9–12)
include the full student book text on each teacher's page as well as lesson
plans and assignments. The teacher's manuals or editions are *absolutely necessary* if you want to teach a formal course, since the student books for
these grades *only* include the reading selections and "Reading Check" questions. The teacher's books are really excellent teaching tools, too, opening
students' eyes to literature's spiritual, moral, and technical aspects through
analysis and discussion of the reading assignments and carefully-chosen
writing assignments. One writing assignment, for example, is to turn a story into a drama. The teacher's manual explains the exact steps students
need to go through to make the transformation.

After grade 10, the upper-grades literature curriculum now switches
over to a chronological study of **American** and **British Literature**, the
same sequence as A Beka presents. Each course examines literary works in
the light of the author's life, the historical period and literary movement to
which he belonged, and what the Bible has to say about the underlying
philosophies of these movements. Lots of *long* reading selections, intermixed
with shorter stories, essays, and poems. Both books include a complete
modern play. These are *not* "fun" books—frankly, I think they would work
well in a college course. *Mary Pride*

**BJUP Literature for Christian
Schools**
Explorations in Literature (grade 7),
Excursions in Literature (grade 8),
Fundamentals of Literature (grade
9), and Elements of Literature (grade
10), $30 each. Teachers Manuals
(grades 7 and 8, 9 and 10), $39 each.
American Literature (grade 11), $30;
teacher's edition, $42.50. British
Literature (grade 12), $30; teacher's
edition $42.50. Various videos, clas-
sic books, and teacher's guides to
the classics also available. Shipping
extra.
*Bob Jones University Press Customer
Services, Greenville, SC 29614.
Orders: (800) 845-5731.
Web: www.bjup.com.*

These books are all wholesome and
enormous fun to read, containing a
great mix of drama, humor, tear-jerkers,
and whatever else appeals to preteen
children. I read several of the stories
and poems out loud at the dinner table,
and every child in our family read
through the books in the next weeks!
You can, then, use the books either as
the basis of a formal study course, or
simply as readers to introduce your
children to famous authors and styles.

When we were using the upper-
grades literature program, my most severe criticism was that the background
political history was so densely packed
that it was not always easy to assimilate.
This is a common failing of upper-
grades material when it deals with history—loading the student with so
many names and dates that he can't
possibly retain them all. All this encyclopedic information is fascinating, but
a broader tracing of background history
would suffice, without distracting student attention from the literature itself.
BJUP says that this criticism is no
longer true, but we haven't seen review
samples of the up-to-date versions, so
we don't know. Other sources of information to acclimate a student to the
time periods he is about to study are
the EDC Publishing or Dorling
Kindersley titles that deal with British
history. These books, which emphasize
how people lived in each time period,
help a lot in avoiding culture shock.

Christian Light Perspective of Truth series

Grades 9–12. Perspectives of Life, grades 9–10: student book, $22.95; teacher materials, $17 (includes teacher's guidebook and test answer key). Perspectives of Truth, grade 12: student book, $22.95; teacher materials, $5; teacher's guidebook, $12. Student materials, $10. Shipping extra. *Christian Light Education, PO Box 1212, Harrisonburg, VA 22801-1212. (540) 434-1003. Fax: (540) 433-8896. Email: orders@clp.org.*

These lovely hardbound books are a bargain in themselves. For 600 textbook pages of this quality of printing, you'd normally expect to pay $40 to $80.

Perspectives of Truth in Literature is an absolutely marvelous literature text that leads your teen not only to discover the different literary forms and styles, but also to evaluate a book's content.

Some quotes from the beginning of Unit 1:

> *We do not go to literature to find truth, but simply to find truth well expressed and illustrated . . .*
>
> *The standard of truth is not the man who writes it or the time in which it is written, but rather, truth is judged by the revelation of God . . .*
>
> *Many men pride themselves on having an open mind. By this they claim to be able to consider any new idea without first rejecting it. They hope they will be able to reject it if it is wrong.*
>
> *Such men consider persons inferior who have already made up their minds about certain subjects and refuse to entertain any further discussion. But such open-minded persons are often in a dangerous position. For if a person opens his mind to anything, he should not be surprised to discover that his mind is harboring a lot of mental garbage and what truth he has is being corrupted.*
>
> *But a closed-minded person is also in danger. Much error is quite probably locked on the inside and much truth is knocking in vain from the outside.*
>
> *How then should we read? We must read with a noble mind like the Bereans of Paul's day. All literature must be tested by the yardstick of God's Word. What measures up is to be accepted and savored; what fails the test is to be rejected without further consideration.*

Reading this text is a treat, because of the exceedingly high quality of the stories, essays, and poems included in the book, and the excellent thought questions at the end of each selection. Comprehension, reading speed, and writing technique are also covered in this text. With some adaptation (e.g., the parent reading the stories aloud and then discussing the questions with the child) I would think you could begin to use **Perspectives of Truth in Literature** with preteens as well. In any case, it is too good a book for any literature-minded *parent* to miss!

The new **Perspectives of Life in Literature** is the second textbook in the CLE high school literature series. It is broken down into five units: short stories, poetry, biography, allegory, and reflections (on the theme of Christian victory). Each of these units is further subdivided. For example, three short stories each are grouped under the headings of Symbolism, Tone, and Unity. Poetry is subdivided into kinds of poetry (blank verse, rhymed and bound verse, and free verse), poetic form (acrostic, triolet, sonnet, and Hebrew poetry), purposes for poems, and poems in four major themes on the subject of joy. The biographical subjects are Menno Simons, John Bunyan, Clayton Kratz, and William Carey. "Reflections" are on the themes of discipline, ambition, faithful Christians, and Bible characters—three or four on each theme. The Allegory section includes most of the text of Bunyan's *Pilgrim's Progress*, plus the Bible parable of the ten virgins and a couple more. By the time you finish the book, you will not only be familiar with the terms and methods of literary analysis, but you'll also have developed a good understanding of how to evaluate literature in the light of eternity.

Also included in both books are exercises for vocabulary, comprehension, and writing. The Student Packet for grades 9 and 10 includes five

Lightunits in a workbook, plus five tests. The Student Packet for grade 12 includes a workbook with 10 Lightunits, plus 10 tests.

If you're looking for an excellent literature course with a biblical worldview, and don't mind missing out on the worldly authors covered in the SAT II and AP literature tests, there isn't a better set of books around. *Mary Pride*

What's black and yellow and read all over? **Cliffs Notes**! Yes, those helpful little books that saved your bacon when you forgot to read the tomes your high-school Lit teacher assigned you are still around. Over 200 are now available, for titles from *Absalom, Absalom!* to *Wuthering Heights*.

But we homeschoolers are too noble and pure to ever "cheat" by using Cliffs Notes, right? We *always* read the entire assigned book, don't we?

Well, not always. Here's one good reason to invest in some Cliffs Notes: an increasing number of nihilistic, politically correct, sexually explicit, and otherwise dubious literary works are being hustled into the literary "canon" on which standardized tests of literature are based. You don't want to slog through these if you can help it, but on the other hand you don't want to flunk the test. The solution: zap through undesirable books with Cliffs Notes!

Here's another good use for Cliffs Notes: as a mini-literature course of their own. Cliffs Notes do more than just summarize the plot. They also include a brief life of the author, a list of characters, an introduction to the book's themes and historical context, character analyses, perhaps an essay or two related to the book, a list of topics for essays you can base on the book, and a bibliography for more study, should you feel so inclined. If you *do* read the book, you'll get much more out of it after reading the accompanying Cliffs Notes. If the book uses difficult language, foreign phrases, dialects, or words that have gone out of use, the Cliffs Notes translates these into modern English, chapter by chapter. (Complete Study Editions, available only for Shakespeare and Chaucer, include the complete text, a running commentary, and glossary, side-by-side in three columns per page.)

A book may be famous and influential, but life is too short to read books you don't like, or whose viewpoint you hate, or that you have to struggle too hard to understand. Look at it this way—*they* read *Lord of the Flies* (a book I would not recommend to *anyone,* let alone a sensitive teenager) so *you* don't have to! *Mary Pride*

When you decide to start reading the classics of the ancient world, you will discover you have a problem. Many of them refer to mythology, or to other classics which you have not yet read. It can literally take years before you piece it all together—and then you almost need to start at the beginning again, so you can finally read your way through with understanding.

These books from the Cliffs Notes people may solve your problem.

Cliffs Notes on Mythology presents the basic gods and myths of Egypt, Babylon, India, Greece, and Rome, plus the major Norse gods and myths, and a section on Arthurian legends. Refreshingly, the Old Testament is *not* included, nor are we treated to the spectacle of Abraham and Samson being handled as mythological figures. If you can manage 200 well-written pages, you can quickly come up to speed on ancient mythology. If this is too much for you, you can use the index to look up myths and mythological beings as you encounter them in literature. The book also includes recommended reading lists of both primary sources (actual myths) and sec-  ondary sources (books about myths), plus geneological charts to help you straighten out which "deity" begat who or what, and a few review questions.

Be aware that all was not tea and biscuits back in ancient days. In all these books, stories of lust, murder, torture, betrayal, and unnatural family relations are common. Zeus, for example, could never keep his hands off any pretty girl. Oedipus killed his father and married his mother. Not that the flesh-and-blood people were all that much better. I need only mention Nero and Caligula, as two examples of Roman emperors whose antics were X-rated. These Cliffs books handle such topics as matter-of-factly as possible, without seeking to exploit any prurient interests. Even so, it's often like reading the ultimate soap opera.

Covenant Home Classic Critiques

Grades 5–12. $12.95 per set; $24.95 for both. Shipping extra.
Covenant Home Curriculum, 17800 W. Capitol Dr., Brookfield, WI 53045. (414) 781-2171. Fax: (414) 781-0589. Email: educate@covenanthome.com. Web: covenanthome.com.

Cliffs Notes on Greek Classics is about twice as fat and covers an enormous amount of territory. For "Greek Epic Poetry," you get summaries of works by Homer and Hesiod. A "Greek Drama" section explains the structure of your typical ancient Greek play. You then get summaries of 32 Greek tragedies (by Aeschylus, Sophocles, and Euripides) and 10 Greek comedies (by Aristophanes and Menander). For Greek prose writers, you get Lysias, Demosthenes, and Aesop. For lyric poets, Sappho, Pindar, Alaeus, and a bunch of "lesser" poets. For Greek historians, Herodotus, Thucydides, and Xenophon. For Greek philosophers, summaries of 10 works by Plato and Aristotle. All this plus a glossary, timeline, selected bibliography (which includes both primary and secondary sources), and index.

Cliffs Notes on Roman Classics is another tome, just slightly smaller than Greek Classics. This one is laid out in chronological order, starting with "Early Roman Literature" (summaries of four works by Plautus), "The Roman Republic" (an introduction to Roman drama, plus summaries of a humorous play by Terence and a multi-volume history of Rome by Ennius), "The Golden Age" (Cicero, Julius Caesar, Lucretius, Catullus, Virgil, Livy, Tibullus, Propertius, Horace, and Ovid), "The Silver Age" (Seneca, Longinus, Pliny the Elder, Pliny the Younger, Josephus, Martial, Plutarch, Tacitus, Epictetus, Juvenal, Suetonius, and two minor writers), and "The Late Empire" (Marcus Aurelius, Apelius, St. Jerome, and St. Augustine). Again, each writer is introduced in historical context, and his work is summarized and commented on. Again, you also get a glossary, timeline, genealogy (this time of Roman emperors), selected bibliography, and index. *Mary Pride*

How about a homeschool publisher who does the book reports for you? **Classic Critiques** from Covenant Home Curriculum provide a roadmap through classic literature. Each Critique includes a story summary, with attention to the author's worldview. The summaries themselves are rather exciting, and could well serve as interest-sparkers enticing families to read those books. Some Critiques also feature discussion questions; others have suggestions for topics to discuss.

Each Classic Critique is printed on a single sheet, usually folded in the middle. We're not talking about overwhelming you with tons of data here! They are also attractively printed on parchment-style paper, with a line-drawing illustration of a scene from the book on each cover.

List A includes *Great Expectations, Treasure Island, Macbeth, The Red Badge of Courage, Captains Courageous, Wuthering Heights, Twenty Thousand Leagues under the Sea, Pride and Prejudice, The Call of the Wild, Gulliver's Travels, The Turn of the Screw, Paradise Lost,* and *The Wind in the Willows.*

List B includes *Jane Eyre, A Tale of Two Cities, The Last of the Mohicans, Ivanhoe, Canterbury Tales, Hamlet, The Hunchback of Notre Dame, Julius Caesar, Moby Dick, The Iliad, The Odyssey, Alice in Wonderland,* and *Up from Slavery.*

The Covenant Home Curriculum includes many of these books, plus much emphasis on creative writing and correct grammar. If you consider in-depth study of great literature from a Christian viewpoint important for your child's education, you might want to look into either Classic Critiques or the entire Covenant Home Curriculum program (described in detail in Volume 1). *Mary Pride*

Learn to quickly recognize the "slant" of most books that touch on the subjects of law, history, economics, and literature, with the help of lists of "positive indicators" and "negative indicators," each introduced in a very short chapter in this very short (112-page) book. An "indicator" is a phrase that typically reveals an author's bias. Example of a positive indicator: "Overcome problems and move forward." The associated "recommended reading" list of books and media with this particular positive indicator includes *Island of the Blue Dolphins, Robinson Crusoe,* and the "Little House" books—as well as a plug for the *Star Trek* series! A "negative indicator": "Their motives were corrupt" (referring to the Founding Fathers).

Lists of "misleading terms" are also included in **Evaluating Books**, such as "debt to society," "the economy," and "unregulated" (when used as a cuss word meaning "It oughta be regulated!"). Along with the "statist viewpoint" for each negative indicator, you get "the other side of the story"—e.g., why the statist outlook is wrong in this instance, along with a Jefferson quote supporting the "other side." Not surprising, since the book's subtitle is "Guidelines for selecting books consistent with the principles of America's Founders." Plus you get a list of recommended authors (not all of whom I would recommend—e.g., Robert Heinlein's early novels are great, but his later ones are full of sex and attempts to justify unfaithfulness as a lifestyle), mail-order bookstores, organizations (again, some better than others), and a handy index. *Mary Pride*

Canadian homeschoolers, take heart! Your country's settlement is the clever centerpiece of the first of the **Family Reading Guide series**: a pleasant unit-study approach to *Anne of Green Gables*. The Liesenfelt family has devised "The Canada Game" comb-bound into a charming but primitively-illustrated study guide, and in the course of playing the game your family will learn a lot about exploration and immigration, farming, logging, mining, fishing, and fur trading. You must cut out all the colored-paper and card-stock game pieces yourself, but any family of *Monopoly* nuts should love it. Individual chapters for all three study guides include solid vocabulary study (crosswords, word search, and fill-in-the-blank) and standard discussion questions. A preface to this guide includes such science questions as why Anne did not help Minnie May's croup with a dose of ipecac.

Soften the edges of a mining or geology curriculum with the guide to George MacDonald's *The Princess and the Goblin*. The complex but fascinating "Masterminer" game in this study has players manage mining operations by hiring pickax-wielders, dynamite-haulers, basket-haulers, and cart-pullers; and by investing in various grades of ventilation, support, and lighting systems for the workers. The winner will have made the most profit at the end of the game, and playing pieces include a tidy study of mining and enough on minerals to reinforce your outside study of geology.

Since this review was first written, the reading guide to *The Children of Odin* has been dropped, and five more have been added. Their titles are: *A Christmas Carol, The Prince and the Pauper, The Princess and the Goblin, Alice's Adventures in Wonderland, Anne of Green Gables, Wind in the Willows,* and *The Secret Garden. Cindy Marsch*

NEW!
Evaluating Books: What Would Thomas Jefferson Think About This? An "Uncle Eric" Book

Grade 9–adult. $8.95 plus shipping. *Bluestocking Press, PO Box 2030, Shingle Springs, CA 95682-2030. Orders: (800) 959-8586. Inquiries: (530) 621-1123. Fax: (530) 642-9222. Email: uncleric@jps.net.*

NEW!
A Family Reading Guide series

Grades 5–10. A Christmas Carol, $8. The Prince and the Pauper, $22. The Princess and the Goblin, $20. Alice's Adventures in Wonderland, $18. Anne of Green Gables, $18. Wind in the Willows, $18. The Secret Garden, $22. *Treegate Publications of Wisconsin, 833 Liberty Drive, DeForest, WI 53532. (608) 846-8728.*

NEW!
Great Authors of the Western Literary Tradition

College/adult. Audio series, $399.95 plus shipping. Discount for first-time buyers.

The Teaching Company, 7405 Alban Station Court, Suite A107, Springfield, VA 22150. (800) 832-2412.
Fax: (703) 912-7756.
Email: custserv@teachco.com.
Web: www.teachco.com.

This set contains lectures on half of the "Great Books" as The Teaching Company has put most of the lectures on the philosophically oriented books in the series *The Great Minds of the Western Intellectual Tradition*. They also have a separate set on the plays of Shakespeare that appears quite promising, as well as many other series that provide a wealth of educational opportunities.

The audio series **Great Authors of the Western Literary Tradition** brings to your living room the opportunity to sit at the feet of some of America's finest Ivy League professors as they lecture on the books that form the *corpus* of the Western literary tradition. If you have ever thought that sending your child to an Ivy League college would be a dream come true but were mortified by the current tuition, this set of remarkable lectures might just be the opportunity for which you always hoped. Now available only on audiocassette, the set contains eighty 45-minute lectures. The price of the lecture time in this series ($6.67/hour) compares almost comically with the price of actually going to an Ivy League College and sitting in on the lectures in person (over $60/hour at most of the Ivy League colleges).

The lectures in this series do not focus on such broad topics as "Greek Literature" or "Literature in Venice." Each lecture focuses on a particular book and attempts to prepare the students for an intelligent reading of that text. This format works very well, for you do not have to sit through lectures full of general and vague observations but are given ready aid to set out on your own journeys in the delightful world of first-hand literary exploration.

The lecturers chosen for the "Great Authors" series are the best that one can expect from collegiate academia. The lectures are usually aimed at an audience that is only vaguely familiar with the texts, so much time is spent giving introductory explanations that are helpful to the first-time reader. The themes discussed are usually the stock themes that comprise the standard observations usually given when commenting on these texts. This is a delightful contrast to the trendy college professors who in their interest in staying abreast of the latest literary criticism burden their students with explanations of esoteric scholarly disputes that bear little relation to the core themes that make these texts fascinating reading. Most of the professors chosen to lecture in this series also show themselves delightfully oblivious to the politically correct browbeating served up in the latest dispatches from the Disgruntled People's Studies Department. This video series may have done us the favor of preserving for posterity a remarkable sampling of education before multiculturalism. This series is excellent for those who would like to have an introduction to the books the comprise the "great conversation" that has wound itself down through the corridors of Western history.

Even though this series is not plagued by many of the ills that beset contemporary education, one should not be so naïve as to think that they do not afford some very serious challenges to the fidelity of those wedded to the biblical worldview. Before the advent of the dumbing down of our colleges, most Christians going into the secular colleges understood that there was a serious intellectual challenge to the Christian faith that they would have to face if they were to remain intellectually vital in these institutions. The same challenge will face those who would glean from the teaching in these tapes. Even though it is far beyond the scope of this article to examine in detail the views put forward by each of the lecturers, I would like to give some general observations on the major ones.

S. Georgia Nugent (Princeton)—Nugent provides most of the lectures on the ancient Greek writers. In her light but engaging lecture style she is able to bring out the literary themes that are at the core of what makes the books a delight to read. Even thought she mentions an interest in feminist studies, this only surfaces in her necessary observations regarding the low place for and mistreatment of women in Greek society.

Michael Sugrue (Princeton)—Despite his nervous pacing and vivacious gesticulations, Sugrue's content quickly draws one into the literary panoramas he lays out. He shows tremendous ability in expositing a book's central themes, but he is a caricature of the hard-nosed skeptical intellectual out to champion the secularism found in writers such as Thucydides and

Descartes. His heavy-handed treatment of theological questions in his lecture on the book of Job make his lack of spiritual discernment painfully obvious. In his lecture on Pascal's *Pensees*, he also shows a deep lack of understanding of Pascal's Christian motivations; however, he does have a good number of helpful observations on the disagreements between Pascal and Descartes.

Arnold Weinstein (Brown)—Weinstein's introductory lecture to the series is almost enough to set one against the rest of the tapes to come. Weinstein is a thoroughly modern man whose vague attempts to find a justification for the study of literature could almost be a casebook example for the unprincipled wide-eyed liberal attempting to pull moral phrases out of his own vacuous psyche. He shows a disconcerting ability to find Freudian metaphors throughout the literature he lectures on, no matter what the period. His lectures on modern literature show the fruits of what is obviously his expertise; however, his lectures on the earlier literature have a chaff-to-wheat ratio that is so high that they are often not worth the struggle of listening. One thing that can be said in his favor is that he is so boring to listen to that you need have little fear your children would pay him attention long enough to suffer the ill effects of his teaching.

If you are interested in finding something to put your student in front of while you do the laundry, these tapes will not prove the "child-safe" diversion that you might hope for; however, for those who are willing to take up the hard work of cultural discernment, these tapes offer a remarkable opportunity to acquaint oneself with the works that have shaped our culture's intellectual history. *Fritz Hinrichs*

Have you wanted to tackle the classics but didn't know how? If you feel inadequate, these guides may be just the ticket. Written by a homeschool mom with eleven years of teaching experience in the public schools, the **Great Books Guides** are a thoroughly Christian approach to literature.

The *Scarlet Letter* study guide—the one I reviewed—is a 64-page, spiral-bound consumable workbook, packed with activities to make standard high-school classics more approachable. You will learn about literary terms, drama terminology, the major themes and symbols used in each book and learn something about the author—in this case, Nathaniel Hawthorne. A separate page lists all the unusual vocabulary words. Next are study guide questions, divided by chapters, which help you deal with the plot itself. The critical thinking questions are good enough, although I would have liked to see more of them, and would have appreciated more questions that delved into analytical comparison. Some representative questions:

> *"Is Dimmesdale a weak character? Should he have confessed?"*
> *"Was Chillingworth always an evil man? If not, what led him to become one?"*

You get a short fill-in-the blank, true/false quiz for testing comprehension, creative and expository writing assignment ideas, and enrichment activities.

Don't despair if critiquing your teen's writing is a foreign concept. A complete and detailed check list for compositions is included to guide you in what to look for. And finally, a seven-page unit test rounds out the guide. All answers are included in the back.

Great Books Guides are available for other American and British literary classics and are designed to encompass a full year's study of each. They're also complete enough that they can be used by your teen on their own. But why not share the experience with them? All in all, this would make a solid purchase. *Marla Perry*

NEW!
Great Books Guides
Grades 9–12. Each guide, $18.95.
$2 discount for first-time orders.
Shipping extra.
McJake Enterprises, 110 Leckford Way, Cary, NC 27513. (919) 469-1229.
Email: Karenncary@aol.com.
Web: members.aol.com/mmaddry/.

NEW!
How to Read a Book

Grade 9–adult. $13 postpaid.
*Simon & Schuster, Att: Order Dept.,
200 Old Tappan Rd., Old Tappan, NJ
07675. (800) 223-2348 ext. 6. (800)
445-6991. Web: www.simonsays.com.*

How could a book with the title **How to Read a Book** ever make it onto the New York Times bestseller list? Doesn't that title put it in the same category as *How to Take a Bath*—information about something everyone already knows how to do?

Released in 1940, and in revised form in 1972, this "Classic Guide to Intelligent Reading" is about how to advance intellectually by learning to understand what you read in books of all sorts—especially those that are somewhat "above" you in subject content. What it really is, is a self-study program for intellectual development.

People used to attend four years of college to get instruction similar to what is packed between the covers of this 426-page book. Now they still go to college, usually taking *six* years to graduate, and don't get most of what this book contains. The literary "deconstructionists," who sail perilously close to declaring that no human being can understand what any other human being writes, because we are all just a bunch of chemicals reacting to our environment, and therefore (implicitly) all literature is really good for is therapy or propaganda, infest today's college campuses to such a degree that literature classes have become a series of rants on the authors' supposed politics and sexual preferences, and the classics themselves are an endangered species, most having had the bad taste to have been written by dead white males. For if there is no truth, and no abstract standard of excellence, just various forms of chemical soup striving for evolutionary dominance, why not make literature class (and all other classes) into ethnic, sexual, and racial wars as to whose DNA sequences are best represented?

Authors Mortimer Adler and Charles Van Doren wrote their book before this silliness gained its foothold, and therefore *How to Read a Book* takes the position that you *can* understand what an author meant, although it may take more or less effort, depending on the author. The authors introduce four levels of reading: elementary ("the cat sat on the hat"), inspectional ("you have 15 minutes to read this passage," otherwise known as systematic skimming), analytical ("what kind of book is it, what is the author saying, do you agree or disagree with him, and why?"), and syntopical ("find a number of books that treat the same topic, find the relevant passages, translate them into similar terms, and compare them"). They show how to do this for books both practical and theoretical, books on all academic subjects (math, history, science, etc.), imaginative fiction of classical standing (epics, poetry, novels, drama), reference books, journalistic writing, and even advertising. As a fillup, they also include a suggested reading list (137 authors, from Homer to Solzhenitsyn, most with several suggested works apiece), and an appendix of reading exercises and tests. Quite a lot for the modest price. *Mary Pride*

NEW!
Oxford School Shakespeare series

Grades 6–12. Each book, $7.50–$7.95.
Practical Teaching, $12.95.
*Oxford University Press, 2001 Evans
Road, Cary, NC 27513. (800) 451-
7556. Fax: (919) 677-1303.
Web: www.oup-usa.org.*

The **Oxford School Shakespeare series** allows young readers to study Shakespeare in the original Elizabethan language—and understand it. Introductory scene-by-scene commentary explains the plot. The full play text follows. Wide margins include explanatory notes: what the strange words and phrases mean in today's English, plus helpful hints on character motivation. Each book in the series also includes a description of the leading characters, background on Shakespeare's England, a timeline of Shakespeare's complete works, discussion questions and test suggestions, comments from famous critics, and suggestions for further reading. Just what you need to get a grip on the Bard.

Titles currently available: *Anthony & Cleopatra, As You Like It, Henry IV, Henry V, Julius Caesar, King Lear, Macbeth, Merchants of Venice, Midsummer Night's Dream, Othello, Richard II, Romeo and Juliet, Taming of the Shrew, The Tempest, Twelfth Night,* and *Winter's Tale.* An optional instructor's manual, *Practical Teaching of Shakespeare,* is also available. *Mary Pride*

Perhaps even more useful than Cliff's mythology guides, and covering both the Greek and Roman myths in one book (instead of Cliff's two), **A Short Guide to Classical Mythology** is set up in dictionary style, with entries in alphabetical order. Some entries are brief, simply telling you who a minor character was and in what stories he appeared. Other entries include entire story summaries. For example, the entry under "Odysseus" first tells you who Odysseus was, then narrates his adventures, divided into the geographical regions in which they occurred.

Originally written in 1959, and reprinted in 1995 substantially as is, with only slight corrections, this 109-page, handy-sized book can be a real help to the novice classicist. *Mary Pride*

NEW!
A Short Guide to Classical Mythology
Grade 7–college. $9.50 plus shipping.
Bolchazy-Carducci Publishers, Inc., 1000 Brown St., Unit 101, Wauconda, IL 60084. (847) 526-4344.
Fax: (847) 526-2867.
Email: orders@bolchazy.com.
Web: www.bolchazy.com.

The Writings Themselves

Over the years I've tried subscribing to several different classics-of-the-month collections. One publisher's was less expensive, but the book pages were roughly chopped and the paper was ugly. Easton Press's leather-bound **100 Greatest Books Ever Written** series, on the other hand, are printed on acid-free paper, with gilded edges, and a bound-in ribbon marker.

Titles in this mostly-fiction series sometimes overlap the Harvard Classics (also from Easton). But most are unique to this series such as, Dicken's *Great Expectations,* Dostoevsky's *Crime and Punishment,* and Jules Verne's *Twenty Thousand Leagues Under the Sea.*

Be aware that some books in this series are unedifying. *The Red and the Black,* for example, glamorizes the scurrilous career of a young French clergyman who tries to model his life on Napoleon's, including dalliances with the ladies (whose characters in the book range from pathetic to unconvincing). Boccaccio's *Decameron* is full of titillating tales of seduction.

Bottom line: for books you love, like *Wind in the Willows,* these editions are an investment in a lifetime of reading pleasure. For the others, be sure you send them back promptly, or make sure to request the list of all the titles and tell them you *don't* want the bad apples. *Mary Pride*

NEW!
The 100 Greatest Books Ever Written
Grade 9–college. Each volume, $39.95. You receive a new book approximately each month.
The Easton Press, 47 Richards Ave., Norwalk, CT 06857. (800) 211-1308.
Fax: (203) 831-9365.

The leather-bound **Harvard Classics** from Easton Press is the legendary "Five-Foot Shelf of Knowledge." Why "Harvard" Classics? Because the fellow who had the idea of collecting the most important Great Books ever written into a readable set was Dr. Charles W. Eliot, President of Harvard University.

I'll be honest with you; I own this set. And I paid for it. I cringe as I admit this, because some of you out there will think I must be either rich or extravagant to buy fifty books at the hefty price per book you see above. Actually, I thought of it like this:

"Reading and understanding these books will give my kids the equivalent of four years or more of liberal arts from the finest universities in the world. Plus, since these books are in our home, we, the parents, can discuss these books with them, rather than having someone with an agenda we might not like leading the discussion. Since the cost of even one year at a quality college is over $10,000, and we have nine children, this works out to be a good investment."

The series includes, by book:

NEW!
The Harvard Classics
Grade 9–college. Each volume, $53.50. You receive a new book each month.
The Easton Press, 47 Richards Ave., Norwalk, CT 06857. (800) 211-1308.
Fax: (203) 831-9365.

One last important note for canny shoppers with more time than I have: Sometimes you can find an old set, or at least some volumes, of Harvard Classics for sale. After repeated efforts to get Easton Press to supply a missing volume for our set failed, we were able to pick up an older copy of that volume at a library sale for $2.

Here are just a few of the Harvard Classics

- Volume 1—Benjamin Franklin, John Woolman, and William Penn
- Volume 2—Plato, Epictetus, and Marcus Aurelius
- Volume 3—Bacon, Milton's prose, and Thomas Brown
- Volume 4—Milton's complete English poems
- Volume 5—Emerson
- Volume 6—Robert Burns
- Volume 7—St. Augustine's *Confessions* and Thomas a Kempis's *The Imitation of Christ*
- Volume 8—Nine Greek dramas
- Volume 9—Cicero and Pliny
- Volume 10—Adam Smith's *The Wealth of Nations*
- Volume 11—Darwin's *Origin of Species*
- Volume 12—Plutarch's *Lives of the Ancient Romans*
- Volume 13—Virgil's *Aeneid*
- Volume 14—Cervantes' *Don Quixote,* part 1
- Volume 15—*Pilgrim's Progress,* Donne, Herbert, and Walton
- Volume 16—*The Thousand and One Nights of Scheherezade*
- Volume 17—Folklore and fable: Aesop, Grimm, Anderson
- Volume 18—Modern English drama
- Volume 19—*Faust,* both Goethe's and Marlowe's versions, plus other works by Goethe
- Volume 20—Dante's *Divine Comedy*
- Volume 21—*I Promessi Spose* by Manzoni
- Volume 22—Homer's *Odyssey*
- Volume 23—Dana's *Two Years Before the Mast*
- Volume 24—Burke
- Volume 25—John Stuart Mill and Thomas Carlyle
- Volume 26—Continental drama
- Volume 27—English essays, Sidney to Macaulay
- Volume 28—Essays, English and American
- Volume 29—Darwin's *Voyage of the Beagle*
- Volume 30—Faraday, Helmholtz, Kelvin, Newcomb, and other famous scientific writers
- Volume 31—Cellini's autobiography
- Volume 32—Montagne, Saint-Beuve, Renan, etc.
- Volume 33—Travel literature
- Volume 34—Descartes, Voltaire, Rousseau, Hobbe
- Volume 35—Froissart, Malory, Holinshed
- Volume 36—Machiavelli, More, Luther
- Volume 37—Locke, Berkeley, Hume
- Volume 38—Harvey, Jenner, Lister, Pasteur
- Volume 39—Famous Prefaces
- Volume 40—English Poetry 1
- Volume 41—English Poetry 2
- Volume 42—English Poetry 3
- Volume 43—American Historical Documents
- Volume 44—Sacred Writings 1 (some Bible books, plus Confucius)
- Volume 45—Sacred Writings 2 (some epistles and hymns, plus Buddhist writings, the Bhagavad Gita, and chapters from the Koran)
- Volume 46—Elizabethan Drama 1
- Volume 47—Elizabethan Drama 2
- Volume 48—Pascal
- Volume 49—Epic and Saga
- Volume 50—Introduction, Reader's Guide, Indexes

Every one of the works in these books is available in paperback from some publisher or other, or on CD-ROM, as far as I know, with the exception of Dr. Eliiot's Reader's Guide and the General Index (which, annoyingly, uses Roman numerals to indicate which volume a topic appears in). So if you want to save a lot of money, you can go that route. However, book lovers will understand why I felt it was worth the extra money (and time savings!) to have these lovely, crimson leather-bound books with gilded pages. They will last centuries, with care, and communicate a respect for the subject matter by their very appearance. *Mary Pride*

NEW!
The Norton Anthologies

Grade 11–college. English Literature volumes 1 and 2, $45 (hardcover) or $43.75 each (paperback). American Literature volumes 1 and 2, $45.63 each (paperback). Shipping extra. *W. W. Norton & Company, Inc., 800 Keystone Industrial Park, Scranton, PA 18512. (800) 223-2584. Fax: (800) 458-6515.*

Wow! Are these books big! When Norton puts together an anthology, it's *really* an anthology, not just a wimpy "collection." We're talking over 2,500 pages per book here. Now reading in bed can count as phys ed—just holding the book in place takes serious muscle!

The **Norton Anthologies** are extremely popular with high-school and college literature teachers. It's easy to see why. You get a little bit of everything, from "Native American Oratory" to the almost incomprehensible ravings of James Joyce (some of the cleaner parts of *Ulysses* and *Finnegan's Wake*). There's definitely an attempt at multicultural diversity, with a number of obscure woman authors and racially self-conscious readings. On the other hand, classic readings are not neglected. Jonathan Edwards and other genuinely important Colonial and pre-Colonial writers are included. Historical writings abound: the text of the Declaration of Independence, Tom Paine's *Common Sense,* the *Federalist Papers,* and much more besides. If you want to read letters from Cortez and Christopher Columbus, you're in luck. If you want oodles of poetry, you're even luckier.

I'm willing to bet you *don't* want oodles of poetry. That's OK. The idea of a literature anthology is to give you what wiser heads think you *ought* to read, not what you *want* to read. The authors do have some mercy—you're only assigned 20 pages of James Fenimore Cooper (a writer who defines the word "tedium"). A few goodies sneak in: *The Legend of Sleepy Hollow* and *The Purloined Letter,* to name but two.

Footnotes explain obscure words and references. The boredom index of a reading can be directly correlated to the number of footnotes in most cases, making James Joyce the Boredom King. While some Olde English authors need more translation, Joyce, writing in modern English, went out of his way to be obscure. Just as well, considering the way his mind worked.

Truly ancient English authors are translated for our benefit. You also get a thorough explanation of how language and writing has changed over time. Each reading gets a hefty introduction, to help you make sense of it.

You could read every word of each volume. Or you could just do what English teachers everywhere do, and read the bits you want to study. Either way, these books are value for money. *Mary Pride*

Classics on Cassette

Sometimes it's easier to *hear* a book than to read it. This is especially true of plays and poetry. British Shakespearean actors can present the Bard more vividly and understandably. The pacing and emphasis can make obscure poetry clearer. Plus, with audiocassettes you can study literature while driving, knitting, or washing the car! With all this going for them, you'll definitely want to check out some of the sources below.

Something for everyone in the huge 170-page **Blackstone Audiobooks** catalog. Blackstone Audio Books sells and rents recordings of *unabridged* classics. These range from the gargantuan *Gulag Archipelago* by Nobel Prize-winner Alexander Solzhenitsyn to children's classics (Aesop's fables, the Ramona series, *The Five Little Peppers and How They Grew,* and many more), to classics of the Western world (*Iliad, Odyssey, Aeneid,* and just about every other Great Book) . . . from politics to philosophy . . . from education (including my own book *Schoolproof*) to religion (in this case, Christian and Catholic titles, includ-

ing many of Dr. Francis Schaeffer's works) . . . from humor (Erma Bombeck, P.G. Wodehouse, Jerome K. Jerome) to science fiction (*Starship Troopers,* anyone?) . . . and much, much more. The catalog is heavy on the conservative-libertarian side of things, with works by Thomas Sowell, Ludwig von Mises, Walter Williams, George Gilder, Clarence Carson, Paul Johnson, and other neo- and paleo-conservative luminaries. The religion section is big on Francis Schaeffer and Malcolm Muggeridge, with a smattering of A.W. Tozer, St. Augustine, and Dr. Martyn Lloyd-Jones. Their lit-

NEW!
Blackstone Audiobooks

All recordings are available for purchase **or 30-day rental**. The rental option is a super money-saver for cash-strapped families. To make this even tastier, **Blackstone also guarantees that they have the lowest price available on any unabridged title.** Find a lower published price, and they'll beat it by $2!

NEW!
Newport Classics Libraries

Ages 3–adult. $49.95 each postpaid. *Newport Publishers, 100 North Lake Avenue, Suite 203, Pasadena, CA 91101-1883. (800) 579-5532. Fax: (626) 796-7588. Email: newportpubl@earthlink.com.*

The only thing Kathy didn't mention is the incredible price of these tapes. Forty audiocassettes for $49.95?! "Books on tape" typically run around $7.95 to $9.95 per tape, and this series costs just over $1 per tape and includes a quality briefcase-shaped box with a carry handle. This has got to be the audiotape bargain of the decade, and a super gift. *Mary Pride*

erature selections include generally-accepted classics by Jane Austen, Jonathan Swift, Charles Dickens, Dostoevsky, and so on, as well as more traditional children's books like *Pinocchio*. Travel and adventure. Amazing true stories. Bestsellers of the more edifying kind. Plays. Speeches. Biography. More.

These recordings are literature, not entertainment. You won't find music, dramatization with multiple voices, or other gimmicks. One reader reads the entire book straight through. This can, however, have its lighter side. Frederick Davidson's reading of the poetry in *The Princess and the Goblin* put my children in stitches. (I wonder if George MacDonald intended his character's anti-goblin poems to end with a loud, rude, "Blah!"?)

If you haven't sent for this catalog yet, do it—and be sure to take advantage of the $6-off coupon just inside the front, redeemable for purchases or rentals made within 30 days of receipt of the catalog. *Mary Pride*

Audio tapes have been a big part of our schooling for years, helping us to take advantage of moments spent on those inevitable tasks. This classics collection on tape has been a very popular item around our house since it first arrived.

Each volume contains 40 high-quality, long-playing stereo audiocassettes. The **Children's Classics Library** contains such favorites as *Pinocchio, The Wind in the Willows, Aesop's Fables, The Adventures of Huckleberry Finn* (unabridged), and others, including a tape of nursery rhymes. The **Family Classics Library** contains *A Tale of Two Cities, Call of the Wild, Les Miserables, A Christmas Carol,* and more.

The publisher has been faithful to record most books in their complete form on tape. When my husband, Tim, taped himself reading *A Christmas Carol* to our children it took up three full tapes, which is how many tapes you'll find on this same book in the Classics collection. Unlike our homemade readings, the Classics Libraries are enhanced by music and sound effects, with parts read by several actors.

The quality of the Classics series is not necessarily Christian. You will find some classic fiction contains immoral behavior, e.g., racism in *Huckleberry Finn*. While the sex and violence is not all graphic by today's standards, it is alluded to in some tales, e.g., the *Outcasts of Poker Flat*, which talks about a town casting out its lowlife, consisting of gamblers, charlatans, and prostitutes.

While we chose to skip some tapes, the older children benefited from discussing the issues presented in others. We so enjoyed *Les Miserables* (not the complete book, which is voluminous!) that we found the play on video, read about the production of the play, Victor Hugo's life, and I read the book itself, with my oldest breathing down my neck to get the copy for himself.

Fiction allows children to peek into the characters of people from different walks and times of life. This helps them to gain an understanding of the internal thinking that motivates outward behavior. Great books allow our children to learn independently from thinkers of every age, though with parental and Scriptural guidance. As individuals, they can catch themselves in false thinking patterns, having seen the end result in the fictional characters. As a family, our children will develop that cultural literacy which can take complicated human situations and identify them by one character. "Oh! doesn't his rigidity remind you of Javert?" This builds mental bonds between the children as they develop a code of characters to express ideas, a bond they'll enjoy both now and into adulthood. *Katherine von Duyke*

CHAPTER 11

Speak, Debate, and Perform

The Rhetoric phase of a classical education includes speech presentations, debate, and dramatic readings. Teens are ready for this. But maybe not in school, where classmates and teachers judge you severely. Shy kids *can* gather the confidence to try their wings. Inarticulate kids *can* learn to speak clearly and persuasively. Arguably the greatest Greek speaker of all time, Demosthenes, was shy *and* inarticulate. As a teen, he practiced speaking alone on the beach with a mouth full of pebbles (a technique I do *not* recommend, due to the choking hazard). Ol' Demosthenes wouldn't have had to work so hard if he'd had some of the speech helps below!

Talk to Me

"Who is Christy Farris?" If you have to ask, you probably haven't been homeschooling very long! Christy's dad, Michael Farris, is the founder and president of Home School Legal Defense Association, and Christy is just the kind of daughter to make all homeschoolers everywhere proud. Besides helping with her dad's almost-successful campaign for lieutenant governor of Virginia and serving as a short-term missionary to Russia, the still-teenaged Christy found time to enter debate competitions and, eventually, write this **Introduction to Argumentation and Debate**. In 83 oversized spiral-bound pages, it explains how debate tournaments work, the rules of logic, researching and choosing the best evidence, the main points debaters on the *affirmative* side must bring up and how to construct an affirmative case, how to construct a case for the *negative* side, responsibilities of the various speakers on a debate team, speech and delivery tips, what to expect during a debate round, and a *very* short list of additional resources. Practical, helpful advice just perfect for homeschoolers (or anyone else) who wants to join a debate team. And, by an amazing coincidence, Home School Legal Defense Association sponsors a series of debate competitions for homeschoolers. If the idea of learning to handle yourself professionally and persuasively appeals to you, but you don't know anything about debate, problem solved. Get this book! *Mary Pride*

NEW!
An Introduction to Argumentation and Debate
Grade 9–college. Book, $10. Set of two videos, $20. Postpaid.
Home School Legal Defense Association, PO Box 3000, Purcellville, VA 20134. (540) 338-5600. Fax: (540) 338-2733. Web: www.hslda.org.

An Introduction to

Argumentation and Debate

by Christy Farris

Want to learn the secrets of "Conversation Power"? The six sure ways to strike up a conversation with a total stranger . . . the seven cardinal sins of conversation . . . powerful techniques of persuasion . . . how to silence objections and overcome resistance . . . how to be well liked and popular . . . how to ask questions that get honest answers . . . these are the tidbits offered on the back cover and brochure for **Lifetime Conversation Guide**.

I am sitting here with this 297-page, indexed hardcover. Whatever it promises on the cover, you do indeed find inside. Bear in mind that the advice is pretty much value-free: thus, you will indeed learn "how to have your orders instantly obeyed" and how to "gain power for yourself so you can control any given conversational situation," without any bothersome questions about whether such domination is a good thing or not. The author freely admits that "greed at times motivates all of us," without bemoaning this in the slightest. To his credit, however, he does give common-sense rules for how to have a happy home and family (lots of attention and praise helps), and no sleazy love-life advice or suggestions for how to confuse or exploit others, as I have seen in other books of this type.

Chapter topics include understanding other people's 14 secret motivations, how to strike up a conversation and feel at ease with strangers, how to build friendships, how to be popular, marriage and family improvement, exercising leadership in business situations, how to correct others' mistakes so it sounds like a compliment, employee management, how to get reliable scuttlebutt, body language how-tos, persuasive speech techniques, salesmanship, gaining cooperation from others, how to give a talk or speech, secrets of powerful writing, seven cardinal sins of conversation and how to avoid them, and ways to open or close a conversation or speech.

Most kids grow up avoiding conversational confrontations with adults. Few are well prepared to do business and yet be well liked at the same time. Yet when they cross that boundary from "teen" to "adult," they will suddenly be expected to know how to talk like a take-charge professional. This book's advice, as much as it may sound like a pastiche of cliched business magazine articles, is actually rather good. Sometimes the cliches are true . . . and when a kid hasn't encountered these truths of "what makes people tick" yet, it all seems fresh as the morning dew. Most adults will find helpful pointers here, too, especially those of us with nerdish backgrounds. *Mary Pride*

What do Mother Teresa, Art Buchwald, Erma Bombeck, Oprah Winfrey, and a cavalcade of presidents, politicians, businessmen, and entertainers have in common?

They're all in this book.

By Peggy Noonan, famed speechwriter to Presidents Reagan and Bush, **On Speaking Well** tackles one subject only: "how to give a speech with style, substance, and clarity." Its 212 standard-sized pages include an index, but oddly, no table of contents! No matter, because once you start reading the fascinating anecdotes and real-world advice with which this book is filled, you won't want to stop.

On Speaking Well covers not only the art of presentation—speeches, toasts, tributes, and eulogies—but the art of thinking out, writing, and editing the speech itself. You'll learn from the successes and failures of famous people, while gaining insight into such important topics as "why not to try to write sound bites into your speech." Why has TV news become such a wasteland? How can you find your "voice"? What are the cures for stage fright? Should you pause for applause? This, and much more, awaits you here. Recommended. *Mary Pride*

If you want to read a prepared piece of literature . . . or make a speech . . . or give your Christian testimony . . . **Let's Talk** has the professional advice for a person of junior-high age. Since the author's company sells bunches of prepared scripts for reading aloud, it's no surprise that the section on how to do this is the best and most detailed part of the book. You find out how to play the parts of several characters at once using the "Dramatic V," how to get up on the stage gracefully and escape off it gracefully, what to do if you "freeze" and forget your part, and other essential information usually not provided to the sweaty-palmed set.

Compete with Confidence tells you what you need to know to win a speech competition—specifically, a competition in which each person presents a prepared literature selection. Everything in this "workbook" is included in *Let's Talk*. I say "workbook" in quotes, because while the publisher hopes you will buy one book per student, in real life the few parts that need to be filled in can easily be done on separate paper.

Speak Out! covers the same material as *Let's Talk*, but at a high-school level. It also includes some topics not in the other book, such as interpreting poetry, storytelling, playing a part in a play, how to memorize a piece, and how to read Scripture passages aloud. The whole book is good, but the section on stage deportment is especially good. I might not have hated drama class if I'd had this book! The teacher's guide includes answers to the study questions and tests. *Mary Pride*

> ANNOUNCER 2: *Juliet wishes Romeo had another name, so he would not be a Montague, an enemy.*
> JULIET: *(To herself) O Romeo, Romeo! Wherefore art thou "Romeo"? What's in a name? That which we call a "rose" by any other name would smell as sweet.*
> ROMEO: *(Standing where she can see him, he calls up to her.) Call me but "Love" and I'll be new-baptized. Henceforth I never will be "Romeo"!*

The Bard for 11-year-olds? Besides the Bible, no one else has had a more profound effect on our language and literature than Mr. Shakespeare. The comedy of *A Midsummer Night's Dream*, the madness of *Hamlet*, the political intrigue of *Julius Caesar* . . . Shakespeare's greatest strength was as an observer of human nature. If you love wonderful literature (and what self-respecting homeschooler doesn't?) then sooner or later, you'll probably want to study at least one of Shakespeare's works in depth.

And therein lies the rub: Shakespeare was never meant to be read like a novel, or studied like a science text. His words were meant for the stage! Swan Books has attempted to make these difficult works accessible for younger audiences, and done it with an eye towards performance. Each book in the **Shakespeare for Young People** series is an abridged version of the play. The flavor of the original language has been left intact. Stage directions and narrators have been added, to help explain both the flow of action, and the motivation of the characters. Each book is about 63 pages in length, and also includes tips on simple staging, costuming and props.

The series includes:

- *A Midsummer Night's Dream for Young People*
- *Romeo and Juliet for Young People*
- *The Taming of the Shrew for Young People*
- *Macbeth for Young People*
- *Julius Caesar for Young People*
- *Henry the Fifth for Young People*

- *Hamlet for Young People*
- *Much Ado About Nothing for Young People*
- *Twelfth Night for Young People*

The weakness of these books is also their strength: they are meant for staging, not simply reading. Not all homeschoolers will find material in this script format useful. However, a unit study group, support group, or even a group of friends could use one of these plays for the ultimate hands-on experience. After all, how many 11-year olds do you know who've "done Shakespeare?" These books make him "do-able", and they do it well. *Michelle Van Loon*

Bridging the gap between the simplified approach of their Shakespeare for Young People series that I reviewed above and the full-tilt, unabridged "Real Thing," Learning Links has a series of script books for high schoolers. Listen to a few lines from Juliet's famous balcony scene, presented the **Shakespeare on Stage** way:

> **Juliet:** *(Murmuring) O Romeo, Romeo! (Full of love, she cannot understand why he should be an enemy to her house.) Wherefore art thou "Romeo"? (Either he should leave his family or she should reject hers.) Deny thy father, and refuse thy name! Or . . . if thou wilt not, be but sworn my love, and I'll no longer be a Capulet!*

The original language is there, with the added illumination of acting direction, which helps to explain Juliet's motivation for her tormented words.

Diane Davidson, the author of this series, writes: "Sometimes, in our desire to appreciate Shakespeare properly, we forget the obvious: that Shakespeare was not a schoolteacher, not a classical scholar, but a professional entertainer." Though ivory-tower academics write endless papers trying to crawl into Shakespeare's mind and analyze (as only academics can) what he was really trying to say, the average student simply wants to understand what all the complicated language means in modern English. By trimming the original text and adding lots of stage and character direction, Davidson attempts to make Shakespeare entertaining for high-school age students. Her direction is not of the ivory-tower variety, and she edits these classic works with a light, commonsense hand.

Books in the series include *Macbeth, Julius Caesar, Romeo and Juliet, The Merchant of Venice, A Midsummer Night's Dream, Hamlet, Prince of Denmark, As You Like It,* and *Othello.* As with the Shakespeare For Young People series, these works are meant to be staged, not simply read, which would seem to limit their use with the average homeschool family. However, any one of these scripts can be used as a part of a literature study if you're looking to give your high school student an intelligent introduction to these cultural building blocks. The play's the thing . . . indeed! *Michelle Van Loon*

NEW!
Shakespeare on Stage

Grade 8–12. $6.95 each, plus shipping. Discounts available for larger orders.
Learning Links, 2300 Marcus Ave, New Hyde Park, NY 11042.
(800) 724-2616. Fax: (516) 437-5392.
Web: www.learninglinks.com.

NEW!
Speak Up

Grade 7–adult. $12.99 plus shipping.
Don Aslett Cleaning Center, PO Box 700, Pocatello, ID 83204.
Orders: (800) 451-2402.
Inquiries: (208) 232-3535.
Fax: (208) 232-6286.
Email: tobih@aol.com.
Web: www.donaslett.com.

The inimitable Don Aslett, "America's Greatest Cleaning Expert," shares his years of public-speaking experience with you in this book. Don's claim to speaking fame is that he has personally made over 5,000 speeches to groups of all sizes all over the world in the past 40 years. These groups have ranged from TV and radio talk-show audiences, to wealthy businessmen, to housewives, to Cub Scouts, to you name it!

Like Don's other books, **Speak Up!** is packed with eye candy in the form of cartoons, lists, jokes, quotes, and other fun stuff designed to help you overcome intimidation. He takes you through all stages of preparing a speech, from the moment you are first trapped into it to the last moment of triumphal applause. Unlike other speaking books, he handles the details (e.g., how to set up your microphones and avoid possible disruptive influences) and all sorts of special situations as well (e.g., dealing with interpreters, speaking at funerals and weddings). There's lots on how to pick a topic and deliver your speech, with none of the silly "make the butterflies fly in formation" or "imagine your audience in their underwear" nonsense that you'll find in other books on public speaking. Instead, you get advice on how to prepare like a pro, deliver like a pro, get on the media like a pro, and even become a speaking pro, if you so desire. All this and more is interwoven with examples from Don's wide experience, plus brief fill-in-the-blank exercises at the ends of every chapter to help you remember what Don just told you.

Let's make it simple: if you want to speak, this is the book to get. Highly recommended. *Mary Pride*

I once got suckered into taking a "drama" class in high school. This intensely embarrassing experience might even have been fun had I read **Acting & Theatre** first. I would have known enough to expect the (to me) sappy "theatre games." (I'm not the type who loves to sit in a circle holding hands with strangers.) I would have known the basics of improvisation and characterization. I would have known my way around sets, props, costumes, and stage makeup. I would have been able to impress the teacher with my knowledge of theatrical history and styles, from Japanese Kabuki theatre to the most modern influences. Even better, I might have known enough about what theatre was about to skip the course in the first place. (As an actor, I make a nice houseplant.) As it was, I ended up trying to play Mercutio in green tights—one of the low points of my life. Save yourself this stress. Get the book. *Mary Pride*

Do you suffer from poor enunciation? Rapid-fire speech? Soft, breathy speech? Nasal or monotonous delivery? Do you pepper your speech with "uh," "um," or even worse, "like" or "you know"? Is your speech "sloppy," with lots of word endings dropped or mumbled? Do you have a noticeable regional or ethnic accent? Do you have trouble being heard in a large area?

Or let's turn it around. Do others hang on your every word? Is your speech filled with variety and emphasis on the points *you* want to make?

If you have any problems listed in paragraph one, or a lack of success as mentioned in paragraph two, here's a resource from a voice coach who has worked with prominent figures in the worlds of business, government, and entertainment. His 238-page indexed **Vocal Advantage** paperback and accompanying 56-minute audiocassette strike directly at the roots of the most common voice and speaking problems. If you have the discipline to do the exercises—most of which involve taping yourself with a view to working on specific problem areas—this is a relatively quick and inexpensive way to improve your speaking performance. Add in some written work and a speech or two and you could call this a semester of high-school Communications 301. *Mary Pride*

CHAPTER 12

Spelling & Vocabulary

You can become a good speller. Or you can learn to use your computer's spellchecker. This won't help you when you write by hand, but if you cultivate awful handwriting, people won't be able to read it, and won't know how badly you spell.

You can develop a good vocabulary. Or you can use your word processor's built-in thesaurus. This doesn't work as well as a spellchecker, since you still have to know what the word you substituted *means,* or risk looking like a bumptious fool.

Then again, depending on your chosen career, you may not need a quality vocabulary. For example, you could become a Hollywood scriptwriter. Then you only need to know four words well: the F word, the S word, the D word, and the B word. If you don't know what words I'm referring to, good for you. We'll just call them all "blankety-blank." Then you can perform deft verbal surgery like this:

- **Sentence before scriptwriter gets it:** "You rambunctious simpletons have destroyed my experiment!"
- **Sentence after scriptwriter's first pass:** "You blankety-blank simpletons have destroyed my experiment!"
- **Sentence after scriptwriter has finished polishing it:** "You blankety-blank blankety-blanks have blankety-blanked my blankety-blank experiment!"

With practice, fifty percent of your dialog can consist entirely of "blankety-blank," thus placing it squarely in range for an Academy Award for Best Screenplay.

While 100 monkeys in a room with 100 typewriters could not actually type a single poem of Shakespeare no matter how much time you gave them (they'd wreck the typewriters almost immediately), one monkey with a typewriter could write dialog like this. So don't be a monkey; improve your vocabulary before it's too late and Hollywood comes banging on your door with a banana in one hand and a contract in the other.

Rebecca Sealfon, a homeschooled student, won the Scripps-Howard National Spelling Bee in 1997

A Beka Vocabulary/ Spelling/ Poetry Books

Grades 7–12. Student books: (grades 7–9), $7.20 each; grades 10–12, $8.55 each. Teacher's editions and tests available for some grades. Shipping extra.
A Beka Book, Box 19100, Pensacola, FL 32523-9100. (800) 874-2352. Fax: (800) 874-3590. Web: www.abeka.com.

NEW! Calvert Spelling and Vocabulary

Grades 5–8. Each grade, $20.
Calvert School, 105 Tuscany Road, Baltimore, MD 21210. (410) 243-6030. Fax: (410) 366-0674. Email: inquiry@calvertschool.org. Web: www.calvertschool.org.

Spelling and Vocabulary Together

A Beka Books integrates **Vocabulary, Spelling, and Poetry** in its line of books for grades 7–12. Students memorize poetry, learn vocabulary words from the A Beka literature texts they are supposed to be studying at the same time, and learn the "Five Spelling Rules to Master" along with correct spelling of frequently misspelled words. New vocabulary words are analyzed according to their Greek and Latin prefixes, suffixes, and roots, using the handy Word Analyzer included in each book. Books are slim and not terribly expensive.

Teacher's books, where available, include the entire student text plus answers to all the exercises and explanations for the verbal analogies exercises.

If you're planning on using the A Beka literature series, it won't hurt to get the *Vocabulary/Spelling/Poetry* books as well, especially since I gather this series is being revised, starting with grade 7, to include integrated literature/vocabulary/spelling test booklets. *Mary Pride*

Although I resolved not to include software in this edition of *The Big Book of Home Learning,* for every rule there must be a few exceptions. **Calvert's Spelling and Vocabulary CD-ROMs** are an exception because (1) this is a major product from a major homeschool supplier that many families will use, and (2) it teaches both spelling *and* vocabulary at once.

Each of Calvert's Spelling and Vocabulary CD-ROMs is a complete one-year course. The program is not designed to be a game, but to be a teacher. Graphics and sounds are used to liven things up, but mostly the program quietly and patiently drills you in the words of each lesson.

After an initial animation, the program starts at the login menu. You enter your name. If the program doesn't recognize you, it asks if this is your first time and starts a record of your progress if so. Once the program knows who you are you move on to the main menu. You have three choices: Spelling, Vocabulary, and the Grammar Game.

If you choose spelling, the program displays a list of lessons by week, i.e., Lessons 1–4, Lessons 6–9, Lessons 11–14, etc. The four numbered lessons are for Monday through Thursday. Friday of each week is for the weekly review.

The student selects a week on the lesson menu. On this menu you have a choice of each of the four numbered lessons, the weekly review, or your study lists. The study lists menu gives you the opportunity to study either your current weekly word lists, your review list (compiled out of the words you missed on your weekly review quizzes), or your personal list of words to practice that your teacher put into the program. If the student wants to, he can select one of these lists and practice it in the "lab."

A spelling lesson consists of up to ten words. First you do a pretest on the words. The program pronounces each word, says a sentence that defines the word in context, then repeats the word. You then type the word and press "return." The program goes on to pronounce the next word, etc. When you reach the end of the list, the "check" button appears. You can click it to check the words, or you can change any word that doesn't look right to you first, and then click "check." The program puts a check mark on the numbers of words that are correctly spelled and an X on the numbers of the ones that are wrong.

You must correct the words that are wrong before you can go on. You do this by clicking on the "ear" symbol that will be placed next to one of the Xs. The program displays the word spelled correctly, and the word as you spelled it. It speaks the word, and spells it out loud for you. You have to click on the letters in your version that are wrong, then press the "type again" button and type the word from memory. If you spell it right, you can go on to the next word. Otherwise, the program spells it for you again, and you type it again. Once you have corrected all the words, you go on to the lab.

In the lab, you interact with each of the words you got wrong on the pretest. In order to get through the lab, you have to do at least one activity with each of the words. The activities are: 1. Write—fill in the blanks by clicking on a letter, then clicking on the blank in which to put it. When you are done, you get to type in the word from memory; 2. Look—find your word in a large array of letters and click on each of the letters; 3 Touch—move scrambled letters to blanks for the word in the right order. Once you have done an activity on each of the words, the "Exit" button appears and you can go to the post-test. If you get any wrong on the post-test, you have to correct them. Once you have done that you are done with that lesson.

When you have done the four lessons, you can do the weekly quiz, consisting of 20 of the week's words. Any words you miss in the posttest go into your practice word list.

As you can see, this process gives the words a good workout. You should know them better at the end of the week than you did at the beginning.

The vocabulary program consists of 16 units of 8 lessons and two activities apiece. Lessons are either teaching lessons or review lessons. Each teaching lesson consists of up to four words. You pick a word to review. The program puts up three possible definitions for the word. You choose one. If you are right, the program congratulates you with a little graphic animation. If you are wrong, the program blats at you. Ether way, the program displays a screen defining the word, illustrating the word (sometimes animated), and giving an interesting derivation of the word.

Review lessons give a definition and three possible words. Click on one of the answers and either be congratulated or blatted at.

Activities consist of giving a definition and you either fill in the blanks or descramble the letters, as in the "Write" and "Touch" activities from the spelling lab.

The grammar game is designed to correlate with the spelling lessons. The program displays a sentence with one of the vocabulary words in green, and a dart board with the balloons labeled with names of the parts of speech. Throw a dart at the balloon that's labeled with the part of speech corresponding to the green word in the sentence. It's kind of fun actually, but I ran into an answer I didn't agree with on my first try. Please decide this for me.

The sentence is: Please leave the book over *there* on the table. They said "there" was a pronoun. I say it's an adverb and I still can't figure what noun it is in the place of. Who's right?

Let's face it, this program is not the most exciting educational program in the world. On the other hand, it does have enough bells and whistles that a child will enjoy playing it and will learn to spell a whole lot of words in the process. If you're already using the Calvert course, you definitely should get this program. *Bill Pride*

Spelling for Success

5 Minutes a Day to Perfect Spelling is unique among spelling programs. Why? Because it's based on research into how good spellers spell. Program co-developer Kevin Trudeau, a bad speller, had a good friend, J. Mark Dufner, who was an excellent speller.

Mark also had the habit of constantly correcting Kevin's spelling mistakes. This eventually sparked Kevin's curiosity, and he began asking lots of people, "What steps do you go through when you spell a word?"

NEW!
5 Minutes a Day to Perfect Spelling
Grade 10 and up. $65 postpaid.
The Wetzels, Rt. 1, Box 73A, Seneca, MO 64865. (888) 890-9313. Phone/fax: (417) 775-2847.

Here's what he found. Good spellers "see" the word in their heads. Bad spellers tend to try to "sound out" the word. That's because, while learning to "sound out" words is essential for learning to *read,* the irregularities of English guarantee that phonics alone *cannot* teach you how to spell correctly. The word *phonics* itself, for example, would be spelled "fonix" if it were totally phonetic.

Refining these insights further, the pair found some simple techniques, involving eye movement and learning to "see" the word well enough to spell it forwards *and backwards,* that could be *taught* to bad spellers, making them good spellers.

They put what they learned together in a six-tape series, collected in a cassette binder along with a very brief "action guide" to the lessons and a 3000-word list of commonly misspelled words.

Now enter the Wetzel family. Their fifth grade son, Travis, had to have vision therapy since the end of second grade. The vision therapist explained Travis' problem to them with the analogy that he was "learning like a blind man" because his brain could not make sense of information sent through his eyes. Reading, writing, and spelling were impossible for him, even though he was very bright.

As Travis' therapy progressed, his skills drastically improved . . . except for spelling. But when the Wetzels introduced Travis to the 5 Minutes a Day program, after only two weeks of practice Travis was spelling words like *phenomenal, bouillon,* and *monumental.* His eight-year-old sister experienced similar results.

The Wetzels were so excited that they decided to distribute this program, published by Nightingale-Conant, to other homeschool families. So they sent me a review sample.

Aside from Lesson 2, which supposedly is on phonics, but doesn't really have anything to do with the rest of the tapes and furthermore simply groups sounds by the mouth and tongue positions used to create them (so *r* and *w* are in the same category, for example), and the "stress reduction" techniques mentioned on another tape, this series rings true. It can provide new hope for those who think of themselves as "hopeless" at spelling. *Mary Pride*

Memory Techniques for Spelling

Grades 7–12. $39.95 plus shipping. *Arthur Bornstein's Memory Training Programs, 11693 San Vicente Blvd., Los Angeles, CA 90049. (800) 468-2058. In LA: (310) 478-2056. Fax: (310) 207-2433. Email: abornstein@aol.com. Web: www.bornsteinmemory.com.*

Sample Card

Arthur Bornstein, famous memory training lecturer and educational consultant, has developed yet another flashy and entertaining memory program, this one for poor spellers. Based on Bornstein's memory techniques, **Memory Techniques for Spelling** provides 20 techniques for remembering odd and unusual spellings, as well as spelling rules, study tips, and memory devices for many commonly misspelled words. You get a set of 56 oversized, full-color flash cards, each illustrating a memory technique for recalling a specific word on the front and with teaching instructions on the back; an Instruction Manual/Spelling Guide; and an instructional cassette tape.

As an example of Bornstein's approach: the flash card for technique one, "Exaggeration of Letters," shows the word *separate. Separate* is in capital letters, with the troublesome *A* extending from floor to ceiling and flashing red. Your students will certainly pay attention to these flash cards! Spelling will become one of your most enjoyable subjects, instead of a tedious exercise in frustration. Bornstein has given us a program designed for success. *Mary Pride*

What happens when you immerse your sixth-grade daughter in an intensive phonics program to jump-start her reading ability? Beverly Adams-Gordon discovered what other parents who begin homeschooling older children have learned: *phonics works!* However, Adams-Gordon's daughter Angie continued to struggle mightily when she was called on to express herself in writing. Angie's reading scores jumped four grade levels, but her spelling ability had improved only slightly. Frustrated with the lopsided, single learning modality approach of available spelling products, Adams-Gordon developed "Angie's spelling program." Though Adams-Gordon did not reinvent the spelling wheel, she worked with the mind of a Detroit engineer to combine and refine what was out there. **Spelling Power** is the welcome result.

The 338-page spiral-bound, non-consumable text consists of an 88-page teaching manual, followed by tabbed sections that make it easy to locate the resource you'll need. You are coached thoroughly through the three main components of the program: Systematic Spelling Study, Integrated Functional Writing, and Discovery Activities. You'll begin by administering a placement test to your child, the results of which will target his individual instructional level. Spelling words and rules are attacked with a variety of visual, auditory and kinesthetic tools, then applied to the writing process, all in about 15 minutes a day. Dictation and proofreading help your child cement spelling words, not as isolated lists, but as part of the bigger goal of making him a better communicator. Constant testing and review and simple-to-prepare learning games round out the program.

The **Spelling Power Activity Task Cards** box comes jammed full with over 360, 4 x 6" cards, each containing a hands-on activity to reinforce the spelling and language arts learned with *Spelling Power* (but the cards could be used with any spelling program). Your child will be asked to complete activities such as, "Tape record the spelling of your study words. Say each word and then spell it. Play the tape back and check the spelling of each word," and, "Write a story using all of your study words. After you have written your story, proofread the story and find each study word. Be sure that you have spelled each one correctly." Each of the five tabbed sections (Drill Activities, Skill Builders, Writing Prompters, Dictionary Skills, and Homonyms and More) focuses on an overall learning goal. Within these sections, the cards are color-coded by specific interest and ability level. The included teacher's guide gives instructions on how to use the cards, indexes of activities, answer keys, and a narrative of the *Spelling Power* rules. The practice and review provided by these activity cards will be invaluable to your child's long-term language skills.

The only weakness in this program is that the teaching manual section tends to read a little like a master's thesis. (This is basically alleviated in the video presentation.) Know that you'll have to put some time in learning the program before you can teach it. If you're willing to do that, *Spelling Power* offers your child the academic equivalent of a daily trip to the gym: a well-balanced workout that pumps up those spelling muscles. *Michelle Van Loon*

Vocabulary

Educators Publishing Service is serious about vocabulary development. Their **Analogies** series combines practice in solving analogy problems with opportunities for vocabulary study. Books 2 and 3 are designed to build skills for the Scholastic Aptitude Test and other standardized tests. All three workbooks sharpen students' reasoning powers and their ability to see the relationships between ideas. Accompanying removable quiz booklets with pre-perforated pages are available for each *Analogies* worktext. Each quiz booklet includes six analogy quizzes and six vocabulary quizzes. *Mary Pride*

NEW!
Spelling Power

Grade 1–adult. Spelling Power, $49.95. Spelling Power Activity Task Cards, $29.95. The Basic Approach To Daily Spelling Lessons video, $24.95. Add 10% shipping, minimum $5.
Castlemoyle Books, 6701 - 180th St. SW, Lynnwood, WA 98037. Orders: (888) 773-5586. Inquiries: (425) 787-2714. Fax: (425) 787-0631. Email: beverly@castlemoyle.com. Web: www.castlemoyle.com.

Analogies series

Grades 7–12. Book 1 (for grades 7 and 8), 2 (for grades 9 and 10), and 3 (for grades 11 and 12), $6.25 each. Analogy and Vocabulary Quiz Books 1–3, $7.10 each. Add shipping.
Educators Publishing Service, Inc., 31 Smith Pl., Cambridge, MA 02138. (800) 225-5750. Fax: (617) 547-0412. Email: epsbooks@epsbooks.com. Web: www.epsbooks.com.

BJUP Vocabulary for Christian Schools

Grades 7–12. Student worktext, $9. Teacher's edition, $10. Shipping extra.
Bob Jones University Press Customer Services, Greenville, SC 29614. Orders: (800) 845-5731. Fax: (800) 525-8398. Web: www.bjup.com.

BJUP's vocabulary series is not integrated with its other courses, so you can use it regardless of what resources you are using for literature study. Some text selections do refer to stories in the BJUP literature program, but you don't need to read the original stories to do the exercises.

NEW!
English Vocabulary Quick Reference

Grade 7–adult. $39.95 plus $3.50 shipping.
LexaDyne Publishing, Inc., PO Box 4498, Leesburg, VA 20177-8564. Orders: (888) 599-4700. Inquiries: (703) 779-4998. Fax: (703) 779-4960. Email: vocabulary@quickreference.com. Web: www.quickreference.com.

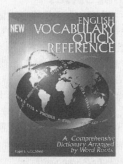

BJUP's Vocabulary for Christian Schools series for grades 7–12 is divided up into levels, one level per grade. Levels A–C focus on Latin prefixes, roots, and suffixes. Level D introduces Greek word parts. This is also the book where you find *ack-ack, flip-flop, riffraff, shilly-shally,* and all those other delightfully bumptious words formed by duplication of a sound within a word. Level E continues with the Greek and Latin, while adding a few words from the French (e.g., *connoisseur*). It also has several chapters on words that allude to the Bible (*shibboleth*), to people in history (*Pyrrhic victory*), to places in history (*marathon*), to literature (*Lilliputian*), and to myths (*jovial*). Those word histories are fascinating! Level F focuses on how words change over time and different types of words (e.g., euphemisms). All levels teach how to discern a word's precise meaning, and how words relate to each other (synonyms, antonyms, homonyms, compounds, etc.).

Words are introduced in a variety of ways. Sometimes they are carefully taken apart and each part defined. Sometimes you are given synonyms for each new word. Sometimes the words are introduced in the context of a text selection. Sometimes an individual word is highlighted and its history given—e.g., *checkmate* comes from the Persian *Shah mat,* meaning "the king is dead."

Each level contains 15 lessons plus cumulative lesson reviews, games, puzzles, and additional enrichment activities. Lessons are designed to only take 10–15 minutes each. From level B on, each book has a cumulative list of word parts learned in the earlier levels. This setup is ideal for every-other-week Friday-morning lessons.

The teacher's edition for each level includes the student text, with additional material, answers to exercises, and so on also included.

I like the tone of this series. It is friendly without being patronizing or silly. Although it is not as strictly organized as it could be—for example, students aren't put through a systematic program of learning Latin roots, then Greek, then French, then Old English—it captures the interest better than such an strict approach is likely to. Every lesson has something new and fresh. *Mary Pride*

Don't be put off by the less-than-thrilling book title. **English Vocabulary Quick Reference: A Comprehensive Dictionary Arranged by Word Roots** is an amazingly clever, colorful, and fun approach to developing a massive and impressive vocabulary.

Like a few other products, this one aims to teach you Greek and Latin word roots—260 of them. All are listed in the Primary Root Index at the beginning of the book. But that only accounts for 14 of the book's 378 oversized hardbound pages.

In the 220-page Dictionary section, every root is followed by a comprehensive list of color-coded words containing that root—complete with pronunciations, definitions, and simple etymologies (what the word parts mean separately and what languages they come from). If the entry is in red, it can be found in one of the major student dictionaries, and is likely to appear on the SAT.

Within each definition, "keywords" are colored blue. These are often really key *phrases,* the meat of each definition, such as *fluid in a body cavity* or *flower cluster.* (In case you're interested, the words that go with these key phrases are *hydrocele* and *inflorescence.*) These key phrases are then arranged in alphabetical order in a 108-page Keyword section, each with the word and page number of the basic Dictionary entry. If the main entry definition was printed in red, its keyword will be, too.

The Main Entry Index follows with each main entry word (again, color-coded in red or black) in alphabetical, rather than root, order, and the page number within the Dictionary section in which it can be found.

Finally, a Secondary Root list of over 500 additional roots for which no lists were made rounds out the book.

The color-coding makes *English Vocabulary Quick Reference* so easy and fun to use. You can see at a glance if a word is common or obscure, zero in on its core definition (the key phrase), and learn groups of words together. For example, for the root *crypt/o,* meaning "hidden," the main entries in red are *Apocrypha, apocryphal, crypt, cryptic, cryptogam, cryptogram, cryptography, decrypt,* and *encrypt.* Less important words in the list were *cryptanalysis, cryptoclastic, cryptocrystalline, cryptogenic, cryptomeria, cryptozoite,* and *procryptic.* Learning the meanings and spellings of all these words could easily be accomplished during the course of a school day, thanks to the clever page design. With a little effort, a student could learn *every single one* of the thousands of vocabulary words in this book in a couple of school years. Way to go to ace the SAT!

Want to know more? You can check out sample full-color pages from *English Vocabulary Quick Reference* at the web site listed above. Or you could just take my word for it that this high-quality, hardbound book can be an entire vocabulary course in itself for every high-schooler in your family. Highly recommended. *Mary Pride*

Increase your student's vocabulary and/or prepare for the SAT I, with **Visual Vocabulary**. Each book contains 150 high-school and college words on cut-out flashcards.

One word is presented on each card. On the front of each card is the word and a picture that represents the word. On the back of the card is the word again, the phonetic pronunciation, the definition, and a sentence showing the proper word usage. For the word *gastric,* a labeled picture of a stomach is on the front. The back has *gastric* written again, the phonetic pronunciation (GAS trihk), another picture of the labeled stomach, and the definition, "(adj.) referring to the stomach." The sentence that shows the proper usage is, "The Thanksgiving meal caused the gastric juices in the children to start flowing."

Use these as a family or independent study. I like the idea of studying vocabulary with cards. Once the word is mastered, just remove it and put in another card. Make sure you or the student maintains a record of which words have been mastered. This method allows you to track your students easily. Use the Visual Vocabulary flashcards as you would any other flashcards and watch your student's vocabulary soar. Encourage your students to utilize their new word in everyday situations. One day per month could be set aside to write sentences using the new words. In the group (A) card set I did not notice any words that I would not want my kids to learn or use. *Lynn Smith*

Now these are *interesting* books. The **Vocabulary from Classical Roots** series is intended for students in grades 7–11. Each book can be used at several grade levels. Book A is for grade 7, Book B is for grade 8, and so on.

The premise: teach kids the Greek and Latin roots they need to decode zillions of English words, especially those lurking on the SAT and in the more literate works of literature. The method: roots are grouped by themes and sub-themes. In Book C, for example, the first part, "Who Am I?," has two lessons each on The Person (with roots like *humanus, vir, gyne,* and *anthropos*), Personal Relationships, Feelings, and Creature Comforts. After each root and its definition come a number of English words based on the root. Each English word is defined and used in a sentence. A variety of exercises at the end of each lesson provide practice with the words.

The team of English, computer science, medical, biology, mineralogy, and theology professionals that compiled *English Vocabulary Quick Reference* is now working on *The Medical Vocabulary Quick Reference.* It will have the same design as *English Vocabulary Quick Reference,* but contain only medical words. When it's ready, it should be a big help for you pre-med types.

NEW!
Visual Vocabulary
Grades 7–12. $18 plus shipping. *Little River Press, 109 Amelia Court, Yorktown, VA 23693. (757) 865-8652. Fax: (770) 271-2967.*

Vocabulary from Classical Roots series
Grades 7–11. Each book, $8. Each teacher's guide and answer key, $6.25. Shipping extra. *Educators Publishing Service, Inc., 31 Smith Pl., Cambridge, MA 02138. (800) 225-5750. Fax: (617) 547-0412. Email: epsbooks@epsbooks.com. Web: www.epsbooks.com.*

Also available from Covenant Home Curriculum, with their lesson plans and texts added

Vocabulary Mastery Study Course

Grade 5–adult. Course textbook, $22.50. Complete course with textbook, study guide, and tape, $29.50. Shipping extra.
Arthur Bornstein's Memory Training Programs, 11693 San Vicente Blvd., Los Angeles, CA 90049. (800) 468-2058. In LA: (310) 478-2056. Web: www.bornsteinmemory.com.

NEW!
Vocabulary: Greek I

Grades 7–12. $11 plus shipping.
Wordsmiths, 1355 Ferry Road, Grants Pass, OR 97526. (541) 476-3080. Email: frodej@jsgrammar.com. Web: www.jsgrammar.com.

NEW!
Vocabulary: Latin I & II

Grades 7–12. Latin I, $11. Latin II, $11. Shipping extra.
Wordsmiths, 1355 Ferry Road, Grants Pass, OR 97526. (541) 476-3080. Email: frodej@jsgrammar.com. Web: www.jsgrammar.com.

This is not as dull as it sounds. Old woodcuts and engravings liven up the pages, while the sentences and exercises abound with literary, historical, and geographical references designed to improve students' cultural literacy. Example: "In *Pride and Prejudice,* Mrs. Bennet's crude efforts to marry off her five daughters *mortify* Elizabeth Bennet." A classical quotation also introduces each lesson, while special "Nota Bene" sections provide valuable background information about the words being studied.

This series has a definite paleofeminist flavor (we hear about tons of famous females in the example sentences), but stops short of actual preachments (thank you). Easy to use, will definitely increase vocabulary and aid in social climbing if taken as prescribed. *Mary Pride*

"Would you be willing to spend as little as 20 minutes a day to learn 40 new words without the grind and repetition?" Scott Bornstein, son of the internationally famous memory expert Arthur Bornstein, has developed a **Vocabulary Mastery Study Course** based on memory techniques, the use of root words, and putting your new vocabulary words to work in daily conversation. The course is designed to "assure your retention of more than 1,600 words," plus increase your reading comprehension of thousands more, thanks to your study of root words, suffixes, and prefixes. Each day's vocabulary lesson ends with a review. You get a deluxe hardcover wire-bound textbook including 84 full-page illustrations. An optional 30-minute cassette tape and study guide round out the program. Excellent preparation for the verbal part of the SAT exam. *Mary Pride*

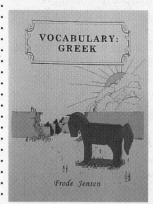

Frode Jensen's **Vocabulary: Greek I** is not intended as a conversational Greek course. The focus is on learning the Greek roots, prefixes, and suffixes which are part of many English words. For this it is fine. It would benefit anyone interested in learning modern, *koine*, or classical Greek, and also anyone interested in increasing his English Vocabulary. There are no lessons on Greek grammar and conversation, and no attempt is made to teach the Greek alphabet. The course should take 18 weeks. Lesson plans, suggestions, and tests are included. *Anne Brodbeck*

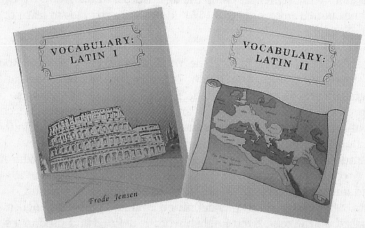

Vocabulary: Latin I (oversized self-cover, 90 pages) from Wordsmiths is a worktext covering 18 weeks of regular vocabulary study. As "a systematic program of learning English words containing Latin roots, prefixes, and suffixes" it includes almost everything you need: learning tips, tests and exercises, exercise answer key, and alphabetized lists of words with their Latin parts. Lacking are regular tests (you get a sample test with suggestions for how to create more of your own) and any teaching helps except a couple of pages listing the roots and affixes. If you want flashcards—an essential review tool, in my opinion—you will have to make your own.

This is more of a self-study course than a teacher-oriented course. Exercises consist of matching English words to their definitions (which are nowhere given in the book), finding the Latin roots of English words, and doing the same thing from Latin to English. The student is supposed to solve all these exercises by consulting the roots and affixes pages. Exercises don't introduce just a few of the Latin word parts at a time, either. Right from the beginning the student is constantly forced to search through all the dozens of Latin word parts over and over again. Contrast this with a teacher-oriented course, where the teacher would introduce a few new Latin word parts each lesson, drill them with flashcards, and then have the student work the exercises.

I'm not saying the Wordsmiths approach can't work. It just requires much more work from the student. At first he'll be working extremely hard for very little observable reward. If this would create a motivation problem for your student, I suggest you either select a more traditional program or make flashcards and introduce the Latin word parts over a month or so before beginning the course.

Vocabulary: Latin II continues where Latin I left off, and adds many more vocabulary items to that basic list.

Free quarterly language-arts newsletter with every order. *Mary Pride*

From the people who produce the best-selling SAT preparation course, here are some vocabulary study aids.

Contending that most vocabulary books contain too many absurd, unnecessary, and rarely-used words, **Word Smart I** (no relation to the excellent "WordSmart" computer software from SmarTek) is a guide which presents what Princeton Review terms "an educated vocabulary." The editors entered into a computer all word lists from past SAT 1 exams, as well as a broad base of common words from publications such as newspapers, best-sellers, and classics. *Word Smart I* is the end result, containing 823 of the toughest words found in these mass-market publications.

Parents will be pleased with the amount of instruction given. Techniques for learning—and retaining—new words are thoroughly covered in the first chapter of the book. The point-by-point methods can be structured into several lessons for younger students, while older children should catch on fast with little assistance. Use of a dictionary is explained in detail, as is the use of a thesaurus. Words are introduced in alphabetical groups with accompanying sentences. A few of the sentences used apply to public school situations or carry themes related to politics and may promote further parent/child discussions. Drills and exams are included, though parents may wish to check retention levels more often than *Word*

NEW!
Word Smart

Grades 7–12. Word Smart I and II, $12 each.

Princeton Review, Random House, 400 Hahan Rd., Westminster, MD 21157. (800) 733-3000. (410) 848-1900 ext. 2000. Fax: (800) 659-2436. They prefer you to order from bookstores. Web: www.randomhouse.com.

Smart I allows. Not only is there an answer key in the back of the book, but parents will be thrilled with additional word lists which contain common usage errors, science and computer terms, word roots, and many other lists. The book also provides a "Hit Parade" of words found most frequently on various achievement exams.

Word Smart II picks up where *Word Smart I* finishes, so parents need not worry they will run out of vocabulary words anytime before graduation. *Lisa Mitchell*

CHAPTER 13

Classical Languages

Interest in classical languages has grown tremendously during the last few years in homeschool circles. I suspect this is largely due to the influence of the Classical Education method. For many families, high school at home has become prep school at home, complete with Latin, Greek, and possibly Hebrew as well.

Oxford, move over! Cambridge, watch out! The homeschoolers are coming!

Hebrew

The most overlooked classical language among homeschoolers today is Hebrew. This Bible language *is* harder to learn than Greek or Latin. However, even a small effort to learn a few rudiments of Hebrew (its alphabet and word structure) enables a high-school student to use seminary-level Bible study tools.

If this still seems too hard, you can try some of the resources in the next chapter for learning *modern* Hebrew, and then pick up biblical Hebrew as a *dialect* of the same. Try this if it is easier for you to learn by *listening* then to learn by *reading*.

The large **Behrman House** catalog is chock-full of Hebrew language resources for learners from preschool through adult; Jewish heritage courses by grade level; books on rabbinical wisdom; and more. Some choice items: *Sam the Detective's Reading Readiness Book* ($5.95) teaches kindergartners the Hebrew letters. *Ivrit Alfon: A Hebrew Primer for Adults* ($6.95) teaches the Hebrew letters, phonetic reading, and a basic 100-word vocabulary. Much, much more, all from a Reform Jewish perspective. *Mary Pride*

A careful study of the Hebrew Bible will reveal what Martin Luther called a "special energy" in its vocabulary. Luther discovered what many Hebraists of the twentieth century have recently come to affirm with him: it is impossible to convey so much so briefly in any other language. Luther concluded the following: "The Hebrew language is the best language of all, with the richest vocabulary ... It has therefore been aptly said that the Hebrews drink from the spring, the Greeks from the stream that flows from it, and the Latins from a downstream pool."

—*Pinchas E. Lapide,*
Hebrew in the Church,
translated by Erroll F. Rhodes
(Wm B. Eerdmans Publishing
Company, 1984)

NEW!
Behrman House Hebrew Resources

All ages. Free catalog.
Behrman House, Inc., 235 Watchung Avenue, West Orange, NJ 07052-5520.
(800) 221-2755. Fax: (973) 669-9769.
Web: www.behrmanhouse.com.

EKS Hebrew Language Gear

Grade 9–adult. The Beginner's Dictionary of Prayerbook Hebrew, $15.95. Teach Yourself to Read Hebrew (5 cassettes and book), $31.95; Book only, $9.95. Prayerbook Hebrew the Easy Way, $18.95; Teacher's Guide, $8.95. The First Hebrew Primer for Adults, $31.95. Tall Tales Told in Biblical Hebrew, $16.95. Hebrew Alphabet Poster set (3 posters), $12.95. Sounds of Hebrew Flashcards, $8.95. Verb Charts, $12.95. Shipping extra. Other products available. *EKS Publishing, 1029-A Solano Ave., Albany, CA 94706. (510) 558-9200. Fax: (510) 558-9255. Email: eks@wenet.net. Web: www.ekspublishing.com.*

NEW!
The First Hebrew Primer, 3rd Edition

Grade 9–adult. First Hebrew Primer, $31.95. Teacher's Guide, $8.95. Answer Book, $9.95. Shipping extra. *EKS Publishing, 1029-A Solano Ave., Albany, CA 94706. (510) 558-9200. Fax: (510) 558-9255. Email: eks@wenet.net. Web: www.ekspublishing.com.*

EKS is one-stop shopping for all kinds of great Hebrew language gear. **Teach Yourself to Read Hebrew** is a pronunciation/letter recognition guide using Sephardic pronunciation. It does not teach translation skills, just how to make the proper Hebrew sounds associated with the words. Each cassette tape has one lesson per side. You would be smart to get the cassettes. **Prayerbook Hebrew the Easy Way** is designed for those who can already read the Hebrew words in the prayerbook but don't understand their meaning. The 21 chapters provide a simplified introduction to grammar, oral reviews, and lists of new vocabulary, and each ends with a prayerbook selection. The Teacher's Guide provides answers to the exercises and teaching tips. **The First Hebrew Primer for Adults** (reviewed below) is a complete course of 33 lessons requiring no previous language experience. You get some heavy-duty grammar here—all seven regular conjugations and three of the most common variations on same. Exceptions are presented in the same chapters as the basic rules, making for completeness but somewhat impeding easy learning. You will have much more success with this course if you first study through *Teach Yourself to Read Hebrew*. **Tall Tales Told and Retold in Biblical Hebrew**, designed to accompany *The First Hebrew Primer for Adults*, expands and supplements the *Primer* with familiar fairy tales translated into the style and vocabulary of Biblical Hebrew. This you gotta see, right?

The Beginner's Dictionary of Prayerbook Hebrew is a very attractive, easy-to-use, large-format book. Unlike all other prayerbook Hebrew dictionaries, here words are listed in the same grammatical forms as they appear in the prayerbook. This is wonderful for those who struggle to remember the Hebrew roots, which often are so different from the words made from those roots. For ease of use, the dictionary contains only words encountered more than 50 times in the prayerbook. A pronunciation guide for every word is appended after the dictionary. At the bottom of each page are simple instructions for finding the words you want (e.g., disregard beginning *vav*). Truly a wonderful resource for beginners!

The remainder of EKS's line is study aids and games. *Mary Pride*

The First Hebrew Primer, subtitled "The Adult Beginner's Path to Biblical Hebrew," is a major textbook (400 pages!), not just a primer as we may normally think of them. A 76-page answer book and a 64-page teacher's guide are also available. It will cover a full year of diligent study. All three books are softcover.

This course assumes that we are already motivated to learn to read Biblical Hebrew and so spares us cutesy motivational devices. It works on the motivational principle of success with a challenge spurring greater effort. This works well with people who choose the course for themselves, but I don't think it will overcome a reluctant student.

Although sold as a course for adults, my 14-year-old daughter loves it (and is learning a lot). It is especially satisfying to be able to read the Hebrew she finds in grocery stores or movies and in the Bible.

The course features English words written in Hebrew as an introduction to the Hebrew alphabet and rewards diligent students with a list of *bona fide* Hebrew words and names, which are also familiar to those who love the Scripture. From words and sentences we progress to narratives, tall tales, and Bible stories. Grammar lessons are distributed throughout, with additional charts, lists, and appendices at the back. *Anne Brodbeck*

Not One Jot . . . A Christian Meditation on the Hebrew Alphabet is more like a treasure chest than a meditation. The 119th psalm itself is a treasure often overlooked, its richness and beauty unrecognized. The team of author David Mulligan and illustrator Mike Schumacher illuminate its secrets, revealing rich multiple meanings of each Hebrew letter.

The acrostic poem, the longest of all the psalms, has an eight-verse stanza for each letter, in which each verse starts with the same Hebrew letter. The Hebrew alphabet itself frames each double page. The left-hand side has an eight-verse stanza in beautiful Hebrew book-print (without modern vowel pointing), as it is in scribe-written copies of the Hebrew Bible. The right-hand page describes the symbolism of numbers, objects and implicit ideas. Victorian style illustrations help the reader interested in memorization of Scripture and the *aleph-bet*. It is not a grammar or reading text, but makes an excellent additional resource for the study of Hebrew.

A lovely 98-page book, *Not One Jot* is wire-bound and opens flat for study. *Anne Brodbeck*

Greek

While Latin study is soaring among homeschoolers, Greek is not. This should not be so.

Traditionally, prep schools taught both Latin *and* Greek, and they did this for a reason. Greek is the language of the classics and of the New Testament. It is also beautifully simple to learn, once you get past learning the alphabet. You could be reading the New Testament in its original language sooner than you think!

Alpha Omega Publications has LIFEPAC worktexts for one full year of **New Testament Greek**. This elective high-school course covers the essentials of grammar, with plentiful exercises for translating both Greek to English and English to Greek. *Mary Pride*

Subtitled *New Testament Greek for Laymen*, **Basic Greek in 30 Minutes a Day** is a book for people who don't need to be Greek scholars, but do want to study the New Testament in the original. After completing it, you will feel at home with the Greek alphabet, pronounce Greek words fluently, know the meanings of hundreds of New Testament words, understand theological terms that came from Greek, see connections between Bible words that are not obvious in English translations, be able to use Greek dictionaries and other valuable reference tools, and understand the basic principles of Greek grammar.

How is this possible in 30 minutes a day? Author Jim Found uses cognates (words that resemble English words of similar meaning), introduces Scripture quotes very early on, and avoids long-winded grammatical explanations and convoluted terminology. The book is laid out like a junior-high-

NEW!
Not One Jot
Grades 7–adult. $12.95 postpaid. *Messenger Publishing, P.O. Box 251, Marshfield, VT, 05658. (800) 886-0496 or (802) 426-4018.*

Alpha Omega Greek LIFEPACs
Grades 9–12. $38.95 for complete boxed set including LIFEPACs, answer keys, test key, and Greek Manual. Textus Receptus (Greek New Testament), $13.99. Greek/English Lexicon, $29.95. Shipping extra. *Alpha Omega Publications, 300 N. McKemy, Chandler, AZ 85226. Orders and inquiries: (800) 622-3070. Web: www.home-schooling.com.*

Basic Greek in 30 Minutes a Day
Grade 7–adult. $15.99 plus shipping. *Bethany House Publishers, 11400 Hampshire Ave. S., Minneapolis, MN 55438. (800) 328-6109. Fax: (612) 829-2503. Email: info@bethanyhouse.com. Web: www.bethanyhouse.com.*

school workbook and is about as easy to use. Designed for Real People, not scholars who dote on tiny print and footnotes, *Basic Greek in 30 Minutes a Day* can either be used as a stand-alone introduction to Greek study through reference aids, or the gateway to serious Greek study. *Mary Pride*

As you'll see later in reference to **Bolchazy-Carducci's** classical Latin *Pronunciation and Reading* guide, their **ancient Greek program** also comes with a booklet and two cassettes. It explains how to pronounce the vowels, consonants, and pitch accents of ancient Greek. The booklet has demonstration texts and practical exercises, and presents a method of reading Greek poetry that integrates the pitch accents with the rhythm.

Bolchazy-Carducci has several classic Greek selections on audiocassette, all read by Stephen C. Daitz, the same man whose voice is on the tapes of *Pronunciation and Reading*. Choices include *A Recital of Ancient Greek Poetry* (four cassettes), Aristophanes' *Birds*, Euripides' *Hekabe*, *Selections from the Greek Orators*, and *Plato's Portrait of Socrates*. Each of these three programs includes, besides its two cassettes, an accompanying booklet with the complete Greek text and a facing English translation. *Mary Pride*

"I'm barely able to cover English grammar. How could I ever teach my child Greek grammar?" If you are looking for an answer to that question Trivium Pursuit could well have the answer.

Homeschool Greek doesn't assume knowledge of English grammar. It introduces English grammatical concepts and then proceeds to the Greek. The student is expected to know the Greek alphabet and phonetic system. (Covered separately in *A Greek Alphabetarion*.)

You are expected to keep a detailed language notebook of technical terms, vocabulary, examples, and idiomatic expressions, nouns, verbs, particles, etc. You get a 350-page text, New Testament reader with English translation, about 300 vocabulary cards, and three audiocassettes.

In a typical lesson, you cover the page below a designated line, read the material, and answer the questions orally or on a piece of paper. When you have answered the questions, you move your cover sheet to the next marker line and check your answers. If you are correct, you move your cover sheet to the next marker line and continue.

Volume I, titled "Mostly Nouns and Such," is 18 chapters divided into 95 lessons, with 14 comprehensive tests. The lessons start out easy but progress rapidly to more and more difficult material. The last five lessons would be challenging for anyone.

Bolchazy-Carducci Greek Readers

Grade 11–college. Pronunciation and Reading of Ancient Greek (second edition), $34.95. Selections . . . tape series, $39.95 each. Shipping extra.
Bolchazy-Carducci Publishers, Inc., 1000 Brown St., Unit 101, Wauconda, IL 60084. (847) 526-4344. Fax: (847) 526-2867. Email: orders@bolchazy.com. Web: www.bolchazy.com.

UPDATED!
Homeschool Greek

Grades 7–12. $88, including vocabulary cards, test booklet, reader, and pronunciation tapes. Shipping extra.
Trivium Pursuit, 139 Colorado St., Suite 168, Muscatine, IA 52761. (309) 537-3641. Email: trivium@muscanet.com. Web: www.muscanet.com/~trivium.

This course will provide any student with a strong foundational knowledge of Greek grammar. *Volume II: Mostly Verbs & Such* should be available soon. *Terri Cannon*

Boy, oh boy! An "easy, self-study" course in New Testament Greek that really is easy and self-study!

It's Greek to Me, Volume 1 (98 pages, spiral-bound) puts the rudiments of New Testament Greek at the fingertips of any learner working at the junior-high level or above. Written by a Moody Bible Institute professor, its 20 illustrated lessons start with the Greek alphabet and pronunciation. You practice these with easy and fun transliteration exercises, many of which have you matching Greek names with the descriptions of notable Bible characters. (Bible references are provided for those non-scholarly types who don't know who "Agrippa" is.) After conquering this first step, you immediately begin translating simple Bible verses. By the end of the book you have mastered the present tense and have a 184-word vocabulary, not counting all the Greek names you now can read!

It's Greek to Me couldn't be easier to use. You need no additional Greek study tools, and an answer key is built in. Technical grammar is avoided. Instead, "Word Keys" strengthen English vocabulary by creative discussions of Greek word roots, and "Word Treasures" shed light on the meaning of some simple New Testament phrases. "Help Notes" explain exceptions and details. Cartoon characters Barnabas, Phoebe, and Sheepskin liven up the text while making abstract ideas easier to understand.

Volume 2 of *It's Greek to Me!* is due out eventually. I can hardly wait!

Figure this as a four-and-a-half-star resource only if your student does not know his Bible all that well, as in that case he'll be spending a lot of time looking up the answers to the transliteration exercises. If he knows who's who in the Bible, *It's Greek to Me* is a five-star resource. *Mary Pride*

Kaegi's Greek Grammar is a straightforward, well-organized Greek grammar first published in the 1800s in German and translated into English in the early 1900s. This reprinted edition is easy to read and reference.

I never have been a great fan of grammar texts. There is something so detached in a discussion of hortatory and deliberative subjunctives.

But if you want to really learn Greek and be able to read Homer in the original, you will need a reference. This one would do nicely. *Terri Cannon*

A colorful revision of the original program introduced over 30 years ago. **A Reading Course in Homeric Greek** helps students quickly tackle selected undoctored passages from Homer's *Odyssey*. Contains "stimulating essays on aspects of Greek art and culture which highlight humanistic values and increase literary appreciation." Includes a special supplement, "Transition to Attic Greek," to help the student read more recent versions of Greek, whether classical or *koiné*. *Mary Pride*

Latin

Latin study at home is becoming common for homeschoolers. Don't forget that many of the Latin courses reviewed in volume 2 are equally suitable for a first course for junior high!

Whatever remnants of Oxonian thinking still survive in the American graves of academe find their home at the **American Classical League**. ACL offers its members *The Classical Outlook* magazine, teaching tips and materials, info on new products, the National Junior Classical League (open to homeschoolers), the National Mythology Exam for students grades 3–9, national Latin and Greek exams, teacher and student scholarships, fraternal support, and an annual Institute.

The Institute mainly concentrates on pedagogical issues, although you will find the occasional workshop on multicultural and feminist issues. Lest the attendees be overcome by their mental exertions, the Institute program includes such things as picnics, riverboat rides, sing-a-longs, social hours, and tours. For students, there are competitions, workshops, and social events as well. Students must be accompanied by the adult leader of their chapter of JCL. For the last few years, Dr. Jukka Ammondt, the voice behind *Elvis in Latin,* has performed at the Institute.

You don't have to join ACL to order their products; the catalog and general information about their competitions is free. *Mary Pride*

The *Artes Latinae* program reviewed in Volume 2 of the Big Book actually was developed for teen students. Don't rule it out just because it is so much easier to use than regular teen-and-adult Latin courses!

Or, if you want to know whether Caesar said "Vainy veedy veeky" or "Wainy weedy weechy," **Bolchazy-Carducci's Pronunciation and Reading Guide to Classical Latin** comes with two cassettes and a booklet with demonstration texts and practical exercises. You'll find out how to pronounce the vowels, consonants, and diphthongs of classical Latin, how and why Latin is accented, and how to read Latin poetry by integrating its natural word accents with a rhythm based on the number of syllables in a line.

Other Latin readings available on cassettes from Bolchazy-Carducci: selections from Cicero, Virgil, and a combined set of selections from Catullus and Horace, all read in Restored Classical Pronunciation by Robert P. Sonkowsky. Each of these three programs includes, besides its two cassettes, an accompanying booklet with the complete Latin text and a facing English translation. This is fascinating stuff, too, let me tell you. The whole world would watch C-Span if our modern Senators had one-tenth of Cicero's oratorical gifts! You haven't seen negative campaigning until you've experienced Cicero's oration against Catiline.

Bolchazy-Carducci also has a tremendous line of Latin and Greek texts, readers, and supporting materials, including some in medieval and Renaissance Latin, the form of Latin recommended for study by Dorothy Sayers, author of "The Lost Tools of Learning" and many famous literary works, fictional and otherwise.

Let's mention just one reader useful for teen students: **Latin Stories**. This little book is designed to accompany Wheelock's *Latin (An Introductory Course Based on Ancient Authors).* The first 18 of the 38 Latin stories are tales from classical mythology. The last 20 are adaptations of passages from famous Latin authors. The book has vocabulary lists with each story, plus a list of the grammar required to read the story and a capsule description of the story theme in English. Interesting reading! *Mary Pride*

American Classical League

Parents. Membership (includes The Classical Outlook magazine), $25.
American Classical League, Miami University, Oxford, OH 45056. (513) 529-7741. Fax: (513) 529-7742. Email: AmericanClassicalLeague@muohio.edu. Web: www.umich.edu/~acleague.

Bolchazy-Carducci Latin Readers

Grade 5–college. Pronunciation and Reading of Classical Latin, $34.95. Selections from . . . tape series, $39.95 each. 38 Latin Stories, $10.50. Shipping extra.
Bolchazy-Carducci Publishers, Inc., 1000 Brown St., Unit 101, Wauconda, IL 60084. (847) 526-4344. Fax: (847) 526-2867. Email: orders@bolchazy.com. Web: www.bolchazy.com.

The **Cambridge Latin** course is the same used at English prep schools, revised for North American students. In Unit I, you meet the family of Lucius Caecilius Iucundus, a merchant living in (of all places) Pompeii. As you progress through the 12 stages of Unit I, you learn about Roman civilization (through English text, illustrated with graphics). You also study Latin grammar and vocabulary. Lots of humor and interesting cultural sidelights.

In Unit II, we are following the adventures of a Roman official in Britain.

Each unit has an accompanying Language Information booklet. This includes more language information and exercises, and also the invaluable Latin-English dictionary of words used in the unit. The units themselves feature high-interest stories (some illustrated).

Short Latin Stories, a separate reader correlated with the Cambridge Press series, is really fun! Starting with easier stories, and progressing to the more difficult, *Short Latin Stories* offers a mix of fables, history, myths, and humor, all selected for entertainment value.

This excellent series is designed for middle grades and up, although I see no reason why motivated, intelligent preteens couldn't use it. *Mary Pride*

Latin Grammar for Christian Private and Home Schools (199 pages, spiral-bound) starts somewhat differently. It begins with pronunciation and parts of speech and quickly moves on through the typical

material of a traditional Latin course, all the way up to the fourth conjugation and fifth declension. Christian content is found in the translation exercises, e.g., translating the phrase "Christ is God" from English to Latin. This book includes explanations of what you are studying, so no separate teacher's manual is required. The accompanying solution key has answers to all the exercises.

Latin Grammar is much simpler to use than other traditional school Latin courses I have seen (e.g., Cambridge Press and Longman's). The streamlined format, with everything in one spiral-bound book and accompanying solution key, is a lot easier to use than juggling the teacher's editions, textbooks, workbooks, and readers from other publishers. The course teaches sentence translation only, with no long selections to work through, so you still will need a set of Latin readers eventually. Maybe this can be Canon Press's next publishing project! *Mary Pride*

Now this brings new meaning to the word "classic"! When I first heard about this **Elvis Songs in Latin CD** via an online chat, I just *had* to get it. So I tracked down the gentleman who had mentioned it, and asked him to buy me one next time he was in Finland. Why Finland? Because the incredibly talented Dr. Jukka Ammondt (a professor of Literature at the University of Jyvaskyla, believe it or not) whose rich voice sings these Elvis songs in Latin, is Finnish, and that's where the CD was recorded.

The kids and I were wondering just how "Hound Dog" would come across in Latin. We're still wondering, because all the songs on this CD are Elvis *ballads*. Remember "Love Me Tender?" Now it's *Tenere Me Ama*. "Can't Help Falling in Love" is *Non Adamare Non Possum*. Plus many more!

Cambridge Latin Courses

Grades 7–12. Unit I: student book, $22.95; workbook, $7.95; teacher's manual, $16.95. Unit II: student book, $24.95; workbook, $7.95; teacher's manual, $17.95. Short Latin Stories, $10.95. Also available: units III and IV. Shipping extra. *Cambridge University Press, 110 Midland Ave., Port Chester, NY 10573. Orders: (800) 431-1580. Inquiries: (914) 937-9600. Fax: (914) 937-4712. Email: order@cup.org. Web: www.cup.org.*

NEW!
Canon Press Latin Grammar

Grades 6–12. Latin Grammar, $20. Solution Key, $8. *Canon Press, Community Evangelical Fellowship, PO Box 8741, Moscow, ID 83843. (800) 488-2034. Fax: (208) 882-1568. Email: canorder@moscow.com. Web: www.canonpress.org.*

NEW!
Elvis in Latin

All ages. $20 plus shipping. *Bolchazy-Carducci Publishers, Inc., 1000 Brown St., Unit 101, Wauconda, IL 60084. (847) 526-4344. Fax: (847) 526-2867. Email: orders@bolchazy.com. Web: www.bolchazy.com.*

NEW!
Fabulae Romanae
Fabulae Graecae

Grade 9–college. Fabulae Romanae,
$24.08. Fabulae Graecae, $24.44.
Shipping extra.
*Addison Wesley Longman, One Jacob
Way, Reading, MA 01867.
(800) 822-6339. Fax: (800) 367-7198.
Web: www.awl.com.*

NEW!
Jenney's Latin

Grades 9–12. Jenney's First Year
Latin, $47.45. Second Year Latin,
$48.97. Third Year Latin, $52.47.
Shipping extra.
*Prentice Hall, 4350 Equity Drive, PO
Box 2649, Columbus, OH 43216.
(800) 848-9500. Fax: (614) 771-7361.
Web: www.phschool.com.*

Something this unique can't be kept a secret. Not only is this CD now a hot seller in Europe, but for several years now American Classical League has hosted an enthusiastically-received "Elvis in Latin" concert with Dr. Ammondt. (Picture a group of classical scholars screaming for multiple encores—the mental image is alone worth the price!) Our "Artes Latinae" friends at Bolchazy-Carducci Publishers were there at the first concert and couldn't resist. So now this painless way to pick up Latin vocabulary (and fit into the *frigidus* Junior Classical League in-crowd!) is available right here in America, complete with a little booklet of the Latin lyrics and their English translation. What a gift for that Latin student in your life! *Mary Pride* (P.S. *Frigidus* is Latin for "cool.")

Fabulae Romanae: Stories of Famous Romans is a series of stories for students who have already had the equivalent of 1½ to 2 years of high-school Latin, or at least a year of college-level Latin. Its 31 readings, all adapted from ancient authors, follow the history of Rome from its founding to the death of Cicero in 43 B.C.

To make it easy for students to translate the stories, each Latin paragraph has a "running vocabulary list." This means the words are translated when they occur in the text next to them, rather than you getting an alphabetized vocabulary list at the end of the reading. Good grammar notes, a time line, indexes of people and places, and an English/Latin vocabulary also help. The teacher's guide for each book includes translations of all the stories, plus questions to ask your students, and references to standard Roman history texts for those inclined to further study. Grammar topics are outlined in the order in which they appear in the text, and there is also a list of audio-visual resources.

Now also available, **Fabulae Graecae** is stories of famous Greeks, but written in Latin. Meant as a bridge for third-semester Latin, it includes running vocabulary list on the left-hand page of each two-page spread. These lists include only words that have not been studied in **Ecce Romani** books 1–4. (Obviously, the publisher is hoping you have used this Latin program, which was reviewed in Volume 2 of the *Big Book*.) Lots of grammar helps, plus complete English/Latin and Latin/English vocabularies, are also included, making it easy for students to figure out the stories "on their own." *Mary Pride*

Popular among Latin teachers for years, the **Jenny's Latin series** offers a traditional, well-organized approach to the language. Roman history, culture, and literature are highlighted throughout. Study passages are carefully designed to only use vocabulary and syntax the student has already been taught. English vocabulary is deliberately increased by the systematic study of Latin word roots used in English words. A neat "Traces of Roman Civilization Today" feature shows the influence Roman culture continues to exert, while proverbs "From the Philosopher's Handbook" help build a vocabulary of classical sayings. All lessons have ample oral and written exercises, and frequent review lessons ensure material is retained.

The thrust of the course is to enable the student to study classical Latin writings, which in fact are introduced as early as Second Year, with readings from Caesar, Nepos, Ovid, Martial, Plautus, and Livy. Third Year you will be translating Cicero's orations, Sallust, selected writings of Pliny, Ovid (more works), plus writings from later Romans and quite a bit of medieval Latin writings, from the Venerable Bede to Roger Bacon.

The First Year book introduces each chapter with a culture feature entitled "If You Lived in Ancient Rome." The presumption is that you are a pagan Roman—the contribution of Christianity is not discussed in the section on Roman religion. Topics include your house, the rooms in your house, your furniture and accessories, your kitchen, your food, your meals, your water supply, your birth and infancy, your day, your education, your wedding, the role of women, the toga, your clothing, other fashions, public baths, theatre, chariot racing, gladiators, transportation, traffic and accommodations, roads, sea travel, the *numina,* the gods, official cults, personal worship, Roman medicine, funeral customs, business and industry, import-export trading, manufacturing, government contracts, architecture, the Circus Maximus, and palaces. As you can see, there is a *lot* of cultural information here! Text is accompanied by many lush photographs, and the reading and exercise selections teach more culture and history.

This format is not followed in the other books. Instead of having a cultural introduction to each chapter, each book begins with an introduction to background history and culture. A detailed biography and literary analysis of each writer and piece precedes the literary selection to be translated. Extensive grammar appendices and helps, and of course a lengthy Latin-to-English dictionary, help your student with translation.

We personally have used the first- and third-year Jenny's books in our children's online Latin courses. The handsome hardbound texts are pricey, but can be used with child after child. They are quite suitable for high school. For middle-school use, I suggest taking two years with the First Year book. This pace helps ease the younger student into these unfamiliar waters. *Mary Pride*

The publishers of Artes Latinæ also carry a huge line of classical texts in the original languages. You know, get-down stuff like Euclid, Plutarch, Cicero, Ovid. For those not quite ready for the Big Time, here come the **Latin Easy Readers**! The first, exotically titled *Elementary Latin Translation Book,* introduces students to Roman history and Greek mythology. The second, a Latin translation of Vergil's *Æneid* (books I & II) by none other than Artes Latinæ developer Waldo Sweet, substitutes an easy Latin paraphrase for the usual student notes in English. Lots of other readers are available. *Mary Pride*

Trademarks aside, this book would have been better named *Latin Made Organized.* Like other "Made Simple" books, the explanations and practice sets in **Latin Made Simple** are not actually simpler than those in a regular textbook. However, this book has some handy features that do make it easier to use for self-study than a typical textbook.

For example, all the practice exercises are right in the book. You don't need a textbook *and* a workbook. The practice readings have the translation directly opposite, so you can cover it with a piece of paper and then check your work without flipping pages. Answers to the practice exercises, plus a Latin/English vocabulary and all the grammar charts, are in the back of the book.

Aside from this, the book follows the sequence of a typical Latin course, roughly equivalent to two years of high-school Latin or one year of college Latin. The instructions are straightforward, and the book itself is usable for self-study, as advertised. *Mary Pride*

Also available in the Jenny's Latin series:
- Teacher's resource books, cassettes, and tapescripts
- Lesson guides, review exercises, and a testing package
- Workbook with answer key
- *Cursus Honorum,* an honors program of challenging passages for advanced students to translate from Latin to English and English to Latin
- *Writing Latin Prose,* a set of passages for composition and translation practice

Latin Easy Readers
Grades 7–12. $14–$18 each.
Bolchazy-Carducci Publishers, Inc., 1000 Brown St., Unit 101, Wauconda, IL 60084. (847) 526-4344.
Fax: (847) 526-2867.
Email: orders@bolchazy.com.
Web: www.bolchazy.com.

NEW!
Latin Made Simple, Revised Edition
Grades 9–12. $12.95 plus $2.50 shipping per order.
Bantam Doubleday Dell Publishing Group, Inc., 2451 S. Wolf Road, Des Plaines, IL 60018.
Inquiries: (800) 323-9872.
Can order by mail only.

Longman Publishing Group Latin Readers

Grades 7–12. The Romans Speak for Themselves: Book 1 and 2, $16.28 each; teacher's handbook, $16.28. *Addison Wesley Longman, One Jacob Way, Reading, MA 01867.* (800) 822-6339. Web: www.awl.com.

NEW!
Oxford Latin Course

Grade 9–college. Part I, $20.95. Part II, $15. Part III, $22.95. Teacher's books, $14.95 each. Shipping extra. *Oxford University Press, 2001 Evans Road, Cary, NC 27513.* (800) 451-7556. Fax: (919) 677-1303. Web: www.oup-usa.org.

The Phenomenon of Language (2nd edition)

Grades 7–12. Book, $26. Teacher's manual, $17.24. Shipping extra. *Addison Wesley Longman, One Jacob Way, Reading, MA 01867.* (800) 822-6339. Fax: (800) 367-7198. Web: www.awl.com.

Vis-Ed Biblical Hebrew, Modern Hebrew, Latin, Biblical Greek, and Classical Greek Flashcards

Grade 9–college. Each set, $10.95. Shipping extra. *Visual Education, 581 W. Leffel Lane, Springfield, OH 45501.* Orders: (800) 243-7070. Web: www.vis-ed.com.

You want to read Latin? You've got it! **The Romans Speak for Themselves** contains short readings adapted from genuine Roman authors and correlated to Longman's **Ecce Romani** program. *Mary Pride*

Just as Cambridge Latin is the classic high-school Latin text, **Oxford Latin** is the classic college text. Again, you have the typical life-in-Roman-times scenarios built into the readings and culture notes. Each lesson starts out with captioned cartoons showing a bit of Roman life. The captions demonstrate the grammar you'll be learning in this chapter. A grammar lesson comes next, followed by English-to-Latin and Latin-to-English exercises that drill the grammatical principles. You then get a Latin story to translate, with words you are not yet expected to know appearing in the margin right next to the lines they're used in. Don't get sloppy, though—words you are already supposed to know are *not* provided, except in the small Latin-to-English dictionary in the back of the book, and the Latin II dictionary doesn't include the words you learned in Latin I, etc. New vocabulary words to memorize appear separately, with even more grammar lessons, reviews, and exercises following.

With 20 lessons per book, and each book meant as a one-year course, you should count on a pace of a lesson completed every other week. That's about a page a day.

Oxford Latin is streamlined enough to use for self-study, but easier to follow with the help of someone who knows the language. Additional workbooks are available, but you don't need them for anything. There's plenty to do in the student book all by itself. *Mary Pride*

What do you get when you cross Latin with an introductory course in linguistics? It sounds awful, like pasta with barbecue sauce, but really it's good enough to deserve a separate review of its own. It's **The Phenomenon of Language**, a sprightly text that uses Latin as a vehicle for giving students a method for learning all languages quickly and efficiently. Besides the charming Roman-style cartoons and clever activities, the student spends a lot of time discovering how languages work. The exercises are designed according to the Platonic method: students are gently led to draw the correct conclusions on their own.

The *Phenomenon* approach takes more time than other vocabulary courses, but teaches more Latin. Since it does *not* teach Greek, Old English, or Norman French roots, you might want to follow it up with, say, levels D–F of the Bob Jones University Press program. *Mary Pride*

All Languages

Bill's constant seminary companion was a box of **Vis-Ed vocabulary flash cards**. Each set contains approximately 1000 cards, 1½ x 3½" in size, plus a very useful study guide with index. For example, the Biblical Hebrew study guide shows words in frequency of occurrence and by grammatical categories. Each card has the target language word on the front and both its English meaning and pertinent grammatical info on the back. Recommended if you're seriously studying any of these languages. *Mary Pride*

CHAPTER 14

Foreign Languages

Spanish and French are still the most popular homeschool foreign languages, among Americans at least. This is as it should be, with French-speaking Quebec to the north, and Spanish-speaking Mexico to the south. Spanish is increasingly useful right here in the good ol' USA too, with more and more of our fellow citizens speaking it at home and elsewhere. Meanwhile, a study of French, and to a lesser extent German, yields immediate dividends in increased English vocabulary, since many English words are borrowed from, or share roots with, words from these languages.

The case for studying languages such as Italian, Swahili, and Japanese is less pragmatic. Lots of people study them just for fun. Learning a new language *is* fun. It gives your family an instant "secret code" for talking in crowds. It makes you feel smarter. It may even come in useful in business or travel someday—who knows? And don't forget that a few colleges still insist on a foreign language requirement for either entrance or graduation.

If you pick

- French
- German
- Latin
- Spanish

and do a good job of learning it, you can take an Advanced Placement exam and attempt to earn college credit for your knowledge. SAT II tests, which may gain you the right to take more advanced courses in the subject, and/or impress a college counselor with your level of scholastic achievement, but do *not* earn you possible college credits, are available in:

- Chinese
- French
- German
- modern Hebrew
- Italian
- Japanese
- Latin
- Spanish

Other languages—such as Russian or Swahili—may be fun to study, but at present there are no standardized tests commonly used by colleges to validate your knowledge of these languages. Just a little something to keep in mind when picking a language to study . . .

How to Learn

Penton Secrets of Learning a Foreign Language
Grade 7–adult. $15.95 plus shipping. *Penton Overseas, Inc., 2470 Impala Drive, Carlsbad, CA 92008-7226. Orders: (800) 748-5804. Inquiries: (760) 431-0060. Fax: (760) 431-8110. Web: www.pentonoverseas.com.*

Secrets of Learning a Foreign Language is a three-hour audiocassette program with accompanying informative booklet. Written by a man who learned 16 languages in the foreign service, its mission is to help first-time language students, and those who have failed at languages in the past, learn the tips and techniques necessary to master another language.

Learning foreign languages is different than other disciplines in that you can't just tack on the knowledge to what you already know. To become fluent, you must learn to *think* in the target language, literally replacing your normal thought patterns while you're talking, reading, or writing in that language. *Secrets of Learning a Foreign Language* explains how to do this, as well as concepts like how to discover the roots of words, the way to master proper pronunciation, how to pick up grammar skills, and lots more. The book has received rave reviews from the experts. *Mary Pride*

A Beka Spanish

Grades 7–12. Spanish I text, $30.80. Teacher's guide, $23.35. Pronunciation/Scripture cassette, $10.20. Vocabulary manual, $13.80. Teacher's edition of manual, $16.35. Vocabulary tape, $10.20. Spanish II text, $32.20. Teacher's guide, $23.35. Vocabulary manual for II, $15.45; teacher's edition, $18.65. Test booklet for either I or II: student, $4.20; teacher, $8.85. Songbook, $9.20. Shipping extra.
A Beka Book, Box 19100, Pensacola, FL 32523-9100. (800) 874-2352. Web: www.abeka.com.

Alpha Omega Spanish LIFEPACs

Grades 9–12. $94.95 for boxed set including LIFEPACs, answer keys, test key, and tapes. Basic Spanish Ready Reference Card, $.99. Shipping extra.
Alpha Omega Publications, 300 N. McKemy, Chandler, AZ 85226. Orders and inquiries: (800) 622-3070. Web: www.home-schooling.com.

Audio-Forum Foreign Language Courses

Grade 9–college. Prices range from about $100–$300. Languages: Spanish (including Business, Medical, Spanish for Policemen and Firemen, Spanish for Health Professionals, and Pastoral Spanish, plus FSI Spanish), FSI French, Haitian Creole, German, Italian, Modern Hebrew, Arabic (several dialects), Chinese (several dialects), Portuguese, Japanese, Polish, Russian, Modern Greek, Classical Greek and Latin, Scandinavian languages, Eastern European languages, Turkish, Urdu, Thai, Vietnamese, Khmer (Cambodian), African (several dialects), and English. Living Language Videos:

Foreign Language Courses

Por Todo el Mundo and *Mas Que Vencedores* are the titles of the two **A Beka Spanish** high-school courses for Christian students. Strong emphasis on witnessing for Christ includes Bible memory verse for every week, practice lessons from the life of Christ, and a missionary motif.

Each course has two texts—books A and B— loaded with lots of grammar drill and practice exercises. A separate vocabulary-building program is found in the Vocabulary Manual for each course. Vocabulary and Pronunciation/Scripture cassettes coordinate with the texts. Plus there is a songbook with Christian praise songs in Spanish.

A Beka's French I and **II** courses, entitled *Nouveaux Chemins* and *Langue et Lovange*, have a similar format and prices

Both French and Spanish are also available as video courses through A Beka Video School. See Curriculum Buyers' Guide in Volume 1. *Mary Pride*

Alpha Omega Publications has 10 LIFEPAC Gold worktexts for one full year of high school Spanish. The Spanish course comes with a set of 10 cassette tapes. Along with the dialogs and grammar, each LIFEPAC in the series of 10 Spanish worktexts has sections on Cultural Activities, The World of Music, and a What Does the Bible Say? translation exercise. LIFEPAC titles include Introduction to Spanish, In the School, The Family and Home, Around the Town, Pastimes, In the Restaurant, Personal Care, Traveling, Idioms, and Let's Use Our Spanish.

The optional 8½ x 11" laminated and three-hole-punched **Basic Spanish Grammar Ready Reference Card** costs less than a buck and makes grammar review a breeze. *Mary Pride*

Audio-Forum does not develop their own courses. As they say, "We have drawn on the expertise of our academic advisory board to help us identify and locate the most effective courses in use anywhere in the United States or abroad. We then obtained the rights to offer these by mail throughout the English-speaking world."

Most Audio-Forum courses are duplicates of the **Foreign Service Institute** courses used to train U.S. diplomats and overseas personnel. These are the full-length, in-depth courses. Unlike others' language programs, Audio-Forum FSI courses do not all follow the same basic format. They do, however, offer a wider variety of languages than anyone else, including Arabic, Cantonese, Hungarian, Hebrew, and Vietnamese, to name just a few. If you want to dig down to your family's "roots" and learn the language of your non-English ancestors, Audio-Forum probably has it.

How does it work? Repetition, repetition, repetition . . . FSI students normally memorize the dialogs, and one can understand why, since you hear the same one over and over and over. I was surprised to hear the street French of the French I series: *Juizreux* or some such mangled remnant for *Je suis hereux*. That may be the way they talk in France, but it puts a stumbling-block before beginners to not hear extremely distinct pronunciation. We don't mumble at babies, after all!

FSI courses come with culture notes and big, fat textbooks. Make no mistake about it, FSI is the heavy artillery of language instruction.

The **Living Language video courses** from Crown Publishers are also offered by Audio-Forum. These consist of real-life tourist situations—hotel, airport, restaurant, store. A friendly emcee explains what's happening in between the adventures of our totally-fluent tourist couple. Phrases and words are introduced at conversational speed, then repeated slowly with English subtitles. The emcee then shows how to use the sentence structures you just used to create more new sentences. You're learning to speak, not to read, since the target language never appears on screen. A booklet with additional vocabulary and dialog transcripts would add a lot to this program. *Mary Pride*

The **Berlitz** organization is, according to itself, "the world's leading publisher of books for travellers . . . plus Cassettes and Self-teaching courses." Berlitz, as you may recall, started as a you-attend-the-classes language school. The company has wisely decided to put together inexpensive courses using the Berlitz method. These are aimed mostly at the tourist market.

The bottom of the line is **Berlitz's one-hour cassette course**. You get basic phrases spoken in four voices and a little booklet with the text of the recordings, plus translation. I don't think much of these phrasebooks as a serious learning tool. If all you want is a taste of the language, that's all you'll get.

The **Berlitz Basic Home Study Cassette Course** looks more promising. You get a 90-minute "zero" or beginner's cassette with ten basic lessons in four voices. These are not just random phrases, but follow a grammatical plan. This is followed by two more 60-minute cassettes. You also get two illustrated books with the text of all lessons plus helpful notes, a rotating verb finder, a Berlitz phrase book, and a pocket dictionary.

The **Berlitz Comprehensive Cassette Course** includes all the above, plus two more C-60 cassettes, six CDs, and four more illustrated manuals.

I believe in "baby-talk"—slow, exaggerated pronunciation—for beginners, and Berlitz apparently does not. The Spanish cassette I heard didn't quite race along at Puerto Rican speed, but was pretty brisk nonetheless. *Mary Pride*

The **Bob Jones University Press** *Praktisches Deutsch* two-semester high-school **German** program uses the "total immersion" approach. Each of the student texts has nothing, *nichts*, but German in its pages. Translation is avoided; rather, teens are expected to build vocabulary through "association, description (in German), and illustration." BJU is trying to get you *thinking* in the language, as well as reading it, writing it, and speaking it.

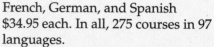

What are your chances of teaching this course at home? Slim, unless you already know German. In fact, even the Customer Service Rep at BJUP told us, "If you don't know German, don't order these." You can't lean on a teacher's edition, because there isn't any. Instead, BJUP provides sets of cassette tapes for language practice.

Student lessons, as in other Bob Jones material, cover a wide range of topics: German history, art, literature, daily life, travel, amusement, songs, politics, and, of course, religion. Students learn German Bible verses, and the program has an evangelistic bent.

French, German, and Spanish $34.95 each. In all, 275 courses in 97 languages.
Audio-Forum, division of Jeffrey Norton Publishers, Inc. 96 Broadstreet, Guilford, CT 06437. (800) 243-1234. Email: info@audioforum.com. Web: www.audioforum.com.

Berlitz Foreign Language Courses

Grade 9–college. One-hour course, $18.95 (Arabic, Chinese, Dutch, Finnish, French, German, Greek, Hebrew, Italian, Danish, Japanese, Norwegian, Portuguese, Russian, Serbo-Croatian, Spanish, and Swedish). Basic Home Study Cassette Course, $59.95 (French, German, Italian, Spanish). Comprehensive Cassette course, $225 (same 4 languages).
Berlitz Kids, PO Box 3239, Princeton, NJ 08543. (800) 9-BERLITZ. Fax: (800) 452-0466. Web: www.berlitz.com.

UPDATED!
BJUP French, German, and Spanish

Grades 7–12. German 1: student worktext, $15.50; set of five audiocassettes, $59.95. German 2: student worktext, $17.50; set of five audiocassettes, $59.95. French 1: student text, $30; teacher's edition, $39; student activities manual, $12; student activities manual teacher's edition, $15.50; set of nine audiocassettes, $65. French 2: same prices. Spanish 1: similar materials and prices except set of 12 cassettes, $91. Spanish 2: similar materials and prices except set of six audiocassettes, $48. Shipping extra.
Bob Jones University Press Customer Services, Greenville, SC 29614. Orders: (800) 845-5731. Web: www.bjup.com.

You have to be careful with this total immersion stuff. They tried it in my seventh-grade French class, and everyone in my class agreed that we didn't understand what we were supposed to be learning. Memorizing dialogues is fine *as long as they are explained*. BJUP, to their credit, does expect the teacher to clear up confusion and explain what the students can't figure out for themselves.

BJUP's **French** courses are more traditional in approach. Activities, dialogues, grammar exercises, and pronunciation exercises are the backbone of of these two semesters of high-school French. Unlike the German courses, materials are presented in English. However, it is necessary that the teacher have a good command of basic French in order for the student to make progress.

Materials for both semesters are similar: a hardbound student text, an oversized spiral-bound teacher's edition that includes the student pages plus marginal teaching notes and answers to exercises at the bottoms of the pages, an activities manual with cassette scripts and additional exercises, a teacher's edition of same, and a set of audiocassettes for pronunciation training and listening comprehension. You will have best success if you purchase *all* of these.

French cultural facts from a Christian perspective are included mostly through following the fictional adventures of the Dupont family, American missionaries working in France.

High-quality, durable materials, systematic treatment, and interesting vignettes make the BJUP French courses a fine choice for Christian families where one parent knows some French.

BJUP also offers two semesters of high-school **Spanish**. Materials are the same as the French courses (student text, student text teacher's edition, student activities manual, student activities manual teacher's edition, audiocassettes), and the teaching approach is also similar. *Mary Pride*

EMC/ Paradigm Foreign Language Products

Grades 7–12. Easy Readers, $3.75–$8.95 each. Mystery Readers, $3.95. Spanish for Business (Beginning or Intermediate versions), $11.95 each; complete kit (with three cassettes, textbook, and teacher's guide), $59 each. Lander und Sitten (3 videos and teacher's resource guide), $195. Shipping extra. *EMC/Paradigm Publishing, 875 Montreal Way, St. Paul, MN 55102. (800) 328-1452. Fax: (800) 328-4564. Email: educate@emcp.com. Web: www.emcp.com.*

This colorful catalog of foreign language materials for public and private high schools includes courses in Spanish, German, Italian, French, Russian, Japanese, and Greek.

EMC Easy Readers series, available in Spanish, French, German, Russian, and Italian, are classics originally written in those languages, condensed and simplified for easy reading. Reading levels are marked as A, B, C, or D. A-level books contain a 600-word vocabulary (about what you can expect after a semester of high school or a year of junior-high study). B-level is 1,200 words; C-level, 1,800 words; D-level, 2,500 words. EMC/Paradigm also has hi-lo mystery thrillers in some languages.

For most languages, **EMC/Paradigm** offers **BBC learning kits** or adaptations. Its BBC Spanish series, *España Viva*, digs into the culture and everyday life of Spain. (Accompanying videocassettes for these and other BBC programs from EMC/Paradigm are available from Films Incorporated.) Lots of easy-read mystery thrillers in different languages.

The **Spanish for Business** series (not the same as Audio-Forum's) follows the trials and tribulations of the Commercial Hispana, a fictional Spanish import/export firm with connections in Latin America, with a "striking variety of unconventional exercises." Two levels, not terribly expensive for a business language course.

These are just a few of the Spanish materials. I wouldn't have space to list all materials for the other languages either. Each has one or more beginning programs and cultural introductions, except Portuguese and Greek. Taking those for granted, let's look at some of EMC/Paradigm's more interesting products.

Buongiorno Italia! is a BBC program for beginners that features conversations and interviews with Italians filmed and recorded in Italy.

Lander und Sitten sounds absolutely fabulous, but unfortunately is too expensive for me to check out for you. This is a three-video visit to Germany, Austria, and Switzerland, narrated in both German and English. It hits all the historical (and tourist!) hot spots: the Black Forest, the Bavarian Alps, the Rhine, Frankfurt, Munich, Salzburg, Innsbruck, Vienna, Lausanne, Zurich, and more.

EMC/Paradigm's **Russian line-up** includes an adapted BBC series (textbook, workbook, study guide, cassettes, teacher's guide) with optional accompanying video series; and seven Russian Easy Readers (three at level A, two each at levels B and C). *Mary Pride*

All About Language, a collaboration between Douglas Moore and Harris Winitz, is for late-beginning and early-intermediate language learners. Students should understand the vocabulary and sentence structure of books 1 and 2 of the Learnables (see review in volume 2) before tackling this program.

Each book in the program teaches a "lexical field." What's a lexical field, you ask? It's "a group of words that reflect a common core of meaning." In other words, a bunch of words related to a single topic. These are taught both visually and auditorally. Each double-page spread has pictures on the left-hand side and text on the right. Meanwhile, the cassette(s) that come with each set ensure you are practicing the correct pronunciations.

The entire series is available for ESL. Some sets are also available for Spanish and German.

The Spanish series: *La Comida* (eating), *Medios de Transporte* (transportation), *Colocando* (verbs of place), *Caminando* (verbs related to walking). Each is a single book with a single cassette.

For German: *Gehen* (verbs of walking): *Stellen, Legen, und Setzen* (verbs relating to putting, placing, and setting); *Essen* (eating); *Beförderung* (transportation); *Hauser und Gebauder* (houses and buildings); *Telefon* (telephoning); *Berufsleben* (occupations); and *Wetter* (weather). These book/cassette combos are similar to those for Spanish in their format.

These are great for kids or adults. *Mary Pride*

VocabuLearn from Penton Overseas is a popular vocabulary-development program available in 21 languages. These are *not* standalone programs. Think of them as "audio flash cards." Each VocabuLearn course includes two 90-minute audiocassettes and a word list containing over 1,500 words and expressions used on the cassettes. The words are not in any particular order, except that nouns, verbs, and other parts of speech are presented separately.

Here's how it works. On one side of the tape, an American voice says a word in English, followed by a pause long enough for you to vocalize the word in the target language, if you know it. Then a native speaker of the target language says the word slowly in that language. Halfway through the tape, the process is reversed. The target language word or phrase comes first, followed by a pause, then by the word in English. This "reversible" feature means non-English speakers of the target language can also use these tapes to learn or improve their English. The word lists are different for both sides of the tape, by the way, to allow more vocabulary on the tapes.

VocabuLearn courses come in three levels. Level I is basic skills—simplest words and phrases. Level II includes more words and expressions. Level III includes more complex and sophisticated vocabulary. The tapes are super-crisp, thanks to Dolby Stereo, and the packaging is nice.

VocabuLearn/ce, a computer enhanced version of VocabuLearn for both IBM-PC and Macintosh users, is also now available in both levels I and II for Spanish, French, Italian, German, Japanese, Russian, and Hebrew. Each level comes with the same cassettes and booklet as regular VocabuLearn courses, but also has computer disks that allow you to drill yourself on the written words using your computer.

Levels I and II are available in Arabic, Armenian, Mandarin Chinese, Danish, Dutch, French, German, Greek, Hebrew, Italian, Japanese, Korean, Polish, Portuguese (South American), Russian, Spanish, Swedish, Vietnamese, and a special French/Spanish course. Level I also has Swahili, Tagalog, and Ukranian. Level III is now available for Chinese, French, German, Italian, Japanese, Russian, and Spanish. Sets including all three levels of a language are available for all Level III languages.

Foreign language teachers, libraries, and bookstores seem quite fond of this system, judging by how the courses sell. Remember, this is more of a *testing* device than a teaching program. What's the difference? Typical teaching programs group the words together that go together, like emotions, parts of the body, days of the week, and months of the year. These words *are* taught on the first VocabuLearn tape, but they show up in no particular order and spaced widely apart. This deliberate randomness is designed, like the deliberate highway curves in the middle of flat prairie country, to "wake you up." You are forced to associate words *only* with their meanings, not with the surrounding words. This can have its advantages over systems that associate lists of words. Consider how many of us still have to run through the entire ABC song to find which letter comes before V! VocabuLearn, in contrast, forces you to *think* about which word means what. Its publishers claim this results in significantly quicker vocabulary learning.

VocabuLearn's big selling point is that "it is the first audio language system that concentrates on simple vocabulary and helpful expressions." In other words, *no grammar studies*. As the authors correctly point out, grammar is what foreign-language students fear. Grammar is just a way of arranging your speech in orderly patterns, which we all picked up by osmosis at the ages of 3–5 after we learned a basic vocabulary in our native tongue. In languages like Hebrew where the word roots are heavily changed when you change tenses and cases, you are not going to be able to escape grammar study of some sort. However, any such study will be a lot easier if you already have a basic vocabulary to begin with. *Mary Pride*

NEW!
The Standard Deviants
Spanish Videos

High school and college level. Each video, $19.99. Workbook, $11.95. *Cerebellum Corporation, 2890 Emma Lee St., Falls Church, VA 22042. (800) 238-9669. Inquiries: (703) 848-0856. Fax: (703) 848-0857. Web: www.cerebellum.com.*

I explain how the **Standard Deviants Video Series** works in the Basic Math chapter—and why it has nothing to do with "deviants" and everything to do with "deviating from the standard," i.e. how to become a curve-wrecker (a grade A student, to those of you who never took statistics). These fun videos demystify the "tough" subjects for college students . . . and smart high-school students, too!

The Salsa-riffic World of Spanish is their two-tape series on this language. Like other Standard Deviants products, these concentrate on sorting out the problem areas, the stuff students tend to get wrong on tests. You'll review pronunciation, the Spanish alphabet, cognates, diphthongs, written accents, capitalization, counting through the millions, basic conversational gambits, gender, pronouns, *ser* and *estar, -ar/-er/-ir* verbs, negations, and lots more, including plenty of vocabulary. A lot is covered in the approximately three hours running time, replete with zany characters in skits designed to draw your attention to language principles.

As far as I know, this series is *not* available in the Edited For All Audiences edition yet. You might want to check on this before purchasing.

Although it won't be around after the stock sells out, an excellent workbook is available to accompany the Spanish videos. It is a course book in itself, explaining the material covered on the three videos. Time codes and video notes sections cross-reference the videos. Practice exams and quizzes double-check what's been learned. Fun activities and simple one-person games (we're talking crossword puzzles and the like) add yet more reinforcement. There's some humor, but it's mostly of the "funny names in the word problems" sort. Chatty educational content outweighs humor about 20 to 1. *Mary Pride*

If your learning style is "aural," meaning you learn best by listening, Sybervision may have the language course for you! Instead of studying a textbook or filling out workbook pages, you are expected to learn your new ("target") language by listening to carefully constructed cassette dialogs.

NEW!
Sybervision Language Courses
Grade 7– college. $345 each plus $12 shipping.
Sybervision, 1 Sansome St., Suite 810, San Francisco, CA 94104. (800) 888-9885 ext. 5108. (800) 606-8255. (415) 981-8021. Fax: (415) 433-3047. Web: www.sybervision.com.

The **Sybervision Language Courses** use the "Pimsleur method." Similar to Saxon's approach to math, this system features incremental recall and repetition of words and phrases at carefully timed intervals in the dialogs, rather than traditional drills. Sybervision language courses are characterized by light cultural humor throughout, clear pronunciation guides, and useful dialogs.

First, you hear a dialog in foreign speech. It sounds like gibberish! Were you foolish to buy this course? Don't despair. Help is on its way. The cassette instructor breaks down the sentences into words and the words into syllables. You are asked to repeat these words and syllables. Then, using what you have learned, you are asked questions in the target language. The correct response is then given, so you can see if you answered correctly. The course also repeats previous matter at scientifically-determined intervals to reinforce your memory. By this means, you actually learn to think in the target language.

Most courses come with 15 one-hour tapes (30 lessons in all), in a sleek binder, plus a 50-odd-page study guide that explains the teaching method and includes reading exercises, grammar notes, and a selected English/target language vocabulary list. The foreign vocabulary is presented in its own script—e.g., Russian in Cyrillic, Greek in Greek— instead of in "romanized" script.

Let's talk about the Pimsleur method for a minute. Unlike other methods which teach pronunciation, grammar, and vocabulary separately, Pimsleur courses ask you to "anticipate" a correct answer, based on what you've already learned. In other words, you have to *interact* with the tapes, not just "repeat" what is said. Second, with "Graduated Interval Recall," the tapes keep reminding you of each new word or grammatical construct at ever-lengthening intervals, until you have heard it so often it resides in your long-term memory.

An experienced American language teacher is your tutor on the tape, providing you with all the instructions you'd normally have to read in a textbook. During each half-hour lesson, you also engage in conversations with two people, one male and one female, using the dialect and accents favored by educated citizens of the target country.

Reading lessons, which appear on a tape of their own, can be done in conjunction with the other lessons, or separately later on. You may need to exercise the latter option if you tend to listen to the tapes in your car, since quite obviously the reading lessons require you to follow along with the words in your study guide.

Dozens of courses are available, in a wide variety of languages. We reviewed a representative sampling; here's what we found.

Italian 1. This is the best Sybervision course I have seen, with beautiful music to begin, punctuate, and end every of the thirty half-hour units. At the end of the 15-tape set is a tape with reading rules and exercises. After finishing the course, several of us were highly complimented on our Italian elocution. We did not feel competent, but others were impressed. The lesson content stresses socializing, conducting business, and traveling. We are not sure if the emphasis on alcoholic beverages in the dialogs is humor, cultural reality, or reflects Sybervision's usual young-executive audience.

Other courses we have personally reviewed include
- German I and II
- Russian
- Modern Hebrew (the study guide, to its credit, introduces both handwritten and printed forms of the Hebrew letters)

All followed the same format outlined above, and were excellent in both packaging and presentation.

Also in this series:
- German III
- Spanish I, II, & III
- French I, II, & III
- ESL for Japanese speakers
- ESL for Spanish speakers
- Italian
- Portuguese (Brazilian)
- Japanese
- Mandarin Chinese
- Arabic
- Modern Greek

Vis Ed "Think" Language Flashcards

Grade 7–college. Think Language series, $18.95 each level (cassettes only). Levels available: Spanish I and II, French I and II, German I and II, Russian I, English I and II (for foreign students and remedial). Shipping extra.
Visual Education, 581 W. Leffel Lane, Springfield, OH 45501.
Orders: (800) 243-7070.
Inquiries: (937) 325-5503.
Fax: (937) 324-5697.
Web: www.vis-ed.com.

Spanish 1. Fifteen hour-long cassette tapes should take one month to complete and leave the student with a basis of conversational ease and some self confidence. An 18-page booklet accompanies the tapes, with commentary on how to learn foreign language and reading exercises. Reading is introduced in Unit 2 (the second day of class) after intensive practice in pronunciation. Because Castilian Spanish is the language of the upper class and business in many places, Sybervision teaches Castellano. You may notice that the Castilian pronunciation does not use the exaggerated lisp taught by some high-school Spanish teachers but is a very natural and unaffected sound. Spanish pronunciation differs from English, in subtle ways, and these differences are emphasized, especially in the reading lessons. The use of native speakers on the tapes helps the student get a natural fluency and feel for the language.

Spanish 2. This course follows Spanish 1, and assumes you know basic Spanish pronunciation and conversational usage. It is a good review for those who completed a year of high school or college Spanish years ago but isn't, by itself, comparable to a good year's course on a high school or college level. Although you should achieve better fluency than with a typical college or high-school course, you will need additional resources to bring your Spanish writing and reading up to speed.

Spanish 3. We are thrilled that Sybervision is introducing its Spanish 3 materials. This course is an almost effortless extension of Spanish 2 vocabulary and grammar through conversational usage. The conversations are practical and realistic and deal with travel, business, friends, and family life. Several of the past tenses are used, until they become a natural part of your thought and speech patterns. Changes in the conversations are frequent enough to avoid the boredom of either repetitive drills or memorized dialogs.

Nine out of 10 people who take a Sybervision course learn to speak at the "intermediate high" level established by the U.S. Government's Foreign Service Institute. If you follow course instructions, Sybervision guarantees you will reach that level in 30 to 45 days, or you get your money back. Good deal! *Anne Brodbeck and Mary Pride*

For older children or adults, the Best Inexpensive Language Program award goes to **Visual Education's Think English/French/German/Spanish/Russian** series. Each language comes in two levels (except Russian), each corresponding to a year of high-school language instruction or a semester of college. You get a set of white Concept Cards flash cards with cartoons illustrating the sentences, phrases, or words introduced on the card, a set of correlated green Structural Pattern or Usage cards giving grammar principles and drill, a cassette with both male and female native speakers of the language repeating an hour's worth of phrases from the Concept Cards, and an accompanying booklet with all the vocabulary translated alphabetically into English, plus study tips and an outline of the lessons, all neatly packed in a sturdy box for just *$18.95 per level!*

Each of the Think languages has its own unique program design. The Spanish cards are different from the German cards, etc. Maria and Juan, our friends in Spanish Level I, start right in dancing, but Käte and Erich, from German Level I, are more interested in studying. Make of this what you will!

The Think series starts right in with complete but simple sentences, so for young children you are better off with the more expensive but slower-paced Learnables from International Linguistics (reviewed in detail in Volume 2). Otherwise, anyone with a basic grasp of English grammar and sentence structure can, thanks to the illustrations and patterned approach, learn to *think* in the target language, as opposed to merely mentally translating words from one language to another. Hint: If you are unacquainted with the target language try looking through the cards first, translating words you can't figure out from the cartoons, before studying with the cassette. *Mary Pride*

Sign Language

Say It by Signing is a 60-minute video course with subtitles in English. Dramatized lessons include greetings, introductions, time expressions, transportation, eating out, shopping, sports, and recreation. Dialog-based "survival" approach. *Mary Pride*

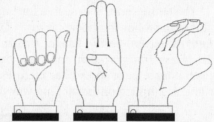

English as a Second Language (ESL)

Audio-Forum has a vast array of ESL helps, as you can see from the list at left! Let me briefly capsulize these programs.

Ingles en Tres Meses is a programmed basic English course. All instructions and drills are recorded with Spanish translation. Volume 1 is for total beginners. Volume 2 is for brushing up and refining your English. Volume 3 is for those who can speak in English but "lack the native *feel* for it." This last volume concentrates on idioms and idiomatic expressions.

The **Survival English** series consists of three or four cassettes with accompanying phrasebook of vocabulary necessary for everyday living in the USA. Language groups served are Khmer, Hmong, Cuban Spanish, Cantonese, Lao, and Vietnamese.

The **Living Language** courses, distributed by Audio-Forum and published by Crown Publishers, Inc., are brief two-cassette courses with a two-way dictionary/phrase book and conversations manual. Covers rudiments only. Language groups served are native speakers of French, German, Italian, Spanish, and Chinese.

Ingles Para Emergencias is all the English you hope you will never need to use. Discover basic questions and answers useful when chatting with the telephone operator, fire department, ambulance service, medical attendants, and police.

The **British Broadcasting Corporation**, or BBC, has both audio and video courses for English as a second language. The basic audio courses are available only in bilingual editions. *Let's Speak English* comes in Arabic, Chinese, German, and Indonesian. *Calling All Beginners* is in Arabic, Chinese, French, Greek, German, Italian, Portuguese, and Spanish. Intermediate versions are English-only and specialize in areas such as business, international trading, technology, travel, international meetings, medical practice, and aviation. The BBC video ESL courses are all for business people, and come only in intermediate and advanced levels.

For those who know English up in their heads but have trouble making it sound like English when they say it, there's the **Speechphone** audiocassette series. This three-course program helps overcome the problems of incorrect stress and faulty rhythmic patterns, enabling those listening to the speaker to make sense of what is being said. A worthy mission, as those of us who have suffered in college under the ministrations of foreign teaching assistants will testify.

This list is itself only a subset of what Audio-Forum offers. Write for their free ESL catalog. *Mary Pride*

Audio-Forum Say It by Signing video
Grades 9–college. $34.95 plus shipping.
Audio-Forum, division of Jeffrey Norton Publishers, Inc. 96 Broadstreet, Guilford, CT 06437. (800) 243-1234. Fax: (203) 453-9774. Email: info@audioforum.com. Web: www.audioforum.com.

Audio-Forum English Courses
Ingles en Tres Meses, $165 (volume 1), $215 each (volumes 2 and 3). Survival English, $35–$50 (cassettes and book); Book alone $9.50. Living Language, $29.95 each. Ingles Para Emergencias, $19.95. Speechphone courses, $39.50 each. Shipping extra.
Audio-Forum, division of Jeffrey Norton Publishers, Inc. 96 Broadstreet, Guilford, CT 06437. (800) 243-1234. Fax: (203) 453-9774. Email: info@audioforum.com. Web: www.audioforum.com.

NEW!
International Linguistics "All About Language" series

Grades 7–12. Full set of *All About Language* series, $199. Most *AAL* book/cassette combos, $22–$32 each. Shipping extra.
International Linguistics Corp., 3505 East Red Bridge Road, Kansas City, MO 64137. Orders: (800) 237-1830. Inquiries: (816) 765-8855. Fax: (816) 765-2855. Email: learn@qni.com. Web: www.learnables.com.

NEW!
International Linguistics "Using Verbs" series

Grades 7–12. Full set of Verb books/cassettes, $65. Each Verb book plus cassette, $22. Additional Verb books, $12 each. Grammar Smart Sets (Reproducible) $85 each. Shipping extra.
International Linguistics Corp., 3505 East Red Bridge Road, Kansas City, MO 64137. Orders: (800) 237-1830. Web: www.learnables.com.

NEW!
Sybervision English as a Second Language

Grade 7– college. $345 each plus $12 shipping.
Sybervision, 1 Sansome St., Suite 810, San Francisco, CA 94104. (800) 888-9885 ext. 5108. (800) 606-8255. (415) 981-8021. Fax: (415) 433-3047. Web: www.sybervision.com.

NEW!
Audio Forum Radio France programs

Grade 10–adult. Price: $39.50 plus shipping.
Audio-Forum, division of Jeffrey Norton Publishers, Inc. 96 Broadstreet, Guilford, CT 06437. (800) 243-1234. Fax: (203) 453-9774. Email: info@audioforum.com. Web: www.audioforum.com.

All About Language, a collaboration between Douglas Moore and Harris Winitz, is for late-beginning and early-intermediate language learners. Students should understand the vocabulary and sentence structure of books 1 and 2 of the Learnables (see review in volume 2) before tackling this program.

Each book in the program teaches a "lexical field." What's a lexical field, you ask? It's "a group of words that reflect a common core of meaning." In other words, a bunch of words related to a single topic.

The entire series is available for English as a Second Language. It includes the following book/cassette combinations: *Business I and II*, *Entertainment (Movies)*, *Family*, *Houses & Buildings*, *Post Office*, *School*, *Telephone*, *Transportation*, and *Weather*. Some sets come with two cassettes. Each double-page spread has pictures on the left-hand side and text on the right. A simple, nonthreatening way to increase ESL vocabulary. *Mary Pride*

For the critical skills of using English verbs properly, Harris Winitz, the author of the Learnables foreign-language program written up in *Big Book* Volume 2, has created a **Using Verbs series** of books and cassettes, with one volume each for verbs of walking, eating, and placement. On the left side of each page are 12 numbered

By the author of the popular Learnables series pictured above

pictures, correlated with 12 sentences on the right side of the page. The accompanying audiocassette for each book affords the student the opportunity to improve his pronunciation and reading. *Mary Pride*

English as a Second Language/Ingles Esencial is designed to provide basic English, usable in travel, social circumstances, and business. You are taught to pay careful attention to the difficult English sounds that are foreign to the Spanish speaker. The lessons on the first cassette are very easy but move forward rapidly as the course proceeds through the 15 one-hour tapes. The English speaker speaks a generic form of English without regional variants. The Spanish speaker does not attempt to speak English as a native and uses a standard, not regionalized, form of Spanish. This course stresses ear training. Beginning with lesson 3, you also get reading exercises. These emphasize differences in pronouncing Spanish and English. This covers the famous "Pimsleur Method" described in the Sybervision review in the Foreign Languages section of this chapter. *Anne Brodbeck and Mary Pride*

Additional Help & References

Parler au Quotidien is a selection of 30 short radio programs taped from **Radio France Internationale.** Fast-paced and interesting, these everyday conversations in French are not intended as an introductory course. Beginners can hear what the language sounds like while advanced students of French will thoroughly enjoy the spirited conversations. The publishers transcribed these conversations for us, so we can follow along, discuss the issues and dissect the language patterns.

Most of the programs are about language, but they touch on issues such as sexism, the environment, and history too. No heavy-handed propaganda, just light intellectual banter.

A great supplemental resource for those who want to go a few steps farther. *Anne Brodbeck*

Perspectiva: World News Monthly in Intermediate Spanish for Language Learning and **Standpunkt: World News in Intermediate German for Language Learning** are geared for adults who have a basic grasp of everyday Spanish or German. *Perspectiva* usually runs 22 pages per issue while *Standpunkt*, has a similar but larger format at 30 pages per issue.

With each issue you can sit down to a well-balanced mix of cartoons, editorials, news stories, and other articles in intermediate Spanish or German as it is used in normal adult life. Subjects may include health, music, books, cooking, personalities, ecology, science, politics, and travel.

The print is fine enough so that you feel you are getting your money's worth of information, and the paper quality is good enough so that you may not even need your reading glasses. Each issue also includes a glossary (which defined every word, phrase, or idiom I was unsure about), a review of several different points of grammar, and a selection of spoken idioms with sample sentences to help build conversation skills.

New subscribers receive a free gift: *Spanish Grammar at a Glance* or *German Grammar at a Glance*, a small summary booklet (16 pages) of essential items of Spanish or German grammar. This is a fine way to brush up on language skills in your sit-down moments. Now, when you get to have a conversation in Spanish or German you will have something to talk about, the current subjects, oriented vocabulary, and grammatical reminders. *Anne Brodbeck*

Foreign Languages and Your Career is the fourth edition of a book that tells you how to make some moola if you know how to *parler, sprechen, hablamar, lego, gavaritsiya,* or so on. Sounds good! As long as it doesn't involve translating German for international bankers in the deeps of New York City, that is! *Mary Pride*

So you've taken French before. So you know how to say, "The pen of my aunt is on the table." But do you know how French people *really* talk?

If you were to overhear, *"Oh, la vache! Le voleur s'est faith épingler par le flic!"* would you think the speaker was trying to say, "Oh, the cow! That thief got stapled by the cop!" or would you realize what was actually being said, namely, "Wow! That thief got nabbed by the cop!"?

These books are serious teaching tools, even though they include many humorous thoughts and phrases. The 10 lessons in French 1 each include vocabulary, dialogs, and grammatical notes that take you from "street" contractions (lots more letters missing than they told you about in French 101!) to how to tell the world you're sick, and of what. Two review tests (with separate solution keys) check your mastery of the material. The book also includes an appendix and a glossary. The layout is attractive, with vocabulary words in boldface, boxed examples, and visuals that include charts and cartoon-style illustrations. Previous French study is a must—this book is not a substitute for French instruction, but a follow-up to it.

The "Street Language" series so far includes:

- **Street French 1**—The Best of French Slang
- **Street French 2**—The Best of French Idioms
- **Street French 3**—The Best of Naughty French (this one I'd skip, unless you feel that for self-preservation you need to understand the epithets others use around you)
- **Street Spanish**—How to Speak and Understand Spanish Slang
- **Street German 1**—The Best of German Idioms

A number of "street English" and "business English" books are also available, with the odd jargon of these two venues. At this time I haven't seen any of them. *Mary Pride*

This is so cool! Imagine putting your foreign-language lessons to work in the real world.

These are not instruction manuals. You will still need a course in your target language. They *are* a way to make foreign-language practice way more interesting than flash cards or listening to uninspired "dialogs" in the dreaded Language Lab.

Each **Surf's Up! Website Workbook** has about 200 spiral-bound pages, with 50 "activities" designed to get students using their new language skills right away, by connecting to and interacting with sites on the World Wide Web.

I put "activities" in quotation marks, because a typical "activity" will involve researching the answers to a number of questions, by connecting to several sites. For example, Activity 13 in the German workbook has as its goal, "Get acquainted with Martin Luther! Students will read a short text and answer some questions in German." This is an "intermediate" level activity, so the instructions are in German, as follows:

Geben Sie auf die folgende Adresse ein: **http://www.wittenberg.de** Clicken Sie auf den Namen **Martin Luther**, und lesen Sie seine Biographie!

A number of true-false and sentence questions follow.

Beginner-level activities have instructions in English.

Each activity has a theme (in this case, Famous People/Religion), a main web address, a goal, a level, comments about how to teach it, and a list of related website. Some activities also have "Techno-Tips," e.g., "You may want to have students turn off the 'Auto Load Images' option in the 'Options' menu. This page [about German cars] contains a drawing of a car that is uninteresting and may be more distracting than helpful, especially since the writing on the drawing is difficult to make out due to its small size."

In the course of practicing your German, you research the cultures of East Germany, Liechtenstein, Germany proper, and Switzerland; Oktoberfest; German cars; the European Union; the Romantic movement;

NEW!
Surf's Up! Website Workbooks

Grade 8–college. $16.95 each. *Audio-Forum, Duc. 96 Broad Street, Guilford, CT 06437. (800) 243-1234. Fax: (203) 453-9774. Web: agoralang.com/audioforum.html.*

Activities are arranged in alphabetical order by topic. I suppose this makes sense, but I personally would have preferred to have beginner activities grouped together, intermediate activities together, and so on. An answer key would also be great to have, for the busy parent or teacher who doesn't have time to figure out all the answers herself. (The Basic French and Basic Spanish workbooks do have stickers on their covers, listing a Web address where you can find updates and answers.)

Mozart; Luther; German art, including the Bauhaus movement; the German family; German food; German entertainment; German Americans, such as the Amish; Germany history; housing; jobs; movies; music; news; politics; sports; TV; transportation; weather; and more.

Each workbook closes with a list of links, by topic. For example, under "Austria," you'll find 13 sites, including indexes of Austrian links, tourist info, video archives, and other *sehr* useful resources.

Surf's Up! Workbooks are currently available for Basic French, Basic German, and Basic Spanish. English as a Second Language is in production.

I would strongly recommend these workbooks to who has a computer and who is studying one of these languages. *Mary Pride*

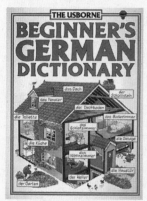

To pick up a lot of phrases and vocabulary quickly, the illustrated **Beginner's Dictionaries** (now available in French, German, Italian, and Spanish) are a better buy than either the "Learn" series or the "Essential" series reviewed below. Not only is the art less murky than in the "Essential" series, but the scenes are less teenager-ish, include more labeled illustrations, and don't overwhelm you with too many phrases to learn at once. A pronunciation guide in the back helps, but a cassette tape would have been a great help here. Even lacking the tape, though, these are a great value, containing over 2,000 illustrated words and phrases grouped into everyday scenes. *Mary Pride*

NEW!
Usborne Beginner's Dictionaries
Grades 6–12. $12.95 each plus shipping.
EDC Publishing, Division of Educational Development Corporation, 10302 East 55th Place, Tulsa, OK 74146. (800) 475-4522.
Fax: (800) 747-4509.
Web: www.edcpub.com.

Usborne's "Essential Guides" series, which includes editions for French, German, and Spanish, as well as a book entitled *Survive in Five Languages*, is also being outfitted with accompanying tapes. This makes these "essential phrases for traveling abroad" books much more usable. Designed for teens traveling alone, the dialogues are family-friendly and not overloaded with business terms. Best as a quickie prep for traveling; not really usable as a separate language course. You *can* get the books alone, but I'd go for the book/cassette combos. *Mary Pride*

NEW!
Usborne "Essential Guides" Language Series
Grades 6–12. Essential French, Spanish, German, $6.95 each. Survive in Five Languages, $7.50. Shipping extra.
EDC Publishing, Division of Educational Development Corporation, 10302 East 55th Place, Tulsa, OK 74146. (800) 475-4522.
Fax: (800) 747-4509.
Web: www.edcpub.com.

Also new, but available right now, are the new **Learn French**, **Learn Spanish**, and **Learn German** packs, with book plus tape. These illustrated language introductions include basic vocabulary and dialogs, grammar, and pronunciation notes, as well as background notes on European culture. For motivational value, each book has a mystery plot, in the same vein as the Puzzle Adventures series.

As how-to-learn-it guides, they are not (in our view) terribly successful, as they throw tons of new material at you on each page. What you really need is a little material carefully introduced at a time, with plenty of review. Think of these more as language reference books or mini brush-up courses for those who have already had some exposure to the target language. *Mary Pride*

NEW!
Usborne "Learn" Language Packs
Grades 6–12. $19.95 each plus shipping.
EDC Publishing, Division of Educational Development Corporation, 10302 East 55th Place, Tulsa, OK 74146. (800) 475-4522.
Fax: (800) 747-4509.
Web: www.edcpub.com.

Vis Ed Foreign-Language Flashcards

Grade 7–college. Vocabulary Flashcards, $10.95 each language. Compact Facts Flashcards: Conversation, Grammar, Verbs, $10.95 each. Available in English, French, German, Russian, and Spanish. Shipping extra.
Visual Education, 581 W. Leffel Lane, Springfield, OH 45501. Orders: (800) 243-7070. Inquiries: (937) 325-5503. Fax: (937) 324-5697. Web: www.vis-ed.com.

Vis-Ed is your premier source for flash cards. **Vocabulary Flashcards** are 600 to 1,000 small cards plus study guide with index: available also in classical languages. Cards have English word on one side, target language word on the other. These are extremely handy for vocabulary drill; a batch can even fit in your shirt pocket, for drill "on the road." I suggest you drill batches at a time, rubber-band the ones you are working on, and don't leave the box anywhere that little people can knock it over. Putting 1,000 cards back in alphabetical order is no joke! **Compact Facts** are prime ideas, rules, and grammatical formulas in plain speech on 60 pocket-sized cards. *Mary Pride*

PART 4

Math

Sarah Pride, age 14, earned the title Grand
Champion for the second year running in the
International Quarter Mile Math Game Tournament.
Sarah placed first in both high-school categories (which
covered addition, subtraction, multiplication, division,
integers and mixed operations). Sarah, who has been
homeschooled all her life, also scored better than all adult
participants. Homeschoolers comprised about four percent
of the more than 1,000 tournament participants. (And
yes, Sarah is Mary Pride's daughter!)

These homeschooled girls from Arkansas competed in a national Stock Market Game, coming in second among 18 teams at the local level. They were given 100,000 simulated dollars to invest. The sponsor tracked their investments, just as if they were real. In 10 weeks, they made $10,000! Pictured, from left to right, are: Natalie Anders, Vickie Allison, Kristen Ruth, and Kelly Furr.

CHAPTER 15

Basic & Remedial Math

The math covered in this chapter is the kind you need every day in real life. Naturally, the resources you'll find here tend to be straightforward and down-to-earth.

If you were a math whiz in elementary school, taking fractions, decimals, and percents in your stride and zipping through measurement and interest problems, you don't need this chapter. But if, like so many others, you're a little fuzzy on how to proceed when facing a complicated word problem, this chapter is for you.

Helps for Parents

When this book first crossed my desk, I was skeptical. In these days of pop psychology responses to fear and anxieties, I expected to see smiley faces and teddy bears on every page.

You cannot tell a book by its cover—or its title! After reviewing **Math Anxiety Reduction**, I recommend that this book be added to every home education library.

The first seven chapters teach the home educator how to prevent math anxiety in the student and how to help the student deal with existing anxiety. While the book was written for the school setting, the home educator can assimilate these techniques and adapt them to the home school. If the student has a negative physical reaction to math, it will interfere with the learning process. This concept is explained in depth in Chapter 6. It contains an excellent description of "Benson's Relaxation Response" which helps the math student can get past the physical reaction and get on with the learning.

There are a few math problems in Chapters 6 and 7 but the bulk of the math is found in Chapters 8 through 10. These math problems are presented on a middle to high school level. "Focus ovals" on many pages carry hints when a new idea is introduced. The examples are clear and the explanations are short and very clear.

Every home educator should read at least the first eight chapters. After reading and digesting these techniques, home educators will not create math anxiety and they will know how to deal with existing math anxiety in a calm and compassionate manner.

Students with math anxiety in middle and high school should read the entire book and slowly review the math concepts presented in the last chapters.

NEW!
Math Anxiety Reduction (second edition)

Grades 7–12. $29.95 plus shipping. *H & H Learning Systems, 1231 Kapp Dr., Clearwater, FL 33765.*
Orders: (800) 366-4079.
Inquiries: (727) 442-7760.
Fax: (727) 442-2195.
Email: hhcompany@aol.com.
Web: www.HHPublishing.com.

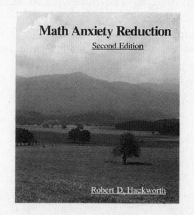

Math Anxiety Reduction
Second Edition

Robert D. Hackworth

I would use this text along with any current math curriculum. When reading this book, please do not skip any of the chapters and remember that Chapter 6 is the most important chapter in dealing with the existing anxiety.

I wish I knew about this book before I ever taught math as home educator. Some home educators can be overpowered by math curriculum; this book helps prevent disaster. *Michele Fitzgerald*

Strong's Math Dictionary & Solution Guide is the type of book that should be on the shelf of every homeschooler preparing for the PSAT and the SAT. Instead of the normal, sequential approach to learning math, author Chris Kornegay drew on the time-proven approach offered by an encyclopedia or dictionary. You can look up exactly what you need.

I am very fussy about diagrams, especially math diagrams. These diagrams are clearly labeled and exceptionally explained, even for people who are not especially crazy about math. Once I have a math concept, I am dangerous, but for me getting the concept is hard. In this book, the concepts are explained clearly.

I have used many different math publications in the last ten years. There were times when I wanted to pull my hair out because I felt the text was going around in circles using vocabulary or an idea that was just not clearly explained. This will *not* happen with this book.

This reference text excels in providing a clear understanding of a wide range of mathematical concepts: Basic Math, Algebra, Geometry, Trigonometry, Basic Statistics, and Beginning Calculus. My son is currently preparing to take the PSAT and this book has proven invaluable. *Michelle Fitzgerald*

Basic Math Courses

Basic Mathematics I and **Pre-Algebra** review the math children were supposed to have learned in grades 1–6. Gazillions of practice exercises—the publisher says there are more exercises in these books than in any other math books written on this level for Christian schools. Pre-Algebra pushes on to beginning work in advanced math topics like algebra, geometry, and trigonometry.

Teacher's keys and tests are available for these books. *Mary Pride*

NEW!
Strong's Math Dictionary & Solution Guide
Grades 5–12. $39.95 plus $4 shipping.
Strong's Publishing, 7212 Christy NE, Albuquerque, NM 87109. Orders/Fax: (505) 821-0736. Email: cckkmm@aol.com.

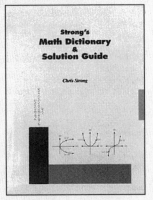

A Beka Mathematics
Grades 7–8. Basic Mathematics I, $15.40. Teacher's guide, $19.65. Pre-Algebra, $18.75. Teacher's guide, $23.75. Shipping extra.
A Beka Book, Box 19100, Pensacola, FL 32523-9100. (800) 874-2352. Fax: (800) 874-3590. Web: www.abeka.com.

BJUP Math for Christian Schools
Grades 7–8. Student worktexts, $30. Teacher's editions, $42.50. Test Packet, $8. Answer key, $4.50. Shipping extra.
Bob Jones University Press Customer Services, Greenville, SC 29614. Orders: (800) 845-5731. Fax: (800) 525-8398. Web: www.bjup.com.

BJUP's new seventh- and eighth-grade math courses, **Fundamentals of Math** (grade 7) and **Pre-Algebra** (grade 8), emphasize the use of math in real-world jobs. As usual for math courses at this level, much time in the seventh grade book is spent in reviewing elementary math. *Mary Pride*

Is math a practical subject? Adults say it is. Children are supposed to agree: **Math at Work** is a book that *proves* it!

To produce this book, people in a variety of occupations contributed math problems they actually encountered in their work. The result is a 67-page book with over 300 math problems grouped by skill area (e.g., fractions, decimals, percent) and an answer key in the back. Problems cover a range of difficulty and include skills usually taught in grades 5–8.

High-school students will enjoy Part 3, in which the student gets to work through a real-life sequence of problems in which he often needs the information from previous problems to solve the present one. These include sequences such as "Carpenter Nathan Patches Mrs. Sauder's Slate Roof," in which he has to figure out how much slate to use, what it will cost to repair the roof with new slate or used slate, how much labor expense is added to the used slate by the time it takes Nathan to remove it from Richard Eby's house, how much the slate chosen will cost after standard markup, and how much interest Mrs. Sauders has to pay Nathan if he carries a six-month loan on her work at 9.5 percent interest. As the book introduction points out, in this way the student learns that "real-life math does not come prepackaged as fractions or percent."

Problems throughout *Math at Work* are labeled by occupation, such as automobile mechanic, baker, carpenter, electrician, farmer, printer, and so on. This is a refreshing change from the paper-pushing professions or welfare math usually featured in a book of this kind.

The book format is letter-quality dot-matrix printing, double-spaced, with almost no illustrations. But then, real-life math problems often appear in scribbled handwriting on leftover scraps of paper. It may not be fancy, but I like this book. *Mary Pride*

From the people who produce the best-selling SAT preparation course, **Math Smart** uses a playful approach to show how all operations of math are related. Basic math procedures such as multiplication, division, and fractions are covered, as well as more intimidating topics. Exponents, square roots, geometry and algebra are explained in easy-to-use terms. Hints and tips are provided, which help to make the more difficult areas of math easier to understand and enjoy. There are drills throughout the book, and an answer key is provided.

While *Math Smart* is not a curriculum, it is a very effective, non-threatening resource that both parents and children will be eager to use. This teaching tool has the capacity to become a homeschooling favorite. *Lisa Mitchell*

Why does it take over 270 pages to make math simple? That's because **Mathematics Made Simple** covers a lot of ground, from basic arithmetic to pre-algebra, basic geometry, basic probability, and even pre-trigonometry. After all, it is advertised as "a complete introduction to algebra, geometry, and trigonometry."

Most of the book's space is devoted to definitions and explanations. "Practically Speaking" boxes appear now and then, to show how you can actually use the math you are learning. Lots of examples are worked for you, plus there are multiple-choice quizzes at the end of every chapter to test your understanding, with answers provided in the back of the book. A comprehensive test may also be found at the end of the book.

Christian Light Math at Work
Grades 5–12. $6.95 plus shipping. *Christian Light Education, PO Box 1212, Harrisonburg, VA 22801-1212. (540) 434-1003. Fax: (540) 433-8896. Email: orders@clp.org.*

NEW!
Math Smart
Grades 7–12. Math Smart, $12. ISBN# 0679-74616-1. *Villard Books, Random House, Inc., 400 Hahn, Westminster, MD 21157. (800) 793-BOOK. Available in bookstores.*

NEW!
Mathematics Made Simple, Fifth Edition
Grade 8 and up. $12.95 plus $2.50 shipping per order. *Bantam Doubleday Dell Publishing Group, Inc., 2451 S. Wolf Road, Des Plaines, IL 60018. Inquiries: (800) 323-9872. Can order by mail only.*

The attractive two-column format includes many illustrations and very decent explanations. If you feel you missed anything on your first pass through math class, this book might be just what you're looking for. Since the public schools are doing such a great job of teaching math these days, perhaps that's why over 2 million copies of this book have been sold to date. *Bill Pride*

This program was especially designed for students "where traditional methods have failed." It consists of ten 64-page worktexts, diagnostic placement and mastery tests, a separate answer key, and a teacher's resource guide.

Number Sense is a revision of the original program, *Programmed Learning*, which attracted some favorable attention in homeschool circles, as well as in classroom situations. The original program had more workbooks, fewer graphics, and a less sizable teacher's resource guide. In its present form, Contemporary Books is touting it as the ideal introduction for their best-selling *Number Power* adult math program for GED preparation.

Number Sense was originally designed for use by school teachers who need individualized math help for lots of students, especially those who were already having trouble with math. The "adult" format of the program makes it usable for all ages (each booklet of the original program had "Grades 4–12" printed on its cover), even though the entire program is designed at an easy reading level. Word problems focus on questions like figuring out how many pounds of roast beef you can afford, making change, or reading a thermometer.

Areas covered by Number Sense are:

- Whole Numbers—with one workbook for *Addition & Subtraction* and one for *Multiplication & Division*
- Decimals—with one workbook for *Addition & Subtraction* and one for *Multiplication & Division*
- Fractions—with one workbook for *The Meaning of Fractions*, one for *Addition & Subtraction*, and one for *Multiplication & Division*
- Ratio & Proportion
- Percent: *Meaning of Percent* and *Percent Applications* are the two workbooks.

The teacher's resource guide has simple, sensible activities for each skill area (e.g., practicing place value by playing a game with straws for "points" and bundling the straws by tens when you have enough) and an "Item Analysis Chart," which helps you find the exact lesson to assign for extra help in a given area. It also includes some basic math pedagogy (e.g., the necessity of moving students through the concrete, semiconcrete, semiabstract, and abstract levels of thinking, and what this means), and some good common teaching sense (e.g., don't overdo the praise— praise only genuine success, no matter how small).

You start by giving the student a simple diagnostic test in a particular area (Whole Numbers, Decimals, Fractions, or Ratio/Proportion/Percent). The results of this test show you where to start in the Number Sense series, or which particular "gaps" to fill by assigning specific pages. You work your way through the workbook, checking your work against the answer key. After all assigned pages have been completed, the student takes a mastery test, to see if he really has mastered it all.

Everything is spelled out and every possible difficulty is anticipated; you don't have to know how to teach math to use this program.

Number Sense series

Grade 4–adult. Complete set, $72 (includes one copy of each student workbook, one copy of each diagnostic test, one answer key, and one teacher's resource guide). Individual workbooks, $7.44 each. Answer key, $7.44. Teacher's resource guide, $13.44. Shipping extra. *Contemporary Books, Inc., 4255 West Touhy Ave., Chicago, IL 60646. (800) 323-4900 x 147. Fax: (800) 998-3103. Email: ntcpub@tribune.com. Web: www.contemporarybooks.com.*

If your student is having trouble in any particular area—say, fractions—you might find it well worth your while to get the workbooks for fractions, along with the answer key and teacher's guide. It's too bad that Contemporary only sells single copies of the tests as part of a complete set. If you want the tests (an integral part of the Number Sense system) you have to buy a set of 10 fractions tests or 10 decimals tests, for example. In the long run, you may find it simpler just to get a complete set of Number Sense materials, or to skip the tests. The workbooks aren't all that long anyway, and it won't hurt for your student to do a few extra pages.

The main strength of this program is its excellent explanations. Allan Suter, the program's author, has a real gift for making the complex simple. Problem areas, such as subtracting from a number that contains lots of zeros, or solving multi-step problems, are separated out and attended to separately. Nobody has to fail at math with this kind of material.

I could wish that along with the excellent explanations and step-by-step skill building came a continuous review of skills already learned. Homeschoolers would be wise to provide some homemade "incremental" review problems from previous lessons along with the new skill of the day, to ensure that our students not only understand, but can't forget what they've already learned. Alternatively, if your child is having special trouble with math, you could try using Number Sense in tandem with one of the Saxon basic-math courses (*Math 54* or *Math 65*). Number Sense has better explanations, and Saxon provides the review! *Mary Pride*

Applied Math/Consumer Math

For older students, A Beka's **Consumer Mathematics** covers what you'd expect, with an emphasis on free enterprise and biblical use of money. Topics covered are buying a car, travel, income, budgeting, housing, food, clothing, calculators and computers for business and personal use, federal taxes and records, banking, investments, and small business. Teacher's editions and tests are available. *Mary Pride*

As you recall, the Alpha Omega system is set up with 10 LIFEPACs per grade. These are consumable workbooks, fairly slim, with full instructions and how-to examples built in.

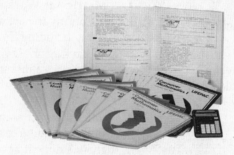

Alpha Omega's **Consumer Mathematics LIFEPACS** take the same form—10 LIFEPACs, with the last LIFEPAC as a course review. It has a heavy emphasis on family finances, construction and building trades, service occupations, transportation math (figuring currency exchanges and car operating costs, for example), plus some basic business math. One interesting feature is the LIFEPAC on "Occupation Diagrams," such as how to read maps, scale drawings, and house plans, and make calculations based on these diagrams. No separate teacher's handbook. *Mary Pride*

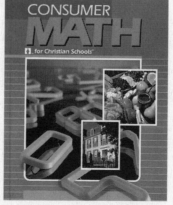

BJUP's **Consumer Math** begins by reviewing elementary math: adding, subtracting, multiplying, dividing, fractions, simple algebra, percent, and measurement. You spend 125 pages on those topics. Next you learn the math you need to cope with income statements, taxes, borrowing, banking, buying and owning a car, food and clothing, housing (including information on renting or leasing versus buying), home operation and maintenance (utility bills, property taxes, home improvements and repairs), and insurance. Big, thick, hardbound book, over 500 pages—a whole year's course for schools, but you shouldn't need to spend this much time on it at home. *Mary Pride*

Number Sense does not teach the arithmetic facts. You should spend some time working on those before beginning this program. What it does offer is:

* clear, easy-to-follow explanations of each math skill, broken down into bite-sized bits (one skill per page)
* a logical sequence of skills
* highly visual page design, with plenty of white space
* minimal reading load (grade 3–5 reading level)
* and plenty of practice.

A Beka Consumer Mathematics

Grades 9–12. $21.20, paperbound. Solution key, $34.90. Test booklet, $12.20. Answer key, $20.20. Shipping extra.
A Beka Book, Box 19100, Pensacola, FL 32523-9100. (800) 874-2352. Fax: (800) 874-3590. Web: www.abeka.com.

Alpha Omega Consumer Mathematics LIFEPACs

Grades 7–12. Complete boxed course (LIFEPACs, 2 Answer Keys, Test Key, 5 Solution Keys), $42.95. Shipping extra.
Alpha Omega Publications, 300 N. McKemy, Chandler, AZ 85226. Orders and inquiries: (800) 622-3070. Fax: (480) 785-8034. Web: www.home-schooling.com.

BJUP Consumer Math

Grades 9–12. Student book, $30. Teacher's edition, $42.50. Activity book, $13. Teacher's activity book, $17.50. Test Packet, $8. Answer key, $4.50. Shipping extra.
Bob Jones University Press, Greenville, SC 29614. Orders: (800) 845-5731. Fax: (800) 845-5731. Email: lgrover@wpo.bju.edu. Web: www.bju.edu.

NEW!
Everyday Math for Dummies

Grade 9–adult. $14.99 plus shipping. *IDG Books Worldwide, Inc., 7260 Shadeland Station, Suite 100, Indianapolis, IN 46256. (800) 762-2974. Fax: (800) 550-2747. Web: www.idgbooks.com.*

Like the other books in this series, most of which are on computer topics, **Everyday Math for Dummies** is visually exciting, loaded with funny cartoons, and written in a friendly, slightly irreverent style. Its 343 pages cover personal finances (checkbook balancing, time payments and interest, taxes, etc.), business math (markups and margins, projecting trends, debt and taxes), basics of high school math (algebra, geometry, and trig), tipping, gambling, sports statistics, and statistics in the news. Sixty-five pages are devoted to math tricks.

Like other books in its category, this one is mainly directed to providing survival math skills to people who took math in public school but didn't really "get it" the first time around. It wouldn't work as a math course all by itself, but could be a dose of motivation for a math-hostile student. *Bill Pride*

NEW!
Metrics at Work

Grades 7–12. $7.95 plus shipping. *Garlic Press, 605 Powers Street, Eugene, OR 97402. (541) 345-0063. Fax: (541) 683-8767. Email: garlicpress@pond.net. Web: www.garlicpress.com.*

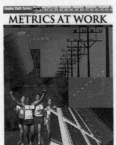

Metrics is the system of measurement used in scientific circles. Because in metric measurements everything comes in units of 10, it's easy to do scientific calculations. Trouble is, most of us still think in feet, pounds, inches, and miles, and most math texts only spare a few minutes for the task of teaching us how to think in a foreign scale of measurements..

Metrics at Work is just long enough (80 pages, not counting the answer key) to thoroughly teach the use of metric measurements, including how to convert from metric to English measurement and back again. If you're weak on hectometers and decimeters, this book may be a wise investment, especially if you plan to take high-school or college science courses anytime soon. *Mary Pride*

NEW!
Real-Life Experiences Using Classified Ads

Grades 6–12. $9.95 plus shipping. *Midmath, Ellen Hechler, PO Box 2892, Farmington Hills, MI 48333. (248) 855-2895. Fax: (258) 737-6917.*

Ellen Hechler seems to have a gift for taking a complicated subject and making it simple and appealing. She's done it again with **Real-Life Experiences Using Classified Ads**. In five unit-study scenarios, students imagine they are 18 and have finished school. Using the classified ads, they must find a job, set up a budget, get a car, and locate an apartment. Next they discover how much money they have left over to buy the "extras"—like food! If enough students participate, they discover naturally that it would have been wise to spend less and save more. A good application of sowing and reaping.

While these lessons contain nothing objectionable, you will need to add practical applications of principles like praying for God's will, finding your calling, and tithing. Good presentation. Lots of springboards for discussion when done with a group. *Kim O'Hara*

NEW!
Rod & Staff Applying Numbers

Grade 8. Student Edition, $15.40, Teacher's Edition, $18.45. Worksheets & Tests, $1.65. Shipping extra. *Rod and Staff Publishers, Box 3, Hwy 172, Crockett, KY 41413. (606) 522-4348. Fax: (800) 643-1244.*

Have you ever wished you could find a math curriculum that teaches both pre-algebra/geometry and business math? It seems that most publishers make us choose one or the other. **Rod & Staff** shows us they realize both are necessary. Matter-of-factly, their new **Applying Numbers** calmly proceeds through everything an eighth grader should know, whether he or she is going on to study algebra or start a business or both.

For those who like the Saxon continuous review approach, you will be delighted to find the same kind of coverage in *Applying Numbers*, except that there are more problems from the newest topic, and the review problems are in a separate section. (You'll especially like the notes that tell you which lesson to flip back to if you can't remember how to do a review problem!) Explanations are clear enough that my fourth grader grasped how to add fractions from the half-page explanation, where his fourth-grade math text befuddled him in six pages.

The teacher's manual has copies of student pages, teaching tips, and answers (on the same page as the problems). The worksheet/test booklet is well worth its price even if all you use are the blank business forms. *Kim O'Hara*

Soon after your child's first job comes the first checking account. The real-life skill of managing a checking account is a crucial area that need not be neglected by homeschoolers. Author Victoria W. Reitz deserves a hearty thanks for a workbook full of practical experience! Lessons in **Your Checking Account** teach how to set up and control a checking account. Students become familiar with basic banking terms, procedures, and general policies. Everything is provided to give your child a valuable representation of a real banking experience. Divided into two parts, the student activity text uses the first section to address steps in finding the best bank, opening a checking account, using a register, dealing with lost checks, and balancing your checkbook. Further practice in part one prepares your child for a real checking experience. Part Two is the six-month banking simulation. Students will enjoy practicing buying clothes, paying doctor bills, and even winning a church raffle! There are plenty of blank checks and deposit slips for practice, and a full glossary in the back of the book is perfect for a vocabulary list. The handy teacher's guide is available at a nominal price and includes answers for each lesson of the banking simulation, pre-tests and post-tests, as well as follow-up activities. *Lisa Mitchell*

Basic Math Videos

This little company has created quite an impressive lineup of math instruction videotapes, all of which are among the best presentations of their type available. You'll find this less surprising when I tell you that Dana Mosely, the teacher featured on these **Chalk Dust Basic Math** tapes, and all their other series, has over 15 years of classroom teaching experience. For over 10 years, Mr. Mosely has been under contract with the college division of D.C. Heath and later Houghton Mifflin (when they purchased Heath) to create and produce math videos that correspond with some of their best-selling math textbooks. These videos are jointly copyrighted by Chalk Dust and Houghton Mifflin. Houghton Mifflin uses these videos as a part of their program of marketing their textbooks to colleges. But they are not set up to sell them to homeschoolers.

Enter Chalk Dust, a family company owned by Dana, Richard, and Minerva Mosely. When you call to order, you may hear their 14 cockatiels, Quaker parrot, and pet duck chirping or quacking in the background!

In a day when educators put on clown costumes and play rap music in a desperate attempt to grab student interest, Mr. Mosely still sticks to the classic "teacher" image. White shirt. Patterned ties. Conservative haircut. What

NEW! Your Checking Account: Lessons in Personal Banking
Grade 10–adult. Activity text, $9.27. Teacher's guide $4.95. Shipping extra. *J. Weston Walch, Publisher, PO Box 658, Portland, ME 04104. (800) 341-6094. (207) 772-2846. Fax: (207) 772-3105. Email: customer_service@mail.walch.com. Web: www.walch.com.*

NEW! Chalk Dust Basic Math Course
Grades 5–12. Five videos, $25 each. Textbook, $44. Solution guide, $25. One tape or solution guide free if you prepay for book and tapes for a full course. Free 30-day evaluation period (you are sent 1 videotape and literature). Shipping extra. *Chalk Dust Company, 11 Sterling Court, Sugar Land, TX 77479. (800) 588-7564. Fax: (281) 265-3197. Email: sales@chalkdust.com. Web: www.chalkdust.com.*

you're getting here is solid instruction and explanations, plus some impressive blackboard drawings, not "Ronald McDonald Goes to Math Class."

There is no farbling around, no stuttering, no erasures. Every line is drawn right the first time. Every word is readable. None of your time is wasted watching the instructor preparing elaborate grids—those are drawn in advance. And since these are not classroom lectures, but delivered directly to the video camera, no time is wasted panning cameras across the classroom or listening to foolish student questions.

Chalk Dust courses are comprehensive and thorough. These are not "summary" or "review" courses. They teach you everything you need to know, not just the high spots.

What's more, you're not just buying a "videos plus textbook" course. Individualized tutoring help is available for each Chalk Dust student, at no extra charge beyond the course purchase price. Here's how it works. You email the instructor with your questions. He then will respond via email, phone, or fax—whatever is most helpful in your case.

On top of this, Chalk Dust offers:

- A free 30-day evaluation period. They'll send you a videotape from the series that interests you, plus literature about the series. You have 30 days to evaluate and return the video.
- A 30-day money-back guarantee on any course you purchase.

Now, the facts about Basic Math. The textbook used is *Essential Mathematics, Fourth Edition,* by Barker and Aufmann, published by Houghton Mifflin. Six major topics are covered on the five videos:

- Video 1—Whole Numbers, from "What is a whole number?" and "How do you write and read the big ones (millions, billions)?" through the four major operations (addition, subtraction, multiplication, and division), to exponential notation, order of operations, prime numbers, and factoring. I've found that children in grade 5 and up can jump right into this tape with adult supervision and assistance, while it's a great review for teen and adult students.
- Video 2—Fractions, from Least Common Multiple and Greatest Common Factor through the four major operations with fractions and mixed numbers, to order/exponents/order of operations.
- Video 3—Decimals: introduction, four major operations, comparing and converting fractions and decimals
- Video 3 continued—Ratio and Proportion
- Video 4—Percent: what it is, equations and problems with percents
- Video 5—Applications for Business and Consumers: A Calculator Approach. This chapter is almost 100 percent word problems. It covers topics found in both business math and consumer math texts: purchasing, percent increase and decrease, interest, real estate expenses, car expense, wages, and bank statements.

If you break your viewing up into 15-minute segments or thereabouts, you end up with 39 lessons. Obviously, a lot of the beginning material can be gone through quickly. However, even if you did just the amount of work corresponding to 15 minutes' worth of tape each week, in a year you would finish this course. The recommended method of viewing is:

(1) Watch the segment with notebook and pencil in hand. Read the section of the textbook.

Chalk Dust's lineup includes Basic Math, Prealgebra, Algebra I, Algebra II, Geometry, SAT Math, Trigonometry, College Algebra, and Precalculus.

Coming by the time you read this: Calculus I (spring 1999) and Statistics (summer 1999).

(2) A day or two later, watch the video segment again. This time pause the tape where appropriate and try to work the sample problems along with the video instructor. Work some more problems in the textbook.

(3) (Repeat if necessary and as necessary) Watch it again! Reread the textbook section and do some more problems.

This method practically *guarantees success* with older students who just did not "get it" from their school math courses. That's why hundreds of junior colleges and four-year colleges have purchased Basic Math and Pre-Algebra courses from Chalk Dust! Recommended. *Mary Pride*

Take (1) a huge number of confused college students who (2) desperately need to do well in their courses and (3) are willing to pay for help, and what do you get? In this case, the **Standard Deviants Video Series**. ("Standard Deviant" in this context is a word play referring both to how your grades will improve—i.e., *deviate* from the *standard*—and to the fun-loving rule-breakers today's college students fondly imagine themselves to be.) Designed to make tough college subjects easy to understand, the videos in this series mix solid instruction with offbeat humor in a mostly successful attempt to make the facts and concepts you need to remember memorable. Because they work hard at making the subject matter fresh and understandable, high-school students will understand them just fine.

Employing the something-new-to-see-every-10-seconds style of MTV, this series doesn't just *present* information: it socks you in the eye with it! Off-the-wall comedy skits illustrate (and sometimes parody) course concepts. Serious content is often delivered in a droll way, via a lineup of dozens of characters that range from Captain Helium (a flying superhero) to a male and female janitor with attitudes. Cartoon bits that remind you of Monty Python mingle with snatches obviously inspired by Saturday Night Live.

The faces you'll see are young. Most people involved in this company are recent college graduates. Genuine college professors are paid to edit the videos for accuracy, but the videos themselves are designed by the young, for the young.

So, these tapes are fun to watch and hold your attention. What about their content? Amazingly, they are all well-organized and quite complete in what they cover. This means some subjects require two, or even three, tapes of two hours or more duration. This also means that savvy kids and teachers are discovering you can use these tapes for more than just review. Some profs are even showing these videos in class!

Available for basic math is an EFAA video, **The Zany World of Basic Math.** It begins with integers, decimals, and addition. When I say "begins with," I *mean* "begins with": you're watching the tape for a while before you get to addition with carrying and subtraction with borrowing! Then on to multiplication, division, order of operations, scientific notation and exponents, rounding, fractions, ratio, and percent.

Keep in mind this is designed as a *review* tape. It's not a "teaching" series, like Chalk Dust. Use it to cement topics that didn't stick the first time around.

Although it won't be around after the stock sells out, an excellent workbook is available to accompany the *Zany World of Basic Math* video. It is a course book in itself, explaining the material covered on the three videos. Time codes and video notes sections cross-reference the videos. Practice exams and quizzes double-check what's been learned. Fun activities and simple one-person games (we're talking crossword puzzles and the like) add yet more reinforcement. There's some humor, but it's mostly of the "funny names in the word problems" sort. Chatty educational content outweighs humor about 20 to 1. *Mary Pride*

NEW!
The Standard Deviants Basic Math Videos

Grade 9–college. Video, $19.99. Workbook, $9.95.
Cerebellum Corporation, 2890 Emma Lee St., Falls Church, VA 22042. (800) 238-9669. Inquiries: (703) 848-0856. Fax: (703) 848-0857.
Web: www.cerebellum.com.
Direct mail sales are not available.

Important note: the high school subjects have recently been edited to make it suitable for all audiences. The first editions of these tapes, which were originally designed with secular college students in mind, did include quite a few mildly naughty bits. The new "Edited For All Audiences" (EFAA) versions of high school titles, which will now replace the old versions, should be just fine. If you're buying from a retailer, or directly from Cerebellum, be sure to ask for the Edited For All Audiences version. These can be identified by the yellow video shell. Just turn the tape over and check the bottom.

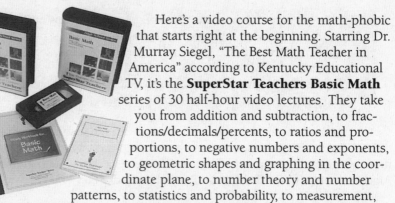

NEW!
SuperStar Teachers Basic Math

Grades 9–adult. $99.95 plus $10 shipping. Workbook included. *The Teaching Company, 7405 Alban Station Court, Suite A107, Springfield, VA 22150. (800) 832-2412. Fax: (703) 912-7756. Email: custserv@teachco.com. Web: www.teachco.com.*

Here's a video course for the math-phobic that starts right at the beginning. Starring Dr. Murray Siegel, "The Best Math Teacher in America" according to Kentucky Educational TV, it's the **SuperStar Teachers Basic Math** series of 30 half-hour video lectures. They take you from addition and subtraction, to fractions/decimals/percents, to ratios and proportions, to negative numbers and exponents, to geometric shapes and graphing in the coordinate plane, to number theory and number patterns, to statistics and probability, to measurement, and so forth, right up to an introduction to Algebra I. Many concepts are presented with computer-generated graphics and printed transparencies, with an occasional hike to the blackboard or flipchart thrown in. *Mary Pride*

Video Tutor Real Life Math Series

Grades 5–12. 7 videocassettes (4 on Fractions, 3 on Decimals), $39.95 each plus shipping. *Video Tutor, Inc., 2109 Herbertsville Road, Point Pleasant, NJ 08742. (800) 445-8334. (732) 295-7019. Fax: (732) 295-7020.*

Colorful, loaded with computer graphics, and hosted by two insufferably vivacious TV-newsroom-style hosts, the **Video Tutor Real Life Math** series consists of five video cassettes (three on fractions, two on decimals), plus two correlated workbooks covering all the work in these areas tested by college entrance and GED tests. Occasional skits featuring math used in real-life settings, such as shopping and checkbook balancing, attempt to both entertain and motivate your student. The shopping sequence I saw utterly failed at this—its main message seemed to be that if you are obnoxious to the grocery man and refuse to round your numbers, you'll get a better deal! The meat of the format, however, is the back-and-forth lecture format, which does cover a lot of teaching but is not tremendously entertaining.

This series would be of most value for people who love chatty evening news shows and feel overwhelmed by trying to explain these subjects to their children. Tapes are suitable for use by anyone, child through adult, who has mastered basic arithmetic. Available videotapes: *Fractions 1* (intro to fractions, word problems), *Fractions 2* (adding and subtracting fractions), *Fractions 3* (multiplying and dividing fractions, word problems), *Decimals 1* (intro to decimals; adding, subtracting, multiplying, and dividing), and *Decimals 2* (real life uses of decimals, calculator skills, checkbook balancing). Also available: Algebra and Integrated Math series for high school through adult. *Mary Pride*

Math Tricks

NEW!
Math Magic

Grade 7–adult. $13 plus shipping. *HarperCollins Publishers, Inc., Direct Mail Department, 1000 Keystone Industrial Park, Scranton, PA 18512. (800) 242-7737. Fax: (800) 822-4090. Web: www.harpercollins.com.*

Scott Flansburg, the "Human Calculator," covers pretty much the same ground in this book as Professor Ed Julius does in his Rapid Math series (reviewed later in this section). **Math Magic** includes tricks to speed up your addition, subtraction, multiplication, and division; estimation tricks; tricks for figuring tips and taxes, and to make sure you're getting the right change. It even ends with a final exam, same as the other books.

Where *Math Magic* differs from *Rapid Math* is mainly in its chattiness and lack of practice problems. Its "Math in Real Life" section also includes good stuff on longitude and latitude, time zones, military time, and area ("How Big Is the Back Forty?"). The Human Calculator also throws in "nine steps to algebra" and a glossary of arithmetic terms. So your main decision will be whether you need the practice problems, or whether you'd rather pay less and have most of the same tricks in one smaller book. *Bill Pride*

Mental Math in Junior High is an easy-to-use large-format book designed to help you teach or learn the techniques of figuring math problems out in your head. It picks up the techniques of the two earlier books in this series (*Mental Math in the Primary Grades* and *Mental Math in the Middle Grades*) and adds on some flashy junior-high stuff as well. You'll be using a few visual aids: dominoes, a ten frame and counters, and a 100 chart. You'll also be learning all kinds of useful strategies for working with everything from addition problems to fractions, decimals, and percents. Here's one little example of front-end multiplication: "Multiplying in your head is easier if you break a number into parts and multiply the front-end numbers first." So 524 x 3 becomes 500 x 3 + 20 x 3 + 4 x 3 = 1500 + 60 + 12 = 1572. No sweat, right? If this seems too hard, it's only because you missed the first 14 lessons of this very helpful book. Each lesson has two reproducible pages: a lesson page for introducing new math strategies and a Power Builder page with two sets of practice problems. The book has 50 lessons, enough for one per week for a year. Again, the answers are in the back. *Mary Pride*

Rapid Math in 10 Days by Edward H. Julius teaches you four simple math techniques per day for 10 days. This is not just a set of tricks: the book also includes lots of problems for you to practice your new tricks, with answers in the back of the book. You will learn how to do basic addition and subtraction quickly in your head. The book's "excell-erat-ed" techniques will also speed up your multiplying, dividing, and estimating, provided the numbers you are trying to divide or multiply fall into certain "tricky" categories. For example, multiplying by 5 is the same as dividing by 2 and adding a decimal place.

Learning these tricks not only speeds up your mental math—a useful skill, since math computation is the one test subject homeschoolers tend to fall behind on—but also inculcates a certain amount of mathematical thinking. It wouldn't hurt you any to get this easy-to-use book, and it might even help. *Bill Pride*

Rapid Math Tricks and Tips is subtitled "30 Days to Number Power." That's because the professor wants you to learn two math tricks per day for 30 days. Many of the tricks from *Rapid Math in 10 Days* are included, plus you also get some flashy parlor tricks, over 2,000 sample and practice problems, weekly quizzes, and a final exam.

More Rapid Math Tricks and Tips is subtitled "30 Days to Number Mastery" and picks up where *Rapid Math Tricks and Tips*

leaves off. The format is the same—including sample problems with solutions, weekly quizzes, and final exam—and the pace is similar—one or two math tricks per day. Learn cool stuff like how to multiply two four-digit numbers without writing down any intermediate steps—just the answer! I bet you'll be able to *feel* your brain cells growing. *Bill Pride*

CHAPTER 16

Algebra

John Maynard Keynes called economics the "dismal science," and thanks to him, today it often is. But I know a subject that strikes even more fear into the hearts of students from junior high through college. It's spelled A-L-G-E-B-R-A!

If you suspect algebra is not terribly useful in daily life, consider this: How frequently do you need to calculate the point at which two trains running on parallel tracks will end up side by side, given that Train A starts 50 miles behind Train B, but is traveling at 1.4 times Train B's speed? Every day, right?

I can get away with saying this stuff to the teens reading this book because I was a math major in college before I switched to engineering. But unfortunately, *you* can't. You just have to take it on faith that algebra is Terribly Useful. And it *is*, if you ever plan to study

- higher math
- chemistry
- physics
- statistics
- engineering
- banking
- business math

and a bunch of other stuff that probably sounds as exciting to you as having a tonsillectomy.

Forget, if you can, for the moment about how wonderful a mastery of algebra will be for your future career path. Think instead of how much fun it is.

"Fun? Are you out of your mind?"

No. You just need to adopt a different state of mind. **Algebra is a type of puzzle.** Once you learn the rules, you can figure out those pesky little *x*'s and *y*'s without any trouble at all.

The Saxon Algebra textbooks, reviewed in this chapter, are by far the most popular choice for homeschool algebra students. After all, John Saxon pioneered the "incremental learning" technique for math courses, which introduces new skills step by step and reviews them lesson after lesson. But

The main secret of algebra success is to obtain a curriculum that
- explains each step clearly and completely, with plenty of examples to illustrate how it's done
- constantly reviews each previous skill learned, so it becomes automatic

you could also use any well-written algebra program and add in your own extra review problems. Some students benefit from courses that incorporate extra hands-on activities with math manipulatives, algebra software, or other clever instructional methods. So really, it's up to you. Admit that there's no escape from the big A, but be glad there are so many easy-to-use and imaginative products designed to help you learn it at home.

Algebra Curriculum

I can best describe **Advanced Algebra Through Data Exploration** as "Star Trek math." Just as the crew members on the Starship Enterprise use "tricorders" to analyze the world around them, students of this course use the graphing calculator to analyze numerical data and come up with usable results previously far beyond the reach of a high-school course.

Take a look at the chapter titles: Introducing the Calculator, Patterns and Recursions, Sequences and Explicit Formulas, Introduction to Statistics, Data Analysis, Functions, Parametric Equations and Trigonometry, Exponential and Logarithmic Functions, Topics in Discrete Mathematics, Systems of Equations, Polynomials, Probability and Statistics, Functions and Relations, and Trigonometric Functions. As you can see, some areas of study traditionally considered separate courses—probability, statistics, geometry, and trig—are integrated into this course. Other areas usually considered too difficult for high school—discrete math, data analysis, and recursive functions—are also included. Additional optional activities based on Key Curriculum Press's groundbreaking *Geometer' Sketchpad* software are also woven into the course.

This all sounds pretty intimidating, but actually the opposite is true. Once you learn how to use the graphing calculator, the exercises and problem sets make a lot of sense. Although written for classrooms, the "group" activities usually can be completed by just a parent and child working together.

You'll need the 816-page, hardbound student textbook, the 392-page softbound (and three-hole-punched) teacher's guide with answer key, and the solutions manual. Be sure to purchase the *Calculator Notes* for your particular brand of calculator; these are invaluable when using this course at home. Also nice to have are the quizzes, tests, and exams (all available as one 160-page reproducible book). At home, I doubt you'll have time to make much use of the teacher's resource book, although classroom teachers will doubtless find it inspiring.

If you're just taking Advanced Algebra for brownie points before getting into college, this is overkill. But if your future career plans lie in any scientific, engineering, or mathematical field, including any business field that routinely requires data analysis, Key's *Advanced Algebra Through Data Exploration* is an exciting new choice. *Mary Pride*

A "gradual, progressive development of algebraic concepts, skills, and applications," **Algebra: An Introductory Course** takes nothing for granted. The first three chapters don't assume the student knows anything more than simple arithmetic with whole numbers. If even these skills are lacking, Appendix I presents a complete review of whole-number arithmetic, and Appendix II reviews arithmetic problem-solving skills. This step-by-step, review-first-and-teach-second approach is followed throughout the book. For example, fractions are reviewed in chapter 4 before algebraic fractions are introduced.

Author Morris Bramson tries to avoid "excessive abstraction and rigorous theory" in favor of concrete terms and everyday scenarios. Realizing some college-bound students do need a more rigorous, theoretic approach, he has added an appendix that introduces set theory.

NEW!
Advanced Algebra Through Data Exploration

Grades 10–12. Textbook, $42.07. Teacher's guide with answer key, $29.95. Teacher's Resource book, $49.95. Solutions Manual, $24.95. Quizzes, tests, and exams (includes CD-ROM), $59.95. Blackline masters for Calculator Notes (you need to specify calculator model), $4.95. Complete package (includes Calculator Notes), $199.61. Shipping extra.
Key Curriculum Press, 1150 65th St., Emeryville, CA 94608-1109. (800) 995-MATH. Fax: (800) 541-2442. Email: customer.service@keypress.com. Web: www.keypress.com.

NEW!
AMSCO Algebra: An Introductory Course, One-Volume Edition

Grades 7–10. Hardbound, $24. Paperback, $13. Workbook, $10.80. Shipping extra.
AMSCO School Publications, 315 Hudson St., New York, NY 10013. (212) 886-6500. Fax: (212) 675-7010. Web: www.amscopub.com.

Graphing Calculators

Fully realizing that college entrance tests of the future will undoubtedly all force the student to prove his or her proficiency as the operator of a graphing calculator, I would like to lodge my protest against the proliferation of math courses designed to cater to the use of this device.

As an engineer, I must say that the interface design of the typical graphing calculator is appalling. There is no way you can look at a graphing calculator and figure out how to use it without the huge, thick manual. (The manual for the Texas Instruments TI-85 is 352 pages long—as long as my high-school algebra textbook.) Even keys that could be made easy to use are laid out in a fashion designed to conflict with everything you've learned so far about how to input data. For example, let's look at the TI-85:

- Although most adding machines, telephones, and numeric keypads place the "0" under the "2," here it is under the "1"

- Where would you expect to find the "Escape" key (here, the Quit/Exit key), considering that in computer programs it's almost always at the top left or right of the screen? Here it's in the middle of the top row.

- The arrow keys on a computer keyboard are on the lower right. Here, it's the upper right.

- On a keyboard, "Delete" will never be found in the middle of the second row from the top, as it is here.

If the designers had color-coded the keys for sine, cosine, and tangent ; if they had color-coded the operators (+, -, x, ÷); if they had placed the "mode" keys (On/Off, Enter, Store, Exit, Delete, and so on) together instead of all around the keypad; if they had used a narrower font or the available space and actually spelled out the words *insert, recall, store,* and *matrix* (among others); this would have been a help. For starters.

However, these calculators are *not* designed to be "human friendly." This means that, at the same time a student is struggling to learn the course material, he or she has to master an innately confusing electronic instrument. One that does not print out the steps you have taken, so you can't double-check your work. One with a tiny screen.

What is the benefit of learning to use a graphing calculator?

- **You no longer have to graph functions yourself.** Of course, in the past drawing your own graphs on graph paper was considered a learning experience. You *knew* why functions came out looking the way

they did. You could do it yourself. Too, in the real world, most complicated graphing is done on computer, using programs with more sensible and friendly interfaces.

- **You can solve and graph much more complicated functions.** Of course, you don't need to do this to learn the course material. If you don't routinely work with huge, hairy functions you aren't necessarily ignorant of how to graph or factor polynomials, any more than if you don't routinely add dozens of numbers in the trillions by hand you are necessarily ignorant of addition.

- **You can learn to do what a technician does**. Type in the function correctly and you will get a correct answer, even if you don't have a clue as to *how* that correct answer was calculated. This is "learning algebra" or "learning trigonometry" or "learning calculus" only if being the person who types in the programs that the computer programmer wrote is the same thing as knowing how to program computers.

- **Calculator manufacturers get to make lots of money,** as students are required to buy their expensive products. This is a benefit to the manufacturers, not to the students or their parents.

- **Teachers get to spend more time on "calculator literacy"** and less on topics that require actual abstract thought and understanding.

Since your student is going to have to learn to use a graphing calculator, the best approach educationally is probably to get him one when he is in sixth grade. Go through the manual together, and learn how to type in all kinds of problems. He doesn't have to understand what these problems *are*: he is just getting familiar with the device. Then, when he takes his high-school math courses, he won't be distracted by trying to learn how to handle the calculator, and will be able to concentrate on the subjects themselves. Added benefit: he might become curious earlier about what the functions on the graphing calculator—sine, cosine, logarithm, matrices—actually mean, and decide to investigate some of them on his own.

Einstein's Theory of Relativity was not developed using a graphing calculator; it was developed in his mind. The scientists and engineers of tomorrow need to know how to *think* in algebraic, trigonometric, and calculus terms. Let's make the extra effort, at home, to make sure our students do just that.

As well as everything you'd expect in a high-school Algebra I course, the text even includes some geometry: linear measurement, area, and volume, plus an appendix on geometry terms and concepts. Finally, you also get some basic trig and probability and statistics.

The explanations and illustrative problems are pretty much what you'd expect: not particularly chatty or friendly, but not stuffy and off-putting either. You get *lots* of problems to solve: exercise sets following every skills section within a chapter, chapter reviews, and "Check Your Skills" problem sets. Taking a leaf from Saxon's method, cumulative reviews are included, with answers and page references so you can restudy the parts you didn't quite master. Unfortunately, these cumulative reviews only appear every few chapters instead of being included in the daily problem sets, as is the case with Saxon Math.

You will need a separate answer key, since answers to all exercises except the cumulative reviews are not provided. *Mary Pride*

Algebra the Easy Way kicks off Dr. Douglas Downing's series of math storybooks. Would you believe that you can learn equations, negative numbers, exponents, roots and real numbers, algebraic expressions, functions, graphing, quadratic equations, polynomials, permutations and combinations, matrices and determinants, mathematical induction, imaginary numbers, and more by following the adventures of some fictional folks, including a dragon and a gremlin, in a fantasy kingdom? Believe it. In spite of the gremlin (Our Villain), these stories are short on magic and zero on occultism, but long on math motivation and methods.

In this attractive, oversized paperback you get not only the stories, but over 100 drawings, graphs, and diagrams, plus problems to work at the end of every chapter. Solutions to problems are in the back of the book.

If this sounds like Frode Jensen's "Journey to Grammar Land" applied to math, you are right. If you liked one, you should love the other.

Barron's guarantees that this book will improve your grades in 30 days, or you can return it to them for a full refund. *Mary Pride*

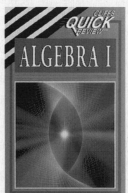

Cliffs Quick Review: Algebra I recognizes students' limitations by starting with a quick hike through pre-algebra—good stuff like the associative principle and square roots. It then works through all topics of a normal Algebra I course by proposing problems, and immediately providing the worked-out solution.

If you like to try to think of the answer before looking at the book's solution, you can see if you "got it" or not; but that is not always easy when the answer is on the next line or on the same page.

What this book is best for is as a quick read to make sure you understand and remember all the topics—say before you have to take a major standardized test that includes algebra, or before your online algebra final. It's also about the quickest and cheapest "refresher course" available for parents who plan to teach their offspring algebra. I would only recommend you use it this way if you were good in math during your school days, though. For relearning algebra from scratch, a deeper treatment is needed. *Bill Pride*

How "quick" a review can a 318-page book be, even if it is a small and handy size?

Cliffs Quick Review: Linear Algebra covers vectors, matrices, linear systems, real euclidean vector spaces, determinants, linear transformations (ooh, kernels and ranges!), eigenvalues and eigenvectors. No, I am not making these terms up. Real mathematicians actually study these things, as do engineering students.

Believe it or not, I see no reason why any reasonably astute student who has already gone through algebra couldn't pick up a lot about linear algebra from this book alone. Practice problems (which this book doesn't provide) would be nice, but they are not strictly necessary. Perhaps less (one quick explanation) may be more (better grades and less confusion) when it comes to this subject.

As to whether learning linear algebra is worth anything—if you plan on going to engineering school, working through this book first will make many classes a lot easier for you. At least that's what Mary says. *Bill Pride*

Looking for an algebra course that is super easy to use, pleasing to the eye, and in which every page stands alone? Here it is: the **Key to Algebra** series. Since I last wrote this up for *Big Book*, the series has grown to 10 consumable workbooks, plus answer keys/teacher notes and reproducible tests. It used to be more of an "Algebra ½" course; now it covers most of a first-year algebra course, though it's still not as advanced as the courses taken by honors students.

In a typical algebra course, students are given a rule, then shown some exercises worked out that follow that rule. In the Key to Algebra series, students often "discover" rules by working out simple problems, then applying the pattern to form the rule.

No math teaching experience is required to use the Key to Algebra series. *Everything* you need is in the inexpensive workbooks. Each page contains only one concept. Sample problems are now typeset, but the text still talks directly to the student, to reduce intimidation. Visual models are used wherever possible, such as shaded-in areas when studying fractions. Examples are worked out step by step. New terms are explained and underlined. Exercises gradually increase in difficulty. An end-of-book review helps insure that new concepts are remembered.

You write directly in the workbook, and there's plenty of space in which to write! Each page has an airy, open format, with few exercises per page and lots of visuals whenever possible.

The series now includes:

Book 1: Operations on Integers
Book 2: Variables, Terms and Expressions
Book 3: Equations
Book 4: Polynomials
Book 5: Rational Numbers
Book 6: Multiplying and Dividing Rational Expressions
Book 7: Adding and Subtracting Rational Expressions
Book 8: Graphs
Book 9: Systems of Equations
Book 10: Square Roots and Quadratic Equations

Unlike some of the earlier series, the *Answers and Notes* books include extensive and helpful teacher notes, as well as answer keys to the exercises

in the workbooks. Possible student difficulties are anticipated and dealt with immediately. When you consider how inexpensive these books are, it makes sense to get them as well. If you need to save money, you can skip the Reproducible Tests, as long as your student's daily work shows continuing mastery.

This series is so well designed that your fifth-grader can start on it, yet your twelfth-grader can use it without feeling dumb. Perhaps that's why this has been the best-selling algebra workbook series for over two decades!

The *Key to . . .* lineup also includes Key to Fractions, Key to Decimals, Key to Measurements, Key to Metric Measurements, Key to Percents, and Key to Geometry. All but Key to Geometry are reviewed in Volume 2; Key to Geometry's review can be found in the Geometry chapter of this book. *Mary Pride*

Mastering Algebra—An Introduction is a dynamite book of 500 pages of basic algebra problems. This text presents the problems in a concise manner in a step-by-step detailed approach. As you work through the problems, the solutions are right there to provide positive motivation. After working through numerous problems in a designated section to gain a concept, there is a series of ten practice problems to work to ensure the idea has been understood. The answers to these problems are in the back of the text and are each worked out in clear logical steps. So here you have one text that contains everything. There is no answer key to misplace! As a home educator I am always looking for ways to reduce misplaced texts.

This text is laid out ideally for both the student and the teacher. Each chapter opens with a "Quick Reference to the Chapter." This reduces preparation time. You know immediately what you are going to cover. My preparation time has been cut in half because of the way the material is presented. For the student the text provides great explanations and there are not an overwhelming number of practice problems. If the student is an independent learner, this text is ideal. The student can work at his own pace and not get off track.

This text could use a section that contains extra practice problems for those students who might need more help or need to refresh old skills. There are no tests or review sections.

Other books in this series: *Mastering Fractions* (reviewed in Volume 2), *Mastering Algebra: Intermediate Level*, and *Mastering Algebra: Advanced Level*. This is a comprehensive series that is great for the student who likes the step-by-step approach. *Michele Fitzgerald*

Cornerstone's **Principles from Patterns: Algebra I** is designed to follow Cornerstone's *Making Math Meaningful*. Starting with pre-algebra and ending by solving equations with radicals, this one-book course presents the patterns of Algebra I by helping the student understand the principles that underlie them, with very simple step-by-step explanations and lots of hands-on activities.

Take raising to a power, for example. *Principles from Patterns* doesn't merely state that raising a value to a power is the same as multiplying that value by itself a number of times equal to the exponent. Instead, it reminds students how multiplication works. Just as multiplication is a short way of adding a number to itself again and again, raising to a power is a short way of multiplying a number by itself again and again.

The concept of the Pythagorean theorem is taught using squares that are placed so their corners touch and their sides form the legs of a right trian-

NEW!
Mastering Algebra—An Introduction

Grades 9–12. $49.95 plus $4.50 shipping.
Hamilton Education Guides, PO Box 681, Vienna, VA 22183.
(703) 620-3960.

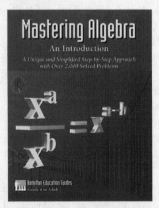

NEW!
Principles from Patterns: Algebra I

Grades 7–9. $45 plus shipping
Cornerstone Curriculum Project, 2006 Flat Creek, Richardson, TX 75080.
(972) 235-5149. Fax: (972) 235-0236.
Web: www.cornerstonecurriculum.com.

gle. A third square is placed so that it completes the triangle. Count the little squares in one of the first two squares and add this to the count of the little squares in the second square. Compare the result to the number of small squares in the third square and—*voila*—they are the same. Express this relationship in terms of the length of one side of each square and you have $a^2 + b^2 = c^2$.

This book makes every concept it introduces understandable to anyone. Question: How many of you got thrown for a loop the first time someone stuck an "x" into an equation? The way this program sneaks up on the concept of variables, I would be surprised if anyone doesn't get it right away. And for parents who *still* don't get it, there's an answer key in the back!

Chapters cover Math Sentences (basic arithmetic and orders of operations), A New Number (arithmetic with negative numbers), Seven Fundamental Principles (inverse, identity, associative, commutative, distributive, and transitive properties, plus real numbers), Equations with One Variable, Equations with Two Variables, Polynomials, The Quadratic Formula, Factoring, Fractions Involving Variables, and The Pythagorean Principle.

If your math student is confident and anxious to progress to new mathematical challenges, he would probably get frustrated with the slow, careful pace of this 336-page oversized book. On the other hand, someone who is fearful or hesitant about math or who has difficulty with the abstract concepts of algebra would likely enjoy *Principles from Patterns. Bill Pride*

Algebra at home? Calculus? One math series has had much to do with making upper-level math a homeschooling possibility—**Saxon Math**.

It's not that Saxon books include different content from other mathbooks, because they don't. What's different is the *method*.

Saxon books employ

- **Self-teaching.** While the assistance of a teacher doesn't hurt, the instructions in the books are clear enough for kids to teach themselves.
- **Incremental learning.** Only a little new material is introduced in each lesson.
- **Continuous review**. Once a concept is introduced, it isn't ignored until the final exam, as in virtually every other math textbook for the upper grades. Instead, problems based on it are included in the problem sets for the following lessons, until the concept is not only understood, but unforgettable.
- **Personality.** While most problems are just straight computations, Saxon stretches himself when it comes to the word problems. Historical figures and vocabulary words pop up to surprise you, while simultaneously (Saxon hopes) getting you interested in some of the subjects mentioned. Humor creeps in from time to time, too, as do little jabs meant to challenge students to work harder and more honestly.

Each book provides daily lessons, each followed by a set of 30 problems. The student is expected to work all these problems, plus any practice problems that may be included in the lesson itself.

NEW!
Saxon Algebra

Grades 7–12. Algebra ½ (2nd edition): Home Study Kit, $52.95. Algebra 1 (2nd edition): Home Study Kit, $53.95. Algebra 2 (2nd edition): Home Study Kit, $53.95. Solutions Manual, $25/course. Shipping extra.
Saxon Publishers, 2450 John Saxon Blvd., Norman, OK 73071. (800) 284-7019. Email: info@saxonpub.com. Web: www.saxonpub.com

The Solutions Manual for each course shows step-by-step solutions to each of the problems in the problem sets. A good purchase if you're not confident in your own ability to "backtrack" where your students went wrong in homework problems done incorrectly. Not included in The Home Study Kit; must be purchased separately.

The only complaints I've ever heard against Saxon's algebra-and-beyond sequence are that (1) it's lacking when it comes to geometry, which up to this point has been spread out through the books without a separate book of its own, and that (2) kids who aren't abstract thinkers may not "get it" without additional hands-on instruction.

More geometry has been added to the revised editions of Algebra 1 and 2, but compared to a good geometry course, this remains a weak area for Saxon.

The Home Study Kit for each Algebra course includes a short textbook, answer key for exercises and assignments, and a booklet of tests with answer keys.

Since skills, once introduced, are repeated in every subsequent lesson, you don't have to be overly concerned if your student doesn't "get" one of these difficult math concepts right away. It will be repeated and reinforced again and again, until sooner or later his mind makes the breakthrough and it all starts to make sense to him. It helps, of course, if you know enough of this math to explain any sticky points.

Algebra ½, so called because it's mostly an introduction to algebra and review of basic math, builds a foundation for basic algebra skills and concepts, with emphasis on signed numbers, positive and negative exponents, linear equations, and word problems.

Algebra 1 continues these topics while emphasizing systems of linear equations. Most problem sets include area and volume problems, and many include problems involving similar triangles. Starting with this book, geometry is fully integrated with algebra.

Algebra 2 goes back to the beginning. Starting with signed numbers, it quickly reviews all of the topics of Algebra 1. The purpose of this course is to fully prepare students for the advanced algebra concepts—such as logarithms, the complex plane, probability, and conic sections—that they will encounter in advanced math and applications courses. Topics from geometry, including proofs, are introduced and practiced throughout the book. You will be amazed at how much geometry your students learn from the new edition of this algebra book!

Saxon Math is still the most popular junior-high and high-school homeschool course. It's what I have chosen to use with my own children. *Mary Pride*

Each of the **Straightforward Math** algebra workbooks starts with a brief review of material that should have been covered in a previous course. Then you get chapters with the basic format of *instruction . . . examples . . . practice exercises . . . instruction . . . examples . . . practice exercises.* A cumulative review follows the first few chapters. The next few chapters are also followed by a review covering them, and finally there's a cumulative review covering everything you studied in the entire book. Nice large print and an open page design make the workbooks easy to follow. Answers are meant to be written on separate paper and checked against the answer key in the back of the book. Extra points to Garlic Press for doing it this way, since it means each of these inexpensive workbooks is *reusable*.

What these books cover, they cover nicely. What they're missing: (1) word problems (2) any topics more advanced than quadratic equations. For the word problems, you can try Garlic Press' *Applying Algebra* worktext. For the rest, you'll have to look at some of the more advanced algebra resources in this chapter. *Mary Pride*

Algebra Videos

For a basic description of how all the Chalk Dust courses work, see the review of Chalk Dust Basic Math in the Basic Math chapter. Points to note: free tutoring on demand via email, fax, or phone from the video instructor; extremely thorough in content (not just the "high spots"); courses use standard textbooks, many written by the man (Ron Larson) who has written about 40 percent of college math texts sold today; you get to keep, not just rent, the tapes; evaluation tapes and literature available; 30-day money-back guarantee.

Chalk Dust Prealgebra starts with a review of basic math. The reference text is *Prealgebra: A Worktext,* second edition, from Houghton Mifflin. In the second "chapter" of this course (each chapter corresponds to a videotape), you're already getting into algebraic-like expressions. The sequence is as follows: whole numbers and exponents, integers, prime numbers and fractions, fractions and mixed numbers, decimal numbers and square roots, percent with applications, algebra topics I, algebra topics II, statistics, and geometry and measurement. Some of these same topics are covered in Basic Math, but here the coverage is much more robust. However, an honors student—one who grasps concepts quickly and generally scores 95 percent or better on assignments—can skip directly from Basic Math to the next course we are about to discuss.

Chalk Dust Essentials of Algebra I again starts with about two hours of arithmetic review. The tapes cover algebra fundamentals, linear equations, graphing linear equations, exponents and polynomi-

als, factoring and solving equations, functions and their graphs, systems of linear equations, rational expressions and equations, radical expressions and equations, and quadratic functions and equations, for a total of 11 videotapes. The optional reference text is *Elementary Algebra, Second Edition* by Larson and Hostetler, published by D.C. Heath in 1995. However, the course can be used with any standard school algebra text.

Chalk Dust Essentials of Algebra II opens with a two-hour-plus review of Algebra I. It then goes on to introduce equations/graphs/functions, linear functions/equations/inequalities, sys-

tems of linear equations and inequalities, rational expressions and rational functions, radicals and complex numbers, quadratic functions/equations/inequalities, additional functions and relations (including polynomial functions, circles, ellipses, and hyperbolas), exponential and logarithmic functions, and winds up with a potpourri of additional topics including sequences (arithmetic and geometric), the binomial theorem, and a brief introduction to probability and statistics. The reference text for this course is *Intermediate Algebra: Graphs and Functions* by our old friends Larson and Hoststetler, published by D.C. Heath in 1994.

NEW!
Chalk Dust Algebra Videos
Grade 7–college. Prealgebra, 10 tapes. Algebra I, 11 tapes. Algebra II, 10 tapes. College Algebra, 10 tapes. $25/tape postpaid. Textbooks, $69 each except Prealgebra, $64, plus $8 shipping/book. Solution guides, $25/course. One tape free if you prepay for book and tapes for a full course. Free 30-day evaluation period plus $5 shipping/tape. *Chalk Dust Company, 11 Sterling Court, Sugar Land, TX 77479. (800) 588-7564. Fax: (713) 265-3197. Email: sales@chalkdust.com. Web: www.chalkdust.com.*

Chalk Dust recommends the following course sequences:

- If your child is headed for a career in the sciences, do Basic Math, Algebra I, Geometry, Algebra II or College Algebra and then Precalculus followed optionally by the soon-to-come-out Calculus course.
- A somewhat less demanding sequence is Basic Math, Prealgebra, Algebra I, Geometry, Algebra II, and an optional course in Trigonometry. If you start in grade 7 and do one course per year, you wind up with Trigonometry in grade 12.

NEW!
Firebaugh's Algebra on Videotape

Grades 7–12. Three "phases," each available in choice of three tape qualities. "Good" quality (extended play, 2 tapes, 12 hours), $49.95/phase. "Better" quality (6 tapes, 12 hours), $69.95/phase. "Best" quality (6 tapes, 12 hours, commercially recorded), $89.95/phase. Add $5 shipping per order.
Keyboard Enterprises, 5200 Heil #32, Huntington Beach, CA 92649.
Orders: (800) 362-9180.
Inquiries: (714) 840-8004.
Web: www.cyberbrokers.com/algebra/

The brochure for these "phases" suggests five ways to use them: (1) As a core curriculum. For this, the tapes are complete *in what they cover.* Some of the more advanced topics you'd find in, say, Saxon Algebra I are missing. (2) As a curriculum supplement, to provide additional explanations of tough concepts. (3) As a tutoring tool. (4) As a way to add a little variety to what for many kids is a boring subject. (5) As additional practice exercises. Firebaugh has thoughtfully provided thousands of worked-out sample problems throughout the course, plus more than enough practice worksheets.

Whatever use you choose, it is suggested that a parent or someone else monitor the student, to provide additional motivation and encouragement.

Chalk Dust College Algebra starts with a 2½ hour review of everything from real numbers and polynomials to fractional expressions and probability. Then you tackle algebraic equations and inequalities, the Cartesian plane and graphs, functions and graphs, zeros of polynomial functions, exponential and logarithmic functions, systems of equations and inequalities, matrices and determinants, sequences and probability, with an appendix on conic sections. As you can see, this is basically Algebra II plus a few extra goodies. If you have your heart set on AP credit, you may well choose this course in preference to the high-school Algebra II. Reference text: *College Algebra Concepts and Models, Second Edition* by (who else!) Larson and Hostetler, plus a new face, Hodgkins. Again the book is a D.C. Heath production, this time published in 1996.

Remember, the key to success is to watch each lesson *several* times and work the problems on screen and in the textbook. You can't just leave your student in front of the VCR and assume they will learn advanced math. But if they are willing to make the effort, and you are willing to follow up and make sure they do, the Chalk Dust math courses will prepare them well for college. *Mary Pride*

Algebra baby step by baby step. That's what you get in this series of **Algebra Videotapes** by math teacher **Leonard Firebaugh**. All three "phases" combined cover about a year of junior-high or high-school Algebra I. To arrive at the finish, you have to watch 36 hours of video instruction and complete hundreds of pages of handwritten worksheets.

Firebaugh clearly doesn't expect his students to "get it" the very first time he introduces a topic. Lesson after lesson covers the same topic. For examples, there are six video lessons on "addition of fractions with different denominators" and four on "multiplication of polynomials." While this might frustrate a math whiz, the more common "math-phobic" student will be reassured by this approach.

Don't expect fireworks from Firebaugh. His delivery style is dry and straightforward—in fact, downright wooden at the beginning, when he is trying to convince you of the benefits of studying algebra. He loosens up some when he get into the teaching, so don't judge the entire tape series by the first 10 minutes. It's just good solid instruction from an experienced teacher who knows all the ways kids can possibly mess up in algebra and how to prevent them.

The lectures are aimed directly at the camera. Most of the time Firebaugh is demonstrating concepts and working problems at the whiteboard, asking himself the questions a clueless student would ask and immediately answering them. This saves *beaucoup* time, compared to boring video courses where the teacher interacts with actual clueless students, and we have to wait for them to painfully struggle out their questions, or cutesy courses with kid models pretending they are having tons of fun and asking phoney, staged questions.

Each phase comes with the tapes, plus about 250 pages of worksheets, tests, answers, and solution keys. These printed materials do *not* include algebra instruction—that is all on the videotapes.

For kids who struggle with math, Firebaugh's patient, step-by-step explanations could help. *Mary Pride*

If you're committed to using the Saxon Math algebra series, and

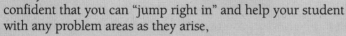
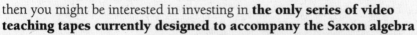

- your student could use extra help, or
- you don't personally feel confident that you can "jump right in" and help your student with any problem areas as they arise,

then you might be interested in investing in **the only series of video teaching tapes currently designed to accompany the Saxon algebra texts**. I say "accompany," because these tapes are not a substitute for the texts, but a visual add-on from an entirely different publisher.

State-certified teacher Paige Singleton, who has had several years of experience helping homeschoolers with their Saxon studies, is your video instructor. In each video lesson, you see Miss Singleton presenting new concepts and working every problem set in that chapter. In the **Algebra ½** and **Algebra 2** series, she writes out the problem steps in marker on large notebook pages. In the **Algebra 1** tape series, she uses a classroom-sized whiteboard. In both cases, the problems and graphs usually are already written out, so your time is devoted solely to learning how to reach the solutions. Her handwriting is large and neat. Her verbal explanations tend to be on the "how to solve this problem" side, rather than concentrating on explaining why the solution works or anticipating student difficulties. For that, you need the Saxon text itself. *Mary Pride*

I explained how the **Standard Deviants Video Series** works in the Basic Math chapter—and why it has nothing to do with "deviants" and everything to do with "deviating from the standard," i.e. how to become a curve-wrecker (a grade A student, to those of you who never took statistics). These fun videos demystify the "tough" subjects for college students . . . and smart high-school students, too!

Currently available for algebra is a two-video Edited For All Audiences set, **The Adventurous World of College Algebra**. Together, they run about three and a half hours. As usual, madcap skits and characters abound: the crazy General Polynomials, Bones and his adversary Weinercroph racing to find the Golden X of Algebr, Martians, and more. Abstractiana, the goddess of imaginary numbers, is just that—imaginary—but with gods and goddesses erupting all over the fiction and even *non*-fiction shelves in the bookstore, I would have been happier if she were the "queen" of imaginary numbers.

Be that as it may, you can be sure that these tapes everything in a standard college algebra course, and that it won't put you to sleep.

Although it won't be around after the stock sells out, an excellent workbook is available to accompany the algebra videos. It is a course book in itself, explaining the material covered on the three videos. Time codes and video notes sections cross-reference the videos. Practice exams and quizzes double-check what's been learned. Fun activities and simple one-person games (we're talking crossword puzzles and the like) add yet more reinforcement. There's some humor, but it's mostly of the "funny names in the word problems" sort. Chatty educational content outweighs humor about 20 to 1. *Mary Pride*

SuperStar Teachers Series: Algebra I and Algebra II

Grade 7–adult. $149.95 each plus $10 shipping.
The Teaching Company, 7405 Alban Station Court, Suite A107, Springfield, VA 22150. (800) 832-2412.
Fax: (703) 912-7756.
Email: custserv@teachco.com.
Web: www.teachco.com.

What happens when you take the best high school math teachers across the country and put them on video? You get the **SuperStar Teachers Algebra** series from The Teaching Company.

Each course is designed to teach the basics in an easy-to-understand way. There are 30 lessons per subject, and each class is 30 minutes in length. Included with the four videos are two booklets per course, which outline the material taught. They tell us that workbooks with problem sets will be available soon.

Algebra I, taught by a public school teacher from New Jersey, covers real number systems, sets and venn diagrams, number lines, order of operations, factoring polynomials and all things polynomial, rational expressions, and the slope of lines to name just some of the topics. If you are diligent in watching and listening to the demonstrations, you should have no problem conquering the concepts taught.

Algebra II is a continuation and includes review, linear equations and solving linear inequalities, slope and intercepts, the equation of a line, graphic linear equations, solving by using elimination, functions and quadratic functions, the quadratic formula, imaginary numbers, polynomial division and sketching, square and cube roots and solving matrices. There is too much to list it all! Murray Siegel, who teaches Algebra II, has a list of credentials the length of your arm and is an engaging teacher. Special praise for this class comes from our high school son who says "he makes learning fun."

The quality of these courses is high and each lesson is laid out in a way that makes sense, leading from one subject to the next. All the SuperStar teachers take advantage of the visual opportunities and use plenty of diagrams and examples to explain their points. Use these videos for reinforcement, to explain those problems that the book just can't seem to nail down, and for your visual learners. Our family has used these courses for over a year and can attest to their usefulness and value. *Marla Perry*

NEW!
Video Tutor Algebra I

Grades 7–12. Each tape, $29.95.
Complete set of six, $149.95.
Video Tutor, Inc., 2109 Herbertsville Road, Point Pleasant, NJ 08742. (800) 445-8334. (732) 295-7019. Fax: (732) 295-7020.

Running from 30 minutes to 103 minutes apiece in length, the six **Video Tutor Algebra I videos** go all the way from combining like terms to solving quadratic equations with the quadratic formula.

However, as they themselves admit, these videos are not meant to stand alone. They are meant to "supplement school math instruction." This becomes obvious even in the first couple of lessons on tape 1 where the instructor, John Hall, assumes the student already knows what "like terms" and "reciprocal fractions" are.

In each lesson, Mr. Hall solves several problems in a cheerful yet careful manner, showing the steps on a whiteboard. Problems are chosen to illustrate certain points. As he moves through the steps needed for each problem, he describes what methods are needed, though not *why* those precise methods are needed. For example in lesson 1, the first problem is $9x + 3x$. He tells you to check first if they are like terms, but he does not state how you are to know this.

After he is finished with the on-screen problems for a lesson, you are instructed to finish the additional five to ten assigned problems for that lesson in the small included booklet that accompanies the videotape.

Each lesson is designed to cement previously-learned concepts rather than to teach absolutely new ones. For this purpose, these tapes would be irreproachable. *Sarah Pride*

Replacing Algebra

As if the "New Math" for grades 1–6 didn't make life confusing enough, now there's a movement in math teaching circles to replace the entire Algebra/Geometry.Trigonometry/Calculus curriculum. In the New Upper Math, kids would be introduced to "real world" problems and work as teams using graphing calculators to solve these problems. Along the way they are supposed to pick up the skills they would have learned in traditional courses.

Below is a review of the first course we've seen based on these theories.

When I first looked at Key Curriculum's **Interactive Mathematics Program** (IMP for short) series of books, I was amazed at the amount of material there was to read. I started with the *Introduction and Implementation Strategies* and soon decided this was for administrators and not the homeschooling family. Next in the series was the *Teaching Handbook,* a discussion of teaching philosophy and classroom management issues. This book was interesting but also not necessary for homeschooling teachers. The *Teaching Handbook* stressed the philosophy that the traditional teaching model used for many years has not been successful because children do not learn that way. It goes on to say that the IMP curriculum is intended to replace the traditional program of Algebra I, Geometry, Algebra II/Trigonometry, and Pre-Calculus. Being trained in the old (i.e. "traditional") school, I was confused at first by this approach. But, as I read the Teacher's Guides, I became more familiar with the philosophy of breaking math instruction into types of problems found in the real world—problems that often require mixing techniques from the different "traditional" courses. The key elements are all there and the students will become familiar with them and review them periodically.

The Student Text for Year 1 is broken into five sections and covers variables, positive and negative numbers, some basic geometrical concepts, probabilistic thinking, algebraic expressions, graphing equations, normal distribution, standard deviations, and at the end of the year, basic trigonometric functions (sine, cosine and tangent) are introduced. This curriculum develops writing, reasoning, and calculator skills and if used in a group setting will promote constructive interaction.

I worked through several of the problems and found them challenging. I also had a ninth-grade volunteer work on additional problems. He found the problems challenging, but because he was trained in the old (traditional) mathematical philosophy, he found that it took a while to adjust his way of mathematical thinking.

NEW!
Key Interactive Mathematics Program (IMP)

Grades 9–12. The IMP Student Textbook, Year 1, $35.95. Teacher's Guides, $18.95 each (five are necessary for each year). Teaching Handbook for IMP, $9.95. Introduction and Implementation Strategies for IMP, free. Shipping extra.
Key Curriculum Press, 1150 65th St., Emeryville, CA 94608.
(800) 995-MATH.
Fax: (800) 541-2442.
Email: orders@keypress.com.
Web: www.keypress.com.

The material is well laid out. The Teacher's Guides provides useable lesson plans and direction. Blackline masters and a glossary are included in each Teacher's Guide. Five Teacher's Guides are needed for each year and are necessary to convey the mathematical ideas presented in the IMP Student Textbook.

Although this is a complete and well-thought-out math program, it is important for the homeschooling teacher to be aware that mathematical philosophy presented in this curriculum is different than mainstream homeschooling math texts. *Michele Fitzgerald*

CHAPTER 17

Geometry

George Washington, the first American president, used geometry a lot. In his younger days, George worked as a surveyor. This noble profession, which enables neighbors to settle boundary disputes without killing each other, is based entirely on geometry. In his later years, George took an interest in the plans for the city of Washington, D.C., and also had some involvement in land speculation—both of which again required him to know geometry.

We can find **geometry in the Bible** as far back as the Flood. Noah had to build an ark—a large boat—whose exact dimensions were provided by God. After the Flood, the Tower of Babel undoubtedly required some geometry to construct. Moving on into later recorded history, the ancient **Egyptians** had an ongoing need for surveyors, since the annual Nile flood tended to inundate boundary markers. They also needed geometry to build their pyramids and temples. The **Greeks,** as usual, took the subject a step farther. Euclid, who is to blame for much of what you'll have to study in geometry class, was a Greek. The **Romans**, as usual, snitched from the Greeks. Later on the **Arabs**, who were real mathematical whizzes, not only gave us Arabic numerals (e.g., 1, 2, 3, 4 as opposed to I, II, III, IV), but applied geometry in many satisfying ways to both architecture and architectural decoration. Now, in our **modern world**, geometry has gone far out, with fractals, recursive patterns, and other new geometric constructs.

You don't have to learn all of this in high school, of course. What you'll actually study will be **basic geometric shapes** in two and three dimensions: circles, squares, parallelograms, triangles, cones, cubes, and so on. You'll learn **how to construct them** using ruler and compass, and how to perform cute operations such as bisecting an angle. You'll learn **how to calculate area and volume** of various shapes. In more advanced classes, you'll also learn how to create **geometric proofs**.

Proofs are fun, if you like that sort of thing. They follow rigorous rules of logic—a great chance to increase your thinking skills! In order to do proofs, you have to learn certain geometric rules, called *postulates*. These usually are real knee-slappers, such as, "The sum of the angles in a triangle is always 180 degrees." Armed with these postulates, and basic logic, you can prove an amazing number of geometric facts. This is valuable, because it proves that (1) math is not just a bunch of random rules and (2) the more math you know, the more math you can derive from what you already know. Frightening, isn't it?

George the Geometer

Key to Geometry

Grades 6–12. Complete Set, $40.40.
Set of 8 workbooks, $27.40.
Answer s and Notes for books 1–3,
4–6, 7, and 8, $3.25 each. Circle
Master compass, $2.60. Plastic
straightedge, $3.85 per set of 12.
Shipping extra.
*Key Curriculum Press, 1150 65th St.,
Emeryville, CA 94608.
(800) 995-MATH.
Fax: (800) 541-2442.
mail: orders@keypress.com.
Web: www.keypress.com.*

Basic Geometry

Key to Geometry is another great workbook series from Key Curriculum Press. Each page contains only one concept. Sample problems are printed in large type to reduce student intimidation. Visual models are used wherever possible. Examples are worked out step-by-step. New terms are explained and underlined. Students get plenty of workspace and lots of exercises which gradually increase in difficulty. An end-of-book review helps insure that new concepts are remembered.

No math-teaching experience is required to use the series. *Everything* you need, except a compass, pencil, and straightedge, is in the inexpensive workbook. However, if you think you'd like a little extra help, the *Answers and Notes* books include foolproof teaching instructions, as well as answer keys for the workbook exercises.

Key to Geometry covers basic geometry, and includes no proofs. Much of the course is spent making geometric constructions. You start by drawing lines and bisecting angles, and go on to eventually make sophisticated constructions requiring up to 12 steps. You also learn geometric terms: 134 in all.

Like the other "Key to" series, you learn by doing. After working with a type of geometric construction, students are lead to deduce the rules that apply. This is completely backwards from most geometry books, which first tell you a rule, then give you examples to work to illustrate the rule.

The series covers:

Book 1: Lines and Segments
Book 2: Circles
Book 3: Constructions
Book 4: Perpendiculars
Book 5: Squares and Rectangles
Book 6: Angles
Book 7: Perpendiculars and Parallels, Chords and Tangents, Circles
Book 8: Triangles, Parallel Lines, Similar Polygons

Key to Geometry is not a full pre-college geometry course, but it works well as a high school or junior high "alternative" course for those not pursuing higher math, or as a supplement to traditional full-menu high-school geometry courses. Younger students can also use it, thanks to the wonderful job the authors have done of simplifying this work, while their basically serious approach won't make even a twelfth-grader feel "dumb." *Mary Pride*

This reusable workbook (answers to problems are written on separate paper, instead of in the book) doesn't cover proofs. What you get in **Straightforward Math: Geometry** is coverage of congruency; properties of polygons; the Pythagorean Theorem; similarities of polygons; and calculations of perimeter, area, and volume. Each of the five chapters ends with a review and some "application" problems. A final two-page assessment test helps you determine what you've learned (or failed to learn).

Due to the limited space (one workbook instead of two), this isn't quite as simple and step-by-step as the Straightforward Algebra books. There's more to cover per page, so things get complex pretty soon. For kids who are abstract thinkers, that may be OK, but if your student struggles with spatial concepts or math, the Key to Geometry series would be a better choice. *Mary Pride*

College Prep Geometry

All the major homeschool curriculum publishers offer Geometry courses. Some, like A Beka and School of Tomorrow, have videos to accompany these courses. Others simply offer textbooks, workbooks, answer keys, and teacher manuals.

These courses all follow more-or-less traditional outlines, and are similar in format to typical materials from school publishers. So, to conserve space, we're *mentioning* but not *reviewing* them here. Look to the right!

If you're looking for something different . . . a "quickie" course or refresher, or a whole new way to teach geometry . . . then eyeball the reviews below.

Geometry the Easy Way totally lacks the cute characters and plots of *Algebra the Easy Way* and *Calculus the Easy Way*. Instead, you get a pretty standard treatment of basic high-school geometry, including formal proofs, with hundreds of step-by-step examples and over 700 drawings, graphs, and diagrams. You could actually call this book "Geometry the Traditional Way."

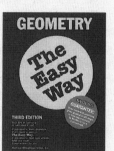

So why pick it instead of a "regular" textbook? Because it is clear, logical, easy to follow, and Barron's guarantees that this book will improve your grades in 30 days, or you can return it to them for a full refund. *Mary Pride*

Cliffs Quick Review: Geometry covers points, lines, planes, segments, midpoints, rays, angles of all sizes, parallel and perpendicular lines and planes, triangles, polygons, perimeter and area, similarity, right triangles, circles, geometric solids, and a tad of coordinate geometry. The book states, but does not prove, the basic postulates and theorems you expect to see in a typical high-school geometry course. No exercises for you to complete, but a lot of worked-out examples to study. Simple, straightforward, good for a "refresher" or as an aid to understanding whatever geometry materials you are using. *Bill Pride*

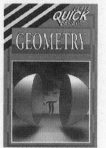

Discovering Geometry by Michael Serra is subtitled "An Inductive Approach." The foreword to this 834-page oversized hardbound textbook says, "This book is unique in that the students actually create geometry for themselves as they proceed through the activities and the problems. Concepts are first introduced visually, then analytically, then inductively, and, finally, deductively."

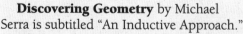

First *visually*, then *analytically*, then *inductively*, finally *deductively*? What on earth does all that mean?

The book attempts to capture your interest immediately with many examples of geometry in nature and geometry in art. True, these are visual examples. However, this is not what the foreword is talking about. Here's how the book's unique teaching approach works out in practice.

NEW!
Barron's Geometry the Easy Way, Third Edition
Grades 9–12. $12.95 plus shipping. *Barron's Educational Series, Inc., 250 Wireless Blvd., Hauppauge, NY 11788. (800) 645-3476. Fax: (516) 434-3217. Web: www.barronseduc.com.*

NEW!
Cliffs Quick Review series: Geometry
Grades 9–12. $7.95 postpaid. *Cliffs Notes, Inc., PO Box 80728, Lincoln, NE 68501. (800) 228-4078. Fax: (800) 826-6831. Web: www.cliffs.com.*

UPDATED!
Key Curriculum Press Discovering Geometry, Second Edition
Grades 7–12. Student text, $41.17. Teacher's guide and answer key, $29.95. Teacher's resource book, $49.95. Quizzes, Tests, and Exams, $59.95. Shipping extra. *Key Curriculum Press, 1150 65th St., Emeryville, CA 94608. (800) 995-MATH. Fax: (800) 541-2442. Email: orders@keypress.com. Web: www.keypress.com.*

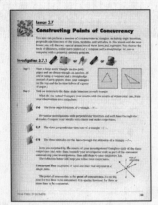

Note the hands-on format . . .

. . . and the many "thinking" activities

Answer to the Container Problem: Pour the full contents of the 4-liter container into the 9-liter container twice, thus making it contain 8 liters. Then fill the 4-liter container up again and pour into the 9-liter container until it's full. Since only 1 more liter can fit, you'll end up with 4-1=3 liters in the 4-liter container.

Every concept is introduced with numerous diagrams illustrating the definitions, both of things that meet the definition and things that don't. This is your *visual* introduction.

Say the problem is: "Define *right angle*." The text shows three illustrations with right angles—two with a little square drawn inside the angle and one labeled 90°—and two illustrations of angles labeled as *not* right angles—one labeled 46° and the other labeled 105°. The student is supposed to *analyze* these particular examples, and then to come up with a general principle—by logical *induction*—that a right angle is one that makes a square corner, indicated by a little square in the angle, and measures exactly ninety degrees. Likewise for *acute angles,* the text shows as acute angles three angles all of measure less than 90° (one of 89°). The not acute angles are a right angle, a 91° angle and a 100° angle. From this we can infer that an obtuse angle is one that has a measure less than 90°. This is the inductive approach—generalizing definitions and principles from examining individual examples. This approach of discovering definitions for oneself is bound to cement the concepts better than just handing a kid a definition and saying, "Learn this." Finally, the answers to the exercises are *deduced* by applying the principle you just figured out.

After you have been using inductive reasoning to discover geometry rules and using those rules to deductively solve problems for 733 pages, you finally get to the place where most geometry texts start—the fearsome and dreaded geometric proof. The difference is, that by the time a student has gotten this far in this book, formal geometric proofs are a cakewalk. In normal geometry, doing proofs is taught at the same time the student is wrestling with the concepts and definitions of geometry. In this book you can learn the proof process much more easily since you are already familiar with the concepts and definitions from the chapters before.

Chapter titles are Geometric Art, Inductive Reasoning, Introducing Geometry, Using Tools of Geometry, Line and Angle Properties, Triangle Properties, Polygon Properties, Circles, Transformations and Tesellations, Area, Pythagorean Theorem, Volume, Similarity, Trigonometry, Deductive Reasoning, Geometric Proof, Sequences of Proof. That's a lot of geometry!

In addition to the straightforward geometry, you get occasional "Improving Skills" exercises for reasoning skills, visual thinking skills, algebra skills, etc. Try this one on for size:

Container Problem 1 (from page 231) You have an unmarked 9-liter container and an unmarked 4-liter container, and an unlimited supply of water. In table, symbol, or paragraph form, describe the process necessary to end up with exactly 3 liters in one of the containers.

The second edition of *Discovering Geometry* has been upgraded to full color illustrations. Nice! Also, *Quizzes, Tests, and Exams* is now separate from the *Teacher's Guide and Answer Key.* You need both. The *Quizzes* material is 390 oversized pages, perfect-bound, with a handy CD-ROM tucked inside a back pocket. For your convenience, the CD-ROM includes all the quizzes, tests, and exams in Microsoft Word format for both Macintosh and Windows computers. The *Teacher's Guide and Answer Key* is 370 oversized perfect-bound pages with the course overview and philosophy, course outlines, suggestions for cooperative learning (not useful in most homeschool settings), lesson guides, lists of conjectures/postulates/theorems, glossary, and of course answers for all the exercises, puzzles, projects, and activities in the book. The *Teacher's Resource Book* (280 perfect-bound pages) will be of most use to those also using Key Curriculum Press's nifty *Geometer's Sketchpad* software. Besides activity masters for *Sketchpad* demonstrations, and *Sketchpad* demos on disk (tucked inside the back cover) for both Windows and Macintosh computers, it does offer a slew of transparency and worksheet masters (not needed for home classes with one or two students and no busywork time). All these books are nonconsumable and can last through dozens of kids.

The only thing that bothers me about this course is that you could take a lifetime to teach it. There is just *so much* to do! And if you get a copy of *Geometer's Sketchpad*, the playtime can end up taking your whole school day for weeks! The wise teacher (classroom or home) will spend as much time planning what to leave out as what to teach. *Mary Pride*

Cool Geometry Activities

Want a really neat crafts project that increases spatial thinking skills and provides a foretaste of advanced geometry? How about a bunch of those projects? Then **Geometric Playthings** is the book for you! In the line made famous by the TV show *Star Trek*, "It's like nothing I've ever seen before!" You get an oversized (9¾ x 12½) book with eight double-page spreads of unusual objects to color, cut, and fold. You start from the centerfold (three attractive Moebius strips) and work your way out. By the time you're done, you will have constructed deltahedra, hexaflexagons, and polyhedra of all sorts. If you don't know what these are, don't worry—you will by the time you finish these enjoyable projects! Each geometric object is decorated to the hilt with attractive designs that you can color in, for added crafts value. The price is also right. I've seen glitzy catalogs for yuppies offering make-it-yourself geometric playthings for considerably more than Dale Seymour is asking. *Mary Pride*

Euclidean geometry, the kind you learned in school, happens on a plane. No, not the kind that flies through the air. "Plane" or "Euclidean" geometry (so named after Euclid, the ancient Greek responsible for opening up this field of study) takes place in two dimensions, on a theoretical flat sheet of no depth extending out to infinity. It's a world of lines and line segments, triangles and rectangles.

But there's a whole other world out there. That's where Key Curriculum Press's Lénart Sphere Construction Material and the accompanying book, *Non-Euclidean Adventures on the Lénart Sphere,* come in. Imagine a world in which lines are never parallel and a triangle can have three right angles. Tough? Then imagine geometry on the surface of a sphere, instead of on a plane. As on the surface of our planet (yes, I know it's not smooth or perfectly round, but it approximates a sphere).

The **Lénart Sphere Basic Set** comes with all the construction material you need: a transparent plastic 8-inch sphere, a ring-shaped support for the sphere, hemispherical write-on/wipe-off transparencies that fit over the sphere, a spherical ruler you can use to draw and measure arcs/angles/great circles, a spherical compass and center locator for drawing circles on the sphere, a set of wipe-off markers, a hanger from which you can dangle your spherical constructions, a four-color polyconic projection of the earth you can cut out and make into a globe, and the 16-page booklet *Getting Started on the Lénart Sphere.*

The booklet is nice, but **Non-Euclidean Adventures on the Lénart Sphere** (available separately or as part of the **Lénart Sphere Package**) is better. This 224-page three-hole-punched softbound book of blackline masters can be a complete course in spherical geometry, or you can pick and choose your favorite activities. No previous experience with spherical geometry is needed to teach that course or activities; the book explains everything very clearly. It's yet another way Key Curriculum Press is introducing students to the math of the future. *Mary Pride*

Geometric Playthings
Grades 7–12. $11.95 plus shipping. *Dale Seymour Publications, PO Box 5026, White Plains, NY 10602. (800) 872-1100. Fax: (800) 551-7637. Web: www.cuisenaire-dsp.com.*

NEW!
Lénart Sphere Math
Grade 6–college. Non-Euclidiean Adventures, $15.95. Lénart Sphere Package (includes book), $69.82. Lénart Sphere Basic Set (no book), $59.95. Shipping extra. *Key Curriculum Press, 1150 65th St., Emeryville, CA 94608-1109. (800) 995-MATH. Fax: (800) 541-2442. Email: customer.service@keypress.com. Web: www.keypress.com.*

Geometry Videos

For a basic description of how all the Chalk Dust courses work, see the review of Chalk Dust Basic Math in the Basic Math chapter. Points to note: free tutoring on demand via email, fax, or phone from the video instructor; extremely thorough in content (not just the "high spots"); courses use standard textbooks written by the man (Ron Larson) who has written about 40 percent of college math texts sold today; you get to keep, not just rent, the tapes; evaluation tapes and literature available; 30-day money-back guarantee.

Chalk Dust Geometry is a set of 11 videotapes, ranging from about one hour to over two hours long, and covering all of a typical high-school geometry course. Teacher Dana Mosely attempts to capture the student's attention right from the start by dedicating the first video to topics of student interest—optical illusions, shapes, congruence and similarity—before proceeding to the more typical—introduction to coordinate and noncoordinate geometry, measurement, and how to make geometric constructions with a ruler and compass.

As in the other Chalk Dust math series, the silver-haired and energetic Mr. Mosely varies his time between addressing the student directly with vigorous word pictures and examples, and writing on and pointing to the blackboard. Lots of hand motions. Especially impressive: Mr. Mosely can draw a perfectly straight line freehand! His geometric drawings are neat and easy to understand, with no messy erasures.

The remaining 10 videotapes cover geometric reasoning (patterns, structures, basic rules about angles and segments, etc.), lines in a plane, congruent triangles, properties of triangles, polygons, transformations, similarity, right triangles, circles, planar measurements (area and perimeter), space measurements (volumes and surface areas), loci (point equidistant from a given point), and proofs. Tapes include classroom lectures and blackboard demonstrations, plus some computer animations for illustrations in the first seven tapes.

The optional reference for this course is *Geometry: An Integrated Approach* by Larson, Boswell, and Stiff published by D.C. Heath in 1995. However, the course can be used with any standard high-school geometry text. *Mary Pride*

What happens when you take the best high school math teachers across the country and put them on video? You get the **SuperStar Teachers** series from The Teaching Company.

Each course is designed to teach the basics in an easy-to-understand way. There are 30 lessons per subject, and each class is 30 minutes in length. Included with the four videos are two booklets per course, which outline the material taught. Workbooks with problem sets will be available soon.

Geometry covers fundamental geometric concepts, angles, inductive and deductive reasoning, two-column proofs, triangles, polygons, congruence of triangles, ratio, proportion and similarity, the pythagorean theorem, tangents and arcs, applied theorems, and prisms, pyramids, and polyhedra among its many lessons. This is taught by Jim Noggle, a high-school teacher from Indiana with 25 years experience. He uses a blackboard, easel flipchart, and a few physical models of geometric objects to present geometry from angles to solids, plus a tad of trigonometry, in 30 lectures. This course even covers proofs.

The quality of these courses is high and each lesson is laid out in a way that makes sense, leading from one subject to the next. All the SuperStar teachers take advantage of the visual opportunities and use plenty of diagrams and examples to explain their points. Use these videos for reinforcement, to explain those natty problems that the book just can't seem to nail down, and for your visual learners. Our family has used the Geometry course for over a year and can attest to its usefulness and value. *Marla Perry*

NEW!
Chalk Dust Geometry Video Course

Grades 9–12. 11 tapes. $25/tape postpaid. Textbook, $69 plus $8 shipping/book. Complete solution guide, $50. One tape free if you prepay for book and tapes for a full course. Free 30-day evaluation period plus $5 shipping/tape. *Chalk Dust Company, 11 Sterling Court, Sugar Land, TX 77479. Orders: (800) 588-7564. Fax: (281) 265-3197. Email: sales@chalkdust.com. Web: www.chalkdust.com.*

NEW!
SuperStar Teachers Series: Geometry

Grades 8–11. $99.95 plus $10 shipping. *The Teaching Company, 7405 Alban Station Court, Suite A107, Springfield, VA 22150. (800) 832-2412. Fax: (703) 912-7756. Email: custserv@teachco.com. Web: www.teachco.com.*

CHAPTER 18

Trigonometry

A lot of people are snowed by calculus and trigonometry. Actually, these subjects aren't that tough. You just need to remember that calculus is about curves and trigonometry is about angles. In calculus you're trying to sneak up on the curve (approximating it closer and closer), while in trig the angles stay put.

I trust this brief explanation has made everything perfectly clear? Good. You are now ready to tackle any or all of the resources in this chapter.

Complete Trigonometry Courses

Would you believe **Trigonometry the Easy Way** is the "Gilligan's Island" of trigonometry? Starring Marcus Recordis, Gerard Macinius Builder, the king, the professor, and Trigonometris, this tale of mirth and woe is divided into 15 episodes.

Our gallant crew start off with a rather stilted introduction to terminology, but the novel format perks up when they start calculating the height of Christmas trees and the distance to a star. Using the story format, author Douglas Downing takes you from triangle problems to conic sections and polynomial approximations, revealing the "how" and "why" of trigonometry along the way. It's not all high jinks, though—each chapter ends with problems for you to solve (solutions are in the back of the book). Over 100 charts and graphs make all clear.

This is not as hokey as it sounds. Traditional trigonometry texts fail dismally at conveying exactly why anybody needs to know the subject. Even in fantasy novel form, the problems in this book seem more real than in the average text. Subject coverage is quite thorough, explanations are quite detailed, and the entire presentation is quite winsome.

Consider this book as at least a supplement to whatever trig course you may choose, or even for the trig course itself. *Bill Pride*

NEW!
Saxon Advanced Mathematics

Grades 11–12. Home Study Kit,
$57.95. Solutions Manual, $25.
Shipping extra.
*Saxon Publishers, 2450 John Saxon
Blvd., Norman, OK 73071.*
(800) 284-7019.
Email: info@saxonpub.com.
Web: www.saxonpub.com.

The Solutions Manual shows
step-by-step solutions to each of the
problems in the problem sets. A
good purchase if you're not confident in your own ability to "backtrack" where your students went
wrong in homework problems done
incorrectly. Not included in The
Home Study Kit; must be purchased
separately.

Saxon Advanced Mathematics,
previously known as *Geometry-
Trigonometry-Algebra III*, is the
fourth book of the high-school sequence. Think of it as the "precalculus" book, or as the final course of a
less-demanding college prep sequence.

Saxon Advanced Mathematics reviews fundamental algebra and
geometry, while introducing and
continually practicing new topics. These include logarithms, determinants,
arithmetic and geometric series, conic sections, roots of higher-order polynomial equations, and functions, including curve sketching. The geometry
in this volume includes terminology and proofs. You also get a lavish helping of word problems, as in all Saxon books.

The book provides 125 daily lessons, each followed by a set of 30 problems. The student is expected to work all these problems, plus any practice
problems that may be included in the lesson itself.

The Home Study Kit includes the hardbound student text, Answer Key
for practice sets and problem sets, and a booklet of tests with answer keys.

Since skills, once introduced, are repeated in every subsequent lesson,
you don't have to be overly concerned if your student doesn't "get" one of
these difficult math concepts right away. It will be repeated and reinforced
again and again, until sooner or later his mind make the breakthrough and
it all starts to make sense to him. It helps, of course, if you know enough of
this math to explain any sticky points. *Mary Pride*

NEW!
Cliffs Quick Review series: Trigonometry

Grades 11–12. $7.95 postpaid.
*Cliffs Notes, Inc., PO Box 80728,
Lincoln, NE 68501. (800) 228-4078.*
Fax: (800) 826-6831.
Web: www.cliffs.com.

Extra Trigonometry Help

This slim book does a decent job of covering the
subject. The explanations are crisp, the visual design
is clean, and the problems are all worked out for
you.

If you need a complete course, with lot of problems to solve, you'll need more than this. But for a
quick review, or even a quick introduction, **Cliffs
Quick Review: Trigonometry** is just fine. *Bill Pride*

NEW!
Straightforward Math: Pre-Calculus

Grades 11–12. $7.95 plus shipping.
*Garlic Press, 605 Powers Street,
Eugene, OR 97402. (541) 345-0063.*
Fax: (541) 683-8767.
Email: garlicpress@pond.net.
Web: www.garlicpress.com.

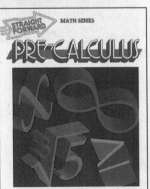

You might want to think of **Straightforward
Math: Pre-Calculus** as "Trig 2" and "Not All
That Advanced Algebra" mixed. This workbook
does *not* start with a review of previous math.
You jump right in to seven chapters covering
advanced arithmetic, functions, inequalities,
graphings polynomials and rational functions,
trig functions and equations (the stuff we were
lonely for in the Trigonometry workbook), and
exponential and logarithmic functions.

Nice, open format, much easier to follow
than your typical Advanced Math textbook. A
little extra help for those who need it. *Mary Pride*

Everything about triangles, the **Straightforward Math: Trigonometry** workbook covers. Anything having to do with tangents, cotangent, secants, cosecants, and trigonometric identities, it doesn't. Everything is in degrees, not radians. With that in mind, this is a good little workbook. You get a brief review of triangle geometry, three chapters (each ending with a set of review questions), a cumulative review quiz covering all three chapters, and an appendix on "non-right triangles," plus answer key in the back. Not fancy, but a good accompaniment to your first textbook chapters on trig. *Mary Pride*

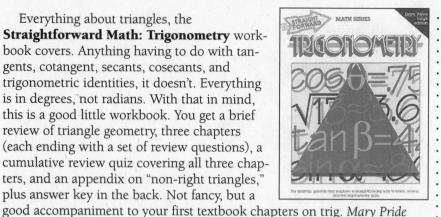

Trigonometry Videos

For a basic description of how all the Chalk Dust courses work, see the review of Chalk Dust Basic Math in the Basic Math chapter. Points to note: free tutoring on demand via email, fax, or phone from the video instructor; extremely thorough in content (not just the "high spots"); courses use standard textbooks written by the man (Ron Larson) who has written about 40 percent of college math texts sold today; you get to keep, not just rent, the tapes; evaluation tapes and literature available; 30-day money-back guarantee.

Chalk Dust Trigonometry is a set of 10 videotapes that cover all of a typical high-school or college trig course. Assuming the classroom teacher makes it all the way through the book—most don't. The course is subtitled "A Graphing Approach" (meaning you get to experience the horror of a graphing calculator), and you can purchase (which I strongly recommend) an optional reference text by that name, e.g., *Trigonometry: A Graphing Approach*, written by Larson, Hostetler, and Edwards, and published by D.C. Heath.

Your video instructor is Dana Mosely, a man with over 15 years' classroom teaching experience and eight years' experience as D.C. Heath's video instructor in mathematics. As always, he divides his time between addressing you directly and drawing on and pointing to the blackboard. When possible, grids are prepared in advance, so no time is wasted watching him set up his blackboard. Mr. Mosely's sine curves are just as beautiful as his straight lines—unlike other instructors, his blackboard work is a joy to watch. He also is clearly comfortable with the topic, to the point of calling sine function values "these rascals." No stuffy, unintelligible mystique here!

The tapes on this trig course are mostly longer than those in other Chalk Dust courses. Tape 1, "Prerequisites," is almost 4 hours long. It goes from a lecture on the real number system, through graphing in the Cartesian plane, to inverse functions. Tape 2 is a whopping 4 hours and 26 minutes, and covers measurements in radians and degrees, basic trig functions as they relate to unit circles/right triangles/any angle, graphing trig functions and inverse trig functions, and trig applications. The remaining videotapes cover "additional topics in trigonometry," complex numbers, exponential and logarithmic functions, and topics in analytic geometry. This is where you get into the fun stuff, such as parabolas, ellipses, hyperbolas, and polar coordinates.

As you may have surmised, to many students trig is deadly stuff. Only future engineers and scientists really enjoy trig, or even half-understand it at the pace it's presented in class. These videos, each tape of which corresponds to a chapter in the reference text, are just the help a struggling trig student can use. *Mary Pride*

NEW!
Chalk Dust Precalculus Videos

Grades 11–12. Precalculus, 20 tapes. $25/tape postpaid. Textbook, $79 plus $8 shipping. Solution guide, $25. One tape free if you prepay for book and tapes for a full course. Free 30-day evaluation period plus $5 shipping/tape.
Chalk Dust Company, 11 Sterling Court, Sugar Land, TX 77479.
Orders: (800) 588-7564.
Inquiries: (281) 265-2495.
Fax: (281) 265-3197.
Email: sales@chalkdust.com.
Web: www.chalkdust.com.

> You can substitute this Precalculus course for *both* the Chalk Dust Trigonometry *and* the Chalk Dust College Algebra Courses.

NEW!
The Standard Deviants Trigonometry Videos

Grade 11–college. Each video, $19.99.
Cerebellum Corporation, 2890 Emma Lee St., Falls Church, VA 22042.
(800) 238-9669.
Inquiries: (703) 848-0856.
Fax: (703) 848-0857.
Web: www.cerebellum.com.
Direct mail sales are not available.

Chalk Dust Precalculus is a heavy-duty course that you can easily substitute for both their Trigonometry and College Algebra courses. The reference text is *Precalculus with Limits, A Graphing Approach*, second edition, from Houghton Mifflin. Unavoidably, a graphing calculator is required for this course, and you are taught how to use it. The authors recommend you use the TI-82 or TI-83; however, there is an appendix that explains how to get the same results with 13 other models, as well as a guide to graphing calculators intended to teach you how to use them.

The first two tapes review the cartesian plane, graphing and graphing, lines in the plane, solving equations and inequalities, and how data is represented graphically. Topics then introduced and studied are functions and their graphs, polynomial and rational functions, exponential and logarithmic functions, trigonometric functions, analytic trigonometry, additional trig topics, systems of equations and inequalities, matrices and determinants, sequences/probability/statistics, topics in analytic geometry (yea, conic sections and polar coordinates!), analytical geometry in three dimensions, and finally, what we have all been waiting for: limits and an introduction to calculus. Cathy Duffy says, in her excellent review you'll find both in her book and on the Chalk Dust web site, "A student should not consider taking an 'AP' high-school calculus course following this but a college calculus course," and I concur.

The entire Precalculus course costs about what you'd have to pay for one credit hour at a major university. But the amount covered is what you'd find in a three-credit course, and with way better instruction than you'll get from the typical college professor or (more realistically) the typical teaching assistant. Deal! *Mary Pride*

I explained how the **Standard Deviants Video Series** works in the Basic Math chapter—and why it has nothing to do with "deviants" and everything to do with "deviating from the standard," i.e. how to become a curve-wrecker (a grade A student, to those of you who never took statistics). These fun videos demystify the "tough" subjects for college students . . . and smart high-school students, too!

They may call these two videos **The Twisted World of Trigonometry**, but rest assured, they are available in Edited For All Audiences editions. Like other Standard Deviants videos, these employ wacky characters and situations to prod your memory and engage your interest. Trig being trig, there is also quite a bit of serious computer-generated charts, graphs, and explanations. Remember, you're *reviewing* trig, not *learning* it, from these tapes. Their best use is as a motivational jolt or extra review along with a regular trig textbook or video course. Total running time for both tapes combined: three hours. *Mary Pride*

CHAPTER 19

Calculus

There are only three reasons for studying calculus:
(1) You want to be an engineer, scientist, doctor, mathematician, or M.B.A.
(2) The college of your choice is "selective" in its choice of student, and the Algebra 1-Geometry-Algebra 2-Trigonometry-Calculus sequence will impress them.
(3) You just adore solving puzzles and think math is fun.

If you fall into categories (1) or (2), here are some courses and refresher courses that might ease your pain. If you fall into category (3), you are Scotty from *Star Trek* and you're feeling no pain at all. "What could be more fun than a whole new bunch of math to learn?" you enthuse. Well, we've got your birthday shopping list right here. Beam it up, Scotty!

Complete Calculus Courses

Written for high schoolers, but covering everything taught in a college calculus course, **Calculus: Concepts and Applications** aims kids smack at the Advanced Placement Calculus AB and BC exams. While you don't have to use it as an AP course, author Paul Foerster's years as an AP reader and his contacts with leaders of the AP reform movement mean this course is right on top of the latest AP requirements.

Like Key's *Advanced Algebra Through Data Exploration* (see review in Algebra chapter), this course makes extensive use of the graphing calculator throughout the year, right along with teaching students how to also solve problems on paper or in their heads. The first chapter of the book overviews the entire course. Precalculus review is included as each topic is introduced, rather than all at once at the beginning of the course. Timed review questions and a "calculus journal" in which students write out what they've been learning are other special features of the course. The usual photos of women truck drivers and Navy pilots, etc., are about all the political correctness this course allows—the problems mostly concentrate on real-world applications. Finally, you'll find touches of humor throughout, as in the question about "Lee Per" and his bungee cord. (Read the last sentence aloud if you don't "get it" right away.)

NEW!
Calculus: Concepts and Applications
Grade 12 and college. Student textbook, $54.95. Instructor's guide, $29.95. Solutions manual, $28.95. Instructor's resource book, $49.95. Complete package, $131.04. Shipping extra.
Key Curriculum Press, 1150 65th St., Emeryville, CA 94608-1109. (800) 995-MATH. Fax: (800) 541-2442. Email: customer.service@keypress.com. Web: www.keypress.com.

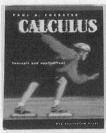
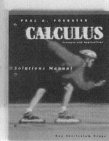

The student text is a hefty 792 hardbound pages. Answers to odd-numbered problems are in the back of the book, for self-checking purposes. You'll need the 312-page Solutions Manual if you want to check every single problem.

For a course like this, the Instructor's Guide is also a good idea (for one thing, you'll get answers to the projects and exercises), but you'll likely not have time to pursue the additional ideas in the Resource Book.

Not as easy to use for self-teaching as *Saxon Calculus*, but perhaps more interesting for the mathematically-minded, this course is a possibility if an adult well-versed in math and the use of the graphing calculator is available to help the student. *Mary Pride*

NEW!
Saxon Calculus with Trigonometry and Analytic Geometry

Grade 12–early college. Home Study Kit (includes student book, answer key and tests), $67. Book only (student edition), $68. Answer key and tests, $18. Solutions manual, $25. Shipping extra.
Saxon Publishers, 2450 John Saxon Blvd., Norman, OK 73071. (800) 284-7019. Email: info@saxonpub.com. Web: www.saxonpub.com.

Don't count on the math review in the beginning of *Saxon Calculus* to make up for serious deficiencies—it's designed to refresh kids on what they already know, not teach them basic algebra. Even kids who were strong in algebra might want to slow down the pace and take several days for each of the beginning lessons.

John Saxon makes learning genuine college calculus more painless than anyone else, in my opinion. His **Saxon Calculus** text is designed to do most of the teaching, using the techniques of "incremental development and continuous review." Each concept is introduced bit by bit (that's "incremental development") and problems based on it appear in problem sets for days afterwards (that's "continuous review"). This step-by-step, practice-it-over-and-over approach gives students enough time to digest even the most difficult math and become comfortable with problems that terrify those using traditional "bungee math" courses. ("Bungee math" is my own term—it refers to math books that show you the concept once and then snatch it away until the final exam.)

On the day a new topic is introduced, only one or two problems in the problem set are on that topic. The rest review material from previous lessons. However, the new topic will be reviewed and added to from now on for dozens of problems sets.

For example, the first lesson on limits is Lesson 16. You get at least one problem involving limits in every problem set for the next 111 lessons. Derivatives appear in Lesson 27, and problems involving derivatives are in each of the next 90 problem sets. These problems are carefully designed to incrementally increase the student's proficiency and understanding, not just haphazardly thrown at the student.

Beginning with a thorough review of the math you need to tackle this course, the *Saxon Calculus* book takes you up through all the topics you can expect to find in the Advanced Placement AB-level calculus test, as well as many on the tougher BC level. Problem sets include types of problems typically found on these tests, as well as many applications in the areas of physics, engineering, business, and chemistry. In all, you get 117 lessons. This works out to four lessons a week, with Friday for testing and math enrichment.

Saxon's famous sense of humor and wide erudition shines through occasionally on the word problems, but not as frequently as in the other Saxon math books, due to the graphical nature of so many of the problems. It's hard to be humorous when asking students to sketch the graph of $y = x$ divided by $(x - 2)(x + 3)$.

Your job as a parent is simply to make sure the student does every step of every problem in every problem set. For this, you need the Solutions Manual. Even if you're the sort of person who enjoys solving complex differential equations for fun, you really don't want to grind through all those problems by hand in order to check Junior's work. With the Solutions Manual, Junior can check his own work—not just if he got the answer right, but if he did each step correctly, since the Solutions Manual shows all the problem-solving steps for each problem. This makes it easy to pinpoint and correct trouble areas. *Bill and Mary Pride*

About those prices—no, there are no typos. The Home Study kit actually costs less than the student book alone. And the Solutions Manual is not another name for the answer key. While the answer key contains just the answers, the Solutions Manual shows you each problem worked out step by step. While you might be able to live without a solutions manual for Algebra ½, my advice is, don't do calculus without it.

Quickie Calculus

The storm struck my ship with devastating suddenness. Something hit me on the head, and my memory was completely knocked out. The next thing I remember was being washed ashore on a strange land called Camorra. The farmer who first met me . . . decided to take me to the capital city. There it proved to be a time of crisis. Nobody was able to figure out the speed of the new train, which was powered by a friendly giant named Mongol.

So begins the most unusual calculus text I have ever seen. Characters in this fantasy story proceed to solve problems they encounter in the mythical land of Camorra by using calculus. We follow their logic, written as conversations, as they determine the number of roses to get for the elliptical rose garden and the length of banners to be draped from poles for their upcoming celebration.

A substantial amount of the book is dedicated to mathematical explanations. The story serves as glue to hold it all together and keep things moving rather than as a riveting adventure.

Alexander the Great died in 323 B.C. **Calculus the Easy Way** ends on page 323. Is there a connection? No, but now you might remember these two factoids more easily. In a similar fashion, *Calculus the Easy Way* employs story vignettes to illustrate the principles of calculus. Following the antics of characters such as Recordis, Trigonometeris the (female) professor, the Builder, the king, and so forth, the book manages to cover all essential first-year calculus topics. You get not only the stories, but over 150 drawings and tables, plus problems to work at the end of every chapter. Solutions to problems are in the back of the book, where they belong.

Calculus the Easy Way requires a basic knowledge of algebra, geometry, and trigonometry, since it is designed as an introduction to calculus. However, it does not include rigorous proofs and all of the background theory that would normally be included in a calculus text.

Practice exercises, tests, and answers are included in one book.

The fun format of this book makes it a natural for homeschoolers who need more motivation or who want an alternative to Saxon for some reason.

Students who will be taking more advanced calculus courses will need further study, but others will find this sufficient and will certainly have more fun learning calculus. *Bill and Mary Pride*

Forgotten Calculus is a book you won't want to forget! Modestly claiming to only be a "refresher course" for those who have already taken calculus in school, this 455-page, oversized paperback is great for teaching you calculus from scratch. Starting with the question, "What is a function?" this book tells you what each mathematical term means, provides you with tons of examples, and offers problem sets at the end of each chapter with answers in the back—perfect for self-study. With the subtitle "A Refresher Course with Applications to Economics and Business," the MBA type is clearly targeted, but anyone who appreciates systematic instruction, a nice clear visual design, and thorough coverage of topics up to and including integration and partial derivatives will appreciate this book. *Bill Pride*

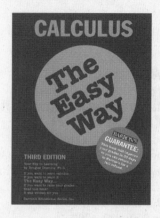

NEW!
Cliffs Quick Review series: Calculus

Grade 12–college. $7.95 postpaid. *Cliffs Notes, Inc., PO Box 80728, Lincoln, NE 68501. (800) 228-4078. Fax: (800) 826-6831. Web: www.cliffs.com.*

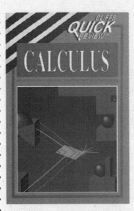

Can the Cliffs Notes people do for calculus what they did for classic literature? Not quite: you can't whiz through this slim 132-page book and pass the AB or BC Calculus test. However, if you have already taken a calculus course, or are having trouble understanding the course you are taking, **Cliffs Quick Review: Calculus** slices and dices the subject down to its understandable essentials. The section on limits is very good, for example. You get lots of definitions, explanations, and examples of calculus basics, but no problems for you to work. *Bill Pride*

NEW!
HarperCollins College Outline series: Introduction to Calculus

Grade 12–college. $14 plus shipping. *HarperCollins Publishers, Inc., 1000 Keystone Industrial Park, Scranton, PA 18512. (800) 331-3761. Fax: (800) 822-4090. Web: www.harpercollins.com.*

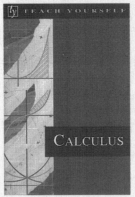

Much more affable and personable than its sister *Calculus with Analytic Geometry* book, the **HarperCollins College Outline Introduction to Calculus** book is 250 pages of basic calculus. Covering approximately the same ground as *Cliff's Quick Review: Calculus*, it includes more explanations, plus it has problems for you to work. Answers immediately follow each problem set. As a self-study text, this could work, even though it is mainly meant to accompany a regular course. *Bill Pride*

NEW!
Teach Yourself series: Calculus

Grade 12–adult. $14.95 plus shipping. *NTC Publishing. 4255 West Touhy Ave, Lincolnwood, IL 60646. (800) 323-4900 x 147. Fax: (800) 998-3103. Email: ntcpub@tribune.com. Web: www.ntc-school.com.*

Originally published in 1940 in Britain, this handy-sized 400-page book does not appear to have been visually updated since, although it has been recopyrighted several times. **Teach Yourself Calculus** presents the subject in bite-sized pieces. Some problems are worked in the text—far less than in the *Forgotten Calculus* book, for example. Each chapter ends with exercises for you to work, with answers in the back. The graphs are scruffy, but the diagrams are good. The new edition includes problems you can work with a calculator or solve with simple home computer programs.

You could in fact teach yourself calculus with this no-nonsense book, though it wouldn't be much fun.

The same authors have also produced *Teach Yourself Algebra* and *Teach Yourself Trigonometry*, which presumably follow a similar format. *Bill Pride*

NEW!
Wiley Quick Calculus, 2nd Edition

Grade 12–college. $17.95 plus shipping. *John Wiley & Sons, 1 Wiley Drive, Somerset, NJ 08875. (800) 225-5945. Fax: (800) 597-3299. Web: www.wiley.com.*

The first edition of this book sold over 250,000 copies. That's a lot of copies of a book "designed to teach you the elementary techniques of differential and integral calculus with a minimum of wasted effort on your part." A *lot* of folks out there must be suffering from "calculus anxiety," and eager for a book that promises to teach you the subject all by itself.

So how quick is **Quick Calculus**? About half the size of the College Outline books from major publishers, which are merely designed to *supplement* a calculus course, this book not only presents definitions and examples, but re-explains what you might have missed, after you try to solve a problem on your own. On the other hand, if you got the problem right, you are directed to skip the additional explanations. This "hand-holding" feature, which makes you feel like a teacher is actually helping you figure it all out, is probably what accounts for the book's phenomenal sales success. The chatty tone and simple, clear visuals also don't hurt. *Bill Pride*

Extra Practice

The 544 pages of **The Calculus Tutoring Book** give you four semesters of calculus in one book (thus explaining its price). It covers all of introductory calculus, and calculus with analytic geometry, with a practical engineering flair that's only natural considering it's published by the Institute of Electrical and Electronics Engineers Press. It's supposed to be useful either as a course supplement, or for self-study. Dilbert would love the design: integration tables adorn the inside covers. You get exactly 1,151 problems with detailed solutions, plus instruction that covers the standard calculus sequence.

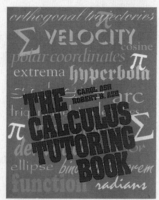

Personally, I doubt the average student could use this for self-study, unless he is the type who enrolls in engineering school and then skips all the classes in order to have more time to program his computer. *Bill Pride*

Bill says I should have been calling the books in this series "thin textbooks" instead of "workbooks." True, they aren't designed to be written in and thrown away—you write the answers on separate paper and can therefore reuse the books. True, they also include lessons, not just practice exercises. Let's compromise and call them "worktexts."

The two **Straightforward Math: Calculus AB** books should have been expanded into four books, in my opinion. Because of the amount of information to cover, trying to jam it into two books meant sacrificing some of the openness of the other books in this series. In their present form, what you get is similar in appearance to a regular textbook, albeit in larger print. Three chapters in the first book, two in the second, each with practice exercises and answers, cover all the topics in a typical Calculus AB course. More white space and visuals would have been nice, as would have been a slightly more step-by-step approach. *Mary Pride*

Calculus Videos

For a basic description of how all the Chalk Dust courses work, see the review of Chalk Dust Basic Math in the Basic Math chapter. Points to note: free tutoring on demand via email, fax, or phone from the video instructor; extremely thorough in content (not just the "high spots"); courses use standard textbooks written by the man (Ron Larson) who has written about 40 percent of college math texts sold today; you get to keep, not just rent, the tapes; evaluation tapes and literature available; 30-day money-back guarantee.

Chalk Dust Calculus I is in production. As I write this, the first five tapes are available. The entire course should be ready by the time you read

NEW!
The Calculus Tutoring Book
College. $39.95 plus $4 shipping. *IEEE Press, PO Box 1331, Piscataway, NJ 08855. Orders: (800)701-4333. Inquiries: (732)981-0060. Fax: (732) 981-9667. Email: customer-service@ieee.org. Web: www.ieee.org.*

NEW!
Straightforward Math: Calculus AB
Grade 12. Book 1 and 2, $7.95 each. Shipping extra. *Garlic Press, 605 Powers Street, Eugene, OR 97402. (541) 345-0063. Fax: (541) 683-8767. Email: garlicpress@pond.net. Web: www.garlicpress.com.*

NEW!
Chalk Dust Calculus Videos
Grade 12. Calculus I, 10 tapes. $25/tape postpaid. Textbook, $79 plus $8 shipping. Solution guide, $25. One tape free if you prepay for book and tapes for a full course. Free 30-day evaluation period plus $5 shipping/tape.

Chalk Dust Company, 11 Sterling Court, Sugar Land, TX 77479.
Orders: (800) 588-7564.
Inquiries: (281) 265-2495.
Email: sales@chalkdust.com.
Web: www.chalkdust.com.

NEW!
The Standard Deviants Pre-Calculus and Calculus Videos

Grade 11–college. Each video, $19.99.
Cerebellum Corporation, 2890 Emma Lee St., Falls Church, VA 22042.
(800) 238-9669.
Inquiries: (703) 848-0856.
Fax: (703) 848-0857.
Web: www.cerebellum.com.
Direct mail sales are not available.

this review. It will cover an entire year of high-school calculus, and be an excellent preparation for college courses in advanced mathematics. In fact, there's a good chance your first college math course will start out using the same book you'll be studying in this course! *Mary Pride*

I explained how the **Standard Deviants Video Series** works in the Basic Math chapter—and why it has nothing to do with "deviants" and everything to do with "deviating from the standard," i.e. how to become a curve-wrecker (a grade A student, to those of you who never took statistics). These fun videos demystify the "tough" subjects for college students . . . and smart high-school students, too!

Their pre-calculus course is two videos, entitled **The Dangerous World of Pre-Calculus**. For calculus, there are also two videos, entitled **The Creepy, Crawly World of Calculus**. All are available in Edited For All Audiences editions.

The pre-calculus course only goes as far as exponents and logs. In other words, you'll need a separate Trig or Advanced Math course as well. Calculus covers a standard college sequence, but of course, not in a standard way. See how the evil Doctor KnowWay is thwarted in his efforts to confuse and frustrate hapless students such as yourself. Meet other wacky characters acting out, emphasizing, or punning on pre-calc concepts. Be enlightened by computer-generated graphs and explanations. It's like an edgy Sesame Street of hairy math, right down to the odd characters in the funny costumes.

If pre-calc and calculus scare you to death—and after the build-up these courses get, who wouldn't be scared?—just remember you can't be scared while you're laughing.

Again I remind you: these aren't *teaching* tapes, they are *review* tapes. You're supposed to be attending class (online classes and sessions at the kitchen table count), and *then* watching the appropriate parts of these tapes. Of course, they also work as an introduction, but just to swish the new concepts through your brain for the first time. Don't expect to learn calculus and whip out a "5" on the Advanced Placement test from these tapes alone. You'll need a lot more in-depth instruction and practice before you'll become proficient—just what a regular textbook or video course offers. But for under $40 a set, you may find the extra help and motivation these tapes offer is worth it. *Mary Pride*

PART 5

Practical Sciences

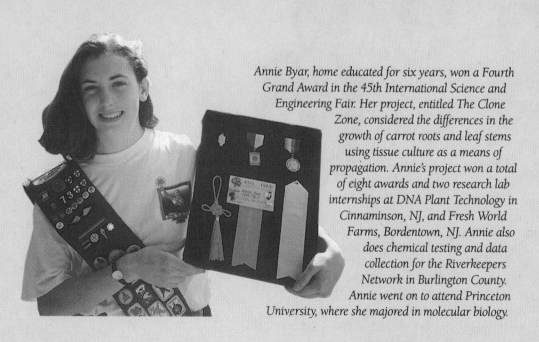

Annie Byar, home educated for six years, won a Fourth Grand Award in the 45th International Science and Engineering Fair. Her project, entitled The Clone Zone, considered the differences in the growth of carrot roots and leaf stems using tissue culture as a means of propagation. Annie's project won a total of eight awards and two research lab internships at DNA Plant Technology in Cinnaminson, NJ, and Fresh World Farms, Bordentown, NJ. Annie also does chemical testing and data collection for the Riverkeepers Network in Burlington County. Annie went on to attend Princeton University, where she majored in molecular biology.

At 17, Nathaniel Bluedorn of New Boston, IL, won a trip to the Johnson Space Center! Nathaniel was a regional winner in an essay contest sponsored by the National Aeronautic and Space Administration and the National Science Teachers Association. The challenge was to create a 20-page planned trip to Mars, complete with experiments, that would balance technical and practical concerns with a clear writing style. In Houston, Nathaniel gave a presentation based on his paper, and had the opportunity to speak with NASA scientists. Here Nathaniel is flanked by his mother, Practical Homeschooling columnist Laurie Bluedorn, and a NASA judge.

CHAPTER 20

Junior High Science

Life Science (Grade 7), Earth Science (Grade 8), Physical Science (Grade 9). That's the typical junior-high science curriculum. Alternatively, kids at these grade levels may study "General Science"—courses that combine topics from Life Science, Earth Science, and Physical Science.

These junior-high courses are what I call "holding pattern" science—snippets of what high-school students learn in their Biology, Chemistry, and Physics courses, and what they'll be studying *again* in their college science courses. There's something to be said for skipping straight to the high-school courses—provided your student has studied Algebra before tackling Chemistry and Physics. However, if your student's elementary science education wasn't that stellar, these junior-high courses may be just what he or she needs to "catch up."

- **Life Science** = cell biology, botany (plants), zoology (animals), anatomy, and ecology
- **Earth Science** = geology, oceanography, meteorology (weather), and astronomy
- **Physical Science** = electricity, magnetism, simple machines, and some simple chemistry
- **General science** = all the above, in any order the publisher prefers

General Science

A Beka's General Science series covers three grades (grades 7–9), with one textbook for each grade. Instead of separate courses in, say, earth science and life science, you get a "building-block" approach, with similar topics presented each year in a "spiral" fashion. This constant repetition, with a little bit new added every year, is supposed to help students digest and remember more.

All books in this series challenge the evolutionary hypothesis, include lots of colorful art and photos, introduce new scientific terms in bold print, and include student experiments and activities. Each gives significant space to creation science and encourages students to both learn and apply the basic principles of science. The books also have a wealth of "in-text learning aids," A Beka's term for sidebars on important concepts, interesting facts, chapter outlines, worked-out examples, and the like.

A Beka General Science

Student text: Grade 7, $16.20; Grade 8, $14.75; Grade 9, $23.15. Teacher's guide: Grade 7, $24.95; Grade 8, $20.95; Grade 9, $20.20. Student tests, $4.35-$6.20 each grade. Teacher key for test booklet, $8.85 each grade. Student quizzes, $4.60 each grade. Teacher key for quiz booklet, $8.85 each grade. Shipping extra. *A Beka Book, Box 19100, Pensacola, FL 32523-9100. (800) 874-2352. Fax: (800) 874-3590. Web: www.abeka.com.*

The grade 7 book, **Science: Order and Reality**, touches mostly on field biology (with pictorial sections on wildflowers, trees, birds, fish, insects, and weeds), simple physics (with an emphasis on how everyday appliances work), basic principles of science, and scientific creationism.

Science: Matter and Motion, the grade 8 book, has the broadest coverage, with sections on earth and space science, human and cellular biology, chemistry, and physics, as well as the general series emphasis on basic scientific principles and creation science.

Science of the Physical Creation, the ninth-grade book, repeats the grade 8 topics with the exception of human biology, which is not covered in this grade.

The section on earth science is greatly expanded, with topics such as atmosphere, weather, oceanography, earthquakes, volcanoes, rocks, and fossils, as well as an extended discussion of why uniformitarian geology (everything happening very slowly over a long time) is wrong. The physics section shows physics at work in modern electronic devices such as computers and lasers.

For each grade, the teacher's curriculum guide includes the lesson plans and teaching information, but not a copy of the student text. *Mary Pride*

All three of **Alpha Omega's** grade 7–9 **Science LIFEPACs** could be considered basic science. These workbook-based courses come in slim LIFEPACs including the lesson text, exercises, and tests.

Grade 7 starts off defining science as a discipline and a career. The second unit covers measurement and graphing. Next come two units on astronomy, one on the atmosphere, one on weather, one on climate, and two on human anatomy. The review unit tries to lend a "careers" viewpoint to the areas studied. Altogether a decent little course.

Grade 8 is more concerned with the interplay between science and technology. After this topic is introduced, we move to two units on basic chemistry (the structure of matter, elements, compounds, mixtures, how matter changes, acids, bases, and salts) and one on health and nutrition. Physics is then introduced by two units on energy (mechanical, thermodynamics, magnetism, electricity, and present and future energy sources) and two on machines (simple machines and Newtonian physics). All of this is fine, aside from the environmentalist doomsaying in the latter parts of unit 1. The previous version of the last unit introduced biology from a strongly environmentalist point of view, as natural cycles disrupted by boorish humans (all of us) who need strong government regulations to force us into more Spartan lifestyles. According to Alpha Omega, this slant has been rewritten out of the current version.

The **grade 9** course is actually named "General Science." Rather than reviewing the material in grades 7 and 8, it introduces several new topics. Our Atomic World is the first unit, followed by a unit on volume, mass, and density. Two new topics then come up: physical and historical geology (creationist viewpoint). Body Health I, the fifth unit, is an introduction to microbiology from the viewpoint of human health. Body Health II is more of a standard "health" unit (disease prevention, institutional health agencies, and how your body fights disease). Following are units on astronomy (emphasis on telescopes and space exploration) and oceanography. Science and Tomorrow, the ninth unit, then looks at ethical and technical issues in science, while the review unit gives practical applications of the topics studied, from what a libertarian friend of mine likes to call a "statist quo" point of view.

The straight-science units are quite well done. Unlike other workbook-style science programs, the Alpha Omega offerings actually do a good job of blending teaching with experimentation and observation. *Mary Pride*

Alpha Omega Science LIFEPACs

Grades 7–9. LIFEPACs, $3.50 each or set of 10 for $34. Teacher Handbooks (includes two answer keys and test key), $9.95 per course. Complete Boxed set, $41.95 each grade. Elementary Science Kit, $209.95 (includes supplies for middle-grades experiments). Shipping extra.
Specialty items and individual replacement items also available.
Alpha Omega Publications, 300 N. McKemy, Chandler, AZ 85226. Orders and inquiries: (800) 622-3070. Fax: (602) 785-8034. Web: www.home-schooling.com.

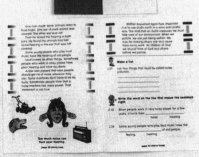

Christian Light Education's General Science course, like other CLE courses, was originally licensed from Alpha Omega Publications. Like the AOP course, it has 10 worktexts (CLE calls theirs "LightUnits").

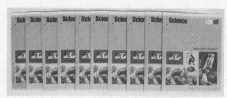

AOP combines their answer keys into one "teacher's guide" volume, while CLE has one answer key for each two LightUnits. The CLE version has heavier-duty kivar covers, brown print, and has been gently edited in conformity with Mennonite beliefs. Not as beautiful as the four-color LIFEPAC Gold Physical Science II/Health edition from Alpha Omega on which it is based, but about $7 less expensive. Also, CLE lets you purchase all the science supplies needed for the experiments either as a kit or individually. Their order form lists science supplies by grade number (in small print, to the right of each alphabetical item), whereas AOP does not offer their own science supplies. *Mary Pride*

Imagine a junior-high *lab* science curriculum for homeschoolers, written by a homeschool dad with B.S. degrees in Biology and Chemistry, an M.S. in Environmental Microbiology, and a Ph.D. in Microbial Ecology. **Rainbow Science** is the curriculum and Durell C. Dobbins is the dad.

Mr. Dobbins is a scientist, but take one look at the lab kit and you know he is at least part engineer as well. The durable materials lab kit comes in a molded transparent plastic case so that every piece of equipment has a place in the kit, and you can immediately see if any piece is missing. The consumables kit is partitioned so that each small bottle of chemicals has a little hole for itself, the batteries have their own place, the styrofoam balls have a compartment, and all the rest fits in the space that remains. The small items all come in a small resealable bag. Everything is easy to find, in a logical place, and should be easy to keep that way.

The list of materials in the lab kit takes up two full pages, so I can't list everything, but here is a sampling: cups of various sizes and configurations (straw in the rim of one, holes in the side of another, etc.), magnifying glass, a steel rod and an aluminum rod, a lab grade thermometer, two small bar magnets, a measuring tape, safety goggles, a baseball, and much, much more.

The consumables package has all the chemicals, batteries, tape, styrofoam balls, balloons, colored dot stickers, felt-tip pen, pencil, etc., you will use up while doing the experiments. The chemicals, measured to the right amounts into individual little bottles, are all common household materials, with the possible exception of potassium chloride and the iron filings. The rest are things like sodium bicarbonate (baking soda), sodium chloride (table salt), acetic acid (contained in vinegar), soil, vegetable oil, shortening, etc.

The flat paper supplies—paper towels, waxed paper, filter paper, tin foil, etc.—are all in the "cardboard protector," a cardboard folder in its own resealable bag. You will also find a game board, a list of the elements, a periodic chart, and the "money" for the game in this packet.

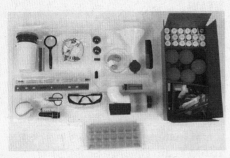

Rainbow Science Curriculum consumable materials

Rainbow Science Curriculum textbooks and study manuals

So the lab kit is great. What about the course that goes with it? The text for the course is designed to cover two years. The Two-Year Text Package includes:

- a 347-page text beautifully illustrated with full-color photos, complete with bibliography, glossary, and index
- comb-bound Teacher's Helper book (only year one so far)
- one page "Parent Fortification" against having your faith wounded by the assertions of modern science. The author sounds like he divides truth into Science and Bible types of truth when he says, "The Scriptures . . . were not intended to be 'scientific,' because they preexisted the discipline of modern science." His basic message, "Don't let your faith rely on the pronouncements of modern science; rely on the word of God," comes through clearly.

The textbook is divided into a Red section for Physics, a Yellow section for Chemistry, and a Blue section for Biology. In Year 1, you cover the red and yellow sections of the textbook. In Year 2, you cover the blue section. Each year provides 32 weeks of science instruction with two textbook lessons and one lab lesson each week—enough for a typical school year, with some weeks off at your discretion. After the blue section, the text contains a rainbow-colored applications section about earth science, weather, and astronomy.

Each lesson of the textbook has a one- or two-page narrative on the day's topic, followed by exercise questions. Every third lesson is a lab. The lab lessons are contained in *The Rainbow Home Laboratory Manual*. Each lab lesson starts with a list of everything you need, then tells the student what experiment or experiments to perform. The author is careful to point out any hazards involved in the experiment and always has "Put on the silly looking glasses from the kit" as step one. If a chart is needed to record the results of the experiment, the chart is supplied.

The teacher's guide lets the teacher know that day's lesson concept, the scientific truth it will illustrate, and any new terminology introduced in this lesson. It also contains an answer key for the exercise questions. Occasionally a lesson will give a suggestion for a field trip to supplement the lesson. For lab lessons, the teachers guide tells what the experiment was about and what should have happened with troubleshooting tips to help your student understand what went wrong if he didn't get the expected result.

This course looks like a winner to me. I highly recommend it as an all-in-one science curriculum for the middle school years. *Bill Pride*

Grade 7 Life Science

BJUP Life Science for Christian Schools

Grade 7. Middle-Grades Science series, $30. Teacher's edition (grade 7), $42.50. Student activities, $13 per grade. Teacher's activities edition, $18.50. Shipping extra. *Bob Jones University Press Customer Services, Greenville, SC 29614. Orders: (800) 845-5731. Fax: (800) 525-8398. Web: www.bjup.com.*

Like A Beka, **BJUP** has a series of three textbooks for middle-school general science. Unlike A Beka, these are separate courses in life science (grade 7), earth science (grade 8), and basic science, e.g., an introduction to physical science (grade 9). All three courses are solidly creationist, richly illustrated, well organized and laid out, and loaded with interesting sidelights and supplemental materials. The teacher's edition for each grade includes a complete student text with special added teacher's notes, provides a master list of materials needed, gives sources for supplemental audiovisual aids, leads the teacher step by step through each chapter with teaching philosophy and methods, and provides answers to the discussion and short-answer questions in the student text. Each teacher's edition comes with a sturdy three-ring binder with labels to identify the subject taught. The teacher's guides are printed on beige paper, so you can easily differentiate between them and the teacher's text in your binder (they fit together in one binder).

In the grade 7 **Life Science for Christian Schools** course, you begin with a Bible-based philosophy of science. The book then gets into classification, cells, creationism, life processes of organisms, and their reproduction. Genetics and evolution are both discussed, followed by a fairly well-balanced unit on ecology.

The only thing wrong with the ecology unit is the usual "Man does this" and "Man must do that" collective emphasis that crops up when discussing it; otherwise, the authors maintain a healthy distance from the eco-hysterics, firmly stating that people have a right to live and work on the earth. Finally the book ends with a section on human anatomy and physiology. The section on transplanted organs in this section unfortunately echoes the secular medical position, which promotes any and all transplants while ignoring the fact that some major organ transplants are taken from persons whose hearts are beating and who are breathing (biblically alive persons, in other words) who have *for the purposes of legally cutting out their essential organs* been labeled "brain dead." This is a major problem, on a par with abortion, that Christian texts have yet to acknowledge or deal with. (It takes up little space in the textbook, but I felt it was important enough to mention.)

The student activity manuals for each grade include experiments, worksheets, reports, and projects. For example, in the life science course you dissect leaves and earthworms, make an insect collection, make observations using a microscope, and make a notebook featuring different kinds of animals, among many other things. *Mary Pride*

Unique among science curricula for homeschoolers, **Lyrical Life Science** teaches through the ear. Students listen to the songs (sung by popular "Songs of the Confederacy and Union Armies" artist Bobby Horton) until they know them by heart. They read the text, which has complete lyrics and music for the songs, plus lots of other background information. Then they fill in the blanks and do the exercises in the workbooks. That's it!

Other educational song tapes are fun, but may spend an entire song teaching one or two words. Textbooks present lots of words and concepts, but tend to be a snore. Lyrical Learning's songs are fun *and* thorough. They pack in tons of terminology, in easy-to-remember fashion.

Each chapter of each volume begins with a song. The tune is borrowed from a song that nearly everyone will already know (example: "Dixie," "If You're Happy and You Know It . . . "), but the new words really pack an educational wallop. Here's an example, "Viruses cause many different infect-ious diseases! Influenza, common colds with fevers, coughs, and sneezes—AAAHHHCHOOO!" (Sing this to the tune of "Yankee Doodle" and see if you can do it without a giggle or two! We couldn't!)

Following this lyrical introduction to the material, the main text continues with several pages of textbook-type information which expands upon and reinforces what the student has learned in the song, and ends with a bibliography of resources for further study and an index. The accompanying workbook tests your student's memorization of the knowledge presented in the chapter. Comprehension of the presented material is evaluated with a set of short essay questions. Your student is then given the chance to apply what he or she has learned in the "Digging Deeper" section. The activities in the Digging Deeper area range from discovering what the difference is between a "theory" and a "law" to reasoning out why you would not

I would definitely urge you to purchase the teacher's editions for each grade along with a student text for your student. The teaching instructions are absolutely excellent— well worth the price—and you need to have the answers in a separate place from the questions.

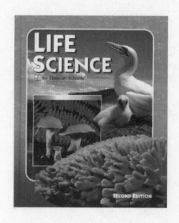

NEW!
Lyrical Life Science, Volumes 1–3

Grades 5–9. Each text/cassette set, $19.95. Each text/cassette/workbook set, $25.50. Add $3 shipping for first set, $1 for each additional. *Lyrical Learning, 8008 Cardwell Hill, Corvalis, OR 97330. Phone/fax: (541) 754-3579.*

likely "find a snake crawling on the snow in Alaska in the winter." Answers to questions are found in the back of each workbook.

Volume 1 of Lyrical Life Science is divided into eleven chapters (The Scientific Method, All Living Things, Invertebrates, Cold-blooded Vertebrates, Birds, Plants, Algae, Fungi and Nonvascular Plants, Vascular Plants, Protozoa, Genetics, Viruses and Bacteria).

The 15 chapters of **Volume 2—Mammals, Ecology, and Biomes** cover Mammals, Monotremes & Marsupials, Carnivores & Pinnapeds, Ungulates, Primates, Rodents, Rodent-Like Mammals, Bats, Insectivores, Toothless Mammals, Whales, Sirenians, Single-Family Orders, Ecology, and Biomes.

Volume 3—The Human Body covers this topic in 13 songs. It includes a song about each major body system: Introduction to the Human Body, Skeletal System, Muscular System, Nervous System, Sensory System, Reproductive System (tastefully done), Digestive System, Excretory System (again, tastefully handled, nothing gross), Circulatory System, Immune & Lymph Systems, Respiratory System, Endocrine System, and an interesting song entitled "Ologies" that teaches what the name of each science is that involves anatomy (histology, cardiology, neurology, etc.).

Memorization of complicated terms and classifications is a very important part of serious science study, but is often considered the most difficult and boring of tasks by students and teachers alike. Hats off to Lyrical Learning for adding some fun to the process—and making it so much easier! *Teresa May and Mary Pride*

Grade 8 Earth Science

BJUP Earth Science for Christian Schools

Grade 8. Middle-Grades Science series, $30. Teacher's edition (grade 8), $42.50. Student activities, $13 per grade. Teacher's activities edition, $19.50. Shipping extra. *Bob Jones University Press Customer Services, Greenville, SC 29614. Orders: (800) 845-5731. Web: www.bjup.com.*

The grade 8 **Earth Science for Christian Schools** text is really about both space and earth science. After the introductory chapter on science and origins it explores the solar system and universe in seven chapters, including a chapter on space exploration. Next the weather sciences, geology, and oceanography are introduced, with chapters on the Bible and geology, minerals, rocks, volcanoes and earthquakes, mountains, weathering/mass-wasting/erosion, groundwater, glaciers, and oceanography. The final chapter challenges students to apply their Christian beliefs in the scientific world, giving a list of specific areas in which Christians can contribute positively to scientific investigations (e.g., new investigations in creationism and new methods for obtaining minerals from seawater). The book is 469 pages in all, including indexes and glossary, but they go by quickly because the text is so interesting and well organized.

The student activity manual includes experiments, worksheets, reports, and projects. In the earth science activity manual a few of the things you do are: draw an ellipse using string and thumb tacks, make a shadow board and record its readings, calculate the distance to the moon using your own homemade equipment, and write an essay on the uniformitarian theory of geology.

I would definitely urge you to purchase the teacher's edition along with a student text for your student. The teaching instructions are absolutely excellent—well worth the price—and you need to have the answers in a separate place from the questions. *Mary Pride*

Just what the world has been waiting for—an astronomy trivia game. Lots you never knew about comets, meteors, and other relatively small denizens of the sky. The 54 playing cards each include a question, answer, and informative paragraph as well as (aren't they tricky!) a list of *possible* answers to questions on other cards. You can guess and bluff, but you do better if you really know something. **Good Heavens** also includes a 24-page booklet with tips on celestial observation that introduces you to "the solar system's minor members." Evolutionary viewpoint. *Mary Pride*

Janice VanCleave's A+ Projects for Young Adults series so far includes three titles: *Biology, Chemistry,* and *Earth Science.* According to the author herself, there is hope for a *Physics* volume as well, sometime in the reasonably near future.

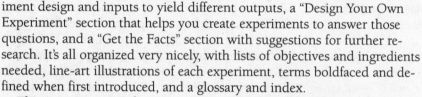

Each book has the same subtitle: "Winning Experiments for Science Fairs and Extra Credit." All books have the same format. First, you are given insider advice on picking and arranging a science fair project. Then you are given 30 topics related to the book's academic area. Each topic comes with one simple "cookbook" experiment, a set of questions about how you can vary the experiment design and inputs to yield different outputs, a "Design Your Own Experiment" section that helps you create experiments to answer those questions, and a "Get the Facts" section with suggestions for further research. It's all organized very nicely, with lists of objectives and ingredients needed, line-art illustrations of each experiment, terms boldfaced and defined when first introduced, and a glossary and index.

This is not a series of weenie experiments. The **Earth Science** book, for example, is divided into these parts: Mapping the Earth, The Earth & Space, Physical Composition of the Earth, The Earth's Lithosphere, The Earth's Hydrosphere, and The Earth's Atmosphere. Some of the chapter topics include heliocentrism, layering of regolith particles, the hydrologic cycle, and hygrometers. The nomenclature may be scary, but here's where Mrs. VanCleave's genius appears. By the time you've finished each chapter introduction, you will actually understand what the chapter title means and what you're about to do!

No complicated or expensive equipment is required for the experiments. For Earth Science, this is fine, since it is usually a middle-school subject and colleges aren't expecting a serious lab component. Without a doubt, you'll learn more earth science from this helpful book than from most pricey textbooks. The book meets and exceeds its stated purpose: to help you understand earth science and come up with good science fair ideas. *Mary Pride*

Latch on to an issue of **Sky & Telescope** magazine and you'll have *no* trouble locating astronomy books and supplies. The ads are often worth more than the articles in a publication of this sort, leading you on to dazzling vistas and brilliant ideas that you would never have discovered on your own. The magazine itself is not overly glitzy; it just has a good mix of readable technical articles, a mixture of spectacular black-and-white and full-color photos, reviews of telescopes and accessories, and a detailed calendar of celestial happenings to watch for. Amateur astronomers do occasionally make serious discoveries, it turns out, and this is certainly the magazine for the serious amateur. *Mary Pride*

The Weather Book

Grade 7–adult. $20 plus shipping.
*Order Entry Dept., Random House,
Inc., 400 Hahn Rd., Westminster, MD
21157. (800) 726-0600 ext. 3700.
Fax: (800) 659-2436.
Web: www.randomhouse.com.*

Packed with many illustrations, **The Weather
Book** struts the talents of the *USA Today* staff.
Impressive 3-D style illustrations, and equally impressive photographs, leap out at you from every
page. The feature writers gave it their best shot,
too, with lucid descriptions of every weather fact
you're likely to ever need, plus lots of human interest stories about people who fool around with
weather.

The good-looking magazine-style table of contents really tries hard to sell you on the book,
with chapter titles such as "The USA's Wild Weather." Other chapters include *How the Sun causes weather, Why the winds blow, Storms and fronts,
What makes rain?, Floods and droughts, Snow and ice, Thunderstorms and tornadoes, Sky watching, How to predict the weather,* and *The future of Earth.*

Appendices include state-by-state records for extreme weather, a glossary, and an index. *Mary Pride*

Grade 9 Physical Science

"Matter" is the theme of the entire ninth-grade **Basic Science for
Christian Schools** course. Units are: What Matters to the Christian, A
Description of Matter, The Structure of Matter, The Chemistry of Matter, the
Motion of Matter, The Energy of Matter, The Energy of Waves, and Some
Matters of Technology. "Christian Men of Science" sections dotted here and
there cover Lord Kelvin, Robert Boyle, Johannes Kepler, Michael Faraday,
Samuel F. B. Morse, James Clark Maxwell, and Sir John Ambrose Fleming.
"Facets of Basic Science" sidebars introduce interesting topics like space
stations and how air vehicles fly. Lots of cartoons, graphics, and photos.
Environmental issues are raised throughout the book as examples of scientific areas requiring moral decision-making. To BJUP's credit, though they
mistakenly repeat the collective-stewardship terminology that has become
popular, they stress the importance of technological answers that meet people's needs. Consider this your basic intro to high school science.

BJUP Basic Science for Christian Schools

Grade 9. Middle-Grades Science
series, $30. Teacher's edition
(grade 9), $42.50. Student activities,
$13 per grade. Teacher's activities
edition, $16.50. Shipping extra.
*Bob Jones University Press Customer
Services, Greenville, SC 29614.
Orders: (800) 845-5731. Fax: (800)
525-8398. Web: www.bjup.com.*

The student activity manual includes experiments, worksheets, reports,
and projects. The investigations in the basic science course are more difficult to do at home, as many of them involve observing a teacher working
with specialized equipment and chemicals. "Observe closely as your
teacher demonstrates the electrolysis of water" is not quite the same as performing an experiment yourself.

I would definitely urge you to purchase the teacher's editions for each
grade along with a student text for your student. The teaching instructions
are absolutely excellent—well worth the price—and you need to have the
answers in a separate place from the questions. *Mary Pride*

NEW
School of Tomorrow Physical Science

Grades 9–12. Workbooks and score
keys, $4 each. Additional activity
pacs, $2.80 each. Each set of 2
videos is $55 to purchase. Video
rental options: $74.95 per quarter to
keep worktexts and scorekeys and
rent 6 videos, or $59.95 per quarter
to rent the videos only. Optional

School of Tomorrow has courses in Physical Science, Biology,
Chemistry, and Physics that you can use three ways:

- Watch the videos together as a family. Thanks to the TV-quality production, even little kids will gladly watch the Physical
  Science and Biology tapes, thereby getting a real head start on
  the science concepts and terminology they will later encounter
  in formal courses. Everything possible is done to illustrate
  what you are learning. If you are studying birds, for example,
  you will see dozens of examples of different varieties of birds
  in real-world settings—so instead of just learning "bird anato-

my" from diagrams, you see a duck's webbed feet as he walks and swims, a heron's long, sticklike toes, and so forth. It's like watching a TV nature special, only *without* the evolutionary content and *with* well-organized learning units, labs, and accompanying worktexts.

- Use the worktexts and videos together as a formal high-school-level course. The material is presented carefully, thoroughly, and entertainingly, plus there are "labs" on the videos so you can see experiments in action, whether or not you choose to duplicate them at home.
- Go the computer route. This option allows the computer to control the video, and provides you with interactive exercises as well.

Character lessons and creationism are built into these series, as are vignettes from the history of science. The Physics series, for example, includes Thales and a plethora of other ancient Greeks, plus Galileo, Newton, Kepler, Boyle, Benjamin Franklin, and Maxwell.

Each course has 12 workbooks and 4 score keys. Workbooks include both the colorful teaching text and a pull-out "activity pac" that includes all the fill-in exercises and student work. Additional activity pacs are available for a bit less than a complete new workbook, but personally I don't see the point of saving a few pennies and making all the kids share the outer text pages. Each course has two optional videos per workbook, for 24 videos in all per course. Each course has 12 optional computer disks, available in your choice of low-density or high-density for PCs only. To use the disks, you'll need the CVI upgrade kit or their computer with CVI built in. With the CVI option, you watch the videos lesson by lesson and the computer automatically asks questions and grades student answers at the appropriate spots.

We tried using the **Physical Science** course with five of our children at once. The fifth- and sixth-grader weren't quite up to the level of study skills needed to follow and take notes on the videos, but the older kids had no trouble. For younger children, I'd suggest just watching the videos together as a fine preparation for their future junior-high and high-school science studies.

This entire science series deserve a five-heart rating. It's the easiest to use, most exciting, best organized, and most thorough high-school science curriculum I have yet seen. *Mary Pride*

The two **Physical Science** courses available from **University of Nebraska-Lincoln Independent Study** are true correspondence courses. What makes them special? Complete lab supply packages are available for each course! This is a huge time-saver. Too, the fact that you took your lab science courses from a fully accredited correspondence program operated by a state university can't hurt when you send in your college applications.

As with all correspondence programs, you send in papers and tests (fax and email options are now available for quicker service), which are graded and returned to your "local supervisor." This person can not be a family member without special permission. He is responsible for proctoring closed-book tests and receiving correspondence from UNL. He is also supposed to supervise the coursework and make sure you stay on track. If you are not interested in the correspondence option, in other words you just want the course materials, you don't need a local supervisor. As a compromise, UNL will send course materials directly to the student, only requiring that tests be proctored by an "approved person," which can include a librarian (we all go the library, don't we?).

You find your assignments in the course syllabus. You then read the assigned textbook pages, write the answers and essays in the syllabus, do the projects (complete lab supplies are available for both Physical Science courses), and take the pretests. There is a lot of study and writing; these are not Mickey Mouse courses. Although you are allowed to finish a course fairly swiftly (in as little as three weeks, with special permission), in real life a semester course takes about a semester to finish.

Our oldest son took both of UN-L's Physical Science courses, and pronounced them "pretty interesting." Which, from him, is a huge round of applause. *Mary Pride*

Smaller print and bigger words than other Usborne books this size, and lots more "real" science (including math), make it clear the **Usborne Starting Science series** is aimed at the junior-high and high-school crowd. The terrific, detailed illustrations make it clear that kids will read it. Parents, too.

If it's possible to explain science or engineering principles with full-color drawing, you can bet it's been done in these 32-page, double-page-spread format books. Whether you're looking at pictures of the combustion cycle or 3-D illustrations of a battery-powered electrical circuit, there's always enough detail to show how it works and enough lush eye candy (highlights, textures, blends) to make the pictures pretty. Each book ends with a glossary and index.

Books in this series include:

- **Machines**: the basic physics of how machine parts work, engines (including the internal combustion engine), flying machines, floating machines, space rockets, time-telling devices, robots, and lots more. For each machine type, again you're told how it works, e.g., how does water hold a ship up? How do propellers move a ship? How can submarines rise and dive? Consider this an introduction to mechanical engineering for the young and young at heart.
- **Atoms and Molecules**: history of atomic theory, parts of an atom, energy of the electron, the nucleus of an atom, the elements (stuff that is made up of atoms of the same type), mixtures and compounds, how molecules move, polymers, the periodic table, electricity, radiation, nuclear reactions, uses of radioactivity, quantum theory, and unusual particles. You could consider this a mini introduction to chemistry, as all these topics are covered in much more detail (with many fewer helpful visuals) in any high-school chemistry course.
- **Electricity and Magnetism**: electrical energy, static electricity, thunder and lightning, magnetism, magnetic compasses, cells and batteries, electric circuits, resistance, heat and light, electromagnetism, electric motors, generators, transformers, and electricity in the future. Includes a number of simple experiments you can do with batteries, wire, and household ingredients, plus additional fun facts about everything from fish that generate electricity to electric cars.
- **Astronomy**: looking at the night sky, the solar system, the sun, the planets one by one, comets and meteoroids, the Milky Way and beyond, the Big Bang theory, telescopes, how to become an amateur or professional astronomer, a very brief history of astronomy, and speculation about the future of astronomy. Great illustrations, as usual, with just a few actual space photos thrown in.

These are fine books to get you started. Recommended. *Mary Pride*

CHAPTER 21

Biology

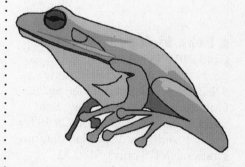

Q: Who first said, "The proper study of mankind is man?" (This is another trick question.)
A: A frog waiting to be dissected in biology class!

If that makes your flesh crawl, I'm with you! I refused to take biology in high school just so no frogs would have to die on *my* account.

Today, thanks to plastic models and dissection simulations in software, no frogs must die. In fact, most current biology texts spend more time poking around cells than messing with frogs and other animals visible to the naked eye. We are the DNA Generation, comin' at ya, goin' strong. With all the excitement about genetic engineering, naturally biology textbooks feel they have to cover the topic to some extent.

Biology is also the class where students typically learn about the birds and the bees, leading up to a discussion of human reproduction presented with all the charm of assembling a paper box. "Put Tab A into Slot B and out comes a baby." My personal feeling is that, since humans aren't animals except according to Linnaeus's classification scheme, human sexuality belongs under Marriage and Family Life, where it can be placed in context with all the emotional and spiritual commitment that should go with it.

Secular biology texts tend to be packed with:

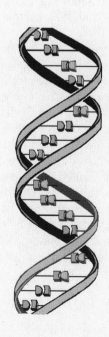

- Disproved evolutionary "facts," such as the hoary old idea that the embryo passes through evolutionary stages, from fishlike creature with gills to human. No respectable geneticist holds this view; Ernst Haeckl, the man on whose work the theory was based, faked his data.
- A basically evolutionary "cell-to-man" approach, with far more emphasis on the cells than the men, and almost none at all on plants and animals.
- An approach to human reproduction that focuses more often than not on how to *prevent* it, with no mention of marriage as even a factor in the decision to have sex and/or reproduce.

All the above, plus the deliberately opaque writing method favored by textbook authors, tends to make secular texts unacceptable to most homeschoolers. Unfortunately, *this is the material that college placement tests cover.* From the SAT II to the AP to the CLEP, they will all expect you to be up on evolutionary terminology and super-saturated in genetics, reproduction, and the parts of the cell. So if you use a resource, such as A Beka's excellent biology text, that actually teaches you what you might need to know about plants, animals, anatomy, and what you might call "everyday biology," you might *flunk* a college placement test, like the son of a friend of ours did. After this debacle, our friend bought the young man a biology book from the bookstore and had him study that, after which he passed the test with a very high score.

The moral is this:

- If you don't plan to go to college, and want to learn useful biology, or your religious convictions make you unhappy about being forced to study evolutionary theories and sociological sexuality, go ahead and use whatever biology resource suits you best.
- If you plan to go to college, you may in fact use a Christian text to prepare you, but you should plan on supplementing with books that reflect what the public schools teach and the placement tests test.

Biology Curriculum

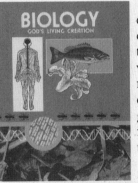

A Beka's enormous Biology text (649 pages!) is quite different from other biology courses. Instead of introducing science topics with philosophy and theory, **Biology: God's Living Creation** starts with the concrete (plants, animals, etc.) and then moves to theory. Again, instead of following an evolutionary sequence (enzymes, to cells, to single-celled organisms, to invertebrates, to fish, etc.) it presents the created world in the order traditionally followed by naturalists.

For example, in the Botany section, students first learn about the familiar flowering-seed plants, then leaf structure and function, flowers/fruits/seeds, stems and roots, and finally less well-known plant varieties. Human anatomy is studied before zoology, and familiar animals are studied before the less familiar animals. In this way, A Beka hopes to avoid the conflict caused by teaching creation science along with evolutionary classification categories.

Other features: a built-in set of transparent overlays of the human body, to aid in detailed study of body structures and organs. Easy-to-follow outline format with distinctive typefaces for sections, subsections, etc. Frequent sidebars on "Wonders of the Living Creation" draw attention to God and the marvelous way in which He made things. Lots of excellent drawings, photos, graphs, and charts, many in full color, explain difficult concepts.

The book is divided into logical sections: botany, human anatomy and physiology, life science methodology and philosophy, zoology, and cellular and molecular biology. The subsections are equally well organized. For example, under Zoology you find chapters on mammals, birds, reptiles and amphibians, fish, arthropods (invertebrates with jointed feet), and a final chapter on less-familiar invertebrates. The chapter on less-familiar invertebrates includes sections on mollusks, echinoderms and rotifers, hollow-intestined invertebrates, worms of various types, and single-celled protozoa. Underneath the section on mollusks you find subsections on bivalves (two-shelled mollusks), gastropods (stomach-footed mollusks), and cephalopods (head-foot mollusks). The subsection on bivalves is divided up into series of para-

A Beka Biology

Grade 10. Biology text (paperbound), $30.20. Teacher's guide, $20.20. Student test booklet, $6.20. Quiz booklet, $4.60. Biology field and lab manual, $12.45 or $20.45 for teacher's edition. Video lab demonstrations (VHS only), $150.20. Biology transparencies available for school classrooms. Shipping extra. *A Beka Book, Box 19100, Pensacola, FL 32523-9100. (800) 874-2352. Fax: (800) 874-3590. Web: www.abeka.com.*

Like other A Beka science books, *Biology: God's Living Creation* is like a cross between an encyclopedia and a regular textbook. The contents are accompanied by as much detailed information and as many visual aids as you could expect to find in an expensive encyclopedia—from a Christian viewpoint, which you wouldn't find in the encyclopedia. Unlike the elementary-grade A Beka books, the textbook information is extremely well organized, making it easy to digest and remember.

graphs, each introduced with a word in boldface. The topics in boldface are shells, locomotion, feeding and respiration, other systems, and edible bivalves. Accompanying the pages on bivalves are a list of study objectives for the section, a three-part line drawing of how clams move about, a beautiful full-color "Anatomy of a Clam" illustration, a photograph of underseas clam shells, and a gorgeous full-page full-color picture of 59 shell types, each numbered, with the name of each given on the side.

I gave this one example to show how well organized the information in this book is, from the section level right down to the paragraph level. The study objectives for each chapter section make it a breeze to learn and review the information. The gorgeous visual aids tempt you to linger over each topic. The fascinating sidebars don't detract from the main text (as so often happens), but rather complement it. Altogether, an excellent job.

A biology course is, of course, more than just the student textbook. A Beka also offers a teacher's edition that includes the full student text as well as a scope and sequence, daily lesson plans, demonstration ideas, chapter summaries, and teaching strategies. The *Field and Laboratory Manual* is also available in both student's and teacher's editions, and includes complete instructions for completing 27 labs and three special projects. *Mary Pride*

Alpha Omega's 10th-grade **Biology LIFEPACs** come to you as a set of 10 workbooks with the lesson text, exercises, and tests all built in. The design of these LIFEPACs is easy to use, with frequent teacher checkpoints and student experiments right in the book. Here's what you get:

- Taxonomy: The Key to Organization—introduction to classifications and creationism, including the history of taxonomy
- Basis of Life—elements, molecules, chemical reactions, organic compounds, and enzymes
- Microbiology—microscopy techniques and various little beasties of importance to scientists
- Cells—what are they made of and how do they act?
- Plants: Green Factories—structure and growth of plants
- Human Anatomy and Physiology—including a *very* restrained explanation of human reproduction that manages not to refer to the sex act at all (instead we hear about eggs, sperm, and the changes pregnancy causes to a woman's body)
- God's Plan for Inheritance—genetics
- Cell Division and Reproduction—asexual and sexual reproduction in cells, plants, and animals
- Ecology, Pollution, and Energy
- Principles and Applications of Biologists

Units 1–8 are really good, super easy to use, and free of trendy new-agey doctrine. Units 9 and 10 in a previous version suffered from uncritically quoting environmentalist doctrine. The publisher assures us that these problems have been addressed. *Mary Pride*

Biology the Easy Way is an even-handed, secular treatment of the material usually covered in a good high-school biology course. Starting in the typical fashion with cellular biology, it doesn't waste the student's whole time on microscopic particles—a common error of many recent biology texts. There's a good section on zoology, a little botany, and one chapter each for nutrition, diseases and immune system, and heredity and genetics. The book winds up with one chapter each on ecology and evolution, rather than riddling the rest of the text with references to these topics.

If you think it would be too complicated to actually get the equipment and materials and work through the labs, A Beka has even provided video labs with step-by-step demonstrations of the dissections and biochemical labs in the *Field and Laboratory Manual*. The video lab might be a wise purchase for those with little time or storage space, since the list of required equipment and materials to do all the labs runs on for pages. If you *do* want to work through the labs, much of this material and equipment is available from the sources in Chapter 27. To be even more specific: if you are willing to really put the time into working through this entire biology book, especially as a two-year course, and have a number of children to whom you plan to teach this course (either all at once or one by one), it would indeed be worthwhile to get the equipment and do all the excellent labs and projects. If you simply want to teach the lab techniques and concepts, even though the video lab initially seems expensive you will save a lot of time and money by purchasing it.

Alpha Omega Biology LIFEPACs

Grade 10. Complete boxed set (including answer key), $41.95. LIFEPACs $3.50 each or set of 10 for $34. Teacher Handbook, $9.95. Elementary Science Kit, $209.95 (includes most specialized biological lab equipment and supplies needed for the lab experiments). Shipping extra.
Alpha Omega Publications, 300 N. McKemy, Chandler, AZ 85226. Orders and inquiries: (800) 622-3070. Fax: (480) 785-8034. Web: www.home-schooling.com.

NEW!
Biology the Easy Way, Second Edition

Grades 9–12. $12.95 plus shipping.
Barron's Educational Series, Inc., 250 Wireless Blvd., Hauppauge, NY 11788. (800) 645-3476. Fax: (516) 434-3217. Web: www.barronseduc.com.

If you've been using a Christian biology text, you might well want to invest in this book, because those topics are tested frequently and often in college entrance tests. Lots of explanations, illustrations, exercises on terminology and concepts, and review tests are included.

Barron's guarantees that this book will improve your grades in 30 days, or you can return it to them for a full refund. *Mary Pride*

BJUP Biology for Christian Schools

Grade 10. Student text, $32. Teacher's edition, $42.50. Biology lab manual, $13. Teacher's Lab Manual, $19.50. Shipping extra. *Bob Jones University Press Customer Services, Greenville, SC 29614. Orders: (800) 845-5731. Fax: (800) 525-8398. Web: www.bjup.com.*

The lab manual was not laid out as well for home use as others I have seen, nor was the visual format as easy to follow. Organizing your lab materials could be a challenge, too, especially if you're trying to live without the teacher's lab manual, which has better-organized materials lists. BJUP sells most of the needed supplies; you can ask for their separate Science Supplies catalog or, even better, get the BJU Grade 10 order form from Home Training Tools. See HTT's writeup in chapter 27.

If you have a fundamentalist/evangelical point of view and want to find answers in controversial areas like eugenics, drugs, abortion, miracles, euthanasia, homosexuality, genetic engineering, AIDS, animal rights, and so on, as well as the normal 10th-grade biology topics, **BJUP** has a book for you. It's a hefty 739 pages, but the pages are smaller than those of A Beka's biology text. To save money, you can get the teacher's edition: it includes all the material in the student text, plus teacher's note and answers to the problems.

Biology for Christian Schools follows the normal public-school textbook sequence, though with a Christian twist. First comes a section on life itself—its chemistry, structure, continuity, and history—all from a creationist viewpoint. Next, the unit entitled "Biology: The Science of Organisms" follows the usual simplest-to-most-complex sequence found in secular biology texts. First there's a chapter on classification techniques. You then start off with bacteria, viruses, and other teeny-tiny organisms; move on to protozoa and algae; follow up with fungi; then move to the plant kingdom, and the animal kingdom. Animals are covered in four chapters: one each for invertebrates, arthropods, vertebrates, and mammals and birds, in that order. Finally man himself is studied: his anatomy, body systems, and spiritual responsibilities for medical and physical decisions.

The accompanying lab manual not only introduces lab techniques and provides assignments, but even has space for writing the answers and making your lab drawings. Some of the experiments involve feeding one critter to another, bothering a critter, opening an incubated egg, or even dissecting a live critter (an anesthetized earthworm, in this case). You'll be spending a lot of time making and observing microscope slides, dissecting, and testing your own and other people's bodily functions and reactions. *Mary Pride*

NEW!
Castle Heights Experiences in Biology

Grades 9–12. Lab Manual, $24.95. Student Data Book, $9.95. Shipping extra. *Castle Heights Press, Inc., 2578 Alexander Farms Dr., Marietta, GA 30064. (800) 763-7148. Fax/Phone: (770) 218-7998. Email: julicher@aol.com. Web: www.flash.net/~wx3o/chp.*

You can't get a school much smaller than a homeschool. Most of us don't have the means to get all the necessary equipment to set up a conventional high school biology lab. Often, we try to modify traditional laboratory experiments to suit our needs. This takes time and effort, especially if you don't have a strong background in science. Castle Heights Press has scaled down a solid biology lab program to suit the needs and the budgets of homeschoolers.

If the words *classification, osmosis,* and *transect* make you nervous, **Castle Heights Experiences in Biology** lab manual will calm your fears. While the vocabulary may be new and challenging for you and your child, Kathleen Julicher's clear, precise writing will make understanding respiration as easy as breathing. She believes that, "The heart of the scientist is built by observing life." Your student will grasp the precepts of biology through activities, and learn the language of the scientist by using it.

The author divides the manual into five sections: Zoology (including observation and dissection), Human Anatomy and Physiology, Cellular Biology, Botany, and Ecology. Most of the experiments are in Zoology and Botany. Each experiment includes a list of materials, step by step procedures, and specific questions and guidelines for writing a report.

Line drawings accompany dissection instructions. The anatomical parts for each animal are well-labeled. Dissection of the earthworm, for instance, includes several drawings of cross-sections, external views, and a cut-away of the digestive system. You will identify the parts in stages, enter your own drawings in your notebook, and answer the questions provided. The questions are often essay questions, such as, "Describe the method of locomotion of the earthworm. Where would the worm's muscles used to do this be located? Are they there? (Look at your worm.) How are they oriented? In what direction is their motion?"

The companion notebook gives you plenty of space to record data and make sketches. The preformatted charts and graphs make reporting your results easy, and set a good example for future reporting.

This lab guide will provide your child with a good, solid lab experience, comparable to a large high school program. *Macbeth Derham*

Christian Light Education's Biology course, like other CLE courses, was originally licensed from Alpha Omega Publications. Like the AOP course, it has 10 worktexts (CLE calls theirs "LightUnits"). AOP combines their answer keys into one "teacher's guide" volume, while CLE has one answer key for each two LightUnits.

The CLE version has heavier-duty kivar covers, brown print, a lower price, and has been gently edited in conformity with Mennonite beliefs. Not as beautiful as the four-color LIFEPAC Gold edition from Alpha Omega, but somewhat more balanced in its tone, in my view.

CLE lets you purchase all the science supplies needed for the experiments either as a kit or individually. Their order form lists science supplies by grade number (in small print, to the right of each alphabetical item). I find their order form much easier to use than other curriculum providers, though you can also order from Home Training Tools, if you wish. *Mary Pride*

Cliffs Quick Review: Microbiology goes in great detail into the only biology that high-school curriculum writers seem to care about anymore. In its 243 pages, you'll learn about:

- Overview and brief history of microbiology
- The chemical basis of microbiology (not to fear—these are your basic simple atoms, molecules, acids, bases, and the like)
- Microscopy (techniques for spotting and staining the wee beasties)
- Prokaryotes (beasties wi' nae nuclei) and eukaryotes (beasties wi' nuclei)
- Microbial metabolism, or how the other 99 percent live
- Microbial cultivation and growth (the care and feeding of small yukky things)
- Control of microbial growth (in which we learn how to employ physical methods, chemical methods, and antibiotics to slow 'em down or kill 'em dead)

This is not a find-everything-you-need-in-the-kitchen type manual. Depending on which 15 of the 34 experiments you choose to do, you may need to have access to a good microscope (essential for any high school bio lab). You must also purchase some stains, animals for dissection, and some glassware (slides, etc.). Most of these items won't set you back too much, and Home Training Tools offers lab kits specific to this manual (see Chapter 27).

NEW!
Christian Light Education Biology
Grade 10. Set of 10 LightUnits, $22.90. Set of 5 Answer Keys, $11.45. 10th Grade Unit Science Kit, $112. High-School Microscope, $188. Shipping extra.
Christian Light Education, PO Box 1212, Harrisonburg, VA 22801-1212. (540) 434-1003. Fax: (540) 433-8896. Email: orders@clp.org.

NEW!
Cliffs Quick Review series: Microbiology
High school. $9.95
Cliffs Notes, Inc., PO Box 80728, Lincoln, NE 68501. (800) 228-4078. Fax: (800) 826-6831. Web: www.cliffs.com.

I hope this doesn't say something strange about me, but I liked this book. It covers a huge amount of information quite well. Students who are thinking about going into medicine, nursing, or biology will find it quite a help, as will parents who want to know what all those magazine articles and medical thrillers are about.

- Microbial genetics (very helpful in understanding Robin Cook's medical murder mysteries)
- Types of bacteria
- Types of viruses, viral structure, and viral cultivation
- Types of fungi
- Unicellular algae
- Protozoa
- Host-parasite relationship
- Development of infectious disease
- Non-specific body defense and the immune system
- Disorders of the immune system
- Diseases of the skin and eyes, the nervous system, the cardiovascular and lymphatic systems, the respiratory system, the digestive system, and the reproductive system
- Aquatic microbiology (keeping them out of what you drink)
- Soil microbiology (the farmer's friend)
- Food microbiology (or, "What died in the refrigerator?")
- Industrial microbiology (or, "How to make money from bacteria in the privacy of your lab")

That's it: no appendices, extra charts, glossary, or index.

Although a few line-art illustrations are included, words make up the vast majority of this book. That's fine with me. The basic microbiology text you'll be using, whatever it is, will have plenty of eye candy (if you can call photos of diseased tissue "eye candy"). This book is about putting it all together in a small package and having it make sense. *Mary Pride*

NEW!
Janice VanCleave's A+ Projects in Biology

Grades 7–12. Each book, $12.95.
John Wiley & Sons, 1 Wiley Drive, Somerset, NJ 08875. (800) 225-5945. (732) 469-4400. Fax: (800) 597-3299. Web: www.wiley.com.

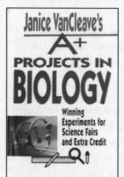

Janice VanCleave's A+ Projects for Young Adults series includes a **Biology** book, divided into three parts: botany, zoology, and the human body. Some of the 30 chapter titles under "botany" include: "Cell Homeostasis: A Steady State," "Apical Dominance: Growth Inhibitor," and "Geotropism: Plant Movement Due to Gravity." The titles may be scary, but here's where Mrs. VanCleave's genius appears. By the time you've finished each chapter introduction, you will actually understand what the chapter title means and what you're about to do! (For more info, see the series review under "Earth Science" in the Junior High Science chapter.)

No complicated or expensive equipment is required for the experiments. This means that, while you will learn a *lot* if you do all the experiments, instead of just picking one for a science fair, it might not sufficiently impress college officials to count as the "lab" portion of a science course. However, the book meets and exceeds its stated purpose: to help you understand the subject and come up with good science fair ideas. *Mary Pride*

NEW!
Schaum's Outline Series and Solved Problems Series: Biological Sciences

Grade 9–college. Biology, $14.95 (888 solved problems). Zoology, $13.95 (1050 solved problems). Biochemistry, $16.95 (830 solved problems). Organic Chemistry, $14.95 (1806 solved problems). Genetics, $14.95 (209 solved problems). Human Anatomy & Physiology, $13.95 (1470 solved

Think your life is full of problems now? Just wait until you get ahold of these books!

Schaum's approach in its **"Outlines" series** is to give you a mess of carefully solved problems, in the logical order in which such problems come up in a course, as well as some instruction in the subject. Generally problems outweigh instruction by about 4 to 1. Schaum's **"Solved Problems" series** is nothing but solved problems.

With this approach, a logically-organized table of contents and complete index are a must, and Schaum's has them. Diagrams, charts, and other illustrations also help, and these oversized books have them, too.

In all, the various series, which cover everything from English grammar to foreign languages to advanced science and engineering, include 147 books which between them have sold over 30 million copies, thus averaging about 200,000 copies sold of each book. That's a lot of desperate students who need help!

Use these books to help you with your homework, or "unlock" a type of problem you just don't get, but please do try to *understand* the answers. Otherwise, you'll only be cheating yourself. *Mary Pride*

The **School of Tomorrow Biology** course has 12 workbooks and 4 score keys. Workbooks include both the colorful teaching text and a pull-out "activity pac" that includes all the fill-in exercises and student work. Additional activity pacs are available for

a bit less than a complete new workbook, but personally I don't see the point of saving a few pennies and making all the kids share the outer text pages. Each course has two optional videos per workbook, for 24 videos in all per course. Each course has 12 optional computer disks, available in your choice of low-density or high-density for PCs only. To use the disks, you'll need the CVI upgrade kit or their computer with CVI built in. With the CVI option, you watch the videos lesson by lesson and the computer automatically asks questions and grades student answers at the appropriate spots.

While this course is *very* complete in the subjects it covers, you will have to supplement with studies of evolutionary dogma in order to score well on college entrance and achievement tests.

The last two tapes on the Biology series sadly partake of eco-hysteria, with phrases such as "airborne pollution is slowly suffocating us" and uncritical promotion of every environmental bogeyman, from acid rain to ozone depletion, from the idea that fertilizer and pesticides have "contaminated" virtually all U.S. farmland to the notion that government regulations are the sole solution to all environmental problems. I'd supplement that last Biology unit with the book *Facts not Fear,* reviewed in the Ecology chapter.

That last Biology unit aside, this is a really fun, inspiring, and academically thorough course. *Mary Pride*

I explained how the **Standard Deviants Video Series** works in the Basic Math chapter—and why it has nothing to do with "deviants" and everything to do with "deviating from the standard," i.e. how to become a curve-wrecker (a grade A student, to those of you who never took statistics). These fun videos demystify the "tough" subjects for college students . . . and smart high-school students, too!

Available for biology is an Edited For All Audiences video, **The Dissected World of Biology**. As is often the case in biology courses these days, this is mostly microbiology—noth-

problems). 3000 Solved Problems in Biology, out of print. 3000 Solved Problems in Organic Chemistry, $27.95. Shipping extra.
McGraw-Hill, Order Services, PO Box 545, Blacklick, OH 43004-0545. (800) 338-3987. Fax: (614) 755-5645.
Web: www.mhhe.com.

NEW
School of Tomorrow Biology
Grades 9–12. Workbooks, $4 each. Score keys, $4 each. Additional activity pacs are $2.80 each. Each set of 2 videos is $55 to purchase. Video rental options: $74.95 per quarter to keep worktexts and scorekeys and rent 6 videos, or $59.95 per quarter to rent the videos only. Optional computer disks, $7.25 each. CVI upgrade kit, $780. Shipping extra.
School of Tomorrow, PO Box 299000, Lewisville, TX 75029-9904. Orders: (800) 925-7777. Inquiries: (972) 315-1776. Fax: (972) 315-2862.
Email: info@schooloftomorrow.com.
Web: www.schooloftomorrow.com.

NEW!
The Standard Deviants Biology Videos
High school and college level. Video, $19.99. Shipping extra.
Cerebellum Corporation, 2890 Emma Lee St., Falls Church, VA 22042. (800) 238-9669. Inquiries: (703) 848-0856. Fax: (703) 848-0857.
Web: www.cerebellum.com.
Direct mail sales are not available.

ing you can actually dissect!). In just two hours, you cover genes, atoms, protons, electrons, neutrons, covalents bonds, polarity, ions . . . Wait a minute! Isn't this supposed to be a *biology* video? Yup, you get stuck with introductory chemistry when you take the "molecules to man" route. Pressing on, you tackle proteins, DNA, RNA, everything you ever wanted to know about cell anatomy and behavior, then on to plants and a tiny bit on animals and people. Exactly the stuff covered in college achievement tests.

Moral: if you want to use a Christian biology course, but still do well on the SAT II or AP, then a close encounter with this tape is probably the least painful way to fill the bill. *Mary Pride*

University of Nebraska-Lincoln Independent Study offers **Biology** courses as well.

As with all correspondence programs, you send in papers and tests (fax and email options are now available for quicker service), which are graded and returned to your "local supervisor." This person can not be a family member without special permission. He is responsible for proctoring closed-book tests and receiving correspondence from UNL. He is also supposed to supervise the coursework and make sure you stay on track. If you are not interested in the correspondence option, in other words you just want the course materials, you don't need a local supervisor. As a compromise, UNL will send course materials directly to the student, only requiring that tests be proctored by an "approved person," which can include a librarian (we all go the library, don't we?).

You find your assignments in the course syllabus. You then read the assigned textbook pages, write the answers and essays in the syllabus, do the projects, and take the pretests. There is a lot of study and writing; these are not Mickey Mouse courses. Although you are allowed to finish a course fairly swiftly (in as little as three weeks, with special permission), in real life a semester course takes about a semester to finish.

Biology 1 is mainly cell biology. It includes five assignments (sections of work to complete and send in) and three exams. The text is *Living Things* from Holt, Rinehart and Winston (1985 edition). **Biology 2** continues with the same text, covering classification of living things, characteristics of plant and animal kingdoms, some human anatomy and physiology, and nutrition, drugs, and disease. Neither course includes lab materials.

Biology 3 (otherwise known as Advanced Biology) covers the same topics as Biology 1 and 2, but this is a lab science course. The text is *Biology: A Systems Approach* (Addison-Wesley, 1988). Separate kits are available for students using microscopes and students not using microscopes.

All courses have evolutionary outlook and present typical public-school treatment of lifestyle topics. *Mary Pride*

EDC Publishing has introductions to electronics, chemistry, biology, and physics that actually *explain* these subjects. Since parents often choke at the point of advanced science instruction, I know you'll like these!

Each book in the series is wholesome and well-balanced. The **Introduction to Biology**, for example, has a much better-balanced perspective on ecology (as the study of small, mostly closed systems) than the newer Usborne titles on conservation and ecology. They also got the story of the pepper moths straight, although they missed the boat slightly on mutations, where the text gives the impression that beneficial mutations have actually been observed, and mixes the phenomenon of natural selection (e.g., penicillin-resistant bacteria surviving) into the topic of mutations (not fair, since some of the bacteria were immune to the penicillin in the first place).

NEW!
University of Nebraska-Lincoln Independent Study Biology courses

Grades 9–12. Nonresident, $94/course. Resident, $90/course. Biology 1 materials, $57. Biology 2 materials: $26 if you have the book from Biology 1, $57 otherwise. Biology 3 materials: with microscope, $207; for microscope work but not including the microscope, $111; without microscope, $114. Handling fee, $21 per course.
University of Nebraska-Lincoln, Independent Study High School, 269 Clifford-Hardin, NCCE, Lincoln, NE 68583-9800. (402) 472-4321. Fax: (402) 472-1901. Email: unldde1@unl.edu. Web: www.unl.edu/conted/disted

Usborne Biology

Grades 7–adult. Introduction to Biology, $7.95. The Usborne Book of Science (combined volume, also includes chemistry and physics), $16.95. Shipping extra.
EDC Publishing, Division of Educational Development Corporation, 10302 East 55th Place, Tulsa, OK 74146. (800) 475-4522. Fax: (800) 747-4509. Web: www.edcpub.com.

Cheerful cartoon people and critters demonstrate chemical principles throughout the book. Simple experiments and science puzzles are provided, along with gorgeous illustrations (full-color in the first 32 pages, black-and-white in the last 16) and simple explanations of difficult concepts.

Topics include: Definition of biology. What living things have in common. What living things are made of (intro to cell biology). Making food (includes an experiment to prove plants need light and chlorophyll to make starch). Feeding (how different animals do this). What happens to food (includes a jelly-and-pineapple experiment). Getting energy (an experiment with mung beans). How substances move around the body (a "potato chip" experiment which will *not* work unless you remember that the British consider french fries to be "chips"). Plant transport systems (more experiments). Waste disposal. Skeletons and movement. Sensitivity (growing bent-over plants to show how they turn towards a light source). Coordination. Reproduction (birds and the bees emphasis). Life cycles and growth (watch a fly's life cycle—yuk!). Genetics and heredity. The plant kingdom classified. The animal kingdom classified. BASIC computer program to classify living organisms. Ecology and the environment. Mutations and natural selection. Using a microscope. Answers to puzzles found in the book. Short index. A lot in 48 pages! *Mary Pride*

It sometimes seems like half of the work in a science course is learning the *names* of everything. Taking science courses can increase a young person's vocabulary by 50 percent—meaning there's a *lot* of terminology to learn!

The Usborne dictionaries of science are wonderfully designed to serve both as 128-page visual reference works and as explanations of the vocabulary associated with each scientific discipline. Arranged by themes, they present each scientific term in its context, explained with words and full-color pictures. The complex is made simple, justifying the series' slogan: "The facts you need to know—at a glance."

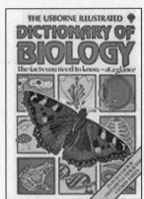

The **Dictionary of Biology** starts off with ecology, including this realistic definition of an ecosystem: "An ecosystem is a self-contained unit, i.e., the plants and animals interact to produce all the material they need." That sounds like the old, sensible ecology we all knew and loved. Next come life and life cycles (brief mention of evolution here), the structure of living things, and cell division. Plants, Animals, and Humans are the three major sections. Each covers anatomy, reproduction, and growth. A final general section in black and white touches on types of reproduction (including cell division), genetics and heredity, fluid movement, food and how it is used, metabolism, energy for life, homeostasis, hormones, digestive juices and enzymes, vitamins and their uses, plant classification, and animal classification. A fairly lengthy index rounds out the book.

You'll find a drawing of naked teens standing side by side in the section on human reproduction, and a rather unflattering picture of a baby in the womb. Aside from these minor points, there's nothing in the book to object to, and lots to be thankful for!

Recommended. *Mary Pride*

The handy-sized 64-page **Usborne Essential Guides** are very dense in information compared to other Usborne books. Touted for their uses in reviewing for exams, and as reference books, I'd like to suggest they are actually most useful when used along with your normal textbook. The concise

Usborne Dictionary of Biology
Grade 7–adult. $12.95 plus shipping.
EDC Publishing, Division of Educational Development Corporation, PO Box 470663, Tulsa, OK 74147. (800) 475-4522. Fax: (800) 747-4509. Web: www.edcpub.com.

I suggest that you use the *Dictionary of Biology* both as a reference work *and* as a handy desk aid for when you run across a concept in your science book that you just don't get. It's also is a great review tool and study aid, since it's so well organized by topic.

NEW!
Usborne Essential Guides
Grades 7–12. Essential Biology, Essential Chemistry, Essential

Physics, $6.95 each. Essential Science, $15.95. Shipping extra. *EDC Publishing, Division of Educational Development Corporation, 10302 East 55th Place, Tulsa, OK 74146. (800) 475-4522. Fax: (800) 747-4509. Web: www.edcpub.com.*

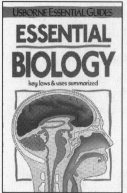

definitions generally come with pictures that illustrate the concepts, helping you understand what may be a bit obscure in your textbook. You wouldn't want to use them as a course text, though, since each concept is presented only once, with no review, and there are almost no practice exercises.

Unlike almost all concise guides to basic sciences, an attempt is made in this series to include laboratory science. For example, the **Chemistry** book has sample lab setups for common experiments, and outline drawings of common lab apparati. This is very nice as a supplement if the course you're taking at home doesn't include lab work.

Books available in this series are *Essential Biology*, *Essential Chemistry*, and *Essential Physics*. *Essential Science* is these three guides in one volume. *Mary Pride*

NEW
School of Tomorrow Biology Videos

Grades 11–12. Each set of 2 videos is $55 to purchase. Video rental options: $74.95 per quarter to keep worktexts and scorekeys and rent 6 videos, or $59.95 per quarter to rent the videos only. Optional computer disks, $7.25 each. CVI upgrade kit, $780. Workbooks also available. Shipping extra. *School of Tomorrow, PO Box 299000, Lewisville, TX 75029-9904. Orders: (800) 925-7777. Inquiries: (972) 315-1776. Fax: (972) 315-2862. Email: info@schooloftomorrow.com. Web: www.schooloftomorrow.com.*

Biology Videos

School of Tomorrow Biology Videos are friendly and well produced. There are 24 in all. For a complete course, add the computer-video interactive (CVI) option or the workbooks. For more details on the full course, see writeup earlier in this chapter. *Mary Pride*

CHAPTER 22

Creation Science

When Charles Darwin came up with the idea of evolution, this is what it looked like:

- Acquired characteristics are inherited. As a monkey hung from a tree, for example, his arms stretched out. So his descendants would be born with longer arms.
- Natural selection tends to weed out the "less fit" species and members of species in favor of the "more fit" in a slow, gradual process of change.
- The fossil record would eventually show gradual change from every old species into the corresponding new ones, once more fossils were uncovered.

Modern science has disproved Darwin in every point. We now know DNA controls inherited characteristics. We now know that floods, volcanoes, and earthquakes bring sudden, violent change, and that it's preposterous to imagine millions of years without these events. We also now know that the fossil record does not show gradual change from one species into the next. Rather, it shows distinct species without intermediate stages.

However, while scientists are busy disproving Darwinism, most still tend to be shy about embracing its obvious opposite, creation science. Not that they actually bother to *disprove* creation science, mind you. I ran across a really great example of this in Michael Crichton's sequel to *Jurassic Park,* called *The Lost World.* By the time we reach page 208 of the hardback version, Crichton's fictional mathematician, Ian Malcolm, has spent page after page arguing that life could not have developed randomly. Life has a form and pattern, he states. He takes up one argument after another for classical Darwinism and demolishes them. Then comes this exchange:

Thorne said, *"Are you saying evolution is directed?"*
"No," Malcolm said. *"That's Creationism and it's wrong. Just plain wrong."*

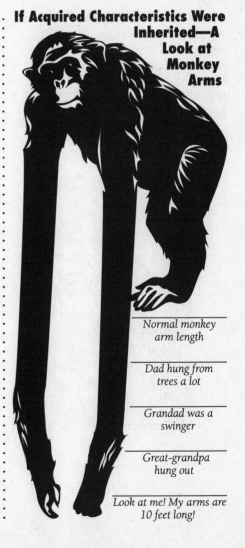

If Acquired Characteristics Were Inherited—A Look at Monkey Arms

Normal monkey
arm length

Dad hung from
trees a lot

Grandad was a
swinger

Great-grandpa
hung out

Look at me! My arms are
10 feet long!

Life is a . . . What?

By the way, you may be curious what Michael Crichton *does* believe about origins, if he doesn't believe in either Darwinism or creationism. Keeping in mind that Crichton hangs out with cutting-edge scientists, and what his characters say is what you're going to be hearing from the secular scientific community in the near future, here's his answer: "Life is a crystal." In other words, life has a mystical built-in need to form regular patterns. But no Designer built in the built-in patterns. We know this to be true, because . . . um, because . . . because "Creationism is just plain wrong." Not very scientific, that. Why not be a true scientist and form your own opinion, using the resources available below?

NEW!
Answers in Genesis

All ages. Free catalog. "Max Pack," $899 plus shipping.
Answers in Genesis, PO Box 6330, Florence, KY 41022-6330.
(800) 778-3390. Fax: (606) 727-2299.
Email: cservice@AnswersInGenesis.org.
Web: www.AnswersInGenesis.org.

That's all Malcolm has to say about creationism in the whole book. "It's wrong." Nothing about *why* it's wrong. No arguments disproving it. Just an incorrect assertion three pages earlier that "it's fair to say that every scientist in the world agrees that evolution is a feature of life on earth." (This is incorrect because lots of scientists do not believe in evolution, and in fact the way the sentence is stated, Malcolm would be wrong if only *one* scientist disbelieved in evolution.)

If you follow the debate about whether creation, evolution, or both should be taught in the public schools, you find that the arguments against teaching creationism boil down to these:

- All scientists know evolution is true. (This is false.)
- Creationism is religious. (Actually, so is evolution.)

Rarely, if ever, do the proponents of creationism-free science courses bother to make a case against creationist arguments. On the other hand, creationist texts spend a lot of time and space explaining the various hypotheses of evolution. The moral? If you want to know both sides of the issue, purchase and study some creationist texts. If you prefer to opt for censorship of the opposing view, study standard school texts.

Creation Science Resources

Write these people. Ask for their catalog. Ask to be put on their newsletter mailing list. As the current **Answers In Genesis** catalog says, thy are "more than just a Creation v. Evolution ministry." These are the people who bring you the excellent *Creation* magazine, and its companion, *Creation Ex Nihilo Technical Journal.* The staff travels widely, giving seminars in churches and other venues, and debating evolutionists. Tapes and videos of these seminars and debates are available through them, as are creationist children's materials, Christian biographies, a nice selection of worldview and science materials for homeschoolers, creationist books for family study, tracts, technical materials, books on the relevance of Creation, and tons of books and videos for laymen on theology, history, biology, geology, archaeology, and astronomy. The catalog even carries neckties, t-shirts, sweatshirts, and Christmas cards, all with a Christian or creationist message!

All right, I'll admit it; the neckties don't send me. However, AIG, as they are fondly known, have more going for them than fashion neckwear. These are the people trying to build a creation-science museum in Kentucky. As I write this, it look like the zoning approval is finally going to come through, after a long battle with anti-creation zealots from inside and outside the local community. AIG has a million bucks' worth of exhibits ready to go (many picked up for pennies on the dollar from other science museums), so this should be something to see when it's finally ready.

What's all the theology and such doing in their catalog? It's there because AIG considers their mandate to be "Defending the Bible from the very first verse!" This gives them a well-balanced outlook, as much of their work involves convincing people that the Bible is relevant today. This worldview emphasis means that their catalog is a great resource for worldview materials.

You might be interested in this: Answers In Genesis offers an instant library of their best, most current books, videos, CDs, and cassettes, called their "Max Pack." Individually, these titles retail for $1,635.40, but as a set you can get them for $899. This is not a motley assortment of leftovers; I've read most of them, and can testify that this is a good, wide selection for all ages that covers all the major areas of creationist and worldview controversy. A super support-group purchase, and not unreasonable for the well-stocked home library of the well-heeled homeschool family. *Mary Pride*

Back to Genesis is a series of video seminar tapes. Most are for teens and adults.

The videos in this series include:

- **Mount St. Helens: Explosive Evidence for Catastrophe** Multi-media presentation of the St. Helens explosion and its significance for the Biblical flood (by Steve Austin)
- **A Geologist Looks at Noah's Flood** Evidence for the flood and Ice Age (by John Morris)
- **Dinosaur Mystery Solved** Dinosaurs and their significance in the Bible (by John Morris)
- **A Geological Perspective on the Age of the Earth** Scientific evidence for recent creation (by John Morris)
- **Challenge of the Fossil Record** Evolution? The fossils say no! (by Duane Gish)
- **Origin of the Universe** Critique of the Big Bang and other theories of cosmic and stellar evolution (by Duane Gish)
- **Origin of Man** So-called "ape-man" and the impossibility of human evolution (by Duane Gish)
- **Introduction to Biblical Creationism** An introductory overview of the strong evidence for creation v. evolution (without reference to science) (by Henry Morris)
- **Introduction to Scientific Creationism** An introductory overview of the strong evidence for creation v. evolution (without reference to scripture) (by Henry Morris)
- **The Long War Against God** The long history and deadly worldwide impact of evolution (by Henry Morris)

A good buy for your church or home school support group. *Mary Pride*

Phillip Johnson created a splash in the academic world a few years back with his book *Darwin on Trial*. Johnson, a professor of law at the University of California at Berkeley, systematically dismembered the body of bad science known as the theory of evolution. His follow-up book, *Reason in the Balance*, continued the assault. Both books are masterpieces of scalpel-sharp critical thinking.

They are, however, not light reading. In **Defeating Darwinism**, Johnson simplifies his approach a bit, making the depth of both his research and his analysis of evolutionary naturalism accessible to a broader audience. He uses the 1960 film *Inherit The Wind* (the historically inaccurate fictionalized treatment of the Scopes Monkey Trial) as a jumping off point to dissect the academic world's entrenched and inflexible thinking about evolution as Fact. This 131-page paperback uses the basics of logical argument to highlight the flaws in this thinking, and to present the Creationist/Intelligent Design platform.

Knowing how to dismantle a fallacious argument is only part of Johnson's thesis in writing this book. He writes, "Every history of the twentieth century lists three thinkers as preeminent in influence: Darwin, Marx

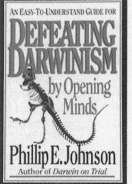

AN EASY-TO-UNDERSTAND GUIDE FOR
DEFEATING DARWINISM by Opening Minds
Phillip E. Johnson
Author of *Darwin on Trial*

Back to Genesis video series
Grades 7–12. Back to Genesis video series, $14.95 each (except Mount St. Helens, $19.95) or $125 for all 10. Relevance of Creation video series, $14.95 each or $73 for set of 6 videos. Shipping extra. *Institute for Creation Research, 10946 Woodside Ave. N., Santee, CA 92071. (800) 628-7640. (619) 448-0900. Fax: (619) 448-3469. Web: www.icr.org.*

Another video seminar series, **Relevance of Creation**, is a dramatic presentation of the conflict in the public schools between the evolutionary and creationist worldviews, with Ken Ham and Dr. John Morris defending creationism against the typical classroom dogmatic propaganda for evolution. Topics:

- **Creation Evangelism** Importance of creation for true evangelism.
- **Creation and the Last Days** Exposition of II Peter 3 and what it says about evolution.
- **Genesis 1–11** Survey of Genesis and its importance.
- **Genesis and Decay of the Nations** Impact of evolution on society.
- **The Genesis Family** Significance of creationism for family life.
- **What Really Happened to the Dinosaurs?** Children's video on dinosaurs.

NEW!
Defeating Darwinism by Opening Minds
Grades 9–adult. $9.99 paperback. $15.99 hardback. *Inter-Varsity Press, PO Box 1400, Downers Grove, IL 60515. Orders: (800) 843-9487. Inquiries: (630) 734-4000. Fax: (630) 734-4200. Web: www.ivpress.com.*

and Freud. All three were regarded as 'scientific' (and hence far more reliable than anything 'religious') in their heyday . . . Marx and Freud have fallen, and even their dwindling bands of followers no longer claim that their insights were based on any methodology remotely comparable to experimental science. I am convinced that Darwin is next on the block. His fall will be by far the mightiest of the three."

It is books like this that will help to hasten the end of Darwinism. This is a must-read. *Michelle Van Loon*

In the Beginning: Compelling Evidence for Creation and the Flood, 6th edition

Grade 7–adult. $17.95 paperback. Shipping extra.
Center for Scientific Creation, 5612 N. 20th Pl., Phoenix, AZ 85016.
Fax/Phone: (602) 955-7663.
Web: www.creationscience.com.

In the Beginning is a great creation science book for teens and adults. It's easy to read, carefully researched, meticulously documented, and offers answers to the most important questions of the origins controversy.

Besides the usual creation-science approach to questions about the historicity of Genesis and what happened to make the dinosaurs extinct, the book is unique in explaining for the first time how 17 major earth features—including mountains, volcanoes, the Grand Canyon, and "ice ages"—resulted from a worldwide flood. At the same time, it reveals serious yet little-known problems with many evolutionist ideas about earth history and the origin of life—including many ideas that evolutionists themselves have discarded, but are still taught as fact in children's textbooks.

In the Beginning's author, Dr. Walter Brown, has had rather an interesting history of his own. Dr. Brown, who retired from the Air Force in 1980 as a full colonel, received his B.S. from West Point, M.S. from New Mexico State University, and Ph.D. from M.I.T. During his 21 years of military service he served, among other positions, as Chief of Science and Technology at the Air War College, associate professor at the U.S. Air Force Academy, and Director of Benet Research, Engineering, and Development Laboratories in Albany, New York. He is not, in other words, your basic half-baked, undereducated nut. His "hydroplates" theory, whereby he attempts to explain continental drift and a host of other worldwide phenomena more convincingly than the plate-tectonics people do, is absolutely fascinating. Not that you have to be a degreed scientist to follow his thinking—it's laid out in outline form, with charts, graphs, maps, and unobtrusive footnotes.

If you've ever suffered through a mainstream geology course, wherein the profs tried to explain how long, slow, uniform processes caused veins of rock to buckle back on themselves, rivers to dig huge canyons, and marine fossils to appear on the top of the Himalayas, you owe it to yourself to get this book. Everything the profs had trouble explaining is explained more neatly, convincingly, and understandably right here in this wonderful book. *Mary Pride*

Scientific Creationism (2nd edition)
Gish/Doolittle Debate (VHS video)

Grade 9–adult. Scientific Creationism (2nd edition), $10.95. Gish/Doolittle Debate (VHS video), $14.95. Shipping extra.
Institute for Creation Research, 10946 Woodside Ave. N., Santee, CA 92071.
Orders: (800) 628-7640.
Inquiries: (619) 448-0900.
Fax: (619) 448-3469.
Web: www.icr.org.

Institute for Creation Research is a major source of creation-science materials, all produced by scientists and writers associated with ICR. Large catalog, attractive and professional materials. ICR now has a strong line of creation science books for children.

Adults and older teens might want to start off with the excellent **Scientific Creationism** and some of the juicy creationist v. evolutionist debates featuring the hard-hitting Dr. Duane Gish. You'd better send for the catalog, which also includes several audiocassette series and tracts, plus a large number of other good books, if you're trying to build a strong home science library. Or subscribe to ICR's free periodical *Acts and Facts*. Find out what the ACLU is afraid to let into your public school classrooms! *Mary Pride*

Unlocking the Mysteries of Creation

grew out of author Dennis Petersen's creation science seminars, and thus has both lots of visual impact and an interactive, talk-to-the-reader style. Mr. Petersen evidently likes to keep his audience on the edge of its seat. Let's take a look at the "mysteries" he unlocks.

Section One, "Unlocking the Mysteries of the Early Earth," starts with an explanation of why it matters whether you believe in creation or evolution. It then proceeds to explain what really happened "in the beginning" according to the Bible . . . why the early earth's climate could have been radically different . . . why volcanoes *weren't* present at the beginning . . . and why radiometric dating methods aren't reliable (nor do they verify the approved geologic chart). "What Do Processes in Nature Tell Us About Earth's Age?" is an excellent section, showing the evidence from "geological clocks" such as interplanetary dust buildup, juvenile water, comets, oil deposit pressure, erosion, topsoil, coral reefs, the wearing away of the edge of Niagara Falls, stalactite growth in caves, igneous crust buildup, population studies, the magnetic field, dissolved minerals in the ocean, atmospheric helium, and so on. The section closes by giving evidence against the "Gap Theory" of creation.

Section Two, "Unlocking the Mysteries of Evolution," challenges the Big Bang theory, the idea that non-living matter produced life, the use of time as the magic factor to make evolution plausible, the idea that random chance can produce increasing complexity, and the idea that simple forms develop into complex forms. In this section, the author examines some famous "fossil links" such as the horse series, and the way geologists date rocks by the fossils while evolutionary biologists date fossils by the rocks. The section concludes with a look at three creatures—the bombardier beetle, the woodpecker, and the giraffe—each of which could not possibly have evolved, since they needed *all* their complex body systems at once in order to survive.

Section Three, "Unlocking the Mysteries of Original Man and the Missing Links," examines the famous "missing links" you learned about in school, and what's happened to this chart since. Why have some ancient human skeletons been ignored? What happened to the dinosaurs? Could man and dinosaurs have lived together? Were there really such things as dragons?

Section Four, "Unlocking the Mysteries of Ancient Civilizations," is my favorite part of the book. The "mystery" seems to keep cropping up: "Why were ancient peoples *so advanced*—when in theory they should be just one step up from cave dwellers?" This section includes amazing information on the technological achievements of ancient man, from the electric battery used by the Mesopotamians to 4,500-year-old examples of electroplating. How did ancient peoples like that race of giants in the Andes Mountains of Bolivia move 100-ton stones across rough terrain from a quarry 60 miles away? That, in turn, pales next to the building stones used in the temple at Baalbek, Lebanon, one of which weighs over 2,000 tons. Even with power equipment, modern engineers can't move anything that big! The list goes on and on, from the achievements of the Maya to those of China, Babylon, Egypt, Greece, and so on. Could it be that, instead of our modern doctrine of "continual progress," our ancestors actually knew more than we did about a lot of things? This section includes a time line showing how long the Bible patriarchs lived, making it clear at a glance that the wisdom of previous generations was around for a *long* time!

Unlocking the Mysteries of Creation

Grade 6–adult. Book, $22.95. Videos, $22.95 each, or entire set of 12, $275 (includes free workbooks). Workbooks, $5.75 each. Shipping extra.
Creation Resource Foundation, PO Box 570, El Dorado, CA 95623. Orders: (800) 497-1454. Inquiries: (530) 626-4447. Fax: (530) 626-3221. Email: info@awesomeworks.com. Web: www.awesomeworks.com.

This is an incredible creation science book. The engaging format combines illustrations, cartoons, text, and graphs; illuminating text unlocks the mysteries of the early earth and early civilizations. A wonderful book for preteens and up, or for reading aloud while your children look over your shoulder. Also available as a video series—see photo below.

A 12-part video series is also available. Four workbooks are available for accompany the video series. Each workbook covers the contents of three or more videos.

None of the stuff in this book is weird *Chariots of the Gods* phoney baloney. Every fact is cited and sourced, often from sources as mainstream as *Reader's Digest* and *National Geographic*.

Unlocking the Mysteries of Creation will profoundly challenge your thinking, even if you already believe in creation science. If you *don't* already believe in creation science, it'll blow you away! *Mary Pride*

NEW!
The Young Earth
Grade 9–adult. $14.95 plus shipping.
Master Books, PO Box 727, Green Forest, AR 72638.
Orders: (800) 999-3777.
Inquiries: (870) 438-5288.
Fax: (501) 438-5120.
Email: mbnlp@cswnet.com.
Web: www.masterbooks.net.

Is the earth billions of years old? Did God create a world full of suffering and decay before He created man and woman? Starting with an overview of fossil and rock dating methods, Dr. John D. Morris' **The Young Earth** decimates the "old earth" viewpoint that has become trendy among a segment of the creationist community. In this oversized book, 141 pages are devoted to these and other dating methods you never encountered in your college geology course, such as why human bones are so scarce when people have supposedly been on the earth for millions of years, how worldwide physical processes really work, the decay and reversals of the magnetic field, the percentage of helium in the atmosphere, and many others, all well-diagrammed and illustrated. The illustrations and diagrams appear again in larger size in the back of the book, so you can copy them onto transparencies and use them in a class presentation, if you are so inclined. Recommended. *Bill Pride*

CHAPTER 23

Ecology

Ecology and conservation are two separate subjects. But they are often mingled together and confused with each other in school materials.

Ecology is a *science*. Conservation is a form of *etiquette*. Ecology is the study of biological systems. Conservation is training in wilderness manners and polite waste management.

All this is very nice and proper. Who could argue with science and politeness?

Mix politics and religion in with ecology and conservation, though, and you get a very different animal. Let me provide you with just one example, commonly cited in school materials. It's called the "Butterfly Effect." The Butterfly Effect doctrine states that when a butterfly flutters its wings in California, it can cause a hurricane in Tokyo. The idea is that even the smallest cause may lead to an enormous effect, since every single creature on this planet is interdependent with every single other creature. From there, the point is usually made that world government is necessary, since all countries are interdependent ecologically with all other countries.

This is mumbo-jumbo. As engineers know, local effects tend to damp out locally. Effects tend to decrease according to the inverse square or inverse cube of their distance from the cause, depending on whether the cause is surface-bound or airborne. Also, no effect can be greater than its cause. To prove this point, just put that butterfly in a wind tunnel and see what difference flapping its wings makes. Turn up the wind force and see if you even still have a butterfly!

We can learn many important and useful facts from the science of ecology, but the Butterfly Effect isn't one of them. Let's now discuss some of the other false statements commonly found in ecology materials.

Man is destroying the planet. What about Woman? And Children? What do you mean here by "destroy"? The fictional planet Krypton was "destroyed" when it exploded. Is the Earth about to blow up?

The statement that "man is destroying the planet" is designed to maximize the reader's guilt; by assigning blame equally to all of us. This is ridiculous on its face, as well as being a transparent substitute for the Christian doctrine of original sin. Now, instead of recognizing our unworthiness before God, we are supposed to feel unworthy that we pollute the planet merely by existing.

- **Ecology is a *science*. It is also a *religion* and a *political philosophy*.**

- **Conservation is a form of *etiquette*.**

- **"Stewardship" doctrine can go either way— but typically it follows the political and religious assumptions of ecology-as-religion and ecology-as-politics.**

The statement is also designed to generate panic, as we are supposed to believe that Doom is Imminent and The End Is Near. Actually, even Lake Erie, a real pest-hole if there ever was one, is getting better. With the exception of some extremely poor people in the Phillipines, few of us live surrounded by garbage. In laymen's terms, this means The End Is Not Yet and the Rumors of the Planet's Death are Greatly Exaggerated.

This does not mean that every bit of real estate smells like a rose. Disasters happen. If we start to ask, "Exactly who *is* responsible for major ecological disasters?" the answer almost always is Mother Nature (*one* volcanic eruption spews forth more contaminants than the entire human race puts out in a decade), Big Business, and Big Government. The Chernobyl disaster, not to mention the entire polluted country of Poland, stand as testimony to what government elites can do when they are given full powers to run everyone else's lives. And we are all familiar with oil tanker spills and other such disasters. But somehow the action message at the end of every ecology text always tells us to lobby our politicians for *more* government control of the economy and the land.

Everything is interdependent. This is an irresponsible statement, scientifically speaking. It is more correct to say that *some* things are interdependent with *some* other things, and the amount of interdependence varies according to a number of conditions. We have already seen that butterflies in Ohio don't actually have much effect on the weather in Tokyo. On the other hand, sewage pumped into Narragansett Bay will definitely have effects on the neighboring seashore communities.

If everything I do on my property affects your property, you now have an excuse to control my behavior, or take away my property rights. If, on the other hand, you have to demonstrate I am creating an actual nuisance that drifts onto your property—too much noise, smell, mess, or whatever—then we can each enjoy our property as long as we have reasonably good manners.

The "everything is interdependent" doctrine is implicitly a call for a one-world government exercising total control over all property and behavior. It's both bad science and bad politics.

There are too many people in the world. Not in Iowa, there aren't. I can see how people who live and play exclusively in major cities could get this attitude. Actually, *cars* take up more land and stink up more air than all the people on earth combined.

For centuries, gloom-and-doomers have been saying the human race will soon outstrip its ability to feed and house itself. For centuries, the promised apocalypse has never come. That's because human beings are not just "consumers." We are *producers* as well.

We're using up all our resources! The Earth is a closed system. With the exception of a few satellites we have shot off into space, every resource that ever was on the planet is still right here. Many of these resources are renewable—trees, for example. The way some people talk about recycling paper these days, you'd think nobody ever heard of planting *new* trees. As for "nonrenewable" resources such as gas and oil, we can either (1) find new deposits using better searching methods, (2) recover material from previously uneconomical sites using new techniques, and (3) invent or discover substitutes. Nuclear energy, for example, can easily substitute for dirty coal in creating electrical power. If you don't like the idea of huge, dangerous nuclear plants, then how about small, safe ones like those on a nuclear submarine? In years of operation, no nuclear submarine has ever had a core meltdown. A tiny nuclear plant like this can power a whole small town. Even smaller nuclear plants could be devised, cutting the danger from leaks and meltdowns down to the point where the risk is negligible. Simple, sensible solutions such as this are available right now, once we have the political will to implement them.

Here's one for my fellow Christians: **We must be good stewards of God's creation.** Again, this implies we all have property rights in each other's property. If you think you own the whole world, you are suffering from delusions of grandeur. If you think that government bureaucrats should own the whole world, you are just plain suffering from delusions. "We must be good stewards of the part of God's creation that belongs to us, and act nicely when visiting the part that doesn't" is more like it.

Time fails for me to speak of the Gaia Hypothesis (briefly stated, the idea is the Earth is a sentient entity and we are the acne on her skin), the Ozone Hole Hypothesis (aerosols and freon are wiping out our protection from Deadly Sun Rays—actually, sunlight acting on the atmosphere constantly creates ozone, which is why "ozone holes" appear periodically in areas the furthest from the sun), the Global Warming Hypothesis (cut pollution *now* or the ice caps will melt and New Yorkers will drown—two problems here are that we are now actually experiencing a short cycle of Global *Cooling,* and volcanoes alone produce way more pollution than all of mankind combined), the Helium Balloon Scare (birds and animals supposedly mistake balloon scraps for food, scarf them down, and choke—except nobody has ever observed this happening even *once*), and many more notions peddled as *proven facts* in today's textbooks and popular media.

Here are some of the questions we asked as we reviewed ecology teaching materials. Does the material treat mankind as one lumpy, guilty mass, or recognize individual responsibility? Is it alarmist or balanced? Does it provide both sides of the scientific arguments for and against topics such as global warming, or not? Does it call for ever-shrinking freedoms and a more stringent lifestyle, or does it inspire students to come up with new solutions that respect human freedom?

At the moment, few resources available are accurate scientifically and free of political propaganda. We've done our best to find them for you. We've also provided reviews of some less-than-perfect materials which either include good information or are heavily promoted to homeschoolers. Hopefully, more good material will become available in time, since customer demand has a lot bigger effect on what is published than butterfly wings have on hurricanes. It's up to you—keep the planet safe for humans by demanding better ecology books!

Ecology for Teens

I might be prejudiced, but I kinda figure folks who *live* in the country understand it a tad better than city-dwelling greenies who only venture out on backpacking trips. For a *real* taste of the country, you won't find anything better than **Country** magazine. Each issue is a work of art, with gorgeous pictures on glossy paper. Great features include:

- A "Timely Homesteader Tips" section, with tips like how to peel an onion the no-tears way.
- "Let's Head for the Country"—a 10-page scenic photo-tour that let's readers visit backroads places that likely aren't on any map.
- Wholesome, lively humor "Overheard at the Country Cafe."
- An encouragement section, in which readers send in photos and facts about the folks they think are the "greatest country father-in-law" or "greatest country teen."
- "The Way it Was"—photos of country life from the old days.

Country Magazine
Country Extra
Farm & Ranch Living
Reminisce
Reminisce Extra
Country Woman
Grade 3–adult. Sample issue of any magazine, $2.99. One year (6 issues) of any magazine, $17.98.
New subscriptions: Reiman Publications, Subscription Fulfillment, PO Box 5294, Harlan, IA 51593.
Sample issues: Reiman Publications, Circulation, PO Box 992, Greendale, WI 53129. (800) 344-4566. Fax: (414) 423-3750. *Web: www.reimanpub.com.*

I love the "marginal notes," short wise or humorous sayings lining the margins of many pages. There's also crafts, recipes, a helping-hands forum where people can write in with information requests, a Country Inns & Farm Vacations section that introduces a number of hospitable country bed-and-breakfasts and inns in each issue, and lots more!

If this all sounds kind of cornball to you, you've been breathing smog for too long. These magazines are folksy, but brother, they are *slick*. You could frame any of the photos, and the amount of real-life information in each issue is astonishing.

Country is the most relaxing magazine I know . . . except maybe for **Country Extra** and **Farm & Ranch Living**. *Country Extra* is for people who want *Country* more than six times a year. It comes out in the in-between months, and has some special features of its own (many of which eventually cross over into *Country*). *Farm & Ranch Living*, as the name implies, is about farm and ranch living. It's not a professional journal about the best breed of hogs or how to maximize profits, but another gorgeous photo-'n-life-stories magazine like *Country*. If you subscribe to it, you'll end up touring over 70 farms and ranches a year without leaving your living room. As the blurb says, "Read the others for profit, read ours for pure pleasure."

I might add to this, "Read these magazines to find out what it's *really like* out there, according to the people who take care of the land and animals." This isn't agribiz; it's agrilife. *Mary Pride*

NEW!
Facts not Fear

Grades 5–12. $14.95 plus $3 shipping.
Home Life, Inc., PO Box 1190, Fenton, MO 63026. Orders: (800) 346-6322. Inquiries: (636) 343-7750. Fax: (636) 343-7203. Email: orders@home-school.com. Web: www.home-school.com.

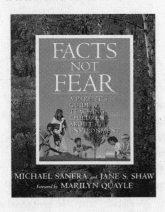

Facts not Fear should be mandatory reading in ecology classes . . . if I believed in mandatory education in the first place! Unlike the unscientific doom-mongering found everywhere from school texts to TV shows, here are the scientific facts that debunk all the common ecology apocalypses. Written in consultation with a distinguished academic and scientific advisory professional, this book presents both the "fears" (what school kids are taught) and the "facts" (what the research really says.

Part 1 explains the problem—how "phony science" and eco-activism have become entrenched in schools. The book then devotes a chapter each to these questions:

- Will Billions Starve?
- Natural Resources on the way out?
- Are Our Forest's Dying?
- The Rain Forest—One Hundred Acres a Minute?
- American Wildlife—On the Edge?
- Where Have All the Species Gone?
- The Air We Breathe
- A Hotter Planet
- Sorting Out Ozone
- Acid Rain
- Not a Drop to Drink!
- Don't Eat the Apple!
- A Garbage Crisis
- The Recycling Myth

Easy-to-read format, plus booklists for further study, make this an indispensable homeschool tool. *Mary Pride*

Usborne Environmental Books

Grades 5–12. Ecology, $7.95. Protecting Endangered Species, Protecting Trees & Forests, out of print. Protecting Rivers & Seas, $4.50 each. Protecting Our World

Usborne has done us all a great favor by showing us, in full color and with lovely artwork, just exactly what the greenie movement believes and hopes to accomplish. From pages 4 and 9 of **Ecology:** "The connections between all living things stretch into a vast web . . . All life on earth is interlinked in one vast, continuous web." From page 13: "We are upsetting the fine balance of nature, and the results may turn out to be disastrous." From page 22:

In the natural world there is a fragile balance in plant and animal populations [so fragile it supposedly has already lasted millions of years!—MP]. There are several ways that their numbers are naturally kept in check . . . However, this is no longer true of the human population, the growth of which is fast destroying nature's balance, with alarming consequences for our planet.

From page 31, under the heading "The living planet":

Some scientists argue that the whole planet and its atmosphere works like a living organism. The idea of a "living" planet is known as the Gaia hypothesis, after the Greek Goddess [capital G in the original] of the Earth [capital E in the original].

On page 3 in **Protecting Endangered Species**: a "Wanted" poster with a smiling man on it, with an arrow pointing to "Human—the most dangerous species."

From page 14:

On the following pages you can find out about some of the ways humans can protect endangered species. The best way is to set aside areas of land or water where animals and plants can live safely. These are called protected areas. They are places such as bird sanctuaries and national parks.

In other words, property rights for animals. On page 22 of that book—and also on the end pages of every book Usborne is now publishing on these topics —are pitches for conservation groups ranging from the World Wide Fund for Nature to Greenpeace. Children are urged strongly to join these groups.

Every environmental bogeyman is trotted out in these books—from the great menace of acid rain, which a $500 million government study now assures us has always been there and doesn't really hurt anything anyway—to the famous "evolutionary embryology" sequence, now scoffed at by every reputable embryologist, where the human embryo in its development is supposed to "mirror [the changes] that took place over billions of years, in which life evolved from tiny, single-celled organisms into the complex structures of today." (It turns out, though the book doesn't tell you, that the guy who invented this theory faked his data.)

So there you have the ecology movement in a nutshell: insulate your water heater, campaign for massive one-world government, dismantle industry, discourage human fertility, property rights for animals, the pantheistic "one vast continuous web" of nature, and Gaia, the earth goddess. Nowhere in all this is the merest suggestion that private property should be respected or that farming of endangered species is one possible way to save them. *Mary Pride*

In 32 full-color indexed pages, each of these **Usborne Understanding Geography** books introduces an area of geographical or scientific study in two-page-spread format, highly illustrated.

Newer Usborne books tend to end with a whimper, namely a double-page-spread of alleged ecological problems related to the book's topic and a pitch for One World Government-type solutions. These books have that, all right, but end on a more upbeat note, with a page of what people are actually doing in their real lives to improve conditions. Bill's impression was, "The *Seas* book makes it sound like saving the seas is pretty hopeless. The other books give us more hope."

(combined volume), $10.95. Shipping extra. *EDC Publishing, Division of Educational Development Corporation, 10302 East 55th Place, Tulsa, OK 74146. (800) 475-4522. Fax: (800) 747-4509. Web: www.edcpub.com.*

NEW!
Usborne Understanding Geography series
Grades 5–12. World Farming, $7.95. All others, $6.95 each. Shipping extra. *EDC Publishing, Division of Educational Development Corporation, 10302 East 55th Place, Tulsa, OK 74146. (800) 475-4522.* Web: *www.edcpub.com.*

The *Seas and Earthquakes* books both start with an evolutionary glance back over billions of year. *World Farming* merely harkens back to Stone Age man.

When it comes to our own time period, as usual the books are excellent, laden with fun facts presented with exciting visuals and captivating text.

Volumes in the series so far include , *Earthquakes and Volcanoes*, *World Farming*, *Seas and Oceans*, and *Storms and Hurricanes*

To me, some of these sound more like they belong under "Ecology" than "Geography." Which is why I put them in this chapter! *Mary Pride*

Usborne's The Young Naturalist

Grades 5–12. $6.95. KidKit, $18.95. Shipping extra.

EDC Publishing, Division of Educational Development Corporation, 10302 East 55th Place, Tulsa, OK 74146. (800) 475-4522. Fax: (800) 747-4509. Web: www.edcpub.com.

If any one book can introduce the entire field of nature studies to kids aged 10 and up, **The Young Naturalist** is the one. With the usual lively Usborne mix of text and illustration, facts and experiments, it covers:

- Observing and recording—keeping a bird notebook, making a tree chart, and mapping mole hills, among other activities.
- Collecting natural objects and displaying them.
- Collecting and observing bugs.
- Breeding and observing the life cycles of tiny critters such as butterflies.

Projects include making nesting boxes and bird blinds, building an aquarium and formicarium (ant house), resurrecting an urban plot, pressing leaves, collecting and displaying spider webs, making plaster casts of animal tracks, and lots more.

The Young Naturalist is particularly strong on teaching nature observation skills. Simply reading through the book (not an easy task, with the wealth of information and illustration continually tempting you to browse!) will give you new eyes with which to view the natural world around you.

Don't underestimate this book. All the projects and activities, though worthwhile, require a fair degree of commitment. Country dwellers will also find it easier to do the activities, although the book includes indoor and urban activities as well. *Mary Pride*

NEW!
What Do We Know About Grasslands

Grades 7–12. $15.95 paperback plus shipping. ISBN: 0872-26-3592. *Peter Bedrick Books, c/o NTC Contemporary Publishing, 4255 W. Touhy, Lincolnwood, IL 60646. (800) 323-4900. Fax: (800) 998-3103. Email: ntcpub@tribune.com. Web: www.contemporarybooks.com.*

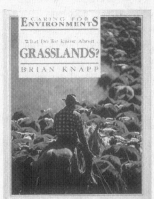

What Do We Know About Grasslands? is a well-balanced and interesting read. Author Dr. Brian Knapp realizes that people have a right to live on the earth, and that their future success at least partly depends on keeping the land they live on from drying up and blowing away. In this context, *Grasslands* presents not just stunning photos and useful facts, but the ongoing drama of how people, animals, and plants have come and gone on the various grasslands of the world. Eschewing the almost useless (educationally speaking) double-page-spread format so overused nowadays, the book offers instead intelligent chapters with apt photos and illustrations. Its oversized 44 pages are enough to cover the subject in a way readers will remember. I heartily recommend *Grasslands*. *Mary Pride*

CHAPTER 24

Chemistry

"Better Living Through Chemistry" has gotten a bum rap lately. Our all-natural, preservative-free age tends to associate "chemicals" with "cancer" and other ugly words. But we still drink H_2O and sprinkle NaCl on our french fries. We still take O_2 into our bloodstream and breathe out CO_2. Without Tn filaments, our light bulbs would not light. Without $NaHCO_3$, our biscuits wouldn't rise. If life is just a bowl of cherries, without chemicals you wouldn't have either a bowl or the cherries.

Chemistry class usually starts with a study of the elements of which all matter is made. Then you get into some serious math while studying measurements and chemical reactions. You learn to take lab notes, too, which is an excellent exercise in logical thinking and scientific honesty. You also get to play with fire, water, earth, and air, plus acids, bases, and small nuclear explosions. (Just kidding about the small nuclear explosions, to see if you were paying attention.) All this can be done quite easily at home, or if you prefer, you can watch a teacher perform the more dangerous experiments on video.

In case you forgot your high-school chemistry:

H_2O = water
NaCl = table salt
O_2 = oxygen
CO_2 = carbon dioxide
Tn = Tungsten
$NaHCO_3$ = baking soda
R_2D_2 = small droid

Chemistry Courses

A Beka believes in giving you a *lot* of pages for your money, and their **Chemistry: Precision and Design** text for 11th-graders is no exception. Its hefty 655 pages include enough information to take you through high-school chemistry and through the Advanced Placement exam. Most on-site high-school classes won't get through the whole book in one year.

Let's start with the book's content first. Chapters are:

- Chemistry: An Introduction.
- Mathematics in Chemistry. Your typical introduction to scientific notation, significant figures, precision and accuracy, and dimensional analysis (making sure you always end up with the proper units, e.g., feet or inches or ml or kg).
- Matter: The Substance of Chemistry. Properties of matter, how matter changes, ways to separate matter, elements, subatomic particles, the periodic chart, and a fascinating section called "Chemical Elements in Bible Times."
- Stoichiometry: Elements and Compounds. Writing chemical formulas, learning about moles and percentage composition, etc.

A Beka Chemistry

Grade 11. Chemistry text (paperbound), $25.20. Teacher's edition (includes student text), $35.45. Solution key, $31.75. Student test booklet, $6.20. Teacher key for test booklet, $9.20. Student quiz booklet, $4.60. Teacher key for quiz booklet, $9.20. Chemistry lab manual, $12.45; $20.45 for teacher's edition. Video lab demonstrations (VHS only), $150.20 each for first and second semester. Shipping extra. *A Beka Book, Box 19100, Pensacola, FL 32523-9100. (800) 874-2352. Fax: (800) 874-3590. Web: www.abeka.com.*

- Stoichiometry: Chemical Reactions. In which you learn to balance chemical equations and do various things with them.
- Gases. Everything you are likely to need to know on this subject unless you take a college course in thermodynamics.
- Chemical Thermodynamics. Did I mention thermodynamics? Here it is—but not everything you'd get in a college course (e.g., no adiabatic containers or engineering applications).
- Electronic Structure. Waves! Quantums (quanta?)! Orbitals! The hydrogen spectrum!
- The Periodic Table. Now we really get into it: its historical development, classification, periodicity, electron configurations, atomic sizes, ionization energy, electron affinity, and electronegativity.
- The Chemical Bond and Intermolecular Forces. If the words "ionic" and "covalent" mean anything to you, this is the chapter for that sort of thing.
- Selected Nonmetals and Their Compounds. Hydrogen, oxygen, nitrogen, phosphorus, sulfur, halogens, noble gases. Balanced sidebar on the ozone-layer controversy.
- Selected Metals and Semimetals. Metallurgy, alkali metals, alkaline earth metals, iron, copper, gold and silver, aluminum, and silicon and germanium (very important in manufacturing electronics).
- Solutions and Colloids. You start with definitions, learn everything you can about the properties of soaps and colloids, and end up looking at soaps, detergents, and other common colloids.
- Chemical Kinetics. Reactions, in a nutshell.
- Chemical Equilibrium.
- Acids, Bases, and Salts.
- Ionic Equilibrium in Solution.
- Oxidation-Reduction Reactions: Electrochemistry.
- Nuclear Chemistry.
- Organic Chemistry. Thirty-one pages take you from a definition of organic compounds through chemical bonding, structural formulas, functional groups, alkanes, alkenes, alkynes, aromatic hydrocarbons, alcohols, aldehydes and ketones, carboxylic acids and esters, amines, amides, proteins and amino acids, carbohydrates, and fats.

A lot of the text is taken up with worked examples, exercises keyed to the examples, separate explanations of key concepts, review exercises, chapter summaries, and key term glossaries at the end of each chapter. These all help a *lot,* especially the chapter summaries, which are definitely needed since the text itself is not written in the most uncomplicated language. Let's put it this way—it's obvious that the author is a real scientist!

Chemistry: Precision and Design is not overly rich in graphics. It has more of a normal textbook appearance than, say, A Beka's biology text. In many respects, it reads like a college textbook.

A Beka also offers a teacher's edition that includes the full student text as well as a scope and sequence, daily lesson plans, demonstration ideas, chapter summaries, and teaching strategies.

The *Chemistry Laboratory Manual* is also available in both student's and teacher's editions, and includes complete instructions for completing 36 labs. Be forewarned: the list of required equipment is long (most of it is standard lab equipment readily available from various sources), but the list of required chemicals is *long*!

An alternative to taking the time and money to set up your own home lab and work through the experiments is to purchase A Beka's video chemistry labs. These are video demonstrations of the actual experiments in the

Chemistry Laboratory Manual. Although the video labs aren't inexpensive, if added to a home school support group library the cost per family would become reasonable. Then you could perhaps just do one or two of the most interesting experiments on-site, for the hands-on experience. *Mary Pride*

Alpha Omega presents **chemistry** as its 11th-grade science course. This is designed as a set of 10 workbooks with the lesson text, exercises, and tests all built in. The boxed set also includes the teacher handbook and answer keys. LIFEPACs are easier to use than textbooks, in my opinion, with frequent teacher checkpoints and student experiments right in the book. Here's what you get:

- Introduction to Chemistry—metric units, length/volume/ mass, the scientific method, scientific notation, and careers in chemistry. The careers subunit is taken from a brochure prepared by the Manufacturing Chemists Association, and (oddly) introduced by a bit of eco-hysteria: "Technology that has brought us hybrid grains has also given us the population explosion." *Au contraire, mes amis*: it's *God* who blesses people with children. "Chemicals for killing pests are now often more feared than the pests." So why are there bags of pesticide for sale down at my local nursery store? "Everything in this universe is tied to everything else"—a classic statement of pantheism. The careers subunit itself presents the usual skewed picture of all races and sexes equally represented, when in real life most individuals working in professional, chemistry-related fields are white or Asian and male. (Actually, my mother is the only woman I know who has ever worked as a professional chemist.)
- Elements, Compounds, and Mixture—some neat "kitchen science" experiments in this unit
- Gases and Moles
- Atomic Structure and Periodicity—including brief bios of the scientists who discovered all this
- Chemical Formulas, Bonding, and Molecular Architecture
- Chemical Reaction, Rates, and Equilibrium
- Equilibrium Systems
- Two units on introductory organic chemistry
- A review unit

This is mostly a straight science course, and quite a good one at that. Explanations are uncomplicated and everything is well organized. You can figure out what the text is talking about with very little headscratching.

You need a certain amount of lab equipment and supplies to do the lab experiments—e.g., Erlenmeyer flasks, Bunsen burner, ring stand, tubing, beakers, filters, wire gauze, rubber stop for flask, metal samples, chemicals, test tubes, vacuum apparatus, and so on. Some of this specialized equipment is available in Alpha Omega's Elementary Science Kit. You should get the chemicals from specialized vendors who know how to ship hazardous materials (see Chapter 27).

Wherever feasible, Alpha Omega suggests household objects you can use in place of expensive lab equipment. For example, you may use a hot plate for some experiments instead of a Bunsen burner, or a coin instead of a prepared metal sample. The experiments slack off as you approach the end of the course, since the last units mainly concentrate on number-crunching and memorizing vocabulary and concepts. *Mary Pride*

Alpha Omega Chemistry LIFEPACs
Grade 11. Complete boxed set, $38.95. Elementary Science Kit, $209.95 (includes some specialized apparatus necessary to do the chemistry lab experiments). Shipping extra.
Alpha Omega Publications, 300 N. McKemy, Chandler, AZ 85226. Orders and inquiries: (800) 622-3070. Fax: (480) 785-8034. Web: www.home-schooling.com.

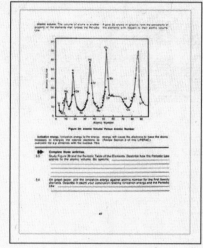

LIFEPAC Sample Page

BJUP Basic Chemistry for Christian Schools

Grade 11. Student text, $30. Teacher's edition, $44.50. Chemistry lab manual, $13. Teacher's lab manual, $16.50. Shipping extra.
Bob Jones University Press Customer Services, Greenville, SC 29614.
Orders: (800) 845-5731.
Fax: (800) 525-8398.
Web: www.bjup.com.

BJUP's 11th-grade chemistry course is called **Basic Chemistry for Christian Schools**, not just Chemistry for Christian Schools, because, in the words of its own introduction, "it explains complicated theories with simple ideas and it uses an understandable format." The biggest difference you'll notice between a course like this and one like A Beka's is that concepts are explained most frequently with words, not with mathematical equations. The author also does an excellent job of explaining complicated processes in everyday terms, using everyday examples and analogies. Line drawings and cartoons make concepts memorable, while the text is also rich in photographs, graphs, and charts. Again, the teacher's edition includes all the pages in the student text, plus teacher notes and answers.

Let me give you an example of how clear and straightforward the writing in this book is. From the chapter on chemical equilibrium:

> *A chemical equilibrium results when forward and reverse reactions proceed simultaneously. This idea ranks as one of the premier concepts in chemistry. Like the kinetic theory and the atomic theory, it helps to explain many observations. While the study of thermodynamics tries to answer the question "Can the reaction occur?" and kinetics seeks to determine "How fast will the reaction occur?" the study of equilibria seeks to answer "How far will the reaction go?"*

All the concepts mentioned in this paragraph, except for chemical equilibrium, have been studied in previous chapters. Yet, although the student already knows about kinetics and thermodynamics, the author provides him or her with the best one-sentence definition of all three topics that I have ever seen.

A little later, chemical equilibrium is illustrated by the fable of Betty and Bob each scooping punch into the other's punch bowl in an attempt to escape their duties as punch servers at Mrs. Tisdale's garden party. (The one who emptied a bowl first could take time off while the other would have to remain and keep serving punch.) When their rates of transfer become equal, they reach dynamic equilibrium and give up the contest. This example is easy to understand and hard to forget —just like the opening definitions in the chapter. The whole book is as good as this!

Don't think for a minute that because the author doesn't indulge in egghead gobbledygook that you're getting anything less than a comprehensive high-school chemistry course. *Basic Chemistry for Christian Schools* has it all, with chapters on:

1. Science, Chemistry, and You. The scientific method, history of chemistry, and what chemistry can mean to a student taking the course.
2. Matter—its classification, energy in matter, and measurement.
3. Atomic Structure—the development of atomic models, including the quantum model.
4. Elements—the periodic table and types of compounds formed by groups within the table.
5. Chemical Bonds.
6. Describing Chemical Composition—how to write the names of compounds, and introducing the mole.
7. Describing Chemical Reactions—writing equations, etc. It's typical of the BJUP approach that "stoichiometry" is a subsection of this chapter rather than the chapter's title, and that the author takes pains to describe exactly what stoichiometry is before launching into the math of how to do it.

8. Gases.
9. Solids and Liquids.
10. Water—as a molecule and in compounds and reactions.
11. Solutions—stuff with other stuff dissolved in it, not "solutions" as in "answers to problems." Colloids are a section in this chapter.
12. Thermodynamics and Kinetics.
13. Chemical Equilibrium.
14. Acids, Bases, and Salts.
15. Oxidation-Reduction.
16. Organic Chemistry. In this chapter you meet all the aromatic hydrocarbons, alkenes, etc. introduced in other textbooks— with the important difference that the minute they are introduced they are defined. E.g., the subsection heading reads "Alkenes: Chains with Double Bonds" not simply "Alkenes."
17. Biochemistry—carbohydrates, proteins, lipids, cellular processes.
18. Nuclear Chemistry.

Note that in the final chapters advanced chemical topics are *introduced*, not beaten to death. I heartily applaud this, as there is no profit in throwing more information at students than they can reasonably be expected to retain. These final chapter topics, from organic chemistry on, are all separate college courses, and even separate degree majors. What high-school chemistry students really need is to find out whether they will want to take any of these college courses later on, rather than to learn half the college material in high school.

The real-life examples in this book are fascinating and the writing is the best I have seen in any chemistry course.

Now what about the lab manual? It's straight lab science, not a mixture of kitchen science and lab science, like Alpha Omega's experiments. The lab manual is just excellent for home use, with a list of all personal lab equipment needed at the beginning of the book and pictures of all the lab equipment at the end, plus illustrated instructions on general safety procedures and how to use the lab equipment. The experiments parallel the textbook. Some have historical significance. For example, the experiments in which you synthesize mauve dye and soap both are repetitions of the original historic experiments. All the regular "book" experiments give you full instructions on how to set up your equipment and step-by-step procedures for doing the experiments. A Special Labs section at the end provides lab problems *without* procedures, so you have to figure out your own equipment setup and experiment steps.

In all, this looks like an excellent course. *Mary Pride*

Most of us don't have the means to get all the necessary equipment to set up a conventional high school chemistry lab. Often, we try to modify traditional laboratory experiments to suit our needs, and this takes time and effort; especially if you don't have a strong background in science.

Author Kathleen Julicher's **Experiences in Chemistry** manual brings highschool chemistry within the grasp of most homeschoolers. Again, this is not a kitchen-type experiment manual. You must buy equipment and chemicals. Home Training Tools can supply these for somewhat less than $150. For chemistry, knowledge is not cheap! Nevertheless, Julicher's lab course is thorough, and includes 36 experiments. Your student will study density, gasses, balancing equations, synthesis, titration, and more. The author includes special warning symbols for your child's safety, and she rec-

NEW!
Castle Heights Experiences in Chemistry
Grades 9–12. Lab manual, $24.95.
Student activity book, $9.95.
Shipping extra.
Castle Heights Press, Inc., 2578 Alexander Farms Dr., Marietta, GA 30064. (800) 763-7148.
Fax/Phone: (770) 218-7998.
Email: julicher@aol.com.
Web: www.flash.net/~wx3o/chp.

ommends that you cut out the safety rule chart and post it. I recommend that you have your student copy it; he will know the rules better having done this.

A typical experiment includes a procedure, lots of questions about observations, and observation data charts. Like the biology questions, the chemistry questions require thinking. A question in the Gas, Temperature, and Pressure experiment asks, "Explain the use of a pressure cooker to speed the cooking of foods." Clearly, Julicher does not care for easy answers!

Since this is a high school course, your student should be familiar with algebra. Geometry wouldn't hurt, either.

This lab guide will provide your child with a good, solid lab experience, comparable to a large high school program. Julicher provides no bells and whistles, and requires no-nonsense answers to real questions. Add the chemistry text of your choosing, and your child will be well prepared to pursue high school science. *Macbeth Derham*

NEW!
Christian Light Education Chemistry

Grade 11. Set of 10 LightUnits, $22.90. Set of 5 Answer Keys, $11.45. Core Unit Science Kit (materials for all grade levels), $197. 11th Grade Unit Science Kit, $89. Elementary Microscope, $106. Triple-beam balance, $107. Shipping extra.
Christian Light Education, PO Box 1212, Harrisonburg, VA 22801-1212. (540) 434-1003. Fax: (540) 433-8896. Email: orders@clp.org.

Christian Light Education's Chemistry course, like other CLE courses, was originally licensed from Alpha Omega Publications. Like the AOP course, it has 10 worktexts (CLE calls theirs "LightUnits"). AOP combines their answer keys into two volumes, while CLE has one answer key for each two LightUnits. The CLE version has heavier-duty kivar covers and brown print. It has been gently edited in conformity with Mennonite beliefs and is less expensive than the AOP course.

CLE lets you purchase all the science supplies needed for the experiments either as a kit or individually. Their order form lists science supplies by grade number (in small print, to the right of each alphabetical item), and is quite easy to use. The experiments are real high-school lab science, not kitchen science. *Mary Pride*

NEW!
Janice VanCleave's A+ Projects in Chemistry

Grades 7–12. Each book, $12.95.
John Wiley & Sons, 1 Wiley Drive, Somerset, NJ 08875. (800) 225-5945. (732) 469-4400. Fax: (800) 597-3299. Web: www.wiley.com.

Janice VanCleave's A+ Projects for Young Adults series includes **Projects in Chemistry**. (For more info about the series, see the review under "Earth Science" in the Junior High Science chapter.)

This is not a series of weenie experiments. The 30 chapter topics are weather, humidity, air, biochemistry, calories, fatty acids, vitamin C, minerals, proteins, carbohydrates, indicators, acids and bases, phase changes, colloids, electrolytes, chromatography, coloring and color-fastness, viscosity, crystals, floatation, hard water, molecular motion, polymers, megaabsorbers, water, oxygen, carbon dioxide, thermodynamics, thermometers, and insulators.

As you can see, the emphasis is on the practical. You will learn a great deal of terminology and scientific method, but a standard chemistry text is also needed if you plan to cover all the standard chemistry subjects.

No complicated or expensive equipment is required for the experiments. The *Chemistry* book relies heavily on eye-droppers, tincture of iodine, and household ingredients for its experiments, rather than the pipettes, graduated cylinders, chemical balances, and Bunsen burners found in a typical high-school chem lab. This means that, while you will learn a *lot* if you do all the experiments in a book, instead of just picking one for a science fair, it might not sufficiently impress college officials to count as the "lab" portion of a science course. However, it meets and exceeds its stated purpose: to help you understand the subject and come up with good science fair ideas. *Mary Pride*

The **School of Tomorrow Chemistry** course has the same format and material types as their Biology course—videos, workbooks, score keys, and a computer-video interactive (CVI) option. See the Biology chapter for more details.

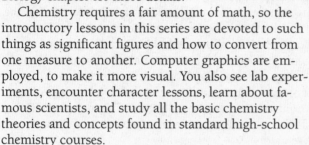

Chemistry requires a fair amount of math, so the introductory lessons in this series are devoted to such things as significant figures and how to convert from one measure to another. Computer graphics are employed, to make it more visual. You also see lab experiments, encounter character lessons, learn about famous scientists, and study all the basic chemistry theories and concepts found in standard high-school chemistry courses.

The presentation is friendly, not stuffy. The camera moves around in similar fashion to a network TV show; you aren't stuck watching "talking heads." Wherever possible, you are shown, not just told.

If your student has any fear of chemistry, or needs extra help with the math, this is *the* course you should use. *Mary Pride*

University of Nebraska-Lincoln Independent Study offers two types of chemistry courses: standard lab correspondence courses and innovative Web-based courses with plotlines and characters.

Chemistry 1 and **Chemistry 2** are standard lab courses. Each is available with complete lab supplies or (for less cost) with only dry labs and virtual experiments. Special packages of lab supplies are available for students living overseas.

The Chemistry 1 and 2 regular correspondence programs require you to send in papers and tests (fax and email options are now available for quicker service), which are graded and returned to your "local supervisor." This person can not be a family member without special permission. He is responsible for proctoring closed-book tests and receiving correspondence from UNL. He is also supposed to supervise the coursework and make sure you stay on track. If you are not interested in the correspondence option, in other words you just want the course materials, you don't need a local supervisor. As a compromise, UNL will send course materials directly to the student, only requiring that tests be proctored by an "approved person," which can include a librarian (we all go the library, don't we?).

You find your assignments in the course syllabus. You then read the assigned textbook pages, write the answers and essays in the syllabus, do the

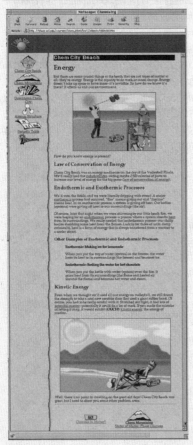

projects, and take the pretests. There is a lot of study and writing; these are not Mickey Mouse courses. Although you are allowed to finish a course fairly swiftly (in as little as three weeks, with special permission), in real life a semester course takes about a semester to finish.

In contrast to these lab courses, Basic Chemistry: Chem City and Chemistry 1: Voyage of the Democritus are Web-based courses that require students to solve puzzles, learning chemistry concepts along the way.

In **Chem City**, you role-play an investigative reporter who uses chemistry to track down the causes of environmental problems. This course is extremely basic, intended for an introduction or review before a student is ready for a regular Chemistry 1 course. And I mean *basic*. Lesson 1, for example, has you clicking on a seashore visual to identify all the matter in the picture—even the air! Further lessons take you to the mountains, downtown, and other locations, learning about such things as the states of matter and properties of acids and bases. This is material usually covered in elementary school, but a lot more fun. The Atomic Structure lesson, in which you get to click on each important figure in the development of the theory to discover his contribution, is especially cool. The included CD-ROM makes the visuals and the animations much faster than if these components were on the Web alone.

In **Voyage of the Democritus**, which also comes with a CD-ROM, you are a crew member on a spaceship searching for a new planetary home. Something goes wrong with your suspended animation, and when you wake up, the entire crew has lost its memories. You have to rediscover your knowledge of chemistry so you can figure out if a planet is worth living on. Topics you'll be researching are food, transportation, energy, air and atmosphere, shelter, and clothing. Crew dialogues set up the questions. You get information from the computer, which sticks lessons up on your screen as needed, and the Holographic Imager. This device shows some fictitious expert explaining a concept. The Memory Bank also shows up every third lesson or so. It's a heavily illustrated lesson with "check-ups" (problems you have to solve), sidebar factoids, and links to related web sites. Web-based communication with the teacher and your fellow students is also possible.

At the end of each Web-based lesson module, you complete the assignment and send it in to your teacher. Grades and other info are also available to you through the Web.

Ecological political correctness abounds in both Web courses. The Democritus left Earth because of overpopulation. Some of the sites for you to link to include topics such as acid rain, global warming, open-pit mining, and rainforest deforestation. For nuclear energy, you get a site on the Chernobyl disaster. You get the idea.

Both Web-based courses run on Macs and PCs. You'll need a fairly recent model computer with fairly recent system software and web browser. The specs in the manual for Macs only mentioned "System 7," but it turns out you need System 7.6.1 in order to run Netscape 4.0.4, which is required for these courses. In all, it ended up taking us about four hours to install and set up and necessary software.

Don't expect the Web courses to have the fun factor of a typical computer game. The plotline basically sets up the scenario, but does not build from there, and you won't find Hollywood-quality animations and movie clips, either. However, they are much more involving than the typical dry chemistry textbook. As for those dry Chemistry 1 and 2 courses: we're using them ourselves, since we need the labs for college prep. May the day come soon when even the lab-based courses are as innovative and involving as UN-I's current web-based courses! *Mary Pride*

Self-Study Texts

Chemistry the Easy Way is "all the essentials in one clear volume." Along with basic instructions on everything covered in a good high-school chemistry course, from atomic structure to equilibrium to laboratory set-up, you get hundreds of step-by-step examples, five practice achievement tests (for those planning to take the Chemistry SAT II or the Regents Chemistry test), and a glossary. It's not pretty, or amazingly easy to follow or fun to use, but it *is* methodical. Barron's guarantees that this book will improve your grades in 30 days, or you can return it to them for a full refund. *Mary Pride*

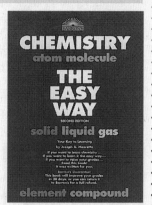

The blurb on the back says **Chemistry Made Simple** is a "self-study guide for a college general chemistry course or high-school-level chemistry." It includes "58 clear diagrams and figures" and "53 useful tables." (After reading this, Bill asked me how many *unclear* diagrams and *unuseful* tables were also included. The "Made Simple" marketing wordsmiths strike again!) Speaking of wordsmiths, the introduction assures us,

> *As to the flow of words, every effort has been made to keep the phraseology and style as simple as possible.*

If you ask me, more effort should have been made to cut down the flow, as the sample above amply illustrates.

Where is this book strongest?

"Elementally, my dear Watson."

The book is very strong on elemental properties, introducing elements by families and spending most of the book on this. However, it doesn't spend nearly as much time on problem-solving as other chemistry books I'm familiar with. You get a *few* problems worked, but considering how difficult it is for most students to master measurement conversions and equations involving these, and equations involving equilibrium, more help here would have been a good idea.

There is no cumulative review; all problems of one type occur only in the chapter on that topic. A fair number of problems are worked in the text, and each chapter ends with a set of problems for you to work, with answers in the back. As a plus, the book does include some simple experiments for you to do—which as a minus generally require apparatus and ingredients you don't have on hand. A list of materials used in the experiments would have been very helpful.

I see no reason to use this book, as opposed to a typical chemistry textbook. It might be helpful as a supplement, especially in the early part of your course that deals with elements and the periodic table. *Mary Pride*

Review and Reference

Cliffs Quick Review: Chemistry is 174 pages with no index. It does have a glossary of chemical terms, and an appendix to the problems given in the text, of which there aren't all that many. As a quick review, it covers everything in your basic high-school chem course, from elements, atoms, and the periodic table, to equilibrium and thermodynamics.

Now, for a book like this, clarity of style is essential and a tiny touch of humor is desirable. What you get is sentences like these:

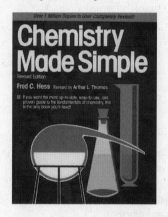

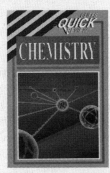

NEW!
Schaum's Outline Series: Beginning Chemistry

Grade 11–college. Analytical Chemistry; College Chemistry; and Organic Chemistry $14.95 each. Beginning Chemistry, $13.95; Biochemistry, $16.95; General, Organic, and Biological Chemistry; Physical Chemistry, $15.95 each. Add shipping.
McGraw-Hill, Order Services, PO Box 545, Blacklick, OH 43004-0545. Orders: (800)262-4729. Inquiries: (800) 338-3987. Fax: (614)759-3641. Web: www.schaums.com.

Usborne Introduction to Chemistry

Grades 7–12. Introduction to Chemistry, $7.95. The Usborne Book of Science (combined volume, also includes biology and physics), $16.95. Shipping extra.
EDC Publishing, Division of Educational Development Corporation, 10302 East 55th Place, Tulsa, OK 74146. (800) 475-4522. Fax: (800) 747-4509. Web: www.edcpub.com.

> *The anamolous electronic configuration of chromium and copper is interpreted as the displacement of one electron from an s orbital into a d orbital; these two elements have only one electron in the 4s subshell because the second electron was promoted into a 3d subshell. This example warns you that there are exceptions to the general pattern of electronic configuration of the elements.*

It also warns you that this book is no laugh riot. Condensed it may be, but simplified it is not. *Mary Pride*

The "beginning chemistry" we're looking at here is a college chemistry course. High-school kids study a lot of the same stuff, but probably won't finish everything covered in this book.

It amazes me that a course "outline" can be 372 oversized pages, including the glossary and index. Like other "outline" books, **Schaum's Outline Series: Beginning Chemistry** is long on worked problems. Since answers are given directly below the problems, you need to cover the page with a piece of paper and move it down as you read, if you want to work any of the problems yourself.

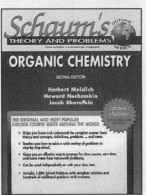

The explanations are step-by-step, as are the problems, which are generally worked out in some detail. The design is functional, but short on diagrams, and lacking in such expected features as bold typeface treatments, grey boxes, and other visual helps. In this day of desktop design, I'd hope for something a lot better looking in the next edition.

Also available from Schaum's in the outline department: *Analytical Chemistry; Biochemistry; College Chemistry; General, Organic, and Biological Chemistry; Organic Chemistry;* and *Physical Chemistry.* You better believe you're going to need help if you take courses with those names, so why not try Schaum's? *Mary Pride*

EDC Publishing has great introductions to electronics, chemistry, biology, and physics that actually *explain* these subjects. Each book in the series is wholesome and well balanced. The **Introduction to Chemistry**, for instance, is pro-industry. It talks about "new, useful substances," which is refreshing to read in an era when all man-made substances are coming under attack.

Cheerful cartoon people demonstrate chemical principles throughout the book. The book also takes a humble view of the history of science, noting how a hypothesis "cannot be conclusively proved true, but if it is never disproved, it comes accepted and can be used in explaining discoveries and forming new hypotheses." Simple experiments are provided, along with gorgeous illustrations (full-color in the first 32 pages, black-and-white in the last 16) and simple explanations of difficult concepts.

Topics include the following (remember, the whole book is only 48 pages long): What is chemistry? Looking at chemicals. What things are made of. Looking at particles (including why a saucepan boils over and how a refrigerator works). Physical changes (includes four separate lab-style experiments for separating substances). What is a chemical reaction? (make a simple compound). Looking for patterns in chemistry. Why chemical reactions happen. Looking at compounds (simple apparatus for testing whether substances conduct when dissolved in water). Valences. Fast and slow reactions (more experiments). Catalysts (lab experiment with hydrogen peroxide, and a simpler one with saliva and starch). How metals react (the flame test is fun!). Acids, bases, and salts (lab and real-life experiments). What is organic chemistry? (Answer: no, it's not about recycling, being the study of compounds containing carbon. Experiments include making wine, then turning it into vinegar.) Organic families (no, it's not about folks who subscribe to *Mother Earth News*—make some molecular models!). Useful organic compounds (make your own plastic out of household ingredients!). Splitting compounds. Identifying substances. Computer program (BASIC text to type in for a program that identifies unknown substances). Formulae and equations. Doing experiments. Answers to puzzles included in the book. Glossary of chemical terms. Short index. Safety instructions are buried on page 45, for some reason: read that page *first!*

This is just a super book. The experiments are super. The text is super. The illustrations are super. Buy it! *Mary Pride*

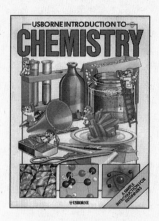

Chemistry Videos

School of Tomorrow Chemistry Videos are friendly and well produced. There are 24 in all. For a complete course, add the computer-video interactive (CVI) option or the workbooks. For more details on the full course, see writeup earlier in this chapter. *Mary Pride*

I explained how the **Standard Deviants Video Series** works in the Basic Math chapter—and why it has nothing to do with "deviants" and everything to do with "deviating from the standard," i.e. how to become a curve-wrecker (a grade A student, to those of you who never took statistics). These fun videos demystify the "tough" subjects for college students . . . and smart high-school students, too!

Currently available for chemistry are:

- (Edited For All Audiences edition) **The Super-Charged World of Chemistry** (three videos)
- **The Deep Fried World of Organic Chemistry** (three videos)

Although it won't be around after the stock sells out, an excellent workbook is available to accompany the EFAA Chemistry videos. It is a course book in itself, explaining the material covered on the three videos. Time codes and video notes sections cross-reference the videos. Practice exams and quizzes double-check what's been learned. Fun activities and simple one-person games (we're talking crossword puzzles and the like) add yet more reinforcement. There's some humor, but it's mostly of the "funny names in the word problems" sort. Chatty educational content outweighs humor in the workbooks about 20 to 1.

I really enjoyed watching these chemistry videos. From the introduction to states of matter (Volume 1 starts off easy), to the inside story on molarity and molality (at the end of Volume 3), here is everything I studied in high school chem class and forgot in the 29 years since. What a great, time-efficient refresher . . . or introduction! And what a super way for kids who have taken other courses to review for the SAT II or AP tests. Go, Helium Man! *Mary Pride*

NEW!
Superstar Teachers
Chemistry

Grades 11–12. $149.95 plus $10 shipping.
The Teaching Company, 7405 Alban Station Court, Suite A107, Springfield, VA 22150. (800) 832-2412.
Fax: (703) 912-7756.
Email: custserv@teachco.com.
Web: www.teachco.com.

Part of the **SuperStar Teachers** High School Series, **Chemistry** is 30 lessons that cover all of high-school chemistry, captured for you on four long-play video tapes, plus two small booklets that provide a bare-bones outline of each lecture. I hear a workbook is now available, but have not yet seen it.

Chemistry teacher Frank Cardulla, the presenter of this course, has years of experience teaching high-school chemistry and has won several major awards for his teaching. His enthusiastic presentation begins by asserting "chemistry is the easiest class in school." Throughout the course, he shows students how to solve chemistry problems by relating them to real-world problems they already know how to solve. For example, the frightening world of "stoichiometry" becomes much more manageable when he shows you how the exact same principles work with a raisin-bread recipe. No stuttering or false starts here—the man is a professional, smooth at what he does.

Don't expect to see spectacular lab setups or lots of green fizz and fireworks. The emphasis in this course is on understanding how chemistry works, and applying that understanding to problem-solving, not on flashy visuals. Mostly what you'll see is Mr. Cardulla using an easel and blackboard. Some computer-generated graphics are also used to illustrate concepts.

About a dozen chemical demonstrations are also included. In spite of what Mr. Cardulla says about the need to do your own lab work, I do wish the course included many more experiments. My favorite memories of high-school chemistry were the exciting experiments the professors did in the front of the room—and many homeschoolers find it difficult to find a safe place to set up chemistry labs at home. Perhaps the Teaching Company could be persuaded to either add a "lab" videotape, or do a separate "Chem Lab" tape set? *Mary Pride*

Games and Goodies

How would you like to win first prize in the Virginia Young Author's Contest at both the regional and statewide levels? And, after that, how would you like to have the book published that you wrote as your contest entry?

Such is the true story behind **A Gebra Named Al**. Author Wendy Isdell began writing it when she was in the eighth grade. Apparently this first contest-winning book of hers did well enough that its companion, **The Chemy Named Al**, which Wendy began writing as a high-school senior, also was published by the same company.

If you have figured out that *Al* and *Gebra* spell *Algebra*, and *Al* and *Chemy* spell *Alchemy* (which, in its experimental side, was the precursor to modern chemistry), give yourself a gold star. Both books follow the fictional adventures of a struggling student named Julie, who travels to the Land of Mathematics and the Land of Science. There, she and the friendly creatures she meets (most named after Periodic Table elements) save the lands using Julie's increasing knowledge of chemistry. (Even the *Gebra* book teaches more chemistry than algebra.) The stories are fun to read and would be a great warm-up to a real chemistry course.

To make these into unit studies, you'll want the accompanying inexpensive oversized teacher guides, **Using a Gebra Named Al in the Classroom** and **Using a Chemy Named Al in the Classroom**. Each includes activities and questions related to each chapter in the book, vocabulary lists and activities, possible answers for the chapter-related questions, and suggested lesson topics to expand the book's teaching value.

If you enjoyed *The Phantom Tollbooth*, you'll probably like these books. If you've never read *The Phantom Tollbooth* or seen its animated video, check it out—and then you'll know what I'm talking about! *Mary Pride*

The **ElementO** board game teaches you about elements and the periodic table . . . and makes it such fun that your eight-year-old will beg to play (mine did!). The simple and elegant game plays a little like Monopoly—you're trying to "buy" the elements you land on, so you can charge other people the number of protons in that element if they land on it. If you have the

whole family of that element, whoever lands on one of them has to pay you the total number of protons in the whole family. You'll learn the element symbols and names without thinking about it. What a great way to give kids a head start on chemistry! *Mary Pride*

NEW!
Friendly Chemistry

Grades 7–12. $95 plus $7 shipping (NE residents add 5% sales tax). Parent's and Leader's Guide (includes video and 200 page supplement), $45 plus shipping. *Hideaway Ventures, HC 68, Box 20, Westerville, NE 68881. Phone/fax: (800) 774-3447. Email: hideaway@nctc.com. Web: www.custercounty.com/ friendlychemistry.*

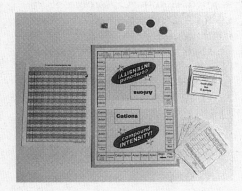

Friendly Chemistry: A Guide to Learning Basic Chemistry is chemistry the homeschool way. You learn the periodic table from flashcards and several board games. The niceties of electrons and atomic structure are introduced with a manipulative device that has you putting little red and white balls into cups in a "Doo-Wop Board." Simple, twaddle-free explanations in the spiral-bound book make chemistry concepts crystal clear, while just enough charts, graphs, and exercises help you cement what you have learned.

Aimed straight at the heart of homeschool moms and dads everywhere, Friendly Chemistry includes 11 student-tested manipulatives (love that hands-on learning!). These include the aforementioned flashcards and Doo-Wop Mania game plus Element Bingo, Ion Bingo, Polyatomic Bingo, Radius Ricochet, The Friendly Neighborhood (a periodic-table game), Compound Intensity, and Teamwork (chemical equations).

Fourteen chapters plus two appendices (300 pages in all) cover chemical concepts that include atomic structure, quantum mechanics, ionizations and compound formation, reactivity, periodicity of the elements, chemical reactions, balancing equations, and stoichiometry. Practice exercises and a glossary are included; unfortunately, an index and an order form for reordering individual manipulatives are not.

The scope of Friendly Chemistry is intended to be comparable to a high-school chemistry course; the goal is to give you a "deep understanding of chemical principles." The "deep understanding" part is right, but you'll need to supplement with the last few chapters of a high-school chemistry text and a book of chemistry experiments to get the full treatment. But why wait until high school? This is probably the only chemistry course that would be great for junior-high kids. Anyone completing this course would have a real jump on either high-school or college chemistry. *Mary Pride*

NEW!
MIT Periodic Table accessories

All ages. Periodic Table T-shirt, $14.95 (specify S, M, L, XL, or XXL). Periodic Table mug, $12.95. Periodic Table mousepad, $16.95. *MIT Museum Shop, 265 Massachusetts Ave., Cambridge, MA 02139. (617) 253-4462. Fax: (617) 258-6563. Email: dangarcia@mit.edu. Web: web.mit.edu/museum/shop/ shop.html.*

This is all just too cool. Thanks to the people at MIT, you can wear the periodic table in the form of an 100-percent-cotton T-shirt, and the entries for the radioactive elements even glow in the dark! Or you can drink out of a mug that has the metals and gases in full-color table form on one side, and a complete table of the elements on the other side. Or, for the ultimate in elemental geekiness, you can combine computing and chemistry with a periodic table mousepad. It's better living through chemistry. *Mary Pride*

CHAPTER 25

Physics

Physics produces deep insights into the nature of the universe that only other physicists can understand. (This is "non-Newtonian" physics.) It is also useful for knowing how far a 1000 kg polar bear will slide on the ice if you smack him with a bowling ball of known weight and velocity. (This is "Newtonian" physics.) Physics is great for making pretty patterns in a homemade or store-bought ripple tank (this is "optics") and playing with homemade circuits (this is "electromagnetism"). Physics is also good for getting government grants that let you buy huge amounts of land, so you can build your particle accelerator. Finally, physics is a rich source of geek jokes, especially when you're pulling an all-nighter in engineering school. (No, I won't tell you any. They are too stupid to repeat. That's why nobody tells them until after midnight, when common sense is at its lowest ebb.)

Everyone who designs in any medium except fabric and paper uses physics. Car designers use it. Bridge builders use it. Construction engineers use it. If you're concerned about what will happen to something when you hit it, twirl it, suspend it, bounce light off it, or take it up to lightspeed, you need physics. Or if you just want to know why Scotty *can't* beam you up, physics is essential. It's the ultimate hands-on science—especially if a lot of your best friends are polar bears who bowl on ice floes.

One thing you need to know: college placement tests distinguish between physics course that do not require calculus as a prerequisite, and physics courses that do. Scientist and engineer types who desire advanced college placement should plan on taking calculus *before* physics, and then using the toughest physics course available. There is some debate over whether the Saxon physics book will meet this goal. It should work fine for the "Physics B" Advanced Placement exam, but if you're thinking of taking the "Physics C" series, you might want to supplement with a college physics textbook.

If you're *not* a scientist or engineer type, you can take it easier . And whether you're a budding physicist or not, you all can have fun with some of the more light-hearted physics resources below!

A Beka Physics

Grade 12. Physics text (paperbound), $25.20. Teacher's guide (does not include student text), $16.20. Solution key, $31.75. Student test booklet, $6.20. Teacher key for test booklet, $9.20. Student quiz booklet, $4.60. Teacher key for quiz booklet, $9.20. Physics lab manual, $12.45. Lab manual teacher's guide, $16.10 Video lab demonstrations (VHS only), $150.20 Shipping extra. *A Beka Book, Box 19100, Pensacola, FL 32523-9100. (800) 874-2352. Fax: (800) 874-3590. Web: www.abeka.com.*

Physics Courses

Did I mention that **A Beka** believes in giving you a *lot* of pages for your money? It's true of their **Physics: The Foundational Science** text for 12th-graders. It's about the same size as A Beka's chemistry text (649 pages) and includes enough information to take you through high-school physics and through the Advanced Placement exam. (Most on-site high-school classes won't get through the whole book in one year.)

My husband Bill previewed this book for me before I reviewed it myself. His comments were, "It has good explanations, well illustrated; lots of biographical sketches of famous physicists who were Christians; examples are worked out in the text; a logical sequence within each chapter; in sum, the book is all business." To amplify on this a little, what you get are the following sections:

1. Basic concepts in physics. This introduces the nature of science, matter and energy, particles, and the branches of physics, plus a chapter on scientific notation, significant digits, and the other math you need to solve physics problems. (This is the same type of math introduction as in A Beka's chemistry text.)
2. Three states of matter. One chapter each on the liquid, gaseous, and solid state. Consider this a chemistry review.
3. Mechanics. Excellent chapters on velocity and acceleration, Newton's laws and friction, vectors, motion in two dimensions, work and machines, energy and momentum, rotary motion, and gravitation.
4. Thermodynamics. Two chapter that make plain what my expensive one-semester thermo course (which half the class flunked) failed to explain. Good everyday applications of thermodynamic principles.
5. Wave phenomena. Waves, sound, and music.
6. Light. Everything normally studied in a physics course on this topic: the nature of light, the electromagnetic spectrum, color, reflection, refraction, and wave optics.
7. Electricity and magnetism. Includes fields, current, circuits, capacitance, resistance/inductance, and electrical devices.
8. Modern physics. Here's where the rubber really meets the road and all the non-physicists start scratching their heads. I remember the good ol' days when scientists didn't study this stuff until college—and if you're older than me, you might remember the days when even college *professors* didn't claim to understand this stuff! The first two chapters, on quantum theory and special relativity, do what they can to make the invisible and theoretical make some sense. The last two chapters will probably bring a sigh of relief, as they are on technological subjects (modern light and electronics technologies) with which we are familiar from reading popular magazines.

Like the other upper-grades A Beka science courses, the physics course has a wealth of teacher's aids and supplemental resources. The teacher's guide includes daily lesson plans, demonstration ideas, chapter summaries, and teaching strategies. The *Physics Laboratory Manual* includes instructions, record-keeping sheets, equipment lists, etc. for 16 physics labs paralleling the topics in the book. These are not nearly as complicated to set up as the biology and chemistry labs. Besides, the book explains how to make your own experimental devices. A ripple tank, for example, can be as simple as a hole in the ground lined with a plastic sheet with brick side walls holding it in place, or a child's wading pool, or a concrete mixing tub, while you provide the wave action with a simple lattice strip rather than a fancy wave generator. Or, if you really don't want to take the time to set up your own home lab and work through the experiments, you can purchase A Beka's video physics labs. These are video demonstrations of the actual experiments in the *Physics Laboratory Manual*.

Physics: The Foundational Science is an excellent choice for intelligent, well-prepared students who are willing to work steadily through it. Anyone contemplating a future in engineering, technological applications, or science should consider it.

Twelfth grade means **physics** in the **Alpha Omega** science curriculum. Each science course is a set of 10 workbooks with the lesson text, exercises, and tests all built in. The design of these LIFEPACS is easy to use, with frequent teacher checkpoints and student experiments right in the book. You get a unit each on:

- Kinematics—scalars, vectors, velocity, acceleration, and other basic mathematical methods for describing motion. Build your own balance for measuring small items, measure the thickness of a molecular layer, use a percussion timer to measure changes in distance, make a scale model of part of the solar system. You do a report on Galileo and solve problems that involve a caterpillar crawling up a wall.
- Dynamics—Newton's and Kepler's laws. You report (of course) on Newton and Kepler's lives, test Newton's Second Law using your old friend the percussion timer, twirl a rubber stopper around on a string, play bumper cars with two steel spheres (you need tracing and carbon paper plus a bunch of other stuff for this experiment), and so on.
- Work and energy—not human work and human energy, but energy, power, heat, and thermodynamics. You'll need your percussion timer again, to measure the kinetic and potential energy of a homemade pendulum. You'll measure calories (the latent heat of fusion of water) using either a calorimeter or an aluminum tumbler inside a styrofoam cup.
- Wave theory. Play with a Slinky, build your own ripple tank, make a torsion wave apparatus out of a flexible wire strip and metal rods with weighted ends (they don't tell you this, but you can make weighted ends by soldering on coins or lumps of metal), fiddle with sound, and more!
- Light—refraction, reflection, etc. Write a report on Christian Huygens. Compare waves to particles (the famous steel-ball-bearing experiment). Lots of experiments with optical equipment: prisms, light pipes, filters, mirrors, etc.
- Static electricity—charges, fields, potential. As you might expect, you'll be rubbing various materials on rubber wands and learning to sketch electrical fields. Some interesting meditations on biblical applications of the ideas of attraction, charge, insulation, and so on.
- Current electricity—resistance and circuits. Write a report on Coulomb, Ampère, Volta, and Ohm. Learn to decipher some simple circuit diagrams and understand simple circuits (serial and parallel). Lots of math. Surprisingly, I didn't see any elec-

Alpha Omega Physics LIFEPACs
Grade 12. Complete boxed set, $38.95. Shipping extra.
Alpha Omega Publications, 300 N. McKemy, Chandler, AZ 85226. Orders and inquiries: (800) 622-3070. Fax: (480) 785-8034. Web: www.home-schooling.com.

trical experiments in this unit.
- Magnetism. Experiments with magnets and iron filings, sketching magnetic fields, simple electromagnetic experiments.
- Atomic and nuclear physics. Lots of terminology, history, and math. No experiments (not that anyone expects you to have radioactive isotopes lying around your house!).
- Review unit.

All these topics are logically presented along with student experiments. The material is at an easier reading level than either the A Beka or Bob Jones University Press courses, and the experiments are easier to set up at home.

If you like to build things and solve math problems—or just like to buy things and solve problems—you'll love this course. *Mary Pride*

Here's another **BJUP** science course we like! Once you get past the first paragraphs of the introduction, in which the authors attempt unconvincingly to reassure the student that physics is not "a form of academic torture" (better not to raise the issue in the first place—it always makes me nervous when the doctor says it isn't going to hurt!) what you have here is a well-written textbook with fascinating sidelights on the history of physics. The teacher's manual includes the student text, plus notes and answers.

Physics for Christian Schools features excellent explanations, examples, and problem sets. The Facets of Physics sidebars make physics real with explanations of the physics of how things work, from fuel cells, to ice skating, to particle accelerators, to diesel trains. Cartoons spice up the text and make the examples more memorable. It's all in two colors: no full-color fancy graphics.

Now, I'm not going to kid you. There's a lot of math here. However, it could be worse. You get a lot of examples worked for you, and the authors do try to make it all make sense in English, using lots of word pictures. Consider this example, introducing the concept of momentum:

> *Momentum measures an object's motion. For example, an object with large momentum is harder to stop than an object with small momentum. What properties do you think affect momentum?*
>
> *The first property affecting momentum should be obvious, after a little thought. Which is easier to stop—a 10,000-kg truck moving at 50 km/hr. or a 0.05-kg tennis ball moving at the same speed? You can stop the tennis ball with one hand, but your whole body would not stop the truck! Therefore, the mass of an object affects its momentum.*

The book is divided into units, each made up of several chapters. Unit 1 introduces the scientific method, scientific notation, measurement (the same stuff you studied at the beginning of your chemistry course). Unit 2, on mechanics, covers motion in one, two, and three dimensions (vectors and scalars), dynamics, circular motion, Newton's laws (with lots of word problems), work and energy, conservation of energy, momentum, and periodic motion. Unit 3, on thermal energy, covers properties of matter, expansion and temperature, thermal energy and heat, and the laws of thermodynamics. Unit 4, on electricity and magnetism, introduces fluid mechanics (I don't recall seeing this topic in other high-school courses), electric charge and fields, electrodynamics, magnetism, electromagnetism, and electronics.

BJUP Physics for Christian Schools

Grade 12. Student text, $23. Teacher's edition, $42.50. Physics lab manual: student edition, $13; teacher's edition, $15.50. Shipping extra.

Bob Jones University Press Customer Services, Greenville, SC 29614. Orders: (800) 845-5731. Fax: (800) 525-8398. Web: www.bjup.com.

Unit 5, optics, is the usual light-and-wave properties: reflection, refraction, and so on. Unit 6, on modern physics, introduces relativity, quantum physics, and nuclear physics. Every other chapter or so is followed by a one- or two-page biography of some famous physicist.

The physics lab manual is pretty standard, with illustrated experiments keyed to the book's chapters. Each experiment has a goal, materials list, explanation, step-by-step procedure, photo or line drawing of the equipment setup, and tables to fill in or calculation sheets to fill out. Yes, you write your tables, calculations, and conclusions right there in the lab manual.

The teacher's manual does not tell you how to construct any of this equipment, but does has a general equipment list for the year. Some of the equipment is intended to be homemade, judging from the setup illustrations.

The excellent teacher's guide to the text does tell you how to make a bunch of lab equipment (Leyden jars, van de Graff generators, etc.) for in-class demonstrations of the chapter concepts. It also includes teaching objectives and notes for each chapter and answers to all the questions. You absolutely should get the teacher's edition, which includes a regular copy of the student text (no special teacher notes) as well as the teacher's guide to the text, if you plan to use this course. *Mary Pride*

Christian Light Education's Physics course, like other CLE courses, was originally licensed from Alpha Omega Publications. Like the AOP course, it has 10 worktexts (CLE

calls theirs "LightUnits"). AOP combines their answer keys into two volumes, while CLE has one answer key for each two LightUnits. The CLE version has heavier-duty kivar covers and brown print. It has been gently edited in conformity with Mennonite beliefs and is less expensive than the AOP course.

CLE lets you purchase all the science supplies needed for the experiments either as a kit or individually. Their order form lists science supplies by grade number (in small print, to the right of each alphabetical item), and is quite easy to use. The experiments are real high-school lab science. Supplies include materials to study electricity, inertia and acceleration, collisions in two dimensions, the speed of sound, and more. You can even purchase a ripple-tank apparatus to study the properties of waves and light. Everything we did in my high-school Advanced Placement Physics course is right here. *Mary Pride*

The new **Exploratorium Science Snackbook** books are great physics resources for older students. These science snacks are quick and fun to cook up, but don't let that fool you—they definitely are *not* educational junk food!

A science "snack" is a guide to help your students create a small reproduction of one of the interactive exhibitions housed at the Exploratorium Museum in San Francisco. Twenty-six "snacks" in each of these first two books explore the properties of light. Let me take a typical snack from *The Magic Wand* and we'll briefly run through it.

The title of this science snack is "Blue Sky—now you can explain why the sky is blue and the sunset is red." After this introduction is a rundown of the property of light (scattering) being demonstrated. After this comes the list of materials needed, most of them common household items. Only one item—a polarizing filter—may need to be purchased, although using

NEW!
Christian Light Education Physics
Grade 12. Set of 10 LightUnits, $22.90. Set of 5 Answer Keys, $11.45. Core Unit Science Kit (materials for all grade levels), $197. 12th Grade Unit Science Kit, $262. Triple-beam balance, $107. Ripple Tank Apparatus and Wave Generator, $218. Shipping extra.
Christian Light Education, PO Box 1212, Harrisonburg, VA 22801-1212. (540) 434-1003. Fax: (540) 433-8896. Email: orders@clp.org.

NEW!
Exploratorium Science Snackbook series
Grades 6–12. $10.95 each plus shipping.
John Wiley & Sons, 1 Wiley Drive, Somerset, NJ 08875. (800) 225-5945. (732) 469-4400. Fax: (800) 597-3299. Web: www.wiley.com.

an old pair of polarized sunglasses is suggested as a workable solution. According to the directions, assembly takes about 15 minutes (it's only three easy steps) and observation is expected to take another 15 minutes or so. Some suggestions are given for manipulating the resulting contraption during observation in order to give the best viewing results, and a very thorough explanation of what we are seeing ensues in the "What's Going On?" section. Under "Etc." at the end of the chapter, the principle of light scattering is explained even further!

The series includes

- *The Cheshire Cat, and Other Eye-Popping Experiments on How We See the World*
- *The Magic Wand, and Other Bright Experiments on Light and Color*
- *The Cool Hot Rod, and Other Electrifying Experiments on Energy and Matter*
- *The Spinning Blackboard, and Other Dynamic Experiments on Force and Motion*

The Exploratorium Science Snackbook Series is very solid in content, and each principle is so well explained that parents should be able to successfully complete a "snack" with their kids even if they are a bit rusty in their knowledge of physics. (Parents and kids learning and re-learning together—I love it!) For the most part, the projects are easily put together with readily available items. For some projects, however, you will need to plan ahead and purchase special materials from a science supply house. *Teresa May*

You don't need a background in physics to supervise this course. A helpful parent needs only to have finished the equivalent of Saxon's Algebra 2 book, as far as the math goes. Dittos for the student, who also needs to have completed Algebra 2.

To make it easier, the text itself will hold your hand a bit, thanks to "incremental development and continuous review." This means that instruction goes bit by bit and the same type of problem pops up day after day in the problem sets, until you get so comfortable solving it that it seems easy.

Saxon is acutely conscious of how desirable it is to pass an Advanced Placement exam, and the book is designed to make this possible, covering all the topics you'll find on the easier exam. Suitable for either high school or college, it deals with Newton's laws, statics, dynamics, thermodynamics (a topic I have always found conducive to sound slumber), optics, DC circuits, waves, electromagnetism, and even special relativity, with a visual layout that will appear friendly and familiar to those who have used any of Saxon's math books. Loaded with simple, helpful illustrations, this monster book (796 indexed pages) will undoubtedly be the top choice of many Saxon fans.

Finally, about the prices—no, there are no typos. The Home Study kit, which includes the student book plus answer keys and tests, actually costs less than the student book alone. Would I be wrong in deducing that Saxon is gently urging you to get all the tools you need to actually succeed in this course?

While we're at it, the Solutions Manual is not another name for the answer key. While the answer key contains just the answers, the Solutions Manual shows you each problem worked out step by step. Very handy. Considering what it would cost you to take a college physics course (in the neighborhood of $1,000 to $3,000), and that if you finish Saxon Physics and do well on the AP exam you might get credit for a college physics course, thus saving the $1,000 to $3,000, why not splurge and get the Solutions Manual? *Mary Pride*

NEW!
Saxon Physics
Grade 10 and up. Home study kit (includes student book, answer key and tests), $61.95. Book only (student edition), $62.67. Answer key and tests, $18. Solutions manual, $25. Shipping extra.
Saxon Publishers, 2450 John Saxon Blvd., Norman, OK 73071. (800) 284-7019. Email: info@saxonpub.com. Web: www.saxonpub.com.

The **School of Tomorrow Physics** course has 12 workbooks and 4 score keys. Workbooks include both the colorful teaching text and a pull-out "activity pac" that includes all the fill-in exercises and student work. Additional activity pacs are available for a

bit less than a complete new workbook, but personally I don't see the point of saving a few pennies and making all the kids share the outer text pages. Each course has two optional videos per workbook, for 24 videos in all per course. Each course has 12 optional computer disks, available in your choice of low-density or high-density for PCs only. To use the disks, you'll need the CVI upgrade kit or their computer with CVI built in. With the CVI option, you watch the videos lesson by lesson and the computer automatically asks questions and grades student answers at the appropriate spots.

The Physics videos start off with quite a bit of math, but you don't need anything beyond algebra to understand them. Computer animation of the functional sort (no pictures, just moving text) shows how the math is done.

Character lessons and creationism are built into these series, as are vignettes from the history of science. The Physics series, includes Thales and other ancient Greeks, as well as Galileo, Newton, Kepler, Boyle, Benjamin Franklin, and Maxwell.

The presentation is friendly, not stuffy. The camera moves around in similar fashion to a network TV show; you aren't stuck watching "talking heads." Wherever possible, you are shown, not just told.

If you're going the Advanced Placement route, you'll need more than this course. But if you just want a solid high-school physics course that's way more involving than most others, consider this one. *Mary Pride*

University of Nebraska-Lincoln Independent Study offers a full year (two semesters) of lab-style **Physics** courses. Complete kits of all the lab materials you'll need are available along with the courses.

These are your standard high-school physics courses. Topics are similar to those you'll find listed in the review for Alpha Omega Physics, although of course taught with different source materials and from a completely secular perspective. The textbook for both Physics 1 and 2 is *Conceptual Physics*, third edition, from Addison-Wesley. You should be well prepared for the SAT II Physics test upon completion of these two courses.

You need to have completed one year each of algebra and geometry before UN-L will allow you to sign up for Physics 1

As with all correspondence programs, you send in papers and tests (fax and email options are now available for quicker service), which are graded and returned to your "local supervisor." This person can not be a family member without special permission. He is responsible for proctoring closed-book tests and receiving correspondence from UNL. He is also supposed to supervise the coursework and make sure you stay on track. If you are not interested in the correspondence option, in other words you just want the course materials, you don't need a local supervisor. As a compromise, UNL will send course materials directly to the student, only requiring

NEW
School of Tomorrow Physics

Grades 9–12. Workbooks and score keys, $4 each. Additional activity pacs, $2.80 each. Each set of 2 videos is $55 to purchase. Video rental options: $74.95 per quarter to keep worktexts and scorekeys and rent 6 videos, or $59.95 per quarter to rent the videos only. Optional computer disks, $8.90 each. CVI upgrade kit, $855.90. Shipping extra. *School of Tomorrow, PO Box 299000, Lewisville, TX 75029-9904. Orders: (800) 925-7777. Inquiries: (972) 315-1776. Fax: (972) 315-2862. Email: info@schooloftomorrow.com. Web: www.schooloftomorrow.com.*

NEW!
University of Nebraska-Lincoln Independent Study Physics courses

Grade 12. Nonresident, $94/course. Resident, $90/course. Physics 1 materials, $232. Physics 2 materials, $291. Handling fee, $21 per course. *University of Nebraska-Lincoln, Independent Study High School, 269 Clifford-Hardin, NCCE, Lincoln, NE 68583-9800. (402) 472-4321. Fax: (402) 472-1901. Email: unldde1@unl.edu. Web: www.unl.edu/conted/disted*

that tests be proctored by an "approved person," which can include a librarian (we all go the library, don't we?).

You find your assignments in the course syllabus. You then read the assigned textbook pages, write the answers and essays in the syllabus, do the labs, and take the pretests. There is a lot of study and writing; these are not Mickey Mouse courses. Although you are allowed to finish a course fairly swiftly (in as little as three weeks, with special permission), in real life a semester course takes about a semester to finish. *Mary Pride*

Basic Physics: A Self-Teaching Guide by K. F. Kuhn has a nice cover and a slightly different mix of topics than the other physics books we've reviewed. Missing are chapters on relativity and nuclear physics. You might not mind too much, because as some wag has said, just reverse the first two letters and "nuclear physics" becomes "unclear physics." Included are basic Newtonian physics, a smidgin of physical chemistry (more than most other books), waves, electricity, magnetism, and optics. This is all my high-school AP Physics course covered, and it was good enough to get me into engineering school.

Bill loved the well-organized and attractive layout, which includes lots of chart and diagrams. Math is not neglected; you get problems worked for you and problems to work with answers immediately following each problem set. The text talks directly to you in a friendly, uncomplicated fashion—again setting it above its competitors. There are appendices on scientific notation and the metric system, and an index, but no glossary. The author may justly feel he defined each term well enough in the text, but if you miss a definition the first time, or start your reading in a following chapter, a glossary is very helpful. However, I'd rather have a good book with no glossary than a lousy book with a great glossary. *Mary Pride*

NEW!
Wiley Basic Physics, 2nd edition

Grade 12. $17.95 plus shipping.
John Wiley & Sons, 1 Wiley Drive, Somerset, NJ 08875. (800) 225-5945. Fax: (800) 597-3299. Web: www.wiley.com.

NEW
School of Tomorrow Physics Videos

Grades 9–12. Each set of 2 videos is $55 to purchase. Video rental options: $74.95 per quarter to keep worktexts and scorekeys and rent 6 videos, or $59.95 per quarter to rent the videos only. Optional computer disks, $8.90 each. CVI upgrade kit, $855.90. Workbooks also available. Shipping extra.
School of Tomorrow, PO Box 299000, Lewisville, TX 75029-9904. Orders: (800) 925-7777. Inquiries: (972) 315-1776. Fax: (972) 315-2862. Email: info@schooloftomorrow.com. Web: www.schooloftomorrow.com.

NEW!
The Standard Deviants Physics Video

Grade 12–college. Video, $19.99. Shipping extra.

Physics Videos

School of Tomorrow Physics Videos are friendly and well produced. There are 24 in all. For a complete course, add the computer-video interactive (CVI) option or the workbooks. For more details on the full course, see writeup earlier in this chapter. *Mary Pride*

I explained how the **Standard Deviants Video Series** works in the Basic Math chapter—and why it has nothing to do with "deviants" and everything to do with "deviating from the standard," i.e. how to become a curve-wrecker (a grade A student, to those of you who never took statistics). These fun videos demystify the "tough" subjects for college students . . . and smart high-school students, too!

A family-friendly Edited For All Audiences edition of **The Unbelievable World of Physics** is available. This covers the material in a standard college course, assuming the staff of Monty Python is teaching the course. Not that John Cleese and company are on this tape; I'm just trying to give you a feeling for what to expect. The unexpected. You won't snore through *this* two-hour condensed presentation of everything you need to learn, or already forget, about physics!
Mary Pride

Cerebellum Corporation, 2890 Emma Lee St., Falls Church, VA 22042. (800) 238-9669.
Inquiries: (703) 848-0856.
Fax: (703) 848-0857.
Web: www.cerebellum.com.
Direct mail sales are not available.

Review and Refreshers

Not to be confused with the amusing *Guide to Cartoon Physics*, which introduces "rules" of physics as seen in animated cartoons (e.g., any cartoon character can run on air until he looks down, at which point he drops like a stone), **The Cartoon Guide to Physics** covers mechanics and electricity, no optics, and just a tad of Einsteinian physics. The book's tone can be gleaned from the chapter on relativity, which is titled, "Run! It's an Escaped Chapter from an *Advanced Physics Book!*" Cartoonist Larry Gonick and physicist Art Huffman strive mightily to make physics fun and understandable. Every one of the 213 pages is loaded with cartoon illustrations and hand-lettered text. A series of cartoons explains each concept. The examples are funny and memorable, in a sophomoric sort of way.

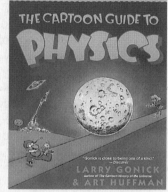

Owing to its total lack of practice exercises, this book fares best as either an introduction to physics for physics' sake (by those who will never have to take a test on it), a companion to the usual incomprehensible physics text, or a refresher to use after you've struggled through a physics course.
Mary Pride

NEW!
The Cartoon Guide to Physics
Grade 9–college. $15 plus $2.75 shipping and sales tax for your state.
HarperCollins Publishers, Inc., 1000 Keystone Industrial Park, Scranton, PA 18512. (800) 331-3761.
Fax: (800) 822-4090.
Web: www.harpercollins.com.

Cliffs Quick Review: Physics does for high-school physics what a checkbook register does for your financial affairs: it gives you a structured way to make sense of data that otherwise might overwhelm you. In this case, your physics course. The people at Cliffs don't actually put it this way, but they could: "We'll help you organize and systematize the unstructured mess you're being taught in high school."

All that good Newtonian stuff is here: mechanics, waves and sound, thermodynamics, electricity and magnetism (even a smidge of active circuits), light and optics. There's even a tad of modern physics: relativity (as if you were going to understand it in just three pages!), quantum mechanics, atomic structure, and nuclear physics. Like the other Cliffs books, you get examples, but no practice exercises, and just enough illustrations to help you make sense of it all. Nice and streamlined, a real help to budding physicists everywhere.
Mary Pride

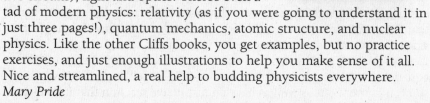

NEW!
Cliffs Quick Review series: Physics
Grade 12–college. $7.95
Cliffs Notes, Inc., PO Box 80728, Lincoln, NE 68501. (800) 228-4078.
Fax: (800) 826-6831.
Web: www.cliffs.com.

Instant Physics

Grade 9–college. $10.95 plus $3 shipping.
Order Entry Dept., Random House, Inc., 400 Hahn Rd., Westminster, MD 21157. (800) 726-0600 ext. 3700.
Fax: (800) 659-2436.
Web: www.randomhouse.com.

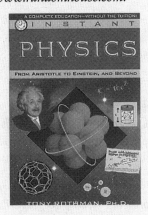

Instant Physics is a lighthearted look at the history of physics, with a lot of good information thrown in. This is not what the cover blurbs lead you to expect. *They* say it's "a complete education without the tuition." But a complete education in *what?*

With the help of this book, you will learn that "Time flies like an arrow, but fruit flies like bananas," and Kepler's undiscovered Fourth Law of Daily Planetary Motion is, "Clark Kent may never be seen in the same room as Superman." You may think the author, Dr. Tony Rothman, threw these "jokes" in as a desperate attempt to make his book more readable. Actually, it's all part of a clever plot to determine who out there is true physicist material. If you think this sort of thing is funny, especially after 2 A.M., then you qualify.

But enough of this buffoonery. Obviously nobody writes a 250-plus-page book complete with index just to tell physics jokes. (We hope.) Along with the amusing patter comes a boatload of instruction in story form. True stories, as in "Plato said this," and "Planck did that." For those of you equipped with basic math skills, accompanying "demos" illustrate how the laws of physics each bunch of scientists and philosophers discovered, debunked, or faked up actually work. Technical vocabulary is carefully defined. Famous fysics folk are introduced in "Who's Who" boxes. All the important topics are covered: Newtonian physics, thermodynamics, electromagnetism, nuclear physics, atomic and subatomics physics, cosmological physics, quantum mechanics, and just a tad on waves (but no optics, light, or sound). It all adds up to a lot more understanding, told in more memorable style, with a lot less pain, than the typical textbook. We like this book, and suggest you read it before, during, or after you take physics. *Mary Pride*

Thinking Physics

Grade 9–college. Thinking Physics, $25.95. Relativity Visualized, $17.95. Add $2.95 shipping.
Insight Press, 614 Vermont St., San Francisco, CA 94107-2636.
Web: www.appliedthought.com/InsightPress.
They only accept orders via mail.

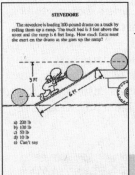

If your name was "Lewis Carroll Epstein," would *you* write physics books? Apparently so. Just as Lewis Carroll helped us "see" Alice's Wonderland, L.C. Epstein wrote **Thinking Physics** to teach us to "see" how physics works. The idea is that you should be able to intuitively know what an answer should be *before* you do a particular experiment, because you understand the principles involved.

Here's an example:

The stevedore is loading 100-pound drums on a truck by rolling them up a ramp. The truckbed is 3 feet above the street and the ramp is 6 feet long. How much force must she exert on the drums as she goes up the ramp?

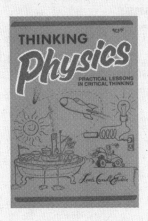

So I've read the problem. So I've tried, and failed, to visualize a female stevedore who actually handles 100-pound drums instead of standing around holding the "Men at Work" sign. (Feminists, lock and load now. But keep in mind I'm the only woman I know who can get up to the "10" level on the Universal Back Machine, and *I* wouldn't be stupid enough to take this job). Luckily, the author gave us a picture of this mighty female at work. He also provided some multiple-choice answers, and (on the opposite page) an explanation of how it all works. Aside from the obvious fact that the cute little pony-tailed blonde is about to be crushed by the drum, since she stupidly isn't wearing shoes with gripper soles, I can now visualize how much force she needs to exert to get the drum up the ramp. The equation for solving this problem is provided, as well as the force vectors, so I can figure it out as well as have an instinctive reaction that it takes less effort to push it up a ramp than lift it straight up from the ground. So from now on, every time I run into a problem like this, all I have to do is think of "Betty v. the drum" and I've got it.

The 562-page, indexed book covers mechanics, fluid dynamics, thermodynamics, wave theory, optics, electromagetism, relativity, and quantum mechanics. All that good stuff.

Also available from the same author: *Relativity Visualized*. This one we haven't seen yet.

As I'm sure you've figured out, this is the kind of stuff *The Flying Circus of Physics* asks you but doesn't give you detailed answers about. Combine the two for a great course in "physics thinking," but be sure to add a workbook with beaucoodles of physics math problems if you plan to use your physics course for college prep. *Mary Pride*

EDC's **Dictionary of Physics** is great for learning or reviewing scientific terminology and basic concepts. The book is organized into full-color sections on mechanics and general physics, heat, waves, electricity and magnetism, and atomic and nuclear physics. The final black-and-white section includes quantities and units, equations/symbols/graphs, measurements, accuracy and errors, fields and forces, vectors and scalars, numbers, circuit symbols, elements and constants, properties of atomic substances, a glossary, and a fine general index.

I suggest that you use the *Dictionary of Physics* both as a reference work *and* as a handy desk aid for when you run across a concept in your science book that you just don't get. It's also is a great review tool and study aid, since it's so well organized by topic. Recommended. *Mary Pride*

Topics in EDC's **Introduction to Physics** include the following (remember, the whole book is only 48 pages long): What is physics? All about energy (includes a neat rubber-band experiment to surprise your friends). Light energy (make a sundial!). How a camera or other lens works. Reflection and refraction. Color (make a color wheel!). Heat energy. How does heat travel (including an experiment on which type spoon handle makes the best conductor). Sounds, noises, and music (sound waves, how to produce them and store the data for replay). Mechanics. Electricity and magnetism (including the ol' lemon-storage-battery experiment and plans for making your own electric motor). Electromagnetic spectrum. BASIC program for calculating how much electricity your appliances use. Glossary. Answers to puzzles. General index.

A lot for your money, and a good browse for anyone thinking of taking or reviewing a physics course. *Mary Pride*

Usborne Dictionary of Physics

Grade 7–adult. $12.95 (paperbound). Shipping extra.
EDC Publishing, Division of Educational Development Corporation, 10302 East 55th Place, Tulsa, OK 74146. (800) 475-4522.
Fax: (800) 747-4509.
Web: www.edcpub.com.

Usborne Physics

Grades 7–12. Introduction to Physics, $7.95. The Usborne Book of Science (combined volume, also includes biology and chemistry), $16.95. Shipping extra.
EDC Publishing, Division of Educational Development Corporation, 10302 East 55th Place, Tulsa, OK 74146. (800) 475-4522.
Fax: (800) 747-4509.
Web: www.edcpub.com.

CHAPTER 26

Engineering

While scientists sit around figuring out hypotheses, engineers are responsible for making something that actually works. That is why scientists look down on engineers.

Seriously, scientists and engineers really are different. Not just from normal people, but from each other, too. As just one example, you've heard of "science fiction." But have you ever heard of "engineering fiction"? That's because engineers aren't into fiction—they're into reality.

Let me tell you a story that illustrates this principle.

A scientist, an engineer, and a mathematician were each led in turn into a room with a fire burning in the wastebasket and a cup of water on a nearby table. The engineer walked in, spotted the fire and the water, and immediately doused the fire with the water. The scientist spent several minutes puttering around the wastebasket, examining it from every angle, then finally picked up the cup of water and put out the fire. The mathematician walked in, took one look, said, "The answer is intuitively obvious," and walked back out! (I don't know how the mathematician sneaked into this story, but trust me, they really *are* that way.)

Here's a true-life story that makes the same point. (I once met the professor who the story is about.) A science professor is driving, with a student in his car. Directly in front of the professor's car is a truck with a load of lumber hanging out the back. The professor starts talking to the student, listing his options for avoiding the lumber. "I could stop the car," he says. "Or I could pull over to the side of the road. Or I could pull out and pass the truck." Etc. While the professor is enumerating all the ways he could avoid the lumber, *he drives right into it!*

Enough about scientists. You now know enough to do the driving when you and a scientist are together in the car—just one of the many valuable lessons you get from reading the *Big Book*. Let's talk about engineers some more.

The first thing they teach you in engineering school is, "List your assumptions."

The second thing they teach you is, "List your assumptions."

The third thing they teach you is, "List your assumptions."

What they are trying to tell you, besides the fact you are a simpleton who needs everything explained three times, is that outcomes depend on input, and if you assume something false about your input, the results

Laws of Engineering

1. List your assumptions.
2. Garbage in, garbage out.
3. If anything can go wrong, it will, so include failsafes.

If actual engineers had designed Jurassic Park according to these laws . . .

1. They would have enjoyed a good laugh at the assumption that huge, dangerous animals will never be able to break through electrical fences.
2. Critical systems design would not have been left to an unsupervised, disaffected employee.
3. They would have *known* electrical power *always* goes out sooner or later, so the dinosaurs would have been confined with huge moats, keepers with trank guns would have been available at all times, and the raptors would have been destroyed.

won't be pleasing. For example, if you are developing a tunnel through a mountain, and one of your assumptions is, "Every car is driven by a good driver," you will forget to provide a way for wrecks to be cleared out of the tunnel without duly impeding traffic. Or if you are designing a computer fabrication facility, and you assume, "All components we receive will be defect-free," you can bet a lot of the computers you ship *won't* be defect-free.

After you have mastering listing your assumptions, you are now ready for your next engineering lessons:

"Check if the power cord is plugged in before calling tech support."

"The thingie goes into the whatzit, but don't force it, or it will break."

"Never mistake your soldering iron for your curling iron."

"Ask everyone what they got on the physics test. This is the way to ensure permanent popularity."

Oh, I might as well admit it. Engineering is more of a subculture than a mere academic subject. You just have to be there to appreciate it. So if you wear white socks and Dilbert is your favorite cartoon character, you might just qualify to use some of the resources in this chapter.

Books

When you stop to think about it, our lives are woven around the buildings we live, work, and play in. This highly illustrated series, then, is a splendid way to get a "you are there" feeling for several historical eras. More than a "how it was built" or "what it's made of" type book, each of these books also displays the *life* that went on in and around the building in question. What did the people do? How did they dress? What did they believe? Whenever possible, you are shown, rather than told, via the ever-popular two-page-spread format. Each spread is loaded with both large and small realistic colored illustrations, many labeled to show you the fine points of the building, clothing, or whatever you are examining. (Warning: some male nudity is noticeable in the Greek Temple book.)

The **Bedrick Inside Story series** includes *A Frontier Fort on the Oregon Trail, A World War Two Submarine, A Viking Town, A Greek Temple, A 16th Century Galleon, A Shakespeare's Theater, A 16th Century Mosque, An Egyptian Pyramid, A Samurai Castle, A Medieval Cathedral, A Medieval Castle, A Renaissance Town, A Roman Fort, A Roman Villa,* and *A Roman Colisseum. Frontier Fort, Egyptian Pyramid,* and *Medieval Castle* are also available in paperback.

Although readable by fifth-graders on up, this kind of detailed book is likely to appeal most to young teens—and their parents, of course! *Mary Pride*

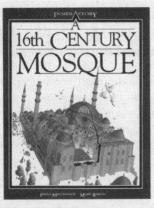

A book to make Dilbert scream with joy. David Macaulay, that British-born fellow who insists on giving us the "inside view" of such items as pyramids and cathedrals, gives us a *deep* look at engineering in **The New Way Things Work**. Assisted by a crew of wooly mammoths (don't ask) he moves quickly from motions and forces to inclined planes and wedges (how to use them for catching a mammoth, for making locks and keys, or in a can opener, plow, or zipper) . . . and that's just the first 22 pages of this massive (dare I say "mammoth"?) 384-page book.

Not to keep you in suspense any longer, this popular book's main parts cover the mechanics of movement, harnessing the elements (from water power to nukes—"flower power" wasn't mentioned), working with waves (light, sound, electromagnetic, x-ray, etc.), electricity and automation, and machines. You'll encounter more "everyday objects" and "high-tech objects" than you can shake a tusk at, each explained and illuminated with wild and wooly text and Macaulay's trademark large cross-hatched drawings, some colored, some not.

Any kid who studies and understands this book has received half of an engineering-school education already. *Mary Pride*

Here's something new: books about the history of engineering, with more than a tad of real how-it-works thrown in. Published by The **Society of Automotive Engineers (SAE)**, these are "coffee-table" engineering books, a species I bet you didn't even know existed.

But what better way to get a taste of engineering than by reading the stories of the men (yup, *men*—feminists must gnash their teeth in vain) who designed the engines that brought us the modern world? From **One Man's Vision**, the life of automotive pioneer Ralph R. Teetor, the inventor of Cruise Control, to **Allied Aircraft Piston Engines of World War II**, a loving look at the technology, these books tell the story of get-down engineering in words and photos. Car fans will be fascinated by **Automobile Design: Twelve Great Designers and Their Work**. Not just biography, the book includes enough of the original engineering designs to give you the flavor of each man's personality. Meanwhile, if you don't understand what makes a car run, **Changing Gears: The Development of the Automotive Transmission** puts it all in perspective, with over 85 years of improving design for you to study. Boats, trucks, buses, and even roads and bridges each get their moment in the sun in this publisher's catalog. *Mary Pride*

Absolutely terrific introductions to basic engineering and its applications, for preteens and up. **Usborne**, an English company represented in the U.S.A. by EDC, has the best, most colorful books around on almost any subject. Each page is artistically laid out with color pictures, diagrams, cutaway illustrations, captions, cartoons, and text to illustrate the principles discussed on that page. All is done with humor and the information conveyed is actually interesting. The overall effect is that of a series of topnotch magazine pieces crossed with a comic book.

If you or your teen don't feel quite ready to tackle heavy-duty engineering, Usborne's **How Machines Work** and **How Things Began** are excellent. Written for ages 7–15, these highly visual books break mechanical processes down into simple, illustrated steps. They're also fun to read! (I should mention that *How Things Began* is a look at the history of inventions, not a treatise on origins!)

People of all ages enjoy Usborne books. I'm 44, and I sneak off by myself to read them when they arrive at our house. On the other hand, our sons, when they were five and six respectively, chose of their own free will to spend hours with the Usborne's engineering series. We hand out these books as prizes to our children for special accomplishments. 'Nuff said! *Mary Pride*

Interested in the physics of engineering—how things work, not just on the snap-this-component-to-that-component level, but in why the components work in the first place? The **Usborne Introduction To series** covers, electronics, lasers, and so on, and actually *explain* these subjects. Each book in the series is wholesome and well balanced. Cheerful cartoon people demonstrate scientific

NEW! SAE Engineering History Books

Grade 9–adult. One Man's Vision, $29. Carriages Without Horses, $32. Automobile Design, $29. History of the Electric Automobile—High-Bred Electric Vehicles, $39. Changing Gears, $29. Allied Aircraft Piston Engines of World War II, $42. Diesel's Engine, Volume 1, $55. Many other books available. Shipping extra.
SAE International, 400 Commonwealth Dr., Warrendale, PA 15096-0001. (724) 776-4970. Fax: (724) 776-0790. Web: www.sae.org.

Usborne Engineering series

Grades 2–10. How Machines Work and How Things Began, $8.95 each. Shipping extra.
EDC Publishing, Division of Educational Development Corporation, 10302 East 55th Place, Tulsa, OK 74146. (800) 475-4522. Fax: (800) 747-4509. Web: www.edcpub.com.

Usborne Introduction To series

Grade 7–adult. Electronics, Lasers, and Robotics, $7.95 each. Shipping extra.
EDC Publishing, Division of Educational Development Corporation,

10302 East 55th Place, Tulsa, OK 74146. (800) 475-4522.
Fax: (800) 747-4509.
Web: www.edcpub.com.

Heathkit Electronics Courses

Grade 10-adult. $99.95–$3,000. May include actual computers and equipment, with additional hardware which simulates "bugs" to fix. *Heathkit Educational Systems, Heath Company, 455 Riverview Dr., Benton Harbor, MI 49022. (800) 253-0570. Email: heathkit@heathkit.com. Web: www.heathkit.com.*

NEW!
K'NEX Construction Kits

Grades K–12. Bridge Technology Pack, $2.25. Comprehensive Bridge Set, $140. Bridge Basics 1, $55. Bridge Basics II, $60. Bridge Basics 1 & II, $90. Bridges Educator Guide, $35. Solar 10, $63. Forces/Energy/ Motion Racer Set, $140. Simple Machines Sampler Set, $35. Elementary Construction Set, $105. K–8 Construction Set, $165. Big Ball Factory, $140. K'NEX MotorPack, $55. Roller Coaster Physics, $275. Roller Coaster Science & Technology, $165. Many other models available. Prices are suggested retail.
K'Nex Industries, Inc., Education Division, PO Box 700, Hatfield, PA 19440-0700. (888) ABC-KNEX. Email: abcknex@knex.com Web: www.knex.com. No retail sales; call for educational catalogers or stores near you that carry their products.

principles throughout each book. Simple experiments are provided along with gorgeous illustrations (full-color in the first 32 pages, black-and-white in the last 16) and simple explanations of difficult concepts. You even get a BASIC program to type in at the end of each book! *Mary Pride*

Kits

Heathkit has home-study courses for the serious student of electronics. The Heathkit course lineup now includes courses in the following categories: basic electronics, digital techniques, surface-mount technology, microprocessors, and programming. The training devices you use to perform the course experiments can be ordered either assembled, or for greater educational value you can get them in kit form and assemble them yourself! You can also purchase tools and test instruments.

New courses added since the last edition of *Big Book* include PC Servicing, PC Networking, PC Monitors, Macintosh Tech Knowledge, PC Multimedia, PC Laser Printers, and PC Troubleshooting.

Heathkit courses are accredited by the DIstance Education Training Council and the Council on the Continuing Education Unit. *Mary Pride*

K'NEX Construction Kits all use the same pieces: rods and connectors. Pieces of one type are all the same color plastic. Rods come in various sizes, all fluted and with knobs on the end to attach to the connectors. Connectors are based on an octagon model. Some are full circle star shapes; others are half circles, quarter circles, or some other fragment of a circle. Straight connectors are also included. Every connector has a hole in the middle, which a rod can slide through and freely turn inside. Specialized pieces, such as gears or pulleys, are included in sets devoted to those types of constructions. All pieces are rugged and easy to snap together and apart.

The Educational Division of K'NEX has created a wide variety of classroom kits. Skipping over those which have small educational value (e.g, the kits that purport to teach language arts or insect kinds), and those meant for 40 students to use at once (and priced accordingly), we find a strong selection of valuable kits priced for the homeschool budget. Each comes with wordless Activity Cards that show pieces required for each build and how to put it together. Best of all, each comes with its own plastic tub or bucket, for easy cleanup.

Just want to check out the K'NEX system? The **Arch Bridge Technology Pack** costs only a few bucks, comes with wordless instructions a five-year-old can follow, and includes the 32 pieces you need to make the pictured bridge. Science and Technology and Math Challenges are also included, for extra value.

K'NEX is perhaps best known for their bridge sets. After all, they sponsor an annual bridge construction competition for students! Their **Comprehensive Bridge Set** comes with a free *Bridges Educator Guide*— 174 pages of systematic lessons, starting with "What Is a Bridge?" and taking you through types of bridges, famous bridges, bridge construction, bridge vocabulary, and a lot more. Student worksheets and answer keys are included. The kit itself includes 945 pieces, and Activity Cards with instructions for 30 different bridge models and designs. These are divided into Easy Builds, Moderate Builds, and Challenging Builds. This is the ultimate bridge set, and the one you should get if you're interested in their competition. For smaller budgets, Bridge Basics 1 and Bridge Basics II are available. **Bridge Basics 1** comes with 353 pieces and Activity Cards for 15 beam, truss, and trestle bridges. **Bridge Basics 2** has 429 pieces and

Activity Cards for 11 beam, supension, cable, and arch bridges. These also come as a less-expensive combined kit, **Bridge Basics 1 & II**, with a total of 635 pieces and 23 Activity Cards.

To investigate solar power, the **Solar 10** kit comes with a solar panel, solar motor, and twelve-foot power cord, as well as 226 rods, connectors, gears, hubs, and tires, and a book with instructions for 10 models. Other solar kits are also available.

The most popular experiments in middle-school Technology classes are those involving model racers. Ostensibly, students use these powered cars to investigate forces, energy, and motion. The K'NEX **Forces/Energy/Motion Racer Set** enables you to build four rubber-band-powered rollers, four rubber-band-powered racers (two designs), or four spring-motor-powered turbo racers (three designs). It comes with 790 pieces, additional rubber bands, lesson plans, an 80-page Educators Guide, and all sorts of school stuff (worksheets, graphs, evaluation forms) so you can will be sure the kids aren't having too much fun.

A variety of classroom-sized Simple Machines kits are available. You don't need these, because the **Simple Machines Sampler Set** has enough components to make one each of the five simple machines: levers, pulleys, wheels and axles, gears, and inclined planes.

If you'd just like to practice building "things," the **Elementary Construction Set** comes with 735 rods, connectors, wheels, tires, pulleys, and hubs, plus instructions on how to build over 40 models. For about 50 percent more cost, the **K–8 Construction Set** has double the pieces, plus a spring motor, battery power pack, and instructions for 82 models. Moving another step up, the 3,100-piece **Big Ball Factory** comes with instructions to build a five-foot tall Rube Goldberg device where you send balls moving in crazy ways throughout the structure with a hand crank. Purchase the **K'NEX MotorPack** if you'd prefer to set the balls in motion automatically.

You may have seen the K'NEX Roller Coaster sets at your local teacher's store. These are the ultimate K'NEX construction challenge. Once built, you can send little racer cars careering around the curves and loops of your own roller coaster. **Roller Coaster Science and Technology** is intended for students in grades 5–9. **Roller Coaster Physics**, which comes with plastic balls for loop and ramp experiments, is meant for grades 8–12. Each comes with its own Educator Guide; each can be motorized with the addition of a MotorPack.

We have personally put together a number of these kits, and can attest to their quality and durability. Great pre-engineering education, too! *Mary Pride*

Radio Shack has for several generations been the home away from home for wireheads. I bet if you polled the entering freshman class at any engineering or polytechnic college, close to 100 percent would say they either made a device of their own design using Radio Shack parts, or put together one or more Radio Shack kits, while they were growing up.

So what does Radio Shack

Calling All Engineers!

K'Nex, manufacturers of yet another unique construction set, are now hosting a national bridge-building contest open to all students, including homeschoolers. The idea is simple. You sign up, you receive specifics on how large the bridge must be, and you try to build as light a bridge as possible, that will hold as much weight as possible, from K'Nex building sets. The winning designs from your "school" will compete against the winners in your district, city, and so on up to the grand prize. Winners at each level will receive prizes such as gift certificates or computer equipment. Naturally, the prizes increase as the level of competition increases.

K'Nex construction tubes and connectors are available in many forms, from roller coaster kits to wind-up vehicles, solar-powered machinery kits, and planetary colonies. They are used in a number of college engineering courses.

Bridges Across America, K'Nex Industries, 2990, Bergey Road, PO Box 700, Hatfield, PA 19440. (800) 822-5639. Fax: (215) 997-8509.

NEW!
Radio Shack Electronic Kits and Books

Grades 4–12 (kit), 9–12 (books). 300 in One Electronic Project Lab (#28-270), $59.99. Basic Electronics (#62-1394), Basic Digital Electronics (#62-1334), $9.99 each.
Radio Shack, division of Tandy Company. Sold in local Radio Shack stores.

Basic Electronics coves the following: learning about electronics, AC and DC electricity, how diodes and transistors work, how amplifiers and oscillators work, radio transmitters and receivers, what digital circuits do, how digital logic circuits work, how electronic memories operate, computers and other digital systems, and how photoelectric devices work. *Basic Digital Electronics* starts by reminding you how common and familiar these systems are (e.g., digital alarm clocks, watches, and calculators), then introduces the various types of digital system functions, how decision circuits work, how temporary storage circuits work, how to couple/convert/compute, more on permanent storage elements, how ICs are designed/made/tested, how to design a simple digital system, and a look at digital communications.

offer for today's budding engineers? No big surprise: a number of "Electronic Project Labs." We picked the 300 in One Electronic Projects Lab to review, as appearing to possess most bang for the buck. We also picked up a couple of really neat books—*Basic Electronics* and *Basic Digital Electronics*. Both books proudly bear the "Radio Shack" emblem, and are ideal choices for your teen's first course on these subjects.

Let's start with the **300 in One Electronics Lab** kit. It comes in a sturdy cardboard box plastered with photos and info about the kit ("the better to sell you one, my dear!"). Inside you'll find a very nice base station with a breadboard built in. Clearly labeled are wire coils to which you can attach wires to hook up various devices: eight light-emitting diodes (better known as LEDs), a "programmable" LED display (programmable in the sense that you can cause the various digits to appear by the way you connect the wires), a double-pole double-throw switch, a bank of eight keys, a tuning knob connected to a variable capacitor and a control-knob potentiometer, a cadmium sulfite cell (CdS cell) that varies its resistance depending how much light you allow to fall on it, speaker outputs, an antenna coil, an output transformer, and two terminals that let you connect external devices, such as earphones, antennae, grounds, etc. Along with this come two plastic containers whose individual bins are full of wires, capacitors of various capacity (both electrolytic and ceramic), resistors of all kinds, two different types of transistors (five of each), a variety of diodes, one earphone (cheap and cheesy type familiar to those of us who once built our own "crystal" radio), a number of standard integrated circuits (ICs), and one semi-fixed resistor. You also get a large, floppy 164-page manual that explains how the kit works and provides instructions for the 300 advertised projects.

The projects themselves are presented in "cookbook" fashion. You are shown a wiring schematic two ways: what is supposed to be connected where on the breadboard, and a classic schematic showing the symbols for the capacitors, resistors, and so on used in the project. The accompanying directions explain what you are going to make, introduce any new terminology, and explain what it is supposed to do. You are also encouraged to play with the finished project, tweaking it in various ways if applicable. From all this, you'll pick up a fair amount of practical expertise with wiring, schematics, and jargon, but not that much deep-down understanding of engineering theory.

For that you need the books. **Basic Electronics** and **Basic Digital Electronics** do a fine job of explaining how these components work and how they are used. With an eye-pleasing two-color format, well-designed chapter structure, chapter questions and problems with answers in the back, glossary, and index in each book, these are a great jump start on the world of electronic engineering. And because they *do* have chapter questions, you can readily use them as self-checking course textbooks. The parent doesn't need to know a speck about electronics.

Science is integrated right into these books. For example, the chapter on diodes and transistors in *Basic Electronics* runs through the nature of atomic structure—valence and so on—that you'd normally learn in chemistry class, in order to make clear how diodes work.

If you buy and work through this kit and these books, and you don't love them, it should still count as two semesters of Electronics 101 and 102 on your high-school homeschool transcript. If you *do* love them, you just might be engineering college material. Recommended. *Mary Pride*

CHAPTER 27

Science Kits & Equipment

I f your child hopes for a career in science or engineering, high-school lab science is a must. What you—and he—may not realize, though, is that selective colleges and universities typically require all applicants to have completed several years of lab science—even if they plan to go into basketball coaching or fine arts!

Lab science has benefits beyond impressing admissions officials. It teaches precision, thoroughness, record-keeping, honesty (it's a huge scientific sin to erase or change any data in a science notebook), self-confidence, and of course, a deeper knowledge of science.

High-School Lab Supplies

The most natural source of high-school lab science is your curriculum provider—assuming they offer lab science. If you use **A Beka**, **Alpha Omega**, **Bob Jones**, or **Christian Light**, you are in luck; your science curriculum already includes lab work. All you have to do is purchase the equipment and supplies. This, however, is not as easy as it sounds. Even if you want to buy every item needed for a grade level, only Christian Light offers a "package" deal. (You need their Core Unit *plus* the unit for the desired grade, by the way.) And if you hope to save a few dollars by only doing the most important labs from your curriculum, you have to spend hours flipping through the lab book to figure out which materials on the price list you can skip.

This is where **Home Training Tools** comes in. They have researched what materials are best for homeschool use with the science curriculum of six different publishers. They have special order forms for each grade level of A Beka, Alpha Omega, Bob Jones University Press, and Christian Light Education. They also have order forms for levels 1–3 of Apologia Educational Ministries and levels 1–3 of the Castle Heights Press "Exploring Creation" series.

I asked Frank Schaner, owner of Home Training Tools, how those special forms work. He told me:

NEW!
Home Training Tools
2827 Buffalo Horn Dr, Laurel, MT 59044-8325. (800) 860-6272.
Web: www.HomeTrainingTools.com.

"The forms list everything you need to do the lab portion of an individual course. You can buy items individually, or in some cases you can buy a kit with all the materials for an entire course.

"When we are researching a form, we buy the curriculum and go through it asking, "I'm teaching this to my children at home. How would I do this?" This is necessary because sometimes a curriculum is written from a school perspective rather than for homeschoolers. We simplify the material needs and suggest low-cost methods for a particular lab.

"The customer decides how much he wants to spend,. For example, he might say, "I want Bob Jones University Chemistry lab, and I only want to spend $100." We send the BJU Chemistry order form out to him for free. He decides which labs he will do and which he will skip so that he only needs to pay $100."

Even if you're not using one of these curricula, Home Training Tools has what you need for lab science at home. They carry a broad range of science equipment and science learning tools: telescopes, microscopes, sphygmomanometers, stethoscopes, barometers, hygrometers, rock collections, chemistry sets . . . just about everything. *Mary Pride.*

A Beka Book
Box 19100
Pensacola, FL 32523-9100.
(800) 874-2352.
Web: www.abeka.com.

Alpha Omega
300 N McKemy Ave, Chandler, AZ
85226-2618. (800) 622-3070.
Web: www..home-schooling.com.

Bob Jones Order Form
Customer Services, Greenville, SC
29614. Orders: (800) 845-5731. Fax:
(800) 525-8398. Web: www.bjup.com.

Christian Light Publications Lab Materials
PO Box 1212, Harrisonburg, VA
22801-1212. (540) 434-1003. Fax:
(540) 433-8896.
Email: orders@clp.org.

School of Tomorrow
PO Box 299000, Lewisville, TX
75029-9904. Orders: (800) 925-7777.
Inquiries: (972) 315-1776.
Fax: (972) 315-2862.
Email: info@schooloftomorrow.com.
Web: www.schooloftomorrow.com.

The major Christian homeschool suppliers all carry lab materials or lab science videos, or both. But it's not always easy to figure out just what equipment and supplies you need.

School Science Suppliers

I don't need to spend much time with these. Schools buy their science supplies from catalogs like these. Bright, colorful, many kit items, some more affordable than others. We've listed contact information for four of the most popular: **Carolina Biological Supply** (their new catalog has Janice VanCleave on the cover!), **Cuisenaire** (also home of the famous Cuisenaire rods), **Delta Education** (very high quality science and math equipment), and **NASCO** (they like homeschoolers enough to occasionally advertise their catalog in homeschool publications). I suggest you pick one person in your support group to request these catalogs, and then pore over them together. Many of their items make more sense as shared group purchases.

Science Catalogs

"Hands on science and technology products" are the stock in trade of **Activity Based Supplies**. Founded by a group with years of experience in school sales, this catalog does *not* include products you can get in stores like Toys "R" Us. They have an entire catalog of LEGO materials, from LEGO PRIMO and DUPLO to the more advanced LEGO TECHNIC. Their second catalog includes model dragsters and race kits (used widely in school "technology education" programs to study physics principles), model planes and rockets (and an entire "rocketry curriculum," plus a book on science fair projects with rockets), engineering kits and books of all kinds

(including K'Nex), plus ingredients to make all sorts of your own creations (e.g., pulleys, fiber optic cables, gearbox kits, motors, etc., etc.). You'll find some classroom bulk kits, but just about everything also comes in individual student packs, for home use. *Mary Pride.*

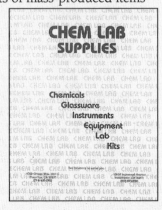

If you'd rather cobble together your lab program using deeply discounted bargains and offbeat items, **American Science & Surplus** offers wonderful widgets from the world of surplus. Some items are military surplus, but a lot are components of mass-produced items that bombed in the market. If they happen to have what you need in stock, it's likely to be the best price available. Common items such as motors, test tubes and glassware, and lots of unique science kits (that nobody else wanted!) are staples of this catalog. *Mary Pride.*

Chem Lab Supplies has been in business for over 15 years, providing lab chemicals, glassware, instruments, equipment, and lab kits to industrial, government, and educational laboratories. They also have you, the homeschool family, in mind, which is why they make single items available that are normally only sold in case lots, and offer discounts off list prices for many standard items. They are also a source for pricier lab items, such as vacuum pumps and professional microscopes. Whether you go the discount route or the pro route, Chem Lab Supplies will help you put together a quality home chemistry lab. *Mary Pride*.

Edmund Scientific's Catalog

Edmund Scientific Company, Consumer Science Division, 101 East Gloucester Pike, Barrington, NJ 08007. Orders: (800) 728-6999. Inquiries: (609) 547-8880. Web: www.edsci.com.

The **Edmund Scientific's Catalog** has all the basic science equipment you need. Microscopes, telescopes, stethoscopes, orotoscopes, binoculars, and the ever-popular sextant. This catalog's main claim to fame is their zany science gifts, from quarters that "blast off" when you tip the waiter, to your personal robot. Plus a pile of science kits with kid-appeal. This is not a catalog designed for homeschoolers per se, but for adults who like science and parents who want to add a dollop of hands-on science to their child's world. *Mary Pride*.

NEW!
Tobin's Lab

Tobin's Lab, PO Box 6503, Glendale, AZ 85312-6503. (800) 522-4776. Web: www.tobinlab.com.

The **Tobin's Lab catalog**, on the other hand *is* designed for homeschoolers. This could be your one-stop shopping source for homeschool science equipment and supplies, especially for the early grades. Produced by the Duby family (Mike, Tammy, Tobin, and Megan), this 88-page catalog has everything from binoculars and microscopes to space games, crystal kits, and dissection specimens. Laid out in the order of the Days of Creation (first day is chemistry, physics, light, color, and solar power, for example), this has everything scientific except the science curriculum itself (though they do offer World Book products and a hefty sampling of Usborne books). Need a Moo Magnet? Some silkworms? A see-through bat model? A triple-beam balance? An Instant Fish kit (just add water)? If you've ever wished for a rock pick for your speleological expeditions, or a dissecting kit for that ginchy KONOS cow eyeball unit study, this is the place to get it. *Mary Pride*.

Lab Kit Rentals

NEW!
Science Labs-in-a-Box

Ages 5 and up. $92.50/month/topic plus $100 deposit. Biology and Chemistry, $102.50/month/topic plus $100 deposit.
Science Labs-in-a-Box, Inc., 13440 Floyd Rd. #7, Dallas, TX 75243. (800) 687-5227 or (972) 644-4452. Fax: (972) 669-1518. Web: www.sciencelabs.com.

A knock at the door. You step outside to be greeted by the friendly UPS guy delivering a *large* box. What's inside? A month's supply of scientific experiments, instructional videos, and lab equipment, all delivered directly to your home. The new **Science Labs In-A-Box** program, offering a convenient "pizza-delivery" approach to science instruction, is one of the most innovative options for homeschoolers introduced in recent years. It is a terrific option for those of you who are serious about science.

As the name implies, every month a box arrives at your house, including all the lab apparatus and ingredients needed for school-quality science— eight monthly boxes containing a total of more than 30 labs. Each box has enough materials for two children to do the experiments. When you finish the experiments in one box, you simply arrange to have that box returned and order the next box in the series. In effect, you're renting up to $2000 worth of equipment and getting all of the materials prepackaged for you, ready to use.

We've received many of these boxes, and can tell you the equipment and materials are all first-class. All necessary materials are included. And I mean all—even down to the roll of tape necessary to repackage the box! For example, the chemistry boxes include a Periodic Table chart, goggles and lab smock, lab instruction videos (hosted by Science Project's own Mr. B in a classroom setting), textbook and teacher's guide, filter paper, various containers (beaker, flask, graduated cylinder, etc.), a broad assortment of chemicals and substances, and much more. All the equipment you need for in-depth hands-on chemistry. Each lab exercise also includes a biblical perspective, highlighting a principle from the lab and applying it to the Christian life.

Available lab courses include:

Topics lab materials

- **Topics** (ages 5–8) includes earth science, weather, physical changes, chemical changes, light, sound, health, magnetism, electricity, and more.
- **Topics II** (ages 5–8) lets you study rainbows, kinetic energy, the water cycle, simple machines, emulsions, airplanes, and more. Available fall 1999.
- **General Science II** (ages 9–11) includes paleontology, life science, physical science, chemistry, biology, and more.
- **General Science III** (ages 9–11) includes earthquakes and volcanoes (make and record your own mini volcano!), astronomy (build and launch your own rocket!), respiratory system, and more.
- **Earth Science** (ages 12–14) includes meteorology, geology, oceanography, astronomy, and more.
- **Life Science** (ages 12–14) includes classification, cells and Biblical creation, life processes of organisms, genetics, and more.
- **Physical Science** (ages 14 and up) includes scientific method, metric system, introductory chemistry, introductory physics, and more.
- **Biology** (ages 14 and up) includes cells, classification, microbiology, genetics, dissection, botany, body systems, and more.
- **Chemistry** (ages 15 and up) includes mixtures and alloys, solvents, water testing, petrochemicals, foods, radioactivity, atmospheric chemistry, consumer chemistry, and more.

Biology lab materials

Chemistry lab materials

If, after you've completed the experiments, you would like to purchase one of the items to keep (e.g. a microscope), just read the price off of the enclosed checklist, and include payment along with the rest of the items being returned in the box. Co-op prices are available—share with a friend if you'd like to save more money and double your fun! *Mary Pride*

Earth Science lab materials

Life Science lab materials

Physical Science lab materials

General Science lab materials

PART 6

Social Studies

Homeschooler Darlene Johnson of Mt. Airy, NC, received commendation at age 13 from Old Sturbridge Village for her three years of outstanding work in the Junior Intern Program. Old Sturbridge Village is a living-history museum with the goal of re-creating life in rural 19th-century New England. Selection into the program is rigorous, followed by extensive basic training in 19th-century life and skills. Darlene hopes to become a veterinarian one day, a direct result of her work with animals at Old Sturbridge Village.

Jennifer Daley, 17, of Crescent City, California, was recently presented with a Congressional Recognition Award from U.S. Representative Frank Riggs. The award was presented "in recognition of her special accomplishments in making a difference in the hopes, dreams, and lives of the people of Del Norte County and the 1st Congressional District of California."

Jennifer volunteered with the American Cancer Society, serving as the Board of Director's secretary and working in the office one day each week.

Jennifer recently became a homeschool graduate, finishing her high school work in just three years.

Virginia Macha, a homeschooled 9th-grader from Virginia, was recently presented with the Bronze Congressional Award for Outstanding Achievement by congressman Walter Jones, Jr. The award is given in recognition of voluntary service, personal development, physical fitness, and educational expeditions. Virginia was the first student from her area to ever receive the award.

CHAPTER 28

Civics & Government

Here's what schools should teach in government classes, but don't.

- How to hold a press conference.
- How to run a meeting according to Robert's Rules of Order.
- Who your state officials are, and how to contact them.
- How to run for political office, or to help elect the candidate of your choice.
- The limits of judges' authority. (In practice lately, there don't seem to be any.)
- What to do if you are accused of a crime.
- What to do if you suspect someone else of having committed a crime.
- The law regarding marriage, families, children, labor and employment, and consumer rights, for starters.
- How to use a law library.
- What the Constitution and Declaration of Independence really say. (Students used to memorize the latter.)
- A tour of the courthouse, the state capitol, your local bureaucracies, and the local jail.

American government was originally designed for citizen participation. It's a good idea for us to learn how to participate. School texts teach very little of what you need to be an active citizen. Fill in the holes with the resources below.

How It Really Works

All the fun of a race for the presidency without the airline meals and Secret Service bodyguards! The **Hail to the Chief** game includes U.S. map game board, pad of 25 Candidate Scoresheets, 36 Campaign Cards, President Cards, State Cards, two dice, four playing pieces, instruction booklet written in the style of the U.S. Constitution, and information about obtaining updates. Two to four players, ages 10 and up, first circulate around the outside of the game board, which is adorned with the pictures of our presidents in chronological order. You amass delegate points in an attempt to

The Saint on Socialism

"To me, the most potentially destructive man of all is the one who really *believes* his motives are based on universal ideals instead of what he'd call more selfish loyalties. Show we a man who claims he bases his actions on the principle that all power is evil, and that human want and inequality can be done away with, and that the world can be persuaded and legislated into eternal peace and brotherhood, and I'll show you a man who's either a liar or a fool ... and most likely a very unstable and dangerous fool at that."

—The Saint Abroad *by Leslie Charteris (Garden City, NY; Doubleday & Company, Inc., 1969)*

Aristoplay Hail to the Chief
Grades 5–12. $25 plus shipping.
Aristoplay, Ltd., PO Box 7529, Ann Arbor, MI 48107. (800) 634-7738.
Fax: (734) 995-4611.
Web: www.aristoplay.com.

25 Questions on the US Constitution

Originally printed i
CHECK newsletter
Used by permission

Do you know what the US Constitution says? Most Americans think they do. However, research has shown that the average American, when confronted with the bullet points in the Marxist Manifesto, is likely to mistake *those* for principles found in the US Constitution. Graduated taxation, to name just one example, is a Marxist principle *not* found in the Constitution, though most Americans consider it as American as apple pie.

To find out what you do and *don't* know, take this little test. Look at the end of this chapter to find out if you got it correct. Good luck!

1) How does the Constitution provide for changes?
a. Congress may pass bills which overrule or ignore the Constitution.
b. Judges may redefine the Constitution.
c. The Constitution can be amended.
d. Public opinion can nullify certain parts of the Constitution.

2) An amendment to the Constitution requires:
a. Over 50% of the vote in both the House and Senate, a signature by the President, and adoption by at least ¾ of the states.
b. Over 50% of the vote in both the House and Senate and adoption by at least ¾ of the states; signature by the President is not required.
c. A ⅔ majority in both the House and Senate, signature by the President, and adoption by at least ¾ of the states.
d. A ⅔ majority in both the House and Senate and adoption by at least ¾ of the states; signature by the President is not required.

3) When the Constitution was first ratified, how were U.S. Senators elected?
a. By a vote of the state legislatures
b. By a vote of the people
c. By election from the House
d. By appointment of the President

4) The Constitution establishes what type of government?
a. A pure democracy
b. A republic
c. An aristocracy
d. An oligarchy

5) In the form of government expressed in the Declaration of Independence and defined by the Constitution, power flows:
a. From God to the elected officials, then to the people
b. From the elected officials to the people; God is not involved
c. From God to the people, then to the elected officials
d. From the people to the elected officials; God is not involved

6) The Constitution requires Congress to be assembled:
a. All year long except for occasional short recesses so that it may address any emergencies which might arise in the states
b. Only once per year
c. Twice per year
d. Three times per year

7) The powers not specifically enumerated in the Constitution as powers of the federal government:
a. Are automatically given to Congress
b. Are automatically reserved to the states or to the people
c. Are given to Congress or the President
d. Are given to Congress or the states by the Supreme Court

8) The only power in the following list which the Constitution does not give to Congress is:
a. The power to borrow money
b. The power to provide for the common defense of the United States
c. The power to create a social security system
d. The power to establish post offices

9) The only power in the following list which the Constitution does not reserve to the states is:
a. The power to create a social security system
b. The power to create a welfare system
c. The power to enter into an agreement with a foreign power
d. The power to build roads

10) Prior to passage of the 16th amendment in 1913, income taxes were unconstitutional. How did the federal government pay for itself before income taxes were collected?
a. Import duties, excise taxes, and taxes divided among the states by population
b. It didn't; the U.S. government was in debt and almost bankrupt
c. A tax was paid to vote (a poll tax)
d. Property taxes only

11) The Constitution does not allow any bills of attainder to be passed. Bills of attainder are:
a. Bills which would allow the Congress to attain any of the rights of the people
b. Bills which allow the president to attain any of the rights of the people
c. Bills which allow the judiciary to attain any of the rights of the people
d. Bills which allow forfeiture of rights or property without trial

12) The Constitution does not allow the passage of any ex post facto law. Ex post facto laws are:
a. Laws which take effect before they are passed

b. Laws which take effect before the people are notified
c. Laws which take effect in the next legislature
d. Laws which take effect after any need for the law exists

13) The Constitution allows the President to make treaties and agreements with foreign powers, providing that:
a. A ⅔ majority of the Senate concurs
b. Over 50% of both the House and Senate concur
c. A ⅔ majority of both the House and Senate concur
d. A ⅔ majority of the House concurs

14) According to the Constitution, the minimum infraction necessary for the impeachment of a judge is:
a. A felony
b. A misdemeanor
c. Treason
d. Bad behavior

15) The Senate and the electoral college share a common reason for their existence, which is:
a. To make government more cumbersome
b. To make government more deliberate
c. To give a greater voice to the larger states
d. To give a greater voice to the smaller states

16) Which of the following phrases does not appear in the Constitution?
a. "A wall of separation between Church and state"
b. "All legislative powers herein granted shall be vested in a Congress of the United States"
c. "No title of nobility shall be granted by the United States"
d. "No money shall be drawn from the treasury, but in consequence of appropriations made by law"

17) The Constitution states that:
a. The right of the people to keep and bear arms for the purpose of gaining sustenance and for self defense shall not be infringed.
b. The right of the people to keep and bear arms shall not be infringed unless Congress shall, by a simple majority, deem it necessary for the safety of the people.
c. The right of the military to keep and bear arms shall not be infringed.
d. The right of the people to keep and bear arms shall not be infringed.

18) The Constitution states that the people have a right to be secure against unreasonable searches and seizures, and requires that warrants specify:
a. What the police want to see
b. The crime that has been committed
c. The place to be searched, and the persons or things to be seized
d. The place to be searched only (anything can be seized)

19) According to the Constitution, a trial by jury cannot be denied if the value of the lawsuit exceeds:
a. $20
b. $2,000
c. $20,000
d. $200,000

20) The Constitution allows the federal government to:
a. Restrict the uses of land for environmental purposes
b. Declare large tracts of land as wilderness areas
c. Take private property without compensation for the building of roads
d. Take private property for public use, but only if the owner is paid a fair price for it

21) The Constitution states that no person may be deprived of:
a. Life, liberty or the pursuit of happiness
b. Life, liberty or property
c. Life, liberty, the pursuit of happiness, or a decent education
d. Life, liberty, the pursuit of happiness, a decent education, or reasonable housing

22) To whom does the Constitution guarantee a right to vote:
a. Citizens
b. Citizens and legal aliens
c. Anyone residing within the U.S. for more than seven years
d. Citizens and all aliens

23) The Constitution forbids slavery or involuntary servitude, except:
a. For individuals in the military
b. For individuals who have not achieved the age of majority
c. As a punishment for a crime
d. Under martial law following a declaration of war

24) The Constitution allows the federal government to promote the progress of science and the useful arts by:
a. Giving tax money to artists and scientific research
b. Giving authors and inventors exclusive rights to their work
c. Establishing an endowment for science and the arts
d. Deciding which of the arts and sciences should be promoted

25) According to the Constitution, who has the right to govern that part of the military employed in the service of the United States?
a. The President
b. The Congress
c. The Senate
d. The Joint Chiefs of Staff

Answers are at the end of this chapter

become the party candidate by correctly answering the questions on President cards. For the benefit of inexperienced players, the four questions on each card are in graduated levels of difficulty. Easiest questions are on the top, hardest on the bottom.

Players choose which level they want to try before starting play. The President Card deck also includes some Bonus Move cards, to "duly increase the Speed at which Young and inexperienced Players do move about the Board and win Points," and Bonus Question cards (questions you must answer about the president on whose space you are sitting). Land on a Select-a-Campaign-Card space and you encounter the pitfalls and triumphs of a real campaign trail, from an endorsement by the *New York Times* (add 5 delegate points) to losing a TV debate (lose 5 delegate points).

Once you have the party's vote, your campaign really starts. You hit the campaign trail, laid out as a series of interlocking routes on the U.S. map in the middle of the game board. In order to win a state's electoral votes, you have to land on the state capital on an exact roll of the dice and correctly answer a question from the State Card deck. You now can enter that state's electoral votes on your score sheet (the number of electoral votes are listed for each state) and nobody else can win that state. After winning the required number of electoral votes, which varies depending on how many people are playing, you can try to be the first to reach Washington, D.C. on an exact roll of the dice, thus becoming president.

Hail to the Chief is really quite easy to play, and the element of chance and graduated levels of question difficulty even things out somewhat between political pundits and their younger brethren. The Campaign Cards have a liberal slant in that you can win points by endorsements from liberal newspapers and groups and lose them by offending the Sierra Club. This is not quite realistic, as Walter Mondale should have won according to these indicators. Otherwise, an admirably crafted, playable game that can really teach you something about presidential history and politics.
Mary Pride

NEW!
KONOS Electing America's Leaders

Grade 7–college. $15 plus $2 shipping.
KONOS, Inc., PO Box 250, Anna, TX 75409. (972) 924-2712.
Fax: (972) 924-2733.
Email: konos@konos.com.
Web: www.konos.com.

Unlike any other government text you have seen, the very first page of **KONOS Electing America's Leaders** asks the question, "What qualities make good leaders?" and answers it from Scripture. A unit on leadership follows, which includes learning the names and eras of the Presidents of the United States, who is on which money bill, which major events happened under which President. constitutional qualifications for and powers of the President, and discussion questions such as "Which President had to make the hardest decision?" Lots of information is provided, so you won't have to look it up yourself.

The next unit in this book is on Government. The two topics are, "What are the different forms of government?" (theocracy, democracy, monarchy, republic, socialism, and dictatorship, mixed in with a bit of history and Scripture) and "What is the structure of the U.S. government?"

The third unit, "How election works," explains everything related to a Presidential race, from the electoral college, to mudslinging, to putting on a mock campaign and election. You then study what a President's life is like, how the electorate has changed over time since the founding of the U.S., how to fill out a voter registration form, and more. Lots of historical tidbits included!

The fourth unit, on the two-party system, describes how parties work, how parties govern themselves, how party conventions work, and lots more.

The last unit, "Campaigning," gets into the nitty-gritties of how to get people to vote for your candidate. From yard signs to hosting a coffee for your candidate, from writing "Dear Neighbor" letters to turning your car into a "Candidatemobile," this chapter gives lots of ways children and families can get completely addicted to the excitement of "politicking," although handing out brochures at the polling place somehow didn't make it on the list. Did you know that every yard sign is considered equivalent to $500 in paid advertising? You will if you work through this excellent illustrated study guide! *Mary Pride*

If you're a Friend of Bill (Clinton, that is), you might not like these parody songs. Then again, who knows? Based on popular songs and show tunes of the 1950's through 70's, **Paul Silhan's political parodies** are enjoyable simply as works of art. After all, it's just *one man* doing *all* the vocals and instruments, yet it *sounds* just like the Beach Boys, or Bob Dylan, or the Beatles, or the cast of "A Funny Thing Happened on the Way to the Forum" . . .

As heard on the Rush Limbaugh radio show, these songs poke fun at liberals (in general) and the Clinton crowd (in particular). Some are sharp-edged, with lines like, "And Hillary has stormy eyes/That flash when she's criticized." . . . Some are enthusiastic but misguided. Conservatives will wince at "Bob Dole Picked Jack," which predicted that Jack Kemp would rocket the Bob Dole ticket to the Presidency—as if. (It's still a good song, though!) Others are just plain fun, like the version of "Hang On, I'm Comin'" as it would be sung by Ross Perot.

- **Running on Empty** songs include *Everyone Knows It's Hillary, Perusin', Bob Dole Picked Jack, Taxes Keep Pilin' on My Head, Eleanor, The Shredder,* many more!
- **Brother's Lib's Traveling Salvation Show** brings you such songs as *Big Gov'ment, Our House, They're Beginning to Try to Look Like Centrists, The Clinton Bash, Yakkity Yak (Don't Cut Back)* . . .
- **Lie-A-Lot** features foot-tappers like *The Little First Lady with Megalomania, The Chipwonks, Tax Man, Whitewater Debacle, Liberals in Disguise (with Taxes)* and many more.
- **The Lippo Tiptoe** belts forth *They Want Newt So Bad, Like a Nixon Clone, We All Live in a Mellow Apathy, Green Scam Machine, The National Hillary Tour,* and 10 others.

I liked these enough to put them in our catalog. Kids love 'em, too! *Mary Pride*

One of the most acute problems when dealing with political issues is recognizing propaganda. The **Propaganda** game, co-authored by Lorne Greene of "Bonanza" fame, consists of definitions of propaganda devices and a series of sample statements, each of which contains one such device. Students play by either challenging the group consensus (in which case the authors' solutions are consulted) or by going along with it. You get points for challenging correctly and lose points for incorrect challenges. You can also play *Solitaire,* checking yourself against the solutions.

Once the basic games have been played several times, students are encouraged to invent their own problems, using the *Congressional Record* or any old newspaper.

Propaganda is an attractive, fun, inexpensive way to bring a little reason to a field that notoriously lacks it. *Mary Pride*

NEW!
Uncle Eric's Ancient Rome: How It Affects You Today

Grade 9–adult. $8.95 plus shipping.
*Bluestocking Press, PO Box 2030,
Shingle Springs, CA 95682-2030.
Orders: (800) 959-8586. Inquiries:
(530) 621-1123. Fax: (530) 642-9222.
Email: uncleric@jps.net.*

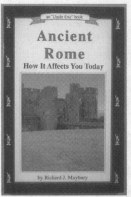

This fascinating book looks back to the Roman Empire to see the start of political problems that not only brought it down, but plague us today. In **Ancient Rome: How It Affects You Today**, author Richard **"Uncle Eric"** Maybury contrasts common law (or Higher Law) with what he calls "the Roman disease"—the idea that the law is whatever the policymakers say it is, with *no restraints* on what policies can be made. He examines in turn our own American coinage (which included the *fasces,* the symbol of fascism, until we entered World War II), the Pax Romana *v.* the Roman Republic, famous fascists Hitler and Mussolini (both of whom sought to recreate a Roman empire), how a strong central government leads to hate-filled factions when there is no common law heritage binding them together, where we got the phrase "vital national interests" as an excuse for outrageous government actions, why the Soviet Union has turned into what he calls "Chaostan," how and why the lovely Roman cities were completely destroyed in the Dark Ages (and why it could happen again to areas we consider "major civilizations" today), why straight lines between countries on the map mean Big Brother has been there, the history of the Byzantine Empire, the Turks, and the Balkans, and what might be coming next if history does indeed repeat itself. The 96-page book includes a number of easy-to-use historical maps and is quite an education in historical and political thinking, unlike anything you'll find in your local public-school textbooks. *Mary Pride*

NEW!
Uncle Eric's Are You Liberal, Conservative, or Confused?

Grade 9–adult. $9.95 plus $3
shipping.
*Bluestocking Press, PO Box 2030,
Shingle Springs, CA 95682-2030.
Orders: (800) 959-8586.
Inquiries: (530) 621-1123.
Fax: (530) 642-9222.
Email: uncleric@jps.net.*

"One of the most dangerous weaknesses in traditional education is that it contains no model for political history." So starts this book, written by a man who is "biased in favor of liberty and free markets, and proud of it."

The fourth book in the **Uncle Eric's** Model of How the World Works series, **Are You Liberal, Conservative, or Confused?** explains what political labels really mean, why school textbooks are all statist these days, why the "left-right" spectrum is inaccurate, and promotes his own "juris naturalis" or "Higher Law" philosophy.

If you can't explain what *socialism, communism, fascism, moderates,* or *statism* mean in a sentence or two, this easy-reading book, written as a series of brief letters from Uncle Eric to his nephew Chris, will help you find your way around the political map—whether you agree with Uncle Eric or not. *Mary Pride*

NEW!
Yes Prime Minister
The Complete Yes Minister

Grade 7–adult. $9.95 each when
they were in print.
*Out of print, but well worth searching
for in your library, through interlibrary
loan, or through out-of-print book
services.*

You will laugh, you will howl, you will startle your family with your wild giggling, while you read **The Complete YES Minister**. Based on the hit British TV show, the only one ever to win a British Academy Award for three years in a row, *Yes Minister* is a fast-paced send-up of bureaucratic statist government, narrated from the diary of fictional Cabinet MP James Hacker, and the best explanation of how government *really* works I have yet seen.

Poor Jim, a politician with an idealistic streak but also a strong wish to survive politically, keeps tackling the bureaucracy in his department, personalized by Sir Humphrey Appleby, the Permanent Secretary. Sometimes Jim wins, sometimes he loses, but he always learns something more about how bureaucracies and governments operate, and you will too. It's all done tongue in cheek, with that delicious British sense of humor.

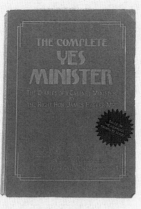

Included are genuine-looking reproductions of official memos, TV news scripts, and other artifacts of day-to-day government life. The authors take care to explain how British Parliamentary government works, which is very helpful to those of us on this side of the sea.

We have read both *Yes Minister* and its sequel, **Yes Prime Minister,** to our children at the dinner table. That way we were able to leave out the infrequent vulgar word that the authors threw in for realism's sake.

I understand there is also a TV series based on these books—or is it vice versa? I've seen the episodes advertised in several video catalogs.

All we need now is a *Complete Yes Senator* version, and people might finally start understanding what has gone wrong with American government as well. *Mary Pride*

How It's Supposed to Work

Alpha Omega's seventh-grade social-studies course tackles a whole bunch of subjects at once: history, geography, economics, politics, sociology, anthropology, you name it. LIFEPAC 6 of this course introduces political science from a historical and philosophical point of view, starting with Jewish and Greek civilization. This is just an excellent unit: you get an introduction to basic philosophy and wind up studying Augustine, Aquinas, Machiavelli, Hobbes, Locke, and Mill! LIFEPAC 9, "The Economics and Politics of Our State," explains how state government is structured and financed.

The first half of Alpha Omega's **ninth-grade** course introduces many aspects of citizenship. LIFEPAC 1 of this course provides the historical and political background of U.S. society, from a (surprisingly) standard public-school viewpoint (good words about those who brought us compulsory public education, huge government programs, and suffragettes). The second and third LIFEPACS explain how national and state/local government work, respectively. Then comes a skippable unit on planning a career (not terribly necessary if you're using Alpha Omega's Bible course, which deals with many of the same issues) and one on the responsibilities and rights of citizens and how to become a citizen.

If you want to find out more about the history of the American political system, the first LIFEPAC of the **grade 11** course has what you want. This traces the history of American democracy (actually, American republicanism) as it developed in the various colonies.

Several LIFEPACS of the **grade 12** course, "Democracy and Christian Challenges," also focus on citizenship. LIFEPAC 1 introduces self, family, education, and discrimination from a political perspective. LIFEPAC 2 talks about how the American party system works. LIFEPAC 4 discusses international relations, while the sixth one presents a standard evangelical view of the Christian under authority (you gotta obey, influence, and vote). *Mary Pride*

Alpha Omega Civics Elective LIFEPACS

Select LIFEPACs from grades 7–12 social studies. Set of 5 LIFEPACs plus teachers guide sold as "LIFEPAC Select Civics set," $19.95. Shipping extra.
Alpha Omega Publications, 300 N. McKemy, Chandler, AZ 85226. Orders and inquiries: (800) 622-3070. Fax: (602) 785-8034. Web: www.home-schooling.com.

BJUP American Government

Grade 12. Student text, $30. Teacher's edition, $42.50. Poster, $4. Test packet, $8. Answer key, $4.50. Shipping extra.
Bob Jones University Press Customer Services, Greenville, SC 29614. Orders: (800) 845-5731. Fax: (800) 525-8398. Web: www.bjup.com.

NEW!
The Challenge of Godly Government
The Challenge of Godly Justice

Grade 9–adult. Study guide, $5.95. Leader's guide, $3. Shipping extra.
The Committee for Biblical Principles in Government, P.O. Box 6031, Aloha, OR, 97007. Fax/Phone: (503) 357-9844. Email: sti@teleport.com. Web: www.teleport.com/nonprofit/committee.

NEW!
Cliffs Quick Review series: American Government

Grade 9–college. $9.95
Cliffs Notes, Inc., PO Box 80728, Lincoln, NE 68501. (800) 228-4078. Fax: (800) 826-6831. Web: www.cliffs.com.

Like all Bob Jones texts, **American Government** is well written and well organized. It's a lovely hardbound text, 465 pages long, designed for serious study. Every chapter section has its own section review questions. Each chapter ends with a list of terms for students to define, content questions, and application questions. Example of a content question: "What five civil liberties are guaranteed by the Constitution?" Example of an application question: "When parents disagree with the state about the disciplining of their children, which has the final authority? Defend your answer."

Now, what does it cover, and from what angle? There are sections on "Foundations" (the philosophy behind the American system), the Constitution, party politics, the powers of each branch of government, and economics. What you won't find in here is much discussion of state and local government. (BJUP does have a *State and Local Studies* syllabus to help teachers develop a state-history course for any state, but not having seen it I'm not sure how far it delves into state and local politics.) What you will find is a conservative (not libertarian) outlook on the place of Christianity in politics, the rights and duties of government, and the rights and duties of individuals. *Mary Pride*

Most homeschoolers are not lacking in political convictions, but many may not be able to articulate the source of those strongly-held beliefs. These Bible study guides (softcover, under 80 pages each) will serve as a starting point for exploring "Just what does God's Word have to say about government and the political process?"

Each of the 12 lessons opens with a short essay, followed by a series of short questions based on a variety of Bible passages. The leader's guide provides you with answers. A bibliography offers suggestions for those who want to read further.

As you can see from these authors quoted in the studies, the stance is conservative: David Barton, Gary DeMar, R.L. Dabney, George Grant, and Charles Colson, to name a few.

The Challenge of Godly Government is an overview of Biblical Law, Economics, Government and the Nature of Man, Pluralism, and Separation of Church and State. **The Challenge of Godly Justice** goes into more depth in the areas of crime and punishment. A new book, **The Challenge of Godly Citizenship,** did not arrive in time for this review.

Even though the studies themselves are brief, they offer much food for thought and topics for discussion. They're not beyond the abilities of most senior high students and would make a good addition to a government course. *Renee Mathis*

Cliffs Quick Review: American Government is 159 pages of power-packed information. Far better organized, and more complete, than any American Government text I have seen, this little beauty covers:

- How we got our Constitution, and a brief overview thereof
- Federalism—where it came from, and how presidents from FDR on have expanded the power of the national government
- Congress: its powers, how it's what we laughingly call "organized," and how a bill way too frequently (in my opinion) becomes a law
- The President: his powers and functions, how the executive branch is organized, what the Vice President can do, and what happens if one of them dies
- The judiciary: state courts, federal courts, and the Supreme Court

- The bureaucracy: where it came from, what it does, how it's organized, and the more-or-less futile attempts in recent years to rein it in
- Public opinion: polls, how opinion is formed, and the spectrum of political ideologies (not including communism, fascism, and other ideas that aren't a significant force in modern American politics—at least, not under their own names)
- Mass media (how it's grown, how it affects politics, attempts to regulate it, etc.)
- Political parties (history and functions)
- Voting and elections
- Interest groups (types, functions, tactics, and possible regulation of same)
- Civil liberties (starting with the Bill of Rights)
- Civil rights (slavery, segregation, the movement, expansion to include more and more groups, trends)
- Public policy (what it is, how it works)
- Economic policy (an excellent short introduction, presenting all the current theories with some political influence)
- Foreign policy

There are no appendices, extra charts, glossary, or index.

I checked this book carefully for bias, and aside from one comment that the Second Amendment "guarantees the right to keep and bear arms *in the context of a state militia*" (emphasis mine), the authors seem to be quite careful to present all points of view. More: they show which view has predominated using specific instances (e.g., NAFTA), and what trends are currently in force. They concentrate on the important stuff and leave out the trivia. Most importantly, they don't seem to have any axes to grind. I especially liked the way they present the world as it really is, rather than as either liberals or conservatives want it to be.

Although it is intended only for "review" of a full course, this book, and a subscription to a few helpful magazines and newsletters, will give you a better political education than any textbook I've seen. Recommended. *Mary Pride*

Want an in-depth introduction to constitutional law for your high-school or college student, or even for yourself? Lawyer Michael Farris, president of the Home School Legal Defense Association and a real nice guy, has what you're looking for! His **Constitutional Law for Christian Students** is a well laid-out, relatively easy-reading summary of constitutional law and theory, written from a sturdy conservative viewpoint. In his own words, "You will find no pretense at neutrality. This book is written to impart what I believe to be the correct views of constitutional law." However, this oversized, 288-page book includes long excerpts from *both* sides of many major decisions.

You get units on the Constitution's historical background, the Constitution as higher law, executive and congressional authority, developing a constitutionally-sound theory of government, and religious freedom. Michael is an acknowledged expert on these areas, especially the area of religious freedom; he has been battling for religious freedom in the courts since 1973, arguing cases before the U. S. Supreme Court and numerous federal and state appellate courts.

The accompanying (and much slimmer) teacher handbook provides questions for each of the book's chapters, along with the correct answers to the questions. These are not discussion questions, but questions like "State

Constitutional Law for Christian Students

Grade 10–adult. Book, $20. Teacher handbook, $5.
Home School Legal Defense Association, PO Box 3000, Purcellville, VA 20134. (540) 338-5600.
Web: *www.hslda.org.*

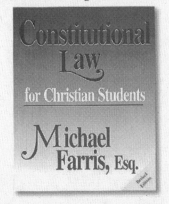

the seven principles of judicial self-restraint" and "Does Congress possess the authority to conduct negotiations of international agreements?" Many questions deal with specific Court decisions summarized and quoted at length in the text. By the time students have finished going through the course, answering all these questions, they will know more about the Supreme Court's interaction with the Constitution than most political shakers and movers do. An excellent way to bring Constitutional studies up to date. Recommended. *Mary Pride*

Elementary Catechism on the Constitution of the United States (Stansbury/Huff— 1828/1993)

Grade 5–adult. Paperback, $20 postpaid. Loose-leaf binder, $25 postpaid.
William H. Huff, 12 Carroll St. #119, Westminster, MD 21157.
(410) 374-4255.
Email: info@lexrex.com.
Web: www.lexrex.com.

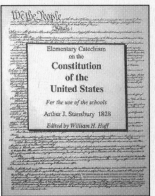

"We prize (our civil institutions), it is true, and are quite in the habit of boasting about them: would it not be well to teach their elements to those whose best inheritance they are?" In 1828, Arthur Stansbury thought it was. He used a catechism (brief question and answer) format to teach citizenship: "Q. Cannot all the people of a country govern themselves? A. If every man was perfectly virtuous, and knew what would be best for himself and others, they might. But this is far from being the case; and therefore the people of every country are and must be governed."

In **Elementary Catechism on the Constitution of the United States**, William Huff has reprinted not only Stansbury's 332 questions on the content and nature of our federal government, but added a few other source documents (Declaration of Independence, the Constitution, a couple of pieces by Franklin, and the Virginia Resolutions of 1798 and 1799). All are compelling snapshots of a young America, and are the strength of this 95-page softcover volume. Laced lightly throughout are Huff's STRONGLY WORDED editorial comments on how FAR our country has fallen from these ideals, emphasized with LOTS of BOLD TYPE. *Michelle Van Loon*

NEW!
Faith of Our Fathers

Grade 9–college. $18.95 paperback.
The Foundation for Economic Education, Inc., 30 South Broadway, Irvington-on-Hudson, NY 10533.
(800) 452-3518.
Inquiries: (914) 591-7230.
Fax: (914) 591-8910.
Web: www.fee.org.

Don't entrust this volume of provocative essays to a bored teen who wants merely to get by with the facts of American history. But if your teen already knows the names Madison and Witherspoon, has a sound biblical foundation, has pondered what "freedom" means, and is prepared to engage in the market of ideas, read **Faith of Our Fathers** together as a taste of what higher education is all about.

The essays in this 394-page quality paperback scrape back the sediment of nineteenth- and twentieth-century philosophies (positivism and materialism) to reveal the rock-solid foundation of the "faith of our fathers"—the God-given natural rights of man and the social contract that naturally arises out of them.

Faith of Our Fathers presents like-minded writers according to their special expertise. The collection is divided into four sections of five to eight essays each by notable writers as diverse as Clarence Carson, Gary North, and Erik von Kuehnelt-Leddihn.

Section I, "The Spirit of '76," outlines the codified ideas and provides character sketches of the generation who set up our nation. Section II, "A Biblical View," explores the job of a prophet in society and includes expected essays like James C. Patrick's "What the Bible Says About Big

Government." Section III, "The Rights of Man," addresses the big questions of freedom, liberty, equality, and justice, ending with Paul Adams' "The Moral Premise and the Decline of the American Heritage." The final section lays out "The Crisis of Our Age" and includes essays on "The Psychology of Cultism" (Ben Barber) and anticapitalism.

While Otto Scott's *The Great Christian Revolution* traces the important Protestant roots of English civilization, *Faith of Our Fathers* picks up after Cromwell and shows what America learned—and today should remember—from her forbears. *Cindy Marsch*

Two classic essays you absolutely must read in order to understand free-market governing and economics. The first is by Colonel Davy Crockett (yes, *that* Davy Crockett); the second, by a lead pencil.

Davy Crockett relates how, as he was campaigning for re-election to Congressman Horatio Bunce taught him that government ain't in the charity biz. (Stripped to essentials; what gives our elected representatives the right to take money *by force* from person A to give to person B? Where is it in the Constitution? Why don't these compassionate congressmen ever give any of their *own* money? How can Ted Kennedy weep buckets for the poor, vote for every tax-and-spend idea in sight, and stay so filthy rich? And why do the voters of Massachusetts keep letting him get away with it?)

The lead pencil relates how he is, perhaps not fearfully, but wonderfully made by the cooperative endeavors of hundreds of people who will never meet each other and whose lives are not coordinated by any mastermind other than God.

The Freedom Philosophy includes both of these essays, and 12 others from libertarianism's best and brightest, but my advice is still to beat your path to Crockett and Pencil first, for indelibly vivid proof that liberty works. *Mary Pride*

The Freedom Philosophy

Grade 10–adult. $9.95. Shipping extra. *Bluestocking Press, PO Box 2030, Shingle Springs, CA 95682-2030. Orders: (800) 959-8586. Inquiries: (530) 621-1123. Fax: (530) 642-9222. Email: uncleric@jps.net.*

The three-volume **God and Government** series together comprise the most comprehensive treatment available on biblical principles of government. Three main areas are covered: The history of government (self, family, civil, and church), the issues of God's governments, and the restoration of the republic. The series is used by hundreds of homeschoolers and several curriculum providers. Over 100,000 copies in print. *Mary Pride*

God and Government series

Grade 7–college. $12.95/volume, $32.95/set. Add 12% shipping. *American Vision, PO Box 724088, Atlanta, GA 31139-9690. (800) 628-9460. Fax: (770) 952-2587. Email: avision1@aol.com. Web: www.avision1.com.*

"Oh, no!" you scream. "Just when I thought it was safe to stay inside! Not another multi-cassette series on The Roots of America and all that boring fighting-fundy stuff!" Well, I must admit that renowned Constitutional lawyer John Eidsmoe's mini-course **Institute on the Constitution** does run to 10 audiocassettes. You won't have cassettes spurting all over your house, though, since they come nicely packed in a cassette binder, and thanks to Mr. Eidsmoe's entertaining style and inexhaustible fund of true stories, you won't most likely be reaching for the Stop button and wishing you'd never sent for these tapes either.

The series provides a systematic education in the history and philosophy undergirding the Constitution, and the history of what has happened to it since then.

Institute on the Constitution

Grade 9–adult. Video series, $69. Audio series, $40. Each set includes a workbook. Shipping included. Ask about 20% homeschool discount. *Michael Meredith, American Foundation Publications, PO Box 355, Bridgewater, VA 22812. (888) 298-8964. Fax: (540) 298-1555. Email: integrity@rica.net. Web: www.afpub.com.*

Institutes on the Constitution includes:

- The Philosophical Background of the Constitution
- Christian Beliefs of the Framers
- The Miracle at Philadelphia
- An Overview of the Constitution (two tapes)
- Biblical Principles in the Declaration and Constitution
- The Bill of Rights and Other Amendments
- The History of Interpretation of the Constitution: Jay to Rehnquist
- Current Threats to the Constitution
- Questions and Answers, and Reclaiming the Constitution (a summation)

The part on reclaiming the Constitution is the weakest, consisting of the usual "learn, tell others, and write your Congressman." Patrick Henry would have been a little more vigorous in his approach, no doubt! *Mary Pride*

NEW!
It's the Law! A Young Person's Guide to our Legal System

Grades 7–12. Book, $12.95.
Facilitator's Guide, $16.95.
Shipping extra.
Volcano Press, PO Box 270, Volcano, CA 95689. (800) 879-9636.
(209) 296-4991. Fax: (209) 296-4995.
Email: sales@volcanopress.com.
Web: www.volcanopress.com.

In **It's the Law! A Young Person's Guide to our Legal System**, author Annette Carrel, patiently, and in language most older kids can understand, explains the laws of this country, and what each person's rights and responsibilities are under those laws. Whole chapters answer questions like "Why do We Need Laws?," "Who Makes Our Laws?," and "What Happens When People Break the Law?"

If you have ever wondered what it was like to be arrested, this book goes into that event in detail. Also, the booking process, arraignment, making bail, going to court, and what happens when one has been placed on probation. Hopefully, that's more information on this topic than most of us will ever need!

The original Constitution is explained in some detail, as are the Constitutional amendments. The last chapter lists games that students can play, using their new knowledge of law. One group discussion activity called "The Case of the Fainting Burglar" talks about an actual case where a burglar cut himself on glass while burglarizing a dentist's office, then sued the dentist and actually won a settlement! Happily, the author points out in the discussion notes that settlements against insurance companies are not "free," but that the costs are passed back to the consumer.

The group discussion scenario in some of the games does disturb me a bit since it is often a tool used to promote a "value neutral" group decision. A Christian parent using this guide can avoid this pitfall by reading Bible passages that address the issues being discussed.

This is a book about the secular side of law. God-given rights are mentioned, but there is nothing here about biblical law, biblical concepts of justice, or the biblical roots of law in this country. The chapter on the colonization of America does not mention the role that religious oppression played in bringing colonists to the New World. To get a well-rounded biblical perspective on law, you will need to supplement this book. *Teresa May*

NEW!
Knowledge Products Giants of Political Thought series

Grade 9–adult. Complete series, $179 postpaid. Individual two-tape sets, $17.95 each plus shipping.

Narrated by Craig Deitschmann, this 12-part audiocassette series is a great introduction to political philosophy—what is sometimes called "civics." It discusses works of political literature and their respective authors, with each writer's voice dramatized to match his region or nationality.

You get a biography of each political writer, along with a brief history of his period, plus extensive readings from his major works, and explanations of what the writers were trying to say. Thoreau, for example, could be taken as advocating anarchy, but actually he did realize government is necessary as long as people are human.

Knowledge Products, 722 Rundle Ave., Suite A-13, Nashville, TN 37210.
Orders: (800) 876-4332.
Inquiries: (615) 742-3852.
Fax: (615) 742-3270.

I especially enjoyed the history portion of the tapes on *Common Sense* and the *Declaration of Independence*. I never understood before why the tea got dumped in Boston Harbor when the tax was so small. (In classic book-report jargon, "If *you* want to find out why this happened, listen to the tapes!")

Like other Knowledge Product series, **the Giants of Political Thought series** has no obvious political or theological axe to grind, making it usable by just about anyone.

Each two-tape set comes in a handy small binder, with a short introduction to the philosopher on the jacket, and includes between 2½ to 3 hours of listening. You can purchase the entire series at once, or do it the easy way, one set per month billed to your credit card.

The series includes:

- *Common Sense*, Thomas Paine; *The Declaration of Independence*, Thomas Jefferson
- *Civil Disobedience*, Henry David Thoreau; *The Liberator*, William Lloyd Garrison
- *Wealth of Nations* (Part 1), Adam Smith
- *Wealth of Nations* (Part 2), Adam Smith
- *On Liberty*, John Stuart Mill; *Vindication of the Rights of Woman*, Mary Wollstonecraft
- *The Prince*, Niccolo Machiavelli; *Discourse on Voluntary Servitude*, Etienne De La Boetie
- *The Communist Manifesto*, Karl Marx, Friedrich Engels; *The Social Contract*, Jean Jacques Rousseau
- *Reflections on the Revolution in France*, Edmund Burke; *Rights of Man*, Thomas Paine
- *The Federalist Papers*, Alexander Hamilton, James Madison, John Jay
- *Leviathan*, Thomas Hobbes
- *Two Treatises of Government*, John Locke
- *Democracy in America*, Alexis de Tocqueville

Extremely well done; recommended. *Bill Pride*

Have you ever read a book and felt that it should be required reading at the high school level or for Supreme Court Justices? Well, **Legislating Morality** by Dr. Norman Geisler and Frank Turek is one of those books. Dr. Geisler and Mr. Turek do not attempt to force their views on you, the intelligent reader. They lead you from beginning to end with logical explanations that only the illiterate could miss.

The book is divided into four parts, plus an epilogue and appendices. The four parts are: Can we legislate morality? How has morality been legislated? Whose morality should we legislate? How should we legislate morality on the tough issues? They include the following in the appen-

NEW!
Legislating Morality
Grade 9–adult. $15.99.
Bethany House Publishers, 11300 Hampshire Avenue South, Minneapolis, MN 55438.
(800) 328-6109. Fax: (612) 829-2503.
Email: info@bethanyhouse.com.
Web: www.bethanyhouse.com.

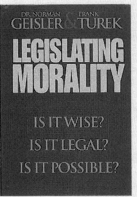

dices: The Declaration of Independence, The Constitution, and excerpts from C.S. Lewis' *The Abolition of Man*.

Geisler and Turek do not just explain their viewpoint. They guide you through the steps to draw the "moral" conclusion in each chapter. In chapter one, *Is it Constitutional?*, they point out that the nation has been making laws concerning morality since its roots. This is not just stated as a fact, but supporting evidence is given to show where and how this was accomplished. They also bring us to the realization that Christianity is *not* necessary to apply moral laws. Yes, moral laws were given to us by God, but an individual's religion, beliefs, or disbeliefs do not affect the existence of moral laws. If the Founding Fathers used this moral law as a basis for our Constitution and civil laws, "We should use the same objective standard when writing laws today."

In the subsequent chapters, we are given both sides of every issue addressed. We are exposed to both the extreme views and the conservative views; and then we understand the only possible moral view. After reading about one-third of the book, I decided it would be required reading for next school year for my oldest son; he'll be fourteen by then. If we want our children to think logically about moral issues, introduce them to *Legislating Morality*; it is a real eye-opener! *Barbara Buchanan*

The Mainspring of Human Progress

Grade 10–adult. $5.95. Shipping extra.
Bluestocking Press, PO Box 2030, Shingle Springs, CA 95682-2030.
Orders: (800) 959-8586.
Inquiries: (530) 621-1123.
Fax: (530) 642-9222.
Email: uncleric@jps.net.

The Mainspring of Human Progress is a little book you never heard of that nevertheless has sold three quarters of a million copies. Who is its author? Henry Grady Weaver (1889–1949), a director of consumer research for General Motors. What's it about? The history of liberty, both its ups and downs, from the Spartan "bee swarm" in which every man's entire life was dictated by state authorities, to the mid-twentieth century. The question: "For 6,000 years people died of hunger. Why don't we?" The style: fast-moving and fascinating, not to mention strongly flavored with the author's own beliefs.

Mr. Weaver contrasts the ancient pagan belief in a static world controlled by statist authorities with what he considers the Christian position—self-government and personal responsibility, with minimum faith invested in any human authority. Along the way we find out why the Moslems were so successful for 800 years, how the English upper classes learned to be jolly good fellows, why the colonists threw the tea into the sea at the Boston Tea Party, why Marx and Engels had absolutely nothing to say that hadn't already been put into practice by the ancient Aztecs, why Spain had the first great trans-world empire and why they lost it, why Good Queen Bess was a better ruler than King George the Third, why of all men the "humanitarian with a guillotine" is most to be feared (and why our bleeding-heart friend always ends up running that guillotine), why even the Pilgrims couldn't make a commune work (they tried!), why advanced thinkers 150 years ago thought the Midwest plains could never be farmed, and so on.

As with any one-person view of history, *The Mainspring of Human Progress* gives you a lot to think about. You can agree or disagree with the author; he does you the honor of saying what he thinks. *Mary Pride*

For a serious introduction to regional world history and government, the **International Government and Politics** Series by Oryx Press is a great place to start. Perhaps you, like me, have trouble keeping the Hutus and Tutsis of Rwanda straight. Maybe you can't remember which Islamic nations of the Middle East are predominately Sunni and which are Shia, and what difference does it make anyway? And what are the historic roots of Islam in Africa? The 200–300-page softcover books in this series serve as reference tools to help you discover answers to questions about the past and the present of the countries of the Middle East or Africa, Western or Central and Eastern Europe.

Beginning with a historical overview to help you understand the roots of today's situations, these books then go on to cover each region, country by country. Besides up-to-date statistical profiles (**Africa** and **The Middle East** were published in 1996) you'll find a political and economic history of each of the 53 nations in *Africa* and the 16 political entities included in *The Middle East*. The authors also deal with themes such as oil, monotheism, the Arab-Jew conflict, refugees, and European colonization. Expect to occasionally encounter typical secular notions such as the assumption of evolution and the problems supposedly caused by Africa's high fertility rate.

Also available: **Western Europe** and **Central and Eastern Europe.**

Though these books are written in greater depth than a typical world political or geography text, they are not difficult to understand. The authors make no assumptions of prior knowledge or background, which increases their value as reference books from which you might just read one portion. I have to admit, though, these books look boring! A few more illustrations added to the scarce black-and-white photos and the line maps would certainly increase the appeal of these rather pricey books. *Anne Wegener*

"The power of collecting and disbursing money at pleasure is the most dangerous power that can be to man. . ." So said a wise, but poor country man to Colonel David Crockett, during his time in the Capitol. This small little book, 206 pages, is full of stories such as this documenting the rise and fall of our economic freedom.

Published by the prolific group, the Foundation for Economic Education, the essays in **The Spirit of Freedom** are divided into four parts: origins of freedom, triumph of freedom, obstacles to freedom, and overcoming the obstacles. Some of the authors you will recognize—Gary North, Clarence B. Carson, and David (Davy) Crockett—while others may be new faces. The book advocates a strong free market, less big government, adhere-to-the-Constitution point of view and gives sound evidence for such thought.

If you are considering a unit on economics, then this book, or something similar, should be strongly considered. Although the topic itself can be a bit dry, the writing and stories lead you along quite nicely. We enjoyed the pieces about the disastrous introduction of the Edsel and the progressive (sic) income tax. And the essay about our dear old postal service was an eye-opener. Read it and weep. Read it and be informed. *Marla Perry*

Anyone interested in law and its written history will benefit from **The Story of Law**. Written from a secular and evolutionary point of view, it starts off with the law of primordial man and continues through recorded international law, the real meat of the book. With various illustrations and charts, we discover Roman and Greek laws, English law, the Code of Hammurabi and just about everything else that lead to the system we have today.

Unless you're a serious student of law, this book will not be an easy read. But for those who are, it will be a real treat. It's not as "heavy" as other law texts and gives an overview that makes it all make sense. *Barb Meade*

NEW!
Oryx International Government and Politics Series.
Grade 9–college. Each book, $34.95. Shipping extra.
Oryx Press, Customer Service Department, 4041 N. Central Ave., Ste. 700, Phoenix, AZ 85012-9759. (800) 279-6799. (602) 265-2651. Fax: (800) 279-4663. Email: info@oryxpress.com. Web: www.oryxpress.com.

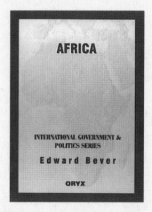

NEW!
The Spirit of Freedom: Essays in American History
Grade 9–adult. $6.95 plus $4 shipping.
The Foundation for Economic Education, 30 South Broadway, Irvington, NY 10533. (800) 452-3518. (914) 591-7230. Fax: (914) 591-8910. Email: freeman@fee.org. Web: www.fee.org.

NEW!
The Story of Law
Grade 9–adult. Paperback, $16 postpaid. Hardcover, $29 postpaid.
Liberty Fund Inc., 8335 Allison Pointe Trail, Suite 300, Indianapolis, IN 46250-1687. (800) 955-8335. (317) 842-0880. Fax: (317) 579-6060. Web: www.libertyfund.org.

A thief robs you of your money, is caught, and ends up in jail. You are still minus your money—and you have to pay taxes to convict and incarcerate the criminal. In some parts of the country, property owners cannot clear brush off their own land lest they disturb the habitat of an endangered rat. Our country mandates compulsory education for children. Laws determine the prices of various goods. Is this justice?

What is justice anyway? What is the difference between common law, natural law, and political law? What two laws should form the basis for every society—two laws upon which people everywhere, of every religion, can agree?

Written in the same format as *Whatever Happened to Penny Candy?* (a series of letters from **"Uncle Eric"** to his nephew Chris), **Whatever Happened to Justice?** explains the basis for true justice, what principles motivated the founders of our country, and what has gone wrong since then.

This excellent book belongs on every family's bookshelf and is must reading for everyone ages ten and over. It will provide the ammunition you need to counter the argument, "You're just trying to legislate your morality." *Rebecca Prewett*

Answers to 25 Questions on the US Constitution

1) **How does the Constitution of the United States provide for changes?**
   c. The Constitution can be amended
   Article V of the constitution states that "The Congress, whenever two thirds of both Houses shall deem it necessary, shall propose Amendments to this Constitution . . ."

2) **An amendment to the Constitution requires:**
   d. A ⅔ majority in both the House and Senate and adoption by at least ¾ of the states; a signature by the president is not required.
   Article V of the Constitution further states that amendments ". . . shall be valid to all Intents and Purposes, as Part of this Constitution, when ratified by the Legislatures of three fourths of the several States . . ." A signature by the president is not required.

3) **When the Constitution was first ratified, how were U.S. Senators elected?**
   a. By a vote of the state legislatures.
   Article I, Section 3 of the Constitution states that "The Senators of the United States shall be composed of two Senators from each State, chosen by the Legislature thereof . . ." This ensured that the states would have a formidable voice in the federal government, thus making it difficult to erode states' rights. It also held down the cost of federal elections, since statewide campaigning for a Senate seat was not required. This Section of the Constitution was modified by the 17th amendment in 1913, which states that "The Senate of the United States shall be composed of two Senators from each State, elected by the people thereof . . ."

4) **The Constitution establishes what type of government?**
   b. A republic
   Article IV, Section 4 of the Constitution states that "The United States shall guarantee to every State in the Union a Republican form of Government . . ." This is not to be confused with the Republican party, which is named after our type of government. A Republican form of government is a representative democracy, where the people elect representatives who cast votes on legislation to be enacted. By contrast, a pure democracy is one in which the people vote directly on all legislation.

5) **In the form of government expressed in the Declaration of Independence and defined by the Constitution, power flows:**
   c. From God to the people, then to the elected officials
   The Declaration of Independence states that ". . . all men are created equal, that they are endowed by their Creator with certain unalienable rights, that among these are life, liberty and the pursuit of happiness. That to secure these rights, governments are instituted among men, deriving their just powers from the consent of the governed." The Declaration of Independence, therefore, states that the rights of the people are endowed by God. The Constitution sets up a Republican form of government, whereby the people elect their representatives.

6) **The Constitution requires Congress to be assembled:**
   b. Only once per year.
   Article I, Section 4 of the Constitution states that "The Congress shall assemble at least once in every year . . ."

7) **The powers which are not specifically enumerated in the Constitution as powers of the federal government:**
   b. Are automatically reserved to the states or to the people
   The 9th amendment to the Constitution states that "The enumeration in the Constitution of certain rights shall not be construed to deny or disparage others retained by the people." and the 10th amendment states that "The powers not delegated to the United States by the Constitution, nor prohibited by it [the Constitution] to the States, are reserved to the states respectively, or to the people."

8) **The only power in the following list which the Constitution does not give to Congress is:**
   c. The power to create a social security system
   Article I, Section 8 of the Constitution describes the powers of Congress in detail so that the power of the various states is not diluted. Article I, Section 8 does not allow the federal government to create a Social Security system. The Constitution could never have been ratified if the federal government had retained the power to collect and disperse vast amounts of money.

9) **The only power in the following list which the Constitution does not reserve to the states is:**
   c. The power to enter into an agreement with a foreign power
   Although states may create programs such as a Social Security system and a Welfare system under the Constitution, Article I, Section 10 of the Constitution states that "No state shall, without the Consent of Congress . . . enter into any Agreement or Compact with another State, or with a foreign Power . . ." The founding fathers were wise to make the states responsible for those powers not enumerated in the Constitution, since competitive state-run programs will be neither insufficient nor excessively generous. The former may cause people to leave a particular state, whereas the latter may cause a large enough influx of people to justify a state tax increase—which may also drive people from a particular state.

10) **Prior to passage of the 16th amendment in 1913, income taxes were unconstitutional. How did the federal government pay for itself before income taxes were collected?**
   a. Import duties, excise taxes and taxes divided among the states by population
   Article I, Section 2 states that ". . . direct Taxes shall be apportioned among the several States . . ." Article I, Section 8 states that "The Congress shall have the Power to lay and collect Taxes, Duties, Imposts and Excises . . . but all Duties, Imposts and Excises shall be uniform throughout the United States . . ." and

Article I, Section 9 states that "No Capitation, [a head tax, or poll tax] or other direct, Tax shall be laid, unless in Proportion to the Census or Enumeration herein before directed to be taken." This means that the only continuous taxation power Congress had was indirect taxes—import duties and excise taxes [luxury taxes]. Any direct tax on a person had to first be apportioned, or divided, based upon the population of each state and, by definition, could only be levied at periodic intervals. Direct taxes were levied sparingly and were used primarily to pay war debts. This was changed in 1913 with the passage of the 16th amendment, which states that "The Congress shall have the power to lay and collect taxes on incomes, from whatever source derived, without apportionment among the several States, and without regard to any census or enumeration."

11) The Constitution does not allow any bills of attainder to be passed. Bills of attainder are:

d.   Bills which allow forfeiture of rights or property without trial

Article I, Section 9 of the Constitution prevents Congress from passing any bills of attainder and Article I, Section 10 prevents the states from doing so. Article I, Section 9 says "No Bill of Attainder or ex post facto Law shall be passed." Article I, Section 10 says "No State shall . . . pass any Bill of Attainder, ex post facto Law, or Law impairing the Obligation of Contracts."

12) The Constitution does not allow the passage of any Ex Post Facto law. Ex Post Facto laws are:

a.   Laws which take effect before they are passed

Therefore, according to the Constitution, the retroactive portion of any law is clearly unconstitutional. Article I, Section 9 of the Constitution prevents Congress from passing any ex post facto law and Article I, Section 10 prevents the states from doing so.

13) The Constitution allows the president to make treaties and agreements with foreign powers, providing that:

a.   A ⅔ majority of the Senate concurs

Article II, Section 2 of the Constitution states that "He [the president] shall have Power, by and with the Advice and Consent of the Senate, to make Treaties, provided two thirds of the Senators present concur . . ."

14) According to the Constitution, the minimum infraction necessary for the impeachment of a judge is:

d.   Bad behavior

Article III, Section 1 of the Constitution states that "The Judges, both of the supreme and inferior Courts, shall hold their Offices during good Behavior . . ." The Founding Fathers were quite adamant that the original intent of the Constitution and its amendments would always be enforced by the judiciary.

Speaking on this issue in Federalist #81, Alexander Hamilton (a member of the Constitutional Convention, later to become Secretary of the Treasury under President George Washington) stated that "In the first place, there is not a syllable in the plan under consideration [the Constitution] which directly empowers the national courts to construe the laws according to the spirit of the Constitution, or which gives them any greater latitude in this respect than may be claimed by the courts of every State."

On June 12, 1823, Thomas Jefferson wrote to Supreme Court Justice William Johnson "On every question of construction, carry ourselves back to the time when the Constitution was adopted, recollect the spirit manifested in the debates, and instead of trying what meaning may be squeezed out of the text, or invented against it, conform to the probable one in which it was passed."

James Madison wrote to Henry Lee on June 25, 1824: "I entirely concur in the propriety of resorting to the sense in which the Constitution was accepted and ratified by the nation. In that sense alone it is the legitimate Constitution . . . What a metamorphosis would be produced in the code of law if all its ancient phraseology were to be taken in the modern sense."

15) The Senate and the electoral college share a common reason for their existence, which is:

d.   To give a greater voice to the smaller states

The Senate was devised as a way to balance the power of the House, where the number of Representatives per state is divided by population. The smaller states, feeling always at the mercy of the more populous states, wanted a check upon this power. Each state, therefore, was given equal power and an equal number of members in the Senate. Likewise, the electoral college was a compromise between allowing the president to be chosen by Congress (too much power for the legislative branch of government) or by a direct popular vote (too much power for large states) or by the state legislatures (too much power for the states over the federal government). The electoral college gives each state a number of electors equal to the number of House and Senate members for that state. Small states, therefore, have a much greater vote than their population would otherwise allow. Since the winner of the presidential election in each state receives all of that states' electoral votes, this system requires the victor to win enough states all across the country to enable him to govern. The electoral college makes it virtually impossible for one region of the country to elect the president of the United States. And although this system also requires the victor to obtain a sufficient popular vote to govern, there are times when the electoral college will elect a president who has not obtained an absolute majority of the popular vote. This was deemed secondary to the ultimate goal of preserving the Union by the founding fathers.

16) Which of the following phrases does not appear in the Constitution?

a.   . . . a wall of separation between Church and state

The phrase ". . . a wall of separation between Church and State" appears in a letter by Thomas Jefferson to the Baptist Association of Danbury, CT, on January 1, 1802. It does not appear anywhere in the Constitution. The eight words contained in that phrase were taken out of context by the Supreme Court in 1947 when it struck down school prayer in the case of Everson v. Board of Education. The Supreme Court, which cited zero precedents for its ruling, stated that "The First Amendment has erected a wall between church and state. That wall must be kept high and impregnable. We could not approve the slightest breach." Thomas Jefferson's letter says, "Believing with you that religion is a matter which lies solely between man and his God; that he owes account to none other for his faith or his worship; that the legislative powers of government reach actions only and not opinions, I contemplate with sovereign reverence that act of the whole American people which declared that their legislature should 'make no law respecting [regarding] an establishment of religion or prohibiting the free exercise thereof,' thus building a wall of separation between Church and State." President Jefferson's meaning was further clarified in a letter to the Reverend Samuel Miller on January 23, 1808 when he said "I consider the government of the United States as interdicted [prohibited] by the Constitution from inter-meddling with religious institutions . . . or exercises."

The First Amendment to the Constitution states that "Congress shall make no law respecting [regarding] an establishment of religion, or prohibiting the free exercise thereof . . ."

17) The Constitution states that:

d.   The right of the people to keep and bear arms shall not be infringed

The 2nd amendment to the Constitution states that "A well regulated Militia, being necessary to the security of a free State, the right of the people to keep and bear Arms, shall not be infringed."

18) The Constitution states that the people have a right to be secure against unreasonable searches and seizures, and requires that warrants specify:

c.   The place to be searched, and the persons or things to be seized

The 4th amendment to the Constitution states that "The right of the people to be secure in their persons, houses, papers, and effects, against unreasonable searches and seizures, shall not be violated, and no Warrants shall issue, but upon probable cause, supported by Oath or affirmation, and particularly describing the place to be searched, and the persons or things to be seized."

19) According to the Constitution, a trial by jury cannot be denied if the value of the lawsuit exceeds:

a. $20

The 7th amendment to the Constitution states that "In Suits at common law, where the value in controversy shall exceed twenty dollars, the right of trial by jury shall be preserved, and no fact tried by a jury shall be otherwise re-examined in any Court of the United States, than according to the rules of the common law."

20) The Constitution allows the federal government to:

d.   to take private property for public use, but only if the owner is paid a fair price for it

The 5th amendment to the Constitution says ". . . nor shall private property be taken for public use without just compensation."

21) The Constitution states that no person may be deprived of:

b.   Life, liberty or property

The 5th amendment to the Constitution states that "No person shall be . . . deprived of life, liberty or property, without due process of law."

The 14th amendment says ". . . nor shall any State deprive any person of life, liberty or property, without due process of law." The phrase "life, liberty and the pursuit of happiness" appears in the Declaration of Independence, not the Constitution.

22) To whom does the Constitution guarantee a right to vote:

a.   Citizens

The 15th amendment to the Constitution, ratified in 1870, states that "The right of citizens of the United States to vote shall

not be denied or abridged by the United States or by any State on account of race, color, or previous condition of servitude." The 19th amendment, ratified in 1920, states that "The right of citizens of the United States to vote shall not be denied or abridged by the United States or by any State on account of sex."

23) The Constitution forbids slavery or involuntary servitude, except:

b.   As a punishment for a crime

The 13th amendment to the Constitution states that "Neither slavery nor involuntary servitude, except as a punishment for a crime whereof the party shall have been duly convicted, shall exist within the United States, or any place subject to their jurisdiction."

24) The Constitution allows the federal government to promote the progress of science and the useful arts by:

b.   Giving authors and inventors exclusive rights to their work

Article I, Section 8 of the Constitution states that "The Congress shall have Power . . . To promote the Progress of Science and useful Arts, by securing for limited Times to Authors and Inventors the exclusive Right to their Respective writings and Discoveries."

25) According to the Constitution, who has the right to govern that part of the military employed in the service of the United States?

b.   The Congress

Article I, Section 8 of the Constitution states that "The Congress shall have Power . . . To provide for organizing, arming, and disciplining the Militia, and for governing such Part of them as may be employed in the Service of the United States . . ."

How did you do?

- 25 answers correct — Were you in Philadelphia when they wrote it?
- 24–21 answers correct — You had a good start, but must have been derailed by network news or reading national news-magazines. Try rereading the Constitution again—it's reprinted in full in the back of Volume 2.
- 20–16 answers correct — Not bad, just a little bit more time and you will be an expert.
- 15–11 answers correct — See the difference between the truth and what the media have been teaching you?
- 10–6 answers correct — Pretty sad. And people who know even *less* than you are allowed to vote!
- 5–0 answers correct — The entire text of the US Constitution, with selected comments, is printed in an appendix of Volume 2. It might be a good idea for you to buy that book and study it.

CHAPTER 29

Economics

There ain't no such thing as "the economy." There's just you, and me, and millions of other people, each making our own decisions about where to work, what to charge for our products, and how to spend our money.

At least, that's the free-market ideal. In today's managed economy, politicians and bureaucrats make more and more rules about how we can hire and fire, work and play, save and spend. Indirectly, so do chain stores such as Walmart. That's because an unnoticed revolution has occurred in the economy: the Age of Mass Distribution.

Ownership of the Means of Distributism

In the last century, Karl Marx thought that the most important economic factor was who owned the means of *production*. In his age, the Factory Age, he was close to right. (Actually, he who controls the most banks beats he who controls the most factories, because bankers foreclose on factories, but who ever heard of a factory foreclosing on a bank?) Marx, the father of Communism, thought the workers would inevitably rebel against the factory owners and take over the factories—the "means of production." Lenin took this one step farther by preaching and practicing that a "revolutionary elite" should take matters into their own hands and free the workers by eliminating the business owners. This little social experiment led to the deaths of millions of people and the misery of millions more for decades.

What would Marx have said if he could foresee our age, in which anyone can create a product, but hardly anyone can get a product *distributed*? Today's technology has made it easy to publish a magazine, build a computer, write a software program, or record a video. But getting it into the hands of customers—that's a serious problem.

Fewer and fewer companies own more and more of the outlets where people buy things. Think of the bookstores, the supermarkets, the Walmarts and K-Marts, the computer stores, and the fast-food restaurants where you shop and eat. Where each community used to have its own locally-owned restaurants, grocery stores, bookstores, and department stores, now chain stores dominate the landscape. What this means is that a handful of chain-store buyers determine what product choices you will have—and which small companies (if any) will be allowed to vend their wares in your local stores.

What is "Value"?

Mr. Dubois had said, "Of course, the Marxist definition of value is ridiculous. All the work one cares to add will not turn a mud pie into an apple tart; it remains a mud pie, value zero. By corollary, unskillful work can easily subtract value; an untalented cook can turn wholesome dough and fresh green apples, valuable already, into an inedible mess, value zero. Conversely, a great chef can fashion of those same materials a confection of greater value than a common apple tart, with no more effort than an ordinary cook uses to prepare an ordinary sweet.

"These kitchen illustrations demolish the Marxian theory of value—the fallacy from which the entire magnificent fraud of communism derives—and illustrate the truth of the common-sense definition as measured in terms of use . . .

"'Value' has no meaning other than in relation to living beings. The value of a thing is always relative to a particular person, is completely personal and different in quantity for each living human—'market value' is a fiction, merely a rough guess at the average of personal values, all of which must be quantitatively different or trade would be impossible.

> "This very personal relationship, 'value,' has two factors for a human being: first, what he can do with a thing, its *use* to him ... and second, what he must do to get it, its *cost* to him.
>
> "Nothing of value is free. Even the breath of life is purchased at birth only through gasping effort and pain....
>
> "I fancy that the poet who wrote that song [about the best things in life being free] meant to imply that the best things in life must be purchased other than with money—which is *true*—just as the literal meaning of his words is false. The best things in life are beyond money; their price is agony and sweat and devotion ... and the price demanded for the most precious of all things in life is life itself—ultimate cost for perfect value."
>
> —*Robert A. Heinlein,* Starship Troopers

A Beka Economics: Work and Prosperity

Grades 11–12. Student book, $16.45. Teacher's guide, $24.90. Student test book, $4.10. Teacher key, $8.85. Student quiz booklet, $4.20. Teacher key/quiz booklet, $8.85. Shipping extra.

Is "Growth" the Greatest Economics Value?

Business magazines now carry articles in which Big Business leaders boast that they will do to a united Europe what they did to America, namely, kill all the mom-and-pop shops and replace them with chains and franchises. This emphasis on "growth," namely, the growth of individual large companies, is promoted as good and wholesome.

Is a good economy one in which big businesses grow ever bigger, buying or destroying hundreds of smaller businesses to add to their market share? If so, then communism is the best economic system, because there you have just one big business—the government—which has successfully destroyed all its rivals. But if communism doesn't appeal, how do we keep the few big businesses from effectively eliminating all their rivals? Aha—we can try a "mixed" economy, in which government controls some industries, and makes a lot of rules for businesses to follow. But that just makes government, the Biggest Business, bigger, and hurts small businesses, because guess who helps the government officials write the regulations? Lobbyists from big businesses, that's who.

Madison Avenue or Main Street?

I hope by now you see what a difference it makes what your goal is for the economy. If you just want lots of people to have lots of consumer products, in the short run you will favor big businesses, which can provide more products cheaper. In the long run, however, you find the big businesses have no national loyalty. If they can save money by moving their factories offshore, they will. Oops! There go millions of jobs. Now you have to ask yourself what good it is to have consumer products if the consumers have no money to spend on them.

Every time a big business makes a major change, it sends big ripples through the economy. So the more your economy depends on big businesses, the more vulnerable it is. Also, the fewer choices people will have about where they work and the fewer chances they will have to make good money at their jobs. Those at the top of the job pyramid, however, get to make obscene profits while throwing whole towns out of work.

So maybe you decide that an economy based on small, more-or-less independent businesses is the best economy. The Bible endorses this viewpoint, with curses on "those who add house to house, and field to field, till they dwell alone in the land," and blessings on an economy in which "each man shall dwell under his own vine and fig tree, and none shall make them afraid." Now, assuming you agree with all this, how do you propose we should get from Madison Avenue back to Main Street?

I hope that the above discussion has shown you that economics is not the "dismal science" that liberal economist John Maynard Keyes dubbed it. Economics is a form of philosophy as much as it is a science. A nation's economic goals determine whose hand is in whose pocketbook, and what shops are on the corner. That's why economics is important—and why it's worth studying.

Economics Courses

I haven't seen this textbook, but Russell Kirk wrote it, so it has to be good. The catalog description of **Economics: Work and Prosperity** says, "Concepts thought too difficult for high-school students are made thoroughly understandable." The theme: America's market economy versus the loser "command" economies planned by central governments. Conservative introduction to topics such as competition, private-property rights, and how the free marketplace works. The Foundation for Economic Education's *Freeman* newsletter gave this book an outstanding review. *Mary Pride*

This text is so new that I haven't seen it! Since it's from BJUP, you can expect it to be hardbound, well written, and conservative (not libertarian) in outlook. You can also expect the course to begin with the philosophy of economics, as informed by BJUP's biblical convictions, and then progress to teaching you economics terminology and applications. You can also expect the teacher's edition to be the best part of the course, giving background information and answers to the fact and thought questions.

The catalog copy says **Economics for Christian Schools** "explains how [economic] principles work in business firms, financial markets, and government. It also includes a practical analysis of the use of economic principles in managing the finances of the household."

This is meant to be a one-semester course, paired with BJUP's *American Government* book in the first semester. Both books have the same format and style of graphics. *Mary Pride*

Basic Economics is an economics text for "reasonably bright teenagers" and up, from the author of *A Basic History of the United States* (see the U.S. History chapter). Solid free-market emphasis with lots of historical nuggets. Lots of handy helps, too: the glossary defines 90 key economics terms, a detailed table of contents tells you exactly what follows what, the index tells you where it is, and a set of 20 profiles of key economic thinkers help you know the players. Almost 400 pages in all. *Mary Pride*

For years, Bluestocking Press has quietly been publishing an entire series of books, written for children and adults, that provide a model of how the world works which is consistent with the vision of America's Founding Fathers. The economic explanations and terms used in the **"Uncle Eric" books** follow the "Austrian" school of thought (so called because its creators were from Austria, not because the Austrian government follows it—they don't). This school emphasizes the importance of the amount and speed of money circulating in an economy.

Using the format of a good-humored uncle writing to his nephew, author Richard Maybury provides a model, that is, a mental picture of how the world really works. Just as a science course will teach you Newton's Laws of Motion and the Law of Gravity, these books will teach you the laws of politics, economics, and justice. You will learn which philosophies fit the way the world really works and which ones don't. All this is in short chapters that don't take much time to complete, in language simple enough for a 10-year-old to read on his own, and for a harried parent to understand!

The tone of the series is refreshingly intelligent and caring, rather than frenzied or despairing, as is sadly often the case when authors with convictions talk about how government ought to work as opposed to how it does work today. That is probably why this series has garnered praise from reviewers as diverse as former U.S. Treasury Secretary William E. Simon and former New York State Teacher of the Year (and frequent speaker at homeschool conferences) John Taylor Gatto, to name just a few of the dozens of luminaries whose endorsements appear in these books.

Books in the "Uncle Eric" series include:

- **"Uncle Eric" Talks About Personal, Career, & Financial Security.** This sounds like a multilevel marketing brochure, but is actually an introduction to the concept of worldview models, with some practical applications for those who would like to live a worthwhile, free life.

A Beka Book, Box 19100, Pensacola, FL 32523-9100. (800) 874-2352. Fax: (800) 874-3590. Web: www.abeka.com.

BJUP Economics for Christian Schools

Grade 12. Student text, $30. Teacher's edition, $42.50. Shipping extra.
Bob Jones University Press Customer Services, Greenville, SC 29614. Orders: (800) 845-5731. Fax: (800) 525-8398. Web: www.bjup.com.

Clarence Carson's Basic Economics

Grade 10–adult. $26 postpaid.
American Textbook Committee, 51054 Hwy. 22, Wadley, AL 36276. (205) 674-3548.

NEW!
Uncle Eric Books

Grades 9–12. Complete set, $77 plus $8.95 shipping. Book 1, $7.95. Book 2, $9.95, teacher support materials 95¢. Book 3, $14.95. Book 4, $9.95. Book 5–7, $8.95 each. Book 8, $15.95. Shipping: first book, $3; additionals, $1 each.
Bluestocking Press, PO Box 2030, Shingle Springs, CA 95682-2030. Orders: (800) 959-8586. Inquiries: (530) 621-1123. Fax: (530) 642-9222. Email: uncleric@jps.net.

- **Whatever Happened to Penny Candy?** The book that started it all! Economics made simple. Covers the origin and history of money, the origin and history of the dollar, the business cycle, inflation, recession, depression, foreign currencies, why governments try to tinker with the market and always fail, and more, with very practical advice on how to tell what's really going on as opposed to how the media might be "spinning" it. Includes glossary of terms, resource list for further reading, and a bunch of great quotes. See separate review later in this chapter.

- **Whatever Happened to Justice?** Covers America's legal system from its original design to the present. Explores the contrast between "higher law" (sometimes called "natural law") and man-made, faddish laws. See separate review in Chapter 28.

- **Are Your Liberal? Conservative? or Confused?** You'll love this book. It explains the entire spectrum of social and economic philosophies, in easily understandable doses, presented with good humor and malice towards none. See separate review in Chapter 28.

- **Ancient Rome: How It Affects You Today.** This book reveals what happens when a society ignores the "Uncle Eric" model. According to "Uncle Eric," ancient Rome was a fascist state. Its rulers believed in "doing whatever seems necessary," with no restraints on their power. In this book you'll see the parallels with modern states, and along the way shed sidelights on Hitler, Mussolini, feudalism, and the Byzantine empire. Not bad for 92 pages! See separate review in Chapter 28.

- **Evaluating Books: What Would Thomas Jefferson Think About This?** Subtitled "Guidelines for selecting books consistent with the principles of America's Founders." Learn how to recognize what a commentator or author's position is on economics, history, law, and more. See review in Chapter 10.

- **The Money Mystery.** This book describes "the hidden force affecting your career, business, and investments," using the historical example of how government and "trigger events" caused the economic downturn of the 1980s, and what this means for us today. The "hidden force" turns out to be what Monetarists call "velocity"—the speed with which money changes hands—and "money demand," or how much people want to hold on to their money. One gem from this book I can't resist quoting: "The economy is not a machine, it is people. When the government makes 'adjustments' to the economy, it is manipulating the businesses, careers, and investments of innocent people."

- **The Clipper Ship Strategy.** How to apply "Business Cycle Management" to your own life, to discover "pockets of prosperity" that exist regardless of the state of the economy. Not a get-rich-quick book, but a practical application of the economic principles in the other books in this series. As a side benefit, you'll also learn how to detect the results of government meddling with the economy in your community and state.

None of my kids are graduating from high school until they've finished reading all these books. Very highly recommended. *Mary Pride*

Economics Introductions

Every now and then a business book comes along which is so classic, so erudite, so accessible, that reviewers such as myself insist that reader such as yourself give it a whirl. **The Dilbert Principle** is that kind of book. Disguised as a comic strip about a hapless engineer, "Dilbert" is actually "a cubicle's eye view of bosses, meetings, management fads, and other workplace affliction." Coincidentally, that is the subtitle of The Dilbert Principle. From the introduction, titled "Why Is Business So Absurd?" to the finale of

NEW!
The Dilbert Principle
Grade 9–adult. $12.95 paperback, $22 hardbound. Shipping extra.
HarperCollins Publishers, Inc., 1000 Keystone Industrial Park, Scranton, PA 18512. (800) 331-3761. Fax: (800) 822-4090. Web: www.harpercollins.com.

true horror stories about management follies, this is the down-and-dirty that they don't teach you at Harvard Business School, or at P.S. 51, for that matter. Scott Adams lovingly explores such topics as humiliation as a business strategy (*not* "looking out for Number One," but what your company is planning to do to Number One), pretending to work, business plans, ISO 9000, downsizing, and my personal favorite, "How to Tell if Your Company is Doomed." These are just a few of the choice topics Adams deals with in prose (with copious examples) and then skewers in pictures (Dilbert *v.* the uncaring corporate universe).

Funnier than Dave Barry, more practical than Charles Schulz, Adams has mastered the art of puncturing the ridiculous. For example, this from the "Budgeting" chapter:

> *Contrary to what you might expect from the word "budget," it is not a fixed amount. It will change many times throughout the year to take advantage of the principle of "Budget Uncertainty":*
>
> *If you change the budget often enough, the employees will begin acting like gophers on a rifle range, afraid to do anything that draws attention. And where there is fear, there is low spending. And where there is low spending, there are huge stock options for senior management, followed by an eventual death spiral of the corporation.*

First you laugh, thinking this is funny. Then you stop and realize it is true. So move over, Tom Peters. This is the 90s, what's left of it. Most of us just want to survive. And nobody is a better survivor than Dilbert. *Mary Pride*

The title says **Economics in One Lesson**. Here's the lesson:

> *The art of economics consists in looking not merely at the immediate but at the longer effects of any act or policy; it consists in tracing the consequences of that policy not merely for one group but for all groups.*

Oh, if only Henry Hazlitt, who penned those deathless words, had been trained as a copywriter. For then the one lesson would have read:

> *If you wanna pass laws that affect how people make and spend their money, Jack, you'd better think about how the laws affect everyone besides the lucky bozo who gets the government handout. And you'd better think about how the laws affect even him, once the first rush from all that cash wears off.*

This has been the curse of libertarianism: cloudy words. Abstract nouns. Long strings of them, holding together undeniable truths that nobody will ever bother to read.

I don't mean to imply that Hazlitt is boring. You just have to be an abstract thinker to appreciate him. He does deserve appreciation, for after uttering his one lesson he goes on to explain how it applies to all sorts of loony-tunes economic policies: public works, full employment, spread-the-work schemes, trade wars, saving dying industries, price and wage fixing, rent control, minimum wage laws, employment-killing unionism, inflation, and more.

Someone who can speak or write with sizzle ought to read this book, take all its ideas, massage them till they come back to life, and send them out conquering and to conquer.

Come to think of it, someone *has.* Vic Lockman's *Biblical Economics In Comics* (reviewed in Volume 2) covers most of Hazlitt's ground, from the bro-

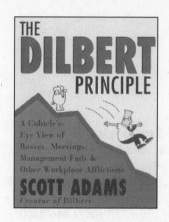

Economics in One Lesson

Grade 11–adult. Book, $10. Cassette, $17.95. Shipping $3.25 extra.
Bluestocking Press, PO Box 2030, Shingle Springs, CA 95682-2030.
Orders: (800) 959-8586.
Inquiries: (530) 621-1123.
Fax: (530) 642-9222.
Email: uncleric@jps.net.

ken-window scenario all the way to why trade barriers don't really help protectionist nations. If you can't bear to descend to the comic-book level, you might consider perusing the prewar speeches of Winston Churchill, which made many of the same points. *Economics in One Lesson* is still considered the classic, though; if you want to impress your intellectual pals, read this book. *Mary Pride*

The Economics of Liberty

Grade 10–adult. $15 plus $3.50 shipping.
Ludwig von Mises Institute, 518 West Magnolia, Auburn, AL 36832.
(800) 636-4737. (334) 844-2500.
(334) 844-2583.
Email: mail@mises.org.
Web: www.mises.org.

Anthologies usually make me itch. I like to read a book written by a person, not a bunch of articles stitched together.

So I was surprised to find myself picking up **The Economics of Liberty** . . . browsing it . . . flipping to an article . . . reading that article, and the next, and the next . . . and finally going back to the beginning and reading the whole thing through, when I was supposed to be doing something else!

What I discovered, to my amazement, is that every one of the writers in this book can *write*. Furthermore, they are pugnacious, combative, argumentative—in short, a joy to read. If you like bland, this is not the book for you. As Patrick Buchanan says about editor Llewellyn Rockwell's work, "It sends a message: 'Hey, fellas, you've been pushing us around a long time; why don't you come outside, and let's get it on?'"

The Economics of Liberty is, in short, a libertarian book—not left-wing retread-hippy libertarianism, but what is sometimes referred to as "classical liberalism," meaning the political philosophy of America's Founding Fathers. If you, reading this book, begin to suspect that the reason the libertarians make more sense on all these issues than the TV pundits and mainstream newspaper columnists is that the libertarians are right, feel free to keep thinking it!

The Economics of Liberty is divided into five sections:

- Economic Truth v. Political Power—in which we learn the truth about the minimum wage, unions, Keynesian economics, supply-side economics, U.S. trade, and Michael Milliken, among other things.
- Debunking the Bankers—in which we find out that all we ever suspected about fractional-reserve banking, S & L loan insurance, and the World Bank is absolutely true.
- Unmasking the Bureaucrats—in which we tour delightful D.C., NASA, and HUD, and discover why the Federal Emergency Management Agency is less helpful than neighbor Charlie and the Red Cross when it comes to little things like hurricanes.
- The Government Mess—in which we examine the principles of statism and find that they only make things worse.
- Threats and Outrages—in which we see what the bureaucrats are planning for our future, and why we don't like it, from compulsory national service for 18-year-olds to elimination of private property through Greenism.
- The Communist Crackup—in which the libertarians say, "I told you so."

No small print, no doublespeak, no scholarly jargon or mind-deadening graphs.

All in all, *The Economics of Liberty* is a very readable introduction to a fresh viewpoint on a host of economic and political issues. *Mary Pride*

Foundation for Economic Education, among other things, carries a fine selection of books from a free-enterprise position. These are classics no educated person should miss, so pick up their free catalog.

Of all the available titles, here is the one to start with:

The Law by Frederic Bastiat explains how, under democracy, special interests can use the vote to "plunder" (his word) others . . . and why the redistribution of income via taxes and government aid (as opposed to private charity) is always wrong. Bastiat, a Frenchman writing in the early 1800s, also predicted the Civil War as an outgrowth of tariffs and slavery, two anti-freedom positions respectively adopted by the North and the South. Very easy to read and understand.

If you never understood economics before, it's probably because of that Keynesian fog that glommed up your school texts. FEE has the antidote. *Mary Pride*

How We Live: Economic Wisdom Simplified uses "The Ten Pillars of Economic Wisdom" to quickly explain how an economy works. While no overt judgment is passed, the description of the parts is sufficient to lead to the conclusion that the whole works best when government takes both an honest and a hands-off approach. This 39-page booklet contains 20 one-page topics, along with plenty of black-and-white photos and graphics. Some of the topics covered are work, unemployment, tools, patents, corporations, individual responsibility, and labor costs. It won't take you long to work through the material and you'll be way ahead of the majority of our population when it comes to understanding how "money makes the world go round." *Renee Mathis*

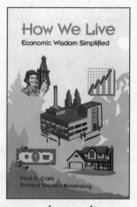

My sixth-grade teacher explained inflation and depression to us, using many historical examples. "Why doesn't our government know this stuff?" I wondered all through my teens. Perhaps because the members of our government took college economics classes similar to the one I later did, taught by people with Marxist leanings.

Richard J. Maybury (Uncle Eric) believes, as did my sixth grade teacher, "You can understand almost anything if it is explained well." And explain it he does, in **Whatever Happened to Penny Candy?**, a book in the form of letters written from **"Uncle Eric"** to his nephew.

If your children (or you) want to understand what is going on with our economy, this book is a must. Recently updated with current information for the 1990's, it is a treasure trove of interesting information and resources for further study. While it paints a realistic view of our future, it is neither frightening nor alarmist. If only I could afford enough copies to send to everyone in Washington D.C. . . . *Rebecca Prewett*

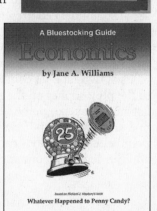

Foundation for Economic Education books

Grade 9–adult. The Law, $2.95 plus shipping.
The Foundation for Economic Education, 30 South Broadway, Irvington, NY 10533. (800) 452-3518. (914) 591-7230. Fax: (914) 591-8910. Email: freeman@fee.org. Web: www.fee.org.

NEW!
How We Live: Economic Wisdom Simplified

Grade 9. $3.95 plus $4 shipping. *Christian Liberty Press, 502 West Euclid Ave., Arlington Heights, IL 60004. (847) 259-4444. Fax: (847) 259-2941. Email: enquire@homeschools.org. Web: www.homeschools.org. They take credit card orders, but not over the phone. Any other contact method will work.*

UPDATED!
Uncle Eric's Whatever Happened to Penny Candy?

Grade 5–adult. $9.95. Bluestocking Guide to Economics (companion book), $12.95. Shipping extra. *Bluestocking Press, PO Box 2030, Shingle Springs, CA 95682-2030. Orders: (800) 959-8586. Inquiries: (530) 621-1123. Fax: (530) 642-9222. Email: uncleric@jps.net.*

Bluestocking Press has now come up with a small companion course in economics, titled *A Bluestocking Guide to Economics*, based on *Whatever Happened to Penny Candy*. This book includes articles from many economists, and many useful references to movies, books, magazine articles, and other media, which would help your understanding of economics as "Uncle Eric" sees it. Discussion questions are included with most passages or references. 125 pages, paperback.

Magazines

Designed to instruct the reader in free market economic and political philosophy, and full of well-researched facts, each issue of **The Freeman** includes a number of reasonably short articles. This handy-sized publication now has extra teaching helps for high schoolers. Articles identified with a "apple" icon ( ) are appropriate for teaching high-school students basic facts of economics, government/civics, history, or philosophy. Sample lesson plans for those articles are now available on FEE's website and may also be requested in print form. What a good idea! *Mary Pride*

Tapes

Narrated by Louis Rukeyser (of *Wall Street Week* fame), this 13-part series discusses works of economic literature and the development of economic thought.

The **Great Economic Thinkers** series includes:

- The Classical Economists
- Karl Marx: *Das Kapital*
- Early Austrian Economics
- Alfred Marshall & Neoclassicism
- The German Historical School of Economics
- The Vision of Leon Walras
- Thorstein Veblen and Institutionalism
- Joseph Schumpeter and Dynamic Economic Change
- Frank Knight and the Chicago School
- The Austrian Case for the Free Market Process
- The Keynesian Revolution
- Struggle Over the Keynesian Heritage
- Monetarism & Supply Side Economics

As you can see, the topics chosen provide you a balanced overview of liberal, conservative, and libertarian economics. All authors covered have seriously influenced present-day economic thought.

A single two-tape set introduction to economics, *Economics in One Lesson*, is also available, also narrated by Louis Rukeyser. It has been called "the shortest and surest way to understand economics."

Each two-tape set comes a handy small binder, with a short introduction to the philosopher on the jacket, and includes between 2½ to 3 hours of listening. You can purchase the entire series at once, or do it the easy way, one set per month billed to your credit card. Great for armchair students, even better for bucket-seat students. Why waste good armchair time when you can soak up economics while stuck in traffic? *Mary Pride*

CHAPTER 30

Geography

I n science-fiction writer Isaac Asimov's blockbuster epic, the Foundation Trilogy, Trantor was a planet that imported all its goods and in return, administered the whole galactic empire.

In our day, America is trying to become Trantor. We are sending all our factory jobs offshore, trading with every country on earth, and mixing it up both diplomatically and militarily in every global scuffle we can get our hands on.

Whether this is good or bad, I leave to your judgment. However, it does mean that a knowledge of world geography is more important in our day than it ever was before. Unless your parents immigrated from Yugoslavia, you likely never even heard of the Serbs and Croats. Yet here we are, with the doings of these people on the other side of the world as daily fare in our newspapers and TV shows.

When it comes to U.S. geography, upper-level courses tend to concentrate on economic geography—exports, imports, population size and density, and other material you can find in any decent atlas. This information changes over time; I don't think it's really worth memorizing. Just get those states and capitals straight, and you'll be better off than the majority of high-school graduates.

Not that I want to discourage any budding geographers, mind you. You can learn plenty about any state and region by

- watching travel videos (the most painless and fun way to go!)
- checking out a state, city, or country's World Wide Web site
- planning a vacation via atlas and travelers' guides
- eating the native cuisine
- subscribing to *Country, Country Extra,* and *Farm and Ranch Living* (see review on page 209)

Well, that's plenty to start with, and it's all more fun than memorizing the size of last year's Idaho potato crop. When you've finished looking over the geography resources below, I'll see you in the next chapter!

A Beka World Geography in Christian Perspective

Grades 9–12. Student book, $17.20. Teacher's guide, $20.20. Student test & quiz book, $4.20. Test & quiz key, $8.85. Map and study book available. Shipping extra.
A Beka Book, Box 19100, Pensacola, FL 32523-9100. (800) 874-2352. Fax: (800) 874-3590.
Web: www.abeka.com.

Alpha Omega Geography Elective LIFEPACs

Select LIFEPACs from grades 7 and 9 History & Geography. Set of 5 LIFEPACs plus teachers guide, sold as "LIFEPAC Select Geography Set," $19.95. Shipping extra.
Alpha Omega Publications, 300 N. McKemy, Chandler, AZ 85226. Orders and inquiries: (800) 622-3070. Fax: (480) 785-8034.
Web: www.home-schooling.com.

BJUP Geography for Christian Schools, 2nd edition

Grade 9. Student text, $30. Teacher's edition, $44.50. Map packet (25 maps), $7. TestBank, $8. Answer key, $4.50. Shipping extra.
Bob Jones University Press, Greenville, SC 29614. Orders: (800) 845-5731. Fax: (800) 845-5731. Email: lgrover@wpo.bju.edu.
Web: www.bju.edu.

Physical Geography

Grades 7–12. $12 postpaid.
American Christian History Institute, PO Box 648, Palo Cedro, CA 96073. (530) 547-3535. Fax: (530) 547-4045. Email: rosebud@c-zone.net.
Web: www.achipa.com.

Geography Courses

A Beka World Geography in Christian Perspective, along with *American Government in Christian Perspective* (see review in chapter 28) used to be offered together as a single course. Now that A Beka has split it into two separate semester-long courses, you can delve a little deeper into the people and places of the world. *Mary Pride*

Alpha Omega doesn't have a geography course for middle or upper grades. Instead, geography is added into the social-studies program in a few workbook units (called LIFEPACS) here and there.

Grade 7 touches on geography twice, once defining it as a discipline and the other time as a unit on the history and geography of the U.S.A. The last half of **grade 9** discusses man's relationship to the earth, world regions, man and his environment, and a useful unit called "The Tools of the Geographer" which introduces globes, maps, graphs, charts, and other ways people have found to represent geographical information.

You can purchase these individual LIFEPACs, with accompanying teacher's guide, as a set entitled "LIFEPAC Select Geography," an elective one-semester course for junior/senior high. *Mary Pride*

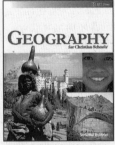

This solid, colorful text was revised in 1998 to reflect the major changes that happened since **Geography for Christian Schools** was released in the '80's. Presentation is the same as in the earlier edition: each chapter is information-packed. Lots of maps and pictures, interesting sidebars and comprehension questions after each section help to illustrate and cement the information in your mind. Each of the 29 chapters in this 662-page hardcover text ends with a comprehensive review. Bob Jones' conservative Christian worldview comes through as the authors endeavor to share a sense of the spiritual conditions in the various parts of the world as they present physical and political geography in those places.

Our family used the first edition of *Geography for Christian Schools* this year and we were pleased with it . . . except that parts of it were out of date. Though that provided some interesting opportunities for discussion, the second edition of the text is very welcome. *Michelle Van Loon*

Want to teach geography using the Principle Approach?
Physical Geography is a reprint of an 1873 work written by Swiss-born geographer Arnold Guyot. Dr. Guyot was Professor of Geography and Geology at Princeton University. His book attempts to teach geography from a Christian point of view. The new edition has an introduction by Katherine Dang, author of the article "Geography: An American Christian Approach" included in James Rose's *Guide to American Christian Education for the Home and School* (also available from ACHI).

The folks at ACHI suggest you use Physical Geography in conjunction with the *Guide to American Christian Education. Mary Pride*

What would happen if you took the best features from Saxon math and put them in a geography curriculum? You'd have a program with an emphasis on regular daily review. You'd make sure the basics were taught, drilled, and frequently applied. You wouldn't need to juggle hefty teacher's manuals and student texts. You'd have clearly written daily lessons that anyone could pick up and teach from. In short, you'd have **Runkle Geography.**

Brenda Brewer Runkle was an associate of John Saxon, and it shows! Her geography curriculum is the most thorough I've ever seen.

You may want to take the recommended three years and work through two units per year, or you may choose to concentrate on just one or two units. The choice is yours, and as a homeschooling mom I like having that flexibility!

To get started, you'll want to jump right in with **Unit 7,** the mapping unit. Learning the place names and capitals of every country in the world, as well as relative location and natural features is the goal here. A few minutes a day is all it takes, but accuracy and correct spelling are required.

Everything you need is in the mapping packet, including full-color maps, blank maps, and detailed teaching instructions for how to break down the material into manageable bites. You'll get a fair amount of cultural and political history here too, making this unit usable as a stand-alone for younger grades.

The next step is a complete grounding in our world's physical characteristics, including latitude, longitude, time zones, map characteristics, etc. **Unit 1,** Physical Geography, is a large-format 213-page spiral-bound book. With its colorful pictures, highlighted "fun facts," photos, diagrams, and illustrations, this book is a visual treat. There are 34 lessons in all, recommended for use in one semester.

Far from tedious or boring, Ms. Runkle writes in a friendly conversational tone and includes a wide variety of critical thinking and hands-on exercises throughout. Geography should be an integrated study, and thanks to this author it is.

I was pleasantly surprised by the complete lack of any evolutionary bias. No groveling to the eco-fanatics in this book! (Not surprising since Ms. Runkle is herself a professing Christian.)

The lessons are bursting with content and conclude with review questions for all material studied thus far, as well as a list of vocabulary words to know. The teacher's guide gives the answers to these as well as five or six concisely worded "review facts" for each lesson. (I can see all sorts of possibilities for using these to create games or dictation exercises.) Tests and answer keys are provided as well.

Runkle Geography is truly an all-in-one program in the best sense of the word. I'm excited about this one! *Renee Mathis*

Cruising the World by Ear

Narrated by Harry Reasoner, Peter Hackes, and Richard C. Hottelet, the 20-part **World's Political Hot Spots** audiocassette series discusses the world regions which historically have been politically unstable. The series includes:

Runkle Geography

Grades 6–8. Unit 1: Physical Geography, $70. Unit 7: Runkle Mapping Method, $52. *Runkle Publishers, 3750 W. Main, 3 Park So., Norman, OK 73072. (877) GEO-TEXT. Fax: (405) 321-9644. Email: brunkle@runklepub.com. Web: www.runklepub.com.*

Unit 1   Unit 7

So far only two units are available:
- Unit 1 includes Teacher's Guide, student book, and test masters
- Unit 7 includes full-color maps, black-and-white maps for exercises, and teaching instructions

Units 2–6 will start being released one at a time in Fall '99.

NEW!
Knowledge Products: The World's Political Hot Spots series

Grade 9–adult. Complete series, $299 postpaid. Individual two-tape sets, $17.95 plus shipping. *Knowledge Products, 722 Rundle Ave., Suite A-13, Nashville, TN 37210. Orders: (800) 876-4332. Inquiries: (615) 742-3852. Fax: (615) 742-3270.*

- *The Middle East*
- *South Africa*
- *Central America*
- *Germany*
- *Ireland*
- *Cuba*
- *The Philippines*
- *Russia and the Soviet Union*
- *Mexico*
- *The Persian Gulf States*
- *India & Pakistan*

- *Ethiopia & East Africa*
- *Poland*
- *Nigeria & West Africa*
- *The Mediterranean Basin*
- *Chile & Argentina*
- *Columbia and its Satellite Countries*
- *The Golden Triangle*
- *China*
- *Central Europe: Hungary, Yugoslavia, Czechoslovakia*

This is a fascinating way to study world history. You can learn the historical background of interesting places while cruising down the highway or doing the dishes! *Mary Pride*

Fact Books

The **Crabtree Lands, People, and Cultures series** is an easy-reading, clear-sighted look at other cultures. With just enough written details, and lots of vibrant large photos and illustrations, these are a great introduction to each of the countries covered.

Most countries have three volumes: *Lands, People,* and *Cultures.* The *Lands* book talks about the landscape, the country's history, and how people live there today. The *People* book introduces the various ethnic and religious groups that share the land and talks about what it's like growing up and living there. The *Cultures* book covers such topics as religions, holidays, clothes, and art.

The series includes *Land, People,* and *Cultures* volumes for Japan, China, India, Mexico, Canada, Vietnam, Greece, and Israel. It also includes a single volume for Tibet, two volumes for Peru (*Land* and *People and Culture*), and a volume entitled *Canada Celebrates Multiculturalism*. One side note of interest (to me, anyway): the teenage girl on the cover of *Israel: The People* looks almost exactly like me at that age!

If you are studying any of these countries, I can highly recommend these books. The entire set would make a wonderful support-group library purchase—or perhaps you could talk your local public library into getting the more expensive set with reinforced library bindings. *Mary Pride*

Operation World began in 1963 as a sheaf of facts, country by country, for use during a week of prayer for the world. Since then, author Patrick Johnstone fell prey to the same syndrome as your humble *Big Book* editor—he kept adding *more* and *more* facts and updating the information while his book got bigger and bigger!

In its present form, *Operation World* provides over 500 pages of densely packed information on every country in the world from a Christian and missionary point of view, plus lots and lots of statistics, historical background information, ethnic information, and prayer needs. This is information you can't find in your *World Book of Facts* or encyclopedia: stuff like, "What is the ratio of missionaries to the number of people in that country?" "How many languages are spoken in the country, and into how many of them is the Bible

NEW!
Crabtree Lands, People, and Cultures series

Grades 4–9. Each book, $7.95 paperback, $19.96 reinforced library binding. Complete set of all 28 books (not including Spanish editions), $221.25 paperback, $558.88 reinforced library binding. Shipping extra.
Crabtree Publishing Company, 350 Fifth Avenue, Suite 3308, New York, NY 10118. (800) 387-7650. Fax: (800) 355-7166. Email: crabtree@crabtree-pub.com. Web: www.crabtree-pub.com.

Operation World

Grade 7–adult. Book, $8.80. Prayer cards, $2.40. 21" x 36" World map, $2.99. Shipping extra.
Operation Mobilization Literature, PO Box 1047, Waynesboro, GA 30830-2047. Orders: (800) 733-5907. Inquiries: (706) 554-5827. Fax: (706) 554-7444. Email: postmaster@omlit.om.org.

translated?" "How are Christians treated in that country?" and "What is the history of Christian missionary activity in that country?" Along with this are geographical, social, population, and other facts. The reader is given specific prayer requests arising from the recent history of each country, plus names and addresses of mission groups operating in that country and a section on "special ministries" such as medical missions and student ministries.

I didn't find it easy to follow the suggested prayer calendar format (which assigns you a country or ministry to pray for each day of the year), mainly because it takes more than one day to digest all the information about a country or mission! A more promising format for homeschool use might be to concentrate on one country per week, or even a country of the month. For behind-the-scenes information on that country from a Christian perspective, *Operation World* is unsurpassed.

To complete your own Operation World "kit," you can purchase not just the book, but also a set of 70 "World Prayer Cards," each with facts and prayer requests about a foreign country, and a world map, for locating your country of the day (or week, or month!). It's a really good deal, and I hope a lot of you take advantage of it! *Mary Pride*

Maps & Globes

The nice folks at Educational Materials Associates have tried hard to find a way to help teachers teach or review plain, unadorned information. Sometimes turning facts into a game can make digesting those facts a little sweeter. They offer materials in history, social studies and science, all with the same basic format: an 11 x 17" cardboard playing board (note that the cardboard is fairly thin; lamination would be a big improvement), a stack of two-sided cards that has information keyed to the board, and a teacher's guide.

The Living Sea is a map game: regions of the sea must be identified by either name or characteristic. (The Mariana Trench can be distinguished by the fact that it is the world's deepest ocean trench, located in the western Pacific, southeast of Guam.) The teacher's guide has game rules, data sheets, a glossary, letter scramble and word search masters and a study guide with pre- and post-test forms you can use to ascertain what you'll need to learn in order to play the game.

Though more of a fact-based unit study than a game, the Living Sea Game does add a splash of competitive interest to an information-heavy study of marine geography. Worthwhile as a supplement to a more in-depth study of our oceans, or if you are simply trying to find a way to spend a short time learning this material without drowning in it. *Michelle Van Loon*

When most of our population can't seem to locate states and capitals within our own country, being able to map the entire world seems like an unattainable goal. What about creating an entire map from memory?
Mapping the World By Heart seeks to teach just that.

In your impressively large kit you'll receive a short introductory video featuring an interview with the author, David Smith. There's a 3-ring binder with 129 pages of instructions, nine blank maps for you to label, and several 17 x 11" world maps which illustrate different map projections. You'll need to provide the atlas, globe, colored pencils, and fine point markers.

The notebook is divided into a "Menu of Lessons." "Appetizers" features seven lessons on basic physical geography. "Entrees" is a series of checklists to use in labeling your different blank maps. "Seasonings" offers instructions for putting together a "World's Fair" exhibition for the students to show off what they've learned. "Dessert" gives the instructions for making the final, memory map.

Here is the suggested teaching plan: After teaching the introductory lessons, you give your child a blank map of, say, South America, along with the checklist of features. Your child labels the map, checks it for accuracy, plays some games (two samples are given), and takes a test that you create. Continue in this fashion throughout the year until the last seven weeks, when you work on the final map.

This is by no means a complete geography program. You will learn where the mountain ranges and rivers are in a country, but you'll learn nothing about the people who live there. Even the author himself uses this for just one or two class periods per week. Neither is it a case of seventh graders whipping out picture-perfect maps in 50 minutes or so. In order to produce gorgeous "by heart" maps at the end of the year, Mr. Smith's students spend 15 class periods creating a detailed world map, using any and all available resources. They spend the next 20 class periods working on the memory maps. No helps are available during class, but each student is encouraged to review at home before coming to class the next day. (I've thought about questioning whether or not this is truly a map "by heart," but I'll leave that decision up to you.) *Renee Mathis*

> Essentially this curriculum is a set of maps and a list of features to label. I've used it myself in a co-op group, but it took some work to plan and gather the additional materials to flesh out the program. If you're up to it, then *Mapping the World By Heart* can be a valuable part of your geography lessons.

Milliken U.S. Map Skills transparency/duplicating series

Grades 4–9. $14.95 each plus shipping.
Milliken Publishing Company, 1100 Research Blvd., St. Louis, MO 63132. Orders: (800) 325-4136. Inquiries: (314) 991-4220. Fax: (800) 538-1319. Web: www.millikenpub.com.

Milliken's **United States Map Skills** transparency/duplicating workbook is a complete course in U.S. geography. With the aid of 12 colorful full-page transparencies, kids learn about time zones, climate, states and capitals, postal abbreviations, population density, state mottoes, major geographic features, and how to use city, state, and interstate road maps. 28 workbook pages and a teacher's guide with answer key round out the book.

This book is much easier to use than a traditional geography textbook, partly because of its highly visual approach. Some of the transparencies are fascinating, like the cutaway view of the heights of the waterways included in the St. Lawrence Seaway. Regions of the U.S.A. are briefly introduced. The individual sets *Eastern U.S.A., Southern U.S.A., Central U.S.A.,* and *Western U.S.A.* have been discontinued. The series still includes a book on Canada. *Mary Pride*

National Geographic Society

Membership, $27, includes the magazine. WORLD magazine (for kids), $10. Maps: $11.95–$92.95 each. Shipping extra.
Subscriptions: National Geographic Society, 3000 University Center Dr., Tampa, FL 33162. Maps: National Geographic Society, Educational Services, PO Box 10597, Des Moines, IA 50340-0597. Educational products (CD-ROMs, maps, books, videos), (800) 368-2728. Membership and National Geographic Magazine, (800) 647-5463. World Magazine: (800) 607-4410. Web: www.nationalgeographic.com.

You know all about **National Geographic** magazine. As befits an originally geographical society, NGS has maps, maps, and more maps. Lands of the Bible today. Bird migration in the Americas. Mural maps to cover your wall. Ocean floor relief maps. Space maps. U.S. regional maps. Canadian provinces. Antarctica (plan in advance for your trip!)

NGS also has a couple of fancy atlases and a quint of fancy globes. *Mary Pride*

I can pretty much sum up the **Odyssey Atlasphere** in three words; it is awesome. Imagine . . . a talking globe that, when you press a stylus to, or even *near*, any point on the globe, tells you the country's name. In a normal human voice, not weird synthesized speech.

But more than that, upon request (by touching a category on the console, or just repeatedly pressing Play) it will tell you all the following:

- **Country**—place name, capital city/cities, type of government, political status, political divisions, date of independence/founding/admitted to a union
- **People**—population, population density, percent urban, population growth rate, population doubling time, life expectancy (males and females), birth rate, death rate, number of people per telephone, adult literacy rate, major religions, common languages
- **Land**—total area, maximum/minimum elevation, maximum depth of oceans and lakes, world circumference and diameter
- **Money**—type of currency, gross domestic product per capita, purchasing power parity, income distribution, energy consumption per capita, energy production per capita, government budget, total imports/exports, import/export partners, average income (U.S. states and Canadian provinces only)
- **Climate**—annual precipitation
- **Sounds**—local music, national anthems (some countries)
- **Time**—set your home location and time/day, then touch any location on the globe to hear the time and day
- **Distance**—between two points, estimated travel time between two points walking/driving/flying, length of a line traced with the styles, total distance between a series of points, estimated travel time between a series of points
- **Compare**—any of the themes above for two places; e.g., population density of USA and Norway

More than that, you can find the location of a country by spelling out its name via touching letters printed on the globe.

More than *that,* you can drill yourself on all the countries of the world with your choice of three games for one to six players (all included in the basic GeoZone game cartridge that comes with your Atlasphere). Each player has an assigned name and can choose a proficiency level of one to four.

- **Eureka** asks you to locate as many countries as possible in four rounds of 45 seconds each
- **Globesurfer** asks you to locate several countries, then answer questions about them
- **Solo Trek** asks you to locate every country on earth in the minimum number of rounds

Even more than *that,* every game gives you verbal hints, such as "Look in Asia" or "Try 2,000 miles northwest."

With the additional "Metropolis" game cartridge, you can learn and test yourself on cities of the world as well.

So far, my family has spent approximately 12 hours playing with the Atlasphere, and we haven't even made it through all its features yet. What we *have* accomplished is to amazingly improve our geographical knowledge. Go ahead, ask my daughter Sarah where Burkina Faso is . . . or the Maldives. We have the Educational Package, which also includes an excel-

lent activity guide and the Metropolis game cartridge, so you can also ask me about capital cities and state/province capitals. And I'll even know how to *pronounce* them correctly!

Any child who can read and understand north/south/east/west can hardly help learning tons more geography than all the other kids on his block with the help of an Atlasphere. Plus, he'll beg you for the opportunity to learn all this! No other product, including software packages, can provide this level of hands-on interactive discovery. *Mary Pride*

Travel Tales

Nobody in the whole history of the world had ever walked around the world alone. It took 33-year-old Steven Newman four years and 39 million steps to complete his 20,000-mile odyssey, during which he traveled through 20 countries on five continents. All along that route Steven wrote letters that were published in *Capper's Weekly*. The best of those letters were put together into this book, **Letters from Steven**.

This is not your typical jock tome. You know, "Forty miles outside of Abilene I developed a humongous blister. Well, I stripped off my Nikes and went for the Dr. Scholls. . ." Steven, a trained journalist, spent his time on the road talking to people, visiting them in their homes, observing the countryside, and doing a lot of thinking. The result is a unique look at the world as it really is, minus the political lenses through which we too often view it.

Steven's letters were written to people he knew wanted to hear about what the places he visited were *really* like. As he chronicles his adventures, from a near brush with death at the hands of bushwhackers to an encounter with a flock of giant birds in Scotland, you get a feel for the contours of our world quite different from the view preached in travel magazines and on the 6 o'clock news. I'll never be able to forget Steven's description of Thailand:

> *"Maybe you like watch American football?" [the Thai waitress] asked. Then pausing as if to wait for my eyes to plunk into my lap, she added, "Today, inside on big screen, we have Super Bowl." . . .*
>
> *Super . . . Bowl—the Super Bowl? In Pakistan and India hardly anyone had ever heard of such a thing. But now, in a land I had expected to be the most primitive yet, I was being offered the most sacred of all American spectacles as casually as I might have been offered a cup of coffee in a Park Avenue eatery . . .*
>
> *Nowhere outside of my own country, not even in London, Rome, or Athens, had I seen such a concentration of consumer and luxury goods from all over the world, particularly America and Japan. It was almost as if those two economic behemoths had found in Thailand a perfect arena in which to do battle for the consumers' bank accounts.*

Steven has a gift for making friends and getting invited to unusual places. He also has a gift of extreme spiritual sensitivity, which in his case has made him open to just about every religion he met on the road, with the sole exception of Islam. (His chapter, "Hell in the Shadow of Iran," is one of the most powerful in the book.) You don't have to buy into his philosophy to get his information, fortunately. And the information is really worth having. Steven helps you *see* and *feel* what life is like for everyday people all over the world—and for the world-walking stranger in their midst, whom they invariably befriended. This is a view of our world you simply can't find anywhere else. Recommended, with reservations only because of the occasional universalistic content. *Mary Pride*

Letters from Steven

Grades 7–adult. Hardcover, $10. Softcover, $5, plus $2 shipping.
Steve Newman, 2799 Logan Gap Rd., Ripley, OH 45167. Fax/Phone (call first for fax), (937) 392-1670. Email: snewman@in-touch.net.

Tour America in 50 weeks, visiting and learning about every state. Make it your goal to interview all 50 governors and get their signatures on a set of T-shirts. Amy Burritt, a 12-year-old Christian homeschooler, is the first person to ever accomplish this goal.

In her book, **My American Adventure**, Amy takes us step by step with her on her journey. With her family and their dog Shasta, we meet the governors and their staffs; visit a variety of educational and fun attractions; learn about each state's geography, main industries, and needs; and share the joys and tears of a sensitive, warm-hearted girl who both enjoys the adventure (most of the time) and misses her hometown friends. We also get to see many of the best moments through the many photos with which the book is dotted.

I read *My American Adventure* from cover to cover in one sitting—and it's 254 pages long! It's great fun seeing which governors win Amy's private awards. Who was the Greatest Challenge? Who won the Quick Quip award? The family's adventures and misadventures strike a responsive chord, and it's fascinating to get "up close" views of so many powerful political figures.

Amy succeeded so well that Michigan governor John Engler wrote the foreword for her book, and six other governors wrote jacket blurbs. She has appeared on CNN, C-SPAN, MTV, and many radio shows and newspapers around the country. Her unique hardcover book is sure to provide not only a painless tour of U.S. geography, but inspiration and food for thought to homeschoolers everywhere. *Mary Pride*

NEW!
My American Adventure
Grade 5–adult. $23, free shipping in U.S.A.
Ironwood Press, PO Box 4651, Traverse City, MI 49685-4651.
Orders: (800) 725-6565.
Inquiries: (616) 275-3505.
Fax: (616) 275-5606.

U.S. History

History is tricky. Unlike mathematics, which follows logical rules no matter who the mathematician is or what his political party, history changes depending on who is telling the story.

We can all memorize (and subsequently forget) dates and places: Columbus sailing the ocean blue in fourteen hundred ninety-two or the Declaration of Independence being signed on July 4, 1776. But even straight-forward memorizing is not without its perils. Do we memorize Susan B. Anthony's birthday or Phyllis Schlafly's? Is Mrs. Rosa Parks' refusal to move to the back of the bus more important to the history of America than John Paul Jones bellowing, "I have not yet begun to fight"? Beyond the few major dates on which all agree, there is room for strife aplenty in choosing which events and people are worth our attention and which are not.

Historians wage skirmishes in the halls of academe over more than the relative importance of Date A and Person B. War also rages over the *interpretation* of events. Even if all sides finally agreed that the Pilgrims landed at Plymouth Rock rather than some less photogenic site, that would not be the end of it. Was the Pilgrims' landing a great step for mankind or a disaster for virgin, Indian-populated America? Historians agree that Custer and his men died at the Little Big Horn. But was Custer a hero or a cad? Name your event and you'll find at least two, but more likely ten, different interpretations of its significance and meaning.

Here's a list of the major theories of history. First, the least popular:

- **Cyclical.** Everything repeats itself, and history goes around in circles. This is one ancient view of history, and it is all tied up with bonds of reincarnation and karma. Nothing you or I do will make the slightest difference. The wheel keeps turning around.

- **Random Chance.** Everything happens by accident. No historical events have meaning or purpose. Existentialists and nihilists like this view.

- **Conspiracy.** A group of clever, evil men have plotted for (take your pick) years/decades/centuries to centralize world power in their hands. They are so very clever, and the rest of us are so very innocent and stupid, that every war, recession, bank failure, and crop failure is their doing. Their nefarious plots almost always succeed. Therefore we are heading into another Dark Age.

A year of U.S. History is typically required for high-school graduation, as is a 2–4 week unit on the history of your state.

A good history course will include source documents and an organized overview of the time period. Biographies and historical fiction, if done well, add details to the picture.

"Time to go to the library, kids!" you call, herding the family into the minivan. "Let's go gather some high quality reading material for our upcoming unit on the Spanish-American War." The children break into spontaneous applause, knowing that you'll again lead them to more mind-enriching reading adventures.

Hmmm. It doesn't work this way for you? (I'll let you in on a secret: I have yet to hear any spontaneous applause from my children, either!) You may not garner applause, but you can build some real excitement in your history study by doing lots of interesting, meaningful reading. A literature-based history study can put some flesh on a skeleton of facts, while at the same time offering you a chance to teach literary analysis of plot, characterization and motivation.

If you want to tackle history this way, the most important thing you need to take to the library with you (besides your card and overdue fines) is an excellent reading list. **Teaching American History Through The Novel** has the potential to be a useful, though not excellent, list. This 178-page softcover resource gives one-paragraph synopses of 300 novels, and organizes these listings in author alphabetical order, chronological order, by theme (such as The Immigrant Experience), and by title. A brief introduction (not brief enough to forego important Politically Correct Warnings about some of the older literature mentioned, unfortunately), a listing of student activities, and a supplementary movie listing round out the text. Books with racist or sexual language are noted as such in the plot synopsis, and there are many, many worthwhile reading choices highlighted.

Not every book listed in here is worth reading, however. If you choose to use a this book to ferret out reading choices, know that it has not been compiled from a Christian perspective, and be willing to take the time to pre-read any book you hand your child.
Michelle Van Loon

- **Modernist** or **Evolutionary.** Things are getting better and better and pretty soon we will end up living in the best of all possible worlds. Why? Cause it just happens that way! Since we are the smartest generation that ever has lived, we don't need to learn from the past. Throw out those history books! Or, if you insist on studying history, make sure it's all stated in terms of today's political program. You know— "The Puritans and Feminism" or "John Adams and Nuclear Disarmament."

Why aren't these more popular? Well, recent sad events such as World Wars I and II have taken the shine off modernist history. Cyclical history appeals mostly to Zen types, and doesn't fit with Western notions of progress. And conspiracy theories and random chance are just too ginchy for most folks. Besides, there's little point in studying history if it's *that* out of control.

We now pass on to the more popular historical theories:

- **Great Man.** Individuals with exceptional ability determine the course of history. Most conservative history books sold in America tend to take this position. Some nihilists like this view, too.

- **Providential.** God controls history and is working out His plans on earth. History in this view is cause and effect. If a nation or an individual sins, it or he can expect trouble. If a nation or individual is obedient to God, then in due course God bestows blessing. Some trouble is part of the normal human condition and necessary to keep us from getting soft, but by and large history has grand purposes that the savvy Bible student can discern. Christian textbooks *should* take this position, to be consistent, but figuring out the eternal message behind specific historical events is hard work. That's why you'll find most "providential" history centers around the American Revolution, when people thought more about these things and source documents are full of well-documented providences.

- **Marxist.** Popular in colleges, which some have dubbed "the last stronghold of real Marxism on earth," Marxism teaches that history is the result of a class struggle between the masses and the wealthy. When class distinctions and religion finally are annihilated, Utopia will arise from the ashes. In the meantime we need censorship and an army of bureaucrats and an army of KGB men and an army of conscripts and an arsenal of nuclear weapons and a first-rate Olympic team. On with the struggle, comrades! Workers of the world unite!

- **Feminist.** In its innocuous form, feminist history tells us what the women and children were doing while the men were out killing each other in glorious wars. You will recognize this as the "daily life" vignettes in many history resources. In its dire form, feminist history teaches that history is the result of a struggle between men and women. When sexual distinctions and religion finally are annihilated, Utopia will arise from the ashes. In the meantime we need sexually unbiased textbooks and an army of bureaucrats and an army of social workers and an army of day-care centers and a third chance at the ERA. On with the struggle, sisters! Women of the world unite!

- **Multicultural.** In its innocuous form, multiculturalism is about studying the cultures of a variety of modern and ancient peoples. In its dire form, increasingly common in school texts and PBS specials, it teaches that history is the result of a struggle between evil white people and noble everyone else. When Western civ courses finally are annihilated, and the books and doings of Dead White European Males are dropped from the curriculum, Utopia will arise from the ashes. In the meantime we need art classes making Aztec masks and social studies classes re-enacting Native American worship rituals and history classes that teach every good thing in the world was invented in Africa and stolen by Europeans. On with the struggle, brothers! Non-Europeans of the world unite!

More on Multiculturalism

Let me take a little more time with multiculturalism. It is the coming wave in school texts today, with a recent attempt to create multicultural national history standards. The standards, when unveiled, created a real brouhaha. Since life is short and brouhahas are long, I will condense it into this: the new standards created a quota system for history. The idea was to create greater representation of women and minorities and simultaneously to cut back on references to important Americans of European descent, such as our first President and the Founding Fathers. Meanwhile, students would be presented with discussion questions that encouraged them to condemn past leaders and generations on the grounds they were all a bunch of worthless racists.

What is *really* insidious about all this are the hidden assumptions behind extreme multiculturalism.

Assumption #1: You can only inherit from your own genetic ancestors.

Supposedly, it's not fair to dwell so much on the achievements of British-Americans, because only those who are members of that ethnic group can take pride in George Washington or Thomas Jefferson. Then we are supposed to line up and start playing "my ancestors were smarter/brighter/kinder/harder working than your ancestors."

This is sheer and utter nonsense. The way civilization works is that we *all* inherit from those whose work we build on. Civilization is a spiritual inheritance, not a genetic inheritance. White people who eat peanut butter benefit from the research of a black man, George Washington Carver. Black people who ride in cars benefit from the assembly-line methods perfected by a white man, Henry Ford. Eastern European immigrants benefit from the freedom and liberties mainly fought for by Western European immigrants. Hispanic factory owners study Japanese management techniques. That's the way it goes.

The criteria for who gets into our history books and who is left out should be as objective as possible, namely, "How much effect did this person have on the lives of his or her generation and succeeding generations?" Dropping an influential person, just because he was white, to add a less influential or practically unknown person, just because he wasn't white, is nothing but a quota system.

A quota system for historical figures is not only wrong, but silly. Should I, who am half Hungarian, have low self-esteem because not a single Hungarian is ever mentioned in most American history textbooks? Should I feel alienated? Should I demand that Hungarian-Americans be represented? This might just end up in Joe Namath making it into the history books—whoop de doo.

Multicultural Madness

Multiculturalism sounds innocent enough. Shouldn't everyone have an open-minded attitude towards other cultures? But the agenda of multiculturalists is far more sinister ... Multiculturalist professors and administrators are not interested in discovering the "beautiful" or the "true" in any culture—instead they preach that all cultures are *equally good*—thereby destroying the concept of an absolute standard. . . . In practice, multiculturalists actually treat one civilization as unequal to other cultures—that is, drastically inferior to the rest of the world. What civilization is so devoid of value? Western civilization, of course!

—Dr. Ronald Nash and Jeff Baldwin, *The Totally Usable Summit Ministries Guide to Choosing a College*

Mary Says

Of course, a lot of modern Western civilization *is* devoid of value. I name gangsta rap and TV soap operas as just two examples. Unfortunately, it's the *good* part of Western civilization that multiculturalists attack: the great classics, Christianity, the biblical family, and so forth. We are being told to substitute a kind of belligerent tribalism for the glories of our shared heritage. Bad idea: history tells us it's one short step from going tribal to going postal with people who aren't in your tribe.

I would also like to point out here that few of us have a pure ethnic background, and even fewer are Daughters of the American Revolution. There is no obvious reason why a person who, like myself, is a mixture of Irish, Polish, French, and Hungarian, should claim George Washington as a proud apple on her family tree. In fact, *none* of us can, because George Washington never had any children.

> **Assumption #2: America is a bunch of piranhas snapping at each other, not a melting pot.**

The other argument for multiculturalism is that there are actually many different cultures in America. Thus, black people have their own culture, white people have their own culture, Asians have their own culture, and so on—and we are being racist and discriminatory if we fail to study all these different cultures equally. Furthermore, if a particular group is lacking in a distinct history of its own, that history needs to be invented, going right back to the Jamestown Expedition.

First, this is a recipe for Balkanizing America, turning the country into a racial battlefield. Instead of learning to work together, cooperate, and ignore racial differences, this doctrine makes race all-important.

Second, the fact that we need to *create* brand-new holidays such as Kwanzaa in order to develop this kind of racial consciousness shows that we are looking at something *imposed* on us, not something that naturally springs out of genuine culture.

Third, this whole enterprise is dishonest, because there are literally thousands of ethnic and racial subcultures in America, all of which are in flux at all times, interacting with the main culture (the one we should be studying) and with each other.

There is no such thing as "white culture" or "black culture" or "Native American culture," except as a subset of the American culture we *all* share. In fact, if you actually started describing the various subcultures, you would immediately be accused of fostering *stereotypes,* as follows:

- Brits drink tea.
- Aussies wear cowboy hats and knee socks.
- Irish like to sing and fight.
- Hungarians put sour cream on everything.
- French like to wear berets.
- Ukranians give each other colorful *pysanky* eggs at Easter.
- Africans wear colorful clothes.

As it so happens, my children make Ukranian *pysanky* every year, tea is my favorite drink aside from Mountain Dew, several of my daughters own French berets, my favorite at-home outfit is an African dress called a dashiki, and in spite of my Hungarian heritage the only food item I put sour cream on is baked potato.

I submit to you that the Olympic team model is more like what America is and has been about. Every Olympic year, we send teams in America's name. These teams have members of all races and ethnic groups. When they win, we all cheer. We are proud of *all* of them, not just those whose skin and hair color matches our own. They belong to all of us and we belong to all of them. Amen to that.

Important Background Information

America's British Culture by Russell Kirk is a relatively short (150-page) lucid work which argues for the necessity of a general culture in answer to the claims of the multiculturalists. Dr. Kirk contends that our inheritance from Britain is so great that to endeavor to root it out would cause the collapse of our civilization.

Kirk covers four areas in which we are indebted to Britain: language and literature, law, representative government, and mores and minds. He praises English as a "terse and forceful" language containing many more words than any other, making it "a swift and accurate means of communication." He explains the guiding role of literature, establishes the source of the freedoms we (used to) take for granted as being the supremacy of law, evaluates what representative government was originally intended to be and was in America, compares British- and European-based law, and traces the origins of American character.

Dr. Kirk contends our British cultural inheritance belongs to all of us, regardless if we are descended from Anglo-Saxons—as indeed many of us are not. It is under severe attack and must be fought for or else we will descend to darkness. We agree and highly recommend this book. While not specifically Christian, it is an excellent treatment of the subjects covered. *Charles & Betty Burger*

America's Christian History: The Untold Story by Gary DeMar is a researched response to the many recent claims, by groups such as Americans United for Separation of Church and State, that America never was a Christian nation in any sense of the words. After first raising the issues, DeMar takes a look at current double standards where "censorship" is concerned (e.g., librarians removing books that have a Christian perspective, but insisting on retaining pornography and making it accessible to minors). He looks at historical examples of nations that have sought to eradicate Christianity from their public life—including recent examples from the USA. He then takes up the historical gauntlet, beginning with the Christian nature of the first American colonies, the debate over the Constitution's lack of overtly Christian content, the Christian roots of our first institutions of higher learning (Harvard, Yale, etc.), and ways the Christian religion has been recognized in our nation's capitol. The rest of the book is devoted to debunking various historical fallacies, such as the misattribution of a line in the Treaty of Tripoli to George Washington, the separation myth, and what various early presidents really had to say about Christianity. Finally, several appendices deal with recent challenges to the idea that America ever was, or ever should be, a Christian nation, and what exactly that means.

If you have uncritically accepted the bogus ideas that the Founding Fathers were all deists, and that they wanted us to have "separation *from* religion" rather than "freedom *of* religion," or if you've ever wondered why courts have taken to ruling laws "unconstitutional" just because the laws reflect Christian values (and where this all might lead—after all, the Bible includes laws against murder, rape, and robbery—will murder, rape, and robbery have to become "Constitutionally protected rights"?), you should definitely consider this book.

While high-school students can read and understand this book, it reads more like something you'd expect to see assigned at the college level. This is more of a comment on our current level of high-school academics than the book, which is clearly written and easy to follow. *Mary Pride*

NEW!
America's British Culture
Grade 9–adult. $34.95 plus shipping. ISBN: 156-000-066X. *Transaction Publishers, 390 Campus Dr., Somerset, NJ 08873. (888) 999-6778 or (732) 445-1245. Fax: (732) 748-9801. Web: www.transactionpub.com.*

Please note that you do not have to be of British extraction to understand the premise of this book: that what is best in America has been built on a substructure reaching back through Britain. I myself do not have a single drop of British blood—in fact, my French and Irish ancestors hated and fought the British—but that does not prevent me from claiming Magna Charta and John Wycliffe as part of my heritage. *Mary Pride*

NEW!
America's Christian History
Grade 9–adult. $10.95. Dramatized audio cassette, $6.95. Shipping extra. *American Vision, PO Box 724088, Atlanta, GA 31139-9690. (800) 628-9460. Fax: (770) 952-2587. Email: avision1@aol.com. Web: www.avision1.com.*

A dramatized audiocassette, which combines music and narration with reenactments of many of the historical quotes in the book, is also available. This is a good choice for younger students, and those who will sit still for a cassette played during supper, but not for a whole book filled with footnotes. *Mary Pride*

UPDATED!
FACE "America's Christian History" books

Parents. Christian History of the American Revolution, $42. Christian History of the Constitution, Volumes I and II, $40 each. Teaching & Learning America's Christian History, $35. American Dictionary of the English Language, $65. Rudiments of America's Christian History & Government, $15.

Foundation for American Christian Education (FACE), PO Box 9588, Chesapeake, VA 23321. Orders: (800) 352-FACE. Inquiries: (757) 488-6601. Fax: (757) 488-5593. Web: www.face.net.

FACE is reviving the "Principle Approach" to government, an approach based on biblical law, on which they say the U.S.A. was founded. Their material traces America's roots through source documents. Political freedom begins with self-government, FACE says, and self-government begins in the home.

A complete curriculum based on the Principle Approach—the Noah Plan—is now available. See review in Volume 1. However, you can also purchase individual books separately. Many of you who never plan to use the Principle Approach for your basic curriculum will nonetheless be interested in **FACE's offerings on the subject of government and American history.**

Before we proceed any farther, let me make it clear that these are not workbooks for young children. The theory is that you are going to work through this information yourself and then present it according to a set of complicated teaching suggestions that require you continually to flip back and forth between books.

The Christian History of the Constitution, Volume 1, formerly entitled *Christian Self-Government* (this is now the subtitle) documents that America is a Christian nation (that is, it was dedicated to Christ once upon a time) with a Christian Constitution (that is, one based on Christian principles). The "Chain of Christianity" is traced westward to America, as the gospel spread from Israel to the Roman Empire and thence to the uncouth white tribespeople who, once Christianized, spread it over the world. An oversized book, hardbound in red cloth, beautifully gold-stamped, 545 pages, consisting almost entirely of quotes from source documents.

Volume 2, previously titled *Christian Self-Government with Union* (again, this is now the subtitle) is red vellum, gold-stamped, eagle-embossed, illustrated, indexed, and 660 pages. More history from source documents, emphasizing the colonist's voluntary union that led to self-government.

Teaching and Learning America's Christian History is the original how-to manual of the Principle Approach. Each principle is spelled out, precept on precept, line on line. Likewise beautifully bound and gold-stamped, likewise large, likewise red, 414 pages long.

Rudiments of America's Christian History and Government is a workbook for students filled with source quotes from distinguished American Christian leaders of the past and questions designed to develop both Christian thinking and an awareness of our Christian heritage. For teens and adults.

The Christian History of the American Revolution, previously titled *Consider and Ponder* (this is now the subtitle) covers the Constitutional Debate period of 1765–1775, during which Americans wrestled with the question of what an ideal government should look like. Its 736 pages nestle between blue vellum covers. *Mary Pride*

NEW!
Issues in American History

Grade 9–adult. $10 plus $1.50 shipping.

Dwight D. Murphey, 2412 Hathway Circle, Wichita, KS 67226. (316) 682-7387. Fax: (316) 978-3263. Email: DVMurphey@msn.com.

Issues in American History: A Conservative Scholar's Perspective by Dr. Dwight D. Murphey, Professor of Law at Wichita State University, gives another side of the story to issues commonly used in textbooks to make American children despise their country's past. Topics include:

- **The Historic Dispossession of the American Indian.** Dr. Murphey doesn't condone or underestimate the amount of wrongdoing on either side. He does try to help the reader understand the historical context—how both the settlers and the Indians felt about and acted towards each other. He also deals with Sand Creek and Wounded Knee, two "massacres" that he has found evidence were more like pitched battles initiated in both cases by the Indians. His concern here is to dispel modern sentimental notions about the "evil" settlers *v.* the "noble" Indians, and show the real complexity of the historical situation in which neither side was above reproach.

- **The Relocation of the Japanese-Americans During World War II** answers two questions: "What exactly was done regarding the persons of Japanese ancestry" and "Why was it done?" Instead of simply assuming this was a racist act, equivalent in some ways to Nazis interning Jews in concentration camps (the typical textbook view), Dr. Murphey shows that the whole thing started as an attempt to (1) incarcerate about 3,000 Japanese aliens who had been classified as dangerous, due to their connections to anti-American Japanese groups, and (2) to relocate Japanese-Americans inland, to keep them out of a "Pacific Coast military zone." He delves into the nature of the camps, the military reasons for establishing them, whether or not the reasons were excessive or invalid, why German-Americans weren't interned, and finally the aftermath of it all ($20,000 apiece paid to each of the evacuees, including those detained as "dangerous aliens," those who left for Japan, and those who attended American universities during the war).

- **Kent State.** An amazing recital of the revolutionary violence, arson, and threats that had already occurred at Kent State before the events of May 1–5, 1970. Also a look at the amount of revolutionary and violent participation—or non-participation—of each of the dead or wounded students. The point he makes here is that, up to the point where the firing began, far from being easily provoked, the authorities in Ohio and elsewhere had been almost unbelievably lenient in the face of escalating physical and verbal abuse. Far from a characteristic event, Kent State was an anamoly—and one that, in context, can be seen as an unsurprising, if undesirable, outcome of the increasing (and unreported) leftist mob violence.

- **The Hollywood Blacklist.** Were the blacklistees communists and communist sympathizers, or noble martyrs? Were they using the considerable power of the entertainment industry to attempt to turn America communist, and if so, is that a good thing? Were they the only blacklistees, or did those who *opposed* communism get blacklisted "behind the scenes"?

- **The J. Robert Oppenheimer Case.** The head of the Manhattan (atom bomb) project, he later had his security clearance revoked. Was this a mistake, or was he really a communist agent? As the author says, "The Soviet Union's rapid development of the atomic bomb immediately following World War II . . . had an incalculable effect upon the military and diplomatic history of the postwar ea, and would merit considerable study for that reason alone. What interests us most here, however, is how the case illustrates two of the more important facts about American society in the twentieth century . . . the liberal-Left intellectual culture in its long infatuation with . . . the Soviet Union . . . and the pathology of the mainstream of 'educated' Americans, whose overweening desire to be 'politically correct' (even though it wasn't called that yet) settled them into a comfortable and smug 'moderation' toward one of history's bloodiest totalitarian dictatorships and the people who supported it."

- **Lynching: History and Analysis.** No, he is *not* defending lynching. This chapter deals with questions such as, "How does it rank among mankind's enormities? Was it unique to American history? What caused it to disappear? Was lynching primarily—or even significantly—racist?" Again, he's done the research, and the answers about lynching, and vigilantism in general, are surprising. *Mary Pride*

The Story of America's Liberty

Grades 7–12. $19.95 plus $3.95 shipping.
Reel to Real Ministries, PO Box 19266, Cleveland, OH 44119.
Orders: (800) 736-4567.
Inquiries: (216) 531-8600.
Fax: (216) 531-8355.
Email: amport@ix.netcom.com.
Web: www.amport.com.

Reel to Real Ministries, an outgrowth of Maranatha Campus Ministries has produced a video, **The Story of America's Liberty**, that takes you on a tour through the nation's capitol buildings. Your attention is directed to the large number of conspicuously Christian inscriptions, artworks, and so on that surround our devoted legislators and Supreme Court justices while schoolchildren are hermetically sealed off from the same. Learn about the historic events that inspired each of the works of art in our nation's capital and find out why those events so profoundly affected the founding of America. *Mary Pride*

U.S. History Courses

A Beka's upper-grades American history book, **Heritage of Freedom** is another winner. I stayed up until 2 A.M. reading it—couldn't put it down! This morning I came down to find my nine-year-old son attempting to eat breakfast with this book on his lap! Written in a narrative style, it has all the good features that researchers have discovered help students to remember what they have read: crisp writing, interesting anecdotal "nuggets," and lots of interest-building photos, illustrations, maps, and charts. Positive, patriotic approach without hype or overdone flag-waving. The plight of the Indians, for example, is treated fairly. The final 17-page *Study Guide for Reading the Constitution* presents the entire text of the U.S. Constitution side by side with good, brief explanations of what each section means. There's a wealth of fascinating information here in these pages! *Mary Pride*

A Beka Heritage of Freedom (2nd edition)

Grade 11. Student book, $22.20. Student test booklet, $6.20. Teacher's key/test booklet, $8.85. Student quiz booklet, $4.60. Teacher key/quiz booklet, $8.85. Teacher's guide, $20.20. Shipping extra.
A Beka Book, Box 19100, Pensacola, FL 32523-9100. (800) 874-2352.
Fax: (800) 874-3590.
Web: www.abeka.com.

Alpha Omega American History LIFEPACs

Grades 8 and 11. Complete boxed set, $41.95 each grade. Shipping extra.
Alpha Omega Publications, 300 N. McKemy, Chandler, AZ 85226.
Orders and inquiries: (800) 622-3070.
Fax: (480) 785-8034.
Web: www.home-schooling.com.

Grade 8 of the **Alpha Omega American History** course is an American history course, from the European explorers to the modern day. Units include European backgrounds, colonization, the War of Independence, becoming a united nation, the westward movement, the Civil War, industrialism, the early twentieth century, and World War II and its aftermath. The ninth LIFEPAC ends with a section on "challenges in the United States today" in the areas of technology, society, government, and religion.

Some of this history is visited again in greater depth in **grade 11**. After two units on the birth of our constitutional government, there are units on national expansion (from federalism through Andy Jackson), the emergence of slavery and sectionalism dividing the nation, the Civil War and Reconstruction, industrialism and isolationism, the Depression years, "A Nation at War" (World War II, Korea, and Vietnam), and contemporary America from the Kennedy administration through the Ford administration. The units on earlier American history are absolutely fascinating, giving a wealth of insight into the temper of those times; from Hoover on, you get pretty much the typical public-school view of things. *Mary Pride*

America: The First 350 Years

Grade 7–adult. Complete set of 16 tapes, notebook, and study guide $69.95 plus shipping.
Covenant Publications, 224 Auburn Ave., Monroe, LA 71201.
(318) 323-3061: Fax: (318) 387-5135.

If you think you've been getting the straight scoop on American history from textbooks—even Christian textbooks—think again! Steven Wilkins, another man with an obvious love of history, has uncovered some fascinating (and forgotten) facts about God's providential guidance of early American history, the Christian roots of the Declaration of Independence and the Constitution, and the *real* issues behind the Civil War— issues we continue to struggle with today.

The lecture format of **America: The First 350 Years** will appeal more to parents and older children. Mr. Wilkins is a master storyteller, so with the exception of the tapes on the Constitution you will find yourself listening with interest to the stories of the men who shaped our history. Did *your* history books, for example, ever tell you that Squanto's first words to the Pilgrims were "Welcome, English! Give me some beer!"? Or that Roger Williams was really an insufferable pest who couldn't work together with *anyone?* Or that Lincoln is on record as saying he didn't care whether the slaves were freed or not, he just wanted to save the Union?

Unlike other history treatments, this audiocassette series neither puts historical figures on a pedestal nor drags them in the gutter. It is by far the best attempt I have seen to approach history with both realism and a Christian sense of reverence for the God behind it. The optional outline is very handy, and the study guide is a dream—just enough questions to get the hearers really thinking.

America: The First 350 Years is divided into four segments, one each on the Founding Era, the War of Independence, the Constitution, and the War Between the States (otherwise known as the Civil War), with eight lectures per segment, each lecture more or less filling one side of a cassette tape. Topics are:

- Motives to Discovery I and II—why did the explorers explore? The truth about Cortez and the Aztecs.
- Puritan Foundations I—who were the pilgrims of Plymouth and the Puritans of Massachusetts, what were the differences between them, and why should this matter? Meet Squanto and his beer mug.
- Puritan Foundations II—what six Reformation teachings formed the Puritan worldview?
- Notable Leaders I and II—fascinating background information on colonial leaders.
- The Banishment of Roger Williams—in which we discover that ol' Roger wasn't the 100 percent all-American hero everyone thinks he was.
- The Salem Witch Trials—what really happened?
- The Causes of the War of Independence I, II, III, and IV—economic, constitutional, spiritual, and practical issues.
- The Declaration of Independence I—five things everyone "knows" about the Declaration of Independence which aren't true.
- The Declaration of Independence II—what the Founding Fathers really meant.
- The Pulpit and the War I and II—the part played by preachers, especially Presbyterians and dissenters.
- The Constitutional Convention I and II—the delegates, the historical background, and what it was all about.
- The Text of the Constitution I, II, III, and IV—lectures on what it all originally meant, spiced with explanations of why many modern political institutions really aren't Constitutional.
- The Bill of Rights I and II—In the author's own words, "Why Thomas Jefferson would oppose the ACLU and why Ben Franklin would not like Dan Rather." More surprises.
- The Jeffersonian and Jacksonian Era I and II—when the government had a surplus and the nation looked a lot different.
- Rationalism and Theological Decline—the demise of Calvinism and the rise of theological humanism.

- Humanistic Reform Movements—the ferment of the 1800s that led to all sorts of strange things.
- The Public School Movement—not quite as American as apple pie.
- The Coming of the [Civil] War I—slavery and abolitionism.
- The Coming of the War II—sectional tensions.
- The War and Its Aftermath—what Reconstruction was really like, and how (in the author's view) we're still being reconstructed today.

Loaded with source quotes so you can check things out for yourself, this is one history resource that your family will remember. *Mary Pride*

NEW!
Beautiful Feet Books "History Through Literature" Curriculum for Junior/Senior High

Grades 6–12. Medieval History: Jumbo Pack, Senior High, $169.95; Junior High, $149.95; Study Guide, $12.95. Ancient History, grades 7–12,: Jumbo Pack $164.95; Literature Pack, $64.95; Study Guide, $12.95. Modern History Through Literature (Civil War to Vietnam), Senior High Part I, $124, Part II, $169, Study Guide $13.95. Timelines available: Early American History, Medieval History, California History. Prices for each timeline: single student, $8.95; two student, $13.95; classroom version for 15 students, $49.95. World of Columbus and Sons, George Washington's World, Augustus Caesar's World, $15.95 each. Books also available individually. Shipping extra.
Beautiful Feet Books, 139 Main St., Sandwich Village, MA 02563. Orders: (800) 889-1978. Inquiries: (508) 833-8626. M–F 11–5 EST. Fax: (508) 833-2770. Web: www.bfbooks.com.

Beautiful Feet Books is a Christian publisher offering a "literature approach to history" (and now, to science and geography as well).

Beautiful Feet study guides provide daily lesson plans, with assignments for the student to read on his own (junior and senior high levels). Students construct and color their own timelines, and create their own journals or notebooks, too. A typical notebook will include Bible verses and biblical principles, book reports, vocabulary word definitions, maps, poetry, comments on the character qualities of the people being studied . . . and the student's own illustrations. The goal is to produce a notebook that is a work of art the student will be proud to show to others.

As you can see, more than just history is being studied here. The student is learning and practicing English composition, literary analysis, map studies, character qualities, art, and Bible. As you can also see, this curriculum incorporates elements of both classical education (with its emphasis on history and fine literature) and the Principle Approach (including its basic principles and its emphasis on recording what is learned in a notebook).

Beautiful Feet study guides are now available for most of Western historical studies: Ancient History, Medieval History, Early American History, and Modern U.S. and World History. Other courses are available, too.

Here are the time frames covered:

- **Ancient History** Ancient Egypt, Greece, and Rome
- **Medieval History** Magna Carta in 1215 through Elizabethan England of the 1600s
- **Early American History/Primary** Vikings to the Civil War—see review in Volume 2
- **Early American History/Intermediate** Vikings to the Civil War—see review in Volume 2
- **Modern U.S. and World History** Civil War through Vietnam

- **History of Science** covers from ancient Greece to current times. See review in Volume 2.
- **History of the Horse** will especially appeal to preteen girls. Covering the period from 1700s through early 1900s, you'll read lots of famous "horse" books (e.g., Black Stallion, Justin Morgan Had a Horse), learn how to identify horse breeds, practice drawing pictures of horses, chart blood lines, and learn Bible memory verses about horses in this one-year course.
- **Geography Through Literature** covers most of the regions of the U.S. See review in Volume 2.

I have read almost every book used in these courses, and can recommend Beautiful Feet Book's choice of literature as both well-suited for the indicated grade levels and plain all-around good reading. Their courses are well-designed, easy to use, and should appeal to students who are not allergic to writing. Not every book is "uplifting," as the catalog copy seems to suggest; you'll find a hefty dollop of books about suffering and injustices of many kinds. Thankfully, these are mostly for the older grades.

Beautiful Feet Books is also in the process of republishing the classic Genevieve Foster "World" books. Each oversized volume has chapters about people and events that were going on worldwide at the same time. *George Washington's World,* for example, lets you know about major personalities of George Washington's day, in the U.S., Europe, and elsewhere. It's a fascinating way to make the pieces of the history puzzle fit together. Each book is well written, with each chapter reading like a story, and packed with timelines, charts, maps, and illustrations. The religious outlook is eclectic: Asante myths and Native American shamans are treated with the same respect as Catholic missionaries and humanist thinkers. Currently available: *George Washington's World, Augustus Caesar's World,* and *World of Columbus and Sons.*

The study guides as a whole are markedly Christian, teaching biblical principles and Bible verses galore. Be aware, though, that although these courses are explicitly designed for Bible-believing Christians, not all the books you will be reading come from this viewpoint. In the upper grades, the guides usually alert you to cases where the Christian worldview and the book's worldview conflict.

Thousands of families have bought and enjoyed these books and courses. They are attractive, relatively easy to use (kids still have to take notes and write reports), and the mostly secular books used in the courses are well-written and fun to read. Your students will definitely learn—and remember—more history this way than they would with textbooks alone. I only wish they'd taught history this way when I went to school! *Mary Pride*

BJUP runs through American history twice at this age level: once in junior high and again in high school. The junior-high text, **The American Republic**, is well written but not particularly exciting. It does have some special helpful features. Early in the book students are given a double-page spread on study techniques, and later on there's another one on map reading. The chapter reviews are good, too. Another special feature: the book contains the entire text of the U.S. Constitution and a brief summary of each section made without any particular comments on the virtues or demerits of the section. The last part of the book regrettably takes a "problem" theme just like secular texts, focusing on the issues the media has labeled as contemporary problems. Patriotic, urbane tone (if you've never seen the two mixed, you'll see them in this book).

United States History, for 11th-graders, is prettier and more interesting. Again, it covers the whole sweep of American history, from the Reformation's influence on politics and the settling of America up until the

Beautiful Feet Books lets you buy just what you want. You can purchase individual study guides and try your luck with finding all the books in the library. You can buy just the books you don't already own. Or you can buy complete "packs" for each course.

Jumbo Packs include all the reading books, supplementary material (including timelines, if available), a student composition notebook, and the appropriate study guide. Semester Packs divide the course into two semesters. If you order both semesters, you get exactly the same materials as if you had ordered a Jumbo Pack. The Literature Packs are a little more tricky. For Medieval History and Ancient History, the Literature Pack includes books not found in the Jumbo Pack.

BJUP American History for Christian Schools

Grades 8 and 11. The American Republic: Student text, $30; teacher's edition, $42.50; TestBank, $17.50. United States History: Student text, $30; teacher's manual, $42.50; map packet (25 maps), $6.50; TestBank, $17.50. Shipping extra. *Bob Jones University Press Customer Services, Greenville, SC 29614. Orders: (800) 845-5731. Fax: (800) 525-8398. Web: www.bjup.com.*

late '80s. If you could actually master all the information in this book (here the excellent teacher's guide really helps), you would be culturally literate, at least when it comes to American history! The map exercises (in the map packet) are also excellent—if you do *those*, you'll be geographically literate! The book ends with the same "problems" focus as the eighth-grade book, rather than a call to any specific actions. The second edition has a more upbeat (but only slightly more challenging) ending. In this area, as in its coverage of the history itself, the teacher's guide is far more interesting and challenging than the actual textbook. *Mary Pride*

For the main course, here's help from the ever-clearsighted **Clarence Carson**. Mr. Carson's insightful, if somewhat dour, reading of American history comes from a solidly Christian background, so he is not over-pleased with recent events since, say, the presidency of Cal Coolidge. From the *Freeman* review of this series:

> *For Carson, history is not merely a collection of facts and dates, an account of explorations, settlements, westward expansion, wars, presidents, and elections. History is the product of the actions of countless individuals, each under the influence of certain ideas. And Carson explores those ideas, ideologies, and 'isms.' He shows how they were responsible for the settlement of this continent, the struggle for freedom, the westward expansion, the construction of schools, churches, factories, and the founding of new religious denominations. He explains why our ancestors fought for their beliefs and strove to create a government, limited in scope, with checks and balances, that would not have the power to oppress the people.*

Whereas the first volumes in **A Basic History of the United States** show the flourishing results of Christians in control of the culture, the latter reveal what happens when good men do nothing.

Here's what you get:

- Volume 1: The Colonial Experience, 1607–1774
- Volume 2: The Beginning of the Republic, 1775–1825
- Volume 3: The Sections and the Civil War, 1826–1877
- Volume 4: The Growth of America, 1878–1928
- Volume 5: The Welfare State, 1929–1985
- Volume 6: 1985–1995.

You will never feel the same about FDR or the Civil War after reading these books! I can't agree with all of Mr. Carson's conclusions, but he certainly has the facts. *Mary Pride*

American history for idiots. What a concept. Isn't that what we already get in public-school textbooks? Ah, but textbooks aren't "fun, fascinating, and memorable," as **The Complete Idiot's Guide to American History** claims to be. Loaded with memory aids, such as "The Least You Need to Know" chapter summaries of only a few sentences each, and written in a readable style, this 360-page book gives you what you'll get in school texts, only in a way you might actually remember.

The memory helps are many, including a "Complete Idiot's Reference Card" to "Thirty American Events Worth Knowing," and chapter features such as

- Main Event—a box with information about what the author considers "the most significant or representative single event of an era, ranging from historical milestones to pop culture landmarks"

Clarence Carson's A Basic History of the United States

Grade 11–college. Original 5-volume set, $39.50. Sixth volume, $10. Complete set (volumes 1–6), $46.50. Accompanying teacher's guide, $8. Shipping extra.
American Textbook Committee, 1720 Mayfair Ln., Alexander City, AL 35010. (256)329-2161.

NEW!
The Complete Idiot's Guide to American History

Grade 7–adult. $16.95.
Alpha Books, a division of Macmillan General Reference, a Simon & Schuster Macmillan Company, 1633 Broadway, New York, NY 10019. Information: (800) 428-5331. Available in bookstores. Web: www.mcp.com/mgr/idiot.

- Word for the Day— "buzzwords that defined a time and place"
- Stats— "key numbers relating to an era or event," really fun stuff such as "population statistics, war casualties, costs, and so on"
- Real Life— "biographical sketches of an era's most significant and representative figures"
- Voices from the Past—from a letter by Christopher Columbus to the utterings of Rodney King, here are "memorable statements from historically significant features and documents"

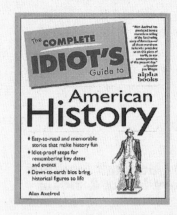

While appearing on the surface to be openminded and fair, you'll not find one positive word about the Christian right, while negative words such as *narrow, coercive, intolerant* and even *threat* appear. This should give you a clue as to the bias of the author, who describes the Puritans as "smart folks you wouldn't want to spend a cocktail evening with" and who seems woefully uninformed about what really went on at Ruby Ridge, Waco, Oklahoma City, and other places where the "mainstream" version of events parroted in this book is in fact not believed by a majority of Americans. It's better on the less recent history, though again you'll notice the author's point of view shining through. It's best on the least-known history, such as various confrontations between Indians and American authorities, which are usually not covered in as much lively detail in school texts. In all, a quick way to brush up on what the public schools are teaching. *Mary Pride*

History texts like to present a single view of history as if it were the infallible truth. Those of us who believe in serious historical studies can get around this by reading real books written about each historical topic and time period. By comparing historian to historian, and reading source documents for ourselves, it's possible to get a more balanced picture of what actually occurred and what it all means.

Following the same method, *Colonies to Constitution,* in the **Critical Thinking in United States History** series, puts serious historical analysis within reach of upper elementary and high-school kids.

The book's 29 historical lessons *all* present differing interpretations of historical events and even disagreements about basic facts. To avoid prejudice, historians are referred to as "Historian A," Historian B," and so on. Kids are encouraged to analyze the historians' writings logically, according to the rules in the "Guide to Critical Thinking" in the front of the student book. By so doing, they encounter "the gathering and analysis of historical data as selective, fragmentary, and open to question and change."

Yet—and here is the genius of the course's author— they are *not* led to perceive history as unknowable or relativistic. Historical analysis is presented as a search for truth, some of which we can discern and some of which we have to leave as open questions until we have more information.

As you may have guessed, *Colonies to Constitution* is as heavy on teaching logic as it is on history. That portion of our history is blessed with many historical controversies, such as what happened to the lost colony at Roanoke, whether Pocahontas really rescued Captain John Smith, who actually fired "the shot heard round the world," the real reasons behind the Salem witch hysteria and the American Revolution, and whether we made a mistake in exchanging the Articles of Confederation for the Constitution.

Colonies to Constitution not only presents the differing historical views, but also leads kids through analyzing each to discover which is most trustworthy. Along the way they learn rules of evidence, true and false cause and effect, rules of comparison, rules of generalization, types of proof, and how to eliminate alternatives.

Critical Thinking in United States History series

Grades 6–12. Each book, $23.95. Teacher's guides, $16.95 each. 4-book set with teacher's manuals, $139.95. Shipping extra.
Critical Thinking Books & Software, PO Box 448, Pacific Grove, CA 93950-0448. (800) 458-4849.
Fax: (831) 323-3277.
Email: ct@criticalthinking.com.
Web: www.criticalthinking.com.

You absolutely need the teacher's guide, as it includes both lesson plans and answer keys.

The Critical Thinking in United States History series contains another three units, each with student workbook and teacher's guide. Like *Colonies to Constitution,* each analyzes differing viewpoints of specific historical events. The series includes *New Republic to Civil War, Reconstruction to Progressivism,* and *Spanish-American War to Vietnam. Mary Pride*

Peter Marshall American History books & videos

Grades 7–12. From Sea to Shining Sea, The Light and the Glory, $13 each (paperbound) or $20 each (hardbound). Study guide for The Light and the Glory, $8. America: Roots of Our Nation video set, out of print. Restoring America, $70/video set or $35/audiocassette set. In God They Trusted, $20/video or $8/coffee-table book with color pictures and text.
Peter Marshall Ministries, 81 Finlay Rd., Orleans, MA 02653.
(800) 879-3298. (508) 255-7705.
Fax: (508) 255-2062.
Email: pmm@c4.net.
Web: www.restoringamerica.com.

Here are two popular long books on American history by **Peter Marshall**, son of author Catherine Marshall and the late Senate chaplain Peter Marshall, and David Manuel.

The Light and the Glory starts with Christopher Columbus and ends with George Washington's last day in office. *From Sea to Shining Sea* picks up the tale and carries it up to the roots of the Civil War.

"Does God have a plan for America?" reads the subtitle in the first book, while the second one continues, "God's plan for America unfolds." American history is read in the light of right or wrong, with the contributions of both Protestants and Catholics noted.

Did you know Christopher Columbus, whose name means "Christ-bearer," thought of himself as a missionary to the Indians? Old Chris was not averse to making big bucks from his discoveries, either, a fact which the book also notes.

Source quotations are skillfully interwoven with some fine storytelling. Take the slavery question, for instance. We hear from the radical abolitionists, the moderates, the plantation owners, the house slaves, and the field slaves. We learn about the hypocrisy of both South and North, and why the voices of reason were drowned by those shouting for blood. We hear Thomas Jefferson's view of New Englanders and his equally unflattering view of Southerners. We learn about the conflict between Puritans, from whom the New Englanders descended, and Cavaliers, the King's men in the English civil wars, who left their mark on the South. This is a lot deeper treatment of the subject than you'll get in any textbook and much more interesting to read besides. Added benefit: no homework questions at the end of the chapters!

The study guide for *The Light and the Glory* does an excellent job of leading students to see the providential workings of God in early American history, as well as what was good or bad about the colonies and explorations.

From the same source are available a lecture series of two videos on the Christian principles behind the Declaration of Independence and the Constitution (*America: Roots of Our Nation*) and *In God They Trusted,* a video dramatization of five important moments in American history. Both will make more sense if you work through these books first. *Mary Pride*

NEW!
Superstar Teachers Early American History

Grade 9–adult. $149.95 plus $10 shipping.
The Teaching Company, 7405 Alban Station Court, Suite A107, Springfield, VA 22150. Orders: (800) 832-2412.
Inquiries: (800) 858-3224.
Fax: (703) 912-7756.

American history the homeschool way! Just as he does in his World History course (reviewed in that chapter), Professor Lin Thompson, a high-school teacher who also has experience as a professional actor, dresses up in period costumes and takes on the persona of historical characters. In **Early American History: Native Americans Through the Forty-Niners,** Professor Thompson portrays both historic figures (Christopher Columbus, John Smith, Patrick Henry, and many more) and "generic" characters such as Goodman Thom, Reverend Thompson, Frenchy Thompson, and XYZ Thompson. The generic characters, easily recognizable by their names, present the common man's point of view, so we can understand not only what those who came before us *did,* but *why* they did it and *what* they thought about it.

The 30 video lectures cover Viking exploration, Columbus, the Virginia colony (what a bunch of misfits!), Pilgrims and Puritans (they are *not* the same), other European colonies, what happened to dissenters in Massachusetts Bay, life in colonial America, the unsavory side of colonial naval exploits (a lecture entitled "Swashbucklers, Smugglers, and Slavers"), the Great Awakening and Enlightenment, wars with France, what brought about the colonists' stand for independence, famous men of the Founding Fathers, the Declaration of Independence, the Revolutionary War on land and sea, the national government and how the war was ended, westward expansion in the new republic, the Constitution, George Washington and the new republic, differences between the French and American revolutions, the beginning of the two-party system (against which George Washington so solemnly warned us), the era of Jefferson, events (including Indian troubles) leading up to the war of 1812, the Industrial Revolution, cities and the transportation revolution, the era of Jackson, how Texas gained independence from Mexico and became a state, westward expansion, colonizing the West with special emphasis on the Mormons (Professor Thompson is a Mormon), Mexican territories and how the borders were settled, and the final push westward to California at the time of the '49-ers. Each lesson is only 30 minutes long, and will leave you gasping for more.

A "workbook," which is actually an outline of each lesson, is included. I find it handy to take notes right in the workbook.

My children Sarah and Joseph used these videos to help them review for the Advanced Placement test. But you don't need to be prepping for AP's to enjoy them. Even sixth-graders will find Thompson's performances entertaining, and his memory for historical details phenomenal. Adult will find there's a lot more to American history than they ever learned in school— even adults who have read hundreds of books on the subject, as I have. Recommended. *Mary Pride*

Source Documents & Stories

George Washington. Robert E. Lee. Clara Barton. Pretty familiar names, right? What about Jacob Riss, Peter Zenger, or Harry Bergh? These little-known names belonged to men who shaped American history in some profound ways. Riss wrote about and photographed the poor in the late 1800's in hopes of stirring public sentiment to help improve the condition of their lives. Peter Zenger's nine months in jail for printing a newspaper critical of the governor of New York introduced the idea of freedom of the press to the American mind. Harry Bergh's crusade against cruelty to animals was the seed for the ASPCA.

This 95-page softcover book presents the stories of 15 **American Heroes 1735–1900** (including the six mentioned above) who made a difference in some way. Each chapter begins with a timeline and a one paragraph "teaser" about the character. An engaging three-page biography follows. Following the story are vocabulary, discussion and group research activities. These are of the critical thinking/open-ended evaluation sort: "Jacob Riss wanted the government to help the poor people in the city. Take one side or the other (of the following statements), and then give all the reasons you can for the side you take. 'The government should do all it can to help poor people.' 'The government should do little to help the poor. (or) Poor people will do better without the help of government.'"

Each biography was very well-written, and there are many creative lesson-extending ideas. *American Heroes* would make a useful supplement for those of you studying history via biography with two caveats: One, there is

NEW!
American Heroes 1735–1900
Grades 4–9. $9.95 plus shipping.
Brooke-Richards Press, 9420 Reseda Blvd., Suite 511, Northridge, CA 91324. (818) 893-8126.

The American Reference Library 1 CD-ROM

Grade 7–college. $99.95 postpaid.
Western Standard Publishing Company, PO Box 780, Orem, UT 84059-0780. (888) 617-4448.
Fax: (801) 426-3691. Web: www.freedomlibrary.com

The creators of the **American Reference Library 1** have compiled a virtual encyclopedia of American history and government into one CD-ROM. You get over 160,000 pages of material, from original source documents to essays and books on American political culture. In all, the disc includes the complete text of 260 books and over 800 research papers, all on the subjects of classic and contemporary history and politics.

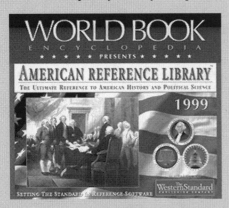

All this makes the American Reference Library 1 a gold mine of resources on U.S. History. With this tool on your shelf, you will be able to confidently teach and study our history, from printing out source documents to read to your preschooler, to getting a teen ready to take the Advanced Placement U.S. History exam. In fact, two of our teens have used it for just that purpose!

It's very easy to use. Organized in a searchable database format, you can easily search and find information throughout the disc. Just type the keyword or phrase you want, and up pops a list of selections that include the word or phrase. It's the easiest way possible to find out what hundreds of great Americans (and foreign visitors) have had to say on a topic. Eye-opening! Or, if you prefer, use this as a super-inexpensive library, and read through one book or article a time at your leisure.

The database is divided into ten major collections:

- **Documents and Histories of American Freedom** 700 first-hand documents and classic accounts, including such original source documents as the *Journal of First Voyage* by Christoforo Colombo, *Democracy in America* by Alexis de Tocqueville, *Narrative of the Life of Frederick Douglas*, *History of the United States* by George Bancroft, *History of the American Nation* by William Jackman, and the *History of the American People* by Woodrow Wilson. All this, plus a guide to the study of U.S. history, and a bibliography of the documents and histories included, so you'll be able to zero in on what to read first.

- **Classics of Western Civilization** Of course you get the *Holy Bible* (KJV), and the complete works of Shakespeare, including his plays and sonnets. Just about every CD-ROM collection includes these. But in addition you get the political writings of St. Augustine, Tennyson's *Charge of the Light Brigade*, *A Vindication of Natural Society* and other books by Edmund Burke, *The Wealth of Nations* by Adam Smith, *Common Sense* by Thomas Paine, *Leviathan* by Thomas Hobbes, *Orthodoxy* by G.K. Chesterton, Bacon and Locke's writings on government, and *The Roots of American Order* by Russell Kirk, plus more by Tolstoy, Bierce, and others.

- **The Constitution Reference Collection** A collection of original founding documents, including the *Mayflower Compact*, *Declaration of Independence*, *Articles of Confederation*, and the *Constitution of the United States of America*. Other collections have

some or all of these, but do they have the debates in the several state conventions on whether or not to adopt the Constitution? Or Supreme Court Chief Justice Story's book explaining the Constitution, in which he states that America is a "Christian Nation"? You will also find other scholarly writings on constitutional questions, including *Church, State and the Constitution* by Edward McLean and *Who Killed the Constitution* by William Eaton. David Barton fans will go wild over this collection!

- **The Founding Fathers** Original manuscripts by Thomas Jefferson, James Madison, and Benjamin Franklin, and biographies of Jefferson, Franklin, and Washington.

- **The Presidential Papers** Not just every inaugural address from Washington to Clinton, but the letters, speeches, and proclamations of note from the chief executives—97,000 pages total.

- **U.S. Congress** A plethora of information for the civics student, including how laws are made, the committee system, listing of all the committees, house rules, members of congress (including email addresses), and even a glossary of congressional terms. No high-school civics course comes close to including this much *accurate* information!

- **The Supreme Court** Amazingly, you get a complete listing of all the key Supreme Court cases and decisions, including an analysis of each case and its interpretation of the constitution.

- **National Party Platforms** Need a laugh—or maybe feel like crying? Check out the campaign platforms of all major parties for every presidential election year from 1840–1996.

The new edition is published in cooperation with World Book. This photo shows the disc from the previous edition

- **Today's Issues, Traditional Values** This is a trove of reference material, with books, newsletters, and articles that provide insightful analysis, from a decidedly conservative perspective, on the political issues that our country continues to confront. You will find *The American Enterprise Institute Newsletter*, *Commentary Magazine*, *Campus*, selections from the *City Journal*, *Congressional Viewpoints*, *Family Voice*, *The Freeman*, *Imprimis*, *Modern Age*, *National Center for Constitutional Studies*, *Human Events: The National Conservative Weekly*, *The Women's Quarterly*, *The Phyllis Schlafly Report*, *The Wirthlin Quorum*, *The WallBuilder Report*, selections from the *National Review*, and many other publications. Writings from prominent Republicans, including Abraham Lincoln, Barry Goldwater, Ronald Reagan, and Patrick Buchanan, are included. Many other articles and books are organized by topic, covering a wide variety of issues: affirmative action, culture wars, the economy, education, the environment, the family, federalism, feminism, big government, health care, immigration, law and order, gay rights, property rights, right to life, science and technology, taxes, term limits, welfare, and more!

- **How to Win an Election** Writings on political campaigns and election issues.

As if that wasn't enough, also included is contact information for over 300 public policy organizations (so you can put your new-found knowledge of government into action) and a collection of over 12,000 topical quotes from figures throughout history.

This CD-ROM collection is almost overwhelming. As a reference program that gives you access to original material, it is excellent. The interface is simple, the data is easy to find, and it's well researched. If you're looking for a U.S. history and civics tool you can use throughout your child's entire education, this is the program for you. *Frank Beeman and Mary Pride*

SYSTEM REQUIREMENTS

PC: 486/33, Win3.1, 8MB RAM, 6MB Hard Drive, VGA, CD-2, SC, Mouse

Mac: 68020 or higher, System 7, 8MB RAM, 6MB Hard Drive

The Robinson Curriculum, reviewed in Volume 1 of *The Big Book of Home Learning*, also includes hundreds of source documents. There is some overlap with the American Reference Library 1 in the area of major political documents. However, the Robinson Curriculum's collection also includes dozens of works of fiction written over 100 years ago. These are excellent for picking up the country's historical mindset, as well as just plain fun to read.

no spiritual content (Robert E. Lee is presented only as a brave statesman, which he was, but no mention is made of his deep faith, which was the wellspring of his courage), and two, some of you may be uncomfortable with the lack of "right answers" to the open-ended discussion questions. That said, this book profiles some compelling and little-known characters that you'll be glad you met. *Michelle Van Loon*

There are the books that you just can't put down and then there are the others. All three of these fall in the first category. Each includes 101 short stories that put flesh on historical figures and give life to dates and places. Written by C. Brian Kelly (former editor of *Military History* and *World War II* magazines), with stories by his wife, Ingrid Smyer, these are chock full of historical postscripts.

Best Little Stories from the Civil War is divided into three sections—beginnings, middles, and ends—with stories reminiscent of those your great-grandpa would tell about his friends or a brief memory he had while marching. All the stories are true and are often about little-known incidents. It might be about a young boy who lost his father at the age of 11 and grew up to become General Robert E. Lee. It might be about foreign military dignitaries who had come over to "see the war," but got more than they bargained for. There is also a longer story about a fascinating woman—Varina Davis—wife of Confederate President Jefferson Davis, included in the back.

Best Little Stories from World War II is similar in tone. The stories tell about spies, the Japanese, a torpedo that narrowly misses the ship carrying the President, and ordinary men that fought on the ground and in the air. Each one is complete in itself, but you won't be able to stop at one!

Best Little Stories from the White House (with First Ladies in Review) transforms our presidents into ordinary men who lived in an extraordinary house. You will read about a White House honeymoon, Lincoln escaping a trap, JFK missing his lunch to talk to a boy, and a president who did some shopping without paying the bill—among other stories. There is a section in the back with short, interesting biographies on all the First Ladies. Yes, even Hillary Clinton.

Since two of the books deal with war, there is a fair amount relating to its violence and horror and the conversations of those involved are sometimes peppered with profanity. There are also a few instances of adult situations. Despite these caveats, my family enjoyed these books immensely. *Marla Perry*

I can't think of a better way to spend 63 minutes than watching **Bobby Horton** sing and play the guitar, fiddle, and banjo and tell stories.

On his **Music & Memories of the Civil War video** you will hear over 18 songs—some that were popular in the North, some in the South, and many in both—that give you insight into the people who fought in the war and those who remained behind and kept the home fires burning. You learn that many of the tunes were sung on both sides, but with different lyrics and that "Dixie" was written by a Northerner. You learn about the town in North Carolina where all men aged 17–45 died in one day. And you learn about the song sung by both North and South, written after the battle of Shiloh Hill.

Bobby Horton is a seasoned professional who contributed to the soundtrack of Ken Burns' series, *The Civil War.* His knowledge of the time period is amazing and will keep you glued to your seat. Throughout the video you see him in different outfits—sometimes the genteel Southern gentleman, sometimes a soldier, and sometimes a common man. The settings add to the appeal as you're taken from the porch of a small, wooden house where he

NEW!
Best Little Stories Series

Grade 8–adult. Best Little Stories From The Civil War, $14.95. Best Little Stories From World War II, $14.95. Best Little Stories From The White House, not available until spring of 2000. Shipping extra. *Cumberland House Publishing, 431 Harding Industrial Dr., Nashville, TN 37211. (888) 439-2665. Fax: (800) 254-6716. Email: Cumbhouse@aol.com.*

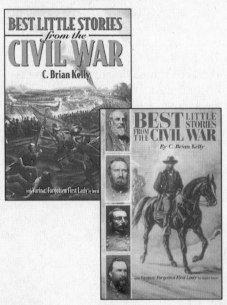

NEW!
Bobby Horton's Music & Memories of the Civil War Video

Ages 5–adult. Video, $25 postpaid. Cassettes, $10 each postpaid. CDs, $15 each postpaid. *Bobby Horton, 3430 Sagebrook Lane, Birmingham, AL 35243. (205) 967-6426. Fax: same number, dial *51.*

plays with his friend, Bill Foster, to a steamboat on the Mississippi. He never loses your attention as you listen to the songs and the stories behind them. These tunes are boastful, optimistic, patriotic, and mournful and they remind you that individual people and lives are forever changed by war.

If you like this video, you're also sure to like **Bobby Horton's Civil War songs on cassette and CD.** Each cassette and CD includes about 18 priceless Civil War songs, plus a paragraph of background info about each song. Complete handwritten lyrics for each song are available separately. The series currently includes

- *Homespun Songs of the Union Army* —Volumes 1 & 2
- *Homespun Songs of the CSA (Confederate States of America)*— Volumes 1, 2, 3, 4, & 5
- *Songs of the Union Army*—Volumes 1, 2, & 3
- *Songs of the CSA*—Volumes 1, 2, 3, 4, & 5
- A video, *Music & Memories of the Civil War,* reviewed in Volume 2
- *Homespun Songs of Faith 1861–1865* is historic Christian hymns performed in the same style as the Civil War recordings
- *Homespun Songs of the Christmas Season* is more Christian hymns in the same style, this time with a Christmas theme
- *Homemade Songs of Vicksburg,* Bobby's latest, is an original instrumental soundtrack of the Vicksburg National Military Park Video Tour

I cannot tell a lie. This is history at its best! *Marla Perry*

Catherine Millard has a reputation for researching the truths about America's history and for presenting these truths in a clear, understandable manner. True to her reputation, here she is again with **Great American Statesmen and Heroes,** a book that brings together 39 of the people who made America what it is.

The book is paperback, 300 pages long, and richly filled with details and information other books often overlook. It deals with well-known figures, such as Thomas Jefferson and John Jay, and virtually unknown people like John Wanamaker and Marcus and Narcissa Whitman. Millard presents these men and women in a fascinating manner, giving excerpts from their own writings as well as sharing what others had to say about them. Millard has also included many of America's foundational charters, compacts, speeches, and sermons. An extensive appendix displays her attention to historical accuracy.

This book contains a great deal of information, but is never dry, and serves equally well for both reference and pleasure reading. I find myself reaching for it often. *Tammy Cardwell*

The books in the **American Family Album series** by Dorothy and Thomas Hoobler are so fascinating you can't put them down. I know. I just spent a half-hour trying to tear myself away long enough to write this review!

To keep the songs historically accurate, volumes 1 and 2 of the CSA tapes each include one strong word pertaining to the everlasting destination of the unrighteous. Even so, the vocabulary is considerably milder than what you'd hear on any prime-time TV show these days.

NEW!
Great American Statesmen and Heroes

Grade 9–adult. $10.95 plus shipping.
Farm Country General Store, 412 North Fork Rd., Metamora, IL 61548. Orders: (800) 551-FARM. Inquiries: (309) 367-2844. Fax: (309) 367-2844. Web: www.homeschoolfcgs.com.

NEW!
Oxford's American Family Album series

Grade 7-adult. Each book (paperback edition), $12.95. All 10 volumes, $199.95 (hardcover) or $99.195 (paperback). Shipping extra.
Oxford University Press, 2001 Evans Rd., Cary, NC 27513. (800) 451-7556. Fax: (919) 677-1303. Web: www.oup-usa.org.

Thus far, books in this series, and the famous people introducing them, are:

- *The African American Family Album*—Phylicia Rashad
- *The Chinese American Family Album*—Bette Bao Lord
- *The Cuban American Family Album*—Oscar Hijuelos
- *The German American Family Album*—Werner Klemperer
- *The Irish American Family Album*—Joseph P. Kennedy II
- *The Italian American Family Album*—Governor Mario M. Cuomo
- *The Japanese American Family Album*—George Takei
- *The Jewish American Family Album*—Mandy Patinkin
- *The Mexican American Family Album*—Henry G. Cisneros
- *The Scandinavian American Family Album*—Hubert H. Humphrey III

In each book you'll find six sections designed to give you a bird's-eye view of American history from the point of view of a particular group. Though the titles may vary from book to book, here are the sections:

- The Old Country—a brief history and a description of what things were like where these people came from
- Going to America—why these people came, what it was like to leave, and how they came
- Ports of Entry—Where they landed and what they thought of their new home
- A New Life—where they ended up in America, what kind of work they did, and how they contributed to the workforce.
- Putting Down Roots—what kind of communities these people formed and what kind of group culture they retained in their families, religion and schools
- Part of America—where these people are today and how much of their heritage they have preserved, spotlighting a particular family from the group

The authors introduce each section. From then on, the text consists mostly of words from the people themselves. The authors briefly introduce each speaker and describe his circumstances at the time his words were written down.

Each two-page spread features two or three pictures with descriptive captions. Sidebars feature individual members, families, subgroups, etc., from the ethnic group. For example, the Japanese book features Manjiro Nakahama, the first Japanese American, and the Mexican book features the vaquero (Mexican cowboy) and the Ronstadt family, etc. Also featured in the wide margins are frequent "How others saw them" quotes from Americans outside the ethnic group, giving their opinions of the ethnic group.

This is a view of American history not often found in textbooks. Although each group's history of persecution, if any, is included, these are not angry politically-correct books, but rather "man in the street" true stories. Great reading, even if you're not a member of the group in question. *Bill Pride*

NEW!
The Spirit of Seventy-Six
Grade 7–college. $29.95.
Da Capo Press, a subsidiary of Plenum Publishing Corporation, 233 Spring St., New York, NY 10013.
(212) 620-8000. Fax: (212) 647-1898.
Web: www.plenum.com.

I am thrilled to announce that a paperback edition of this, the greatest book ever of source documents pertaining to Revolutionary War times, is now in print. I ordered the original hardback version years ago from a "remaindered books" catalog, and it was frustrating to know such a great book existed without being able to recommend it to anyone.

There's a ton of good reading here—well, at least several pounds. Not just another collection of political documents, the 1300-plus pages of **The Spirit of Seventy-Six: The Story of the American Revolution as Told by Participants** contain the written viewpoint of hundreds of people who lived through those exciting times, from Founding Fathers to foot soldiers, from the privileged wife of a Hessian commander to a Philadelphia housewife, from gentle Moravian missionaries to marauding British officers. This is uncensored history at its best, with no axe-grinding for either the politically correct or the conservative hagiographers of American history. A heart-wrenching account of American regiments in Ohio deliberately massacring entire villages of peaceful Christian Indians is balanced by eyewitness stories of brutal British attacks and betrayals and Indian atrocities. Not that any effort was made to "balance" the good and bad of one side against another. What you get in this book is simply what happened, not what anyone wishes would have happened instead.

Chapter 31: U.S. History **311**

The book is laid out in chronological order. Chapters have titles such as "Bunker's Hill" and "Spies, Treason, and Mutiny." Chapters are subdivided into sections, such as "Dr. Church Goes Over to the Enemy," with individual source documents listed under each section. Individual documents are given titles either describing their contents or taken directly from them, e.g., "An Event Which Gives Me Much Uneasiness," written by James Warren. These document titles are well chosen to arouse interest: browsing the table of contents is enough to inveigle even reluctant readers into tackling a source reading or two. Who can resist, "Stupid Fools, They Might Perceive That We Were Officers" or "My Crime Consists in Not Being a New England Man"?

Inside the chapters themselves, sections are introduced with enough historical background to place the documents in historical context. Finally, the documents themselves are amazingly readable, assuming you have the vocabulary of a normal homeschooled high-schooler (e.g., college level or better). A good read that when it comes to early American history will make you well-read. *Mary Pride*

You want a collection of hard-to-find American source documents? Here are two. **That for Which Our Fathers Fought** includes Magna Carta of 1215 (English translation from the Latin), Mayflower Compact of 1620, Declaration of Rights of the Continental Congress of 1754, Virginia Bill of Rights of 1776, the Declaration of Independence, the Constitution of the United States of America, the Bill of Rights and all further Constitutional amendments, and all four stanzas of the Star-Spangled Banner. **That of Which our Fathers Spoke** includes the rights of the colonists, adopted by the Boston town meeting of 1772, Patrick Henry's "Give me liberty or give me death" speech, George Washington's First Inaugural Address, George Washington's Thanksgiving Proclamation, George Washington's Farewell Address, and 60 selected quotations from Washington, Madison, Jefferson, Monroe, Franklin, Adams, and more, in the period from 1750 to 1830. *Mary Pride*

NEW!
That for Which Our Fathers Fought
That of Which Our Fathers Spoke
Grade 5–college. Each booklet, $4 plus shipping.
Trivium Pursuit, 139 Colorado St., Suite 186. Muscatine, IA 52761. (309) 537-3641.
Email: trivium@muscanet.com.
Web: www.muscanet.com/~trivium.

You can eat meat and potatoes for dinner, or you can add handfuls of herbs and splashes of spice to the pot and dine on gourmet cuisine. Adding judicious amounts of entertaining anecdotes to your history study can transform rote information into a full-course dinner.

Sure, you knew that Theodore Roosevelt was a great outdoorsman and naturalist, but did you know that as a boy, he ". . . developed the 'Roosevelt Museum of Natural History' with wee creatures, dead and alive, stuffed into every nook and cranny"? According to **Fascinating Facts from American History**, growing up with Teddy meant that the household "learned to beware of beasties at all times: they didn't put on a hat before checking for frogs; they didn't sit on a couch without looking under the cushions for field mice; they didn't pour from a pitcher without looking for snakes."

This 270-page softcover text is a fun book, plain and simple. Written with a light touch, it is packed with lots of interesting tidbits. The last few chapters, featuring contemporary history, tend toward a slight liberal bias, but the bulk of the book makes a tasty read. *Michelle Van Loon*

NEW!
Walch's Fascinating Facts from American History
Grades 8–12. $18.95 plus shipping.
J. Weston Walch, Publisher, PO Box 658, Portland, ME 04104. (800) 341-6094. (207) 772-2846. Fax: (207) 772-3105.
Email: customer_service@mail.walch.com. Web: www.walch.com.

NEW!
Learning Games History series

Grades 5–9. $12.95 each. Shipping extra.
Educational Materials Associates, Inc., P.O. Box 7385, Charlottesville, VA 22906. (888)362-4263.
Fax: (804)293-5322.
Email: bobt@emagame.com.
Web: www.emagame.com.

Other games reviewed include:
- The *Revolution Game*—same basic format as the *Civil War Game*, but based on the Revolutionary War
- The *Presidents Game*—featuring historical data on all our presidents. One fun fact I learned from this one is that Andrew Johnson's wife taught him to read and write!

NEW!
A Nation Adrift

Grade 9–adult. $20 plus $3 shipping.
Heritage Videos, PO Box 25662, Shawnee Mission, KS 66225.
(800) 578-4409 or (913) 681-1080.

U.S. History Aids

"Just the facts, ma'am." Sergeant Friday on the old TV show "Dragnet" used to gather information about the crime scene with that famous request. Though many homeschoolers are loathe to saw open their children's heads and shovel information into their skulls, there are times when you may want your children to master "just the facts" in history, science or geography.

That's where **Learning Games** comes in. These slim, boxed games strip a subject of all but the bare-bones facts, and require the people playing to recall those facts . . . period. Each game comes with a board (a thin 11 x 17" piece of folded cardboard—the manufacturers should consider laminating it for a bit of extra durability), an informational poster that will help you master the information needed to play the game, playing pieces, instructions, and a teaching guide that is really the heart of the game.

The *Civil War Game* is typical of the series. The playing board is a map of the southern states, with numbers and symbols on the locations of key battles and events. The cards accompanying the game are two-sided: one side has the name of a historical event or geographical area, the other side has a number with the important information about the event or area named on the other side. Play is simple: you win cards by locating and naming the event or area on the board or by challenging the answer of another player.

Where do you find all this information? In the 40-page study guide you'll find not only incredibly detailed battle information (heavy on commanders' names, numbers of troops, combat movement, and casualties), but a couple of puzzles, a chronology, a statistical summary, and pre- and post-test blank forms you can copy.

Educational Materials Associates publishes a number of other games based on history, geography, and science as well.

These games are not really "games" in the traditional *Monopoly* and *Twister* entertainment sense. If you avail yourself of the material in the study guide, you can treat any one of these games as a piece of curriculum.

I appreciated the way the games stayed focused only on facts, without any sort of editorial comment or revisionist hooey. The games function as a flash-card type review of many mastered facts. If you have a data junkie for a student, he might enjoy using these games to learn or review information. If you have a child who has read a lot on a subject like the Civil War, going through the corresponding game might help to cement the names, dates and places in his mind. Though these games will not fit everyone's needs, they offer a creative way for some of you to learn and review "just the facts." *Michelle Van Loon*

Show and tell—a good video should do both. **A Nation Adrift** shows you images of America, from its beginnings (lots of shots of historical paintings) to today (jarring news footage). It also uses lots of direct quotes, many religious and patriotic, to tell the story of a country cut loose from its moral moorings. This 90-minute video also includes lots of lesser known quotes that chronicle the paradigm shift that has occurred in America (George Washington on immorality among his troops, and horrifying racist remarks by Margaret Sanger, the founder of Planned Parenthood). This is not a video to plunk your child in front of unsupervised. Images of a homosexual protest definitely need to be shared with a parent.

Though very professional, the weakness of this product is in the area of solutions/action. Though there is a call to return to America's moral roots, the call comes in the form of more images and lacks specific direction.

The images and content of *A Nation Adrift* should drive you to your knees in prayer. Then again, perhaps that's exactly the call to action the makers of this video intended. *Michelle Van Loon*

A 283-page, spiral-bound teacher's copybook, **Ready-to-Use American History Activities for Grades 5–12** by James F. Silver covers American history from pre-Columbus times to the Challenger accident. Condensing the more important factual information onto one or two pages makes this book a bit terse, but it also eliminates much of the politically correct bias that is often present in secular books of this type.

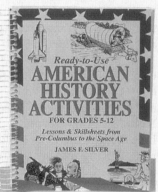

Most of the activities consist of a selected reading of an event, with accompanying essay questions for the student to complete. A sample activity asks students to complete a map of 1715 America, showing the major English, French and Spanish territories and possessions at that time, in order to gain an understanding of why Britain and France eventually resorted to war to settle their claims on this new land. Some surprises in this book include a section on the martyred Whitmans, missionaries to the Cayuse Indians. The desire to spread the Gospel is mentioned as a motivation for the Whitmans to "go west."

Hardly tainted at all by today's prevalent "political correctness," full of interesting (but brief) stories about the men and women who shaped this nation and liberally sprinkled with teacher's notes and suggestions for further study, I'd consider this to be a very useful copybook for supplementing your American History in the upper elementary/high school grades. *Teresa May*

This past month I explored ancient Indian ruins in Canyon de Chelly; retraced the expedition of Lewis and Clark across the Rocky Mountains; climbed down into an Indian kiva at Mesa Verde; rode a merchant wagon on the Sante Fe Trail; stared in awe at the brilliant colors of the Painted Desert; toured 26 historical Civil War Parks; rafted down the Grand Canyon rapids; flew over an active Mount St. Helens; watched Hopi ceremonial dances in the desert Southwest and literally explored our wonderful country from sea to shining sea!

By now you are probably thinking that I have: a) my own jet airplane, b) a time machine, or c) a lot of nerve to think that you would believe a "tall tale" like this! Happily, the correct answer is: d) none of the above! What I do have is a great set of social science/history books from KC Publications.

Solidly filled with glossy, full color photographs, these **Story Behind the Scenery** books pack a real visual punch. The content is as impressive. Each subject is covered thoroughly, including quotes from the logs of the sturdy explorers who first braved each region. These adventure books were literally devoured by my family as quickly as they could be read.

The KC Publications library is divided into four categories. The Story Behind the Scenery category is the largest by far, with 52 books covering National and Historical Parks in all regions of the United States. Special

Interest books deal with forces of nature and famous explorations. The Indian Culture books answered some of our questions concerning the life and religious practices of the Indians of the Southwest. Books can be ordered individually or as a Social Science Collection containing twenty-four books from all categories.

As good as this series is, there are a few problems. Although these books for the most part seem to be uncontaminated by political correctness, the book on Southwestern Indian Ceremonies is overly sentimental about the so-called "environmentally pure" pagan religious views of native Americans and broadly condemns non-Indian (easily read between the lines as "Christian") cultures as arrogant and unconcerned with preserving Creation. Other than that, there is the usual old-earth and evolutionary bias to contend with while reading about the geology of some areas— usually not very noticeable except for the book on Dinosaur National Monument (not surprising . . .) On a more positive note, I felt the book on Lincoln presented one of the more balanced accounts of his life that I have read, it being somewhat kinder to his wife than is the norm in many of today's publications. *Teresa May*

Vis-Ed American History flashcards

Grade 7–college. American History I, II, and III, $10.95 each. World History I and II, $10.95 each. Shipping extra.
Visual Education, 581 W. Leffel Lane, Springfield, OH 45501.
Orders: (800) 243-7070.
Inquiries: (937) 325-5503.
Fax: (937) 324-5697.
Web: www.vis-ed.com.

NEW!
Walch's American History on the Screen

Grades 7–12. $17.95 plus shipping.
J. Weston Walch, Publisher, PO Box 658, Portland, ME 04104.
(800) 341-6094. (207) 772-2846.
Fax: (207) 772-3105.
Email: customer_service@mail.walch.com.
Web: www.walch.com.

Visual Education has a unique product in their three boxes of **American History** flash cards. These 1000-card sets are in chronological question/answer form, with the questions on one side and the answers on the other. They make an excellent pre- and post-test for any real history studies, as well as giving you strongly condensed answers as a starting point for your own studies. Find out what you don't know and *look those subjects up* in the encyclopedia. Presto! Instant history course. (World History I and II also available.) *Mary Pride*

Reading about the past is one thing. Seeing it on the silver (OK, video!) screen can add a whole new dimension to your history study. That is the premise of **American History on the Screen**, a study guide to movies that portray some facet of our nation's history.

This text opens with a mini-course on film analysis and a fairly comprehensive listing of films keyed to the different eras in our country's past. The bulk of this 121-page resource, however, is in-depth units on 17 different films, including a unit comparing and contrasting three different film versions of the O.K. Corral gunfight.

The Civil War unit features the 1989 film *Glory*. A thorough background of the film and plot synopsis are aimed at the teacher, along with discussion ideas. A listing of books and other media resources for the time period are also highlighted. Reproducible student sheets include a listing of the main characters, a "what to watch for" section that offers some editorial comments ("The 54th's 'glory' also raises disturbing questions about the nature of war itself, about the Fort Wagner tactics, and about the pointlessness of such sacrifices as a means of gaining respect"), vocabulary and comprehension questions.

Though some of the background information on the making of the various films is interesting, for most home educators, this sort of formal resource is overkill. If you're involved in watching a movie with your children, following up with discussion and connecting the material to both historical and biblical truths is a natural from the comfort of your living room. *Michelle Van Loon*

If you ever succumbed to the lure of one of the "Choose Your Own Adventure" books, then you are already familiar with the format of this fun-to-read series of reproducible texts. Each 50-page book in the **Choosing Your Way Through America's Past series** has five stories, each featuring a decision point in the life an everyday person from a particular era in our history. For instance, it's 1889 and you're heading for land in Oklahoma. Do you go on foot or on horseback? If you go on foot, the text instructs you to turn to page 43. If you choose to ride a horse, read page 44 to "find out what your fate is" (!). Each situation sets up more choices. If you ride a horse, you find yourself at a starting line with hundreds of other land-hungry folks. Do you run to the creek or stake a claim to your left? If you run for the creek, you eventually find that you've been shut out, and decide to start a dry goods store. At the end of each section are some brief follow up questions and group activity suggestions.

Book 1 offers five story selections from the 1700's. **Book 2** covers the years from 1800–1850, **Book 3** from 1850–1900. **Book 4** features stories through the end of the 1920's. **Book 5** takes you from the 1930's to the 1960's, and **Book 6** brings the series up to the present. Some interesting settings are presented: you can live on a ranch in 1826 California, be a muckraking journalist in 1905, or defend Mr. Widmer, your history teacher, against classmates' accusations that he's a "commie traitor."

Lively writing makes these texts entertaining; however, they are not particularly strong in terms of concrete educational value. You may not agree with all of the choices presented (do you go march with your mother so she can get the right to vote or do you stand against her?), but some of the stories may spark a reluctant reader to keep turning the pages. *Michelle Van Loon*

Magazines

Here is a little-known product that's a real star—a social-studies newsletter of amazing quality and upbeat tone.

Rich Kurz, the editor and publisher of **CHRONOGRAF**, understands the importance of developing an accurate historical and cultural worldview. As he states:

> *The nature of man has not changed in all of recorded history. So, what someone did four thousand years ago can be a lesson for us today. History is not events separated in time and place from each other. The purpose here is to tell history so that it makes sense for today. The "who, what, where, when" are important. The "how and why" are also necessary. The linking of yesterday to today makes it all meaningful. This is a tool to forge that link.*

With an extensive background in graphic design and a Masters degree in cultural anthropology, he is uniquely qualified to produce this elegant and beautiful resource.

CHRONOGRAF is aptly titled, for its very name means "time writing." In each issue's 16 pages, Mr. Kurz writes about the important figures and events of time past and present.

Don't overlook *CHRONOGRAF* because of its deceptively modest size. Rich Kurz manages to summarize an incredible amount of information within its few pages. Throwing out the fluff, Mr. Kurz has sifted through the vast amount of available research to present the reader a complete perspective on the essential issues of American history. This is not just historical storytelling.

NEW!
Walch's Choosing Your Way Through America's Past
Grades 6–12. Each book, $10.60. Shipping extra.
J. Weston Walch, Publisher, PO Box 658, Portland, ME 04104. (800) 341-6094. (207) 772-2846. Fax: (207) 772-3105. Email: customer_service@mail.walch. com. Web: www.walch.com.

NEW!
CHRONOGRAF
Grades 6–10. $20/year (10 issues). Sample issue, $1. Back issues are available.
CHRONOGRAF Productions, 3019 Placer Court, Fort Collins, CO 80526-2651. (970) 226-6282. Fax: (970) 226-1005. Email: richkurz@csn.net.

CHRONOGRAF is laid out beautifully, as you can see.

The format is unique, too. It's like an illustrated book, delivered to your door in serialized magazine format.

But the well-researched text is only part of the package. Highlighting the text are maps, charts, graphs, timelines, and other visual aids illustrating themes covered in the magazine. Here is where Rich Kurz's graphic design experience really shows. His charts aren't just flashy eye candy, as is often the case in mass-market educational publications. Rather, they masterfully summarize what would take paragraphs to explain with words alone. The detailed timelines put events into proper perspective and remind the reader of the "Big Picture."

Even if you just read this newsletter and never pick up a history textbook, you'll be well-versed in early American history and have a good working knowledge of the those people and events that helped shaped our country—"cultural literacy" well beyond what most students are getting from our public schools. This is a way of studying history that really makes sense

So far, *CHRONOGRAF has* produced "The Presidential Series," a series of 10 issues highlighting events from American history by connecting them to what was going on with the Presidents. Detailed biographies are included for each issue's featured President. Plans are also in the works to develop an additional series featuring the 10 most important documents and speeches in American history, but no estimated ship date is yet available.

Chronograf is an impressive piece of work that will be an asset to any home. Highly recommended. *Christopher Thorne*

Cobblestone magazine

Grades 4–9. $26.95 per year (9 issues). $43.95 for 2 years. Back issues $4.95 each plus shipping. Back issue annual sets $48.95 (includes 12 issues, slipcase, and cumulative index).
Cobblestone Publishing, Inc., 30 Grove Street, Suite C, Peterborough, NH 03458. Orders: (800) 821-0115. Inquiries: (603) 924-7209. Email: custsvc@cobblestone.mv.com. Web: www.cobblestonepub.com.

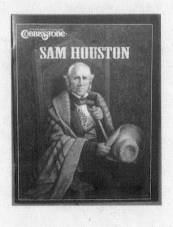

Would you believe a history magazine for kids? This very professionally-done magazine has lots of kid appeal, being loaded with pictures, puzzles, cartoons, and lots of short, zippy stories. Whoever locates the pictures does a terrific job, as they include a lot of rare and apt photos, woodcuts, engravings, and whatnot that truly add to the depth of the stories.

Each issue of **Cobblestone** is organized around one theme. Representative issue themes: Stonewall Jackson, Elections in America, The Monroe Presidency, Geronimo and the Apache Indians, Ann Hutchinson and the Puritans, Our Grand Old Flag, Greek Americans, Tuskeegee Airmen, and Puerto Rico. All are loaded with interesting facts and graphics. An issue on the theme of Newspapers, for example, featured a two-page time line beginning with Roman slaves sweating out newsletters by hand and ending with the Columbus, Ohio *Dispatch* whipping off the first totally electronic newspaper. Articles took off on tangents: Newspaper illustration, war correspondence, rural papers, and specialty presses were some of the unusual subjects covered. The whole issue was held together by several major articles on the history of printing and the freedom of the press. I've described half of that one issue; if it whets your interest, why not send away for a back issue, perhaps choosing one of the themes above?

Topics which will be included under each theme can be found at the *www.cobblestonepub.com* web site.

Back issues, of which there are over 200, are available in boxed annual sets as well as individual copies. The Cobblestone brochure thoughtfully lists them in alphabetic order by topic, rather than in order of publishing. So if you're interested in Civil War Reconstruction or Children Who Shaped History, you can quickly find what you're looking for. Baseball? American Theater? The Amish? Cherokee Indians? Great Depression? Jazz? Laura Ingalls Wilder? As you can see, topics can be cultural, famous people, time periods, or groups of people.

All back issue annual sets include the cumulative index to all previously published issues. *Mary Pride*

State History

State Histories' **In the Light of the Cross** series is a curriculum written to show your student how the Gospel of Jesus Christ has shaped their state's people and past. The set, consisting of text, workbook and teacher's guide, covers state geography, as well as its political, economic, and spiritual history. All the usual state history facts are included here: state bird, state tree, capital, state motto, etc. The addition of a Christian perspective on many historical events, however, distinguishes these books from their secular counterparts. In addition, the customs and manners of native populations of the area are discussed as well as Christian evangelism efforts among these different Indian tribes.

The set is good, but the interest level suffers a bit (as most textbooks do) from its effort to condense hundreds of years of history down to what will fit between the covers of a book. The pictures included were not of very good quality. To maintain interest during this course, students might benefit by reading some carefully chosen, more complete biographies. *Teresa May*

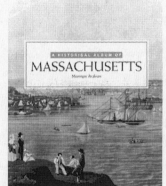

If you live in one of the 20 states for which these **Historical Albums** are available, look no further for a resource to satisfy your state history unit requirement. Each 64-page book is a textbook-style state history, minus the exercises and discussion questions, and plus a "Gazeteer" of important facts about the state: a map, geographical facts, form of government, state flag, state seal, state motto, and so on . . . even the state tree! Plus a timeline of state history, coordinated with a U.S. history timeline, brief bios of notables from that state, and a complete index. Historical Albums are available for those states with the following postal codes: AL, CA, CO, CT, FL, GA, IL, KY MA, MI, MN, NE, NJ, NY, OH, OR, PA, TX, VA, and WA. *Mary Pride*

NEW!
In the Light of the Cross Series
Grades 7–12. Spiral-bound text, $12–$14. Workbook, $7. Teacher's Guide, $7. History worktexts (elementary and high school) available for Arizona, Colorado, Maine, Minnesota, Missouri, New Mexico, Oklahoma, Texas, $6 each. Shipping extra.
State Histories, Route 1, Box 160, Anadarko, OK 73005. (405) 247-2963. Email: achs@tanet.net. Web: www.tanet.net/business/achs.

NEW!
Millbrook Historical Albums series
Grades 7–12. Each book, $23.40 (hardcover) or $6.95 (paperback). *The Millbrook Press, PO Box 335, 2 Old New Milford Rd., Brookfield, CT 06804. Orders: (800) 462-4703. Inquiries: (203) 740-2220. Fax: (203) 740-2223. Web: www.millbrookpress.com or www.millbrookonapproval.com*

CHAPTER 32

World History

A fascinating study was once done on how students learn history. Researchers had students in grade 11 read selections from a regular American history text. Other students read from one of three updated versions of the selections. Linguists (people who teach about the nature of language) wrote one version. English composition teachers wrote another. Two professional writers who had worked at *Time* and *Life* wrote the third.

In the words of Suzanne Fields, who reported this study in her syndicated newspaper column,

> *The results were not ambiguous. Those who read the linguists' version recalled two percent more than the students who read the original; students who got the revision by the composition teachers recalled two percent less.* [That says something about the people we pay to teach our kids to write, doesn't it?—MP] *Students who read the magazine writers' text recalled an astonishing 40 percent more than their classmates who got the original.*

In Suzanne's very words, "Textbooks either condescend to make information ludicrously 'relevant' to the life of a teenager, or they cover too much ground in a dull manner without a connecting perspective."

How did the professional writers, who had never been paid to patronize their readers or bore them, put the pizzazz back into history? They told all in an interview in *American Educator,* the professional journal of the American Federation of Teachers. As Suzanne reports, the writers used a more conversational tone, chose lively verbs, inserted lively anecdotal "nuggets," and "added a sense of drama."

In other words, there's nothing boring about history that a good writer can't fix. History is really *stories,* and who finds stories boring?

Some of the history books and courses below are written by professional writers. Others are presented in dramatic or story form, with an unfolding theme or plot. Still others are—well—textbooks.

Keeping what the researchers found in mind, I think we can safely say that students should fill up on source documents and history stories (biographies, videos, theme-oriented history) before attempting to organize the information with a history textbook. All the better if your history text is written dramatically —although you have to look out for bias once the author starts separating people and movements into "good guys" and "bad guys." (There *are* good guys and bad guys, but it takes a bit of pondering to figure out which is which sometimes!)

Students who have followed our suggested course of study for the elementary years will already be chock-full of historical fiction and biographies. These students will profit more from an organized textbook course than those whose only exposure to history thus far has been textbooks. The latter would do better to take time out for history-as-story before plunging back into formal textbook study.

World History Courses

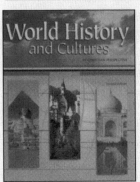

Intended for 10th-graders, **World History and Cultures in Christian Perspective** is the most ambitious of A Beka's world history books. It covers African and Asian cultures, not just the Greek and Roman civilizations. The history of ideas gets good coverage, with A Beka at pains to point out the biblical failings of such theories as evolutionism, socialism, humanism, Communism, and so on. Lots of colorful maps, illustrations, photos, and timelines. The usual encyclopedic amount of textual information. *Mary Pride*

Alpha Omega's grade 10 social-studies course covers ancient and Western history. It starts at Creation, then moves to the Fertile Crescent, Egypt, Assyria, Babylon, and Persia— all in the first unit! The second unit mentions India and China, but concentrates more on the Greeks and Romans. There then is one unit each on the medieval world (its history and culture), the Renaissance and Reformation, the age of mercantilism and empires, the age of revolution, the Industrial Revolution, the two World Wars, the contemporary world (focusing mostly on the Cold War and the atomic age) and a review unit. The workbooks are relatively inexpensive, easy to study or teach, and fast-moving.

Though the course content is somewhat uneven, since you don't get the same author writing all the LIFEPACs, by and large this is a good course. *Mary Pride*

Covenant Home Curriculum has an excellent test series to accompany this BJUP course

World Studies for Christian Schools covers the world's history in chronological order and region by region, starting with the ancient Ur of the Chaldees (Abraham's home town). Under Unit 3, "The Medieval World," for example, you find chapters on the golden ages of China and India, medieval Japan, medieval Islam, the Byzantine Empire, the European "dark ages," and the age of feudalism. The book is fundamentalist, missionary-minded, and anti-Catholic in spots (calling the Roman Catholic Church

A Beka World History & Cultures

Grade 10. Student book, $22.20. Teacher's guide (includes curriculum), $20.20. Student test and map booklet, $6.20. Teacher's key/test booklet, $8.85. Student quiz book, $4.60. Teacher quiz key, $8.85. Shipping extra.
A Beka Book, Box 19100, Pensacola, FL 32523-9100. (800) 874-2352. Web: www.abeka.com.

Alpha Omega Western History LIFEPACs

Grade 10. Boxed Set, $41.95. Shipping extra.
Alpha Omega Publications, 300 N. McKemy, Chandler, AZ 85226. Orders and inquiries: (800) 622-3070. Fax: (480) 785-8034. Web: www.home-schooling.com.

BJUP World Studies for Christian Schools
BJUP World History for Christian Schools

Grades 7 and 10. Student text, $30 each (hardbound). Teacher's edition, $44.50 each. Pre-Made Tests, $8 each. Test answer key, $4.50 each. Shipping extra.
Bob Jones University Press Customer Services, Greenville, SC 29614. Orders: (800) 845-5731. Fax: (800) 525-8398. Web: www.bjup.com.

"Satan's tool" in the last chapter, for example). Written at a seventh-grade level, its emphasis on everyday life and culture makes this text interesting reading and a good background introduction to world history for those who share its general outlook.

World History for Christian Schools, the 10th-grade course, is of course deeper than the World Studies text. It is also more urbane in tone and more interesting to read. The treatment of the Reformation, for example, while it will not thrill Catholics, dwells mostly on historic facts and source quotes. The book does an excellent job of covering the whole of world history from a traditional Protestant and Western-civilization point of view. *Mary Pride*

Christian Liberty Press has done the impossible. They have taken a well-organized, but depressingly leftist-leaning, series of history books and revised them into an excellent, conservative, two-volume world history for Protestant high-school students of the Reformed persuasion.

Streams of Civilization isn't shy about where it's coming from. Right at the start you are presented with various theories of what history is all about and how it should be studied. The authors believe that St. Augustine's concept of a spiritual war between the City of God (a society based on God's laws) and the City of Man (the humanist totalitarian state) is the biblical framework which causes history to make sense. Adopting this framework, they spend a good deal of space on what people were thinking and what were the effects of each new philosophy or theology.

Unabashedly Calvinist, the book sports chapters with titles like "France Under Catholic Despotism" and calls the (self-consciously godless) Enlightenment "The Darkening of the Western Mind." But it's not all philosophy and theology. You get a lot of history here, both political history and cultural history, all well-written. Why not? They're presenting history as a *story,* with "good guys" and "bad guys," which you must admit is more interesting than reading about dialectic materialism.

The books are wider than they are tall, and attractively laid out, with plenty of photos, illustrations, and sidebars. Each chapter ends with questions that can be used for discussion, or as brief essay assignments; projects; a list of vocabulary terms introduced in the chapter (without definitions); and a list of people introduced in the chapter.

Volume I starts at Creation, and goes up to the Renaissance and Reformation.

Volume II starts with the age of European exploration, and goes right up to the Clinton administration.

A teacher's guide, available only for Volume I at the time of writing, provides these helps for each chapter in the text:

- A list of the major concepts in the chapter, with explanations of each
- Explanations of the specialized vocabulary terms introduced in the chapter
- Comments on the suggested projects
- Lesson plan with objectives, step-by-step procedures, and teaching suggestions
- Suggestions on how to evaluate the student's learning
- A paragraph or so about what's coming up in the next chapter

Tests and answer keys are also available—very helpful for the busy home teacher. Finally, a set of **Historical Charts** is available. This is 22 detailed 11 x 17" timelines covering biblical history, church history, political history, intellectual history, history of art, and history of science. *Mary Pride*

NEW!
Christian Liberty's Streams of Civilization
Grades 9–12. Volume 1 & 2, $19.95 each. Historical Charts, $16. Test booklet, $3.50 each volume. Answer key for text and tests, $4.95 each volume. Shipping extra.
Christian Liberty Press, 502 West Euclid Ave., Arlington Heights, IL 60004. (847) 259-4444.
Fax: (847) 259-2941.
Email: enquire@homeschools.org.
Web: www.homeschools.org. They take credit card orders, but not over the phone. Any other contact method will work.

Christian Light: God's World—His Story

Grades 6–8. $19.95 plus $2.50 shipping. Workbooks and teacher's guide available.
Christian Light Education, PO Box 1212, Harrisonburg, VA 22801-1212. (540) 434-1003. Fax: (540) 433-8896. Email: orders@clp.org.

NEW!
The Complete Idiot's Guide to British Royalty

Grade 7–adult. $18.95.
Alpha Books, a division of Macmillan General Reference, a Simon & Schuster Macmillan Company, 1633 Broadway, New York, NY 10019.
Information: (800) 428-5331. Available in bookstores.
Web: www.mcp.com/mgr/idiot.

The Creation and Flood. Sumeria. Egypt. Greece. Rome. Israel and Judah. The Church. Middle Ages. The Reformation. The Inquisition. Age of Exploration. Age of Colonialism. Age of Missions. Russia. China. India. World Wars. Cold War. This one book, **God's World—His Story**, covers the entire history of the Western world. Written from a staunchly Mennonite viewpoint, it makes very interesting reading, as the trials and tribulations of that group are thrown into relief against the background of the great movements of the times.

History is not only presented, but analyzed from a conservative Mennonite perspective—including the mistakes of Mennonites and Anabaptists of the past. Topics are covered in reasonable depth, with many intriguing sidelights on how people lived in each age. Each chapter ends with review questions and Bible exercises, in which you either read about the history of the time period or study passages and apply them to the situations people faced at that time. Good, readable writing, presented with both sobriety and feeling. Lots of character-building emphasis on the frequent necessity of suffering for Christ in this world. No uncritical American patriotism, as in many other Christian textbooks, nor yet any uncritical America-bashing, as in many secular texts.

With all this in mind, I believe *God's World—His Story* provides a good overview of Western world history for this age group while it adds a wholesome balance to the home schooler's history bookshelf, even for those of us who aren't Mennonites. Warning: lots of religious denominations persecuted the Mennonites (e.g., Lutherans, Anglicans, Catholics . . .), so if you're a member of one of these groups and it bothers you to have the failings of your forebears pointed out, don't say I didn't warn you!
Mary Pride

The author of **The Complete Idiot's Guide to British Royalty**, Richard Buskin, is the best-selling author of *Princess Diana: Her Life Story 1861-1997*. Even the foreword is written by a Diana expert: James Whittaker, the reporter who first broke the story of Diana and Charles as a couple and himself the author of a book on the Princess. So it's no surprise that this well-written book starts off with a section on the current ruling house of Britain, including the life and times of Princess Di.

What is a surprise is how educationally sound and helpful this book is. You can consider it a history of Britain, minus the unimportant details that clog history texts and make it impossible to remember anything, and plus lots of juicy stories that will keep you reading.

Like other Idiots books, you get sidebars with additional information, presented in an appealing visual manner. In this case, the regular sidebars include

- Hear Ye, Hear Ye—quotes from the royals or about the royals
- Palace Parlance—definitions of the odd words that describe customs, items, and people related to the monarchy
- Royal Rebuttal—in which the author debunks myths, lies, and rumors about the royals
- On Her Majesty's Service—insider information about the royals
- A Right Royal Tale—juicy tidbits about the royals

When I say "the royals," I don't mean only the House of Windsor. This book covers *all* British royalty, from the ancient Danes and Saxons to Princes William and Harry. After the initial introduction, which briefly summarizes how the monarchy started and grew as well as introducing "royal traditions, trappings, and honors" and the impact of Princess Di, the next five sections follow Alfred the Great through Prince John, the Plantagenet dynasty through the War of the Roses, the House of Tudor through the colonization of North America, the monarch who lost his head through the Hanoverians, and finally Queen Victoria to the present day.

To help you remember all this, the author really goes the extra mile. He has included several quizzes (with answers in the back), plus a chronological list of all the monarchs, a collection of Royal Family trees, a list of recommended books for further reading, a list of famous battles, a list with descriptions of royal residences, and a list of films and selected list of TV dramas about the royals down the centuries. In addition to all this, the book has quite a few photos and portraits of kings, queens, and their residences.

While recognizing the monarchy's current problems and scandals, the author is quick to note that past royalty often did a lot worse. With engaging text spiced with dry British wit (example: "The barons could always be counted on for a quick uprising"), and fascinating subject matter, this is British history at its most readable. Recommended. *Mary Pride*

Here's a novel way to study history! **Milliken's transparency/duplicating books** each contain 12 full-color transparencies to illustrate the geography, history, and important cultural features of a major historical period. They also include background historical information coordinated to each transparency, and between 4–12 duplicating master quiz pages. Answers to the quizzes are found at the end of the teacher's guide section.

The full-color transparencies certainly do engage the attention. Although originally designed for use with an overhead projector, their dramatic appearance and clutter-free design works well as a kind of super illustration.

Try using the workbook pages first as a research aid. Students research the answers and check their work against the answers in the teacher's material. The same workbook pages can then be resurrected later as tests, once the student has worked through the material.

I would also recommend that you skip the silly activities such as "Write a newspaper report of David killing Goliath" or time-consuming busywork such as "Construct a model of the city of Jerusalem" (the book doesn't even contain enough info for you to construct the model). These are not up to the high standards of the rest of these books.

The workbook study pages and essay questions are excellent; kids will really learn the history working through them. Knowledge is stressed; fill-in-the-blanks are kept to a minimum.

Information in these books is generally reliable. Exceptions: the apparent anti-supernatural bias of the writers of the *Hebrews, Phoenicians, and Hittites* book causes them to ascribe Samuel's anointing of David to Saul's "fits of rage which made him unsuitable as a king" (see I Samuel for the true story), and to question David's authorship of the Psalms bearing his name. Otherwise I have to commend the authors of this series for a well-balanced presentation, even of difficult themes such as *Byzantine and Moslems*.

The transparency pages give you a window into these time periods, showing you how people dressed, what kind of buildings they built, how they worked and played, and so on. None of that gruesome focus on violence and the seamy underside of a civilization that mars so many newer public school histories.

Considering that many traditional history textbooks skip over these periods, ignore their cultural side, or distort the entire time period in favor of preaching some faddish new cultural agenda, the Milliken series is an excellent resource. *Mary Pride*

Milliken History
Grade 7–adult. The Hebrews, Phoenicians and Hittites, Byzantine and Moslems, and The Italian Renaissance, $14.95 each.
Milliken Publishing Company, 1100 Research Blvd., St. Louis, MO 63132.
Orders: (800) 325-4136.
Inquiries: (314) 991-4220.
Fax: (800) 538-1319.
Web: www.millikenpub.com.

NEW!
Superstar Teachers World History

Grade 9–adult. $149.95 plus $10 shipping.
The Teaching Company, 7405 Alban Station Court, Suite A107, Springfield, VA 22150. (800) 832-2412. Fax: (703) 912-7756.

A "workbook," which is actually an outline of each lesson, is included. I find it handy to take notes right in the workbook.

Church History

Grade 8–adult. $11.90 plus shipping.
*U.S.: Inheritance Publications, PO Box 366, Pella, IA 50219.
Canada: Inheritance Publications, Box 154, Neerlandia, Alberta T0G 1R0.
Phone/Fax: (800) 563-3594 or (780) 674-3949.
Email: inhpubl@telusplanet.net.
Web: www.telusplanet.net/public/inhpubl/webip/ip.htm.*

Superstar Teachers World History is world history the homeschool way! Professor Lin Thompson, a high-school teacher who also has experience as a professional actor, dresses up in period costumes and takes on the persona of historical characters as he presents 30 lectures covering "The Fertile Crescent to the American Revolution." Major sections, each comprising several lectures, cover early civilizations, the Greek and Roman worlds, the Middle East and Eastern Europe (Byzantium, Islam, and early Russia), medieval life, far Eastern kingdoms, discovery of the New World, and European rulers from the Tudors through the American Founding Fathers. Single lectures introduce the Renaissance, the Reformation, and Africa.

Historical figures portrayed include Ibn Battuta, Marco Polo, Francisco Pizarro, and Patrick Henry, among many others. "Generic" characters include such folks as Olympian Thompson, Barbarian Thompson, Merchant Tompopolus, Peasant Thom, and everyone's favorite, Rolf the Viking . . . among many more. The strangest portrayal is Princess Olga. If you can picture a man with a beard in character as a Russian princess—well, ugh.

Princess Olga aside, these videos are great fun to watch, and chock-full of history, both the kind they teach in school and the kind they don't. You'll learn who did what when, but also *why* they did it, and what it meant to them. For example: did you know that the Vikings were such great warriors because they worked out every day like Sylvester Stallone did for *Rambo*? They rowed their boats for hours every day, and as a consequence had the best upper-body development of any group of men at that time. It also helped that they played "games" like throwing spears at each other, where the object was to catch the spear before it killed you. And that they had guys whose specialty was going crazy in battle, who literally felt no pain while fighting.

Do you think a teenager would find this interesting? Ours certainly did! I bet they remember more of Lin Thompson's lessons than they do of their history text. These videos are so entertaining students might even want to watch them several times . . . which is more than you can say for *any* textbook! Recommended. *Mary Pride*

Church History

Rev. P. K. Keizer (1906–1985) was minister of the Reformed churches of several cities in the Netherlands. Subsequently he served in the "liberated" Reformed Church of Groningen. The liberation occurred as a protest against what the protesters considered unscriptural and illegal actions of Synod during the years of World War II. Without going heavily into Dutch theology, I'll just tell you that the whole thing is explained in the latter part of this book, of which at least two-thirds is devoted to regular church history.

Dr. Keizer also taught church history in high school for many years. His book, **Church History**, shows the fruit of going over the subject again and again, both in its logical outline and in its content. He neither overloads the student nor skips over anything important.

The book is literally outlined, with numbered points, sub-points, and sub-sub points, but all this actually makes it easier to use. The writing is interesting and pious—from a solidly Reformed Protestant viewpoint—and does the teenager the great service of distilling the lives and teachings of many important people in a form he can remember. Take this passage on Erasmus:

At first Erasmus was sympathetic toward Luther. He loathed the papal control over the consciences of the people, exercised relentlessly with the help of the infamous Inquisition. He therefore regarded the collapse of the medieval world as a liberation; indeed, Erasmus believed that this freedom of conscience would allow man to reach full human development. He was, therefore, an optimistic humanist. The Roman Inquisition did not trust this man who ridiculed the monks and mercilessly satirized the shortcomings of the Roman Catholic church. But Erasmus never left this church. "I am not made of martyr stuff," he said. Luther commented, "He is as smooth as an eel; he wants to walk over eggs and not break any."

Note how the well-chosen quotes from Erasmus and Luther bring out the personalities of each man. Note also how the author is concerned to tell you what is right and wrong, not only what happened. Thus his section on slavery not only describes the practice, but powerfully condemns it, citing Bible chapter and verse, so the student can know *why* slavery was wrong.

Church History covers the time from the resurrection of Christ to the 1980s. From 1795 on, the focus is on the Netherlands (Holland), but before then we visit the Gnostics, Marcionites, Edict of Milan, ecumenical councils, Augustine, the Eastern Orthodox Church, the rise and history of the papacy (with attention to Aquinas, Bernard of Clairvaux, and the Cluniac monastic reform, among other things), the Reformation (in Germany, Switzerland, France, Scotland, England, and Netherlands), the Anabaptists and mystics, the Counter Reformation, the Enlightenment, Jansenists, Pietists, and Methodists. These are only about half of the main topics in the main part of the book, giving you an idea of its breadth of coverage. The index helps you find any topic quickly. An excellent resource. *Mary Pride*

Otto Scott has put together a powerhouse of a book on church history and the march of God's Truth throughout time. Written from a Calvinist viewpoint, **The Great Christian Revolution** does not pull punches in its evaluation of the central characters that played a part in history.

Chapters in this 295-page work include: Paganism's Price, The Renaissance, The Reformation, Geneva, Calvin and Servetus, England, Change at the Top, Elizabeth and Mary Stuart, Knox, Mary Stuart and Elizabeth, Shamie Jamie (King James I), Parliament, War, The People Act, The English Republic, The Future Appears, The Protector's End, and The Crown's Revenge. You begin with a discussion on the effects of Greece and Rome and quickly move through time ending with Charles II. In between you hear about all the famous—Luther, Zwingli, Calvin, popes, kings and queens—and the insights that draw it all together.

Mr. Scott tells about the issues he believes enabled Christianity to flourish and grow, and describes them in vivid terms. You learn why Mary of England was called "Bloody Mary," why James I was known as "Shamie Jamie," and why Calvin was villainized over his involvement with Servetus.

This is a fast-paced, dramatic read that summarizes hundreds of years in an easily understood way. Your understanding of these events will never be the same. CAUTION: it contains mentions of some historical figures' abominable behavior. *Marla Perry*

This Canadian Reformed publishing house offers a wide variety of reading materials suitable for use in a homeschool setting. They have quite a broad catalog that carries everything from Dutch hymns on CD to commentaries written from a Reformed perspective. But what may grab your interest (and that of your children) is the selection of **historical fiction published by Inheritance Publications**.

Inheritance offers:

- Brave Dutch youths working to defeat the Nazis during World War II, found in the series authored by Piet Prins

NEW!
The Great Christian Revolution

Grade 8–adult. $14.95 plus shipping
Uncommon Media, PO Box 781, Wauna, WA 98395. (800) 994-2323. Fax/Phone: (253) 851-9150. Email: umedia@the-compass.com. Web: www.the-compass.com.

NEW!
Inheritance Publications historical fiction series

Grade 5–adult, depending on the book. Book prices vary.
Inheritance Publications, US Ordering Information: Box 366, Pella, IA 50219. (800) 563-3594. Canada phone/Fax: (780) 674-3949. Web: www.telusplanet.net/public/ inhpubl/webip/ip.htm.

- Hugeuenots standing for their faith in the face of terrible persecution, as told in Grace Raymond's *How They Kept Their Faith*
- William Rang's *Salt In His Blood*, telling the story of a bold admiral's fighting for the glory of God and King
- A young Indonesian convert standing alone for his faith (the Tekko books, authored by Alie Vogelaar)
- Historical figures such as William of Orange and George Washington, fleshed out for a young audience by Marjorie Bowen and W.G Van de Hulst

Because of the variety of authors, quality and readability also varies. Some of the books were first published in Dutch, which means that sometimes the language in these books may be a bit stiff. ("But Count William and his wife could not sleep. Their hearts were too full of joy and disquiet."—*William of Orange, The Silent Prince*, by Van de Hulst.) Others, most notably the Piet Prins books, though also initially published in Dutch, are such exciting tales that you'll be turning the pages as fast as you can in order to find out what happens next.

Inheritance also publishes other works of fiction. *Captain, My Captain* by Deborah Meroff is a novel in the adventure/romance genre. The interesting twist here is that the romance blooms within the confines of marriage. There are also reprints of older works, such as *Jessica's First Prayer* and *Jessica's Mother*, by Hesba Stretton, that tell a story to make a strong moral point.

The overarching theme in all of Inheritance's children's material is the sovereignty of God. Each book, no matter who the author, brings you back to this truth: God is at work in the affairs of men, and He is to be loved and revered. None of it is world-class literature. But Inheritance does offer some solid supplemental reading that is clean and reverent, and offers it from a unique perspective. *Michelle Van Loon*

Josephus: The Essential Writings

Grade 10–adult. $15.99 plus shipping.
Kregel Publications, PO Box 2607, Grand Rapids, MI 49501-2607. Orders: (800) 733-2607. Inquiries: (616) 451-4775. Fax: (616) 451-9330. Email: kregelpub@aol.com. Web: www.kregel.com

Seminary students have for hundreds of years been assigned to read two books by the New Testament-age Jewish historian Josephus: his *Jewish Antiquities* and *The Jewish War*. In those two books, Josephus covered the history of the Jewish people from the Creation through his own day, including the part the Bible skips, the Intertestamental period.

The problem with studying Josephus' works has always been their length and the obscure language of some old translations. Now all that has changed! Paul L. Maier, Professor of Ancient History at Western Michigan University, has produced a remarkable new translation, entitled **Josephus: The Essential Writings**. Along with a much more readable text, set in a much more readable typeface, you also get 83 photographs of places and people mentioned in this history (I'm talking about photos of their statues, of course!), 12 maps and illustrations, five charts that explain who was related to whom, dates of significant events listed in the margins, a bibliography, and a very helpful index. You and your teens can sit down with this book and read it almost as if it were a novel. Which it is—a novel way to increase your understanding of the vital events up to and after the time of Christ. *Mary Pride*

NEW!
Reformation Overview

Grade 9–adult. $79.99 plus shipping.
Vision Video, PO Box 540, Worcester, PA 19490. Orders: (800) 523-0226. Fax: (610) 584-4610. Email: visionvide@aol.com. Web: www.gatewayfilms.com.

Few can argue that the Reformation was one of the pivotal events in history. However, many—if not most—of us were taught surprisingly little about it in school. The easy-to-use **Reformation Overview** kit includes:

- Leader's Guide
- Student Worksheets
- Two videocassettes, each containing three programs
- 7 Glimpses (short informational articles designed to be used as church bulletin inserts)

The videotapes are an interesting combination of narrative and drama that is well-produced and visually interesting. My husband was so caught up in them that he watched most of them in one marathon session. (The programs were adapted from longer dramatic programs produced by Gateway Films.)

The lessons cover John Wycliffe, John Hus, Martin Luther, the Swiss Reformation, the Radical Reformation, and William Tyndale. Their materials do not delve into the historical only, but include in-depth Bible studies that accompany each lesson and deal with the major issues of the Reformation, from a Protestant point of view.

The Leader's Guide provides suggestions for how to structure the class series (six sessions, twelve sessions, crash course . . .), historical background, biblical background, discussion questions, a chart outlining the Protestant *v.* Catholic views of key theological issues, etc.

While this resource is a bit pricey for many families, it would be a valuable addition for support group libraries and church libraries as well. *Rebecca Prewett*

"Meet ancient man . . . physically superior, mentally sophisticated . . . knowledgeable and capable far above anything most of us have imagined . . . just as the Bible teaches! Discover the secular/humanist researchers who unintentionally lend support to the biblical record of ancient intelligence and the dispersion from Babel. Meet the patriarchs and the pagans who established the thoughts and cultures of mankind, and whose influence still shapes the world today. Delve into the ancient Mystery system that twists biblical truth and traces the dispersion of man throughout the world. Examine evidences of the knowledge and technology that took ancient man to the Americas."

They Came From Babel collects about every contrarian view of origins, ancient civilizations and migrations, and ancient cultures that you have likely never seen before. And as a bonus, you get loads of information about ancient religions and modern philosophies, including what author S.A. Cranfill points out as connections between the two. From "mainstream" contrarians such as Dr. Thor Heyerdahl, whose voyages on the "Ra" and the "Kon-Tiki" are world-famous, to obscure teachings handed down through generations of occultists, you'll find data and theories to challenge ideas you didn't even realize you had accepted. Bibliographies are provided at the end of each chapter, so you can check it all out for yourself with the sources on which the book is based.

Author Shelby Cranfill believes the Bible is literally true where it touches on these subjects. But unlike many Bible-believing authors, Cranfill fills you in on other points of view as well, for the purpose of critiquing them and showing how they differ from, borrow from, or even amplify the biblical version.

I'm not saying I agree with everything in this book. But reading it completes your education, making you aware of what everyone from ancient scholars to New Agers believes about the ancient world. *Mary Pride*

You want a really fascinating church history project? Try watching **Vision Video's Biographies of Famous Christians** in this order:

- John Wycliffe: The Morningstar
- John Hus
- Martin Luther
- Standing in the Storm: The Story of Jan Amos Comenius
- First Fruits

Vision Video, PO Box 540, Worcester, PA 19490. Orders: (800) 523-0226. Fax: (610) 584-4610.
Email: visionvide@aol.com.
Web: www.gatewayfilms.com.

Vision Video has dozens of other videos of interest to thinking Christians. *C.S. Lewis through the Shadowlands*, for example, is the winner of an International Emmy, two British Academy Awards, and 10 other awards from five countries. (I never got to see this one, unhappily; the tape snagged in my VCR and broke it!) *The Cross and the Switchblade* is the classic story of gangleader Nicky Cruz and the skinny white preacher who dared to travel the mean streets of New York and lead desperadoes like Nicky to the Lord. *Hazel's People* is the story of how a visit to Mennonite country changes the life of a bitter fighter for human rights. Many, many more. No need to waste your VCR on watching junk when good stuff like this is around!

NEW!
William and Mary Trilogy
Grade 7-adult. I Will Maintain, $15.90; Defender of the Faith, $13.90; For God and the King, $15.90. Shipping $2.50. (These are US dollars prices.)
Inheritance Publications, Box 366, Pella, IA 50219.
Or in Canada: Inheritance Publications, Box 154, Neerlandia, Alberta, T0G 1R0 Canada.
(800) 563-3594.
Phone/fax: (403) 674-3949.
Web: www.telusplanet.net/public/ inhpubl/webip/ip.htm.

John Wycliffe, the 14th-century leader commonly remembered as "The Morning Star of the Reformation," influenced both Martin Luther, the German reformer, and John Hus, the Bohemian reformer. Jan Amos Comenius was a Hussite, a descendant of Huss's followers. *First Fruits* then takes up the tale of the Moravians, spiritual descendants of Comenius, who blazed the way for modern missions by taking the gospel to the slaves on St. Thomas Island.

From one video to the next, you find church leaders prophesying what will happen to those who follow them—and it comes true on the next video! Hus, who was burned at the stake, said that his persecutors had succeeded in silencing him, a "silly goose" (*Hus* sounds like the word for *goose* in Czechoslovakia), but that the Lord would bring eagles in his place, men of strong and dauntless will. Enter Martin Luther! Hus talks about his debt to Wycliffe's writings; Comenius talks about his debt to Hus, and prophesies that the gospel will be spread abroad by those who follow him (Comenius), as in fact happened.

Fascinating stories, beautifully produced and acted. I would only warn you not to let little kids see the Comenius video, since the Czechs who produced it realistically depicted the horrors of Protestants being slaughtered.

The *Dietrich Bonhoeffer* video features interviews with many people who knew him, including his sister and those who attended seminary with him and studied under him. This is a fascinating look at this man who, although a pacifist, both organized a dissident church in Hitler's Germany and joined a plot to assassinate Hitler. Bonhoeffer was killed in a concentration camp. He continues to increase in influence among theologians, and the issues he faced are brought out clearly as we tour the places he studied and worked. Even Bonhoeffer fans may get some surprises, e.g., the revelation that he developed an interest in civil rights for blacks while studying in America (this was in 1940, remember!) as well as in black gospel music. Truly a man for all seasons. *Mary Pride*

It is not a surprise that most Americans are sadly lacking in knowledge about their own history. If you really want to see people give you a blank stare, just try asking them who **William and Mary** were. (Hint: we're talking historical personages here, not the Prides!) As a matter of fact, you may be wondering that yourself.

European history, with all of its shifting borders and genealogy charting of royalty, has the allure for most of us of a dusty tapestry in a dank old castle. However, if you've been homeschooling for a while and have caught the history bug ("History is cool! God is sovereign!"), and you've studied the Reformation/Renaissance era, you'll have no doubt encountered a lot of strong and often heroic reaction to the use and misuse of power by both church leaders and royalty.

As your homeschooled student gets older, you may find it desirable to spend a bit of time studying the political history of Europe. Inheritance Publications, a small Reformed publishing house, has taken it upon themselves to lightly edit and reprint Marjorie Bowen's historical fiction about William of Orange, originally available at the turn of this century. William, prince of Orange, later King of England, and husband of Mary II, Queen of England, is best remembered for his courageous stand against Catholic France in the late 1600's. William, a staunch Calvinist Protestant, fought political intrigue from within and numerous battles from without, always with his eyes on God. Bowen offers a three-part look at this man's life:

- *I Will Maintain*—a 383-page look at William's young adult-hood
- *Defender of the Faith*—282 pages detailing his marriage to Mary, and their continuing struggle with France

- *For God and the King*—Courage in leadership, through to the end of both William and Mary's lives, 350 pages

Bowen fills in the stark outlines of history with lots of dialogue and incredible detail. In fact, for most readers, this may be the weakness of these carefully researched books: 1015 pages about a man a bit out of the mainstream of your history study may be too much for you to wade through. If, however, you are looking for a detour off the beaten path, you may find these books worth a look. *Michelle Van Loon*

Make Your Own World History Units

Let the Authors Speak is "A Guide to Worthy Books Based on Historical Setting" by Carolyn Hatcher The book begins with an extended essay promoting the Charlotte Mason system of education. But the heart of *Let the Authors Speak* is two book lists. The first "Guide sorted by century/location," lists books by title, author, type (a two-letter code— "RH" for example stands for "realistic historical"), century-location (e.g., "17 NA NE" means "17th century A.D., North America, New England"), and a very brief comment (e.g., "Indian princess, married settler"). This very condensed listing, which is sorted by historical era and location, helps you instantly pick out relevant literature to accompany any geographical or historical studies you may be involved in. The second list contains the same information, only sorted by author. Little codes by each book title lets you know if that book was reviewed in *Books Children Love* or *Honey for a Child's Heart* (two books that write up classic children's books), whether it is on the recommended reading list for Marva Collins' Westside Prep School, and whether it has won the Newbery Medal or the Pulitzer Prize.

This book and an encyclopedia are all you need to plan some really good unit studies. Well worth the price. *Mary Pride*

Sure, everyone knows that the Declaration of Independence was signed in 1776, but did you realize that the Spanish founded San Francisco in the same year? In 1776 Mozart was 20 and Napoleon was seven. And less than a decade later the Montgolfier brothers successfully launched a hot air balloon. **World History and Literature: A Simultaneous Look**, with its extensive timeline lists from Creation to the present, will help you make connections like these between events that occurred concurrently in various parts of the globe. But there is more here. The author, Joni Johnson, also provides you with lists of books, often with reading levels and/or call numbers, divided into Resources (background and reference material), Literature Set in Period (historical fiction, plays, retold myths, and more) and Period Literature (pieces written during that era.) You will also find lists of period art, music, science and people. Mrs. Johnson gives you plenty of space to make your own notes, and as you personalize this book it will become considerably more useful to you.

This is a resource with a lot of potential, but it has some drawbacks. The timeline lists are just that, long lists of dates and events. You may find yourself wading through pages of tiny print trying to discover which events are truly important to you. You might want to color code events from different regions, or highlight those of most interest to you. Also, I was puzzled by the use in this otherwise solidly Christian book of the dating system of BCE/CE (before common era/ common era), which is commonly used to deny the centrality of the incarnation of Jesus Christ.

Nonetheless, if you write your own unit studies or are just looking to beef up your history studies with some good literature, this might be a tool to put on your bookshelf. *Anne Wegener*

NEW!
Let the Authors Speak
Parents. $18.95 plus $2.50 shipping. *Old Pinnacle Publishing, 1048 Old Pinnacle Rd., Joelton, TN 37080. (615) 746-3342.*

NEW!
World History and Literature
Parents. $19.95 plus $3 shipping *Blue Earth Publishing, Joni Johnson, 150 W. Franklin St., Bellbrook, OH 45305. Phone/Fax: (937) 848-3540. Email: terra-blue@mindspring.com. Web: terrablue.home.mindspring.com/ be.html.*

The Ancient World

Scholars. 1-year subscription (2 issues), $30. Single copies, $10–$15 each.
ARES Publishers, Inc., 7406 N. Sheridan Rd., Chicago, IL 60626-2012. (773) 743-1405. Fax: (773) 743-0657. Email: order.arespublishers@att.net. Web: www.arespublishers.com.

Calliope magazine

Grades 4–9. $26.95 per year (9 issues). Back issues, $4.95 each plus shipping.
*Calliope, 30 Grove Street, Suite C, Peterborough, NH 03458.
Orders: (800) 821-0115.
Inquiries: (603) 924-7209.
Fax: (603) 924-7380.
Email: custsvc@cobblestone.mv.com.
Web: www.cobblestonepub.com.*

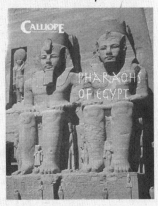

NEW!
The Cartoon History of the Universe, Volumes 1–7 and Volumes 8–13.

Grade 11–college. $19.95 each plus $2.50 shipping per order.
*Bantam Doubleday Dell Publishing Group, Inc., 2451 S. Wolf Road, Des Plaines, IL 60018.
Inquiries: (800) 323-9872.
Can order by mail only.*

Magazines

"An up-to-date current-research library for the student of Antiquity." They said it! **The Ancient World** reports on what's new in ancient history. Some past issue themes: Alexander the Great (the Great One got eight issues!), Ancient Games and Athletics, Corruption in Ancient Greek and Roman Politics, Hellenistic Warfare, and Where Was the Cretan Labyrinth?

Ladislaus J. Bolchazy, of Bolchazy-Carducci Publishers, is one of the editors. *Mary Pride*

This magazine used to be called *Classical Calliope* and focus on the ancient classical world. Now it has been re-christened **Calliope: World History for Young People.** With this wider and more updated focus, it looks like a better bet.

From the blurb:

> *By showing students that world history is a continuation of events rather than a series of isolated, unrelated occurrences,* Calliope *helps young readers understand how and why those events took place.*
>
> *Carefully selected themes explore in-depth circumstances leading up to and following specific events —from ancient times through the Middle Ages and into the Renaissance. Maps and time lines broaden readers' concepts of times and places.*
>
> *In coming issues, readers can visit the Doges of Venice, follow the ancient Phoenician traders on their routes, meet with Peter and Catherine of Russia, and enter the kingdom of Kush and the world of Islam. Complementary articles, activities, puzzles and illustrations—plus recommendations on further reading —involve young readers in the excitement of past events.*

I've looked at a few issues of this magazine, and they've done a good job of putting it together. It's readable, well laid out, and interesting. Relativistic flavor, with equal time and acceptance given to Western, African, and Eastern civilizations and all historic world religions. This means, of necessity, that some uncomfortable facts about ancient pagan civilizations are understated or passed over, since all civilizations and religions are *not* equal (and you think so, too, or we'd have Aztec temples featuring daily human sacrifice in every major city, and you'd have gone back to your ancestors' native countries).

Sample issue themes from previous school years: the Phoenicians, The Doges of Venice, Two Russian greats: Peter and Catherine, The Kingdom of Kush, and Islam. *Mary Pride*

World History Aids

Larry Gonick just can't stop cartooning. His *Cartoon Guide to Statistics, Cartoon Guide to Physics,* and *Cartoon Guide to Genetics* are all reviewed elsewhere in this book or on the CD-ROM version. These projects are small in comparison to his ambitious **Cartoon History of the Universe**.

Now collected in two huge oversized volumes (one each for what used to be seven smaller volumes), the Cartoon History goes from evolutionary prehistory (the Big Bang, the molecule-to-man progression, and assorted fables told as fact about the beginnings of society and money) to the fall of Rome in both East and West. Along the way he manages to dis every major world religion except Islam (which had not yet made the scene). Jesus, for example, is presented as a somewhat schizo teacher who goes totally nuts towards the end, and who may have had a carnal relationship with Mary Magdalene. Oddly by contrast, the early Christians are presented as sincere. But once we arrive at the life of Constantine, it's back to "Christians as hypocrites," the typical tack taken by those who vilify Christ.

"Rude and lewd" is how you'd have to characterize some of the "cartoon history" in these books. The sexual habits of emperors and other historical figures are on display (e.g., Alexander the Great kissing a guy, Tiberius hanging out with little boys, a Chinese queen falling for a fellow with a "big bat"). Of course, stuff like this can be found in many "classics of the Western world," but there you don't have to look at suggestive pictures of it. Not that there's oodles of naked people in these books, but you will find many scenes of clothed people lasciviously clutching each other at orgies, and "primitive people" with breasts and fannies hanging out, as well as pictures such as I have described above.

This is aggravating, because Mr. Gonick's writing and cartooning skills otherwise would make these an excellent introduction to lots of world history and religions for kids. His criticisms are often right on (the undocumented innuendos about Jesus being an exception), and certainly would spark lively discussions. The stories are fascinating, and you don't know them all already. Check out the 100 pages on Chinese history in the second volume, for example. So why, oh why, did he have to stick in so much sex? Do we really need a historian under every bed? *Mary Pride*

> *"That which has been is what will be, that which is done is what will be done, and there is nothing new under the sun."*

Dateline: Troy, a fascinating retelling of the Trojan War, superbly illustrates King Solomon's assessment of life. One night while reading a horrific tale of Hercules to his children, the resemblance between the myth and contemporary headlines impressed author Paul Fleischman. He then conceived the idea for this book which juxtaposes a succinct version of Homer's story with twentieth-century newspaper clippings.

Fleischman's parallel accounts are sometimes amusing, often poignant, and almost always thought-provoking. When in the Greek tale Achilles storms away in a pout because of the forced loss of his female slave to Agamemnon, the alternate page shows the baseball star, Darryl Strawberry, threatening to leave training camp in a similar sulk. Other analogies are drawn between Queen Hecuba's prophetic dream of disaster and the Regan's use of astrologers, and between the Greeks' rout of Troy and the My Lai Massacre. Bits of oddments added to the clippings help create artistic collages in this 79 page hardback.

Though this is a compelling book, it is not one for young children. Sex and violence play a large part in the story-line of the Trojan War. Fleischman's version is light on the former, but has plenty of graphic violence. The story of the Trojan War, however, is great for teaching world-view analysis. Your high school student can compare the worldviews of the Greeks, contemporary society, and the Bible. How does each of these define a hero? What does love mean? And, of course, what does each say about war and death? If you have a teen who has read the original and wrestled with these issues in advance, then he will find this a book which he can't put down. *Anne Wegener*

NEW!
Dateline: Troy
Grade 7–adult. $16.99 plus shipping.
Candlewick Press, 2067 Massachusetts Ave., Cambridge, MA 02140-1340.
(800) 788-6262. Fax: (201) 896-8569.

NEW!
G.A. Henty Series

Grade 7–adult. Each book, $19.99 (hardcover) or $13.99 (paperback). Shipping extra.
Preston Speed Publications, RR #4, Box 705, Mill Hall, PA 17751. (570) 726-7844. Fax: (570) 726-3547. *Web: www.prestonspeed.com*

Books so far in the series include:
- *The Dragon and The Raven (or The Days of King Alfred)*—a look at the battle between the Saxons and the Danes, set in 870 A.D.
- *For The Temple: A Tale of the Fall of Jerusalem*—based on Josephus' narrative
- *In Freedom's Cause: A Story of Wallace and Bruce*—The war for Scottish independence at the end of the 13th century is nothing like the recent movie *Braveheart*
- *By Pike and Dyke*—a late-Reformation era struggle, as discussed above
- *Beric The Briton: A Story of the Roman Invasion*—A time of great transformation for England during the later years of the Roman empire

Additional titles available: *A Knight of the White Cross: A Tale of the Siege of Rhodes, Wulf the Saxon: A Story of the Norman Conquest, The Cat of Bubastes: A Story of Ancient Egypt, Under Drake's Flag: A Tale of the Spanish Main, Saint Bartholomew's Eve: A Tale of the Huguenot Wars, By Right of Conquest: or with Cortez in Mexico, With Lee in Virgina: A Story of the American Civil War,* and *The Young Carthaginian: A Story of the Time's Hannibal.* Coming soon: *Winning His Spurs: A Tale of the Crusades, St George for England,* and *With Wolfe in Canada.* Preston Speed plans to release all of Henty's work at the speed of one volume every four to six weeks. Audio editions of some books will soon be available.

NEW!
Great Cities of the Ancient World

Grades 7–12. Individual videos, 29.95 each. Rome & Athens set, $59.95. Complete set, $79.95.
Questar Video, Inc., attn: John Robey, home education division, 680 N. Lake Shore Dr., Suite 900, Chicago, IL 60611-0345. Orders: (800) 544-8422. Inquiries: (312) 266-9400. Fax: (312) 266-9523. *Email: info@questar1.com. Web: www.questar1.com.*

What do Cindy Crawford, Dennis Rodman, and Arnold Schwarzenegger have in common? All three are 1990's-style American heroes. None have done anything particularly courageous or noble, but the P.R. each receives means that every exploit and project is told and sold with sledgehammer subtlety. If you find yourself looking at their names and sighing, "Celebrity has taken the place of character in our society. Where have all the heroes gone?" you're not alone.

Enter **G.A. Henty**, known in the last century as "The Boy's Own Historian." The prolific Mr. Henty wrote approximately 144 books, plus numerous magazine articles, all with the desire to make accurate history live in the hearts of his readers. Preston Speed Press, the brainchild of a homeschooling family, is lovingly reprinting these classic books in hardcover format, on acid-free paper. These books are meant to kept, and read, and re-read, and handed down to your grandchildren.

Each story uses the device of a fictional boy interacting with real-life historical figures. For instance, *By Pike and Dyke* introduces you to (the fictitious) Edward Martin, a young English sailor who becomes a part of the Dutch struggle for religious independence against Spain in the late 1500s. The text's 351 pages detail Edward's service to William of Orange, and to the cause. You'll watch Edward transformed from a boy into a selfless, courageous man, and you will learn about a period of history that you may not know much about in the process.

Henty is a stickler for detail, and an almost bottomless well of historical knowledge. (One exception can be found on page 6 of *For The Temple*: as part of a meal served to a visiting rabbi, "kid's flesh seethed in milk" was served. No self-respecting rabbi would have eaten this meal, which is specifically prohibited in Exodus 23:19.) That aside, these books are well worth your time. History texts can only outline events; Henty's action-packed narratives fill in the details. And in the process, they invite noble, courageous young heroes into your life. *Michelle Van Loon*

See buildings grow from ruins and dissolve back into ruins before your eyes! See clips from old movies about ancient civilizations! See illustrations, pottery, art, and clothing of ancient days! See all these woven together into the three videos about **Great Cities of the Ancient World**!

The first thing you need to know about this series is that it deserves a PG-13 rating, in my estimation. Christians being burned alive and a Roman actress being thrown off the stage (literally!) because, unlike the other actresses of the time, she refused to strip for the audience after her performance are among the vignettes on these tapes. (Although *that* actress refused to strip, we are shown a nude illustration of another Roman actress who had no such moral reservations.) I mention this because most home-school parents encourage the entire family to watch each educational video they purchase, not expecting scenes such as these.

The narration of these videos also is surprisingly un-family-like, considering their subject matter. When discussing the misbehavior of the ancients, which in itself is not usually the subject of a family video, the narrator expresses no moral censure. At times, it almost sounds like whoever wrote the script *approves* these practices. Yet certainly children are the normal audience for educational videos like there, aren't they?

The most impressive features of these videos is the way they recreate ancient buildings and cities through computer graphics. You'll see a modern city, building, or ruin, and then watch it transform slowly into its ancient counterpart. This was actually rather annoying to watch at times, as you'd think, "Surely this is the final picture at last," just to have yet another building or pillar or whatever appear in the picture. I also didn't see the real point of having to learn so many facts about relatively obscure temples and such, and who cares about what the hillsides or parking lots where they used to stand look like today? I would have been just as happy just to see the ancient world recreated, without any reference to the modern, except for famous ruins such as the Parthenon and Coliseum. I also would have preferred more emphasis on the truly important facts and less on the trivia.

The series includes: *The Pyramids and the Cities of the Pharaohs*, *Athens & Ancient Greece*, and *Rome & Pompeii*

I'd like to see more videos in this series—if the producers can manage to concentrate more on the educational and less on the sensational. *Mary Pride*

What in the blue blazes is a "histomap"? You're gonna love it when you find out! It's a full-color, vertical time line showing the story of civilization.

Unlike other time lines, though, the **Histomap of World History** shows the balance of power at each point in time by the width of the culture's "band" on the chart. See the rise and fall of Egypt's fortunes merely by observing how wide or narrow the pink "Egypt" band is at any time period. Important events in Egypt during that time are printed on its band, too.

Civilizations are presented side by side, so you can easily tell who was more powerful than whom, and what events occurred at the same time but in different places.

The Histomap opens to 11½ x 64" for wall display, and folds to 11 x 8½" if you haven't got that much wall to spare. *Mary Pride*

Usborne's new **Illustrated World History** series is an ambitious attempt to give teen readers an in-depth look at world history and civilizations. The series includes four volumes: *The Viking World*, *Early Civilization*, *The Greeks*, and *The Romans*.

Like other Usborne books, each book in this series is profusely illustrated, with text and illustrations skillfully interwoven to involve the reader. Books are 96 pages each, most in full color. The last 16 pages of each book are given over to black-and-white maps, glossaries, capsule myths and biographies, history outlines with chronological dates, and general indexes.

Each book contains a wealth of information about life in the ancient world—clothes, jewelry, houses, travel, learning, medicine, music, hairstyles, entertainment, and so on—as well as facts about military life and training, religion, the role of women, and other topics generally covered in textbooks.

The Romans is unfortunately unbalanced in its treatment of religion. Christianity, which ultimately conquered the Roman Empire and is of immense historical significance, was presented as one of the "alternatives to the state religion," of equal weight with Mithra-worship, and with a *smaller*

Rand McNally Histomap of World History
Grade 7–adult. $6.95 plus shipping. *Rand McNally & Company, 150 South Wacker Dr., Chicago, IL 60606. (800) 234-0679. Fax: (312) 443-9540. Web: www.randmcnallystore.com.*

Usborne Illustrated World History Series
Grades 7–12. The Viking World, 11.95 (paperbound) or $19.95 (library-bound). The Romans, The Greeks, and Early Civilization, $12.95 each (paperbound) or $20.95 each (library-bound). Usborne Illustrated World History Dates, $22.95 (paperbound) or $30.95 (library-bound). Shipping extra. *EDC Publishing, Division of Educational Development Corporation, 10302 East 55th Place, Tulsa, OK 74146. (800) 475-4522. Fax: (800) 747-4509. Web: www.edcpub.com.*

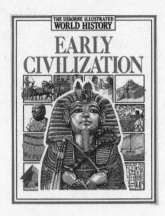

writeup than Cybele-worship. Christians' belief in the resurrection of Jesus—the central tenet of the Christian religion—was not even mentioned in the brief capsule description. Christianity is not brought up as a factor in Roman history until the rise of Constantine. Nor are the martyrs mentioned, except in seven words in this sentence about Constantine: "After his victory he granted tolerance to all religious groups, including Christians (who under Diocletian had been badly persecuted)."

The Romans also includes a totally unnecessary mention of contraceptive use in Roman times (under the heading "Childbirth"). **The Greeks** devotes part of one page, plus illustrations, to describing the custom of *hetairai*, a social class of girls brought up to be mistresses of wealthy men. There is a quite distressing picture of two wailing abandoned babies, and another of a wife holding her newborn baby and arguing with her husband about being allowed to keep it. Yes, these things did happen, as did a lot of other nastiness *not* mentioned, but I question the value of filling kids' minds with it. If you can leave out descriptions and illustrations of Nero's sex life, temple prostitution, and ritual religious torture, you can leave out this other stuff.

There is no criticism of human sacrifice or totalitarian statism, either. Sample quote: "The Scythians were a very wealthy people. Their graves were filled with rich goods, along with human and horse sacrifices." End of quote. Similarly, in **The Viking World**, the custom of killing a servant girl when her master died is mentioned with no moral judgment at all. I don't know about you, but this value-free nonchalance about human life gives me the creeps.

World History Dates, as its name suggests, is big on dates. History is presented in chronological sequence. Side-by-side lists of dates and events show what was happening in different places at the same time: Southern/Western Europe, Northern/Eastern Europe, Africa and the Middle East, Asia, and The Americas. Frequent sidebars present important historical events and cultural features. You'll find, for example, capsule writeups on monasticism and feudalism. Especially important dates are pulled out and highlighted in a separate sidebar of their own. Again, Christianity is slighted. Consider this synopsis of Christianity:

> *Christianity was founded in Palestine by Jesus of Nazareth (c. 5BC–AD29), later known as Jesus Christ. He was arrested and crucified for his teachings. After his death, the faith was spread by his followers . . .*

Bottom line: The Viking volume is usable, and relatively few books cover this subject with anywhere near Usborne's visual depth. However, many other publishers manage to offer books on ancient civilizations, the Greeks, and the Romans without being blatantly offensive to Christians, or dragging in inappropriate sexual topics, or rubbing kids' noses in the pain and suffering of innocents. If Usborne hopes to sell a lot of these volume to homeschoolers, a new edition is needed. *Mary Pride*

World History Fact Books

Once again, the publisher says, "Grades 5 and up," and we say, "Junior High and up." The **History of Everyday Things** series' vocabulary level and text density, not to mention the tiny type used to describe the "everyday things," makes this a definite teen-and-up book.

Far less illustrated than other Bedrick books, this series covers "the everyday things people used at different periods in history." This means this unique series helps you "fill in the blanks" so you can visualize what life was *really* like back then, as opposed to history series which mainly talk about famous people and wars. Chapters are four pages longer, rather

NEW!
Bedrick History of Everyday Things series
Grades 7–12. $10.95 each paperback, $18.95 hardcover. Shipping extra.
Peter Bedrick Books, c/o NTC Contemporary Publishing, 4255 W. Touhy, Lincolnwood, IL 60646.
(800) 323-4900. Fax: (800) 998-3103.

than the usual double-page spreads. In most cases, text fills one column of the left-hand page, while colored drawings of "everyday things," including people in a variety of costumes and activities, fill the second column, as well as the entire right-hand page, of each spread.

There's a lot of reading in each of these books: about eight times as much text as a typical double-page-spread book. Literally hundreds of objects are introduced in each book, as well as a wealth of historic and cultural information. If your student can remember it all, or even a significant amount, he'll have learned a *lot. Mary Pride*

The publisher recommends these lavishly-illustrated oversized history books for grades 5 and up, but Bill and I think they'd be most useful at the junior-high level. Using the two-page-spread format, and replete with illustrations, photographs, diagrams, charts, graphs, and "timecharts" (timelines in chart format), each volume in the **Bedrick Timelink series** is designed to "give young readers an overall view of different peoples and their histories, and the links between states and civilizations across the globe," during the historical period it covers.

Believing as I do in the importance of getting the "big picture" of history, this series is a real find! Beautifully presented, and logically organized, it manages to introduce hundreds of historical figures, events, and customs in a memorable fashion. Best of all, the writing is even-handed, with no obvious ideological axes to grind.

The Time Link series includes:

- *The Age of Discovery*
- *The Modern World* (just a touch of "Saving the Planet" and one-world-governmentism at the end)

This is a great introduction to world history, and a painless review for college-entrance world history achievement tests, too! *Mary Pride*

This project, edited by John Clare, is an example of a series which the publisher recommends for younger ages, but we believe is best for junior high and up. The reason: **Harcourt Brace Living History series**' reading vocabulary level includes phrases such as "The early inventions

used what is called intermediate technology," and it features some true, but unpleasant, facts of history that we think are best saved for older children. Eight-year-olds don't really benefit from hearing the tale of a boy who had his ear nailed to his workbench for working too slow, for example.

With that in mind, what we have here is yet another double-page-spread series. What makes the Living History series different is that instead of drawings, photographs are employed. Most are of models in dramatic "historical reenactment" scenes and poses, with a number of "everyday objects" of the past added in. This lends a feeling of verisimilitude to the books, making

NEW!
Bedrick Timelink series
Grades 7–12. $18.95 each. Shipping extra.
Peter Bedrick Books, c/o NTC Contemporary Publishing, 4255 W. Touhy, Lincolnwood, IL 60646. (800) 323-4900. Fax: (800) 998-3103.

NEW!
Harcourt Brace Living History series
Grades 7–12. Paperback, $9–10 each plus shipping.
Harcourt Brace, 6277 Sea Harbor Dr., Orlando, FL 32887. (800) 543-1918. Fax: (800) 235-0256. Web: www.harcourtbrace.com.

you feel "you are there." See a Greek funeral procession, or Antony and Cleopatra presenting their children to the Egyptian people! Along with the history, you also find out about everyday life in the time periods studied.

Many ancient civilizations were free with nudity in their art. The books include some of these art examples. You will find a Grecian vase with nude men in the form of line-art drawings of Olympic athletes, for example, as well as a couple of pretty graphic male statuettes. However, the posed reenactments are always modest, and you don't get the feeling the nudity is being shoved in your face, as with some other recently-published books for kids.

Series titles include: *Ancient Greece, Classical Rome, Industrial Revolution, Pyramids of Ancient Egypt, Knights in Armor, The Vikings, The Italian Renaissance, Fourteenth-Century Towns,* and *First World War.*

The books we received were fun to read, informative, and memorable. I really like this series. *Mary Pride*

NEW!
Oxford University Press: The Ancient City

Grades 6–12. $32.95 plus shipping.
Oxford University Press, 2001 Evans Rd., Cary, NC 27513. (800) 451-7556. Fax: (919) 677-1303. Web: www.oup-usa.org.

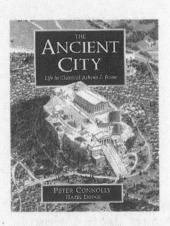

The next best thing to traveling back in time, **The Ancient City: Life in Classical Athens and Rome** will transport you figuratively to the streets of ancient Athens and Rome. Peter Connolly, a respected British classicist, recreates the golden years of both ancient Greece and Rome through superb drawings, engaging maps, reproductions of art, fantastic photos and fascinating text. In this hefty 256-page hardback you will visit public and private buildings and catch a glimpse of the lives lived in them.

The first nine chapters explore Athens, "the shining star of the classical world." Early chapters give a historical summary and explain how the world's first democracy worked . . . which was quite different from ours! The Athenians designed their system first and foremost to limit power and eliminate corruption. If they thought someone was growing too ambitious or powerful, he might be banished for ten years! An intimate look at daily life follows, including birth (unwanted babies were exposed to die—consider if your child is ready to handle this topic), childhood, school, weddings, work and the architecture and function of a typical home. Temples and theater receive ample attention as well.

In the second part of the book, "Rome," Connolly covers similar topics, but he also devotes space to uniquely Roman places such as the baths, the colosseum, the Circus Maximus and Domitian's palace. He helps you see these places by using full-color drawings of reconstructed buildings, floor plans and photographs of the buildings today.

Cautionary note: the Greeks liked to decorate their pottery with nudes, and some examples are included among the illustrations.

This is a marvelous reference book for older students which far exceeds most available for young people today. It is extremely detailed yet non-intimidating, and is so appealing that you may easily spend several hours pouring over it out of sheer enjoyment. *Ancient City* would be an excellent addition to any serious study of ancient Greece or Rome! *Anne Wegener*

NEW!
Usborne Book of Europe

Grades 5–12. $9.95 plus shipping.
EDC Publishing, Division of Educational Development Corporation, 10302 East 55th Place, Tulsa, OK 74146. (800) 475-4522. Fax: (800) 747-4509. Web: www.edcpub.com.

The **Usborne Book of Europe** is big, for an Usborne book. Sixty-four pages introduce you to European history, and a little European politics and culture. It begins with a bit of evolutionary geology and conjecture about Stone Age Europeans. From there on, it proceeds in more-or-less chronological order, to cover Greece, Rome, the Christian church, the Middle Ages, the Renaissance, the Age of Exploration, the Age of Kings, Revolution and Nationalism in France, Industry and Empire, The First World War, Marx/Lenin/Stalin, The Rise of

Fascism, The Second World War, The Cold War, The European Community, Living in the EC, and The Breakup of the Soviet Bloc. Next it switches to a brief cultural history, with sections on education, architecture, and science. Rounding out this highly illustrated volume are a two-page political map of Europe, a chart of statistics by country, a chart of important European historical dates, a glossary, and an index.

This book is enough to whet your appetite, but not enough to really satisfy it. After all, how much can you say about this many different countries in only 64 pages? As a summary of European history, it's OK, but it made me realize that Usborne is missing a really detailed world history series. What is needed is an era-by-era series, with entire books devoted to the Renaissance, the Reformation, the Enlightenment, the French Revolution and Napoleon, and so forth. It also made me wish that Usborne had a series on European countries, or for that matter *all* countries of the world, with an entire 32-page book devoted to each country. *Mary Pride*

Extraordinary courage and ingenuity in extreme circumstances. That's what these highly illustrated true-life stories in **Usborne Real Tales** are about. From British housewife Odette, who was finally released after she was captured and sentenced to death as a spy in Nazi Germany, to the rescue of the Apollo 13 mission crew, here are dozens of true stories, written in taut journalistic style and attractively illustrated with maps, photos, and other embellishments.

People profiled come from all over the world, and from different decades as well (most from the 20th century). Many famous people and events make it into these books. For example, the *Escapes* book includes among its 13 tales the escapes of Winston Churchill from a Boer War camp, Mussolini from mountaintop imprisonment, and Harriet Tubman's thrilling rescues of Southern slaves.

As you can see, it's not always "good guys" who are featured. Soviet master spies' escapes are told with the same zest as Allied prisoners' escapes from Nazi interment. The focus here is really on the escape, survival, heroism, or adventure, not on the morality or politics of the protagonist. The books are not amoral, however. If a French convict was evil, or a spy was a traitor, those words are used.

But you get more than thrilling true stories. The *Survival* book ends with detailed survival tips, and includes important information on how one man (Dr. Alain Bombard) proved that castaways can survive for long periods on the open sea by drinking limited amounts of sea water, fishing, catching rain water, and seining for plankton. The *Escapes* book provides information that could be helpful if you're ever in a prisoner-of-war or hostage situation. All four books provide eloquent testimony to the creativity and durability of the human spirit—something worth remembering in a day and age when political and social theorists preach that men are simply overbright animals. Finally, you can pick up a lot of history here, from details of the French prison colony system to the briefest, most balanced treatment I've yet seen of slavery and the Underground Railroad.

Some of the books end with brief reviews of films you can rent from your video store that are based on the stories covered in the book. All end with several pages of "what happened next?" vignettes, telling you what became of the people in the stories *after* their adventures were over.

NEW!
Usborne Real Tales series
Grades 7–12. $7.95 each. Shipping extra.
EDC Publishing, Division of Educational Development Corporation, 10302 East 55th Place, Tulsa, OK 74146. (800) 475-4522.
Fax: (800) 747-4509.
Web: www.edcpub.com.

The series currently includes

- *Tales of Real Adventure*
- *Tales of Real Heroism*
- *Tales of Real Escapes*
- *Tales of Real Survival*
- *Tales of Real Haunting* (This one you can skip)

Fascinating multicultural historical reading. *Mary Pride*

NEW!
Usborne's The Twentieth Century

Grades 7–12. $10.95 each. Shipping extra.

EDC Publishing, Division of Educational Development Corporation, 10302 East 55th Place, Tulsa, OK 74146. (800) 475-4522.
Fax: (800) 747-4509.
Web: www.edcpub.com.

Inventions. People. Cultural history. Political history. The environment. Technology. Music. Transportation. Medicine. Wars. The Great Depression. Computers and robots. Not in that order. China and Japan. The Middle East. Asia. Africa. Latin America. The United States. The European Community. Dozens of illustrations, two-page-spread format. A glossary, a Who's Who, a "date chart" (a timeline with no lines), and an index. Lots of information in Usborne's **The Twentieth Century**, in a book that tries to pack as much as possible (both visual and textual) into a handy 96-page size.

You won't find any criticism here of Roosevelt and Churchill handing Eastern Europe over to Stalin's tender mercies, or of the Chinese government's "One Family, One Child" program (which includes forced abortions). You will find an illustration of the Chinese government's promotional poster for that program, along with text addressing overpopulation as a major problem. You'll also find some not-so-subtle promotion of world government and other politically correct movements. And with less than 100 people's biographies in the "Who's Who" section, why are Muhammed Ali, Greta Garbo, Coco Chanel, James Brown, and Fred Astaire listed? *Mary Pride*

Chapter 33

Logic & Philosophy

I t's possible to have an illogical philosophy, but I don't recommend it. Logic is to philosophy what supporting beams are to a house; without the support of logic, philosophy degenerates into emotional opinions, and persuasion degenerates into force.

So, who needs philosophy? Everyone! We all have a philosophy, whether we know it or not. Today, the unexamined life is the one we all seem to be leading, and none more prominently than our most prominent leaders. All the more reason to get a grip on wisdom, lest the world get too strong a grip on us.

Logic & Thinking Skills

Introductory Logic for Christian Schools (spiral-bound, 93 pages) is just what the doctor ordered! At last there's an easy-to-use, sequential, even (dare I say it?) logical course on logic for Christian high schoolers. What makes it Christian? Christian vocabulary (statements about Bible characters and doctrinal positions), examples showing the logical fallacies in popular arguments against Christianity, and a lively yet serious tone.

Introductory Logic starts right at the beginning. Students learn to distinguish between true statements, false statements, commands, questions, and nonsense sentences such as, "The round square furiously kicked the green yellowish." From this sound beginning students move on to supported statements and relationships between statements (consistency, implication, logical equivalence, or independence). Next, they learn to translate all statements into sentences using "is." "Paul rebuked Peter at Antioch" becomes "Paul is an Antiochan Peter-rebuker." The reason for mastering this dreadful grammar becomes clear when the text moves on to arguments. Here your student will be learning about premises, conclusions, universals, particulars, abbreviated statements, and a host of other vital logic terms, all of which in this text are simplified into some form of "all/some/many/few A is B." This enables students to make quick work of tough concepts like subimplication, superimplication, syllogisms, and the like. Kids also learn to detect logical fallacies, diagram arguments, and use propositional and symbolic logic.

When I first reviewed this program several years ago, I wished for an answer key. My wish has been granted. For just $4 plus shipping you can have

Logic means "the science of words." It's from the Greek word *logos*, meaning *word* or *discourse*.

Philosophy means "love of wisdom." It's also from the Greek. *Phileo* means *brotherly love* and *sophia* means *wisdom*

Now, guess what nationality invented the sciences of logic and philosophy!

NEW!
Canon Press Introductory Logic

Workbook, $15. Answer key, $4
Shipping extra.
Canon Press, Community Evangelical Fellowship, PO Box 8741, Moscow, ID 83843. (800) 488-2034. Fax: (208) 882-1568.
Email: canorder@moscow.com.
Web: www.canonpress.org.

answers to all the exercises in *Introductory Logic*. This makes the course much more usable. With the answer key and the course's excellent step-by-step layout, adults who have never studied formal logic can easily teach this course to their children. By working your way through one full lesson every other week, you will have covered the entire course in a year. By year's end you and your student will have mastered the vocabulary of logic, and should be able to detect logical errors in the wink of an eye. *Mary Pride*

The four-book **A Case of Red Herrings** series (A-1, A-2, B-1, & B-2) is about "solving mysteries through critical thinking." You may imagine this is what Nero Wolfe and Archie Goodwin do. Actually, these books are full of a type of mind game I used to play when I was a teenager.

You may remember this one: "He was found dead in a room with 53 bicycles." You were supposed to ask questions until you discovered that the "53 bicycles" were Bicycle brand cards. Knowing that a deck of cards has 52 cards, you would then conclude he'd been caught cheating at cards and someone shot him.

Here's one from book A-1:

> *When asked what he wanted to do when he grew up, Igor replied, "I want to shoot people and blow them up." His parents were very pleased with his career choice. How can that be?*

If that flummoxed you, the answer's in the back of the A-1 book. Instructions on how to go about solving these mysteries are also included. Does this really sharpen thinking skills? I believe so, from my own experience of spending hours at this exact kind of puzzle. But thinking skills aren't exactly the same thing as intelligence. Look at me, sitting here writing this review, when intelligent people are asleep in bed. *Mary Pride*

If your student likes puzzles, **Creative Problem Solving Activities** is just the series to develop a good problem solver. Each of the three books in this series contains seven different challenging categories of activities to keep your child interested and learning. Choose from:

- Word Morphs—change one letter of a word to make a new word.
- DooRiddles—are riddles made up of phrases and sentences that contain clues to the answer of the riddle.
- Codeword clusters—words written in code with the code being used throughout that activity.
- Secret Word Puzzles—lists words with numbers after them. You compare and take out letters and finally form one real word.
- Telephone Code Puzzles—lists a category and a sequence of numbers to match to the telephone keypad.
- Shape puzzles—use shapes and information that you need to fill in to generate an answer that does not contradict any of the clues.
- Line Puzzles—figure out from the facts where individuals fall in line.

The content of each book gets progressively more difficult as you go through the series. Choose the book that is not too difficult so you do not frustrate your student. Do all the puzzles in order or hop around doing one type each day. The number of puzzles in each category varies from one book to the next.

Depending on how you use the books, they could last you from two years to just one month. This is a very good supplement to any curriculum. *Lynn Smith*

A source for logic puzzle magazines and books galore. **Dell Magazines** offers:

- *Dell: The Best of Logic Puzzles,* each volume 80 pages of puzzles ranging from easy to expert.
- *Dell Variety Puzzle Spectacular,* 128 pages of cross sums, crosswords, and other variety logic puzzles
- *Best of Math Puzzles and Logic Problems,* 96 pages in size
- *Puzzler's Choice Logic Problem,* over 100 of grid logic puzzles, with solving charts and detailed solutions

Some combo packs are also available at discount prices. *Mary Pride*

It's a kit. It comes in a flip-top box. It includes *Edward de Bono's Thinking for Action,* a 96-page oversized illustrated quality paperback, and all the gameboards, cards, dice, and playing pieces necessary to play all the games in the book. It's Dorling-Kindersley' **Edward de Bono's Super Mind Pack!**

"Learn how to focus your mind and get things done." That's what it says on the cover of the book. The "focus your mind" part leads to activities designed to teach you how to invent patterns for dealing with real-world situations. The "get things done" part takes us into the dreaded world of social skills. This is the part that every other logic and thinking curriculum leaves out. So let's talk about it for a minute.

Those who revel in the pursuit of logic are not normally known for their social skills. The Mr. Spocks of fictional alien worlds (and this world, too) tend to be solitary geniuses, at their best when annoying lower life-forms such as other people are not interrupting their lofty thinking process. Here is where de Bono had his breakthrough. He reasoned,

> *Unfortunately, THINKING for DOING is a messy business. You have to consider other people. You have to have plans and strategies. There are times when you work cooperatively and times when you are forced to be competitive. There may be a need for negotiation.*

So this thinking-skills book entitles its first chapter "Other People." You move right along to chapters on negotiation, guessing, risk and anticipation, planning, resource allocation and trade-off (a topic our free-spending politicians seem to have difficulty grasping), communication, value creation (mostly about economic value), information, possibilities, and cooperation.

Each chapter includes games—14 in all—that can be played with variations, yielding 30 total games. Mostly these are extremely simple simulations of real-world activities. So you get the Clash Game (competition), Communication Game, Negotiation Game, Testing Game, Golf Game, Tennis Game, Driving Game, Soccer Game, Investment Game, Ecology Game, Business Game, Cooperation Game, Information Game, and World-Planning Game. The "sports" games mainly involve planning future actions based on luck and your opponent's actions; a tennis lob or a soccer field position is determined by the throw of the dice.

De Bono is not a proponent of eternal revelation and fixed values, although his presentation allows for the reader to have such values—or not. As long as you're aware of this, and of the fact that fixed beliefs don't always allow trade-offs and negotiations, you should find this "super mind pack" a fascinating exploration. *Mary Pride*

NEW!
Logic by Gordon Clark

Grade 11–college. Paperback, $10.95. Hardback, $16.95. Workbook, $11.95. Answer Key, $2.95. 18-lecture cassette course, $45. Shipping extra.
Trinity Foundation, PO Box 68, Unicoi, TN 37692. (423) 743-0199. Fax: (423) 743-2005. Email: jrob1517@aol.com. Web: www.trinityfoundation.org.

Based on the late Dr. Gordon Clark's college classes, this detailed course (148-page paperback) is best suited to upper high school and college students. It covers not only "argument" logic but formal logic, the history of logic, and symbolic logic at a college level, including Boolean logic and truth tables.

Logic is logically laid out and covers a lot of ground: unfortunately, not in the most organized way. The student is expected to already know, for example, that NaCl is table salt and how to prove the theorem that in an isosceles triangle the angles opposite the equal sides are equal. Information is densely packed and unformatted. It gets better towards the end, but this is a textbook that needs multiple readings

The new **Logic Workbook** (140 oversized pages) and Answer Key (24 oversized pages) add tremendously to the value of this course. For each chapter of the textbook, *Logic Workbook* (1) outlines the chapter, (2) provides a list of terms for the student to define after having read the chapter, (3) provides principles, definitions, and abbreviations, (4) presents a fill-in-the-blanks quiz using the new principles and vocabulary, and (5) gives the student logic examples to work out. The back of the workbook includes chapter tests, followed by quotes from great Christian leaders of the past on the value of studying logic. All the answers to the workbook exercises and tests are found in the answer key. The **cassette course** is designed to accompany the text and workbook.

If you could stand paying as much as $50 total, I would suggest you put your students through *both* the Canon Press logic course and Dr. Clark's logic course. For less than the price of one college credit, you will mightily enlarge their thinking, reasoning, and leadership abilities. (Bonus angle: you might be able to take a college equivalency test and get college credit for your logic courses, too! Save hundreds of $$!) Just make sure you tackle the Canon Press course first. *Mary Pride*

Mind Benders series

Grade K–adult. $7.95 each. Instructions and Detailed Solutions, $10.95. Complete set, $89.95. Shipping extra.
Critical Thinking Books & Software, PO Box 448, Pacific Grove, CA 93950-0448. (800) 458-4849. Fax: (831) 323-3277. Email: ct@criticalthinking.com. Web: www.criticalthinking.com.

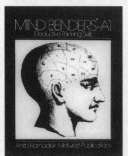

Mind Benders is a series of 12 workbooks featuring deductive thinking skills. Readers are asked to work with sets of clues to reach a logical conclusion. You might want to invest in the *Mind Benders Instructions and Detailed Solutions* for this series. Books are labeled A-1 through A-4, B-1 through B-4, and C-1 through C-3. Novices should begin with the first series book, *Warm-Up Mind Benders*. Mind Benders sets A through C are also available as Macintosh or IBM software (about $60).

This is just one part of Critical Thinking's more than 100-book line. What about Brain Stretchers (two books), Classroom Quickies (three books), and more? *Mary Pride*

Penny Marketing Logic Products

Grade 7–adult. Value Packs, $8.45/7 issues, $15.95/14 issues. Subscriptions: Original Logic Problems, $24.95/9 issues; England's Finest Logic Problems, $11.47/6 issues; World-Class Logic Problems, $9.77/4 issues. Shipping extra.
Penny Marketing, 6 Prowitt Street, Norwalk, CT 06855-1220.

I owe this entry to my mother-in-law, Mrs. Betty Pride. She came to visit us while I was revising the last edition of *Big Book*, and brought along an issue of *Original Logic Problems*, a bimonthly **puzzle magazine from Penny Press.** This magazine has some awesome matrix logic puzzles (if you have to ask what those are, see the Quizzles review on the next page), and Bill and I sat up late one night figuring one of them out. The Penny Marketing lineup includes *Approved Crosswords, Classic Crosswords, Family Crosswords, Merit Variety Plus,* and *Variety Puzzles and Games.* They publish 34 different puzzle magazines including three logic magazines: *Original Logic Problems, England's Finest Logic Problems,* and *World-Class Logic Problems.* Their logic magazines only comes out bimonthly, probably because it takes that long to come up with 45 of these super brain-stretchers in every issue!

For those who like to sample first, Penny Press's Logic Problems Value Pack includes an assortment of seven different Logic Problems magazines—including *Original Logic Problems, England's Finest Logic Problems,* and *World-Class Logic Problems* —for $6.95 plus $1.50 shipping. *Mary Pride*

"You're the detective when you solve . . . **Quizzles**!" Two books with matrix-logic puzzles for seventh-graders and up. Matrix-logic puzzles are this sort of thing:

> Jane, Sue, and Bob each found a job.
> Bob was not the baker.
> The dishwasher was a girl.
> The restaurant needed a dishwasher and a counter manager.
> Jane hated to wash dishes but loved to bake.

I just made that puzzle up, which is why it is so easy to solve! Typically, matrix-logic puzzles come with both the verbal clues and a grid labeled on both sides. In our example above, you'd have a 3 x 3 grid with "Jane," "Sue," and "Bob" across the top and "Dishwasher," "Baker," and "Counter Manager" down the side. You can use the grid to zero in on the answers. For example, since we know Bob is *not* the baker, you could put an "N" in the square for "Bob" and "Baker." We also know Bob is not the dishwasher, since the dishwasher is a girl, so put an "N" in the "Bob" and "Dishwasher" square. That means Bob *must* be the counter manager . . . which means neither girl can be the counter manager . . . and so it goes until you figure the whole puzzle out!

Dale Seymour throws in an extra, though—step by step solutions, so you aren't left wondering how to find out the answers. Lots of fun for teens and their parents! *Mary Pride*

Think-A-Grams are beaucoodles of fun! These oversized books each include 100 visual riddles, plus an answer key. For example: MILL1ON. The answer? "One in a million!" Or try this one:

IN
MY HEAD

"In over my head." Get it?

Great rainy-day activities that really do develop mental sharpness. The series includes three "A"-level books (the easiest level), three "B"-level books, and three "C"-level books (the hardest level). Recommended. *Mary Pride*

Traditional Logic is, just as the brochure says, a systematic course in formal logic, not a sampling of logic topics. That should be "systematic" with a capital "S."

The first three of its 14 chapters are devoted to defining terms such as *simple apprehension, comprehension,* and *extension.* Using these terms, you come to grips with the fact that *truth* and *validity* are two different things, and that you have to know what exactly you're talking about before you can decide if it's logical or not.

The next six chapters of this comb-bound text deal with "judgements" (yes, the word is misspelled this way throughout the entire book). Judgments are assertions about terms. "Chair" is a term. "The chair is brown" is a judgment.

The last three chapters have to do with "deductive inferences" which when written become "syllogisms." These are what everyone thinks of when they think of traditional logic.

> All men are mortal.
> Socrates is a man.
> Therefore Socrates is mortal.

The rest of the text is devoted to defining which forms of syllogisms are valid and which are not.

Each chapter has four days of exercises associated with it. These include your reading assignment, plus questions to answer, charts and diagrams to fill in, and so on. You have to write these on separate paper, since there is no room for most of these answers in the book itself. The answer key contains all the answers for the exercises and you need this key to teach this course.

This is the best exposition of Aristotelian logic I have yet seen aimed at homeschoolers. Easier to follow than Gordon Clark's *Logic* text, more comprehensive (though less mathematical) than Canon Press's *Introductory Logic,* and easy on the eyes with its wide margins and visual diagrams, this course deserves a place in many homeschools.

One unfortunate error: repeated throughout the entire course, in different forms, is the statement *Man is an animal.* As Christians know, this is not correct. Man shares some characteristics with the animals, but he also shares some characteristics with God and the angels. Man is not God, nor an angel, therefore man is also not an animal.

While this is a very thorough and organized course, the exercises seem to be mostly rote echoing back what the student read for the lesson. This text could profit from a larger proportion of the questions requiring the student to think creatively about the material presented, for example creating his own valid and invalid syllogisms. These would be harder to correct using an answer key, but would be of more lasting value for the student. I suggest you create some exercises of this type if you choose to use this text. *Mary Pride*

NEW!
Thirty Second Mysteries

Grade 7–adult. $29.95 plus shipping.
University Games, 1633 Adrian Rd., Burlingame, CA 94010. (800) 347-4818. Fax: (650) 692-2770. Web: www.areyougame.com.

All you need to know about the **30 Second Mysteries** game is (1) it's fun, (2) it's addictive, (3) it encourages creative thinking, and (4) they should sell add-on packs.

What you get are 144 puzzles, like this one on the box: "A group of famous people are always together, even though some have never even met each other. What's more, although outsiders have seen them together, if you could talk to some members of the group, they wouldn't even be aware of the rest of the group's existence." You and your opponent take turns sliding the question card up the card holder. This reveals a different clue to each of you, assuming you are sitting as you should on opposite sides of the card holder. You can also ask each other one question at a time. For example, the first clue here is, "There are four men in the group." If you haven't already figured out that the answer is, "Mount Rushmore," you could ask, "Did they all play team sports?" Your opponent, based on the information available to him, could answer truthfully or say, "I don't know." All this must be done while an enclosed egg-timer is running out its 30 seconds of white sand.

The game requires a peculiar kind of thinking: forming hypotheses and testing them. This is known as "the scientific method." It also requires you *not* to assume too much. For example, if you assumed above that the men were all alive, you would come up with the wrong answer. Listing your assumptions, and discarding those not borne out by the question's information, is known as "the engineering method."

What a great game. I just wish there was some way to get more question cards once you've solved all the original puzzles. *Mary Pride*

"True For You, But Not For Me": Deflating the Slogans that Leave Christians Speechless by Paul Copan is an excellent addition to any Christian's library. This book helps you see past the public's objectable comments on Christianity. It is a must-read for anyone trying to defend the faith against relativists.

So many in today's culture believe that everything is relative. Say what? Exactly. Copan breaks his book out into five parts: Absolutely Relative; The Absolutism of Moral Relativism; The Exclusivism of Religious Pluralism; The Uniqueness of Jesus Christ, Myth or Reality?; and No Other Name: The Question of the Unevangelized. Each part is again broken down into three to six chapters. Each chapter deals with a different aspect of the main topic.

Copan does not just tell us what to say to someone who tosses out one of those sayings. He explains why that someone believes what they said and then he explains why they are in error. Each chapter ends with a summary of what has been discussed. The chapters are fairly short and would be quick reading if it wasn't for some of the confusing terminology. Once you understand the basic terminology, most of the confusion dissipates.

This is a great book to read to understand why some people think the way they do about Christianity, but it also can leave you feeling a little confused. Some of what he says is best left for those who love to discuss philosophy on a higher plateau than I can manage. *Barbara Buchanan*

Philosophy

Trinity Foundation has republished this comprehensive 529-page study of philosophy, by Gordon Clark, who received his doctorate in philosophy in 1929. Dr. Clark was a well-respected philosopher, professor, and writer during his lifetime, and this volume brings his fine work to a new generation. Dr. Clark's writing style is clear and logical, bringing clarity to his complex subject matter.

Ancient Philosophy covers early philosophy, from the Pre-Socratics through the Greeks, including Pythagoras, Heraclitus, Plato, and Aristotle. Both well-known and more obscure

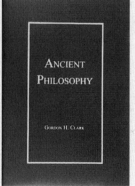

philosophers are carefully introduced and placed in historical context. The reliability of the various source documents is also examined. Dr. Clark uses excerpts from the philosophers' writings, and his own clear explanations to bring these ancient ideas to life. He shows how these ideas developed, how they relate to each other, and their impact on subsequent ages.

Ancient Philosophy is an excellent introduction to important philosophers and their ideas. For the serious high-school or college student, this well-written book provides plenty of food for thought. *Kristen Hernberg*

NEW!
Knowledge Products Giants of Philosophy series

Grade 9–adult. Complete series, $194 postpaid. Individual two-tape sets, $17.95 plus $3 shipping. *Knowledge Products, 722 Rundle Ave., Suite A-13, Nashville, TN 37210. Orders: (800) 876-4332. Inquiries: (615) 742-3852. Fax: (615) 742-3270.*

Narrated in authoritative style by Charlton Heston, the 13-part **Giants of Philosophy** audiocassette series discusses works of philosophy and the men behind them. Written by a professor of philosophy, the narrations include a biography of each philosopher which places his work in its historical context, followed by a good chunk of his major work(s), with commentary and explanations. It's all done very objectively, presenting each philosopher's main points, how he contrasts with other philosophers, and how much of a difference his philosophy made, but no comment on whether the philosophy was right or wrong. This objective approach makes the series usable by just about anyone.

Each two-tape set comes in a handy small binder, with a short introduction to the philosopher on the jacket, and includes between 2½ to 3 hours of listening. You can purchase the entire series at once, or do it the easy way, one set per month billed to your credit card. This amount of listening is easy to get through as you drive around in the car—which is the way I do it.

The series includes:

- *Plato* (c. 430–350 B.C.) Greece
- *Aristotle* (384–322 B.C.) Greece
- *St. Augustine* (354–430 A.D.) Rome
- *St. Thomas Aquinas* (1224–1274) Italy
- *Baruch Spinoza* (1632–1677) The Netherlands
- *David Hume* (1711–1776) Scotland
- *Immanuel Kant* (1724–1804) Germany
- *Georg Wilhelm Friedrich Hegel* (1770–1831) Germany
- *Arthur Schopenhauer* (1788–1860) Germany
- *Soren Kierkegaard* (1813–1855) Denmark
- *Friedrich Nietzsche* (1844–1900) Germany
- *John Dewey* (1859–1952) The United States
- *Jean-Paul Sartre* (1905–1980) France

I have found all the tapes very enjoyable and informative, even the tapes about philosophers I dislike. Recommended. *Bill Pride*

NEW!
Knowledge Products Religion, Scriptures & Spirituality series

Grade 9–adult. Complete series, $194 postpaid. Individual two-tape sets, $17.95 plus $3 shipping. *Knowledge Products, 722 Rundle Ave., Suite A-13, Nashville, TN 37210. Orders: (800) 876-4332. Inquiries: (615) 742-3852. Fax: (615) 742-3270.*

Narrated by Ben Kingsley, the 13-part **Religion, Scriptures, and Spirituality** audiocassette series discusses the origin and practice of several of the world's major religions. The series includes:

- *Orthodox and Roman Catholic Christianity*
- *Protestant Christianity*
- *Judaism*
- *Islam*
- *Hinduism*
- *Buddhism*
- *Shinto and Japanese New Religions*
- *Confucianism and Taoism*
- *The Religion of Small Societies*
- *Classical Religions and Myths of the Mediterranean Basin*
- *African and African-American Religion*
- *Native Religions of the Americas*
- *Skepticism & Religious Relativism*

The series labors mightily to present each and every religion in the best possible light, with the unspoken message that all faiths are equally valid and true. Biblical Christians may find some segments grate. Others that concentrate mainly on presenting the histories or outlining the beliefs of the various groups are interesting and educational. *Mary Pride*

Philosophy based on logic beats philosophy based on political theories any day of the week. The popular college text **Questions That Matter** deserves kudos for taking the logical route. After defining philosophy in four different ways, the book presents a mini-course in logical reasoning, before delving into a historical presentation of philosophy, grouped around the "questions that matter," such as, "What is justice?" The other questions introduced in this book are

- What is reality?
- What is knowledge?
- Is there a God, and if so, who or what is he?
- What is morality?
- What is the purpose of society?

Each of these questions is subdivided into others. For example, the question of Society, after a historical introduction, is broken down into liberalism v. Marxism and the question of justice.

Each chapter ends with a summary, a list of basic ideas covered in that chapter, a Test Yourself section that asks you to recall the facts presented in the chapter (with no answers provided—if you don't know the answers, reread the chapter), Questions for Reflection (your chance to try your hand at a little philosophy), and suggestions for further reading. A number of source readings are included in each chapter, which is very nice and saves a lot of time.

Happily this book does not obsess over modern fads. The behaviorism of B. F. Skinner is the last reading in the book. What you have here is a fair-minded presentation of classic philosophy as it has traditionally been taught—clear enough for a high-school student, broad enough for a college course. Recommended. *Mary Pride*

You told yourself you would read the Great Books someday. You know you ought to. You know your older children should read the seminal books upon which Western civilization is built. But . . . (1) You tried it once and got lost in the old-fashioned language and strange terminology. (2) You once suffered through a class in Western Civ or Philosophy that just confused you. (3) You can't afford to go back to college and pay $10,000 for a two-semester nine-credit course covering everything you missed.

Part of the SuperStar Teachers Series, **The Great Minds of the Western Intellectual Tradition** is a series of 70 lessons. Starring college professors who have received accolades for their classroom performance, this series can help you. In one sense it is pricey, but in another sense, it's a bargain. You get all the college lectures at about one-twentieth the price and you don't have to do any outside reading or write any papers unless you feel like it.

The Great Minds of the Western Intellectual Tradition series starts right at the beginning, with the basic terminology and questions of philosophy. Next you meet the pre-Socratic philosophers, then the Greek triumvirate—Socrates, Plato, and Aristotle. On to a skippable overview of the Old Testament. The lecturer for this segment is into German Higher Criticism, which promotes the idea of an "evolving" Bible cobbled together from sometimes contradictory sources. Yes, this is the way it's usually taught in college. No, it's not worth suffering through, unless you have a nostalgic love for theological liberalism. Next we get a lecture on the writings of Roman Emperor Marcus Aurelius—and that's the end of the first two tapes. You've been through 10 lectures and were presented with more intellectual fare than in all the magazines you read last year (except mine, of course!)

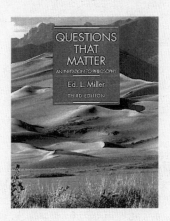

Part 1 is titled "Ancient Philosophy and Faith: From Athens to Jerusalem." Part 2, "The Age of Faith to the Age of Reason," introduces Augustine and Aquinas, More and Machiavelli, Bacon, Descartes, Hobbes, Spinoza, (a guy who must have been a real hit at funerals), and the Newtonian Revolution. Part 3, "The Enlightenment and Its Critics," introduces all the major players whose works our Founding Fathers quoted so copiously, plus Kant (who doesn't belong here chronologically) and Burke (who does). Part 4, "Philosophy in the Epoch of Ideology," brings in the thinkers who ushered in our modern angst. Hegel. Marx (as "the last great Christian heretic"—shades of Francis Schaeffer!). Mill. Thoreau (counterbalanced by Dostoyevsky). Kierkegaard (Mr. Angst himself). Darwin (this lecture is a real loser, touting the discredited theory of "embryonic recapitulation"—e.g., that babies "evolve" through from cell to fishlike being to amphibian to mammal). Weber. Papa Freud. Jung. Part 5, "Modernism and the Age of Analysis," starts off with people most of us have heard of (Nietzsche, James, Sartre . . .) and ends up with a quadrumvirate of deeply confused thinkers—Habermas, Kuhn, Quine, Rorty—into whose pit higher education has currently fallen. (How many words does it take to say, "I don't know what you're really saying and you don't know what I'm saying, either?" Why do people get paid to write books asserting that nobody can truly understand their books?) Finally, the whole series concludes with two lectures entitled "Reviewing the Western Tradition."

The lecturers are a diverse bunch. Some look like college professors. Some don't. One of the more progressive lecturers looks exactly like a Revolutionary War-era British seaman. (His pigtail helps.) More to the point, some stick fairly close to the source material, while others (the seaman among them) are more pushy about promoting their personal views. From least to greatest, though, they all do it with almost no visual aids other than hand gestures. You will be watching profs perambulate from left to right and seeing crowd shots of their studio audiences.

I found the lectures fascinating. Our teenage sons were not as interested, but didn't actually rebel at sitting through these lectures. It would have helped if we had been provided with a vocabulary list (with definitions) and snapshot bios of the thinkers being discussed. Even without such aids, our boys had no trouble understanding the lecturers—a tribute to the profs' ability to make the complex simple.

Would your family benefit from a basic college humanities education? Would you rather send them to college and take potluck? Do you feel up to sorting out the lecturers' bias, maybe even reading the original books for yourself? Your answers to these questions will determine whether you find this course skippable, moderately useful, or essential.

Great Minds of the Western Intellectual Tradition will teach you, more or less, what the "great minds" taught. It will not teach you whether they were right or wrong—although some of the profs clearly prefer some thinkers' theories to others. If you need help with these questions, we suggest you run your students through Dr. Schaeffer's "How Should We Then Live?" video series (reviewed above), which does answer these questions as well as putting the "great minds" in historical perspective, and possibly the Summit Ministries program as well, before turning them loose on the Great Minds. *Mary Pride*

The video series, which is pictures and which I reviewed, is no longer available. Happily, the audio edition can still be purchased.

Be forewarned: the "great minds" were sometimes total losers when it came to personal morality. When Socrates and his friends debate the nature of love, for example, part of the discussion centers on one male guest's lust for Socrates. The lecturer handled this tastefully, but it still isn't the sort of thing you would use to entertain your 10-year-old.

CHAPTER 34

Worldview

Who are you? Why were you born? What is the purpose of your life? Is there a God . . . or gods and goddesses . . . or is the universe run by random chance? Are you really alive, or are you just dreaming that you are? Are good and evil absolutes, or do they change depending on the situation?

A "worldview" is made up of answers to questions such as these. It can be a noble outlook based on serious study and thought, or it could be just an unsuspected mental infection you got from watching too many TV shows and too many violent, abusive movies. You can choose your own worldview, or have other people's worldviews thrust upon you without your knowledge or conscious consent.

No matter where you get your worldview, it will determine how you behave in everyday life. The kind of person you are ultimately depends on what you believe about yourself, other people, God, and the purpose of life—whether you are consciously aware of your beliefs or not.

A noble worldview based on truth is the crowning jewel of a good education. Unfortunately, worldview studies are usually labeled "philosophy" or "theology," and only offered at the college or graduate-school level. This is a grave mistake. If you have never studied philosophy or theology before you get to college, you simply don't have the tools to sift through what you will be taught when you get there. You could quite easily end up with an Infected Worldview based on what you subconsciously pick up from the entertainment world, the prejudices of your teachers, and the fads of your peers, rather than a Chosen Worldview based on knowledge and discernment.

Happily, resources are available for those who want to develop their worldview muscles at home. I suspect this will include many parents, who either never encountered the glories of philosophy in school, or had it presented so poorly they immediately forgot it all. From Plato and Aristotle to the thinkers of our day, here's your chance to join the "Great Conversation" about the most important questions in the world.

Do you have an
- **Accidental Worldview?**
- **Infected Worldview?**
- **Chosen Worldview?**

An **Accidental Worldview** is one you adopt without conscious thought, based on your personal feelings.

An **Infected Worldview** is an Accidental Worldview to which you have added current political and social doctrines, *even when* they initially go against your instincts or your moral training.

A **Chosen Worldview** is one based on logic and awareness of the assumptions *behind* the issues.

Create A Culture
The Great Race to Nome

Grades 5–8; Create A Culture, $9.95.
Grades 3–6; The Great Race to
Nome, $9.95. Shipping extra.
*The Learning Works. PO Box 6187,
Santa Barbara, CA 93160.
Orders: (800) 235-5767.
Inquiries: (805) 964-4220.
Fax: (805) 964-1466.
Email: LESatTLW@aol.com.
Web: www.thelearningworks.com.*

NEW!
Lightbearer's Christian
Worldview Curriculum

Grades 7–10. Complete curriculum,
$795 postpaid. Student workbook,
$14.95. Understanding the Times
abridged textbook, $14.95. How to
Be Your Own Selfish Pig textbook,
$9.95. Student Pack (all three titles),
$35.95. Add shipping to all orders
except complete curriculum.
*Summit Ministries, PO Box 207,
Manitou Springs, CO 80829.
(719) 685-9103. Fax: (719) 685-5268.
Email: Lightbearers@summit.org.
Web: www.summit.org.*

Curriculum

Learning about the Iditarod dogsled race and creating your own culture
from scratch is what these two books are about. Both are unit study guides
with fill in the blank type pages and black and white drawings.

Create A Culture is just what its name implies. With fill-in-the-blank
pages and black-and-white drawings, the book suggests you work in teams
or groups to create a culture from scratch. You name your group, figure out
what habitat you live in, learn about migration, and decide if your group
needs to start a new settlement. You also determine transportation, building and house design, and decide how families are structured—among
many other suggested activities. There are also a couple pages dealing with
religion and deciding what god or gods to worship in your new culture.

This 72-page workbook is designed for the typical public school classroom, but can easily be adapted for homeschoolers. Although qualifying as
politically correct in its strong emphasis on native peoples and the sanctity of
individual cultures, these books could start some interesting conversations.

The Great Race to Nome is a unit study on the Iditarod dog sled race
and things Alaskan. This was our family's favorite. It gives short biographies of mushers, race information and rules, a description of the Iditarod
Trail, record sheets for keeping track of miles traveled and checkpoints
reached, as well as lots of background on the race itself. Maps are waiting
to be filled in, poetry to be written, and a reading race contest is intended
to keep you reading as many pages as the mushers have traveled (a lot!).
Math, language arts, geography, art, science, and social studies are interwoven into the theme.

Both workbooks, from 70–85 pages, are designed for the typical public
school classroom, but can easily be adapted for homeschoolers. Although
qualifying as politically correct in their strong emphasis on the sanctity of
individual cultures, these books could start some interesting conversations.
Marla Perry

You'll hear more about Summit Ministries, a Christian retreat/training camp
in Colorado, in the review of their impressive **Understanding the Times** curriculum for upper-high-school and college students in this same chapter.

Understanding the Times is definitely not a Mickey Mouse course. It's
geared toward students in grade 11 and up, who either are in college already or have colleges breathing down their necks. That's why I recommend the "little brother" to Understanding the Times, namely the brand-
new **Lightbearer's Christian Worldview Curriculum**, for grades 7
through 10.

The components of this course are *not* available separately, except that you can buy additional student materials once you've purchased the complete curriculum.

First, the teaching materials:

- 912-page *Understanding the Times* textbook
- 402-page abridged edition of the *Understanding the Times* textbook
- Large ring-bound Lightbearer's teacher manual with lesson plans and projects and tabs for each topic
- Large ring-bound Lightbearer's student workbook with fill-in-the-blank lecture outlines, and quizzes, with section tabs for Introduction, Theology, Philosophy, Ethics, Biology, Psychology, Sociology, Law, Politics, Economics, History, Conclusion, Log, and Glossary
- *How to Be Your Own Selfish Pig and Other Ways You've Been Brainwashed* by Susan Schaeffer Macaulay, daughter of Dr. Francis Schaeffer (used as a supplementary textbook)

Next, the books:

- *Reaching Kids Before High School: A Guide to Junior High Ministry* by David Veerman
- *Children at Risk: What You Need to Know to Protect Your Family* by Dr. James Dobson and Gary L. Bauer
- Three books by Doris Sanford: *My Friend the Enemy* (first-person story of a child in a Japanese concentration camp), *Lisa's Parents Fight* (about learning to cope with life in an emotionally neglectful family), and *For Your Own Good* (about life in a foster home). These last two are presented as ways for the students to understand the problems of other children their own ages, so as to reach out to them more effectively.
- *World Proofing Your Kids*, by Lael Arrington.

Finally, the videos:

- *The Crossing* is an evangelistic drama in which a class of teens is assigned the speech topic, "What is the most important thing in life?" and one of them finds the answer when his best friend has to face leukemia
- *Pilgrim's Progress* is an animated retelling of the famous John Bunyan allegory, in which Christian travels from the City of Destruction to the Celestial City
- *Passion and Purity* features noted Christian author and speaker Elisabeth Elliot offering biblical perspectives on sex and sexuality
- *False Gods of Our Time*, a docudrama, has Dr. Norm Geisler as host commenting on the conflict between biblical Christianity and atheism, New Age, humanism, the occult, evolution, and false signs and wonders
- *Learn to Discern* is a two-part video series based on Bob DeMoss's "A Generation at Risk" presentation. Meant for parents, *not* for kids, it contains explicit material showing the sorts of things with which today's youth is bombarded. The subject material may be grim, but the genial and humorous Bob DeMoss makes this quite viewable.
- *The American Covenant: The Untold Story,* in which Marshall Foster of the Mayflower Institute dramatically narrates 10

Some of these videos later appear in the Daily Video Package of Summit's Understanding the Times curriculum. It would be nice if they let purchasers of the Lightbearer's curriculum buy the Daily Video selections they want *a la carte*—that could save you a little money when you're considering moving on to Understanding the Times.

The course is designed for 180 one-hour sessions: 15 sessions for the introduction, 15 sessions for each of the 10 disciplines covered, and 15 days to wrap it all up. This can be done with once-a-week sessions for four years in a row (with time for lots of breaks), or daily sessions for a normal school year of 36 weeks.

chronological vignettes documenting America's Christian heritage

- *The Wonders of God's Creation* series (*Planet Earth, Animal Kingdom,* and *Human Life*) is three excellent videos from the Moody Science series, reviewed in Volume 2
- *The Incredible Creatures that Defy Evolution*—if you think, "Which came first, the chicken or the egg?" is a conundrum, check *these* out!
- *In God They Trusted,* a video by the authors of the book *The Light and the Glory,* is five video segments reenacting great moments in America's Christian history
- Two episodes from the TV show *Christy* (*not* including the opening episode!)
- *A Song for Grandmother* video and book combination, about ministering to the elderly
- *When Is It Right to Die?* stars paraplegic writer/speaker/artist Joni Ericson Tada making the case against euthanasia
- *Keys to Good Government* with the ubiquitous and popular David Barton is your introduction to American government as the Founding Fathers intended it
- *William Wilberforce,* a video biography of the British statesmen who led the successful fight to abolish slavery in Great Britain
- The Chickenomics Series, three short separate presentations—*Chickenomics: Basic Economics for Everyone, Chickenpower: Supply and Demand Economics,* and *Chickenfeed: A Fowl Look at Money,* all starring the San Diego Chicken himself, as seen on TV by sports fans everywhere. I don't know how much economics kids will really learn from these videos, but they'll enjoy the Chicken's antics for sure!

The best way to describe this curriculum is, "It will teach you to think like Dr. Dobson." The millions of fans who follow Dr. James Dobson's "Focus on the Family" radio show and its various associated ministries will know what I mean. And though he certainly isn't the only influence felt at Summit (in fact, I'm sure the influence goes both ways), the mainstream evangelical outlook he personifies and popularizes shines through very clearly in these materials.

Now, let's talk price. The Lightbearer's Christian Worldview Curriculum is almost entirely reusable, making it if not an attractively priced buy, at least an achievable purchase for well-off families, especially those with lots of children. Considering that many families are homeschooling primarily in order to raise their children as Christians, the idea that a Christian worldview curriculum should be your highest priority buy (after a Bible course) is worthy of consideration. And if you can't swing the cost by yourself, there's always the chance you can talk your church or support group into clubbing together to get it. Right now, this is the best worldview training available for this age group—let's spread it around! *Mary Pride*

**NEW!
Perspectives on the World Christian Movement (Revised Edition)**
Grade 11–adult. Book, $21. Study guide, $3.99. Shipping extra.
*William Carey Library, PO Box 40129, Pasadena, CA 91114.
Orders: (800) 777-6371.*

Perspectives on the World Christian Movement is a 944-page paperback collection of 95 articles about the Christian movement that, according to the publisher, are "designed to be the missionary platform of essential knowledge for any serious Christian who [has] only a secular education." However, even those with a Christian education are unlikely to have encountered the breadth of learning available in this one book.

The book is divided into four major sections, all tied together by the thread of the Great Commission: The Biblical Perspective, The Historical Perspective, The Cultural Perspective, and The Strategic Perspective.

Articles were contributed by such authorities as John R. W. Stott, Don Richardson, Ralph D. Winter, William Carey, J. Hudson Taylor, Donald A. McGavran, and Andrew Murray, along with many others.

Through this book Christians learn about our scriptural responsibility to be a blessing to others. We explore what has already been accomplished. Cross-cultural missionary challenges are discussed and strategies are mapped out.

Thirty-seven articles are devoted to strategies under the headings Strategies for World Evangelism, Strategies for Church Planting, Strategies for Development, World Christian Teamwork, and World Christian Discipleship.

Every Christian will gain from reading this book. Christians with a weak background in church or biblical history will especially appreciate the summaries of historical events. Others will broaden their understanding of how God has moved ceaselessly through our history as He continues to do today. However, this is not just another book for us to read and be blessed by what others have done. The authors hope to motivate us with practical ideas and encouragement to be part of the effort to reach all men for Jesus Christ.

Since the book is used in college classes, you will find a few study questions at the end of each article.

Although you can easily pick and choose which articles to read, some of us are easily daunted by such a wealth of information. If this is your problem, get the 340-page study guide. It was written to be used as a course (independent study or classroom) book based upon selected readings from the larger book and from Scripture.

Perspectives is not a book to hand to your average teenager. It's for adults, mature young adults, serious Sunday school classes, or for parents to digest and *then* share with their older children.

As the author of the study guide warns, this study is dangerous—it might change your life. *Renee Mathis*

As you can see from the photo, you get a lot with the **School of Tomorrow Missions** course, designed as a high-school elective:

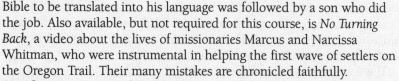

- **Two videos.** *Wings of the Morning* is about the life of missionary David Brainerd. Based on his journal and diary, it gives you a personal look at missions work in early American history. *Beyond the Next Mountain* (not pictured) tells the story of the conversion of the Hmar tribe, and how a man who had prayed for the Bible to be translated into his language was followed by a son who did the job. Also available, but not required for this course, is *No Turning Back*, a video about the lives of missionaries Marcus and Narcissa Whitman, who were instrumental in helping the first wave of settlers on the Oregon Trail. Their many mistakes are chronicled faithfully.
- **Six classic missions biographies,** including these true stories: a Cambridge University man who was one of the founders of Inter-varsity Christian Fellowship; a missionary couple who converted a tribe of headhunters; a couple martyred in China; a husband-wife Bible translation team in Mexico; and a life of David Brainerd.
- ***Give Up Your Small Ambitions!,*** a book about the practical side of becoming a missionary. Sadly, author Michael Griffiths feels it is "responsible" for missionaries to limit their family size.

• **Six PACE worktexts and a score key** to the questions in the worktexts. The worktexts lead students through the books, with mostly fill-in-the-blank questions that are well designed to ensure students understood the main concepts.

Once you've finished this course, you will understand the major terms, requirements, and methods used in missions work today. *Mary Pride*

NEW!
Understanding the Times
Grade 11–college. Basic Teaching Package, $570. Daily Video Package, $425. Four Models worldview poster, $25. Student manual, $15. Textbook, $18.50 (retail $36.95). Abridged textbook, $14.95 (retail $19.95). Teacher manual, $59. Information kit, $15. Preview kit, $25. Individual videos available (Daily Video Package videos only). Shipping extra.
Summit Ministries, PO Box 207, Manitou Springs, CO 80829. (719) 685-9103. Fax: (719) 685-5268. Email: UTT@summit.org. Web: www.summit.org.

Christian high-school kids often turn into . . . umm . . . something else when they have been processed sufficiently in college. Considering this to be a bad result, the staff of Summit Ministries, a Christian retreat/training camp in Colorado, came up with **Understanding the Times**, an intensive curriculum designed to combat the worldviews hapless teens have foisted on them when they hit the groves of modern academe.

The major players out there on the field, according to the Summit staff, are Secular Humanism and Marxism/Leninism. In the most recent edition, these have been joined by New Age (called "Cosmic Humanism" in this course). Offshoots of these philosophies include radical feminism, sexual obsessions as "lifestyle choices," behavioral psychology, redistributionist economics, statist government, sociological law, and relativism in all its guises. Countering these is the "fourth worldview," biblical Christianity.

While the first three worldviews are widely taught on college campuses and disseminated via the popular media, the fourth as we all know is not. Enter Understanding the Times. Originally designed for classroom use in churches and Christian schools, but just as usable in support groups, homeschool co-ops, and individual homes, this includes a slew of books to read and videos to watch.

The entire Understanding the Times curriculum is available only as two complementary packages: the Basic Teaching Package and the Daily Video Package. You can't buy any of the individual items (except as noted below), and you have to have purchased the Basic Teaching Package before you are allowed to purchase the Daily Video Package.

The Basic Teaching package includes:

- 912-page *Understanding the Times* hardcover textbook
- 402-page abridged edition of the *Understanding the Times* textbook
- Large ring-bound two-volume teacher manual with lesson plans and projects
- Large ring-bound student manual with fill-in-the-blank lecture outlines, quizzes, and fact sheets

Note that these four items are also available separately, for those who have already purchased the entire Basic Teaching Package. If you decide to use the entire program for a group, or several children in a family at once, you will want a copy of the student manual and textbook for each student. Only the books (not the manuals) are available separately to people who have not purchased the Basic Teaching Package.

Continuing with the impressive list of materials in the Basic Teaching Package, you'll find:

- Supplementary readings from over 10 authors, such as Thomas Sowell, C.S. Lewis, and John Ankerberg.
- Seven supplemental books: *Children at Risk* (how the retreat from family values has hurt children, especially as it affects the current generation's worldview, by James Dobson/Gary Bauer), *In the Beginning* (an excellent creationist book by Walter Brown, reviewed elsewhere in this volume), *None Dare Call It Treason . . . 25 Years Later* (how the U.S. government has become the playground for world government types, by John Stormer), *Seven Men Who Rule the World from the Grave* (examines the seven thinkers whose views have replaced Christianity as our main cultural force, by Dave Breese), *The Second American Revolution* (a look at the revolution in law, where courts now rule instead of legislatures and traditional values are under siege, by attorney John Whitehead), *America's Christian History: The Untold Story* (by American Vision founder Gary De Mar), and *Reason in the Balance* (the case against naturalism in science, law, and education, by Phillip Johnson)
- Set of 20 video lectures, described below
- Set of three documentary videos (*Evolution Conspiracy, The Search: New Age in a New Light,* and *Assignment Life*)
- Tests and quizzes
- Large (38 x 50") "Four Models of Western Religious Worldviews" poster

Here are the lecture videos in the Basic Teaching Package.

- *Understanding the Times Introduction*
- *Introduction to Worldviews/Secular Humanism as a Religion*
- *The Secular Humanist Worldview/The Marxist/Leninist Worldview*
- *The Cosmic Humanist Worldview/The Biblical Christian Worldview*
- *Reliability of Scripture/Messianic Prophecy*
- *Seven Men Who Rule the World from the Grave I & II*
- *The Empowered Christian Leader/Attitudes of the Christian Leader*
- *The Danger of Deep Ecology/Popular Environmental Myths*
- *Theology and Law*
- *A Biblical Approach to Economics/Socialism v. Capitalism*
- *Radical Feminism*

If you only have time for weekly meetings, Summit suggests you skip the *Introduction, The Empowered Christian Leader, Popular Environmental Myths,* and *Socialism v. Capitalism.* This would give you 18 weeks of meetings. Obviously, with a few more weeks you could cover all the video lessons.

The Daily Video Package (only available to those who have purchased the Basic Teaching Package) includes 20 lecture videos and 9 documentary videos. The lecture videos are:

- *Science and Origin*
- *The Truth about Communism I & II*
- *The Truth about Communism III & IV*
- *Is Communism Really Dead?*

In 1998 Summit added ten more videos. These are:

- *Attitudes and the Christian Leader*
- *Clergy in the Classroom: The Religion of Secular Humanism*
- *Secrets of the World Changers*
- *Love Your God with All Your Mind*
- *Relativism: Feet Planted Firmly in Mid-Air*
- *A Harmony of Differences*
- *The Wonder of God's Creation*
- *The Allure of Rock*
- *The Young and the Restless: Modern Media and the Roots of Teen Rebellion*
- *Pornography: Addictive, Progressive and Deadly*

If you already own the Understanding the Times curriculum, you can get these videos in an update package. The cost of the update depends on whether you have the basic teaching package or the full curriculum and on how long you have owned your curriculum. Call Summit for the current cost of the update packages.

- *The Communist Encirclement/Humanism in Action 1960s*
- *Humanism in Action 1970s/America's War in Vietnam*
- *One Incoming: SDI*
- *What Can I Do? I and II*
- *Moral Relativism: The Attack on Western Civilization I & II*
- *Marriage and Family I & II*
- *Practical Action for the Younger Generation*
- *Challenge to Christians in the 1990s*
- *Immorality of Our Welfare State*

The documentary videos in the Daily Video Package include:

- *America's Godly Heritage*
- *The Case for Creation*
- *The Evolution/Creation Debate*
- *City of the Bees* (from the Moody Science Videos series, reviewed in Volume II)
- *Fatal Addiction* (on the destructive effects of pornography, including Dr. Dobson's famous interview of Ted Bundy)
- *Unveiling the Plague* (on teen suicide)
- *AIDS: What You Haven't Been Told*
- *Hell's Bells* (a rockumentary I suggest you skip, unless your teen is heavily into the hard rock scene or you enjoy being grossed out)
- *Great Inventors*

Some of the non-lecture videos are definitely skippable. The entire segment on rock assumes your youngster has been mired in MTV, and therefore seeks to show the root of this music form via shocking imagery and statements. If your teen has not seen Madonna making out with a preadolescent boy or Alice Cooper's dirty deeds, there is no reason to drag him through this. (I am referring to some of the *milder* excerpts on the three-hour-long *Hell's Bells* anti-rock video.) The videos also are of uneven quality (I am referring to their content), as you might expect with such a varied group of speakers, though Summit is working on improving this.

However, this is certainly not amateur hour. The lecture video speakers include many big names in Christian and conservative circles. Phyllis Schlafly on feminism. Ronald Reagan on communism. Josh McDowell and D. James Kennedy on the reliability of Scripture. E. Calvin Beisner on environmentalism and economics. Homeschool attorney Shelby Sharpe on theology and law. David Barton on America's Christian heritage. Michael Medved on Hollywood. Walter Williams on welfare. Summit's own staff, many of whom are becoming well known in their own right, did most of the rest.

Summit's textbook and manuals may be large, but they are not flabby. This is good material, well up to the standards of a college multidisciplinary course. The nine-credit Western Civ course I took for two semesters umpteen years ago at Boston College (before transferring to RPI) had far less meat to it than Understanding the Times boasts. You're getting an overview of theology, philosophy, ethics, biology, psychology, sociology, law, politics, economics, and history from four different points of view: humanism, Marxism/Leninism, New Age, and Biblical Christianity. Add some composition and speaking practice (which the course includes) and you have what amounts to two years of humanities instruction at the college level.

Combining the Daily Video Package with the Basic Teaching Package will provide enough video sessions for a two-semester Monday-through-Friday course. The videos in the Daily Video Package are also available separately, if you have already purchased the Basic Teaching Package, but I don't necessarily advise this, since the course "flows" best if you run through the videos in both packages in the order Summit suggests, which ends up flipping back and forth between videos from one package and videos from the other.

Obviously, few of us will want to co-op daily. The combined program works best either in large school settings or in single-family settings. But you can still share the costs and advantages with friends, by buying it all together, and then going through it in turns. One family starts, the next starts a month later (using the videos the first family has already finished with), then the next starts a month later, and so on. Even if only two or three families do this, the cost per family is significantly more affordable. Add more, and the price decreases drastically. You only need to add a $15 student manual and one $18.50 textbook for each additional student. For 20 students it is $570 + $425+ $300 + $370 = $1665 = $83.25 apiece . . . for the equivalent of at least one year of college humanities courses. You can see why this is a great support-group library purchase.

Interested, but not willing to shell out that much money without a look-see? Then send for either the Information Kit or the Preview Kit. The Information Kit comes with a 13-minute video overview of Summit Ministries, an audiocassette of a Focus on the Family radio broadcast featuring Summit Ministries, brochures for distribution (handy for talking your friends, support group members, or church into helping pay for and use the program), and a 20-page informational booklet that includes a Curriculum Summary & Syllabus, answers to key questions, overhead masters (again, helpful for persuading a group), and ideas for fund-raising and making a case for the program to all sorts of groups. The Preview Kit contains actual samples of the course: a sample video and its corresponding pages from the teacher manual. Both the Information Kit and the Preview Kit come with certificates that allow you to deduct their entire purchase price from the cost of the curriculum, should you decide to purchase it in the future.

Understanding the Times remains an excellent choice for Christian families determined that their kids shall help the world get better instead of just being swept away on the tide. Try talking your church or support group into buying this program. *Mary Pride*

Magazines

While it may not be to everyone's taste, **Chronicles'** intransigent spirit, strong opinions, and high level of intellectual acumen have made it a "must read" for me. In these pages I first learned about the perils of literary deconstruction and the parlous state of higher education in America. I also got a fresh take on issues from immigration to the Bosnian conflict. Though I know from experience that *Chronicles* doesn't pay its writers much, this magazine consistently attracts the highest quality writers, people who really know their subjects from firsthand experience and research. Most important of all, *Chronicles* consistently seeks for *solutions* to our current social and political problems, and is not afraid to discuss *all* the possibilities. Where other

Chronicles: A Magazine of American Culture

Grade 9–adult. $39/year (12 issues). Foreign subscribers add $12 for surface, $48 for air mail. Back issues available, $7 each postpaid. *Chronicles, Subscription Dept., PO Box 800, Mount Morris, IL 61054. (800) 877-5459. (815) 964-5813. Web: www.rockfordinstitute.org.*

magazines deal with what is "politically possible," *Chronicles* seeks out eternal principles and examines how they should work out if we had the courage to once again act as a nation on our own founding principles. They also poke quite a bit of fun (mixed with with a degree of moral and artistic outrage) at the regnant follies of our current cultural overlords. The feeling here is not grumpy conservatism, but intellectually stimulating conversation with people on the cutting edge of political and social thought. You don't have to agree with everything they print (I certainly don't), but they'll make you think. *Mary Pride*

NEW!
Credenda/ Agenda

Grade 9–adult. Free, but donation accepted.
Canon Press, Community Evangelical Fellowship, PO Box 8741, Moscow, ID 83843. (800) 488-2034.
Fax: (208) 882-1568.
Email: canorder@moscow.com.
Web: www.canonpress.org.

Credenda/Agenda is a monthly publication of Canon Press, whose many fine educational products you have seen reviewed in the *Big Books*. As a ministry of Community Evangelical Fellowship in Moscow, Idaho, *Credenda/Agenda* is sent free of charge to any who request it. (Hint: I suggest you request it by letter or postcard, since it's not polite to make someone pay "800" charges just to give you a freebie!)

The newsletter's purpose is "to apply Biblical principles to the world around us." Features include columns on family life, church affairs, politics, literature, exegesis, church history, and more, all from a traditional Christian perspective. Each article takes up exactly one, or at most two, pages.

Credenda/Agenda is copyright-free, too, so you can snitch all the best bits and publish them in your church newsletter. Such a deal! *Mary Pride*

NEW!
The Moneychanger

Grade 9–adult. $95/year (12 issues). $69 for readers of Big Book of Home Learning includes a Free copy of the Book "Heiland" ($10 value)
The Moneychanger., Box 341753, Memphis, TN 38184-1753.
(901) 853-6136. Fax: (901) 854-5138.
Email: moneychanger@compuserve.com.

I know, the price is ridiculous for an "issues" newsletter. But **Moneychanger** is actually the *best* "what's going on that they haven't told you about" newsletter I've ever seen, disguised as a *precious metals* newsletter.

I don't mean it isn't *really* a precious metals newsletter. You'll find all the complicated charts and discussions of metal prices your little heart could desire. (That's easy for me to say, since *my* little heart has zero $ to invest in *anything!*) However, this "magaletter" (as many words as a magazine, printed tabloid style like a newsletter) also has the best interviews, factoids, and sermonettes (you heard me right) of any publication I read. Perhaps that's because its publisher, Franklin Sanders, a dealer in gold and silver, has been locked in battle with the government for years over his attempts to prove that gold and silver coins are, in fact, legal tender. This may not sound like something you have to go to jail to prove, but weird are the ways of government nowadays.

Anyway, *Moneychanger* is a great way to keep up on the bad things happening out there, without actually having to read about them at length. Best of all, Mr. Sanders' humor and positive spirit make it possible to almost *enjoy* hearing about the latest government absurdities. Meanwhile you're also finding out about unconventional (but sensible) health cures, what the stock market is up to and various investment theories, why we're no longer under constitutional government (FDR asked the states for emergency powers way back in the '30's, and they have never been rescinded, so we're actually under *military* law, which is why the flags in courtrooms have a gold fringe), and lots of stuff of that nature. Solidly Christian throughout. *Mary Pride*

Today's reference publishers are so afraid of offending anyone that they call murderous dictatorships "one-party systems" and refuse to mention the sins of most governments that are currently in power. As for the plight of Christians in other countries, forget it. I bet you don't know that no military personnel, even chaplains, were allowed to wear crosses or show the cross in any way during Desert Storm, at the direct demand of the Saudi Arabians—and that policy affected thousands of Americans directly. If you didn't know that, how likely is it that you know about the Saudi Arabian religious police, called *muttawa*, who go door to door searching for Christian activity? Or that you knew even large compounds of foreign workers in Saudi Arabia aren't allowed to have a church building? Or that beatings, torture, jail, or even death are the lot of any Saudi Christians who are caught worshipping or evangelizing?

The Voice of the Martyrs (VOM) is "a Christian missionary organization dedicated to serving today's persecuted church" around the world. They publish a monthly full-color 16-page newsletter also called **Voice of the Martyrs**. Written at a more adult level than its sister publication, *LINK International* (reviewed in Volume 2), *Voice of the Martyrs* covers the plight of Christians in countries where persecution is practiced. Practical ways to pray and take action are provided. For example, you may be given the address of a prime minister or ambassador, so you can write requesting the release of imprisoned brethren, or perhaps the address of the prison where they are held, so you can write to them directly.

Background information on the world of Islam is a continuing series of articles in this newsletter, as in Islamic countries the penalties for converting to Christianity are very severe. That being the case, why would anyone want to convert? These articles, written by Dr. Saleem Almahdy, a Christian scholar on Islam who was born and raised in a Muslim country, explore what Islam teaches on specific subjects, and how it differs from Christianity. Ways to raise money and gifts for Christians who have been made homeless or deprived of their livelihoods are also explored, and resources for further study are reviewed.

Our 13-year-old daughter, Magda, has been a subscriber to *Voice of the Martyrs* for several years, and likes it very much. It's not the Nancy Drew view of the world. Nancy Drew, as you may recall, visits other countries and always finds the natives to be colorful, helpful, and uniformly members of the dominant religion of their country or tribe. The truth is that, around the world, worldviews are in conflict, and that more Christians have died for their faith in the twentieth century than in all the previous nineteen centuries combined. Even in America, Christians are increasingly portrayed in popular entertainment (movies, books, and comic books) as hate-filled child-abusing bigots and murderers. Oh, right. This makes as much sense as accusing Bangladeshi Christians of poisoning the village wells and stealing the water, or as accusing ancient Roman Christians of having set Rome on fire. But it does not *have* to make sense. Persecutors just need an excuse, not a logical reason.

VOM tells it like it is, without politically-correct patty-caking, and without rancor. The point is to help downtrodden Christians, while cultivating a spirit of steadfastness and forgiveness. And to learn a lot along the way. *Mary Pride*

NEW!
Voice of the Martyrs
Parents. Free, but donations are appreciated.
The Voice of the Martyrs, PO Box 443, Bartlesville, OK 74005.
Credit card orders: (800) 747-0085.
Inquiries: (918) 337-8015.
Fax: (918) 338-0189.
Email: linkinternational@vom-usa.org.
Web: www.persecution.com.

NEW!
The World &I

Grade 9–adult. $36/year, special homeschool rate (12 issues). Canada, $69. All others, $117. Includes 10 teacher's guides
The World & I, 3600 New York Ave., NE, Washington, DC 20002.
Orders: (800) 822-2822.
Inquiries: (202) 636-3334.
Fax: (202) 526-3497.
Web: www.worldandi.com.

If *Time* were less faddish, and *National Geographic* were less politically correct, and you merged the result together, you might end up with something like **The World & I**. Published by the same people who put out the Washington *Times*, each thick issue is a visual and literary feast. You'll voyage to strange new worlds, from discoveries in science to in-depth pieces on other countries. Just about every topic a thinking person would find of interest is covered in here sooner or later: literature, history, art, music, astronomy, philosophy . . .

This is a conservative magazine, but not a Christian one, so Christians should be prepared for the occasional clinker. Still, you'll do a lot less sifting than with other newsstand magazines. *Mary Pride*

Videos

American high school education suffers from an overdose of facts and a shortage of ideas. Or maybe I have that wrong: from an overdose of ideas and a shortage of discernment. How can we pick our way among all the lifestyles and worldviews howling for our attention? How can we even gain enough discernment to realize that modern fads are not eternal truths?
How Should We Then Live?

NEW!
How Should We Then Live?

Grade 9–adult. $99.95 plus $6.85 shipping.
Gospel Communications International, PO Box 455, Muskegon, MI 49443.
Orders: (800) 253-0413.
Inquiries: (616)773-3361.
Fax: (616) 777-1847.
Web: www.gospelcom.net.

Dr. Francis Schaeffer, one of the great philosophers and theologians of our time, has provided a key that can help any high school student, adult, or wide-awake sixth-grader make sense of history, philosophy, theology, and the arts. This three-video series, directed by his son Franky Schaeffer and filmed around the world, follows the history of human thought. It shows not only that ideas have consequences, but what the consequences are. Why the Renaissance? Whither the Reformation? Whence our modern angst? *Pourquoi* Picasso? The answers are all in these twelve 30-minute episodes.

Starting with the Roman Age, Dr. Schaeffer takes us through the Middle Ages, Renaissance, Reformation, Age of Revolution, Scientific Age, Age of Non-Reason, Age of Fragmentation, and today's shining glory, the Age of

NEW!
The Complete Works of Francis Schaeffer

Grade 9–adult. $80 plus shipping.
Crossway Books, 1300 Crescent St., Wheaton, IL 60187. (800) 635-7993. Fax: (630) 682-4785.

If you've had your appetite whetted by Dr. Schaeffer's *How Should We Then Live?* and *Whatever Happened to the Human Race?* video series, picking up this set of his **Complete Works** is a natural. All twenty-two books—Dr. Francis A. Schaeffer's lifework—are included in a beautifully-crafted (and indexed) five-volume set.

I've heard it said that Dr. Schaeffer is "difficult" to read. This might be true if you've never had any training in logic or philosophy. But once a few words like "presupposition" become part of your vocabulary, you'll find that Dr. Schaeffer is crystal clear where the vast majority of 20th-century thinkers are as muddy as a Louisiana bayou.

What's unique about Dr. Schaeffer is that he spent his career interacting with what 20th-century thinkers actually said. He never ducked any arguments flung at Christianity, but instead got right to the roots of what modern man was really saying and showed why it was self-contradictory and didn't work. What's more, he helped hundreds of thousands of people understand where "modern" thought came from, and the historic roots of the modern age. Almost single-handedly, he arrested the "flight from culture" that had afflicted Fundamentalism and Evangelicalism for half a century. As the architect of a historic Christian worldview for the modern world, his importance can hardly be exaggerated.

If you're a Christian, studying these books will greatly increase your faith and devotion. If you're not a Christian, I double-dare you to read them and remain untouched. *Mary Pride*

Personal Peace and Affluence. Yea, all hail the Economy. At each stage, he contrasts historic Christian faith with the errors of the times, and shows what flowed from each belief.

Tape 3 includes two bonus interviews with Dr. and Mrs. Schaeffer, "Living with Suffering and Sickness" and "God's Leading in L'Abri and Our Lives." The former is particularly poignant, since Dr. Schaeffer, who looks hale and hearty on the tape, knew he was dying of cancer at the time.

This series is the ideal foundation for any number of unit studies. If nothing else, it is bound to spark powerful interest in the Great Books and the major historical figures and artworks shown in the video. An ideal "core" course for high school or college level. One warning: a few of the artworks involve non-erotic nudity. Specifically, Michelangelo's "David," Boticelli's "Venus," somebody's "Madonna" which turned out to be the king's mistress (her breast is exposed to nurse the baby), and a few others I forget. Really, it's easy to overlook these parts, although personally I wish they had been filmed more circumspectly.

For less than $100 you can buy this film series, show it to your family, lend it to your friends, and show it to your whole support group. (It's cleared for small-group viewing in "face-to-face instructional settings." In other words, don't rent the local theater to show it.) For considerably less than that, you can buy the book of the same name from Crossway Publishers (1-800-323-3890). For maximum impact, watch the video first, then read the book. Don't hold back; do it. This is a "wisdom investment" that will pay off better than rubies. *Mary Pride*

Famed Rutherford Institute attorney John Whitehead believes discrimination against religious persons is becoming a noteworthy—and nasty— feature of American life. He has written a book, **Religious Apartheid**, with accompanying study guide, to alert us to the problem, and prevailed upon Franky Schaeffer to direct a short accompanying video of the same name.

Whitehead's message is worth hearing. His solutions are not always the best, but until we become aware of the issue, we won't have any solutions. Aimed squarely at church groups, but affordable enough for individual families, the book/study guide/video combo has lots of meat in easy-to-digest form. You'll find out about why we're experiencing this form of discrimination, how it is justified, how it is promoted, and what Whitehead thinks we should do about it. The key word here is *do*: he wants us to take legal, political, and journalistic action to promote religious freedom.

The arty but memorable video is aimed at the MTV generation. Lots of split-screen effects, jerky camera work, and gritty scenes juxtaposed with shots of John Whitehead delivering his comments in locations from college campuses to the Supreme Court steps. Schaeffer is trying to make us *feel* what the book tells us, rather than to convey the book content in typical "presentation" style. One allegorical sequence shows an all-American family happily eating breakfast together. Enter a social worker and bureaucrat, nosing around and writing in their books. The mom is then given a briefcase and hustled out the door. The kids get mesmerized by the TV set and go wild with disco dancing and video games. While she's away from home Mom apparently files for divorce, because some workers come and remove chunks of the furniture. Then policemen come and usher the children onto the school bus. Baby is taken from Dad's arms. Finally the kids are padlocked into the school bus and it drives away, leaving him all alone.

The study guide outlines the arguments in each book chapter, pulls out key quotes from the book for discussion, provides comprehension questions and "devil's advocate" arguments, and summarizes chapter contents. Leading a good meeting with this guide should be a piece of cake.

NEW!
Religious Apartheid

Grade 9–adult. Video/Book/Study Guide combo, $39.95 plus shipping. *Gospel Communications International, PO Box 455, Muskegon, MI 49443. Orders: (800) 253-0413. Inquiries: (616) 773-3361. Fax: (616) 777-1847. Web: www.gospelcom.net.*

Whitehead is great at diagnosis. No question about it. What about his solutions? These involve working within the system, continuing to do good even if it is outlawed (so far so good), and capturing the hearts and minds of the media. Here he's missing the point—we should *become* the media. If all the money Christians had wasted buying ad space in liberal publications had been put into starting our own mass-market, high-quality, general- and special-interest publications, we would *be* the media by now. I mean, if our family can put out *Practical Homeschooling*, with a little money and a lot of work your family could be running the community newspaper, radio station, or cable channel. Get the picture? (If you don't get the picture, show this paragraph to your teenager. He or she will understand.)

Well . . . if it can inspire me to write this passionately, *Religious Apartheid* must be good. Yes. I hear myself saying, "Every support group and church should buy this kit . . . and use it." Before it's too late. *Mary Pride*

Is this a history course, or a philosophy course, or (as its title states) a course in "religions"? All three. Five world religious systems—Christianity, Islam, Judaism, Chinese religion (Tao, ancestor worship, and Buddhism), and the religions of India (which include Buddhism and Islam, but also Hinduism and Sikhism)—each have 10 of the **SuperStar Teachers Great World Religions** lectures devoted to them. One "part" of the course consists of 10 lectures on a particular religious system. The entire course has five parts, for fifty 45-minute lectures in all. There are no special visuals here—just teachers walking about and waving their hands. Typical college lecture fare, in other words. So if you'd like to save money, don't hesitate to pick the audio versions of these lectures.

As is sadly familiar, non-Christian religions are treated with deference, while Christianity, particular in its fundamentalist form, gets rougher handling. Dr. Robert Oden follows the "forms criticism" school of Bible interpretation, which basically ends up finding multiple authors for every Bible book based on "textual evidence." Thus, he says the book of Mark is based on a "Q" manuscript (no example of which has ever been found), just as in his Old Testament lectures in the "Great Minds" series he told us that multiple, contradictory sources had a hand in writing the books purportedly written by Moses. This is standard doctrine as taught in liberal seminaries, so we are not surprised to find Dr. Oden takes a dim view of fundamentalism. What is more surprising is that he believes "fundamentalism" is a religion of its own that crosses traditional religious lines. Thus, an Islamic or Jewish fundamentalist is more in accord with a Christian fundamentalist than with traditional Islam or Judaism, and vice versa, according to him.

Or perhaps this is not so surprising. While *philosophically* those who believe in absolutes definitely share a common ground for argument, *spiritually* the most central tenets of each faith differ. But for those who don't believe in the reality of absolute spiritual truth, the "spiritual" seems fuzzy, while a belief in absolutes is downright threatening.

For that very reason, I was anxious to watch these tapes. This is the view which is being mainlined throughout higher education, and I wanted to see how it played out. It didn't hurt that, as a bonus, lectures on Eastern Orthodoxy, Reformed Christianity and the revivalist tradition, and other topics were also included. It did hurt that Dr. Oden stutters continuously. This made it hard to listen to him for long periods without a break.

For those with limited funds, the parts on non-Christian religions may prove to be a better buy. These include a lot of history and cultural information about the societies based on those religions, and may be helpful in filling in the gaps in your world history studies. Again, don't expect a conservative viewpoint, and you won't be disappointed. This applies especially to the lectures on the religions of India, taught by Dr. Diane Eck of Harvard Divinity School, which promote both those religions and feminism. However, facts do outweigh opinions in these tapes, and with a little discernment, you can easily separate the lecturers' preferences from the genuine historical facts they cover.

In all, very interesting, but not for those who are weak in their faith—whatever that faith might be. *Mary Pride*

Sherilyn Mentes, producer of the Dutch video and the first female president of the International Motion Picture and Lecturers' Association, has struck out on her own. With the assistance of Dr. Dwayne Merry, a professor friend well-versed in anthropology and archaeology, she has produced **Treasures of Peru**, a 75-minute educational documentary under her own "Mentor Productions" label.

Missions-minded Christians would do well to consider this video, as it is a compellingly—even graphically–honest look at the ancient Inca culture of Peru and its modern-day Spanish-Indian-Catholic hybrid offshoot. Visit Machu Picchu, meet Thor Heyerdahl, gaze at pounds of ancient gold jewelry, see the mysterious huge "desert drawings" that are only visible from the air, travel from the Amazon jungles to the snow-covered Andes. See for yourself how the Inca built reed boats just like the Egyptians and ziggurats like the Babylonians, and how their modern descendants resemble the Chinese in some physical features. (If the world was all one land mass once, which some Bible scholars believe, the South American Indians could have simply migrated straight from the Middle East—a theory not ventured in the video!) You get to see the art and architecture of the ancient Incas—and the tribes they destroyed—as well as one horrific scene in which "the Inca" himself, the tribal head of the descendants of the original pagan inhabitants, sacrifices a llama to the Sun God in an only slightly watered-down reenactment of the original human sacrifices practiced by his ancestors.

I could have done without seeing the actual moment of sacrifice (shown on the video), and in my opinion you'd do well to fast-forward by that spot, but I won't forget the sound of the Indian crowd enjoying the animal's suffering in a hurry.

Though the professor makes no Christian comments on the whole weird scene, simply seeing it is enough to banish all thoughts of the sameness and equal goodness of all religions. Not for the squeamish, those without fast-forward buttons, or little children, here is the real face of paganism, along with marvelous photography of the land and history of Peru and its people. *Mary Pride*

NEW!
Treasures of Peru
Grade 9–adult. $24.95 plus $3.50 shipping.
Mentor Productions, PO Box 1148, San Clemente, CA 92674-1148. (800) 521-5104. Inquiries/fax: (714) 498-3954.

NEW!
Whatever Happened to the Human Race?

Grade 7–adult. $99.95 plus $6.10 shipping.
Gospel Communications International, PO Box 455, Muskegon, MI 49443.
Orders: (800) 253-0413.
Inquiries: (616)773-3361.
Fax: (616) 777-1847.
Web: www.gospelcom.net.

Starring Dr. Francis Schaeffer and Dr. C. Everett Koop (back when he was known for his pioneering medical work helping children with severe physical problems and for his prolife views), **Whatever Happened to the Human Race?** is five 50-minute episodes dedicated to alerting the troops to the horrendous inroads pro-death thinking has made in our century.

Koop, as we all know, "grew" in his office as Surgeon General to the point of believing permeable condoms would halt AIDS better than impermeable morals. Dr. Schaeffer, in contrast, died with true dignity in the arms of his family, after an exhausting battle with cancer, from which he never flinched. Although Koop may have waffled so much we are tempted to call him "Aunt Jemima," the wisdom you hear on these tapes is Schaeffer's. Dr. Schaeffer became famous for his ability to explain classic truth in modern terms, without ever compromising. It is oddly comforting to hear him telling us the truth about these issues.

Your teens need to watch these tapes before someone convinces them the kindest thing to do to dear ol' Dad, who has just had a bad auto accident but whose heart is still beating, is to slice out his organs . . . or that aborting babies is just another form of birth control . . . or that old folks are "useless eaters" who should be put to death, following the gloriously multicultural example of certain isolated tribes of Eskimos. Maybe your kids already know better. (I hope so.) Even so, nobody has ever made these points more memorably—and tastefully—than this film series. *Mary Pride*

PART 7

Fine Arts

Mercedes Smith, a 14-year-old homeschooler from Mountainburg, Arkansas, won at the state level for the Junior High Woodwinds Competition, sponsored by the National Music Teacher's Association. She played the flute at the competition, which required all entrants to play a 20-minute program representing three pieces of music, one of which was to be played from memory. For her performance, Mercedes represented Arkansas at the regional competition.

Mercedes also won first place in the Concerto Competition, sponsored by the North Arkansas Symphony Youth Orchestra. She received a plaque and a $100 honorarium, and she has the opportunity to play her selection at the NAS Youth Orchestra's Spring Concert.

Daniel Johnson, a 14-year-old homeschooler from Phelps, WI, won the Best of Show award in the open class photography division at the Vilas County Fair. His photography won numerous blue ribbons in both the 4-H and adult open competitions. His Best of Show photo was of his two-year-old sister Emily peeking out from behind a pink juggling scarf.

CHAPTER 35

Art Skills

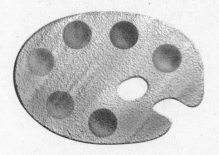

We live in a visual age. The age of naked text has been replaced by the age of four-color, three-dimensional multimedia. If you want to really say something today, you practically *have* to also illustrate it visually, just for it to get noticed at all.

It follows, then, that there is a huge need for noble, uplifting graphics. Here are just a few of the fields that need artists:

- Commercial illustration
- Animation
- Cartoons
- Special effects
- Comic books
- Book illustration
- Magazine graphics

As small as my own company is, two-thirds of the people working there have visual arts training and experience.

Look at it this way—knowing how to draw and design won't ever *hurt* your chances of getting a job!

Another reason for learning the art basics is simply that creating art is enjoyable. Man is made in the image of God, and God is a Creator. For you or me to enjoy painting a picture of a flower is as natural as it was for God to enjoy creating that flower in the first place.

If you can draw, you can communicate in a whole new way. Even if you never become another Rembrandt, the effort you put into learning the skills of perspective, use of white space, color balancing, and so forth will enable you to get that much more out of every piece of art you see for the rest of your life. These skills are easy and fun to learn, with the help of the resources in this chapter.

Alpha Omega Art LIFEPACs

Grades 7–12. Complete boxed set, $43.95, includes 10 LIFEPACs, two Answer Keys, Test Keys, Art-A-Color Plates, and Art Color Swatch Cards. Shipping extra.
Alpha Omega Publications, 300 N. McKemy, Chandler, AZ 85226. Orders and inquiries: (800) 622-3070. Fax: (480) 785-8034. Web: www.home-schooling.com.

The Crafts Supply Source Book, 4th Edition

Parents. $18.99 plus shipping.
Betterway Books, an imprint of F&W Publications, 1507 Dana Ave., Cincinnati OH 45207. (800) 289-0963. Fax: (513) 531-4082.

FLAX Models

Grade 7–adult. Wooden models, $29.90 for 16" or $59 for 20" (choice of male or female). Hardwood hands, $28 each for 8" (choice of male or female, right or left).
FLAX Art & Design, 240 Valley Dr., Brisbane, CA 94005. Orders: (800) 547-7778. Fax: (415) 468-1940. Web: www.flaxart.com.

Art Curriculum & Supplies

It is my policy never to endorse a product I haven't personally seen, and that is the only reason I am hesitant about piling on the superlatives for **Alpha Omega's Art I course** for seventh-graders on up. First of all, the price is right. Secondly, this full-year course hits *all* the bases: fine art, applied art, commercial art, and art appreciation. The course layout, which I have seen, maintains Alpha Omega's usual standards of logic and thoroughness, so each of these areas gets a real workout rather than a passing nod. Thirdly, and this is the part I like the best, the course is designed to provide *practical* art skills, giving the student the tools to use the artistic media (graphics, lettering, layout, cartooning, photography, and printmaking) as well as tools to analyze and improve his personal environment.

AOP says that the fine arts portion of the course can be personalized to fit the student's interests and opportunities. *Mary Pride*

What a bonanza! More than 2,500 suppliers of craft materials are listed in the **Crafts Supply Source Book**, a whopping 298-page oversized paperback. In order to fit that many in, individual supplier descriptions are sketchy, but you do get a treasure trove of addresses and phone numbers for everything from art videos through yarn suppliers—way more than I'd have had room to fit in *The Big Book of Home Learning*. If you can think of a craft, it's probably listed here—from beloved homeschool projects such as Indian and frontier crafts to oddities such as tattooing. Whether your hobby is rubberstamping, building classic cars from kits, metalworking, kite making, scrimshaw, or more ordinary hobbies such as doll-making or any of several dozen fabric and sewing arts, you'll find dozens of great sources for supplies. Any homeschool family that ever does a project or unit study could use this book. *Mary Pride*

Every artist needs a model, right? But brother Dave or sister Janie might not feel like sitting still for two hours or so while you doodle around on your sketch pad. Here's a sufficiently wacky solution for this common problem: wooden models. I mean *really* wooden models, not human models with emotionless expressions.

Flax's **The Perfect Model** series of wooden mannequins are hand carved and fully articulated. This means you can move their joints around in all directions. Get the model into the pose you want, and it can't decide to scratch itself or walk away from you. The smaller models are reasonably affordable and are held up by a wire sticking out of a wooden stand.

Realism in these figures does not extend to facial features or fingers and toes, so that's where Flax's "attractive hardwood hands with light oil finish" come in. Hands are hard for many of us to draw, but not when you can simply pose the fingers of your very own hardwood hand and bend the hand at the wrist, as you can with these fully-articulated models. The catalog says the hands are "ideal for display, sketching, or as a unique gift," but

I'd say price puts these out of range of all but serious artists. A pity, as they are such a useful drawing aid. As for the "unique gift" idea, those grotesque wiggling hands advertised (heaven knows why) in card decks aimed at business execs have reduced the uniqueness of such a gift—unless the gif-tee is an artist, in which case he might appreciate you giving him a hand. *Mary Pride*

Winner of two out of three *Practical Homeschooling* 1998 Reader Awards in the Art category, the **How Great Thou Art** family of art courses by instructor Barry Stebbing has certainly made an impact on the homeschool community. Growing rapidly from one course (the original "How Great Thou Art") to 10 courses for all age levels, and with video lessons and supplies packages now available for many of these courses, it's easy to be confused by the wide range of options available from this publisher.

Here's what I found by examining the How Great Thou Art catalog:

- You can't just go by age level when purchasing these courses, because typically each age level will have two or more courses available.
- Special combo prices are often available when you purchases videos or a teacher's manual at the same time as the course text. So it really helps to know if you'll want any of these additional items *before* you buy.

For the teens, ages 12 and up, two courses are available: **How Great Thou Art I and II** and **The Book of Many Colors**. These are easy to explain: *How Great Thou Art* is a "drawing" course and *The Book of Many Colors* is a "painting" course. Important note: while the courses for the younger children use a cartoony style, the teen courses move to a more realistic style combining line art and texture. I've been told that generally boys at this age level prefer the drawing and draftsmanship lessons, and girls prefer to work with color. However, there's no reason your teen could not eventually complete *both* courses! Video lessons and art supplies are available for both; an addition, a teacher's manual is available for *How Great Thou Art.*

The Book of Many Colors comes with "paint cards." These are sturdy preprinted pieces of oversized cardstock with paintable surfaces. Marker and paint work is done on those cards, instead of on the thinner book pages, so it will turn out nicely. You can purchase extra sets of the paint cards for additional students.

When it comes to Christian content, these courses aren't heavy on theology. You'll find some examples of praise to God for His role as Creator and as the reason for our creativity, and some Bible verses and Bible stories, especially in the products for younger children.

Techniques such as color creation, stippling, cross-hatching, overlapping, and lights and shadows are taught in all the books. More advanced techniques—e.g., 2- and 3-D perspective, anatomy proportions, and composition—are taught in all the series designated for age 8 and up. "Draw what you see" art is brought out in these books for teens.

Now, the big question: is it worth buying the videos, if you purchase a course that has videos available? Yes! On the videos, the affable and energetic Barry Stebbing shows you step by step how to do each assignment, often adding visuals of completed student art. This makes it *so* much easier to see what you're aiming for! Your comfort factor—and motivation—will go way up if you get the videos . . . and while you're at it, make it easy on yourself and get the art supplies from them, too.

NEW!
How Great Thou Art

Grade 7–adult. How Great Thou Art I or II, $14.95 each. Book of Many Colors, $34.95. Videos plus text combos: Book of Many Colors, $89.95; How Great Thou Art I & II, $99. How Great Thou Art I & II Teacher's Manual, $7.95. Extra paint cards, other supplies, text plus teachers manuals combos also available. Shipping extra. *How Great Thou Art Publications, Box 48, McFarlan, NC 28102. Orders: (800) 982-3729. Inquiries: (704) 851-3117. Fax: (704) 851-3111. Email: howgreat@vnet.net. Web: www.howgreatthouart.com.*

To move from cartoons to realism, How Great Thou Art I and II will hone the student's pencil-drawing skills

Your teen will explore more realistic painting methods with The Book of Many Colors

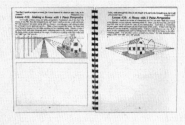

NEW!
Millbrook Arts series

Grades 7–12. $22.90 hardcover, $8.95 paperback.
The Millbrook Press, PO Box 335, 2 Old New Milford Rd., Brookfield, CT 06804. Orders: (800) 462-4703. Inquiries: (203) 740-2220. Fax: (203) 740-2223.

Perspective Without Pain

Grade 7–adult. $19.99 plus $3.50 shipping.
North Light Books, an imprint of F&W Publications, Inc., 1507 Dana Ave., Cincinnati, OH 45207. (800) 289-0963. Fax: (513) 531-4082. Web: www.writersdigest.com.

NEW!
Usborne Calligraphy books

Grade 6–adult. Usborne Guide to Calligraphy, $7.95. Calligraphy Projects, $5.95. Complete Book of Calligraphy (includes Usborne Guide & Calligraphy Projects), $9.95. Calligraphy KidKit, $13.95. Shipping extra.
EDC Publishing, Division of Educational Development Corporation, PO Box 470663, Tulsa, OK 74147-0663. (800) 475-4522. Fax: (800) 747-4509. Web: www.edcpub.com.

Are these the art courses you are looking for? It depends on what you want to spend and what you're looking for. If you want a course that uses modern methods (rather than an "Old Masters") approach . . . if you're looking for a one-book course (rather than one with lots of workbooks) . . . if a Christian tone appeals to you . . . and if you want something that's easy to use, with little time required to set up for a lesson . . . give the How Great Thou Art family a chance! *Mary Pride*

Is this a how-to series or an art appreciation series? The **Millbrook Arts series** is a little bit of both. Each of these 48-page oversized full-color books includes many examples of famous art, plus information on the artists' techniques and simple activities for you to try out these techniques. For example, after studying a Japanese woodcut and an engraving, you try making your own potato prints.

Some activities have their roots in non-Christian religions: making a totem pole, designing your own African mask. Buddha is mentioned as "a prince who gave up all his riches . . . [and] then taught people a better way of life," and Islamic art is also introduced. Christian art is also followed. I don't believe there's any attempt to proselytize for any religion; the authors are just trying to be thorough and respectful of all their possible readers.

The series includes *Nature in Art, People in Art, Places in Art,* and *Stories in Art.* Like other Millbrook books, this series is designed to really *teach* you the subject. It gives you just the right amount of information so you can easily remember it, and just enough do-able activities to make it all feel real. Recommended, with the reservations mentioned above. *Mary Pride*

The 48-page **Perspective Without Pain** workbook is designed to conquer your fears about perspective. Using it in drawings, that is! This workbook covers the basics, gets into boxes and other cubic shapes, and covers curves and indices. Simple language, hands-on exercises, everyday terms. This book was originally part of a four-volume series, but is now a stand-alone book. *Mary Pride*

Calligraphy: From Beginner to Expert is an Usborne book. That means it's highly visual and crammed to the hilt with full-color illustrations. Text serves the illustrations, explaining how the effects are achieved, what the parts of the pen are, and so on. Topics covered are:

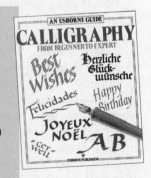

- the history of calligraphy
- basic equipment
- types of letters (capitals, miniscules . . .)
- layout tips
- Gothic and Italic styles
- decoration and illumination
- ways to use calligraphy
- unusual equipment (balsa pens, quills . . .)
- Chinese calligraphy
- stenciling, rubbing, embossing, incising
- careers in calligraphy

The book closes with several pages of sample alphabets, numbers, and borders, and a complete index.

This is an excellent introduction to the "pen arts," and actually provides enough information in its 48 pages for the beginner to get started in the style of his choice. Recommended.

Calligraphy Projects is the follow-up volume. It is 32 pages and provides lots of ideas on how to put your new skills to work. Best deal: **Complete Book of Calligraphy** includes both *Guide to Calligraphy* and *Calligraphy Projects* for less cost than the two purchased separately.

The **Calligraphy Kid Kit** includes *Usborne Guide to Calligraphy* and three Speedball Elegant Writer calligraphy markers—one each of red, black, and blue—all in a handy plastic reclosable pouch. *Mary Pride*

Inexpensive step-by-step guides to media and techniques. Full color, copiously illustrated. As with all Usborne books, the illustrations and layout teach as much or more than the text. This highly visual approach is ideal for visual subjects.

Drawing covers pencil, pen, charcoal, crayon, and pastels, as well as techniques of perspective, measuring and proportion, shading and texture, coloring, and just about anything else you'd like to know. Choosing supplies. Composition. Still life. Portraits. Figure drawing. Animals. Drawing from imagination. How to mount your drawings. How to fix mistakes. Plus an index! An amazing amount of information packed into 32 oversized pages.

Painting, in a similar format, covers oils, watercolors, gouache, and acrylics, plus basic information about painting preparation and supplies as well as techniques. Brushes. Easels. Cleaning materials. How to make your own painting surfaces. Cleanup. Composition, with or without viewfinders. Perspective, measurement, and proportion are just touched on; for detailed instructions in these areas you should consult the *Guide to Drawing*. Like *Drawing*, *Painting* also covers how to paint people, still life, outdoor scenes, painting from imagination, and how to frame and mount your art. A final section on abstract painting is a bonus. The entirely unnecessary picture on page thirteen of a young man painting a technically modest nude (arms and legs arranged to cover the essentials) may cause some to skip this otherwise fine book.

Finally, the **Usborne Young Cartoonist** is a sassy introduction to the art named. Lots of tips and techniques are crammed into less pages than you would expect. The boffo drawings are a bit too uncontrolled for my liking, themselves resembling kid art (perhaps intentionally). The second half of this book, "How to Draw Monsters and Other Creatures," speaks for itself. *Mary Pride*

Learn all the fundamentals of photography with the help of hundreds of good and bad examples. You'll love the guy posed in front of a bush, so it looks like it's growing out of his head. (One of the "bad" examples in **Usborne Photography**.)

If you want to learn to "see" how to make a shot that works, this is the book for you, as most of the book is devoted to this topic. If you want to find out the exact f-stop for a particular photo, check out the tables in the back of the book.

The deepest this book gets into camera tech is the section on how to develop black-and-white film (the authors figure developing color film is beyond most beginners). You also get detailed instructions on how to load and unload a camera, and helpful hints on how to pick a camera and lenses. Fun to read, like most Usborne books, and a good introduction to the subject. *Mary Pride*

Usborne Guides to Painting & Drawing

Grades 7–12. Usborne Guide to Painting and Guide to Drawing, $6.95 each. Young Cartoonist $8.95. Shipping extra.
EDC Publishing, Division of Educational Development Corporation, PO Box 470663, Tulsa, OK 74147. (800) 475-4522. Fax: (800) 747-4509. Web: www.edcpub.com.

NEW!
Usborne Photography

Grade 7–adult. $7.95 plus shipping.
EDC Publishing, Division of Educational Development Corporation, PO Box 470663, Tulsa, OK 74147-0663. (800) 475-4522. Fax: (800) 747-4509. Web: www.edcpub.com.

NEW!
Visual Manna

Grades 1–12. Visual Manna Two: Deluxe (each page is in a plastic protective cover and pages are bound in a binder notebook), $42.95; Economy (pages are shrink-wrapped), $32.95. Visual Manna Drawing Book, $12.95. Visual Manna Real Manna, $10. Complete Art Curriculum: Deluxe version (includes plastic cover sheets), $68.95; Economy version, $42.95. Shipping extra.
Visual Manna, PO Box 553, Salem MO 65560. (888) 275-7309. Fax/Phone: (573) 729-2100. Email: arthis@rollanet.org. Web: www.rollanet.org/~arthis.

Also from Visual Manna: **Bible Arts & Crafts**.

New from Visual Manna: **Teaching English Through Art**. We don't know too much about this brand-new course, except that its section on reference materials includes a series of famous home-schoolers (e.g., Teddy Roosevelt) for children to draw. Each has a brief bio and a line-art, shaded drawing against a background grid.

Visual Manna will send a free copy of their fine newsletter, which includes projects and specific drawing tips, to any reader of this book who encloses an SASE.

Visual Manna's Complete Art Curriculum is a very good resource for the homeschool family serious about art education.

Forty-five lesson plans are provided. All the lesson plans can be adapted to work with grades K–12, and can work with different ages at the same time. This is a big plus when you have children of significantly different ages, because you can work on the same project at the same time with all the children. While the lesson plans list all materials required, and what to do, be prepared to put in the time needed to flesh out the plan by making a project yourself to demonstrate the lesson, and working along with your students.

This curriculum provides a well-rounded art education, touching on the major media (drawing, painting, pottery, etc.) and concepts (perspective, form, shape, color, etc.). An appreciation for different kinds of art is built using illustrations (some in color) of well-known artworks. Projects and suggestions follow each work of art.

Although this curriculum does not make explicit use of biblical themes, the role of art in church history, and the contribution of the church to art are worked in through the lessons (such as in the lesson on stained glass windows). A time line of art history is included.

This curriculum is designed especially for homeschool use, and there is nothing that would be out of place in the homeschool environment (no occult themes for example). *John Nixdorf*

Visual Manna Two is a 25-lesson curriculum that continues the Visual Manna One art curriculum, but with a stronger focus on method. Each lesson introduces a topic such as light (and shading), paper quilling, or sponge painting. The lesson objectives and required materials are listed for each suggested activity, and separate activities are suggested for grades one through six and grades seven through twelve.

While the activities for each lesson provide good ideas, what makes this book really special are its graphics and art reproductions. Each reproduction is accompanied by a discussion explaining its importance and how to study it.

The lessons tie together in fascinating ways. For example, the lesson to teach line concepts includes a Japanese art reproduction. The use of lines in Japanese *sumi-e* painting is discussed, with an explanation that the emphasis is in capturing the essence of something with as few brush strokes as possible. The grade seven through twelve exercise points out how fashion designers use very few lines to capture a figure, and suggests creating a fashion ad.

Visual Manna Two comes two ways: you may either order a shrink-wrapped set of lessons, or a binder with each page inserted in a protective plastic cover. The protected page covers are a great idea for passing the art reproductions around or if you tend to be messy when you create.

The **Visual Manna Drawing Book** is a delightful treat for the student who is serious about their drawing. It is a 73-page consumable drawing book whose purpose is to help students with their drawing skills. The book contains an inspiring set of photographs, drawings, and etchings organized by category and technique, with some explanation and plenty of white space to try out, copy and practice your drawing skills. Topics include shading, landscapes, one-and two-point perspective, drawing people and animals. The examples to copy from include historical sites, famous people through history, and many scenes from nature.

Visual Manna Real Manna is not for everyone. In contrast to the gentle approach taken by the other Visual Manna books, this book is disturbing at times. It is a 46-page spiral-bound book containing mini-posters that were designed to provoke discussion as a means of teaching the Gospel.

Topics include religions of the world, the crucifixion, types of law, arguments against evolution, commercialization of Christmas, etc. It is especially not meant for younger children. One picture depicts Santa Claus flushing himself down a toilet. In one of the write-ups, Buddhism is summarized as "Be disillusioned, annihilate self." Things are balanced somewhat (but not entirely) with some posters inspired by verses of love, peace and joy from the Philippians, Ephesians, and Peter. *Teresa Schultz-Jones*

The Gordon School of Art's "Young Masters" program teaches children (and adults!) to produce art of the same quality as the Old Masters of the sixteenth century. Just as in the sixteenth century, students learn and practice techniques, in contrast to the current fad of encouraging artless "self-expression."

Young Masters program developer John Gordon has broken down artistic technique into a number of minute, sequential steps. Starting with the four basic hand positions for drawing, you move on to techniques for drawing clean and elegant lines.

In the first course, you progress from simple dot-to-dot pictures with ¼-inch intervals, to straight-line grid drawings, to drawings that include regular curves, to those with irregular lines, and finally to those with circular shapes. You also learn basic line inking and pencil shading skills, and some basic color theory.

The Foundation Course is supposed to take between four months and four years to complete, depending on you or your student's age and interest level.

The Foundation Course package includes an excellent teacher training text, two full sets of Level 4 worksheets and related teaching materials, three video tapes (these include introductory info and demonstrations of all worksheets and projects), and two free mail consultations.

The introductory video explains the program's philosophy and shows you the actual work of all 140 students in John Gordon's studio class at the time the video was made. The students range in age from 7 to 16, and to say we were impressed by their progress is an understatement.

The level 5 course is available to Foundation Course graduates. *Mary Pride*

NEW!
Young Masters Art Program

Introductory video, $25 ($20 refundable if returned within 2 weeks). Young Masters Home-Study Foundation Course (levels 1–4), $190 plus $10 shipping. Extra Student Art Books, $15. Supply Packets, $7.50. Add $3 shipping for each book (Canada, add $4; Foreign, add $5).
Gordon School of Art, PO Box 28208, Green Bay, WI 54324-8208. (800) 210-1220. Email: gordon@netnet.net. Web: www.newmasters.com.

Not a photograph; drawn by a Gordon School of Art student!

CHAPTER 36

Art Appreciation

In Timothy Zahn's riveting science-fiction best seller, *Heir to the Empire*, Grand Admiral Thrawn bases his military strategy on insights received through studying his opponent's artwork.

I wonder what strategy the Grand Admiral would employ against us—with art in our museums that ranges from classical and Renaissance masterpieces, to random paint splatters and crucifixes suspended in urine.

I rather suspect the Grand Admiral would consider the classical and Renaissance worlds to be worthy foes. Those who promote the random and disgusting "art" so fashionable today he would expect to fold at the first laser blast. Or, more likely, since they clearly despise their own heritage and culture, he would recruit them to betray us all.

Art Appreciation Curriculum

The Annotated Mona Lisa: A Crash Course in Art History from Prehistoric to Post-Modern is starting to show up in homeschool catalogs. Well organized and appealingly designed, with over one-third of its 300 illustrations in full color, this one-book "course" has both advantages and drawbacks.

First, the advantages. Art periods are covered systematically, in chronological order. Main motifs, works, and artists of each period are cogently presented. Author Carol Strickland succeeds in her goals of demystifying art and teaching the reader enough of the rudiments to better appreciate genuine art.

Next, the drawbacks. Despite its title, this is not a "course." It lacks any closure or feedback mechanism. There are no tests, exams, or exercises to help tamp down all those unfamiliar names and terms. "Facts" are stated which are either inaccurate or unsupported (e.g., the book says that the Easter Island statues were pulled to their final locations on sledges, the Tower of Babel was 270 feet tall, and Ramses was the Pharaoh at the time of Moses). The author is clearly not sympathetic to Christianity, or any religion for that matter. In contrast, "artists" of the 20th century and the 1990s

Some Standards for Great Art

- Does it require technical skill?
- Is the art itself powerful, or does it rely solely on shocking subject matter for its impact?
- Is it beautiful?
- Is it clever or original? ("Shocking" is not synonymous with "original.")
- Is it propaganda? (Great art is universal and speaks to all times and cultures.)

BOTTOM LINE: I would choose the comic-book art of Steve Rude over 99.9% of what calls itself "fine art" today.

NEW!
Annotated Mona Lisa

High school. $22.50 plus shipping. *Andrews & McMeel, PO Box 419150, Kansas City, MO 64141. (800) 826-4216. Fax: (800) 437-8683. Web: www.andrewsmcmeel.com.*

whose "work" consists of raw leftist propaganda and/or raw sexual decadence, with no technical skill included or required, are presented as serious creators. To give you an idea of how offensive they are, some of these "works" have incited the various campaigns to defund the National Endowment for the Arts. Although she spares us any visual examples of the worst offenders, I suspect many of us would be embarrassed to read her descriptions of these "works" aloud to our families.

Plenty of nudes, both paintings and sculpture, are included. That, in fact, is one of the book's recurring messages: good guys like the Greeks emphasized the human body, while bad guys like the medieval Christians felt bodies should be covered and souls should be revealed. The book seems to say that today the body itself is legitimately part of the artist's palette, to be used for its sex-and-violence shock value. How interesting that humanism, having come full circle, ends up dehumanizing us.

A parent who is well versed in art (minimally, having studied Dr. Schaeffer's *How Should We Then Live?*) could use *The Annotated Mona Lisa* to give his or her teens a survey of art history. If you're willing to make some flash cards, or buy a good set of art prints or art cards, and spend some time studying them, maybe the students will even remember most of it. But if you don't have a clue about how art can be good or evil, or don't even believe *any* art can be evil, you are better off skipping this book. *Mary Pride*

NEW!
Bedrick Artists from A to Z series

Grade 7–adult. List price, $14.95 each. At time of writing, on sale for $8.95 each. Shipping extra. *Peter Bedrick Books, 156 Fifth Avenue, New York, NY 10010. (212) 206-3738. Fax: (212) 206-3741. Email: bedrick@panix.com.*

The **Artists from A to Z series** includes one book each on Bonnard, Cézanne, Chagall, Corot, and Matisse. Although the publisher points out, "These are not primarily children's books," the simple styling and A to Z format lend them an accessible feel. Each half-sized hardbound book follows the artist's life and work through a series of two-page chapters. Each chapter title is in French (with English translation beneath), and begins with a successive letter of the alphabet. Some nude artworks are included. *Mary Pride*

Bedrick Masters of Art Series

Grade 9–adult. $22.50 each. *Peter Bedrick Books, c/o NTC Contemporary Publishing, 4255 W. Touhy, Lincolnwood, IL 60646. (800)323-4900. Fax: (800)998-3103.*

If you like oversized (but thin), hardbound, lavishly illustrated "fact" books, take a look at the gorgeous new **Masters of Art** series from Peter Bedrick Books. Books in this series so far include *Leonardo da Vinci, Michelangelo, Picasso, Rembrandt, Van Gogh, Giotto and Medieval Art, The Story of Sculpture* (from evolutionary "prehistory" to the present), and *The Impressionists.* Each book is replete with illustrations (including some impressive "cutaway" illustrations of buildings), photos of famous artworks, and lush historical detail, with most sections following the tried and true "double-page spread" format popularized by Random House's "Eyewitness Books" series. Contents of each book include mini-bios of famous artists of the times, architecture and customs of the times, artistic techniques (e.g., how a fresco mural was made), and lots more—great for unit studies on these art periods. Surprisingly, there is relatively little information on the artists' lives; these books pay most of their attention to art history (including how history in general affects art) and techniques. The reading level is not above a homeschooled preteen. All the books except *Giotto* include some classic nude portraiture or sculpture; the *Story of Sculpture* book abounds in it, including female idols and statues with male genitalia prominently displayed. *Mary Pride*

Masterpieces in Art is an earnest effort, written from a Christian point of view, to enable the home-school teacher to do art appreciation. There is nothing to offend even the most delicate sensibilities. Specifically there are no nudes of either sex. There also are no occult or other objectionable themes.

Over 60 artworks are illustrated and discussed in some detail. In addition to a description of each work, the book provides interesting background information. There are also discussion questions geared to elementary and high-school students.

Regrettably, the book has several major flaws. First, all the illustrations are small (the book itself measures only 5½ by 8½ inches) and done in black and white. Although you get a general idea about the works, it is impossible to gain anything but the most superficial appreciation of them. Second, the selection of artworks is extremely limited, essentially classical European paintings (there is only one sculpture) dating roughly from 1500 to 1900.

Perhaps you could use this book as a companion to color versions of the artwork (which you could find at your local library, or on CD-ROM). By itself it could well have the effect of dampening, rather than heightening, your homeschool student's interest in art. *John Nixdorf*

Here's something more stimulating than crayons and colored paper! The staff at Covenant Home Curriculum think that true art comes from God and that children can learn how to apply biblical thinking to art as well as to other areas, including how to create excellent artworks themselves.

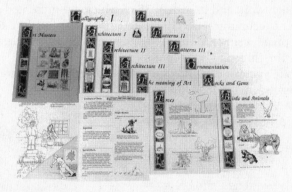

Dale Dykema, Covenant's headmaster and the author of **Art Masters**, practices what he preaches. The layout and design of this series of teaching units is outstanding.

Each lushly illustrated unit is printed on a single 11 x 17" sheet of high-rag-content gray paper and folded in the middle to create a handy four-page booklet. Some units also have an extra sheet tucked in the middle. Text and pictures interweave to explain the concepts taught in the unit. Each unit has a glossary of new words related to the art topic studied and a brief "Plans and Projects" section. Units are:

- The Meaning of Art
- Rocks and Gems
- Birds and Animals
- Poetry in the Bible
- Patterns I (spirals and explosions)
- Patterns II (meanders, branching, vortex streets)
- Patterns III (bubbles, cracking)
- Ornamentation
- Architecture I (introduction)
- Architecture II (houses)

NEW!
Christian Liberty Masterpieces In Art
Grades 7–12. $7 plus $4 shipping. *Christian Liberty Press, 502 West Euclid Ave., Arlington Heights, IL 60004. (847) 259-4444. Fax: (847) 259-2941. Email: enquire@homeschools.org. Web: www.homeschools.org. They take credit card orders, but not over the phone. Any other contact method will work.*

Covenant Home Art Masters
Grades 5–12. $12.95 plus shipping. *Covenant Home Curriculum, 17800 W. Capitol Dr., Brookfield, WI 53045. (414)781-2171. Fax: (414)781-0589. Email: educate@covenanthome.com. Web: covenanthome.com.*

- Architecture III (churches)
- Calligraphy
- Trees

Each subject is approached from at least three ways: what the Bible says about the subject, how artists have handled it before, and techniques for applying it yourself. The Rocks and Gems unit, for example, gives a brief overview of how rocks and gems were used in Bible times and their symbolic meanings in Scripture (e.g., God's people are called "precious jewels" in 1 Corinthians 3:10-13). The unit then goes on to show the 10 most popular styles of gem cuts. Suggested activities include Bible look-ups, rock tumbling, rock identification, and observing gems at home and the jewelry shop, among other things.

The more I look at Art Masters, the more impressed I am with it. The unit on home architecture, for instance, explains the major periods and styles of American home design with more clarity and less words than I have ever seen before—plus you get a line drawing of each architectural style! The same clarity, biblical depth, and range of exercises is maintained throughout the series. Plus the entire series comes with a table of contents and bibliography for further study.

I would definitely recommend Art Masters. *Mary Pride*

NEW!
The Kids' Art Pack

Grade 7–adult. $29.95.
DK Publishing, 95 Madison Ave., New York, NY 10016.
Orders: (888)-DIAL DKP.
Inquiries: (212) 213-4800.
Fax: (212) 213-5240. Web: dk.com.

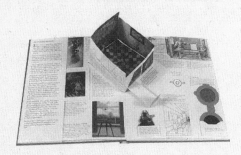

This is a *très* cool book, loaded with pop-ups and a lot more. **The Kids' Art Pack** spotlights 60 masterpieces (providing solid information about each work and its artist), 25 of which are presented as lift-the-flap cut-outs. The techniques used in created art are explored in depth on each two-page spread, using a variety of hands-on goodies: puzzles, a color wheel you can spin, three-D glasses, a mini art student's portfolio, optical illusions, a mobile you can construct on a pop-up pedestal, and more. You even get a 20-page activity book, tucked inside the back cover.

All this is covered:

- Media, from cave paintings to etchings to watercolor to oils to sculpture and more
- Perspective and realism
- Light and color
- Movement
- Pattern and composition
- How art can be used to convey stories and puzzles
- Style and subject

Art examples range from the "prehistoric" through Picasso.

Although the publisher recommends it for age 8 and up, I believe readers of junior-high age and up are most likely to benefit from the high-vocabulary, small-print text with which the book is studded, and less likely to rip this exciting book to shreds while playing with the dozens of activities and hands-on items it contains. *Mary Pride*

NEW!
Showforth Art Videos

Grade 7–adult. $29.95 each. All four, $99.97. Shipping extra.
Showforth Videos, Bob Jones University Press, Customer Services, Greenville, SC 29614-0062.
(800) 845-5731. Fax (USA and Canada): (800) 525-8398. Fax (other countries): (864) 271-8151.
Web: www.bjup.com.

Relatively few people are aware that Bob Jones University has a fine art collection. Putting that collection to good use, these four **Showforth Art Videos**, all hosted by Bob Jones himself, introduce the viewer to topics in art appreciation.

Symbols in Religious Art shows you how to recognize *which* saint or biblical figure you're looking at, by the symbols the artist painted. St. John, for example, has the eagle. *The Symbolists* introduces you to this "school" of art, which followed the Renaissance. *Splendors of the Baroque* and *Glories of Baroque* take you a century further on. The *Splendor* video highlights Italian paintings, while the *Glories* video looks at Fleming, Duth, Spanish, and French painting.

All four videos point out the differences between Catholic and Protestant art, to the benefit of the Protestants. There is some repetition in the paintings you see, but not an excessive amount. They are easy viewing, with captions to help you remember the artists and the paintings, and include a lot of good information. *Mary Pride*

The current ad for **Understanding Comics** says, "There's a big gaping hole in the official history of art, and it's high time somebody filled it!" I agreed with this sentiment as I read it, because I had already bought and read the book. Several times.

Author Scott McCloud, himself a comics professional, is anxious to redeem the comics medium from its undeserved "funny books for kids" image. That's why *Understanding Comics* is not about who's who in comics, or famous comic series, as some might expect. Rather, it is the most insightful and readable analysis of art in general—and "sequential art" in particular—that you will find anywhere.

Just for starters, you'll be looking closely at ancient Egyptian and Aztec sequential art, moving on to the Bayeux Tapestry that chronicles the Norman conquest of England, to medieval death-of-a-saint woodcuts, to Hogarth's famous *A Rake's Progress* and *A Harlot's Progress* (cautionary moral tales of how people fall into sin). You quickly see that sequential art is about more than Donald Duck or Superman—and that there's more to the art of Donald and Superman than you ever guessed!

Along the way you will learn about:

- How words and art have historically been used together
- What happens "in the gutter" between panels, and how your mind translates this into smooth action
- Why your mind recognizes a circle filled with two dots and a line as a "face," and the value of iconic graphics like that v. representational art
- Closure
- Sequence
- Masking
- Panel transitions and panelization
- Suggestion v. depiction
- Ways to convey action and motion
- How line, balloon shape, and lettering are used to convey emotion
- Color
- Japanese art
- How movies were invented
- Why artists create art
- and much more, all presented in comic panel style, with examples that *show* as well as *tell*.

If you're interested in learning about comics as an art medium, I suggest you start with some of Gladstone Publishing's collections of Carl Barks' *Donald Duck* and *Scrooge McDuck*, collections of *The Spirit* by Will Eisner (he is to comic books what Orson Welles is to movies), the Marvel Masterworks collections featuring Jack Kirby's art, and the DC Archives Batman collections featuring the work of Dick Sprang and Jerry Robinson (love those giant typewriters!) and the Silver Age Green Lantern (for fun, and to see how to Gil Kane made a man look like he was *really* flying).

Then, for a look at art in comics today, pick up just about any Image comic (I'm not saying I *like* them, but this is the "hot" trend), anything by Steve Rude (nobody is better on composition and backgrounds—see if you can find the *Nexus* graphic novels or, failing that, his latest *Hulk v. Superman* one-shot), and anything by Alex Ross (his book *Marvels* is a good starting point).

For weird goth art and splatterpunk, look for prestige format Batman one-shots with weird-looking covers. The recent *Predator* mini-series, "Homeworld," is another excellent example.

Your local comics store may have all these in stock, and if not, they can order them for you.

Of course, this is *art* we are talking about. My favorite comic, for both words *and* pictures, is *Astro City,* with covers painted by Alex Ross and amazing storytelling by Kurt Busiek. New issues come out bimonthly, and several collections of back issues are available.

Be aware that much of comics today is *not* G-rated for sex, violence, or vocabulary, and underdressed, big-breasted women remain highly popular. The morality of many (not all) plots ranges from questionable to mistaken. So you don't want to just grab anything you see off the shelf and hand it to the kiddies. However, the same can be said about books and movies. *As an art medium, comics have power and potential—and definitely need more Christian influence.*

NEW!
Usborne Understanding Modern Art

Grades 7–12. $9.95 plus $3 shipping.
EDC Publishing, Division of Educational Development Corporation, 10302 East 55th Place, Tulsa, OK 74146. (800) 475-4522. *Fax:* (800) 747-4509. *Web: www.edcpub.com.*

You will get more out of *Understanding Comics* if you are already familiar with the works of "fine artists" Magritte ("*Ceci n'est pas un pipe*"), Hokusai, Balla, Duchamp, Munch, van Gogh, Klee, Mondrian, Dürer, Rembrandt, David, Ingres, Picasso, Leger, and Monet, as well as the art styles called Classicism, Impressionism, Dada, Surrealism, Futurism, Cubism, and Manga. You will get the most out of it if you are already familiar with the works of comics greats such as Carl Barks, Will Eisner, Moebius, and Art Spiegelmann. But even if none of these names mean anything to you at all, this book will teach you a lot and get you thinking about art in a whole new way. *Mary Pride*

From the Mondrian picture on the front—with a confused student scratching her head trying to figure out what it's about—to the artist biographies in the back, **Usborne Understanding Modern Art** is a great introduction to modern art. Based on the familiar two-page-spread format, it exposes you to dozens of artists, styles, movements, trends, and lots more. You also learn about the modern art world, get to see many famous paintings (including Seurat's "The Models," starring a trio of undressed females), and face all the tough criticisms, such as "It isn't lifelike," "Anyone can do it," and "I can't understand it." Schools covered include cubism, impressionism, expressionism, dada, pointillism, futurism, op art, pop art, constructivism, socialist realism, vorticism, surrealism, primitivism, suprematism, feminist, Bauhaus, ready-mades, even graffiti! Your friends will be amazed when you show them around the art gallery. Good deal. *Mary Pride*

CHAPTER 37

Musicianship

Quick quiz: What has long hair, weird clothes, is followed by screaming preteens and teenagers, and trashes hotel rooms? If you guessed the answer was "a rock musician," you are right.

Let's get this straight before we start. Some of my best male friends used to have long hair, before they went bald (!), and I once employed two guys who wore ponytails. I'm not going to start ranting about hair and clothes. My point is this: music today has been changed in the popular mind from something we all do, to something performed by weird, exotic beings from another planet. Whether the weird beings wear lace and sequins and play at a piano with a candelabra on top, or whether they wear torn clothes and swing their heads around like they're trying to churn what's inside into brain stew, either way they are spreading the gospel of Music as a Freakish Lifestyle.

In this view, your and my proper role is that of the Acolytes with Earphones. We listen. Sometimes, if we're really brave, we sing along in the shower, the car, or at a karaoke setup. That's it. Most of us do not

- compose our own music
- construct our own instruments
- play our own instruments
- sing with our family and friends
- or put on family concerts.

Now, I don't deny that professional musicians have their place, but not one so large that it squeezes out friendly, everyday music. Silence is nice every now and then, too. How many great works have been written because a composer took a walk by a babbling brook or listened quietly to birds singing?

You deserve a chance to become a composer and musician, making music you and your family can enjoy. According to the Bible, we are *all* supposed to be composers and musicians: "Play skillfully on the stringed instruments and shout for joy," "making melody in your heart to God." Regain your inheritance with the resources below.

American Institute of Music Courses

Grade 10–adult. One-time registration fee for new students, $17.95. Preliminary Rudiments Course, Grade I Rudiments, and Grade II Rudiments, $114.95 each. Grade III, IV, and V History, $209.95 each. Grades III and IV Harmony, $219.95 each. Grade IV Counterpoint, $219.95. Piano Pedagogy Level I, $249.95. Textbooks extra.
American Institute of Music, PO Box 2000, Niagara University, NY 14109-2000. (800) 950-8663.

"Qualify for college credit" only applies if *your* college will accept these credits. Make sure of this before you buy.

Davidson Music Courses

Grade 7–adult. Most courses: Textbook, $12.95; Cassette, $10.95; Set, $22.95. How to Play Gospel Music, Play Gospel Songs by Ear, $22.95 each (specify piano or organ). Fills and Runs by Ear, $15.95 for cassette and book. Shipping extra.
Davidson Music, 6727 Metcalf, Shawnee Mission, KS 66204. (913) 262-6533. Fax: (913)722-2980. Web: www.davidsonsmusic.com.

American Institute of Music (AIM) is the U.S. branch of the Tritone Music Group, a private music school based in Toronto, Canada that since 1977 has been providing correspondence courses for students preparing to take the written exams of the major Canadian conservatories. Complete courses range in price from $75 to $239.95, which includes any needed supplementary work. This is a good deal compared to other correspondence schools which charge by the lesson, often costing a lot more.

AIM is accredited by the Distance Education Training Council, and its Target Learning courses qualify for college credit in America. These include Rudiments courses (beginning to advanced music theory), two levels of Harmony, one of Counterpoint, and several of Music History. Plus, AIM offers a "Piano Pedagogy" course for aspiring piano teachers. Please keep in mind that the grade levels are *Conservatory* grade levels, not elementary school grade levels!

These are *correspondence courses,* not just home study courses, so you send in your homework to be corrected and returned to you. AIM lets you work at your own pace, with no deadlines for work completion. If you don't "get" a particular lesson, you will receive additional explanations and supplementary exercises at no charge. Partial refunds are available until the point where you have completed more than half of any course—with a 100% refund if you cancel within five days of receiving your course.

When enrolling, you are asked to fill out a placement quiz, to make sure you are starting at the right level. This is very helpful. You also receive detailed descriptions of each course that includes a complete course outline—also helpful.

I must say that the courses look absolutely fascinating. Keep in mind that these are designed for mature learners—high school and adult—not for young children. Also, the Piano Pedagogy course has several segments promoting the unbiblical "behaviorism" theory of learning. (If you wonder why behaviorism is unbiblical, read Ruth Beechick's *Biblical Psychology of Learning* or my own *Schoolproof!*) Aside from these caveats, what you get (as far as I can tell without actually taking a course) is thorough, easy-to-follow instruction in subjects that many people have found difficult to study on their own, and that you would have to travel long distances (in many cases) to take at a good on-site school. *Mary Pride*

Large newsprint catalog loaded with learn-to-play courses. Keyboard instruments are most strongly represented here. Most **Davidson Music courses** are by Madonna Woods, a lady who has pioneered her own method for learning to play by ear.

Some notable courses in this catalog:

- **Play Gospel Songs by Ear,** a two-course program that teaches you to play the melody line in the right hand and accompany yourself with chords in the left hand. Courses are available for either piano or organ. Uses note names instead of music notation, for the benefit of those who neither know nor want to know how to read standard music. Really good instructional method tells you how to find the right starting notes for the song in the key of C, learn additional keys, add chording, and dress up your playing with some easy tricks. That was all in Course One; Course Two goes on to more advanced stuff. The cassette follows the book's general format but adds additional explanations, and of course it has the musical examples played out for you. All you need to learn to play by ear is to be able to hum a tune!

- **How to Play Gospel Music** starts with a mini how-to-read-music course. Its 20 lessons, designed for both organ and piano, take you all the way through chording, filling out your right hand with 3rds and 6ths, runs, "evangelistic" playing techniques such as cross hands, walking basses, and intros and endings. It uses standard music notation. This is the best-looking Davidson Music book I have seen, with a glossy cover and professionally-printed pages.

- If that sounded a little tame, Madonna also offers a new course, **Fills and Run by Ear**, that explains how to add walking bass line, alternative basses, chord runs, cross hands playing, right hand fills, grace notes, and different rhythms. Other advanced material includes **Learn Chords for Piano, Organ, and Electronic Keyboard**; **How to Play Intros and Endings**; **How to Accompany**; and lots more.

- Several books of **Playing in Church by Ear**, simple arrangements of popular gospel songs written with note and chord names. **Playing in Church** is the same material in standard musical notation. Each also has instructions about music and playing to improve your church piano or organ playing. Also courses on Southern Gospel style playing and evangelistic style piano.

- **Easy Adult Piano** is a three-part method that includes keyboard stickers with note names, chord charts, quizzes, and explanations of eighth, sixteenth, and dotted notes and many musical terms.

- **Home Music Lessons** shows how to set up a music-teaching business from your home. Detailed.

Songbooks include both Christian and pop music. Also available: Electronic keyboard courses. Piano courses for children from different publishers. Chord guitar courses. Learning Unlimited guitar series. Mel Bay Modern Method courses. The "Fun With" series for over two dozen different instruments that is supposed to give you a taste of each.

Intermediate and advanced courses are also available, as is a large selection of easy songbooks in both play-by-ear and standard notations. *Mary Pride*

For total beginners, concert pianist Daniel Abrams has produced a six-audiocassette series that takes you step by step from finding what's what on the keyboard to playing slow blues, diminished chords, and unusual rhythms. **Put Your Hands on the Piano and Play!** includes "beautiful" (as opposed to rowdy) piano pieces in all styles, from classical to pop and blues. You start off slowly with major and minor scales. Plan on working through each tape several times to capture all the information.

Once you've progressed beyond the greenhorn stage, you can add to your piano technique while learning to play pieces by the great classical composers. **Play Your Favorite Piano Classics** includes music scores by Haydn, Bach, Beethoven, Dvorak and others in a spiral-bound book tucked into the cassette binder. Daniel Abrams talks you through each piece on the included audio tapes, pointing out potential trouble spots and giving hints to make your playing more exciting. He also plays each selection, so you can hear what it sounds like. If you're really feeling

NEW!
Homespun Piano Courses
Grade 7–adult. Homespun Tapes Blues Piano course, Instructional Level 2 (assumes basic knowledge): CD & 24-page music book, $19.95. Put Your Hands on the Piano and Play!, Play Your Favorite Piano Classics, $59.95 each. Shipping extra.
Homespun Tapes, PO Box 340, Woodstock, NY 12498. (800) 338-2737 Web: www.homespuntapes.com.

brave, you can play along with the tape, since pieces are separated into left and right channels.

Homespun also has rock and jazz piano courses, plus New Orleans and ragtime piano courses. These are available in audio or video versions. I admit that I've flubbed around with David Cohen's *Beginning Blues Piano* audio course, and found I could actually follow it. (Whether I *want* to play blues is another question—reviewers have to take what they're given!)

If you are an advanced beginning piano player, and would like to get your feet wet in this traditional American blues style, then pick up the **David Bennett Cohen Teaches Blues Piano** mini-course. A professional musician for over 25 years, Mr. Cohen's early training was in classical piano. He later was heavily influenced by early blues masters Otis Span, Professor Longhair, and others.

Many other courses are available in the *Blues Piano* format

Cohen begins his instruction with an explanation of the blues basics, such as the twelve-bar blues, with its I–IV–V progression. All instruction is in the "People's Key" of C natural, for ease of learning and teaching.

Cohen then introduces two basic blues rhythms: the shuffle of traditional blues, and the straight time rhythm of rock and roll. Several alternate and syncopated rhythms are demonstrated, as well as beginning improvisational techniques, including the use of right hand triplets and trills. Included are demonstrations of solos with these rhythms, embellishments, and the use of the diminished chords. This is followed by a treatment of several blues scales—including the very useful five-note blues scale—rounding out with improvisational ideas utilizing full blues scales.

David Cohen's professionalism shines in this course, and he proves himself a worthy teacher and instrumentalist. This is an extremely tasteful presentation of blues piano, purely instrumental, avoiding the possibility of objectionable lyrics often found in the blues style.

The format for instruction is one of Homespun Tapes new "Listen and Learn" packages, which includes a CD and 24-page instruction book, complete with discography.

The CD instruction is much easier to work with than a video or audio lesson, as you can quickly find the track that you are currently working on, and skip over previously mastered material, and enjoy the improved fidelity that a compact disk provides. Highly recommended. *Barbara Petronelli and Mary Pride*

NEW!
Homespun Tapes Learn to Play Irish Tinwhistle

Grade 7–adult. Homespun Tapes Learn to Play Irish Tinwhistle: Teaching Level 1 (no prior experience necessary). 60-minute video, $19.95. Shipping extra.
Homespun Tapes, PO Box 340, Woodstock, NY 12498. (800) 338-2737 Web: www.homespuntapes.com.

Veteran tinwhistler and teacher L.E. McCullough (listen for his background composition on the Ken Burns PBS series, *The American West*) introduces students to the joy of making traditional Irish music on the inexpensive tinwhistle, or pennywhistle, in **Learn to Play Irish Tinwhistle.**

Mr. Cullough begins with a brief history of the instrument and follows with guidelines and sources for choosing an instrument. He believes that the tinwhistle is one of the easiest instruments in the world to play, and suggests that comfort and ease of use settle any technical disputes.

McCullough rapidly teaches fingerings, scales, accidentals, tone production, and correct embouchure. Diatonic and chromatic scales are discussed, as well as phrasing and breathing.

Then, before he gets into the meat of teaching actual tunes, he explains the structure and time signature of several traditional Irish forms of music. McCullough spends a great deal of time teaching the embellishments and ornamentation typical of Irish music: grace notes, triplets, and rolls. He demonstrates these slowly at first; then up to speed, beginning on varying notes (which is quite useful in learning to personalize the tunes). Mr. McCullough strongly believes that melody is the heart of the music, and stresses that embellishments can, and should be mastered after learning the tunes themselves.

The types of tunes presented are airs, polkas, double jigs, hornpipes, and reels. Also included is the hauntingly beautiful harp tune of the late 17th Century, *Tabhair dom do Lamh* ("Give Me Your Hand"), composed in waltz time. The accompanying booklet, which contains fingering charts and written music, also has a discography of recommended Irish music for further study.

Although the Homespun instructional level is 1 (novice), I feel that a beginning student would benefit from a more basic introduction prior to this study; something that incorporates more basic exercises to develop eye-hand-ear correlation. This would make the learning of melodies and embellishments much easier. Perhaps the Clarke Tinwhistle handbook and tape.

Homespun Tapes also sells a very nice, reasonably priced whistle that I would recommend.

Mr. McCullough is a fine player, and his gentlemanly manner makes him a delight to study with. Highly recommended. *Barbara Petronelli*

Homespun, as befits a company started by professional musicians, has a number of courses stressing practical musicianship. Note first the excellent series on **Ear Training**. Matt Glaser does the honors, and I can't think of a better introduction to real musicianship for anyone mature enough to do the exercises. In other words, most five-year-olds won't dig it, but Mozart would have. Consider also The **Homespun Songwriter's Workshop**, a little six-cassette-tape number featuring tips of the trade from notable songwriters Pat Alger, Fred Koller, Steve Gillette, Eric Kaz, and John D. Loudermilk. This

set takes you from the moment of inspiration (and how to hurry it along) to putting together a finished demo. Plus Daniel Abrams's cassette and booklet on **Practice Techniques For All Musicians** and Matt Glaser's three-tape series on developing your musical skills, **Tools For Musicianship**. Lots more: see the other Homespun Tapes listings in this chapter. *Mary Pride*

Homespun has a wide assortment of **video lessons** for adults taught by well-known artists. We're talking the likes of Dr. John, John Sebastian, and Amos Garrett. Instruments covered are acoustic and electric guitar (from basic to advanced), dobro, fiddle, bass, banjo, keyboards, mandolin, autoharp, drums, voice, dulcimer, and flutes of the Andes. These are all recorded on good-quality tape, unlike the cheap stuff some other companies use. This not only helps save your VCR from getting chewed up, but enables you to actually hear the music without strain.

Homespun Tapes, both audio and visual, have an cheerful energy and affability that makes learning from them really fun. You know you're being taught by real musicians who enjoy their work, not by time-serving "educators" who think music is good for you. The tapes are supremely non-threatening. Homespun's teaching musicians typically wear something comfortable, and the set itself often is a room in Homespun founder Happy Traum's house. It's like stepping out to the front porch and asking Artie Traum, who happens to be sitting there, "Hey, how about showing us some of your cool chord progressions?" *Mary Pride*

Homespun Tapes Songwriter's Workshop

Grade 7–adult. Single tapes, $14.95 each. Six-tape series, $49.95 each. Shipping extra.
Homespun Tapes, Box 340, Woodstock, NY 12498. Orders: (800) 338-2737. Inquiries: (914) 246-2550. Fax: (914) 246-5282. Email: hmspn@aol.com. Web: www.homespuntapes.com.

Homespun Tapes Video Courses

Grade 7–adult. Videos, $19.95–$39.95 each. Shipping extra.
Homespun Tapes, Box 340, Woodstock, NY 12498. Orders: (800) 338-2737. Inquiries: (914) 246-2550. Fax: (914) 246-5282. Email: hmspn@aol.com. Web: www.homespuntapes.com.

Learning to Read Music

Grade 7–adult. $14.95 plus $4.95 minimum shipping.
Audio-Forum, division of Jeffrey Norton Publishers, Inc. 96 Broadstreet, Guilford, CT 06437. (800) 243-1234. Fax: (203) 453-9774. Email: info@audioforum.com. Web: www.audioforum.com.

NEW!
Piano for Quitters

Grade 9–adult. $29.95.
Pacific Communications, Inc., 1801 E. Fourth Ave., Olympia, WA 98506-9940. (888) 742-6653.

A self-instructional course, **Learning to Read Music** covers all the basics in only an hour and a half. Pitch. Duration. Rhythm. Note heads. Rests. Dotted notes. Clefs. Sharps and flats. Key signatures. Naturals. Repeats. Other musical symbols and terms. The little booklet *shows* what the cassette *describes,* plus providing some reinforcement exercises. A total beginner would want to listen through several times; a rusty adult wanting to brush up might only need to go through this once. Any wide-awake and motivated person, no matter how young, could pick up a lot of musical notation through this inexpensive course. *Mary Pride*

"Today, it is estimated that over 36 million Americans were once piano students, and quit, making the piano the leading instrument for quitters." So begins the 80-minute **Piano for Quitters** video. Created for those who tried piano lessons and gave up, this unique set of video lessons starts by introducing you to the history of piano instruction. You'll discover that the era of piano prodigies was one in which young students were encouraged to experiment and play around with chords. With the advent of mass-marketed pianos came mass-marketed piano courses.

Unlike the free-flowing methods of the 19th century, these modern methods were highly structured. Students were taught to read *music long before they were taught to* make *music. The resulting boredom, and frustration with lessons, combined with the humiliation of recital play, caused millions of young people, most of whom loved music, to turn their backs on the piano—forever.*

Does that sound like you? If so, you may just want to get that old piano tuned and try out this course. Divided into 10 video "chapters," each followed by a quick review, it will not teach you how to quickly sight-read sheet music. Instead, you'll learn the methods and tricks that composers, arrangers, and improvisational artists use to create music that sounds good. You'll learn how music is *structured,* and be encouraged to experiment. Instructor Mark Almond's philosophy: "When we're practicing major chords and practicing minor chords, we're practicing all the melodies ever written."

You begin by learning three chords: A minor, D minor, and F major. Immediately you begin using these chords, along with the "root" keys for each chord, the latter to be played with the left hand. You'll also be using the "sustain" pedal, to make the music "sing." Next, simple finger exercises are employed to help you learn the names of the keys. You learn how to form any minor or major key, and how to use "altered bass" (different chords in the left hand than in the right hand) to add power and resonance. Major seventh, seventh, and sixth are taught next, in such a simple fashion that I understood them immediately. Ten different chord progressions, included on a foldout card, are also taught. You learn various tricks for adding melody, "expanding" the left-hand part, spreading out the left-hand chord, and finally put it all together in a rendition of "Silent Night."

This is not a course to hand your five-year-old. It will help if you, like so many of us, have struggled with chords and fingering in the past. But previous piano experience is not absolutely essential to master the techniques in this video.

When you've finished, you'll have learned enough to have fun playing around on the piano, making up your own professional-sounding tunes. If you have a good ear for songs and chords, you may even be able to figure out some songs on your own. But you'll still be frustrated. You'll want to apply your new understanding of how music works to sheet music, and to playing consistently by ear. You'll want to see more examples of well-known songs played by this method. In other words, you'll want *Piano for Quitters, Volume 2*, which sadly does not yet exist. Come on, Mark, don't quit now—create the sequel! *Mary Pride*

For those of us who get behind the idea of a homeschool band, the **Christian School Band Method** series has children learning to play hymns and gospel songs while they learn to play their flutes, clarinets, alto saxes, trumpets, trombones, and basses.

Music Invaders, designed for junior-high choir students (but usable by motivated elementary-age home schoolers), is twenty-four 20-minute lessons designed to teach vocal music reading with a "space invaders" theme. You will need the accompanying Teacher's Manual.

The **Hymnplayer** series teaches how to play hymns (surprise!) on the piano. The series has three books for each section: Beginning Hymnplayer, Primary Hymnplayer, Intermediate Hymnplayer, and Advanced Hymnplayer. *Mary Pride*

Leroy Shultz wants to teach you how to play hymns the way you've always imagined with full, rich-sounding chords and embellishments. To accomplish this, three levels of worktexts including cassettes (which are essential to your success) are provided. You should have at least one year of piano before you start, since the program is not meant for novices.

Begin with Level 1 (38 pages) and a study of music fundamentals, signs, intervals, eighth notes, pedaling, and tones as well as lots of music theory and the keys of C, F, and G. Level 2 (48 pages) continues with intervals, leger line notes, syncopation, transposition, tones, major scales and chords, the key of D, and more theory. What you've learned is expanded upon in Level 3 (48 pages) with, among other things, chord inversions, major and minor triads, major and minor keys, three-note chords with octaves, improvisation, and theory.

The accompanying cassettes give instruction and explanation, as well as demonstrations of particular pieces and exercises. The theory is very thorough, but we felt that the sequence of instruction could have been better planned. Scales aren't taught until the second and third levels and some concepts are taught before basic knowledge in key signatures is learned. The selection of hymns included is wonderful—all the great old hymns of the faith.

If you are an intermediate student (Mr. Shultz suggests at least one year of instruction) or have had a good foundation in piano, then this series will develop your skills in the gospel piano style. Though the cassettes demonstrate each page of the books, you probably won't want to tackle it without a teacher available to answer questions. *Marla Perry*

Praise Hymn Band Method, Music Invaders, Hymnplayer

Grades 7–12. Christian School Band Method: Flute, Clarinet, Trumpet, Trombone, Saxophone, and Bass, $2.98 each. Band Director, $8.98. Music Invaders: Student Book, $4.98; Teacher's Manual, $4.98. Hymnplayer series, $4.98 each book. Shipping extra.
Praise Hymn, Inc., PO Box 1325, Taylors, SC 29687. (800) 729-2821. Fax: (864) 322-8284. Email: prazhyminc@aol.com. Web: www.praisehymninc.com.

NEW!
Progressive Gospel Piano: Levels One, Two, and Three

Grade 5–adult. Level 1 book and 1 cassette, $9.10. Level 2 book and 2 cassettes, $14.30. Level 3 book and 3 cassettes, $17.55. All three levels, $37.80. Add $2 shipping.
Progressive Gospel Piano, PO Box 67222, Lincoln, NE 68506. (402) 489-3386.

This charming book made me wish that I were in kindergarten once again, and that Marilyn Moevs Helminiak, the author of **Why Don't You Play LOUD?**, was my music teacher. Who wouldn't love a teacher who comes to class claiming to be Madame Ozankee, a famous opera singer? This class also made me wish I had oodles of musical talent (or could at least play the piano halfway decently) so that I could round up bunches of kindergartners and give music classes. However, although I did learn some things I might try in our own home, and I enjoyed this book immensely, I found that most of it did not "translate" from school to home. Support groups who wish to provide music classes for children might want to consider reading this for ideas. They'll probably end up wanting to kidnap the author so they can have her teach their children! *Rebecca Prewett*

CHAPTER 38

Music Appreciation

This chapter, like all those in this Fine Arts section, is highly relevant even for those with teens in school. Art and music classes are often at the bottom of the public-school priority lists, and even when this is not the case, there's no guarantee class time will be spent on understanding music history and "the classics" as opposed to feel-good discussions of the latest rappers and rock stars.

They say that he who fails to study the past is doomed to repeat it. In the field of music, we should be so lucky. Instead, he who fails to study the past is doomed to simplistic, ever-repeating "tunes" accompanied with throbbing percussion, all backboned by studio highlights played by classically-trained musicians. Yes, even today's pop tunes *still* require background scoring and the help of classical musicians to raise them above the level of "Louie, Louie." Learn to hear what you're *not* hearing with the courses in this chapter.

Music Appreciation Curriculum

The people who put the **André Previn Guide to Music Kit** together say that its purpose is "to challenge 9–13 year olds to find out how musical instruments work and a little about the music played on them." Wrong on two counts. First, no way should this kit be limited to such a narrow age range. As a 34-year-old, I found it fascinating. All our children did too, from ages five on up. For best retention, I believe the ideal age range would be junior high and up. Second, you learn more than "a little" about the music.

The reason the kit is described in such understated terms is, I am convinced, because its makers, not knowing about homeschooling or afterschooling, had in mind to sell it to public schools only. And we all know what priority the public schools put on music instruction. What's the first part of the school budget to be cut when the money supply tightens up? How many hours do schools devote to music training? Good guessing. Add this to the rigid public-school schedule ("Children will learn about music instruments in the second semester of eighth grade, weeks four and five") and we discover why pre-teens are the only group considered likely to use this program.

André Previn Guide to Music Kit

Grade 5–adult. $149.95 plus shipping. *Rhythm Band Instruments, PO Box 126, Fort Worth, TX 76101-0126. Orders: (800) 424-4724. Inquiries: (817) 335-2561. Fax: (800) 784-9401. Web: www.rhythmband.com.*

A pity, because what we have here is a terrific guide to all significant musical instruments and musical forms, presented by a man particularly qualified to do the job. André Previn is famous both as a composer and a conductor, and his career spans the gamut of classical, jazz, and film music. He also (O rare talent!) knows how to communicate what he knows.

Inside the heavy box in which the kit comes you will find four cassettes narrated by André Previn, eight topic books, 24 wallcharts, 24 copies of the activity book, 24 copies of the quiz book, and a teacher's copy of the quiz book with answers. Seven of the topic books cover a type of instrument: one book each for strings, woodwinds, brass, percussion, piano, voice, and electronic and mechanical. The eighth deals with the often-neglected subjects of composing, arranging, and recording.

I didn't expect all that much from the topic books. Sheer naked text was about all I had in mind. So imagine how flabbergasted I was to discover these books match the caliber of Usborne books or Eyewitness books! Just about every instrument known to man is covered in those books, along with fascinating facts about how they work, how they originated, and how they are used. Charts, graphs, photos, and line drawings interweave with carefully-crafted text on each page. Everything is designed for maximum visual impact and memorability. Lots of color throughout.

If the kit were nothing but these topic books, it would already be the best introduction to music via the study of instruments that I have ever seen. But now add to this the four cassettes, whose eight sides each correspond to a topic book. Here's where André Previn's experience really shines. Brilliantly-chosen musical excerpts illustrate the distinguishing features of each instrument and instrument family. He locates a Brahms concerto that shows off the cello's two "voices"—one high and the other low. He presents us with the same Bach piece played once by plucking the notes and once by bowing, in order to illustrate the different sounds of these two techniques. Similar approach to each musical family shows off each instrument's capabilities and foibles. You hear how instruments are used in jazz, classical, pop, and modern styles. (No rock 'n roll, though!) Anyone who has an ear to hear can't help learning how to recognize the different instruments *and* what each is mainly useful for.

Add to this, now, the 24 colorful wall charts. Each highlights an instrument or two, showing where it is placed in the orchestra, detailing its parts, showing how the player holds it, and other useful information, all most attractively presented in full color.

On top of this is the quiz booklet, which tests students on the concepts taught in the topic books, and a teacher's quiz booklet that has the answers. (You get 24 copies of the student's quiz booklet—public school influence, again.)

Add to this the activity book (24 copies of the same book). Here we go far, far beyond anything I have ever seen on the subject of music-making, as students are shown how to construct their own instruments. The teacher's guide expresses the hope that students will actually be given the class time to do this, but an underlying hopeless tone makes it clear that in most cases, they will not. At home you will have the chance to pursue all the activities, which are indeed impressive. Cookbook instructions for science experiments with sound are combined with couldn't-be-simpler step-by-step instructions on instrument construction. Your child will have the chance to make the following types of instruments: strings, woodwinds of the whistle and reed varieties, brass instruments (made from garden hose!), percussion, and mechanical, plus fascinating sound experiments with voice and electronics.

André Previn's Guide to Music is truly the antidote to musical illiteracy. Put this one high on your wish list. *Mary Pride*

True or False: Understanding and appreciating classical music requires formal musical education. Although the answer to that question is false, we often act as if it is a true statement. Author Dhun H. Sethna has become an expert in classical music. His classroom? The operating room! Sethna is a doctor—not of "musicology," but of cardiology.

His 262-page book, **Classical Music for Everybody: A Companion for Good Listening**, is written with the musical novice in mind. If you can't read music, that's no problem. The only requirement Sethna lays out is that the reader come to music with a willing ear. It is written in plain English with no musical notations or symbols. The book is divided into three parts: How to Listen to Classical Music, The Timetables of Music (baroque, classical, romantic, and impressionism), and The Varieties of Musical Experience. Although the book is geared for the novice, it introduces the reader to musical vocabulary such as a "fugue" or the "sonata form" and to the various instruments of the orchestra. My favorite feature of the book is the list of recommended CDs. Whenever possible, Sethna lists inexpensive CDs that don't compromise musical quality. This list makes it possible to build a good, home music library on a budget.

If you're looking for a good overview of classical music written with the novice in mind, look no further! *Rebecca Livermore*

What fun! Two books that take all the stuffiness out of great music and help you get a grip on why regular folks used to pack out music halls to hear it.

Classical Music for Dummies and **Opera for Dummies** have much in common:

- Each book is just over 350 pages long
- Each book comes with an included CD-ROM by the same title, which can be played like a regular music CD or used as a software journey through the music
- Each book is really fun to read. Imagine, for example, learning how operatic lyric writing works by reading a recitative and aria based on the Sandra Bullock movie *Speed*. The writing itself sizzles, and the jokes and similes are really funny as well as educational. Example (speaking of spinto tenors): "Their voices could make a stone weep."
- Each book has lots of "insider" information, from a list of prominent divas' actual outrageous contract demands to how to get an opera singer to invite you backstage
- Each book has oodles of checklists, quotes, tips, and cartoons
- Each book has an index, glossary, and time line
- The music on each book's CD accompanies the text very tightly; music is used to illustrate the book's points, and the book provides step-by-step commentary on each musical piece
- Both books are written by David Pogue ("musical director, orchestrator, and bestselling author of *Macs for Dummies*") and Scott Speck ("award-winning conductor and Fulbright Music Scholar")

Classical Music for Dummies, like other Dummies books, has a Cheat Sheet card bound inside its front cover. On side one of this cheat sheet is a diagram showing the arrangement of an orchestra, plus descriptions of the various instruments. Side two has a timeline of the classics, giving the basic periods (Baroque, Classical, Romantic, and Modern), the composers, and their major works. The book itself starts with the entire history of music in

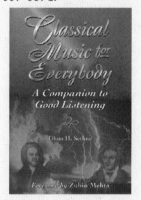

80 pages, followed by brief descriptions of the different types of classical compositions. If you ever wondered what the difference between a fantasia and a rhapsody is, this is your chapter. The field guide to the orchestra, which is next, includes a handy concert survival guide with tips about how to get in for little or nothing and why *not* to eat a huge meal of beans before going. A "Spin Through Your Free CD" follows, with comments on each piece (and each portion of each piece), listed by time played so far, so you can pick up more understanding of what you're hearing. You even get a really good beginning music theory course (called, of course, The Dreaded Music Theory Chapter). Like all Dummies books, it has to end with a section called "Part of Tens," with several more or less useless (but still funny) lists of ten things, such as "Ten Great Classical Music Jokes." In the appendixes, you'll find a good list of suggested titles for your classical music library.

The *Opera for Dummies* Cheat Sheet has an "emergency vocabulary" of common opera terms, an opera timeline, a guide to the ranges of operatic voices, and The Operagoer's Checklist. The book first introduces you to the history and subject matter of opera, which is usually pretty nasty. There's a reason those afternoon TV shows are called "soap *operas*," after all. Like the other book, you are then walked through a concert experience and taken on a spin through the songs on your included CD. A backstage tour follows, where you'll find out what *really* goes on in the opera world. Next, the operas themselves: a guide to the 50 most popular, and "the best of the rest." The same basic lists of tens as in the classical music book wrap up this book. You'll also find tips for getting started on the life of an opera buff: best operas to start with and the easiest way to start.

Aside from the works of P.D.Q. Bach, I can't think of a more exuberant way to introduce a student of any age to the world of great music. *Mary Pride*

NEW!
"For Dummies" Classical Music Series

All ages (listening), grade 5–adult (interacting). $11.99 each.
IDG Books Worldwide Inc., an International Data Group Company, 919 E. Hillsdale Blvd., Suite 400, Foster City, CA 94404. All IDG materials are sold in bookstores. Consumer Customer Service: (800) 762-2974. Web: www.dummies.com.

The new **"For Dummies" classical music series** comes in normal CD jewel cases. It looks like you're just buying a music CD, with a small yellow booklet thrown in. That's not all you get, though. Along with the musical selections on the CD (from the composer's most important works), and a brief booklet biography (with pronunciation guide, glossary, and suggestions for further listening), you also get the following software (also included on the CD, which turns out to double as a CD-ROM):

- Music Workshop, where you can interact with a "midi"-compatible file of the composer's work. "Midi" is a digital music standard that can accept input from a variety of digital musical devices, the most common being midi-equipped keyboards.
- Composer biography
- Jukebox, where you not only can play the music, but also increase your understanding through graphics, pictures, and read-along text.

The For Dummies classical music series is quite extensive. At the time I write this, all these composers were included in the rack in our local Borders store: Bach, Berlioz, Beethoven, Brahms, Chopin, Debussy, Dvorak, Grieg, Handel, Mahler, Mendelssohn, Mozart, Prokofiev, Ravel, Richard Strauss, Rachmaninoff, Rimsky-Korsakov, Sibellius, Stravinsky, Tchaikovsky, Wagner, Verdi, Vivaldi. There were also entries for the following musical styles and instruments: Sopranos, Opera, Waltzes, and Violin. I'm pretty sure there must be at least a "Tenors" CD hiding somewhere. If there isn't, it will likely be added soon.

The software isn't much, sad to say. Unlike the terrific Richard Winters classical-music software (now published by Microsoft, I believe), it doesn't allow you to savor annotated comments while listening to the section of your choice. The composer biography information is scant, the illustrations negligible, and being able to suppress the violins during an orchestral piece just doesn't do it for me. You're just as well off just reading the little booklet and playing the CD on your stereo, in my opinion. *Mary Pride*

Wanna know musical lingo? Wanna know why marches are written in major keys, never in minor? Wanna stop getting confused about sharps and flats, chords and rhythm? Then perhaps concert pianist *cum* composer Daniel Abrams can help.

Homespun's complete **Understanding the Language of Music** tape set tackles both music theory and music history. The music history part is about what you'd expect from an introductory course in Music History. Here's the dope on the music theory part.

Tape 1 is basics of music theory. This is really basic: major and minor scales, intervals, key signatures, sharps/flats/naturals, chords and progressions, and arpeggios. Why major keys sound happy and minor keys sound sad. Lots of discussion of whole and half steps. Better keep the handout in front of you, or this will get confusing. Tape 2 is how music is put together. The place of the I, IV, and V chords in blues, rock, and classical. Seventh chords. Dominant chords. Inversions. Rhythm. Time signatures. Syncopation. Dynamics (playing loudly or softly) and interpretation (subtleties of timing). Plus a history of orchestra instruments.

This introduction to music consciousness is certainly user-friendly. Not terribly time-consuming or expensive, either. Wish Homespun provided more written matter to accompany it, though; the few pages of definitions are not really enough to help a novice become comfortable with all the new terminology. *Mary Pride*

If you've ever wondered how to teach kids to follow along and notice the different themes and instruments in a classical piece, wonder no longer. Pam Enrich has invented something called "Music Maps." Each map outlines a famous musical piece in a totally weird way. Bach's *Brandenburg Concerto #3, First Movement*, for example, takes the form of a curly wig around Bach's head. If you look closely at the wig, you see that the darker curls correspond to the recurring three-note motif which distinguishes this composition. Start at Bach's left shoulder and follow the spiraling curls all the way to the end of the piece. Mussorgsky's *Pictures at an Exhibition* is presented as a map passing by churches and other buildings, crossing and recrossing a river, and ending up at the Great Gate of Kiev. Each sight along the way represents a part of the composition. Look for "fast-moving strings" while crossing the river, while at the churches the style is hushed and hymn-like.

This innovative, visual style of representing music is repeated for all 12 pieces in the original **Music Maps of the Masters**, and for 10 pieces in **More Music Maps of the Masters**. Instructions on the back of each map explain exactly how to use the map to follow—and remember—a composition. You'll also find the recording from which the map was drawn, and its source. Most recordings come from the Bowmar Orchestral Library and Holt, Rinehart and Winston's Exploring Music series. (Many can also be found in the M-L Marketing *Basic Library*, described in Volume 2.)

The twelve composers in *Music Maps* are Bach, Beethoven, Chopin, Gabrieli, Gould, Grieg, Handel, Haydn, Ives, Kodaly, Mussorgsky, and Sousa. The ten in *More Music Maps* are Armstrong, Copland, Gounod, Grieg, Haydn, Mendelssohn, Rossini, Strauss, Tchaikovsky, and Vivaldi. *Mary Pride*

**Homespun Tapes
Understanding the Language of Music**
Grade 9–adult. 6-audiocassette set, $49.95 plus $5.95 shipping.
*Homespun Tapes, PO Box 340, Woodstock, NY 12498. (800) 338-2737 or (914) 246-2550.
Fax: (914) 246-5282.
Email: hmspn@aol.com.
Web: www.homespuntapes.com.*

**Music Maps of the Masters
More Music Maps of the Masters**
Grade 7–adult. Music Maps, $7.95.
More Music Maps, $7.25.
*Rhythm Band Instruments, PO Box 126, Fort Worth, TX 76101-0126.
Orders: (800) 424-4724.
Inquiries: (817) 335-2561.
Fax: (800) 784-9401.
Web: www.rhythmband.com*

NEW!
Music of the Great Composers
Spiritual Lives of the Great Composers, Revised and Expanded

Grade 7–adult. *Music*, $12.99. *Spiritual Lives*, $10.99. Shipping extra. *Zondervan Publishing House, 5300 Patterson Ave. SE, Grand Rapids, MI 49530. (800) 727-1309. (616) 698-6900. Fax: (800) 934-6381. Web: www.zondervan.com.*

Learning about the composers who wrote great music can make your understanding and appreciation of their music richer, especially when the composers had rich spiritual lives. But, like most parents, you probably don't have time to do extensive research into the lives of great composers. Not to worry! With this pair of books, author Patrick Kavanaugh has already done the hard work for you.

In **Music of the Great Composers**, Kavanaugh masterfully presents factual information in a delightfully entertaining way. His book (formerly published as *A Taste for the Classics*) contains the following nine chapters: (1) Getting the Big Picture: Musical Titles or "What's an Opus," (2) Orchestra Music: The Conductor/Instruments of the Orchestra, (3) Choral Music: The Mass, (4) The Concerto: Tempo Indications/Keys and Tonality, (5) Opera: Vocal Types, (6) Chamber Music: The Components of Musical Sound, (7) Song: The Elements of Music Composition, (8) Solo Literature: Sonata Form, (9), Where Do We Go from Here?: Concert Etiquette.

The book also contains appendices which include a listing of the first 1,000 pieces of music you should listen to, an alphabetical listing of the great composers along with basic information about their birth and death, a glossary of common (and not so common) musical terms, and a reading list which will enable you to learn more about the composers which interest you most.

Music of the Great Composers is a 272-page book, filled with fascinating and useful information to help make your voyage into the waters of classical music a pleasant one.

With **Spiritual Lives of the Great Composers**, don't expect a dry, boring recounting of brief moments of spirituality. Kavanaugh is like an artist who, through the medium of words, paints a colorful portrait of each of the featured composers. I savored his well-written biographical sketches, and my kids hung on every word when I read them out loud to them.

This book profiles 20 composers—eight more than the previous edition—including Handel, Bach, Mozart, Beethoven, Mendelssohn, Brahms, Dvorak, Stravinsky, and Messiaen. Kavanaugh points out that although these men were not perfect by any means, they each had a passionate faith in God.

Though each of the twenty chapters contains biographical information, the book focuses not so much on what each composer *did*, but on what he *believed*. If you're looking to add an element to your music appreciation that most books and curriculums neglect—the spiritual aspect—this book can't be beat! *Rebecca Livermore*

NEW!
Superstar Teachers How to Understand and Listen to Great Music: The Greenburg Lectures

Grade 9–ault. Entire Course: Audio, $349.95; Video, $549.95. Add $20 shipping each. Individual parts (I–VI): Audio, $89.95 each; Video, $149.95 each. Add $5 shipping each part. *The Teaching Company, 7405 Alban Station Court, Suite A107, Springfield, VA 22150. (800) 832-2412. Web: www.teachco.com.*

SuperStar Teachers How to Understand and Listen to Great Music is an excellent music appreciation course. Professor Robert Greenburg, a composer and teacher with a very impressive resume that you'll find on the first page of the course booklet, presents you with 48 separate audio or video lessons (your choice), divided into six separate parts:

- Sources: The Ancient World Through the Early Baroque
- The High Baroque
- The Classical Era I
- The Classical Era II and the Age of Revolution—Beethoven
- Nineteenth Century Romanticism
- From Romanticism to Modernism: 1848 to 1913

Although I only received the first set of videos, these introduce the entire course, present the teacher's philosophy and approach, and include

quite a few lessons. So unless something really strange happened in the following lectures, I think Bill and I got a pretty good picture of what this course is all about.

The "great music" covered is Western concert music. By "Western" we mean "European," not Loretta Lynn. By "concert" we mean "played in concert halls." Prof. Greenburg goes into all these definitions in detail, with a "humble apology" (his words) for the oversimplifications and omissions required to cover even this in 48 lectures.

Greenburg proposes "four tenets" of western music:

- Characterized by constant stylistic change
- A mirror of its society
- Searching constantly for new modes of expression
- The rate of stylistic change has increased as per the rate of change in society

He investigates music via a "three-pronged attack":

- Examining the historical, social, political, and religious influences on the composer's world and how musical styles mirror them
- Studying selected compositions as examples and as objects of art, often contrasted with each other—some that Greenburg plays for you on the piano and others played from orchestral recordings
- Developing listening skills and a musical vocabulary

Greenburg appears sound in his historical understanding, with no overt political agenda other than the substitution of "BCE" (Before the Common Era, or Before the Christian Era) and "CE" (Common Era, or Christian Era) for "BC" (Before Christ) and "AD" (*Anno Domini*, Latin for "Year of Our Lord"). Jewish people often prefer the BCE and CE dating. This does not affect his accurate presentation of the role of the church and Christianity in Western music. His energetic presentation is fueled with memorable anecdotes, the kind you want to call the family over to hear. I found it hard to stop watching!

As with other SuperStar Teachers courses, I find the best way to take notes is to write additional comments on the included course outline. Why do the outlining when it's been done for you?

If the goal was to provide you with a music course that rivals or surpasses the best of what you're likely to find in any college you attend, I'd say Greenburg succeeds. This might help influence your thinking about the price. The more people you have watching, the more you save from the cost of college tuition for a similar, but probably worse, course.

If you're a visual learner, I recommend the videos. Although the visuals are few, it's still more involving to see Greenburg in action. If you're an auditory learner who tends to stare into space while listening, then save some money and get the audiocassette version. *Mary Pride*

I don't normally write up products without seeing them. But I received a brochure about InteliQuest Learning Systems' **The World's 50 Greatest Composers Audiocassette Collection** just before sending in the manuscript of *The Big Book of Home Learning*, and I thought this collection looked juicy enough that you'd enjoy hearing what the brochure said about it.

First, what you get. Fifty 60-minute audiocassettes, one per composer. Each cassette provides "a detailed biography of the composer—his life and

NEW!
The World's 50 Greatest Composers Audiocassette Collection
Grade 9–adult. Complete series, $295 plus $14.60 shipping.
Knowledge Products, 722 Rundle Ave.,

Suite A-13, Nashville, TN 37210.
(800) 876-4332 or (800) 264-6641 or
(615) 742-3852. Fax: (615) 742-3270.
Email: kpaudio@edge.net.

the essence of his genius, his contribution to music, and selections of his definitive works." More about those masterworks: you'll learn each work's "form and style, what the composer was experiencing as he composed it, the historical framework in which it was created, how it affected the audiences of the time, and how it influenced music of the future." The idea is that you are going to be able to "identify and interpret over 300 masterworks of classical music," putting you right up there with "only a few who have spent years in serious study."

Composers included are, in the order of the tapes: da Palestrina, Monteverdi, Purcell, Vivaldi, Rameau, J.S. Bach, Handel, Gluck, Naydn, Mozart, Beethoven, Schubert, Von Weber, Rossini, Donizetti, Berlioz, Mendelssohn, Chopin, Schumann, Liszt, Wagner, Verdi, Franck, Strauss, Brahms, Saint-Saens, Bizet, Mussorgsky, Tchaikovsky, Dvorak, Grieg, Rimsky-Korakov, Fauré, Puccini, Mahler, Strauss, Janacek, Debussy, Sibelius, Ralph Vaughn Williams, Rachmaninoff, Schoenberg, Ravel, de Falla, Bartok, Stravinsky, Prokofiev, Gershwin, Aaron Copland, and Shostakovich.

This collection sounds ideal for Knowledge Products' usual "we'll send you a tape or two each month for an affordable monthly price" deal. Why the brochure didn't provide this option, I don't know. I'll tell you more when and if they send me a set for review. *Mary Pride*

PART 8

Real Life Skills

Ninth-grade homeschooler William Estrada of Gilette, PA, won an essay contest for high school students in his county and surrounding counties, sponsored by Students In Free Enterprise. Students were required to write a 3–4 page essay answering the following questions: "What is a major obstacle to free enterprise in America today?" and "What can be done to overcome this obstacle?"

William's essay focused on the decline of the "American Dream" and the loss of the independent, "can do" spirit once common in America. He offered solutions including less government intervention, encouragement of such family values as hard work and perseverance, and community opportunities, such as workshops, to build up free enterprise. The contest prize was either a $1,000 tuition grant or a $500 cash award. Way to go, William!

Jeanel Ward (12) and Tamara Ward (9) of Elkton, MD, both won championships in different baking categories at the Cecil County Fair. Jeanel won the grand championship for her chocolate chip cookies, and likewise Tamara (who had just started cooking that year) won the grand championship for her chocolate cupcakes. Both homeschooled girls won $25 awards from Kraft. Obviously, baking skill runs in the family . . . and the Cecil County Fair judges love chocolate!

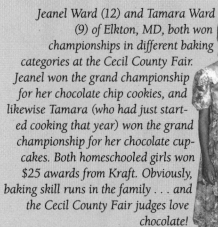

CHAPTER 39

Driver Education

For homeschoolers, getting our kids their driver's licenses has been an especially fraught issue. Home School Legal Defense Association, in cooperation with state homeschool groups, has been fighting for years against the misguided attempts of many state legislatures to "prevent kids dropping out" by denying driver's licenses to all those under age 18 who are not enrolled in school.

Happily, HSLDA has managed to get most states to see the light. But be sure to check with your state homeschool group as to what "proof of enrollment" will be necessary to show that your teen is a full-time homeschool student, should this be an issue in your state.

As to *where* you can get your driver's education instruction, here are some options.

For taking the written test: Go to the Department of Motor Vehicles and get their Driver Laws booklet for the vehicle in question. There are different booklets for cars, motorcycles, and trucks. Most homeschool teens can study the booklet on their own and pass the written test with no problems. One thing to watch out for: one of our sons assumed that, since he'd never be breaking the law, he didn't need to memorize the penalties for each infraction. Wrong! This oversight caused him to take the test twice.

For on-the-road instruction: Studies have shown that teens who are taught by their parents have *far* lower accident rates than those taught by "professionals." The first resource in this chapter shows you how to do just that. Sadly, insurance companies don't recognize the value of this training, so to obtain lower rates your teen may also want to get "official" driving lessons. These are available through:

- **Your local high school.** If they and you both feel comfortable about having your homeschooled teen take just one course, Driver's Ed should be it. Don't expect it to be free. A summer school course at our local high school was around $300. However, the class will cover both the written test *and* on-the-road instruction.
- **A local driver's school.** Sears has driver's education schools all over the country. Local independent schools also may be available in your area. Many will pick up your teen at the door and deliver him back after the lesson. Don't expect it to be cheap: $35/hour is the going rate in our area.

If you, as a parent, don't have time for all of this, or just want to make *sure* your child is getting every bit of instruction he'd receive in a school course, we've also located several correspondence course that fit the bill.

In my opinion, it's better to be as thorough as possible. This is the only school subject that, if you fail to master it, could result in your or someone else's death or disability. Take your time, spend some money, and do it right.

Driver's Education

Written by a driver's ed instructor whose previous work was in the field of auto accident investigation, these books take the unique viewpoint that "no amount of persuasive arguments for safe driving habits can overshadow the repetitive example of parents and/or peers." Aimed at the typical panic-stricken homeschool parent who realizes that doom is now imminent, in the form of a kid old enough to legally pilot a lethal weapon, these two cartoon-packed books provide the detailed, repetitive instructions you need to teach your child to drive safely and with confidence.

As **Help! I Want to Drive** author Charles Lamont Taylor points out,

> *Many insurance companies no longer give a discount for driver's education completion. Even those companies that continue to offer a discount have reduced them to miniscule percentages." Why is this? Because "many drivers who learned through formal education no longer adhere to the principles of safe driving initially taught."*

That ol' demon, Peer Pressure, in this case can lead Junior straight to the morgue.

But there's hope!

> *It now became obvious that the most important person in the training process, outside of the student, was the parent. Yet it is the parent who is all but ignored in most formal programs. This program is an effort to set this straight. By giving the parents the tools necessary to become an effective trainer, they can now affect their child's driving habit for the better . . . for life.*

As he goes on to say,

> *After observing parental involvement in the training process, I have become convinced that most parents can do as good a job (and sometimes even better) for a fraction of the cost that most driving schools charge.*

How is this accomplished? Through a set of two perfect-bound books. The thicker one, for the parent, includes seven lessons. Each has a "classroom" and "behind the wheel" part, a Driver Evaluation Sheet used to score your student's on-the-road driving, a Driver Training Log that includes date, time, remarks, and initials, and a number of overhead-view diagrams of street situations. An answer key and additional tests and forms are also bound in the parent's book. The student's book only includes the "classroom" portion.

Everything I remember from my own Driver's Ed class is in here, plus lots of other helpful safety tips they never told me. Every way the parent or the student can mess up is described in advance, and you're told how to overcome it. The text is highly readable and the cartoons make safety points in a fun, nonthreatening way. But best of all, with this course you can proceed at the student's pace, until he or she is *really* ready to drive. Which in my kids' case, may be age 40, after seeing the graph of highway fatalities *v.* driver's age . . . *Mary Pride*

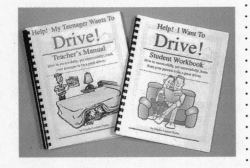

Indiana University's Driver's Education course is directed primarily at Indiana drivers, though it can easily be adapted for other states by substituting your state's drivers manual for the Indiana one. The pouch at the back of the learning guide contains a map of the Indiana state highways published by the Indiana Department of Transportation and an *Indiana Drivers Manual.*

The text for this course is a softback version of *Drive Right,* the same textbook used in the UNL course reviewed below. The authors of this course, however, do not follow the textbook chapter by chapter as UNL and KNHS do, but instead have a good amount of the course content contained in the manual. Supportive readings are taken both from the *Drive Right* book and the *Indiana Drivers Manual.*

Three videos accompany the program. The first, *Lookin' Alive,* comes with the course package and has to be returned before you take the midterm exam. This video is viewed in the lesson about driver responsibilities. The other two videos, *The Game of Your Life* and *Sober Thoughts about Drinking and Driving,* must be requested for loan when you complete the application to take the midterm and must be returned before taking the final exam. These two videos are to be viewed in the lesson about alcohol and drugs.

The learning guide has 10 chapters. Eight are teaching chapters and two are chapters containing tips for taking the exams—one each for the midterm exam and final exam. The chapters are: Driver's Responsibilities; Right of Way Rules; Driving Tips; Different Driving Environments; Drinking, Drugs, and Driving (not just cautionary warnings about how substances affect your driving, but explanations of your legal liability if you drink and drive); Buying and Insuring a Car; Planning a Trip; and Driver's Manuals.

The chapters all start with a brief introduction and an outline of the objectives for that chapter. The teaching part of each chapter that follows is divided into sections, the number of which varies from chapter to chapter. Each section has a reading assignment followed by a discussion and sometimes a written assignment. At the end of each chapter is an assignment review—a checklist to make sure you did all the work for this chapter—and colored pages for written assignments to submit to the instructor at Indiana University for evaluation. A cover sheet is provided to ensure the student provides all the information the instructor needs to identify whose assignment this is and which chapter it is for.

This course gets the award for brevity, doing in eight lessons what others do in 18 or more, yet it covers everything a prospective driver needs to pass his driver's exam (at least in Indiana) and get him ready for his first experiences behind the wheel. *Bill Pride*

Keystone National High School (KNHS) is the newest division of NLKK, Inc. For over 20 years, NLKK has been providing students and their families with distance education courses. Keystone National High School is licensed by the State Board of Private Licensed Schools in Pennsylvania and accredited by the Distance Education and Training Council. They offer a complete course of study providing all you need to fulfill all the requirements for high school driver education.

Here is a list what you get with this course:

- *Responsible Driving* book by American Automobile Association—368 pages, lavishly illustrated in full color
- Driver Education Learning Guide—includes learning guide, "Partner In Safety" parent & teacher practice driving guide, parent/teen driving log, and a list of where to write for state driver regulations.

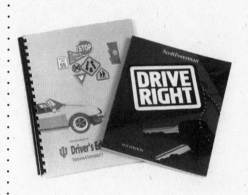

- Envelopes for returning written work
- *Street Smarts* video by General Motors
- An issue of *In Motion* magazine

The book is quite complete. Its sections include: assessing and managing risk, knowing your limitations, handling social pressures (alcohol, drugs, and distractions), signs, signals, and markings, rules of the road, getting to know your car, light and weather conditions, sharing the road, natural laws (physics) and driving, responding to an emergency, buying a car, car systems and maintenance, planning a trip, and getting ready for your state driving test. The format of the text is magazine-like, with many sidebars and pictures. Chapters include case studies, advice from the experts, tips for new drivers, safety tips, "for your information" sidebars, etc. Each chapter ends with a chapter test so you can see if you have mastered the information in the chapter.

The teacher's manual contains a course intro, lesson plans with exams and answer sheets to mail back, driving practice goals based around the *Street Smarts* video, and an answer key for the textbook self-tests. The lesson plans divide the course into four lessons, each spanning a number of chapters in the text. Each lesson begins with a short description and a list of objectives. It then follows along with the text chapter by chapter, dividing each chapter into four sections and a review. For each section it provides a one-paragraph summary of that section from the teacher's point of view, a reading assignment, and a written assignment.

You should figure on each of the four lessons taking two weeks at one hour per day or one week at two hours per day. You would have to vary the number of sections per day, based on the length of each lesson. The first lesson covers three chapters, the second covers five, the third covers six, and the fourth, four.

The 16-minute video is called *Street Smarts*. In this video, Mr. Marshall has taken the job of teaching his son Jesse how to drive. The problem is they can't get through a session without getting into arguments with one another.

> Dad: *"I want to talk to you about your grades . . ."*
> Kid: *"Oh no, not again!"*
>
> Dad: *"Be sure to watch your blind spots"*
> Kid: *"Do you have to tell me this every time we go out?"*

Dad has no patience and isn't giving Jesse room to operate; Jesse has an attitude. Then their "guardian angel" appears and tells them what they are doing wrong. He rewinds the sequence and tells them to do it right this time. They do, and we see what a good driving session looks like.
Items stressed are:

1. The instructor needs to act calm even when he's scared stiff
2. The instructor has to let the student drive. He shouldn't be a back-seat driver, but should keep quiet unless the student driver messes up.
3. Experience counts, so take your student out often, and in all sorts of conditions.

At the end of the video they get people on the street to give their opinions on why teenage drivers have more accidents, the importance of experience, etc. This video's a good little short pep talk to learners and their coaches.

In Motion is an annual magazine for teen drivers sponsored by General Motors. It covers topics like "How do You Rate on Auto Upkeep?," "How to Avoid Car Clashes: Taking Your Parents for a Ride," or "Crash Test Dummies Tell their Story." The tone of the magazine seems to be a little preachy—what teens ought to know about cars and driving as written by an adult. This is a good magazine to accompany a drivers education course, but nothing your student would subscribe to on his own.

KNHS Drivers Ed seems to be a very thorough course at a reasonable price. *Bill Pride*

UNL Driver Education is the only correspondence course we reviewed that does not include videos. The well-illustrated textbook basically teaches the course.

Drive Right, the textbook (a hardbound version of the same text used in the Indiana Driver Education course reviewed above) is divided into four units:

- **The Driving Task** deals with the raw materials of driving and general strategy—basic car controls, street signs and signals, and the IPDE Process (Identify, Predict, Decide, and Execute)
- **Interacting with Traffic** deals with the mechanics of driving—how to turn and where, how to park, dealing with various kinds of intersections, how physical laws affect how you drive, and how to safely share the road with motorcycles and bicycles
- **Driving in Different Environments and Conditions**—city v. country, highway and expressway driving, driving in bad conditions, and handling emergencies
- **Your Responsibilities as a Driver** discusses how to cope with poor vision, fatigue, emotional state, etc., talks about drugs and alcohol and driving, tells how to buy and maintain a car, and shows how to go about planning a trip

The course schedule is designed to allow four or five weeks for each unit, and 18 weeks for the entire course. However, you may take longer if needed.

For the sake of course integrity, UNL requires that you designate a non-family member to be the course supervisor. UNL sends all materials to the course supervisor who then distributes supplies and texts to the student. The supervisor oversees transferring the answers of the unit evaluations to the *CARES* forms, mails the forms to UNL, and receives the evaluation reports back. He also proctors exams and certifies that they were taken with only the resources allowed for that course. Exams for Driver Education are all strictly closed book.

Student materials supplied with this course are:

- *Drive Right*—376-page, hardbound book, full of four-color illustrations and pictures.
- Driver Education Syllabus begins with a course introduction and explanations about how the course is administered and graded. The syllabus has an introduction for each lesson, followed by a reading assignment and a self-test. Answers to the self-tests are in the course handbook.
- Driver Education Course Handbook contains Units I–IV self-test keys and Units I–IV evaluations. Unit evaluations are filled in at the end of each of the four units and are totally open book. The student can use his course syllabus and textbook to answer the questions.

NEW!
University of Nebraska-Lincoln Driver's Education
Grades 9–12. Tuition, $94. Administration Handling Fee, $21. Course Materials, $51. Shipping extra. *University of Nebraska-Lincoln, Independent Study High School, 269 Clifford-Hardin, NCCE, Lincoln, NE 68583-9800. (402) 472-4321. Fax: (402) 472-1901. Email: unldde1@unl.edu. Web: www.unl.edu/conted/disted.*

For the supervisor:

- Manual for the Supervisor, including Form A examinations—Introduction, student progress chart, instructions for using the *CARES* sheets, supervisor's questionnaire, change of status forms, and the mid-term and final exams.
- Supervisor Packet—*CARES* sheets and mailing supplies

The *Drive Right* textbook is uncluttered and easy-to-read. Its numerous illustrations and pictures are well chosen to help the reader understand the text. Pictures of real driving situations are used to help you prepare for on-the-road situations. For example, one page has illustrations/pictures of four situations where a driver has to make an immediate decision: when to brake when approaching a curve, how best to avoid the driver ahead who is braking to maintain control on a dirt road, how to reduce the force of impact with a car blocking your lane when you can't stop, and how to get to the shoulder to avoid a head-on collision when your car is already in a skid.

Drive Right's authors believe in the "Tell 'em what you are about to say, say it, then tell 'em what you just said" philosophy of teaching. Each chapter starts with a brief introduction, and an outline of that chapter's objectives. Then comes the text of the chapter, divided into sections to match the outline of objectives. The chapter ends with a summary recapping what you just read, and a chapter test.

This is a well-organized course that seems like it would be easy for a high-school student to use. *Bill Pride*

CHAPTER 40

Independent Living Skills

Independent living skills include cleaning, cooking, sewing, babysitting, and everything else necessary to live on your own and eventually take care of a family. It also includes training in Honeydew skills, such as carpentry. You know, "Honey, do this," and "Honey, do that."

Why learn how to cook and clean and build the kids a playhouse? Well, when you leave the nest, would you rather enjoy gracious living or live like a pig? If your answer is, "Oink!" you may be reducing your chances in the marriage market. How does that song go . . .

> *I went to your family and asked them for you*
>
> *They all said, "Oh, take her! Oh, take her, please do!*
>
> *She can't cook or sew, she won't scrub your floor . . ."*
>
> *So I put on my hat and tiptoed out the door, saying,*
>
> *"So long, it's been good to know ya . . ."*

Male or female, you can't spend the rest of your life smuggling your dirty laundry home to Mom in plastic trash bags. And you won't enjoy living exclusively on what Chef Boyardee stuffs into his cans, either. These are *survival skills* we're talking about here!

The bad news is that many of us grow up allergic to the word "chores," associating every around-the-house skill with boredom. The good news is that learning to be *professional* at these skills is a lot of fun. As you will see in the reviews below!

NEW!
The Encyclopedia of Country Living: An Old Fashioned Recipe Book

Grade 11–adult. $27.95.
Sasquatch Books, 615 2nd Avenue, Suite 260, Seattle, WA 98104. (800) 775-0817. Fax: (206) 467-4301.

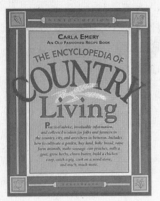

NEW!
Super Sitters

Grades 7–12. Video, $19.95.
Shipping extra.
Super Sitters, 857 West Webster Avenue, Chicago, IL 60614. (800) 323-3431. Fax: (773) 404-0035.

All Around Skills

"But it's not safe! But it's unhealthy! But you need an expert to do that!" Objections to a home birth? No, that's me upon learning my Cajun relatives were planning a "boucherie" (that's a hog butchering to you novices). A country girl I am not, but after reading Carla Emery's book, **The Encyclopedia of Country Living,** I'm ready to head for the hills!

This book is fascinating reading, if for nothing else than to find out where milk, eggs, and hamburger really do come from. Yes, instructions for butchering your own meat are included. Before the squeamish among you write this one off, listen to what else is in this hefty volume: How to buy land; what to build on it; everything you ever wanted to know about gardening, grains, vegetables, fruits, or raising animals; and scrumptious recipes for preparing what you've produced.

The author writes with a sense of humor born of years of experience. This current edition of the encyclopedia was 24 years in the making. Think of Carla as the Mary Pride of the homestead set and you'll get a feel for how many resources are included in this book.

The author's stand on the land and its uses is refreshing in this day and age. While she is pro-stewardship and organic methods (if possible), she takes a no-nonsense approach about the place of animals on your farm. (Persnickety hen? Turn that fowl into fricassee!) There is an excellent rebuttal of some common arguments on land used for raising cows versus grain.

This book is worthwhile just for the recipes, but I'll bet it will inspire even you city dwellers out there to broaden your horizons. *Renee Mathis*

The **Super Sitters** book/video combo begins with the basics: a series of quizzes to find out if your child's got what it takes to be a world champion baby sitter. Questions such as "Could you cheerfully change a messy diaper?" weed out the faint of heart. The book is extremely thorough, containing sections on what to expect from each age group, basics of infant care, ideas for toddler amusements, extensive first aid and safety, and several pages of profile sheets to be filled in on each family (routines, background info, medical information, etc.).

As a parent it was good for me to be reminded not to take things for granted when hiring a new sitter. Be truthful now—do your sitters know where the fuse box and fire extinguisher are located?

The video is 30 minutes long and mostly a recap of the book. There is a demonstration of the Heimlich maneuver, to be used on conscious children over the age of 1, as well as different techniques to use on a conscious infant. I suggest you show this part to the *entire* family, not just the children old enough to be official babysitters. We know of at least one preteen who has used this information (gleaned in a Red Cross class) to save a sibling's life. Secular psychologist Dr. Lee Salk shows up periodically to offer advice on dealing with children's behavior. Pretty innocuous on the whole ("be accepting, friendly, and firm"), although lacking a biblical basis.

What keeps this great program from being a five-star wonderful program is their emphasis on soliciting outside customers for your babysitting business. There are too many potential problems that can arise when you start dealing with strangers—even if you have gone on a screening visit with your parents as advised.

Our homeschool support group has used these materials as a basis for a babysitting class and found them to be well received. A teacher's manual is available, though not necessary. Call the toll-free number for more information. *Renee Mathis*

Carpentry

Now here's a wonderful approach to play structures: let the kids build them! If you've ever played with Lincoln Logs or Tinker Toys as a child, you'll be familiar with the approach in **Builder Boards**. While Jack McKee's wooden pieces more closely resemble giant notched popsicle sticks, the concept is the same. Give your children the basic pieces, some supervision and help if needed, and unleash their architectural creativity.

Although I'm not a woodworker, my husband is. He offered the following comments after reading through the 48-page instruction booklet:

This book was the previous edition of Builder Boards

- Easy-to-follow instructions.
- Drawings, figures, and photographs are helpful, and professionally done. (Would have been better to actually number the figures and reference them in the directions).
- Author includes two options: Using cedar fence posts or ¾" plywood. The plywood eliminates the need for a planer (a plus!) and also gives you a nicer finished product. Because cabinet-grade, finished 2-sides plywood is specified, this won't necessarily be an inexpensive undertaking. Budget approximately $150.
- Among the needed tools are a table saw, sander, hand saw, and router.
- Not a trivial project! Definitely not one for the beginning woodworker, as it is imperative to be accurate in cutting the notches. Too loose and the structure will be unstable. Too tight, and it will be impossible for the kids to put together.

While the author explains how he brings the playhouse pieces to share with schools and day-care centers, I see lots of possibilities for home-schooling families to use these in ministry. (Included with each order is an article about eighth graders building the house for use in a women's care shelter.) Older teens could build this as a senior wood-shop project. Seems like every family has at least one budding builder or architect—*Builder Boards* will be a big hit! *Renee Mathis*

"Great Projects You Can Build." No lie there. **Play Equipment for Kids** is over 30 buildable swings, see-saws, slides, jungle gyms, playhouses, forts, castles, teepees, sandboxes, swimming pools, weekend projects, and more. Complete illustrated instructions start at the beginning, with tools you will need and the various kinds of wood joints you can make. Each project is spelled out in detail, with both metric and English (feet and inches) measurements. Projects vary from the simple to playsets equivalent to those in the Child Life catalog. No wonder this was a Better Homes and Gardens Book Club selection. *Mary Pride*

NEW!
Builder Boards
Grade 8–adult. $12.95 plus $2 shipping.
Hands On Books, 1117 Lenora Ct., Bellingham, WA 98225.
(360) 671-9079.
Email: amckee@az.com.

NEW!
Play Equipment for Kids
Grade 11–adult. $18.95 plus shipping.
Storey Communications, Inc., PO Box 445, Pownal, VT 05261,
Orders: (800)441-5700.
Inquiries: (802)823-5811.
Web: www.storey.com.

Cleaning

UPDATED!
Don Aslett Books

Grade 7–adult. The Cleaning Encyclopedia, $15.95. Who Says It's a Woman's Job to Clean?, $5.95. Is There Life After Housework video, $29.95. Handle 1,000 Things, $12.99. Life After Housework, $10.95. Clutter's Last Stand, $11.95. Not for Packrats Only, $10.95. House do the Housework, $14.95. Clean the Moosehead, $10. Clutter Free, $12.99. Have a 48-Hour Day, $12.95. Office Clutter Cure, $9.99. Stainbuster's Bible, $10.95. #1 with Your Boss, $5.95. Everything I Know About Business, $9.95. Add 10% shipping ($3 minimum). *Home Life, Inc., PO Box 1190, Fenton, MO 63026. Orders: (800) 346-6322. Inquiries: (636) 343-7750. Fax: (636) 343-7203. Email: orders@home-school.com. Web: www.home-school.com.*

The Cleaning Encyclopedia is a reference book you'll turn to again and again. After familiarizing yourself with only a portion of this book, you'll feel like a pro. Not only does "America's Number One Cleaning Expert" **Don Aslett** explain how to clean almost everything under the sun, but you'll learn exactly how the different cleaning processes work. Discover the theory behind cleaning chemistry as well as definitions of those strange-sounding chemicals and ingredients. Boring? Not at all! (You know Don couldn't write a boring book if he tried.)

Take time to flip through the pages and get an idea of how the book is organized. Tools and methods are arranged from A to Z, but not always where you'd expect to see them. I tried looking up "crayon" (a common cleaning problem at our house!) and was stumped. I finally found it under "wax stains." There are plenty of illustrations and cute cartoons, one of which needs to be covered up with a sticker or felt marker. Struggling— and failing—to be funny, the X entry is "x-rated cleaning." In this case it refers to folks who clean house in their "birthday suit" and features a cartoon gal's bare backside.

Other Don Aslett books you won't want to miss:

- *How to Handle 1,000 Things at Once.* How to get it all under control and even do more!
- *Is There Life After Housework?* Don's revolutionary "speed clean" system
- *Clutter's Last Stand.* Sidesplitting! How to tame your "treasures"
- *Not for Packrats Only.* Ideal gift for the junker in your life
- Make Your House do the Housework Design "clean" in and dirt out!
- *How Do I Clean the Moosehead?* Tame your cleaning nightmares
- *Clutter Free.* The sequel to *Clutter's Last Stand.* See review later in this chapter.

- *Who Says It's a Woman's Job to Clean?* Simplified technique. A great first "how to clean" book. Fun to read, too!
- *How to Have a 48-Hour Day.* Humorous, effective advice will get you organized. See review later in this chapter.
- *Office Clutter Cure.* How to get organized and get ahead.
- *Stainbuster's Bible.* Kill hundreds of stains with just a few chemicals. Stain-by-stain directions!
- *How to Be #1 with Your Boss.* The unwritten rules of business success. Really works! See review in chapter 53.
- *Everything I Know About Business I Learned in the Farmyard.* The world's most unusual business book. Also reviewed in chapter 54.

You'll love Don Aslett's wonderful *Is There Life After Housework?* video, in which he combines comic patter with classy cleaning skills. My advice: snap it up. Our kids love the toilet humor (really, it's *clean* toilet humor), and they can't wait to clean windows, vacuum, and wash walls just like Don. *Mary Pride*

Now you can get all the professional cleaning tools and supplies you need from **Don Aslett's Cleaning Center**! Everything from squeegees for your windows and floors to concentrated cleaning supplies (you only need four kinds to do everything in your house). Mops, buckets, sponges, lambswool dusters, dusting cloths, and even the stuff you need to seal your concrete basement floor are all covered in this catalog. Save time and aggravation—get what you need to do it right. Speedy service, good prices. *Mary Pride*

Cooking

If you're looking for a book that surrounds a relatively skimpy amount of helpful information with hundreds of pages telling you what you already know, here it is. The 371 pages of **The Complete Idiot's Guide to Cooking Basics** devotes many, many pages to such topics as how to organize your kitchen (hot questions like whether or not to line pantry shelves with paper), what essential ingredients and equipment you should have on hand, and how to shop. Honestly. How to shop. Complete with hot tips such as, "Never buy food past its expiration date." I kid you not. Round about chapter 10 we finally start sneaking up to the act of cooking itself . . . or so it seems from the deceptive chapter heading. Actually, in chapter 10 the author deals with all your neuroses regarding napkin folds and radish roses, because surely setting the table is more basic then getting anything into the oven.

So here you are at chapter 11. Finally, some instructions in cooking basics. In this and the following chapters you will learn: How and why to measure. How and when to make ingredient substitutions. Definitions of the top 100 cooking terms. Definitions of "catchwords used in recipes." (What makes the "catchwords" different from the "cooking terms"? Beats me.) Cookery techniques (simmering, sauteeing, frying, etc.). How to time your cooking so it all arrives in good shape to greet your dinner guests. How to fix common cooking mistakes. How to choose and serve beverages of all kinds. Tips on how to entertain. Generic buying tips (no actual brand names are mentioned) for pots and pans and small electrical appliances (yes, I know "equipment" was already introduced in an earlier chapter—bringing it up twice in different sections is an example of bad organization). "Over 150 mouth-watering recipes" of all types. I managed not to drool on the pages, but then I find goat cheese or ham and asparagus roll-ups pretty

UPDATED!
Don Aslett Cleaning Products
Grade 7–adult. Free Catalog.
Don Aslett's Cleaning Center, PO Box 39, Pocatello, ID 83204.
Orders or free catalog: (800) 451-2402.
Inquiries: (208) 232-6212.
Fax: (208) 232-6286.
Web: www.cleanreport.com.

NEW!
The Complete Idiot's Guide to Cooking Basics, Updated Edition
The Complete Idiot's Guide to Baking
Grade 7–adult. Cooking Basics, $18.95. Baking, $17.95.
Alpha Books, a division of Macmillan General Reference, a Simon & Schuster Macmillan Company, 1633 Broadway, New York, NY 10019. Information: (800) 428-5331. Available in bookstores. Web: www.mcp.com/mgr/idiot.

NEW!
Cooking For Dummies
Gourmet Cooking for Dummies
Desserts for Dummies

Grade 5 to adult. $19.99 each.
IDG Books Worldwide Inc., an International Data Group Company, 919 E. Hillsdale Blvd., Suite 400, Foster City, CA 94404. All IDG materials are sold in bookstores. Consumer Customer Service: (800) 762-2974. Web: www.dummies.com.

resistible. An index and a bound-in "Reference Card" with cooking tips, measurements, substitutions, and abbreviations round *Cooking Basics* out.

Written by a different author, **The Complete Idiot's Guide to Baking** is a much better book. While it covers some of the same territory (lists of necessary ingredients and equipment, storage tips, baking terms, etc.), you get less of the obvious cliches which plague the first book and more of the insider information and step-by-step instructions you crave. Important stuff, such as food safety advice. Fun stuff, such as how to create quick, spiffy garnishes. The book is very complete, covering all forms of baking, and the recipes are great. I predict a 10-pound weight gain for anyone who seriously studies and uses this book—even if you follow the advice on how to cut fat back in your recipes. *Mary Pride*

"For Dummies" books are usually slicker and more fun to read that their competitors, the "Complete Idiots" series. The humor can be a bit, shall I say "raw," so figure out for yourself whether you would laugh, groan, or be scandalized at a cartoon (titled "Bill and Irwin Make Vichyssoise) where one character encourages another to "Take a Leek." (The riposte? "Let me drink some water first.")

Cooking for Dummies starts off with an exhaustive look at your kitchen: how to arrange it, what equipment to put in it, even what is the best kind of kitchen countertop. Unlike the "Idiots" book, equipment is dealt with lovingly and at length, with pictures to show you what you're reading about. By chapter 3, you're already learning basic cooking techniques: not only "steaming" in general, but how to steam particular foods (rice and veggies, in this example). Each technique gets a chapter to itself. Techniques covered are boiling/poaching/steaming, sauteeing, braising/stewing, roasting/grilling, and the construction of sauces (in which you learn that there is not as much difference as you might think between classic white sauce and library paste). You then expand on your new skills, with techniques for handling eggs, soups, salads, pasta, and one-pot meals. Finally, it's time for Real Menus for Real Life. This part covers necessities you should have on hand, fancy meals you can make for pennies, cooking by the clock, and cooking for one. The inevitable "Part of Tens," which is required by contract to be in each and every "Dummies" book, includes ten recommended cookbooks (*Betty Crocker* and *Better Homes & Gardens* are *not* among them), ten ways to think like a chef, and ten ways to make everyday food look great. The glossary of over 100 common cooking terms, and lists of common substitutions, abbreviations, and equivalents, are in the appendices, where they belong. You can also find a slew of helpful cooking hints on the bound-in Quick Reference Card, and an index in the back of the book.

Gourmet Cooking for Dummies is not just more of the same. Here we enter a whole new world, where foodstuffs have to be not just edible, but super-fresh, and meals have to not just taste good, but taste and look *great*. It's all about extra time, fancier equipment, more money, and more precision. Also more sauces. Author Charlie Trotter, chef/owner of Charlie Trotter's Restaurant in Chicago, knows and loves what he's writing about, and it shows. The same care that went into his restaurant, which earned five stars from *Mobil Travel Guide* and five diamonds from the AAA, shines through in this book. You'll be dealing with advanced techniques such as dry heat versus moist heat, formal knife cuts, and architectural cuisine. Shopping tips are actually important, and included, since obtaining the perfect ingredients is half the battle. Pages and pages of gourmet cooking terms, and their definitions, will help you sound *comme il faut* at your next *soiree*. Sauces, sauces, and more sauces (some incognito as relishes and chutneys). Veggie cuisine (heavy on those herbs and mushrooms). Veggies again (legumes, grains, rice, and pasta). Raw, marinated, and cooked seafood. Poultry. Meat. An entire chapter is then dedicated to layered and formed foods (Charlie calls this "architectural cuisine." My husband Bill calls them "3-D eats.") Foodstyles of the rich and famous follows, with a chapter devoted to such trifles as truffles and *fraises des bois*. A section on desserts to dream of is next (custards, pastries, chocolates . . . *oo la la!*) Next you learn how to orchestrate an entire gourmet meal. Finally, the infamous Part of Tens: ten classic food/wine pairings, ten dining cities and their recommended gourmet restaurants, ten Charlie-endorsed food vendors, ten food/wine books to buy. No appendices, but an index. The "Cheat Sheet" card bound inside has more gourmet tips.

Desserts for Dummies has color photos in the middle ("The better to tempt you with, my dear!"). Here we go ahead with kitchen set-up and equipment, which is admittedly somewhat more complex for desserts than for basic meat courses. We rip into the interesting stuff in chapter 3, with pastries of all kinds from pies and tarts to puff pastries to crepes and blinis. Eggs are next: custards, puddings, and meringues. Easy homemade cakes. Ladyfingers and "the real tiramisu." Awesomely rich cakes. Cold desserts. Special-occasion desserts. Desserts for a mob. The book then dares to ask, "Why not make your own wedding cake?" Having done just that, I would urge you to skip this chapter or face the fate of being the only one present who can't stand to eat your own cake (not that it will taste bad, but you'll have been eating your frosting "mistakes" for weeks already!). You'd think the authors couldn't top making your own wedding cake, but they don't even pause for breath before tackling holiday desserts. Now a 90's type of chapter: reduced-fat sweets. (News flash: what we should be reducing is *sugar* and *carbohydrate*.) Now the Tens: ten ways to make your desserts look great, ten desserts you can make in 30 minutes or less, and ten things you may want to know about chocolate. The appendices include a glossary of dessert and baking terms, common substitutions/abbreviations/equivalents, and mail-order sources for equipment and ingredients. If you believe the way to a man's heart is through his clogged-up arteries, or if you have a quick-burning metabolism like the annoyingly thin Bryan Miller (former restaurant critic for the *New York Times* and co-author of this book) appears to have, *Desserts* will teach you how to pile on the calories in style. *Mary Pride*

The master of Mega Cooking, Jill Bond, has joined forces with the publishing arm of Great Christian Books to publish her popular home arts handbook, **Dinner's in the Freezer**. This isn't a revised edition, so those of you with your original, sturdy, stand-up-on-the-counter *DITF* binders should hang on to them.

Full of anecdotes of her life as a military wife, homeschooling mom of four, and otherwise all-round Professional Mommy, Jill shares her story of how she became determined to use the best tools and create the best methods of serving her husband, family, and community.

"Mega Cooking" is Jill's term for cooking in quantity. Hang on to your chef's hats. . .this woman is serious! She fixes dinners up to six months ahead. Factoring in scratch meals, eat out meals, and leftover meals, this doesn't seem quite as daunting, but you'll still need some hand-holding to pull it off with flair and style.

Some recipes are included for inspiration, as well as plenty of reproducible forms to plan your own shopping excursion and cooking marathon. The author wisely reminds you to customize everything to suit your particular needs and tastes—after all, who wants a six-month supply of something no one will eat?

Minor quibbles that I wish the new publisher had fixed: The chapter/page numbering system is just ridiculous. Each chapter has page numbers beginning with "1", so you're constantly being referred to, for example, "7–3" for chapter 7, page 3. Also, the various hints and tips scattered throughout the book make a well-thought-out index a necessity. Unfortunately there isn't one.

On the plus side, Jill's Master Baking Mix recipe alone is worth the price of the book. Even if you're not a mega-cook yourself, the wealth of information on freezing and storing makes this a handy reference to have around.

The brand-new fourth edition will be three-hole-punched so that it can be put into a binder. *Renee Mathis*

NEW!
Eat Well for $50 a Week

Parents. $12 plus $2 shipping. *Putnam Publishing, 405 Murray Hill Pkwy., East Rutherford, NJ 07073. (800) 788-6262. Fax: (201) 896-8569.*

If your grocery bills are spiraling out of sight and it seems as though there is no hope of ever getting them back down to earth, take heart! **Eat Well for $50 a Week** is a detailed guidebook written by Rhonda Barfield, a homeschooling mother of four, that explains just how possible it is to feed a family of six for just fifty dollars a week.

Sound too good to be true? This family doesn't buy unusual or strange foods, they enjoy dessert once in a while, and they even eat out on occasion. What sets them apart is one hard-working mom who has put to use some money-saving strategies and is willing to share her expertise. The books contains chapters on beating the system at the store, real life examples of shopping lists and menus, easy recipes to try, and resource lists of alternative sources for groceries (co-ops, warehouses, etc.). One of the most enjoyable chapters to read was the fictitious account of Penny Price and her family as they implement one new strategy per week for one year. No need to shock the system all at once. Just take things nice and slow and the savings add up.

If you are willing to do your homework and put in the necessary legwork you are bound to find something in this book that will benefit your family. There is no reason why older children couldn't help keep track of prices, food budgets, and amounts spent. From practical math to spreadsheets there is no end to the possibilities this could awaken in your household. *Renee Mathis*

NEW!
What's for Dinner?

Grade 11–adult. $17 plus shipping. Summer Supplement, $2.95 postpaid. Customized computer printouts service, $20 postpaid. *The Well-Planned Cooking Club, 806 East Hermosa Dr., Fullerton, CA 92835. (714) 381-7398. Email: KElliot01@aol.com. Web: www.timesavers.org.*

If you've never resorted to fast food because you're out of groceries at 5:00 . . . if your grocery bill is not inflated with impulse purchases . . . if you automatically serve your family wonderful healthy meals and snacks . . . then you don't need this book!

But if you're like the rest of us, read on. Kathy Elliot has written one of the most enjoyable, easy to use, clearly written guides to menu and meal planning that I have ever seen. This is the kind of book I wish I had written. Think about it: What is usually the biggest hindrance to using someone else's system? The fact that it was written by someone else! The best thing about **What's For Dinner?** is that it puts the tools you need into your hands. And what delightful tools these are!

You get a binder containing instructions for implementing Kathy's system, sample menu planning worksheets, ingredient checklists, just enough recipes and meal ideas to get you started, and a cute little magnetized menu holder for your refrigerator. Anyone in your family who can read will automatically know the answer to the dinner dilemma.

The beauty of Kathy's methods lies in their simplicity. When you realize that you serve many of the same meals repeatedly throughout the month, and that you spend time making the same grocery list over and over, why not do the job once and for all and be done with it? Why think about this any more than you have too? Follow the step-by-step instructions and make menu plans and corresponding shopping lists. Make them fit whatever shopping/eating style works best for your family. You won't be frustrated by scraps of paper and haphazard lists any longer. For a fee, you can even get your lists nicely printed up on a computer for photocopying.

This one's a winner! *Renee Mathis*

Organizing/Budgeting

It's impossible to review any budget-stretching book without at least a nodding comparison to *The Tightwad Gazette*, whose publisher, Amy Dacyzyn, made "cheap" chic. But, surprise! Pat Wesolowski fares very well when stacked up with her competition. This Christian homeschooling mother of eight has put her newsletter of the same name (**Big Ideas/Small Budget**) into book form. This little volume has a wonderful, homey appeal, especially to those of us who are firmly entrenched in suburbia. In short, Pat's ideas are do-able and practical.

Chapters include ways to save money on birthday parties, eating for free at your favorite restaurants, starting a home based business (including tips for teens), and my favorite: "Ministering Without Much Money."

The *Big Ideas/Small Budget* newsletter costs $12 for a one-year subscription. The sample issue I saw had an article on vacationing cheaply with a large family, homemade doll-house furniture, and travel games on the go.

The only minus: The sans-serif type style and the double spacing in the book make it a chore for the eyes. A little bit of editing would make a big difference! *Renee Mathis*

Larry Burkett's organization, **Christian Financial Concepts,** has prepared a slew of material on personal finances, debt-free living, marriage and money, and the like. Much of this material is now available in your choice of video seminars or audio soundtracks of those seminars.

Both audio and video seminars come complete with the needed workbooks and instructor's guides.

Larry Burkett is generally considered the premier Christian speaker on this topic. He certainly is interesting to listen to, with a wealth of practical and biblical tips on how to get your financial life under control and make it productive for the Lord.

NEW!
BIG Ideas/Small Budget
Grade 9–adult. Newsletter (11 issues per year), $12/yr. Sample issue, $1. Book, $10 plus shipping *D. P. & K. Productions, 2201 High Road, Tallahassee, FL 32303. (423) 570-7172. Email: bisb@juno.com.*

Christian Financial Guides
Grade 11–adult. The Complete Financial Guide for Young Couples, Debt-Free Living, Your Finances in Changing Times, $9 each. How to Manage Your Money (4-tape video set with workbook & manual) $59.99; 6-tape audiocassette soundtrack set with manual $20; With workbook also, $25. The Financial Planning Workshop (3-tape video set) $59.95; 4-tape audiocassette soundtrack including instructor's manual and workbook also, $23. Business by THE BOOK, $12. God's Principles for Operating a Business (11-tape audiocassette series with outline) $39.95. Money Matters for Teens, $9. Shipping extra.

Christian Financial Concepts/Life Pathways Education Office, 5000 Timberview Dr., Flower Mound, TX 75028. Orders: (888) 478-8880. Inquiries: 972-539-1574. Fax: 972-539-4396. Email: rjmarsh@sprynet.com. Web: www.findafuture.com.

NEW!
Clutter Free!

Grade 7–adult. $12.99 plus $3 shipping.
Home Life, Inc., PO Box 1190, Fenton, MO 63026. Orders: (800) 346-6322. Web: www.home-school.com.

NEW!
How to Have a 48-Hour Day

Grade 7–adult. $12.95 plus $3 shipping.
Home Life, Inc., PO Box 1190, Fenton, MO 63026. Orders: (800) 346-6322. Web: www.home-school.com.

His **How to Manage Your Money** seminar, for example, starts out by defining wealth biblically, then delves into God's will for your finances, the perils of money, how to get out of debt, financial planning with a Christian perspective, motives for accumulating wealth, how much is enough, sharing the wealth (including how to tell the difference between those who deserve and *don't* deserve your help), and instruction in a basic Christian approach to making financial decisions.

Sound too philosophical and boring to you? Believe me, it's not! Larry sprinkles his presentation with dozens of true-life examples, good and bad, of the principles he is teaching, and gets *really* specific about the types of behavior that lead to good—or disastrous— financial results. There's plenty for business owners here, as well as for wage earners and homeworkers. That's not to say that I agree with every jot and tittle in this seminar, but that it's an excellent place to start. If you can't afford to buy the video seminar, talk your church into it. *Mary Pride*

Clutter Free! is the first book on de-junking mostly written by the junkers themselves. Find out how real people just like you deal with the agony of packrat relatives, dust-catching "treasures," and all the other detritus of a mass "consumer" culture that never actually "consumes" anything that can be stored in the attic instead. Like all Don Aslett's books, it's warm, human, fun to read, and motivating. *Mary Pride*

The real trick to packing 48 hours into your day is, of course, to be born Don Aslett. Parents, this is what your "hyperactive" kids can accomplish if they just put that energy into something productive instead of swinging from the chandelier. Don exhibits that kind of restless energy, and it's helped him write dozens of books, found and run a multi-million dollar cleaning company, personally build his second home in Hawaii, appear on TV almost everywhere . . . do I need to go on?

However, for those of us without that extra "zip" in our genes, there is now hope, thanks to this book. **How to Have a 48-Hour Day** is dedicated to all us slackers out there who get "workaholic" and "productive" confused. Don first explains why it's nice to get lots more done than you're accomplishing right now; then he tells you how to eliminate the time-wasters *and* add more useful things to your life. He cajoles, preaches, even nags you to make your life count for something besides rest stops and play periods. If this book you're reading ever makes it into print, like it's supposed to, it's because I've started taking Don's advice. *Mary Pride*

CHAPTER 41

Physical Education

By the time you read this, the school-age members of your family may be able to play on their local public-school team. All around the country, school districts are considering whether to allow home-schooled kids to join in extracurricular activities.

I say the answer should be, "Yes!" It's only fair—homeschoolers pay the same taxes as everyone else. Just because we choose not to avail ourselves of the public school's academic classes, that doesn't mean we shouldn't be able to join the school band, the drama club, or the football team.

Even if the local school doesn't invite homeschoolers to join the team, you have other options. In some localities, homeschool groups have started their own teams and leagues. Or you can join Little League, a bowling team, a swim club, or a skating club without having to be affiliated with any school. And there's always the YMCA or the Jewish community center, both of which make many exercise and sports options available.

Let's say you're not all that athletically inclined. Then what? As a well-rounded citizen, you are supposed to know the rules and basic moves of The Biggies: football, baseball, and basketball. Most Americans have at least an idea of what goes on in soccer and hockey, too, and are familiar with tennis, running, swimming, and diving. Golf and skiing are still mostly up-per-middle-class—expensive to play, but not to watch on TV. Most people don't expect you to play polo or know the rules of cricket, although I wish I *did* know the rules of cricket, without which so many English schoolboy stories make no sense. The martial arts are another category, and so are the circus arts.

It's too much to ask a home program to include football, baseball, bas-ketball, hockey, soccer, tennis, running, swimming, diving, golf, and ski-ing. Even kids in those lavish public-school buildings don't do all of this. For our purposes, it's enough to know the rules of the popular sports, and to pick *one* "lifetime" sport to enjoy for yourself.

Of course, homeschoolers can form our own teams, too. Homeschool basketball programs are sprouting everywhere. Here is a photo of the Christian Family Educators team of Grove, KS, taken several years ago to accompany an article in *Practical Homeschooling*.

For information about the annual homeschool basketball championships, see page 422.

Lifetime sports are those, like softball, that you can reasonably expect to still play when you're 45 (or 75!). Boxing, football, and other bone-cracking pastimes are not lifetime sports. Walking, tennis, golf, swimming, and juggling are. Any of these, practiced regularly, provides enough exercise to keep you healthy. With the exception of tennis, which requires another player, all of these lifetime sports can be enjoyed solo.

The Lifetime Sport of Juggling

If you want a specific recommendation, here it comes. Juggling is the ultimate home schooler's lifetime sport. Juggling is fun, impresses your friends, and is great aerobic exercise. The equipment is not expensive, and thanks to the wonderful training and competition videos now available, you can learn at home without an instructor.

Unlike most sports, juggling is very flexible, not only due to the wide range of apparatus used by jugglers (scarves, balls, clubs, rings, unicycles, spinning plates, and balls are just the beginning) but because juggling includes so many sub-sports and styles. You can be a flashy showman, a goofy clown, a technical "numbers" juggler, a balancer, a team juggler (with teams of two, three, four, or more people), a rhythm-stick man, or a club swinger. You can juggle toilet plungers or balance a supermarket cart on your chin! Everyone, whether tall or short, thin or fat, young or old, can find some juggling specialty that fits his style.

Except for numbers juggling—which requires high ceilings—you can juggle almost anywhere. You don't need special shoes or clothes, or an indoor pool or rink. The whole family can juggle at once, so nobody is left out. Even the littlest baby can chew on the end of a club, while toddlers enjoy tossing up a colorful juggling scarf and trying to catch it! Juggling takes no preparation time; just pick up your beanbags! Nor do you need to have superfast reflexes to master many tricks. Many world-class jugglers do most of their act with just three balls!

So do we Prides practice what I just finished preaching? You betcha! My husband Bill can juggle up to five balls, and do many tricks with three and four. I am better with three balls than with four, and can keep three clubs going at once. All of our teens can juggle at least three balls. Before his operation, Ted was practicing passing seven balls with Joe. Joe, our juggling star, has actually performed in public. He has a very professional "devil stick" routine, plus juggles clubs, balls, cigar boxes (a prop popularized by comedian W.C. Fields), and rings.

By the way, for those of you who worry about names, the "devil stick" has nothing to do with the devil. It got its name from the Greek "diabolo," which literally means "throw across." It's also a very difficult prop to juggle, which may also account for the name. Just thought you'd like to know. Other popular juggling props for beginning jugglers include peacock feathers (I am not making this up, and what's more, I know where to get them), scarves, beanbags, and of course diabolos—a sort of giant Yo-Yo that you manipulate on a string between two sticks.

Does juggling peacock feathers and beanbags sound like more fun than you had sitting on the bench in high school, waiting for your two seconds at bat? Then come on, learn to juggle, and no supermarket oranges will ever be safe from you again!

Physical Education Curriculum

Whether you're new to a sport or simply want to learn how to play better, the **Converse All Star series** of books may be the answer for you.

"Let's see . . . Start with the left hand, toss so it flips once . . . How I'll fit two in a hand this size I'll never know . . ."

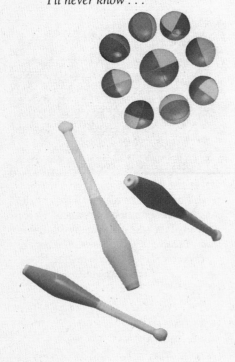

Each oversized paperback book is packed with history, rules, information on how to improve your technique and interviews with some of the stars of the sport. The first few pages of each book explain the background of the game, its rules, regulations and terminology. The main focus, however, is on techniques and strategy. The series makes good use of its many black-and-white photographs and line drawings to clearly illustrate all of the major points.

The technique and strategy chapters in each of the books vary according to the sport:

- *Converse All Star Baseball.* Batting, running the bases, and each of the positions (with infielders, middle infielders and outfielders grouped into three chapters).
- *Converse All Star Basketball.* Dribbling, passing, shooting, rebounding, offense, and defense.
- *Converse All Star Football.* The quarterback, running backs, receivers, offensive linemen, defense, the kicking game, and the game plan.
- *Converse All Star Soccer.* Training, dribbling, passing, receiving the ball, heading, shooting, goalkeeping, putting it all together, and restarts.

The books emphasize what players need to think about as they play. For instance, a football receiver must concentrate on getting in the open to catch the ball, catching it and holding on to it. The books also emphasize what traits are important—in this case, a receiver needs to be "especially courageous," since you'll be catching many balls while you are off-balance and will need to be able to take the "hit." (They do not, however, go into the consequences of what could happen; this is positive thinking all the way!)

At the end of most chapters are games and exercises designed to strengthen your skills in that area. "Keep Focused" lists end each chapter with highlights to the important points.

Each book contains interviews with at least two heroes of the game, including players and coaches. (The soccer book contains an interview with a female player, but everything else—interviews and pictures—appear to be men.) Also scattered throughout the books are little snippets of fun facts and trivia. Key terms are introduced as they come up and are also contained in a glossary at the end of the book.

Even if you'd rather be playing than reading, these books have plenty of appeal for those times that you're on the sidelines. Each section is headlined to make what you need easy to find and the writing style is active:

"He brings the ball under control but the defense is all over him. He takes a quick dribble and sees an opening. His foot flies back, he kicks the ball, and it sails into the corner of the goal. Score!"

I especially like that teamwork skills resound throughout each of the books as a natural accompaniment to technical skills and positive thinking. Rather than stressing the importance of teamwork, each section talks about how that position or skill is performed in relation to the other players. *Teresa Schultz-Jones*

Any book about fun, fitness and food whose author proclaims that she is "far too klutzy for aerobics and would rather die than be seen wearing spandex in public" is okay by me.

Donna and Cameron Partow, the authors of **Families that Play Together Stay Together**, describe the typical American family as running off in many different directions and only coming together to "watch-TV-till-you-sleep." She points out that if we shut the television off and cut back on the amount of outside activities we will have more time together as a family. The book explores healthy alternatives that help a family grow together.

There are 238 pages of information to help your family adopt an active lifestyle. You'll find discussion questions, Bible verses, suggested family activities, and places to record your family's comments and answers. Activities are suitable for all ages and abilities, and range from stargazing

NEW!
Families That Play Together Stay Together
Grade 9–adult. $8.99.
Bethany House Publishing, 11300 Hamshire Avenue South, Minneapolis, MN 55438.
800-328-6109. Fax: (612) 829-2503.
Email: info@bethanyhouse.com.
Web: www.bethanyhouse.com.

and after-dinner walks to dude ranches and adventure vacations in exotic locations. Addresses, phone numbers, and other references help you further plan an activity. The fitness section discusses why regular activity is important, and the food section provides favorite Partow recipes and explains healthy eating. The reference section at the end contains state-by-state listings of places to go (about two per state) and books to read.

Filled with personal anecdotes and insights, the Partows' book reminds us that it isn't how well you do something, but that you made the effort. Donna's descriptions of her experience in-line skating with her teen-age daughter were hilarious and illustrate their point that even unsuccessful activities teach us to try new things, keep a positive outlook, and provide fodder for family legends—when we share the experience as a family. *Teresa Schultz-Jones*

How many times have we sent the kids out to play, called it "physical education" for the day, and felt pretty good about it? When you think about it, we don't approach other subjects in such a haphazard manner, so why should this be any different?

Fitness at Home was designed by author David Kidd (BJU grad., coach, and homeschooling dad) to give children some basic, all-around fitness skills. The goal is not to push or pressure but to provide instruction in a systematic way. Students are expected to exercise five days per week, performing exercises from four different categories: flexibility, abdominal strength, endurance, and arm/shoulder strength. The student training program has a chart to keep track of days and progress, illustrations and descriptions of the different exercises, and a list of memory verses. The chart is reproducible, so the program can be used year after year. The Bible memory verses and discussion topics pertain to self-discipline and perseverance. The program is flexible in that you can substitute other sports activities for the daily requirements.

The parent's manual instructs you on the importance of fitness, how to find your child's target heart rate, and how to administer the pre- and post-tests. The test involves pull-ups (or flexed arm hang), sit-ups, sit and reach, and one-mile run.

The student training chart and a colorful award certificate are included with each Student Training Program. Only one parent's manual is needed per family, and one Student Training Program, but you'll need a new certificate for each participant. The emblem is an optional sew-on patch to identify the student as a participant in this program. There are three different award levels and everyone can earn one. The emphasis isn't worldly at all, rather it is in doing our best for the Lord to take care of the bodies He gave us. *Renee Mathis*

NEW!
Fitness at Home
Grades 1–12. Parent Kit, $4.75. Student Training Program, $2.95. Fitness Emblem, $2.25. Add 10% shipping.
Fitness at Home, 1084 Yale Farm Rd., Romulus, NY 14541. (315) 585-2248. Email: drk3@cornell.edu.

Fun Physical Fitness for the Home
Ages 0–10. $19.95 plus shipping.
Noble Publishing Associates, PO Box 2250, Gresham, OR 97030. Orders: (800) 225-5259. Inquiries: (503) 667-3942. Fax: (503) 618-8866.

Sono Sato Harris' **Fun Physical Fitness for the Home** is an exercise and physical fitness guide that includes an array of indoor exercises to keep your child busy, active and fit during the long winter months. It is also great for the summer months! Not only does it include basic exercises, it also includes creative ideas to make physical fitness more fun.

Sono Harris draws upon her experience as a student, performer and teacher of ballet, modern dance, creative dance and gymnastics. Her love for dance and gymnastics is apparent throughout the book. The book is only 47 pages long, and includes black-and-white line illustrations. There is a lot of material included in a small package. It begins with simple exercises like "The Russian Bear," where your child crawls on hands and feet, working up to straight knees and feet flat on the floor. Also included are stretching and tumbling exercises, as well as basic gymnastics. She gives tips on how to incorporate academics into your physical exercise and music programs through creative expression. A CD done by Craig Bidondo is included to provide motivational background music to the exercises.

The program is thorough and fun. It can be done by older children without a lot of supervision, once they learn the basic exercises. *Maryann Turner*

Physical Education courses designed specifically for homeschoolers are hard to find. This one is top notch! I especially like the "Quick Start" section at the beginning of this spiral-bound 137 page book. This section gives you a jump start when beginning the program. For those of us that get bogged down in the how-tos, this added incentive makes the program very usable.

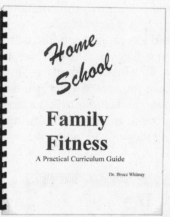

Home School Family Fitness was written by a homeschooling father of seven children, who just so happens to have a Ph.D. in physical education. He uses both areas of expertise to put together an excellent physical education manual for home educators. There are sections on strength, endurance, flexibility and aerobic fitness. The program is very family-friendly, using mostly equipment and ideas that are easily incorporated into your homeschool program. Physical fitness tests, an explanation of the rules, and more than enough activities to keep you busy for 40+ weeks are included. There are both indoor and outdoor activities, and technique checklists for baseball, soccer, volleyball, basketball, tennis, walking, running, and football.

If you need a comprehensive physical education manual that is easy to use, look no further. This one has it all! *Maryann Turner*

Here's why none of your friends can juggle—they started out with beanbags (or balls, or oranges). Here's what you should do; pitch the beanbags and try our **juggling scarves** and **Juggling Step-by-Step** video.

Scarves, the "training wheels of the juggling world," can repair your sagging confidence, and as an added benefit they won't knock over your vases. Once you have mastered scarves, *then* move on to beanbags, but *only after watching the video several times*. Juggling is just too hard to learn from a book for most of us; we need to *see* how it works. Even a juggling friend can't show you the moves in slow motion, but the video can (and does)! You need smooth nylon juggling scarves, not the cheaper kind which disintegrates with use.

In the **Juggling Step-by-Step video** you meet Professor Confidence (a smooth fellow in top hat and tails who introduces the lessons and performs many of the moves), Won Israel (a colorful little clown), Amy (a beautiful Filipino girl), Andrew (an incredibly talented young juggler), John (a great

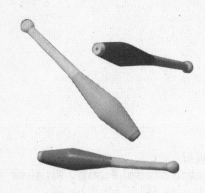

club juggler), and Robert (a Huck Finn-type kid). Each of these has a particular specialty: balls, clubs, rings, scarves, devil sticks, diabolo, and team juggling are some of the topics covered.

Again, after the first lessons on basic moves, you are expected to pick up more advanced moves from simply watching the tape. The lessons and illustrative performances are set to music. As much fun to watch as a stage show!

The *Juggling Step-by-Step* video gives you a basic introduction to juggling scarves, beanbags, balls, rings, and clubs; and then goes on to more advanced routines with clubs and balls, unusual equipment like cigar boxes and hats, and even flaming torches! You'll also be introduced to team juggling, juggling with many objects, multiplex juggling, two-in-one-hand, and lots more. Each instruction sequence includes a routine by some really great jugglers. These videos are a quantum leap in juggling education.

One final word on juggling as the ultimate family sport: When's the last time you saw two guys throwing a football, baseball, soccer ball, or hockey puck back and forth on a street corner, with a hat beside them on the ground, and people throwing money into the hat? Now if they'd been passing *juggling clubs* instead . . . Get the picture? *Mary Pride*

Sports Rules Book

Grade 9–adult. $19.95 ($29.95 Canadian) plus shipping.
Human Kinetics Publishers, Box 5076, Champaign, IL 61825-5076.
Orders: (800) 747-4457.
Inquiries: (217) 351-5076.
Fax: (217) 351-1549.
Email: humank@hkusa.com.
Web: www.humankinetics.com.

Sports literacy between two covers. The **Sport Rules Book** presents the fundamental rules and procedures for 54 sports in its 384 pages.

The new second edition gives the official rules of play as approved by the governing body for that sport, playing area specifications, necessary equipment, and the names and addresses of the governing body or bodies plus the names and addresses of the two top journals for that sport. Some of the more complex rules have been abridged, but most are the complete official rules.

Here's what's covered: Archery (target). Badminton. Baseball. Basketballs. Billiards (pool). Bowling. Boxing. Canoeing. Casting. Cricket (now you can finally find out what those English schoolboys were doing in P. G. Wodehouse's and Rudyard Kipling's schoolboy books). Croquet. Crossbow archery. Curling. Cycling. Darts. Diving. Fencing. Field archery. Field hockey. Flag football (touch). Football. Golf. Handball. Horseshoe pitching. Ice hockey. Lawn bowls. Orienteering. Paddleball. Paddle tennis. Powerlifting. Racquetball. Shuffleboard (get ready for your retirement!). Skiing. Soccer. Softball (separate rules for fast pitch and slow pitch). Speedball. Speedskating. Squash. Swimming. Table tennis (ping pong). Taekwondo. Team handball. Tennis. Track and field (athletics). Trampolining. Tumbling. Volleyball. Water polo. Weightlifting.

I know you're asking yourself, "Why aren't sailing and juggling on this list?" Well, probably you *aren't* asking that, and that's why they aren't in the book. Better luck next time! *Mary Pride*

NEW!
Totally Christian Karate (TCK) Christian Defense System (CDS)

Grade K–adult. TCK book (levels 1–4 and 5–8), $10 each. Corresponding videos, $10 each. CDS book, $25. Add $3.50 shipping.

Every once in a while a product comes along and surprises you. **Totally Christian Karate** is one of those products. I expected karate with a Christian label, a sign slapped on it to make it acceptable to Christians. What I got instead was just what the name implies. *Totally Christian Karate* is, in fact, a new form of karate.

There are many forms of karate and Mitchell Freistat has studied six of them. His studies lead him into eastern religions and when he met Jesus he faced a dilemma. Karate with the usual spiritual content is unChristian, and karate minus the spiritual aspect is merely physical, ". . . sowing only to the flesh with no eternal value." He determined that a Martial Art would only have eternal value if Christ were its foundation, and he set about designing that art. He has taken the physical movements from other Martial Arts, renamed them, and associated them with Bible-based studies. He is intent on preparing your body for self-defense, but even more focused on preparing your spirit for warfare.

The *Totally Christian Karate* course consists of the Bible studies in two oversized comb-bound books and eight video tapes (one for each level). You first purchase the Levels 1–4 book and the Level 1 video (videos for levels 2–4 sold separately). When you are ready for level 5, purchase the Levels 5–8 book and Level 5 video (videos 6–8 sold separately). As you work your way through the levels, you train the techniques physically; do the related Bible studies and spiritual applications; look up, meditate on, and memorize Scriptures; and apply the scriptures in your life. It sounds like a lot, but the layout of the book is so clean and the text so easily understood that the Bible work is not at all intimidating.

The videos themselves are not flashy or high tech; it's just your instructor and a simple background. Freistat demonstrates each move clearly, giving a full explanation of the move itself and its related spiritual truth. For instance, when demonstrating the move "Repent," he gives a concise explanation of what repentance is while showing how to perform the move properly. The spiritual explanation clarifies the necessity of moving in a specific manner, and the move itself is a physical illustration of what it is to repent.

Yes, it is more difficult to learn a Martial Art strictly from video. Without an instructor near to correct your form, it is easy to develop bad habits. On the other hand, this is the best option I've seen for those who must choose between Martial Arts training that offends their religious beliefs and no training at all. Also, Totally Christian Karate is backed by Freistat's declaration that "This is a CORRESPONDENCE course. If you have ANY questions please call. I am here to serve YOU!"

If you already train in some form of karate, or if you are an instructor, you may prefer Freistat's **Christian Defense System**. This 98-page, oversized, comb-bound book contains all of the studies found in *Totally Christian Karate* as well as tables that cross-reference the moves' Bible-based and traditional names, along with advice on integrating the Bible-based studies into your training. The studies, as noted earlier, are excellent; they could easily serve as stand-alone Bible studies for training in spiritual warfare.

Both are excellent new alternatives for those seeking Martial Arts training. *Tammy Cardwell*

Straight from England, the Usborne sports training books answer the question, "Can you really learn anything about a sport from a book?" **Ballet** and **Dance** both teach simple techniques (and the reasons behind them) as well as presenting the history of these art forms. All volumes in the Superskills series do a wonderful job of explaining technique even to someone like me who knows nothing about these fine points.

Athletics, which is really what Americans would call track and field, seems to be an excel-

Totally Christian Karate, 2001 NW 38th Ave., Coconut Creek, FL 33066. (800) 633-7917. Fax: (954) 972-8548. Email: Freistat@aol.com.

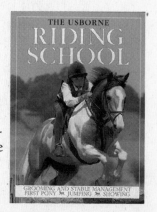

Usborne Physical Education

Grades 6–12. Ballet and Dance, $7.95 each (paperbound) or $12.95 as a combined paperbound volume. The Superskills series: Soccer Skills, Running Skills, Racing Bikes, and Mountain Bikes, $5.95 each; Athletics, $7.95; and Windsurfing, $8.95. Juggling, $6.95. Juggling Kid Kit, $11.95. Riding and Pony Care, $9.95 (paperbound) or $17.95 (library-bound). Shipping extra.

EDC Publishing, Division of Educational Development Corporation, PO Box 470663, Tulsa, OK 74147. (800) 475-4522. Fax: (800) 747-4509. Web: www.edcpub.com.

NEW!
Yes You Can! Surviving a Personal Attack

Grade 9–adult. $19.95 plus shipping.
Curtis Inc., 2025 Reading Road, Suite 130, Cincinnati, OH 45202. Orders: (800) 733-2878. Inquiries: (513) 621-8895. Fax: (513) 621-0942. Email: curtisinc@fuse.net. Web: www.curtisinc.com.

lent description of proper techniques and training methods for those skills.

The diagrams and explanations in **Juggling** were difficult for me to follow and I already know how to juggle pretty well.

Like all other Usborne books, these are lavishly, colorfully illustrated with pictures and text carefully designed to impart information with minimum effort and maximum fun. *Mary Pride*

Being personally attacked is a frightening thought, but according to Debbie Gardner, the founder of Survive Institute, your odds for surviving can be greatly increased if you know how to handle the situation. In **Yes You Can!**, a 110-minute video, she gives you a no-nonsense approach to employ, should you find yourself in a threatening situation. She talks you through various scenarios, and informs you of the choices you could make in each case. She is an energetic and dynamic speaker, who has the ability to make you feel empowered. Of course, this is an adult topic, and discretion should be used when children are around!

Debbie Gardner is outspoken, so sometimes her language is questionable . . . but the techniques and ideas in the video are unique and could prove valuable if you find yourself in a confrontational situation. *Maryann Turner*

National Homeschool Basketball Championships

For many years now, individual homeschoolers and homeschool teams (such as the one pictured on page 415) have been gathering for an annual week-long championship competition. The ninth annual Christian Homeschool Basketball Championship and Family Conference will be held in San Antonio, TX, from March 5–10, 2000. It is sponsored by Family Educators Alliance of South Texas (FEAST). For more info, call them at (210) 342-4674, or visit their website at *www.homeschoolfeast.com.*

CHAPTER 42

Volunteering

Volunteering is a great way to get some real-world experience while serving your fellow man. Colleges love to see volunteer work listed on your application; so do employers. You don't even have to be old enough to drive to volunteer, though it helps.

Schools tend to equate "volunteering" with "community service." But we don't need to think that small! You can serve your church, your homeschool support group, or even start your own organization to meet a need nobody else sees. See the story about Craig Kielburger in this chapter to see what I mean!

Information About Volunteering

If your child would like to spend part or all of his or her summer making a difference in people's lives, **Christian Camping Today: A Complete Handbook for the Short-Term Staff** is *the* book by *the* expert on Christian camping. Author Lloyd Mattson, author or editor of another 20 camping books and former editor of the *Journal of Christian Camping*, gives you a history of Christian camping, explains why it works, the need for short-term staff, what you need to know about campers by age group, meeting expectations (including safety), counseling basics, cabin group basics, and how to make sure the spiritual side of Christian camping remains foremost, both in "program" times and in the daily activities. There's also an appendix of camping resources, of which I will list just one you need to know about here: Christian Camping International/USA, PO Box 62198, Colorado Springs, CO 80962-2189. This is the group that Christian camps belong to; ask for their resource list.

Short-term staff, many of who are teens, outnumber permanent staff in camps fifteen to one. This means lots of opportunity for a homeschooler who is willing to serve. And I bet you didn't know that "In 1996, an estimated 5,720,000 women, men, teens, and children representing 107,000 churches attended CCI/USA camps. Of that number, 268,000 made professions of faith." I bet you also didn't know that "214,800 men and women currently engaged in church-related vocations around the world make spiritual commitments in a CCI-member camp or conference." This deceptively short book is packed with nuggets like that, real-life stories, and the distilled wisdom of years of camping experience. If your son or daughter has an interest in Christian service, buy it! *Mary Pride*

NEW!
Christian Camping Today
Grade 10–adult. $6.99 plus shipping.
Harold Shaw Publishers, PO Box 567, Wheaton, IL 60189.
Orders: (800) 742-9782 x219.
Inquiries: (630) 665-6700.
Fax: (630) 665-6793.
Email: shawpub@compuserve.com.

CHRISTIAN Camping TODAY

Lloyd Mattson

Volunteering

From The Community Service for Teens series, ©1998 Ferguson Publishing Company, used with permission.

Six out of ten American teenagers work as volunteers. A 1996 survey revealed that the total number of teen volunteers aged 12 to 17 is l 3.3 million. They give 2.4 billion hours each year. Of that time, 1.8 billion hours are spent in "formal" commitments to nonprofit organizations. Informal help, like "just helping neighbors," receives 600 million hours.

Each "formal" volunteer gives an average of three and a half hours a week. It would take nearly 1.1 million full-time employees to match these hours. And if the formal volunteers were paid minimum wage for their time, the cost would come to at least $7.7 billion—a tremendous saving to nonprofit organizations.

Teen volunteerism is growing. In the four years between the 1996 survey and a previous one, the number of volunteers grew by 7 percent and their hours increased by 17 percent.

Equal numbers of girls and boys give their time to volunteering.

How voluntary is volunteering? Only 16 out of 100 volunteers go to schools that insist on community service before graduation. Twenty-six out of 100 are in schools that offer courses requiring community service if you want credit for the course.

Six out of ten teen volunteers started volunteering before they were 14 years old. Seventy-eight percent of teens who volunteer have parents who volunteer.

WHY VOLUNTEER?

When teens are asked to volunteer the 1996 survey revealed, nine out of ten do so. Who does the asking? Usually a friend, teacher, relative, or church member.

Teens gave a number of reasons for volunteering, regardless of whether their schools required community service. Their reasons included:

- You feel compassion for people in need.
- You feel you can do something for a cause that is important to you.
- You believe that if you help others, others will help you.
- Your volunteering is important to people you respect.
- You learn to relate to others who may be different from you.
- You develop leadership skills.
- You become more patient.
- You gain a better understanding of good citizenship.
- You get a chance to learn about various careers.
- You gain experience that can help in school and can lead to college admission and college scholarships as well as future careers.

VOLUNTEER FOR WHAT?

You can volunteer in a wide variety of activities. To get a picture of how teen volunteering is spread among various categories, see Exhibit 1.

WHO SAYS YOU HAVE TO "VOLUNTEER"?

Is "volunteering" for community service required in your school? It is if you live in the state of Maryland or in the city of Atlanta, Georgia. In fact, in many school districts across the United States you cannot receive your high school diploma unless you have spent a certain number of hours in community service. The number of hours varies.

Who makes the rule? In Maryland, the only state so far to require every high school student to perform community service, it is the Maryland State Department of Education. In most school districts, it is the board of education, which usually sets policies that meet the standards of the community.

If you have to do it, is it voluntary? And is it legal to make you do it? One family didn't think so. In 1994, the parents of Daniel Immediato, a 17-year-old senior at Rye Neck High School 10 Mamaroneck, New York, sued in federal court to keep Daniel's school from requiring him to spend 40 hours in community service before he could graduate.

Daniel's parents said the requirement interfered with their right to raise their child, that it violated Daniel's privacy rights, and that it was a violation of the Thirteenth Amendment to the U.S. Constitution. That amendment says

> Neither slavery nor involuntary servitude, except as a punishment for a crime whereof the party shall have been duly convicted, shall exist within the United States, or any place subject to their jurisdiction.

The requirement for community service, said the Immediatos, imposed involuntary servitude on Daniel.

In its defense, the Rye Neck School Board argued that what it wanted was to get the students out into the community to see what goes on in the outside world. In the process, said the board, students would find out what it was like to have to dress appropriately for a job, be on time somewhere, and have other people dependent on them. The emphasis was not on what the community would gain, it was on what the student would learn.

The court decided the school system was right. The Immediatos appealed. The U.S. Court of Appeals for the Second Circuit upheld the decision. The Immediatos asked the U.S. Supreme Court to hear the case. It turned down the request, as it does many appeals, without stating its reason for refusing.

"Don't miss an opportunity that is disguised as a requirement." —Karl Methven, Faculty Member and Head Coach, addressing the Class of 1997, Proctor Academy, Andover New Hampshire, at the graduation ceremony May 31, 1997

"If schools are going to demand that volunteering be part of success an a teenager," says Susan Trafford, president, Habitat for Humanity, Central Westmoreland, Pennsylvania, "I think the teens need to have, first, a selection in the volunteerism that they are going to do, and second, an understanding that this is a responsibility. This is the real world. This isn't the high school. This isn't the halls of Central High. I don't think we can just send them off and say, 'Now, here's your volunteer day.' They need a cause to go there, an understanding of someone, of what they will be contributing to. Sure, there are wonderful things that can be done. But don't send me six who have to do this before they can graduate."

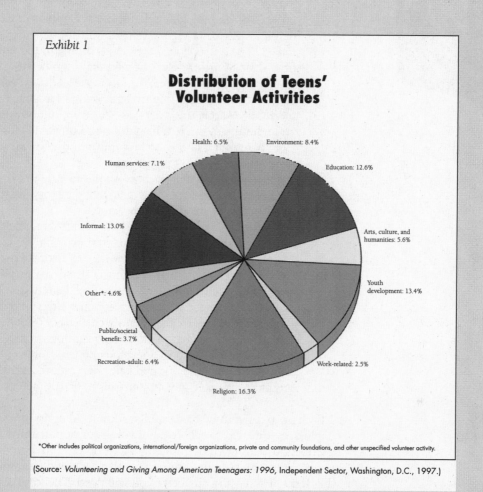

Exhibit 1

Distribution of Teens' Volunteer Activities

Health: 6.5%
Environment: 8.4%
Human services: 7.1%
Education: 12.6%
Informal: 13.0%
Arts, culture, and humanities: 5.6%
Other*: 4.6%
Youth development: 13.4%
Public/societal benefit: 3.7%
Recreation-adult: 6.4%
Work-related: 2.5%
Religion: 16.3%

*Other includes political organizations, international/foreign organizations, private and community foundations, and other unspecified volunteer activity.

(Source: *Volunteering and Giving Among American Teenagers: 1996*, Independent Sector, Washington, D.C., 1997.)

Community Service for Teens is a set of eight hardbound volumes. Each volume looks at a different area of community service compatible with school programs, as their titles make clear:

- *Caring for Animals*—working with vets, zoologists, or animal lovers at animal hospitals, zoos, aquariums, animal shelters and pounds, horse stables
- *Serving with Police, Fire and EMS*—Police Explorers, Junior Fire Corps, Emergency Medical Service Explorers
- *Helping the Ill, the Poor and the Elderly*—hospital volunteering (work with patients and administration); health department;

research and fundraising; battered women's shelters; nursing home volunteering; helping the elderly in their homes (telephone reassurance, food shopping, friendly visiting, escorting); soup kitchen; food banks

- *Participating in Government*—working with the offices of the mayor or city council; the youth commission; helping state legislators; helping U.S. senators and members of Congress; helping with voter registration and turnout
- *Expanding Education and Literacy*—helping in the public library (the homeschooler's home away from home!); school programs, such as Club RIF; tutoring; Headstart; peer leadership and counseling; English as a Second Language
- *Increasing Neighborhood Service*—cleanup; fundraising; office and administration in a neighborhood organization; fieldwork, from neighborly chores to building a house for a low-income resident; public relation and recruiting
- *Promoting the Arts and Sciences*—volunteering in history, natural history, and science museums; living history sites; performing arts; visual arts and art museums
- *Protecting the Environment*—this one has an annoying (but typical of mainstream environmentalism) anti-people tone, talking about how many of us "invade" (their word) the national parks and "force" our waste on the environment. It doesn't mention that land trusts often *sell* the land donated to them to developers, and beats the drums for acid rain, greenhouse effect, and ozone depletion—all of which are seriously challenged by actual scientific research. Some evolution, too. Volunteer opportunities here are recycling and litter collection; study outings; lobbying; staff and administration; scientific and field work; youth leaders; campground hosts; field guides; journalism; Earthwatch; teaching

Each 96-page volume has a similar format. After an introduction, several chapters are devoted to each type of volunteer opportunity. The program is described, usually with examples and anecdotes. You're told what your responsibilities will be if you sign up for that type of community service and what kind of skills and character you will need. The kind of work is described in detail, and you're told what this kind of volunteer opportunity will do for you—skills, character, college and career preparation, job satisfaction, and more.

The amount of detail is excellent, and the quotes from students and their adult supervisors help you feel what it's really like out there. Plus, when possible you are provided with contact information for organizations, or told how to find your local organization, making each volume really practical and useful.

Because the author is from New England, the books use mainly examples of programs in Connecticut (in particular) and the other New England states. So be aware that some of the programs suggested—e.g., EMS (Emergency Medical Service) Explorer—may be common in a state featured in the book, but not available at all in yours.

This series, with the possible exception of the *Environment* book, would be a great purchase for your support group. *Mary Pride*

NEW!
Directory of American Youth Organizations, seventh edition

The Directory of American Youth Organizations is just what its title proclaims. From religious organizations, to sports organizations, to career education and vocational student groups, to science/math/technology organizations, to nonpartisan and partisan political organizations, to "peace and global understanding groups" and a whole lot more, just about everyone is here. Each organization's name, date of founding, and all contact information is listed along with a paragraph or two of detailed description. There are organizations for kids to join, and organizations of interest to those who administer organizations! And it is not limited to only "physical" groups either. There is a brief section of relevant websites, as well as a history of clubs, groups, troops, teams, etc. in general. Basically, if you're looking for something to join, this 207-page, oversized book is for you. *Sarah Pride*

The **Kids' Volunteering Book** has the same format as the **Kids' Business Book** (see review in volume 2). Both are glossy, colorful, paper-bound books, 64 pages long. Each book begins with examples of extremely successful kids, like the boy who voluntarily gathers thousands of socks and sends them to many organizations, using his own money for the postage.

The **Kids' Volunteering Book** informs you how to find the right volunteer job and how to apply for it. It also gives helpful tips on starting your own organization for something you feel strongly about. Tons of photos and true-life stories make the book appealing, but this is not just cute fluff. Lists of organizations, suggested books for further reading, a glossary, and an index provide everything needed to make this the centerpiece of a unit study on volunteering. Or you can do as the author intended, and use it to find your very first volunteer job!

Cleverly written and very interesting reading, no matter what you intend to do. *Sarah Pride*

Grades 5–12 or parents. $21.95 plus shipping.
Free Spirit Publishing, Inc., 400 First Avenue North, Suite 616, Minneapolis, MN 55401. (800) 735-7323. Fax: (612) 337-5050. Email: help4kids@freespirit.com. Web: www.freespirit.com.

NEW!
The Kids' Volunteering Book
Grades 5–10. $9.95.
Lerner Publications, 1251 Washington Ave. North, Minneapolis, MN 55401. (800) 328-4929. (612) 332-3344. Fax: (612) 204-9208. Web: www.lernerbooks.com.

You Can Build Your Own Service! by Raymond Laurita

About four years ago, I watched a CBS "60 Minutes" program about a twelve-year-old Canadian boy who had initiated a personal effort to do something about the exploitation of children the world over. At the time, I was greatly impressed by the energy and thoughtfulness of this bright youngster who was actually achieving positive results in alleviating the suffering of many children. I didn't follow up on the story then, but recently I came across a brief news report about Craig Kielburger and his continuing saga. The headline for the *New York Times* (4/17/99) piece told me that this boy was still involved in trying to stop the problems that interested him first as a twelve-year-old:

A Crusade for Children
Canadian Teenager Enlists His Peers In a Fight Against Child Labor

The reporter related how Craig, who is now 16, had described the start of his quest:

It began while he was fumbling for the comics one day four years ago and he stumbled upon a story that changed his life. The story was about the murder of a Pakistani teenager who had been sold into bondage at age 5 to work in a rug factory.

During an address to an audience of forty eighth-graders from a Long Island, NY, school, who had invited him to speak, Craig related how a story he'd come across accidentally had stirred him to persuade a handful of his friends to start a club that would work against the evils of exploitative child labor. As a result, they wrote letters to companies to urge them not to use child labor. The report of his talk continued:

"We all know there are problems in this world," he said, challenging the students from this lower-middle-class Long Island community to worry about more than Nin-

tendos and going to the mall. "But the question is, are we going to get involved to do something about them?"

It may be hard to believe, but here are a few of the accomplishments of this youngster from Ontario over the last four years:

- He convinced a labor federation to donate $150,000 to the Free the Children foundation, a group which he started to administer incoming funds.
- This foundation now receives $300,000 in donations which go to cover $40,000 in administration with the rest going to build schools overseas and run leadership courses for children.
- Partly because of pressure from Craig and his followers, NIKE began barring its factories from hiring anyone under age 16.
- Carol Bellamy, executive director of UNICEF, says that this young boy "has certainly raised the profile on the issue of child labor."
- As chairman of Free the Children, Craig has visited Asia, Africa, and Latin America, and has met with Nelson Mandela, Mother Teresa, the Dalai Lama, and the Pope. In the Phillipines, he watched very young children scavenging through garbage piles to find things to sell, and in India, he met an 8-year-old girl whose job was dismantling a pile of used syringes. "I asked her, isn't she worried about getting AIDS from the needles?" Craig told the students. "She gave me a blank stare. She didn't even know what AIDS is."
- Through his grass-roots organization and his gift for public speaking, Craig has become North America's leading spokesman against child labor and as a result of his overseas efforts managed to get the government of Brazil to adopt new incentives for education and to discourage children from working on sugar cane plantations, and he and his allies lobbied the Canadian and Italian governments to stiffen laws against adults who use child prostitutes.
- One Free the Children chapter is working on a project that will allow them to send 5,000 medical kits to children from Kosova.

- NIKE's director of labor relations stated, "I applaud his ability to get so much attention for this issue . . . That a 15- or 16-year-old boy can be a symbol for this fight is nothing short of amazing."

Craig appears to be very humble and doesn't encourage being singled out as a phenomenal youth. Rather he tries to share all the credit with his child helpers:

We were very honestly just a group of kids . . . People said we were idealistic, but we were realistic. With school children there was this field out there that was completely empty that was waiting to be built upon. It spread like wildfire.

Where does a twelve-year-old acquire the maturity and self-confidence to undertake such a monumental task . . . and get results? One can get some small insight from his answer to a challenging student in the audience who stood up and asked, "How come you don't get involved in fighting racism?"

After hesitating a few seconds, Craig responded that there are many issues out there, and that he has chosen to focus on child labor. He told Malcolm (the questioner) that if racism was his issue, then he should stand up against it. Then addressing the class, Craig said, "If racism is important to you, please stand up with Malcolm." Almost all the students stood up. "All you have to do," Craig continued, "is have the courage to ask people to stand with you."

As I first watched his story during the CBS report in 1995, I remember thinking how much this youngster's story reminded me of my own and my peers, and later those of my own children's innocent efforts in trying out the adult world . . . starting a newspaper, building a home-made airplane, getting everybody together to have a circus or put on a show, even starting a bank and lending pennies to friends. The list is as endless as a child's imagination. But Craig, for whatever reason, not only had his dream . . . he's living it.

PART 9

The Test Years of Our Lives

Based on his S.A.T. scores, Peter Hernberg, a homeschooler from Rochester, NY, won the state and regional Verbal Abilities Awards in the Johns Hopkins Center for Talented Youth Seventh Grade Talent Search. It's an annual competition for gifted students.

Joshua Casey (17) of Mount Airy, North Carolina, earned his Private Pilot's license. To obtain his license, Joshua had to complete 72 hours of ground school and pass written and oral exams. He also had to complete a check-ride accompanied by an FAA examiner. He was the youngest person the examiner had passed in the last 20 years.

Joshua has been home-schooled for the last 10 years. This year he started taking classes at the local community college, with plans to transfer to Liberty University next fall.

CHAPTER 43

How & Why to Take the PSAT/NMSQT

First, and most importantly, before we begin to discourse of PSATs and NMSQTs, we must bravely confront these two questions:

(1) What do all those letters stand for?
(2) How do you pronounce these unpronounceable names?

If you are patient, we will then get around to the question you really want answered:

(3) How and why should I take this test?

Tackling the PSAT first, we find it stands for "Preliminary Scholastic Assessment Test." It *used* to stand for "Preliminary Scholastic *Aptitude* Test," but when the SAT became an "assessment test," the PSAT followed suit. (You may think the term "assessment test" is a bit redundant. You're right.) Unlike Psmith, which is pronounced with a silent "p," the PSAT is pronounced "pee-sat." It was originally meant as a sort of practice test for the *real* SAT, to be taken usually in the fall of your junior year of high school. However, the SAT is now its own practice test, since you can keep taking it until you get a score you like. So the PSAT is mainly important because of the . . .

. . . . NMSQT, which stands for "National Merit Scholarship Qualifying Test." The National Merit Scholarship Corporation (NMSC) used to offer the NMSQT as a separate test. In 1971 they decided to cosponsor the PSAT and use it as their preliminary screening tool. For those interested, "NM-SQT" is pronounced "en-em-ess-cue-tee," or (rarely) "nimsquat."

The "Goodie Basket" of Tests

Ask not just how NMSQT is pronounced; ask what NMSQT can do for you. This is the goodie basket, dear friends. If you do well on the PSAT/NMSQT, you become a National Merit Semi-Finalist, which impresses college admissions people no end. If you then follow this up with suc-

---

1999 PSAT/ NMSQT Test Dates

Tuesday, October 12, 1999
Saturday, October 16, 1999

2000 preliminary PSAT/ NMSQT Test Dates

Tuesday, October 17, 2000
Saturday, October 21, 2000

For current test dates, call ETS at (609) 921-9000 or visit *www.collegeboard.com*.

Special PSAT Codes for Homeschoolers

For the PSAT/NMSQT *only* (not the SAT I or II), the College Board has now set aside special code numbers for homeschoolers. Each state has a different number, so if you homeschool in Connecticut you need to put down a different code than people who homeschool in Florida, etc. This change was instituted due to the scholarship program requirements. The National Merit people use the code, which normally is the code of the school the student attends, to determine what state you go to school in. Some homeschoolers were putting down the state code for faraway correspondence programs, complicating matters. The test proctor should have the homeschool code for your state, or call the College Board to inquire for it in advance.

Where Do the Questions Come From?

The PSAT is a sort of retirement home for worn-out SAT questions. Questions on the PSAT are taken directly from old SATs, and all the same techniques apply.
—*Princeton Review: Cracking the SAT*

cess on the essay and forms you are asked to fill out, you become a National Merit Finalist, entitled to a chunk of the scholarships granted by the over 600 corporations, foundations, colleges, universities, and other organizations that make up the Merit Program. These range from a one-time National Merit $2,000 scholarship to the real prize, a renewable, four-year Merit Scholarship of up to $8,000 per year. If you're black, you also have a shot at the separate National Achievement Scholarship Program for Outstanding Black Students, also administered by the NMSC. Just check the appropriate space on your test form, and your scores will be entered in this additional competition, where you compete with other top-scoring black students for another bunch of one-year and renewable scholarships.

The scholarship bonanza doesn't end there, either. If you check off the box that says you want to be entered into the scholarship competition, and answer the questions related to it, you have a chance to be among the approximately 14,000 test-takers who end up competing for about 6,500 additional grants financed by corporations, colleges, or the government. You have to individually fill out the paperwork associated with the grants you qualify for, which is a bother, and even if you get all the grants you qualify for, you may not reduce your college costs (see the chapter on Paying for College for an explanation), but winning a scholarship or two always looks nice on your record.

"Hey, Look Me Over!"

Another reason to take the PSAT/NSMQT is that it gives colleges a chance to look you over. For this to happen, you have to enter the scholarship competition, as otherwise only you and NMSC will ever see your scores. (If you went to school, your school would also see your scores.) Colleges that subscribe to NMSC's Student Selection Service get information about students that meet their preselected criteria, such as achieving a certain score level or expressing interest in that college. Do well on the test and you are almost guaranteed to receive many pounds of enticing college promotional material in the mail. You may not choose to attend any of the colleges prospecting you, of course, but it's always interesting to find out tidbits like that Vassar has a bowling alley and RPI is an exceptionally good hockey school. If there's a beach within 100 miles of the college, they'll be sure to tell you that, too.

Lots of Helpful Information

Finally, a really good reason for taking the PSAT/NMSQT is the volume of information you get back. Not only do you get your scores, a test booklet, and a score sheet with the answers you gave on the exam, you also get the correct answers to each question, explanations of how you did on each level of difficulty, recommendations for high school and college courses to take, a list of careers that correspond to the college major you mentioned on the test, and the percentile your scores fell into compared to others who took the test. You don't get nearly as much helpful material returned to you when you take the SAT.

What Is the Dreaded PSAT/NMSQT Like?

You, some form of identification, your test ticket, a test booklet, at least four sharpened #2 pencils, an accurate watch, an optional calculator (lose the calculator and practice your math facts, is my advice), and a score sheet replete with those little ovals you have to darken fully and completely, are in a room with a (probably bored) proctor or two and a bunch of students who actually go to the school. The decor is sweaty palms and t-shirts. The time of the year is October.

Your move:

GO EAST?

GO WEST?

GO SOUTH?

SIT DOWN?

If you, as a veteran of text-only computer games, picked SIT DOWN, you're still in the game. Here's what you have to face:

- Four sections, each 30 minutes long
- A 10-minute break between Section 2 and Section 3
- No food, no chit-chat, and it's wise not to annoy the proctors with unnecessary questions

The Verbal Aptitude part is sections 1 and 3, for a total of 60 questions in 60 minutes. You get 17 sentence completions, 13 analogies, and 30 reading comprehension questions. For Math Aptitude, section 2 is 25 multiple-choice basic math questions. Section 4 is 15 quantitative comparisons, and 10 gridded answers.

About those "gridded answers." These are a step in the right direction. Somebody finally noticed that multiple-choice questions are way too easy to guess, and don't ensure that the student actually knows how to work the problem. So for those questions, you work out the answer and then "grid it in" by filling out the right ovals. So, for example, if the answer is ⅗, you fill in the ovals for "3," "/," and "5" in the last three columns of the grid for that question.

Gridded answers are just one reason you ought to get a PSAT practice book—a *new* one, not one your Aunt Gertie used years ago. They are a recent development not found in old books, and are likely to throw you for a loop if you run across them for the first time with the clock ticking. It's also an excellent idea to take a timed practice test —such as you'll find in a PSAT test-prep book—at home at least once, to get a feel for the speed with which you'll need to fill out your answers.

Important for Homeschoolers!

You may think it's a good idea to take a PPSAT—that is, to have your children take the PSAT before their junior year, just for practice. Don't count on it. You have to sign up for the PSAT at a local high school, and ours said they had such limited space that they were only allowing juniors to take the test.

We found that we *had* to sign up at the school. You can sign up for the SAT by mail or even via the World Wide Web, but not the PSAT. So if you are in a town where the public school people aren't as friendly to homeschoolers as they should be, see if you can sign up at a local Christian or prep school instead.

Preparing for the PSAT

Generally, books and software designed to prepare you for the SAT 1 test also help you prepare for the PSAT. After all, the sections and questions are similar. The advantage of software is that you get instant feedback on your exercises and sample tests. The advantage of books is that you can carry them around with you and use them in any physical location.

About 600,000 sophomores and 1,200,000 juniors take the PSAT each year.

All the PSAT and SAT prep software I have seen is pretty good. The Princeton Review *Inside the SAT, PSAT, and ACT* software, published by The Learning Company, is my personal favorite.

Books on how to take the SAT 1 can be found in the next chapter. The few books I was able to find that specifically tell you how to take the PSAT are below.

Books to Help You With the PSAT

NEW!
Barron's How to Prepare for the PSAT/NMSQT, 10th Edition

Grade 11. $13.95.
Barron's Educational Series, Inc., 250 Wireless Blvd., Hauppauge, NY 11788. (800) 645-3476. Fax: (516) 434-3217. Web: www.barronseduc.com.

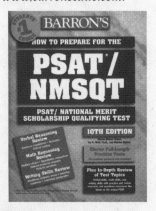

For a few bucks more, Barron's **How to Prepare for the PSAT/NMSQT** gives you about three times the pages (and bigger pages, too) with better information than the Peterson's book reviewed below. You get a diagnostic test, to help determine which areas you need to study in depth, and *ten* full practice tests, as well as over 100 oversized pages apiece on verbal reasoning, mathematical reasoning, and writing skills. Each includes an overview and test-taking strategies for that test section; in-depth explanation, exercises, and answers for each type of test question; and more. The "more" includes:

- a section on building your vocabulary
- a list of words frequently encountered on the PSAT
- a longer Basic Word List, with definitions
- a complete review of the math you need for the PSAT
- test-taking tactics
- how to fight off test anxiety
- whether or not to guess
- what the test is all about and why you should take it

There's a reason this book has survived and thrived through ten editions. It's the best I could find on the shelves. *Mary Pride*

NEW!
Peterson's PSAT/NMSQT Flash

Grade 11. $8.95.
Peterson's, PO Box 2123, Princeton, NJ 08543-2123. (800) 338-3282. Fax: (609) 452-0966. Email: custsvc@petersons.com. Web: www.petersons.com.

Smaller than other books about the PSAT, **Peterson's PSAT/NMSQT Flash** seems intended for students who want to prepare quickly, or at the last minute, to take this test.

Less than 100 pages are spent on test preparation. These are divided into one section each on verbal reasoning, writing skills, and mathematical reasoning—the topics on the test. Each topic section is further subdivided according to the types of questions in that section. For each question type, you are given strategies and practice exercises. The second half of the book is a practice test.

I found the reasoning behind some of the choices in the Analogies subsection to be specious and not in line with questions on the actual test. Typically, if you can substitute "A is a something-or-other or does-something-or-other to B" in the same way with the given analogy, on the test you're home free. You don't have to nitpick between several answers that fit the same structure. I doubt that, given APPLE : FRUIT, you should end up with COLLIE : DOG rather than CARROT : VEGETABLE, for instance, as in one of the book's examples (which also includes PERSIAN : CAT, an exact sister of the COLLIE : DOG "answer").

The book begins in typical fashion, explaining what the PSAT/NMSQT is and the advantages of taking it. This part also includes a suggested study schedule that breaks up the Questions, Strategies, and Exercises portion of the book into 13 session of between 15 and 45 minutes each, and the Practice Test into six sessions, most from 45 to 75 minutes in length. In all, the average student should figure on 10 hours to complete the work in this mostly competent, if unexciting, book. *Mary Pride*

CHAPTER 44

How to Take the SAT I

If you're a homeschooler, a good score on the SAT I or ACT is the most important factor in getting into the college of your choice.

Virtually all colleges require you to provide them with scores from either the SAT I or the ACT as part of their admissions process. For homeschoolers, taking one or both of these tests is close to a necessity. College officials need some way to validate your educational success. While a transcript of your high-school work is important, it's hard for a college admissions officer to believe that dear old Mom or Dad would ever give you a bad grade, whether you earned it or not. A good score on the SAT I or ACT, however, *combined* with a credible transcript; letters of recommendation; and evidence of work, organization leadership, or community service of some kind, works wonderfully well in gaining a homeschooler admission to the college of his or her choice.

While the SAT I has been the best-known test to date, the ACT, which many consider more rigorous, is gaining ground and acceptance. So don't assume you can just take the SAT and be done with it—make sure you check which test the colleges of your choice prefer.

Where Did the SAT I Come From?

Two organizations are behind the SAT I: the College Entrance Examination Board (CEEB) and the Educational Testing Service (ETS). The College Board was founded to represent and provide services for the high schools, colleges, and universities that are its members. ETS is the company that actually creates and administers the SAT I (and many other tests); it was commissioned to do so by the College Board.

What is the SAT I?

The SAT I is a three-hour test, with seven sections. One of the seven sections is a 30-minute math or verbal section used to "try out" new test questions and does not count toward your score. Of course, you will not know which section this is!

In all, here's how the test will look. Keep in mind that the various sections may not, in fact probably *will not,* be offered in the order. Even students taking the same test at the same time may have sections that vary in order.

SAT I Test Dates
October 9, 1999
November 6, 1999
December 4, 1999
January 22, 2000
April 8, 2000
May 6, 2000
June 3, 2000
October 14, 2000
November 4, 2000
December 2, 2000
January 27, 2001
March 31, 2001
May 5, 2001
June 2, 2001

Test dates in the 2000-2001 school year are preliminary dates only and may be subject to change.

Qualifying for Talent Searches via the SAT 1

Most Talent Search programs accept students with high SAT 1 scores. If your student is in grades 3–9 and you think he or she might qualify for a Talent Search program, this is a reason to have him or her take the SAT 1.

A Web page listing many regional and national Talent Search programs, including addresses, phone numbers, and web links, can be found at *www.eskimo. com/~user/ztsearch.html.*

Here are addresses and phone numbers for the two best-known programs:

Duke University Talent Identification Program
1121 W. Main St., Suite 100
Durham, NC 27701
(919) 683-1400

John Hopkins University Institute for the Academic Advancement of Youth
3400 N. Charles St.
Baltimore, MD 21218
For info on their 6th grade talent search: (410) 516-0337 x200
For info on their 7th grade talent search: (410) 516-0337 x100

Verbal Sections
- **Section 1.** You get 9 sentence completions, 6 analogies, and 15 reading comprehension questions based on two reading passages. 30 minutes, 30 questions in all.
- **Section 2.** This one includes 10 sentence completions, 13 analogies, and 12 reading comprehension questions based on one longer passage. 30 minutes/35 questions
- **Section 3.** You should definitely read Princeton Review's *Cracking the SAT* or the *Up Your Score* book before tackling this section, if only to understand how the twisted minds of the people who write these questions work. Two related reading passages, with questions requiring you to analyze them in relation to each other. 15 minutes, 13 questions.

Math Sections
- **Section 1.** Multiple-choice, covering basic math (arithmetic), algebra, and geometry. 30 minutes, 25 questions in all.
- **Section 2.** Quantitative comparisons (15), and 10 "student-produced response questions" that require you to provide our old friends, those "gridded answers" you ran across in the PSAT/NMSQT. 30 minutes, 25 questions in all.
- **Section 3.** Multiple choice, covering basic math (arithmetic), algebra, and geometry. 15 minutes, 10 questions in all.

Plus, of course the bogus section, which may be verbal *or* math.

Simple battery-operated calculators are permitted (check the registration rules carefully, since many fancy calculators are *not* permitted), but if you're smart, you won't use yours much, since many questions will be solved more easily by crossing out common factors, etc., than by lengthy arithmetic. If you do bring a calculator, use it to *check* your answers, not to *calculate* your answers. Students who use their calculators in this fashion tend to do slightly better than those who don't bring calculators at all.

Why Is It Called the "SAT I"?

The SAT has changed quite a bit in the past few years. As of March 1994, it was renamed the "Scholastic Assessment Test" and retitled the "SAT I" (as opposed to the tests previously called "Achievement Tests," which were renamed "SAT II tests"). The SAT I test itself was also redesigned, and its scoring system changed.

All this means that you should throw out any SAT test-preparation material your older brothers or sisters might have used. For the best results, get the latest editions of the test-preparation books of your choice. We've reviewed plenty of them for you.

Test Early, But Not Too Often

Unlike the PSAT, the SAT I is offered many times during the year. You can take it more than once, but this is only worth doing if you think you muffed it the first time and can do a lot better the second time. Even the Princeton Review test-prep people suggest you hold it down to two times: once in the spring of your junior year and again in the fall of your senior year. If you're smart, you'll take the time to work through a good test-preparation book or two *before* you take the SAT the first time.

One exception to the "don't test too often" rule: If you are a gifted student, you might want to take the SAT I *very* early, in the sixth or seventh grade, to see if you can qualify for one of the "Center for Talented Youth" or CTY programs offered by John Hopkins, Duke University, or one of the other Talent Search programs. If you score above a certain minimum, you qualify to attend their special programs, or (of more interest for home-schoolers) take their special distance-learning courses, designed to teach advanced material, such as calculus or physics, to young but very smart students. Needless to say, qualifying for such a program will look great on a college application, plus it might help you knock a few years off your pre-college education.

SAT=Student Attitude Transformation?

One last thing you need to know about the SAT is that the reading passages in recent years increasingly present a worldview that many home-schoolers find offensive. Passages that subtly defame religion or criticize the Christian church's history are not unknown. Negative adjectives never seem to be applied to women or minorities, but are freely applied to men and people of European descent. Other signs of political correctness also appear.

This is all especially bothersome because there are billions of reading passages available that don't comment on anyone's beliefs, mock the traditional family, elevate women *at the expense of* men, and so forth. Writers create pieces about literally millions of topics that don't slice to the heart of anyone's personal beliefs. How to raise roses, the unique quality of the light in Paris (which is why painters have always flocked there), and the motivations of the main characters in Jane Austen's *Pride and Prejudice,* are just three noncontroversial, but college-level, topics.

The SAT designers could choose to use such passages. So why don't they?

One answer could be that colleges increasingly require students to profess political correctness, and thus such reading passages are a good predictor of what you'll face in college. On its surface this sounds plausible, but not all colleges are bastions of P.C. What about Bible colleges? Engineering schools? Conservative colleges such as Grove City and Hillsdale? Shouldn't the SAT be a test of what students might face in *any* college?

A second answer could be that the clueless test designers actually believe no Americans ever listen to Rush Limbaugh. They don't see anything wrong with questions that all but require the student to profess allegiance to the New World Order, because they honestly believe everyone thinks this way already. This is not as strange as it sounds, since the people who construct these questions are not usually grave savants aware of their responsibility. As the authors of *Cracking the SAT* reveal, "Virtually all [SAT] questions are written by ordinary [Educational Testing Service] company employees, or by college students and others who are hired part-time from outside ETS. Sometimes the questions are even written by teenagers. Frances Brodsky, the daughter of an ETS vice president, spent the summer after she graduated from high school writing questions for ETS tests."

Finally, here's one for you conspiracy fans. Did you ever realize what a marvelous brainwashing environment test-taking is? Especially an important standardized test like the SAT I, on which your *whole future* might depend? Consider the requirements for brainwashing: (1) Sleep and food deprivation. (2) Intense emotion. (3) The desire to avoid pain or become "part of the group." (4) An authoritative point of view presented as if it

SAT I Scores Are Pumped Up

SAT scores dropped from a total average of 937 (out of 1600) in 1972 to 902 in 1994.

In 1995, the SAT was "recentered" to give the impression that student scores aren't really that much worse than they used to be. Harder sections of the math and verbal tests were removed, and students were automatically given the points they would have made had they taken these parts and done them correctly. The test time was also increased, so students would have more time to do this easier test. The result: national average scores of 1013, of which 100 points are "freebies" compared to the earlier tests.

were the only reasonable way to think. Now contrast this to SAT test conditions: (1) Most students sleep poorly before the test, and food is forbidden during the test. (2) Most students feel fear bordering on terror as they start the test. (3) Most student intensely desire to join the college crowd, and fear the pain of rejection. (4) The test then presents a worldview to the students under these intense conditions, with *no time* to think about the *ideas* presented in the innocuous form of "reading passages." "Your whole future depends on learning to think like this," the test seems to say.

This may be one reason why more and more students and colleges are switching to the ACT, which doesn't come across so much as a test of political correctness. But you don't always have the choice of which test to take. If you do have to take the SAT I, try *very* hard to remember that answers to the test questions *do not necessarily agree* with what your beliefs say the "right" answer should be. The "right" answer *on the test* is the answer that agrees with the reading passage. So if the test question is something like this . . .

> **14. The main theme of this passage is:**
> A. The church has always persecuted women.
> B. The church could have done more for women than it historically has.
> C. Women need to found a new church of their own.
> D. The church used to teach that the Bible requires complementary roles for men and women.

. . . . don't consult your beliefs; consult the passage, and mark the oval next to the answer that best describes what the author said, no matter how personally insulting you may find it.

The best way to brace yourself for these questions is to practice with similar ones *beforehand*. Either a book of "real SATs" from ETS, or one of the many SAT I test-prep books, is a very wise investment. See the resources below.

Materials to Help You Take the SAT

What makes the **SAT SuperCourse** super? "More practice questions than any other SAT guide." "Lesson-by-lesson instruction from a top test coach." As far as the latter claim goes, author Thomas H. Martinson has developed not one, but *two* courses for expensive SAT-prep schools. His claim is that this book will give you the same benefits as one of those $300–$600 courses.

So what have we here? Starting from the back and working forward, five practice tests. That's nice, because it gives you a chance to find and fix your test-taking mistakes and get very comfortable with the test format. The heart of the book, the "Coaching Program," is almost 430 pages long and requires some serious work on your part. For example, you will be asked to write your own analogies that correspond to example analogies. Here you are either treated to or subjected to "Holmesian thinking," depending on how you feel about using Holmes and Watson to introduce each test-taking strategy. Finally, the first chapters in the book are the usual "what is the SAT and how does it really work?" information.

This book would be a lot more useful if it were better designed. The type is small, compared to its competitors, and the further mistake has been made of using *very* dark grey boxes behind important information, rendering the information hard to read. The Holmes-and-Watson segments fail to amuse. In all, I'd take Gruber's over this book, if you want a complete test-preparation course. *Mary Pride*

NEW!
ARCO SAT SuperCourse, Third Edition
Grades 9–12. Book, $18.95. Book with computer disk, $29.95.
Macmillan Publishing, 135 S. Mount Zion Rd., Lebanon, IN 46052.
(800) 428-5331. Fax: (800) 882-8583.
Web: www.mcp.com.

An amazing number of oversized pages for the price—779 of them, plus 24 pages of yellow cardboard vocabulary flashcards—**Barron's How to Prepare for SAT I** advertises on its cover that this "completely new edition" will explain how to raise your score by answering fewer questions and other test-taking tactics. A new wrinkle is that this huge tome also includes a diagnostic exam, so you can narrow down your study focus to just those areas that actually need work, and that it includes not one, not two, but *seven* model tests.

As promised, the book starts by introducing you to the test itself, with the next part on "Pinpointing Your Trouble Spots." Part III, on "Tactics, Strategies, Practice," first attacks the Verbal test, then the Math. For the Verbal test, it follows a standard sequence of one chapter each on analogies, sentence completion, and reading comprehension. The "Build Your Vocabulary" chapter includes three lists: the SAT I High-Frequency Word List (each word on this list has appeared from 5 to 20 times in questions or answers in SATs given in the '80s and '90s), the 3,500 Basic Word List, and a list of Basic Word Parts. The Math section covers how to answer multiple-choice questions, how to deal with quantitative comparisons, and ends with a math review. Part 4, which makes up the bulk of this bulky book, is the promised seven model tests. Finally, Part 5 adds a bonus, with information about how to get into college and how to write a successful application essay. (Personally, I found the "successful" examples they gave rather scary—it appears that shoving your minority background or sad life experiences into other people's faces is a sure-fire winner.)

With over 5,000,000 copies sold, you can't dismiss this book lightly. But is it a better choice than the various Kaplan, ARCO, and Princeton Review offerings? The others are certainly more approachable and easier to use. Barron's seems to expect a lot from you, even including a list of hundreds of books from which "reading comprehension" suggestions have been taken in the past and suggesting you read them *all*. Clearly, this would not be a good choice for last-minute test-preppers. What this book offers in authoritativeness, it taketh away by its intimidating tone. Still, enough public-school students seem to be attracted by it to make this the #1 SAT-prep bestseller—at least according to the cover. *Mary Pride*

Dana Mosely, the "Silver Fox" of math instructors, is giving you One Last Chance to improve your math skills. This five-video **Chalk Dust SAT Math Review Videos** series is designed to prepare you for the SAT math test, but also can be used to review high-school algebra and geometry in less trying circumstances.

As you might expect from a math teacher, the emphasis here is more on actually *learning* the math than on "beating" the test.

Basically, you get every math topic on the SAT, covered in a logical sequence. You start with whole numbers and integers, and make it as far as fractions on the first video. The second one continues with decimals, percent, ratio and proportion, averages, distance/rate/time calculations, and consumer problems. The third tape reviews algebra, while the fourth covers geometry. The last tape covers "other topics," from sequences to how to interpret graphs and charts, to how to do the "grid-it-yourself" problems now included on the SAT. If you find that SAT-prep books aren't helping you enough with the math, and think a more visual approach with added explanations would help, these tapes might be worth the money. *Mary Pride*

Educators Publishing Service Analogies series

Grades 9–12. Analogies 1, 2 and 3, $6.25 each plus $4 shipping. *Educators Publishing Service, Inc., 31 Smith Pl., Cambridge, MA 02138. (800) 225-5750. Fax: (617) 547-0412. Email: epsbooks@epsbooks.com. Web: www.epsbooks.com.*

NEW!
Gruber's Complete Preparation for the New SAT, 1999

Grades 9–12. $16.95 plus $2.75 shipping. *HarperCollins Publishers, Inc., 1000 Keystone Industrial Park, Scranton, PA 18512. (800) 331-3761. Fax: (800) 822-4090. Web: www.harpercollins.com.*

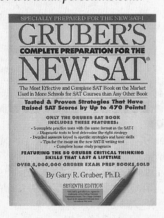

Can you remember back to your pre-college days (for some of us it's *way* back) to the SAT? I remember sweating through that long Saturday in one of the classrooms in my high school. The problems which gave me the most grief were verbal analogies:

> **6. armada : ships :**
>   a. *herd : cattle*
>   b. *magazine : pages*
>   c. *wall : bricks*
>   d. *college : undergraduate*
>   e. *sweater : fabrics*

Here is a way to get a little of the grief out of the way before the test. **Analogies 2** and **Analogies 3** provide strategies and exercises for the potential SAT-taker. Analogies 2 demonstrates techniques such as the bridge sentence, checking for multiple meanings, and handling two-step analogies. Analogies 3 is more of the same with harder problems. Each book contains extensive practice sets with vocabulary lists and answers. (*Analogies 1,* for junior high school, is not really SAT prep, but preliminary practice for this age level in solving analogy problems and adding vocabulary words.)

Anyone who is unfamiliar with the SAT would do well to master these books first. *Bill Pride*

"Five complete practice tests. Diagnostic tests. Detailed answers keyed to specific strategies in basic skills. Tips for the essay on the new SAT II Writing Test. And 50 Gruber critical-thinking skills that last a lifetime!" 941 oversized pages in all, and an impressive 2⅜ inches thick. Is this the baby seat you've been waiting for, or what?

Gruber's Complete Preparation for the New SAT, by test expert Dr. Gary Gruber, includes the best of the "cracking" style books, along with actual instruction in the tested skills. You won't get deep insights into the ids and superegos of the test developers, but you *will* get legitimate help in eliminating the confusion deliberately built into some questions.

If you want "complete," Gruber's has *complete*. When Dr. Gruber tells you about the new grids used in the SAT Math test, he also includes several pages of practice grids for you to fill in, just to get comfortable with them. Instead of *one* diagnostic pre-test, you get *two*: one SAT pre-test, and one test of your mastery of test-taking strategies. Again, instead of *one* math refresher, Gruber's offers *two*—a "Mini-Math Refresher," just 10 pages of rules, concepts, and illustrated examples to memorize, and a "Complete New SAT Math Refresher" broken down into seven sections, each with its own practice test followed by solutions and explanations.

When it comes to vocabulary-building, Gruber's is no slouch. You get instructions in how to extend your vocabulary through prefixes, roots, and suffixes, a list of SAT words appearing more than once on actual SAT exams, the "291 Most Important SAT Words and Their Opposites," the "Gruber SAT 3,400-word list," *and* 100 short vocabulary tests with answers. The idea here is to take each of the tests (not all on the same day!) and then note the words you *missed*. Those get slated for extra study.

The layout is big, bold, and inviting, as are the section headings. Who could resist reading "The 22 Questions that Can Determine Top College Eligibility" (a 19-minute test to determine whether you already have a shot at getting into the top schools)? Or "The 101 Most Important Basic Skills Math Questions You Need to Know How to Solve" (a test to determine your basic math *skills*—as opposed to *strategies*—weaknesses)?

If that's not enough tests for you, the book winds up with an additional four complete practice tests. Dr. Gruber believes that you learn by doing, and by taking *several* practice tests you'll uncover any remaining "holes" in your skills and strategies.

I wouldn't have believed that a book this big could be less intimidating than some of its smaller competitors, but I was wrong. Gruber has the goods. *Mary Pride*

Dr. Douglas J. Paul, Ph.D., a writer of standardized tests, discovered that when students were taught the same way he taught aspiring test-makers, they did significantly better on the tests. Based on his experiences, he developed the strategies used here and in his *Dr. Paul Zaps the ACT* test-prep course.

His **Inside the SAT** course has (and meets) all these objectives:

- To demystify the SAT. He knows all the questions students have, or should have, and provides the best answers I've seen to these questions.
- To reduce test anxiety. The materials' fatherly tone and simple format make you believe, "I can do this!"
- To teach both general and specific strategies for taking multiple-choice tests. At this, Dr. Paul's courses excel. You'll learn how to tackle the PSAT and SAT . . . *and* any other standardized tests you may encounter.

The set includes:

- *Inside the SAT Study Guide.* Here you'll find 178 oversized pages of excellent advice, explanations, strategies, exercises, and answers to the exercises. Appendices include "authentic practice activities," namely sample questions in test format. A vocabulary-building section includes SAT Roots, Prefixes, and Suffixes in charts that show word meaning and give examples of words with those parts (much more useful than bare lists or dictionary-style entries).
- The *Answer Book* has explanations and answers for the practice questions and the questions on all three practice tests.
- Three practice tests. These are not printed in the back of the book. Rather, they are separate test booklets, similar to the ones you'll be using on the real test. Exception: the answer forms are printed in the back of the practice test books, instead of as separate sheets.

This course is perfect for homeschool use. It neither loads you down with extra work nor oversimplifies, and the tone is just right for students who are used to studying on their own. *Mary Pride*

Crisp, efficient, and a great review of skills you supposedly learned in high school, these **Kaplan Books** are a fine investment whether or not you plan to take the SAT I.

Each workbook begins with explanations of how the sections of the SAT it covers are handled in real-life testing. From there, you proceed to a great tutorial section designed to quickly bring you up to speed both on the skills tested and on how to best approach the test. Bill says, "You

could actually learn all your basic math, from whole numbers through advanced algebra and geometry, just going through the Math Workbook!" Finally, you get to try two Practice Tests in the back of each book, which you take by filling out an authentic-looking score sheet, complete with little ovals to fill in. In addition, the Verbal Workbook includes the Kaplan Word List, vocabulary words most likely to appear on the SAT, along with brief definitions and synonyms, plus the Kaplan Root List, definitions of word roots plus several examples for each root of words in which it appears. *Mary Pride*

NEW!
Math Shortcuts to Ace the SAT

Grades 9–12. $12.95 plus shipping.
BookMasters, Inc., Order Dept., P.O. Box 388, 1444 Rt. 42, Ashland, OH 44805. (800) 247-6553.
Fax: (419) 281-6883.
Outside USA call: (419) 281-1802.
Email: order@bookmaster.com.
Web: www.apluspublishing.com.

Would shortcuts for the math section on the SAT benefit your child? Of course they will! Well, **Math Shortcuts to Ace the SAT** is a large, glossy paperback book filled with 34 specific shortcuts that will take some of the stress out of college entrance exams. The 101-page book is filled with diagrams, step-by-step examples, a summary of all the geometry formulas and concepts and explanations of applied math fundamentals. There are answers to all the exercises and easy to understand explanations. The glossary and index are also useful tools for test preparation.

Included in the book are sections on:

- Divisibility
- Comparing Fractions
- Averages
- Quantitative Comparisons
- Algebra
- Geometry
- Word Problems

As a supplement to other SAT test preparation books, this is good for students who need help speeding up on the math section. *Maryann Turner*

NEW!
Peterson's SAT Success, Fifth Edition

Grades 9–12. Book with CD-ROM, $14.95 plus shipping.
Peterson's, PO Box 2123, Princeton, NJ 08543-2123. (800) 338-3282.
Fax: (609) 452-0966.
Email: custsvc@petersons.com.
Web: www.petersons.com.

"No tricks or gimmicks, just the facts for SAT success." That's how **Peterson's SAT Success** bills itself. After an in-depth introduction to the SAT and PSAT, SAT Success starts you off with a diagnostic SAT test—an actual complete SAT. Your grade on this tells you what to concentrate on in the rest of the book.

The authors don't spend much time telling you how to psych out the test. Instead, they spend most of the book's 521 oversized pages drilling you on actual English vocabulary, reading comprehension skills, and math problem-solving skills. Their philosophy seems to be, "If you know the material, you can answer the questions."

SAT Success claims a few unique features. For example, the cover states "RED ALERT sections highlight must-know information." You get the impression the book is periodically interrupted with short, essential information. Actually, there are four "Red Alert" sections, and they just include the same sort of material found in many other books. The first Red Alert section highlights test-taking strategies and includes three study plans: a nine-week plan, an 18-week plan, and a "Panic Plan." The second and third Red Alerts include strategies for the verbal and math tests, respectively. The last Red Alert section is actually a mini-SAT made up of real questions from actual tests.

This book has been significantly updated since its last edition. For one thing, you now get practice exercises after each vocabulary list, to help you cement what you've learned about prefixes, roots, and suffixes, and the words you have learned via 18 small-print word lists full of sample sentences containing the words. The book ends with two practice SATs (as opposed to only one in the last edition), followed by one page each of sample filled-in grids and blank grids for you to fill in. Finally, you now have the option of purchasing the book with a Windows-compatible disk containing Peterson's *SAT TestPrep* software. This includes a short diagnostic test, study plan, and full-length practice test, for immediate feedback on how you did.

In all, substantial improvements have been made in this edition. I still think it's unlikely that most students will wend their way throughout the lengthy (and not particularly friendly) math section. In this case, less may be more—less practice problems could still cover the material, while making the book more approachable. *Mary Pride*

If you start every course by trying to "psych out" the teacher—even if Mom is the teacher— you'll surely love **Cracking the SAT and PSAT**. Unlike other test-prep books, this large (over 600 oversized pages) book does *not* mainly concentrate on teaching and reviewing the actual skills tested. Instead, it focuses on "psyching out" the test—strategies for improving your score by mastering test-taking, and understanding the psychology of the people who created this test. You do get a diagnostic test (with red-outlined pages), and some vocabulary training, but most of the books' effort is directed to help-

ing you simplify problems and learning to eliminate obvious wrong answers in all the types of test questions. For example, they teach you how to "eyeball" angles, how to guesstimate on drawings *not* drawn to scale, how to fake it if you've forgotten the formulas for area and circumference of a circle, etc. Of course, they can't do *too* much without teaching you *some* facts—such as the difference between mean, median, and mode—but you'll have to decide for yourself if you're forgetful enough, or desirous enough of skipping the actual learning the test covers, to bother with a book that just teaches you how to fake out the test. To help you apply your new-found strategies, the book includes two full-length tests, with four more on the CD-ROM. *Mary Pride*

What do you expect when you read the title of this book, **SAT & College Preparation Course for the Christian Student**? I expect something that will prepare my Christian student for taking the SAT, and prepare him to cope with college.

First, the SAT preparation. The back of the book says:

> *The SAT & College Preparation Course for the Christian Student is not a quick fix! The best preparation occurs over a length of time, not just a few weeks. The course is designed to help the student prepare for the SAT without intruding too much into his busy life by doing a few lessons per week rather than a massive "cram" weeks before the exam.*

This is not a bad philosophy for general education, but SAT preparation should be *SAT* preparation.

A normal SAT preparation book takes you through 10–40 hours of practice directed specifically toward the SAT. During those 10–40 hours, you will take sample SAT tests. You will intensively study the vocabulary most

NEW!
Princeton Review: Cracking the SAT and PSAT, 2000 edition
Grades 9–12. Book only, $18. Book/CD-ROM edition, $29.95 (with Mac/Win disc). Shipping extra. *Princeton Review, Random House, 400 Hahan Rd., Westminster, MD 21157. (800) 733-3000. They prefer you to order from bookstores. Web: www.randomhouse.com.*

You get 50 percent off the cost of taking an online SAT with the purchase of this book. You will have to register at *www.review.com/cracking*. Of course, the online test is a *practice* test; the "real" SAT can't be taken online.

NEW!
The SAT & College Preparation Guide for the Christian Student
Grade 9 (since the book expects you to spend three years at it). $39.99 plus shipping. *Great Expectations Book Co., PO Box 2067, Eugene, OR 97402. (541) 343-2647. Fax: (541) 343-0568.*

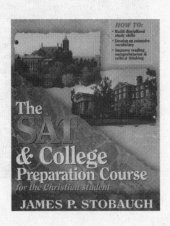

commonly used on the SAT and at the same time learn how to attack words to get their meaning—analyzing prefixes and suffixes and noting the meaning of the root to help you figure out the meaning of a word. You will exhaustively study the strategies for handling analogies. You will learn how to answer comprehension questions, not from your supposed vast knowledge, which may lead you to a wrong answer, but only from the information in the reading passage. You will get a methodical review of the math principles the SAT will be testing. You will learn how to grid in your answers on the freeform answer math questions. Etc. In short, most SAT preparation books' goal is to familiarize you with the test you will be handed in the room on the Saturday you take the SAT test.

This book does none of this. The few questions given in the SAT preparation section of each lesson are not even presented in the format of SAT questions. For example,

> *Define the italicized words in context:*
> *A. While the "Tamara" was avoiding* myriad *submerged reefs and eddies . . .*
> *B. . . . the girls squirmed and greeted us* coquettishly *yet shyly . . .*
> *(from* Kon Tiki *by Thor Heyerdahl)*

This is the *entire* exercise. Such a "vocabulary exercise" is unsystematic, completely lacking in instruction, and will not specifically prepare you for the SAT.

On its cover this book claims it will help you "develop an extensive vocabulary." The main method actually used is to tell you to read lots of classic books (a reading list is provided) and fill out cards on new vocabulary words. No systematic instruction is given in roots, prefixes, or suffixes. No clever mnemonic exercises are employed. Telling you to define words is *not* the same as actual vocabulary instruction.

Like all the exercises, the math questions are not presented methodically and there is little to no instruction. The last very lesson asks:

> *Which of these numbers is divisible by 2? By 5? By 10? By 3?*
> *A. 6   B. 32   C. 3020   D. 99*

Divisibility is a elementary-school concept. Why is it last? Again, this question is presented in math textbook form, not in the form of a SAT math question.

The morality of guessing should be a conscience issue seriously discussed in a Christian SAT preparation guide. Many Christian young people will think that guessing on a test, like gambling, is morally wrong. This book glosses over guessing, first with the erroneous statement in a tip that one should not guess unless he can eliminate one or more answer, and second in his test-taking strategies, by leaving the decision on whether or not to guess up to the student.

The correct pragmatic advice is go ahead and guess, because statistically even random guessing will have zero effect on your score, and if you can eliminate one or more of the answers you will come out ahead by guessing among the ones that are left. Morally? The SAT is trying to test your knowledge and reasoning ability. The only way to measure your knowledge on a question where you are not certain of the correct answer is to measure your knowledge of what is not the correct answer. The only measure of that comes by you eliminating wrong answers and guessing between the two or three that remain. Educated guessing is one of the skills measured by the SAT test. On the other hand, clairvoyance is not and is something

Christians ought not to believe in. As long as you keep the "educated" in the guessing, I believe it is morally right to guess on the SAT. Again, you do not find this discussion in this book.

The mechanics of the SAT are not discussed in any kind of detail. The most important example of this is gridding in answers on the freeform math questions. It would be a shame for a student to get a correct answer on one of these questions, then lose the point for the question because he gridded the answer wrong ($1\frac{1}{2}$ gridded as $1\frac{1}{2}$ will be interpreted as $\frac{11}{2}$). Also, it is a waste of valuable test-taking time for a student to have to learn how to grid answers while taking the test.

Instead of 10–40 hours of SAT preparation time over a period of two to four weeks, *The SAT & College Preparation Course for the Christian Student* is meant to take two to three years. You are supposed to read a book a week, in addition to the readings and devotionals in the lessons, and not just read the book, but carefully note the vocabulary words you do not know meanings for, look them up in the dictionary, write them on index cards, and quiz yourself on them. This is time-consuming, to say the least. Many literature courses have a student read less than this "SAT preparation" course, and I shudder to think of the hours and hours required to write out all the vocabulary words and definitions, which an actual literature guide would provide.

Conclusion: This book is not "SAT preparation" except in the same way that high school or elementary school is "SAT preparation," or that any learning activity is "SAT preparation."

So, what *is* this book really? Almost half of the space for each daily lesson is spent on a Scripture reading assignment and "devotional." A large number of these turn out to be stories about the author, how the author felt about something, and the author's family members. Followed by questions such as "Are there areas in your life that are too close to the edge?" and occasional "Critical Thinking: Worldview" assignments such as "Take a number of publications and discern their worldview or slants on these topics: gun control, capital punishment, and/or abortion," it looks like this book is struggling to be a worldview course. However, it is a poorly designed one, as should be clear from the assignment I just quoted. Whereas an excellent course such as *KONOS History of the World* will provide you with ample data and then ask you to do the assignment, as well as offering suggestions and feedback on potential answers, this one assignment alone could take you hours in the library *before* you even begin writing anything, and no guidance is given to either parent or student as to how to do research, how to discern worldviews, etc.

An excellent worldview/college preparation course will also present alternative worldviews and analyze them in depth. Such is not the case here. The author shares his beliefs and opinions briefly and dogmatically, as if the student *must* agree with him.

Overall, it's surprising how little content or instruction is in this book that costs almost $40.

Judging from what I've heard about this book's sales, there is a large felt need for a SAT and college prep course for Christians. Judging from what I've seen, this book isn't the answer. *Bill Pride*

Unique among SAT-prep books, **Up Your Score** was written by high-scoring students. The first edition was put together by three boys who each scored over 1500. However, as the boys became men, it was felt a fresher, younger writer was needed—namely a graduate of my own high school, Newton North in Newton, Massachusetts, who had scored a perfect 1600. Time wrought its damage on this lad, too, so the very latest version has

Here is a sample page.
This is the entire lesson.

NEW!
Up Your Score, 1999–2000 edition

High school. $8.95 plus $3 shipping. *Workman Publishing Company, Inc., 708 Broadway, New York, NY 10003-9555.* (800) 722-7202. *Web: www.workman.com.*

been *re*-edited by two even newer SAT slayers, this time a girl and boy who each (surprise) got a perfect score.

Why all the emphasis on "new blood"? Because this book is self-consciously brash and irreverent, and therefore the editors want it to stay "in tune" with the latest teen fads and lingo. This may give you a clue as to its tone and style. From comments about "the almighty vocabulary god" to memory tips that require you to connect the word "crass" to an unmentionable rhyming body part, from the sexually androgynous ("His diaphanous dinner dress caused much comment") to cuss words, it's "MTV goes to the SAT."

As is true of the MTV generation, moral ambiguities also abound. Thus, while the original authors advise you to strongly eschew cheating on the test—in fact, to give *wrong* answers to anyone who tries to cheat off you— they hedge on the question of whether it's OK to go back to a previous section if you finish another one early (something which the test makers clearly forbid in VERY LARGE TYPE). They even include suggestions for how to smuggle food into the test (completely against the rules).

I wish—how can I put this?—that the writers would grow up and stop trying to shock us, because aside from these desperate attempts at coolness and wit, the instructional part of the book is more helpful, and definitely more readable, than you'll find in the books by adults.

For the Verbal section, they whiz through the question types, sentence completions, analogies, and those pesky "reading passages" in many less words than the big fat test books, and with more helpful insights. For example, the big fat test books would be afraid to tell you, as this book does, "The ETS tries to be politically correct. So if you see a sentence that mentions women or minorities, it is probably saying something good about them." Armed with this advice, you hardly have to read the obligatory "minority" reading passage that ETS includes in every test. The section on SAT words includes sentences designed to help you memorize the most helpful words (some of which are funny, and some of which are crass). The math tips are great. So are the tips for the SAT II writing test. Best of all, they anticipate how you might muff each question, and head off your mistakes at the pass.

Excellent study tips abound—and kids might actually listen to other *kids* who tell them "nobody studies better with music." Finally, I do have to give them some points for poking fun at a certain other publisher's trademarked (and completely silly) stress-reduction plan.

With more "cracking" tips than a cracking book, and more streamlined cut-to-the-chase remedial instruction than a learn-it-all-for-the-test book, this would be my first choice for a SAT prep book if they could just manage to keep in the levity while leaving out the lewdness. *Mary Pride*

Vis-Ed SAT Prep Set

Grades 9–12. $10.95. All other vocabulary sets also $10.95 each. Shipping extra.
Visual Education, 581 W. Leffel Lane, Springfield, OH 45501.
Orders: (800) 243-7070.
Inquiries: (937) 325-5503.
Fax: (937) 324-5697.
Web: *www.vis-ed.com.*

From Vis-Ed, "The Study Card People Since 1950," now comes a set of their special self-study flash cards called the **SAT Prep Set**, or, more formally, *Preparatory Study Cards for SAT-Verbal.* Inside the box you'll find 340 words-in-context question cards, 290 sentence-completion question cards, and 260 analogy question cards. *Preparatory Study Cards for SAT-Math* is also available.

Each pocket-sized card has a typical SAT-style question on the front, with the correct answer on the back.

The included study guide gives tips on how to analyze each problem type and how the SAT-Verbal test works.

If this isn't enough, you can improve your vocabulary even more with the Vis-Ed *English Vocabulary 1* and *2* sets, *Scientific & Technical Vocabulary* set, *Medical Terminology* set, and *Legal Terminology* set. *Mary Pride*

CHAPTER 45

How to Take the ACT

The A-C-T is put out by the American College Testing Program, which may give you a hint about what the letter in its name stand for. As the only major competitor to the SAT I, it's a test you should consider. The SAT I is better known, of course, Every year about 1.3 millions students take the ACT, while about 6 million take the SAT I. As a rule, colleges in the east and west prefer you to take the SAT I, while many colleges in the midwest and south prefer you to take the ACT.

What is the ACT?

Like the SAT I, the ACT is a three-hour test. Unlike the SAT I, it has four sections:

- **English.** This tests usage, mechanics, and "rhetoric" (basically, good writing v. poor writing). It's all multiple-choice; no essays. Questions cover punctuation (10 questions), grammar (12 questions), sentence structure (18 questions), how to revise or strengthen a passage ((11 questions), word changes that improve style (12 questions), and arranging paragraphs to improve the organization (12 questions). 45 minutes, 75 questions in all.
- **Math.** This includes 24 arithmetic and elementary algebra problems, 18 intermediate algebra and coordinate geometry problems, 14 geometry problems, and 4 trigonometry problems. 60 minutes, 60 questions in all.
- **Reading.** You'll have to answer 10 questions each about four reading passages, one each from the fields of natural science, social studies, humanities, and literature. Princeton Review's *Cracking the ACT* book is particularly helpful with this section, and indeed with any standardized test's reading comprehension (to many of us, "reading with incomprehensible questions following") section. 35 minutes, 40 questions in all.
- **Science.** This is a test of scientific reasoning, not of science facts. You get seven reading passages. These include readings in biology, chemistry, physics, geology, meteorology, astronomy, and/or other physical sciences. Passages fall within the

ACT Test Dates
September 25, 1999
October 23, 1999
December 11, 1999
February 12, 2000
April 1, 2000
June 10, 2000
September 23, 2000
October 28, 2000
December 9, 2000
February 10, 2001
April 7, 2001
June 9, 2001

ACT Registration Information

You must request and fill out the ACT registration folder, and mail it in with your fee payment by the registration deadline. No walk-in or phone-in registrations are allowed.

Pick a test date in the second semester of your junior year, and allow 4 to 7 weeks before the college application deadline for your scores to be mailed to the colleges of your choice.

Here are some phone numbers for additional assistance.

- **ACT Registration Information** (319) 337-1270
- **ACT ID Requirements** (319) 337-1510
- **Special Accommodations** for students with "physical, mental, sensory, or diagnosed learning disabilities who are able to test under standard conditions" (319) 337-1510
- **Testing outside the 50 United States** (319) 337-1448
- **Universal Testing** for students with "physical, mental, sensory, or diagnosed learning disabilities who cannot test under standard conditions" (319) 337-1448
- **TDD** If you have a hearing impairment and have a TDD to call from (319) 337-1524
- **On the web** Visit *www.act.org/aap/*

NEW!
Arco ACT 1999

Grades 11–12. Book only, $13.95. Book with CD-ROM, $29.95. Shipping extra. *Macmillan Publishing, 135 South Mt. Zion Rd., Lebanon, IN 46052. (800) 428-5331. Fax: (800) 835-3202. Web: www.mcp.com.*

categories of "visuals" (testing your ability to understand charts, graphs, tables, and so on), "experimental reasoning" (read the experiment! interpret the results!), and "alternative viewpoints" (questions ask you about how the writers' views conflict, and the evidence that does or might resolve the conflict). 35 minutes, 40 questions in all.

What's Different About ACT Scores?

Also unlike the SAT I, ACT scores range from 1 to 36. What's more, you actually get 12 scores (as opposed to the SAT I, which provides you with only two, a math score and a verbal score). As well as your "Composite Score" of 1 to 36, which measures your performance on the test as a whole, you get a "subject score" from 1 to 36 for each of the four subjects (English, math, reading, and science), and seven "subscores" from 1 to 18 as follows:

- Usage/Mechanics
- Rhetorical Skills
- Pre-Algebra/Elementary Algebra
- Algebra/Coordinate Geometry
- Plane Geometry/Trigonometry
- Reading in Social Sciences & Sciences
- Reading in Arts & Literature

As you may have noticed, there are no science subscores.

Colleges use these subject scores and (in rare cases) subscores for placement and scholarships (occasionally) and to help you pick a major (routinely). This is a lot more help than the SAT I provides.

What About Politically Correct Questions?

You'll find evolutionary passages on many ACT tests. However, the ACT is less likely than the SAT I to include material that insults students' religious and social beliefs, or to carry the flag for anti-male-style feminism. This may be one reason why southern and midwestern colleges are likelier to prefer it.

How Should I Prepare for the ACT?

Try the resources below!

Just how serious are you about getting that really great score? Willing to work through over 500 pages of mind-numbing practice problems and sample tests?

ACT American College Testing Program is not for the faint of heart. Give authors Joan and Norman Levy credit for including, not one, but four sample tests (all with explained answers, by the way).

There's a 10-page section on commonly confused vocabulary words and 15 more pages devoted to test taking strategies. Princeton Review books are much better at gearing strategies to a specific test. This book doesn't get much past "Eat a good breakfast and bring sharp pencils." Beyond that, having to wade through eye-straining newsprint pages, dotted with uneven print quality is just torture.

My advice? Get the Princeton Review book first. If you still need some practice, see how you do on Arco's sample tests. Otherwise Arco is too arduous. *Renee Mathis*

It's not pretty. But does it do the job? Barron's 566-page **How to Prepare for the ACT** starts with "Preparing for the ACT," which inevitably led to a subheading entitled "After the ACT." Moving quickly along, we find a diagnostic examination with answer keys, explanations, and analysis charts. As you're aware, this is supposed to help you avoid wasting time on studying items you already know, so you can intensify your efforts on areas that need it.

"Review and Practice for the ACT" takes up the next 334 pages, with one chapter for each of the four tests. After this, you are presumably ready for the three sample exams at the back of the book.

This book includes strategies right along with the tutorial sections. These are stellar suggestions such as "Concentrate . . . Work carefully . . . Pace yourself . . . Read with a purpose . . . Carefully examine the underlined parts . . . Draw on your knowledge . . . Decide on the best answer." With tips like these, a top score is only moments away. *Mary Pride*

Dr. Douglas J. Paul, Ph.D., a writer of standardized tests and author of *Inside the SAT* (reviewed in chapter 44), is also the creator of **Dr. Paul Zaps the ACT**. This excellent test-prep course has (and meets) all these objectives:

- To demystify the ACT. He knows all the questions students have, or should have, and provides the best answers I've seen to these questions.
- To reduce test anxiety. The material's experienced and personable tone and simple format makes you believe, "I can do this!"
- To teach both general and specific strategies for taking multiple-choice tests. At this, Dr. Paul's courses excel. You'll learn how to tackle the ACT . . . *and* any other standardized tests you may encounter.

The "zaps" part of the course title refers to Dr. Paul's trademarked "zapping" strategies. He also is not afraid to "zap" the ACT test developers for muffing the Science Reasoning Test by making it overreliant on the skill of reading technical charts and diagrams and for failing to allow enough time for reasoning or reflection. When a guy knows enough to criticize the test designers, you know he's a real expert!

The set includes:

- *Dr. Paul Zaps the ACT.* Here you'll find 151 oversized pages of excellent advice, explanations, strategies, exercises, and answers to the exercises. Answers are found in the back of the book.
- Three *PRO-ACT Practice Assessment* practice tests. These are not printed in the back of the book. Rather, they are separate test booklets, similar to the ones you'll be using on the real test. Exception: the answer forms are printed in the back of the practice test books, instead of as separate sheets.

Like Dr. Paul's SAT course, his ACT course is perfect for homeschool use. It neither loads you down with extra work nor oversimplifies, and the tone is just right for students who are used to studying on their own. *Mary Pride*

Getting into the ACT really is the Official Guide to the ACT Assessment, put out by the ACT folks themselves from their world headquarters in Iowa City, IA. In its 556 pages, therefore, you can't expect to find any test-taking strategies more bold than "get a good night's sleep . . . learn as much as you can about the test you're going to take . . . take a sample test." What you *will* get is the inside scoop on what the ACT is all about, plus a surprisingly friendly design, replete with red triangles and black-and-white cartoons.

Someone should have told the book designers that triangles and other pointed objects create an "edgy" mood, while squares and rectangles are authoritative and circles and other rounded objects are seen as friendly. "Edgy" is probably not what they were aiming for. The cartoons, on the other hand, are truly funny and memorable. You'll remember that going to bed earlier than usual may not help, thanks to the cartoon of the girl lying stiff and bug-eyed in bed.

After the normal introductory stuff, which includes such knee-slappers as "Registering for the ACT Assessment" and "At the Test Center," we arrive at your first sample ACT test, disguised as "Format and Contents of the Tests in the ACT Assessment." Actually, it's a set of the individual subject tests, surrounded by explanations of how to handle each test-question type. We then pop out for a look at how to interpret and use your ACT scores; then it's back to the two sample ACTs that close the book. Each of these, of course, has full answers and explanations associated with it.

You'd think that the official guide would use actual ACT tests of ages past. Nope: these are described merely as "sample" tests.

All in all, this is a pretty decent book, but you would do well to pick up a companion volume that reveals the strategies that this book refuses to divulge, such as *Dr. Paul Zaps the ACT. Mary Pride*

Cracking the ACT has the same "fake out the test, don't bother to *really* learn the skills" format as *Princeton Review's Cracking the SAT and PSAT.* However, it's a lot more fun to read. Whereas the *SAT and PSAT* book reads like your football coach is trying to teach you how to take the test designers apart, the ACT book reads like "here's this game, so let's have fun winning it." An example of the prose style:

TRIAGE

This is a medical term that describes a technique used by emergency-room doctors when they have several emergencies at the same time. In order to save lives, the doctors treat the patients with the worst wounds or

NEW!
Getting into the ACT
Grades 10–12. $16 plus $3 shipping. ISBN: 015-600-5352. *Harcourt Brace, 6277 Sea Harbor Dr., Orlando, FL 32887. (800) 543-1918. Fax: (800) 235-0256. Web: www.harcourtbrace.com.*

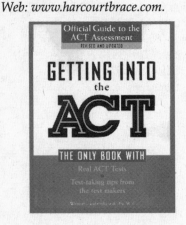

NEW!
Princeton Review: Cracking the ACT, 1999–2000 edition
Grades 10–12. Book only, $18. Book/CD-ROM edition (Mac/Win), $29.95. Shipping extra. *Princeton Review, Random House, 400 Hahan Rd., Westminster, MD 21157. (800) 733-3000. They prefer you to order from bookstores. Web: www.randomhouse.com.*

> illness first, then progress downward in severity until they finally get around to the patient with the scratch on his nose. [This is a bad definition of medical triage, leaving out the third group, namely patients who are so bad off there's no way they'll live, so the doctors ignore them in favor of those for whom there is some hope. But read on nonetheless . . .]
>
> In ACT triage, we want you to learn to do exactly the same thing—in reverse.
>
> See that really tough algebra problem lying over there? Forget it, it's a goner. [Real triage at last!] Send for the chaplain. Now this easy addition problem, on the other hand—this is one to do right now.
>
> See that tough, horrible passage about European authoritarianism during the nineteenth century? Let's see if it's still breathing after we finish the one about Jimmy Carter's election in 1976.

As you have probably guessed, the book starts with instructions on how to guess with style, and how to concentrate on those questions you are most likely to be able to answer quickly. One part each is then dedicated to "how to beat" the ACT English test, math test, reading test, and science reasoning test. You also get to try your hand at the Princeton Review Assessment. This three-and-a-half-hour test is bound right into the book, and winds up giving you a look at how you'll do on both the SAT and the ACT, so you can decide which you'd rather take, if you have a choice.

Because this book is written so much better than its SAT and PSAT counterpart, you can whiz through it much faster and enjoy it more. Since this means you'll have time to work through both this book *and* an actual "how to improve your knowledge" book, and because of the valuable assessment test included, I think *Cracking the ACT* is a good book to get. For more testing practice, get the CD-ROM edition and try your hand at one of the four sample tests on the CD-ROM. *Mary Pride*

CHAPTER 46

How to Take the SAT II

Once upon a time they were known as the College Board Achievement Tests. Then their name was changed to "the SAT II tests." But this series of over 20 tests is still used for the same purpose—to help colleges determine who they want to admit and which courses they want to place you in.

Do not make the mistake of thinking the SAT IIs are optional. Yes, a good score on the SAT I or ACT is a big help—but knowing the parlous state of high school education today, colleges like to be reassured that you actually know something. So, while they use the SAT I to test your reasoning abilities, they rely on the SAT II tests to find out how much you know about each given subject.

Selective colleges typically require you to take at least the SAT II Writing Test, one of the Math tests, and a third test in science or foreign language. Each college is different, so make sure to find out what the requirements are in advance.

You will have to take your SAT II tests no later than December or January of your senior year, in order to meet most colleges' admissions schedules. If you plan to try for early admission, you will need to take them sooner.

The available SAT II tests are:

- Writing (you now can use the new Sample Copy Service to order three copies of your scored essay that you can use to send to colleges)
- Literature (based on what the schools now consider to be "classics," including many overtly amoral and anti-religious works—40 percent of the selections are from 20th-century works)
- American History and Social Studies (the history tested here is weighted towards the onward march of victim groups and one-world statism, and the social studies is likewise geared towards the doctrine that your beliefs and behavior are exclusively a product of your environment and bodily chemistry, as taught in today's public schools)
- World History (previously known as European History and World Cultures)

SAT II Test Dates

Same as SAT I test dates on page 435, *except* no SAT II exams are offered in March or April. SAT II foreign language tests with listening are only available on November test dates.

IMPORTANT!

You may take up to three SAT II subject tests in one day. The Writing Test, if signed up for, must always be taken first.

Score Choice

The new Score Choice option for the SAT II allows you to look over your test scores *before* they are entered into your permanent record. If you release a score, it is entered into the record. You can release none, all, or any of the scores for a particular day. Once released, the score can't be removed. This option slows the process of getting your scores to the colleges of your choice, so plan on taking your Subject Tests earlier if you plan to exercise it.

- Mathematics Level 1
- Mathematics Level 1c (calculator allowed)
- Mathematics Level IIc (calculator with scientific functions required)
- Biology (heavy on evolution)
- Chemistry
- Physics
- Chinese with Listening (the "with listening" tests are not offered at the national test centers on the regular dates, but only at participating high schools—you need a special registration form for these tests)
- French with Listening
- German
- German with Listening
- Modern Hebrew
- Italian
- Japanese with Listening
- Latin
- Spanish
- Spanish with Listening

The more objective and less doctrinaire tests are clearly a better choice for most homeschoolers. The best way to check this out for yourself is to invest a relatively few dollars in some of the test prep books reviewed below. The sample tests enclosed will quickly show you the type of material you can expect on that subject test.

Materials to Help You with the SAT II

The first thing you want to know is, "How many subject tests does it cover?" **ARCO SAT II SuperCourse** "offers 11 full-length practice tests with complete explanatory answers" in "all the most popular subjects," meaning

• American History and Social Studies	• Literature
• Biology	• Mathematics Level II
• Chemistry	• Mathematics Level IIC
• World History	• Physics
• French	• Spanish
	• Writing

By the same author as *ARCO's SAT I Supercourse*, now assisted by Juliana Fazzone, the *SAT II SuperCourse* follows much the same format. After the obligatory general introduction to the SAT II, there's a chapter for each test. Each chapter begins with a brief instructional overview with examples for each question type and strategies for attacking them. A sample test with answers and explanations is also included for each subject test covered.

There is no separate answer key, so you have to skim through pages and pages of explanations in order to score your test. This is annoying if you tend to get lots of answers right. On the positive side, Holmes and Watson are blessedly absent.

More serious than the Princeton Review's *Cracking* series, less silly than the Kaplan "pack your troubles in a plastic pail" approach, more educational than the *Official Guide to SAT II*, this is a decent one-book choice for those considering the tests it covers. *Mary Pride*

NEW!
ARCO SAT II SuperCourse, 3rd Edition
Grades 11–12. $18.95 plus shipping.
ISBN: 067-186-4025.
Macmillan Publishing, 135 South Mt. Zion Rd., Lebanon, IN 46052.
(800) 428-5331. Fax: (800) 835-3202.
Web: www.mcp.com.

Each of the books in **Barron's How to Prepare for SAT II** series starts with . . . mouth-harp lyrics? Recipes? An guide to the Greek vases on display at the Smithsonian? Nope, just like every other test-prep book on the face of the earth, these start with (1) an overview of the test and (2) basic test-taking advice. Why am I not surprised?

After working through this material, you take a diagnostic test that directs you to the exact skills and pages you need to study. Complete explanations of each answer are also included. A huge tutorial section, which could double as a course in the essentials of the subject, then follows. Oodles of practice tests wind up the book. These aren't anything fancy—no explanations, just answer keys.

As of the time of writing, here are the currently available books in this series:

- American History and Social Studies, 9th edition
- Biology, 11th edition
- Chemistry, 5th edition
- French, 6th edition (book and cassette)
- Japanese (book and cassette)
- Literature
- Mathematics Level I, 6th edition
- Mathematics Level IIC, 5th edition
- Physics, 6th edition
- Spanish, 7th edition (book and cassette)
- World History
- Writing

Serious and solid, focused on content, not "cracking," this is the kind of book Mr. Weatherbee would recommend to Archie and Veronica, and that Betty would actually study. *Mary Pride*

Kaplan's SAT II series comes with some unusual features.

The *trademarked* "Kaplan Advantage Stress Management System," about which so much hullaballoo is made on the book cover, combines a couple of list-making exercises (in which you spell out just how stressed you are and list your strengths and weaknesses) with visualization ("Feel how warm the sand is" on your imaginary beach), tensing and relaxing your muscles, positive self-talk, thinking good thoughts, meditating, and transcendental-meditation-style breathing. Nowhere are you told that these are religious practices of Eastern (as in Asian) religions and New Age (as in imported and yuppified) Eastern religions. Prayer was not mentioned as a stress reliever.

Somewhat more useful is the free CD-ROM offer of Kaplan's SAT Digital Test Booklet. This includes a timed practice test with instant scoring, performance analysis, and click-on explanations of why your answers were wrong (if they were).

Each book follows the "stress management" section with a couple of chapters describing the SAT II tests in general and the subject test the book covers in particular. You then get some "cracking"-type test-taking advice mixed with streamlined instruction in the subject, and three practice tests with scoring keys, answers, and explanations.

Like other Kaplan books, these are friendly but basically serious in style—except for the mini-course in New Age thinking. "See yourself walking on the beach, carrying a small plastic pail . . . put your worries and whatever may be bugging you into the pail. Drop it at the water's edge and watch it drift out to sea." And here comes that small plastic pail, bobbing back on the next tide. Sending your troubles out to to sea didn't work for the ancient Greeks (check out the tales of Oedipus and Jason, to name just two), and I doubt seriously that it will do anything wonderful for you. *Mary Pride*

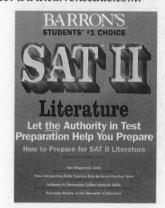
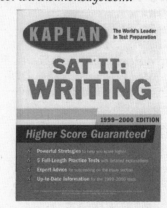

Straight from the hallowed halls of the people who bring you the SAT II, here's the official word on what's included in each test and a whole boat-load of practice tests and mini-tests. Don't expect as complete coverage of each individual test as in books written about just one or a few of the tests. In fact, don't expect *any* serious test-taking tips or instruction in **Official Guide to the SAT II Subject Tests**. Do expect *very* brief explanations of each type of question on each test, plus full-length sample tests in:

- Writing
- Literature
- American History and Social Studies
- World History
- Mathematics Level I and Mathematics Level IIC
- Biology
- Chemistry
- Physics

and mini-tests for these foreign languages:

- Chinese with Listening
- French and French with Listening
- German and German with Listening
- Modern Hebrew
- Italian
- Japanese with Listening
- Latin
- Spanish and Spanish with Listening

You get answer and scoring keys for each tests, but *no* explanations of why your answers were right or wrong. That's why I suggest you use this book along with others more targeted to the tests you intend to take. Use it to "sample" the tests and decide which to take, or to give yourself a final run-through. *Mary Pride*

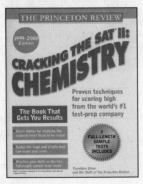

Since the SAT II tests are tests of advanced knowledge, **Princeton Review's Cracking the SAT II** series spends most of its efforts slimming down the available knowledge into the basic facts and strategies you'll need to do well on these tests.

For example, the *Chemistry* book teaches you to associate

Exothermic *with:*	DH *is negative, enthalpy decreases*
Endothermic *with:*	DH *is positive, enthalpy increases*

What is *DH*? What is *enthalpy*? Fear not, all these terms are succinctly explained, so you learn what they mean. What you don't end up studying are all the fussy, distracting details textbooks love to throw in.

In a very real sense, this series spends most of its instructional time *translating* the stuff you supposedly learned in your high-school courses, and stripping off the details that most students never understood and never will. Lots of simple examples and illustrations clarify troublesome concepts. For example, I bet *your* physics teacher never described "potential energy" in terms of a toy airplane with a wound-up rubber-band propeller—"ready, willing, and able to move." Could anything be easier to remember than that? It's the difference between saying, as most textbooks would, "Observe the circuit in the diagram beneath," and saying, as Princeton Review does, "Look at this circuit."

Books in this series cover the following subject areas:

- Biology
- Chemistry
- English
- French
- History
- Math
- Physics
- Spanish

Each book starts with the same basic test-taking strategies, e.g., "Avoiding the Temptation Trap" (a familiar-sounding answer that happens to have nothing to do with the particular question). Beyond that, you get an affable review of basic course material, with frequent practice exercises and excellent explanations of what makes each answer right or wrong. Textbooks should only be this clear! In fact, I could make a case for purchasing these books simply to help translate your textbooks *while* you're taking these courses.

Two practice tests end each book. This is an improvement over earlier editions, which only had one practice test. Typically you'll take the test, then discover you were still weak in some areas. Having at least one more test to take after further study helps you to double-check whether you've filled in those gaps. If you're a testing glutton, you might want to follow up with *The Official Guide to SAT II,* just to have even more practice tests to play with. *Mary Pride*

CHAPTER 47

To GED or Not To GED

I f you're thinking of the General Educational Development Test, otherwise known as the GED, as a handy way to have your child graduate high school early, think again. Homeschoolers do use the GED a lot . . . as you'll see later in this chapter . . . but if you're thinking of having your 12-year-old get a high-school diploma via GED, this is not an option, as I'll explain.

A Brief History of the GED

Although most of us think of the GED just as "the test you take to get your high school diploma," actually it has always been intended solely as a second-chance test for adults.

A couple of years ago I spent a fascinating half-hour on the phone with Jean Lowe, the Assistant Director of the General Educational Development Testing Service. This is the private, non-profit group which owns and leases the GED tests. Let me share some of the history of this organization with you, as Jean shared it with me.

During World War I, a group of university presidents got together and decided to do something to help out the servicemen. Recognizing that the soldiers had their education interrupted by the war, and figuring that surely serving under Uncle Sam was an educational experience, the presidents decided to offer one semester of college credit for every year a man fought overseas. This idea was, of course, a disaster! Many of the soldiers had little more than a fourth-grade education and were totally unable to cope in the college environment.

By the time World War II rolled along, the university community had come up with a better idea. In 1942 they founded the Veterans Testing Service, with the mission of creating and disseminating a test of high-school equivalence. Now servicemen could prove that they had finished out their high-school studies, and colleges would know they were getting acceptable students. This second venture was a huge success, since all the colleges accepted the test from the start.

In the mid-1950s, New York state officials began to see that civilian adults would also benefit from the chance to obtain a "second chance" high school diploma. After some deliberation, the Veterans Testing Service decided to agree to the plan. Its name was then changed to the General Educational

Warning: In September, 2001, a new, very different GED version will be introduced. Make sure you have a copy of the newest version of the GED prep books of your choice if you are taking the test after that date.

In some ways, passing the GED is harder than graduating high school. Every year the people who write the GED try it out on a representative sample of graduating high school seniors across the country. About 30 percent of these high school seniors—and remember, these are people who are just about to get their high school diplomas—*fail* the GED. They get their diplomas anyway, which doesn't seem fair, but that's life. To pass your GED, you're going to need to have more on the ball than a lot of high school graduates.
—*The Princeton Review: Cracking the GED*

GEDTS Essay Scoring Guide

Copyright ©1987, GED Testing Service. Reprinted with permission of the American Council on Education.

PAPERS WILL SHOW *SOME* OR *ALL* OF THE FOLLOWING CHARACTERISTICS.

Upper-half papers have a clear, definite purpose pursued with varying degrees of effectiveness. They have a structure that shows evidence of some deliberate planning. The writer's control of the conventions of Standard Written English (spelling, punctuation, grammar, word choice, and sentence structure) ranges from fairly reliable at 4 to confident and accomplished at 6.

6 The *6 paper* offers sophisticated ideas within an organizational framework that is clear and appropriate for the topic. The supporting statements are particularly effective because of their substance, specificity, or illustrative quality. The writing is vivid and precise, although it may contain an occasional error in the conventions of Standard Written English.

5 The *5 paper* is clearly organized with effective support for each of the writer's major points. While the writing offers substantive ideas, it lacks the fluency found in the 6 paper. Although there are some errors, the conventions of Standard English are consistently under control.

4 The *4 paper* shows evidence of the writer's organizational plan. Support, though adequate, tends to be less extensive or effective than that found in the 5 paper. The writer generally observes the conventions of Standard Written English. The errors that are present are not severe enough to interfere significantly with the writer's main purpose.

Development Testing Service. In due course, all 50 states, all provinces of Canada, and all U.S. territories acknowledged and adopted the GED test as a high-school equivalence exam for adults.

Since the GED Testing Service owns the tests, its board decides who gets to take the tests. Each state leases the tests from the GED Testing Service and negotiates the terms under which it will administer the tests. The GED Testing Service has certain minimum requirements which all states must follow. These terms have traditionally been designed to, in Jean's words, "not subvert the states' attendance laws." In most cases, you can't obtain a diploma from your state via the GED route until you are at least as old as the class in which you would normally have graduated.

Bottom line: if you don't mind waiting until your child is graduation age, the GED is an excellent way to validate your homeschool program's success. If you need this validation earlier, at present you'll have to look elsewhere.

Provisional Admissions and the GED

Many homeschoolers have found that it's possible to enroll your child in college—especially community college—either on the basis of high-school transcripts and test scores alone, or "provisionally," with the understanding that the student will take the GED when he or she comes of age. In such a case, when the student passes the GED the college retroactively grants him credit for the courses he has already taken and passed.

In our area, it's not unusual for a 14-year-old homeschooler to enter community college provisionally, and then take the GED several years later, after which he or she transfers to a four-year college with two years of college credit. This arrangement keeps college costs low, and allows the student to live at home until the age difference between him or her and other college students is not so acute.

What Is the GED?

The GED is a battery of five tests that cover basic high-school knowledge—sort of. It requires you to demonstrate more skills and knowledge than most high-school graduates possess. On the other hand, it doesn't ask you to know a lot of *facts*. You won't be asked for the year the Civil War started, for example. Instead, you might be given a reading passage on the Civil War and asked to answer some questions. If in the science section the test is asking you questions about the light spectrum, you might have a labeled graph of the spectrum that includes all the data needed to answer the questions. A large number of GED questions are based on visuals—charts, graphs, tables, and so forth—so practice in pulling out information quickly from visuals is a must.

The five GED tests are:

The Test of Writing Skills

This test has two parts: 75 minutes to answer 55 multiple-choice questions, and 45 minutes to write an essay. The multiple-choice question presents you with sentences which may or may not contain errors. You have to spot the errors, or state that the sentence has no errors. Error topics include phrases and clauses; grammar; and capitalization, spelling, and punctuation.

The GED Essay is a major topic in itself, with entire books written on how to prepare for this part of the test. In the sidebar you'll find the official GED rules for how they grade this essay.

As you can see, *sticking to the essay topic* is critical, even more so than using correct spelling and grammar. So don't get too creative and "go off at a tangent." This is often a temptation with smart kids who have been home-schooled. Remember, in this case cleverness can be a downright detriment, as opposed to coming up with lots of "supporting statements." Confine your cleverness to constructing zippy sentences; remember to argue *both* sides of the issue before settling down to making your point (for some reason test graders like this); beware of picking a topic angle that might ruffle your grader's political feathers; and you should be OK.

If you're not used to writing this way, I strongly recommend Princeton Review's *Cracking the GED* for inside information on how to handle this part of the test (and all the other parts, too!).

The Test of Social Studies

Here we meet our old friends, reading passages followed by questions about the passage and visual material followed by questions based on the chart, diagram, graph, cartoon, or whatever. A short passage is followed by only one question, while longer passages are followed by three or four questions. Questions break down as follows: about one-quarter on history, one-fifth on economics, one-fifth on political science, one-sixth on geography, and one-fifth on behavior science. The test takes 85 minutes and has 64 multiple-choice questions.

The Test of Science

Reading passages and visuals followed by questions. Science lends itself to visuals, so about one-third of this test is based on visual material. You do ned to know some basic principles of science to do well on this test, but nobody is going to expect you to have memorized the atomic weight of Lithium or anything like that. Half the test cover biological sciences, and the other half covers the physical sciences of chemistry, physics, and earth science. Ninety-five minutes, 66 multiple-choice questions.

The Test of Interpreting Literature and the Arts

As befits a literature exam, this test is solely based on reading passages, including in this case a play, a novel, a magazine-style piece, and a poem. You will have to answer reading-comprehension questions as well as questions that ask you to analyze the passage. Half of the test uses passages from popular literature, a quarter uses passages from literature the schools consider to be classic (which is not at all the same thing as "classical literature," so don't be confused if your GED test-prep book makes the mistake of calling it that), and another quarter uses passages from literary criticism. Sixty-five minutes, 45 multiple-choice questions.

The Test of Mathematics

Mostly word problems and problems based on charts or diagrams. Some very basic algebra and geometry (figuring area and volume, etc.) is required. Half of the test is on problems that use basic arithmetic, thirty percent is on algebra, and twenty percent is on geometry. Ninety minutes, 56 questions.

While it is possible to walk into the GED and ace it without any preparation, and there is no penalty for taking it as often as you like, the wise student will invest in at least one GED preparation book. It's worth it just to familiarize yourself with what's on the test, and *especially* worth it to prepare yourself for the somewhat arcane (to real writers) criteria that govern how the essay is judged. You'll find some helpful resources below.

Lower-half papers either fail to convey a purpose sufficiently or lack one entirely. Consequently, their structure ranges from rudimentary at 3, to random at 2, to absent at 1. Control of the conventions of Standard Written English tends to follow this same gradient.

3   The *3 paper* usually shows some evidence of planning, although the development is insufficient. The supporting statements may be limited to a listing or a repetition of ideas. The 3 paper often demonstrates repeated weaknesses in the conventions of Standard Written English.

2   The *2 paper* is characterized by a marked lack of organization or inadequate support for ideas. The development is usually superficial or unfocused. Errors in the conventions of Standard Written English may seriously interfere with the overall effectiveness of this paper.

1   The *1 paper* lacks purpose or development. The dominant feature is the absence of control of structure or the conventions of Standard Written English. The deficiencies are so severe that the writer's ideas are difficult or impossible to understand.

Note: An asterisk code is reserved for papers that are blank, illegible, or written on a topic other than the one assigned. Because these papers cannot be scored, a Writing Skills Test composite score cannot be reported.

The GED is also available in Spanish, French, braille, and on cassette. To find out more about these options, call (800) 62-MY-GED.

Preparing for the GED

NEW!
Barron's How to Prepare for the GED High School Equivalency Examination, 9th edition

Grade 12–adult. $14.95 plus shipping. ISBN: 07641-0433-0. *Barron's Educational Series, Inc., 250 Wireless Blvd., Hauppauge, NY 11788. (800) 645-3476. Fax: (516) 434-3217. Web: www.barronseduc.com.*

NEW!
Contemporary's GED: The Complete Book

Grade 12–adult. $14.94 plus $5 shipping. ISBN: 08092-37776. *Contemporary Books, Inc., 4255 West Touhy Ave., Chicago, IL 60646. (800) 323-4900 x 147. Fax: (800) 998-3103. Email: ntcpub@tribune.com. Web: www.contemporarybooks.com.*

NEW!
Contemporary's The GED Essay

Grade 12–adult. $9.94 plus $5 shipping. ISBN: 08092-377-25. *Contemporary Books, Inc., 4255 West Touhy Ave., Chicago, IL 60646. (800) 323-4900 x 147. Web: www.contemporarybooks.com.*

Like other GED home-study courses, **How to Prepare for the GED** has the usual brief introduction to the GED, followed by a diagnostic test for each subject area keyed to an evaluator chart (here called a "Self-Appraisal Chart"). By taking the diagnostic test, you reveal which sections of this very hefty 879-page book you need to study. The rest of the book is a series of lessons for each of the five subject tests, followed by two practice examinations. Finally, there's a chart, by American state and territory and Canadian province, of how to register for the GED and under what circumstances it may be taken. (We have that information, updated from the GEDTS people's own materials, right here for you in Appendix 4 of this book.)

A typical lesson format is: a paragraph of instruction, followed by an example, a couple of practice questions, answers to the practice questions, another bit of instruction followed by an example, practice questions, answers to the practice questions, etc., plus an "Important Note" or two thrown in (with a blue background, in a box), and finally a lengthy set of practice questions covering all the bits of knowledge in the lesson, followed by an answer key, scorebox, and detailed analysis of each question.

Personally, I found this format *most* confusing. It feels like you're being interrupted every few seconds, as you switch from instruction to example to question to answer to tip to instruction to example to question to answer . . . Again, I don't see the value in "practice questions" that have the answers right underneath them. With so many other GED programs available, this book wouldn't be my first choice. *Mary Pride*

This one-book study program for the GED does not prioritize and streamline your studies. The unwieldy book features a vast amount of info in its 938 pages, none of which is presented as more or less important than the remaining information.

After the obligatory "what is the GED and what are your most fearful questions?" section, **GED: The Complete Book** gives you one pretest apiece for each of the five subject tests, with answer keys and *brief* explanations of the answers. Headings and subheadings are not arranged in a clear hierarchy, nor is there an obvious plan behind when and where exercises are provided. Answers are at the end of each section. The book then ends with a post-test for each subject area, followed by a practice test for each subject area.

What's the difference between a post-test and a practice test? Each post-test has an evaluation chart, just like the pre-test, which tells you what to go back and study again. The practice test just has answers.

This would not be my first choice for GED prep. Contemporary's individual Satellite series books are much better. *Mary Pride*

The GED Essay: Writing Skills to Pass the Test tells you what the test is like and how the GED staff evaluates essays. Its collection of helpful hints, spelled out in much detail with many examples, includes teaching you how to analyze the assigned topic, brainstorming and planning skills, avoiding common pitfalls, and so forth. The book is designed for you to use with a "partner," someone who will criticize your efforts according to the book's criteria.

This book doesn't highlight the specifics of what the test people are looking for in the same way Princeton Review's *Cracking the GED* does, but it will give you the skills to get A's in English class. *Mary Pride*

"The Breakthrough Approach to GED Math Preparation! Reasoning Skills to Pass the Test!" Do you get the feeling some folks are a teensy bit worried about how they might do on the math portion of the GED—the only part, aside from the written essay, that requires actual knowledge, as opposed to skills in evaluating reading passages?

Written by a former math editor for the GED Testing Service, this excellent, attractive book not only explains how the GED math test works, but could be used by anyone as a course or refresher for basic math, from addition and subtraction through ratios and percents. Each of the 28 chapters of **Contemporary's GED Math Problem Solver** clearly introduces a new concept, while the frequent Skill Maintenance problem sets offer *cumulative* review—so important when a student needs extra help remembering new skills. Naturally, the book also includes a practice test, and answers to all test problems and exercises are in the back of the book.

The accompanying teacher's guide is meant for classroom use, and in most cases can be skipped in the home setting. The math on the GED math test isn't complicated, and the workbook is so clear it practically teaches itself. *Mary Pride*

The attractive **Contemporary's GED Satellite series** study program comes in five oversized, but not bulky workbooks, one for each of the five test areas, plus a corresponding set of five exercise books. Don't let those exercise books confuse you: the basic Satellite series has plenty of exercises and tests built in. The exercise books are just for those who want more exercises.

Each Satellite book starts with some basic information on the GED and a diagnostic pre-test, keyed to the rest of the book so you learn which areas you need to study and can skip the rest. This is followed by, first, step-by-step training in critical thinking skills and test-taking skills, and then training in subject test material (e.g., for the Literature and the Art test, "What is a plot? What is characterization?") Each chapter is followed by practice questions, with answers and explanations in the back. Finally, you get both a post-test (to check how much you've improved thanks to the book) and a practice test resembling the actual GED subject test.

The slender exercise books not only include many more practice exercises, but *complete* explanations of why each correct answer is correct, and another complete subject practice test. In all, a nice little series, quite easy to use, that won't waste your time. *Mary Pride*

NEW!
Contemporary's Pre-GED Satellite series

Grade 12–adult. $12.19 per book. Shipping extra.
Contemporary Books, Inc., 4255 West Touhy Ave., Chicago, IL 60646.
(800) 323-4900 x 147.
Fax: (800) 998-3103.
Email: ntcpub@tribune.com.
Web: www.contemporarybooks.com.

What is a "pre-GED" series? It's a set of five workbooks, one for each of the five GED test subject areas, meant to be used by those who need extra skill development before tackling a regular GED-prep book.

Nicely designed, with a friendly, open format and attractive use of a second color to highlight important words and headings, each book in the **Contemporary Pre-GED Satellite series** begins with a diagnostic pre-test, complete with annotated answer key, and ends with a post-test, again with annotated answer key. Each of these tests comes with an "evaluation chart." This chart tells you which parts of the workbook you need to study to bring the skills you muffed on the test up to par. By comparing your scores on the pre- and post-test, you can observe the progress you made.

The heart of each 300-plus-page workbook is the chapters on actual test material, each ending in a set of practice exercises, with annotated answers to the exercises in the back of the book. These chapters deal both with test-taking skills (e.g., how to get context clues from a circle graph) and with facts and skills covered on the test. The *Pre-GED Social Studies* book, for example, has four chapters on how to think through test questions— "Comprehending Social Studies Material," "Applying Social Studies Ideas," "Analyzing Social Studies Material," and "Evaluating Social Studies Material"—plus a chapter apiece on U.S. history, political science, behavior sciences, geography, and economics. Each of the "subject" sections provides an overview of its topic. For example, the "U.S. History" chapter takes you from "Exploration of the New World" through "U.S. Domestic History: 1945–1990s" and up to "Government's Role in the Economy."

As a quickie review of secular high-school material, these books aren't bad. If your homeschool has used exclusively Christian material, it wouldn't hurt to go through these, since otherwise you are likely to be slowed down by test questions based on material you haven't studied and from viewpoints you don't agree with. Another use for these books is as a quick "hole checker" to see if you've missed anything significant (to the test-makers, that is) over the years. However, if your high-school course hasn't been notably countercultural or academically deficient, feel free to skip these books and go right to a regular GED course. *Mary Pride*

NEW!
New Revised Cambridge GED Program

Grade 12–adult. $16.75 plus shipping. ISBN: 0-835-94726-2.
Cambridge Adult Education, PO Box 2649, Columbus, OH 43216.
(800) ADULT-ED.
Fax: (614) 771-7361.
Web: www.cambridgeadulted.com.

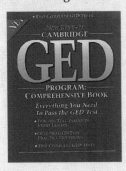

I like the **New Revised Cambridge GED Program** the best of all the one-book GED home-study courses. Like the rest, it is bulky, at over 850 pages. But its attractive two-color design, with thumb indexes, bold headings, and nice large type, is more open than Barron's or Contemporary's, and the instructions are easier to follow than Barron's or Contemporary's (which constantly interrupt lessons to throw lists and questions at you).

What you have here is the usual brief introduction to the GED, followed by a diagnostic test (here called a Predictor Test). The rest of the book is a series of lessons for each of the five subject tests, followed by "Practice Items" and two "Simulated Tests" (the other books call these "practice tests"). One special feature: each chapter begins with a very short "preview test." Answer the few questions and find out just where in the chapter you need to start studying. Continuing this streamlined emphasis, every *brief* lesson within the chapter is followed by a *brief* exercise set, instead of the lesson being interrupted with strings of questions. If you want to sweat more questions, you can play with the Practice Items. Better yet, use the Practice Items as a mini-review before taking a "Simulated Test." Aside from that, there's not much more to say about this flawless, user-friendly book. *Mary Pride*

Notable for its fresh, irreverent tone, **Cracking the GED** does not try, like some other GED-prep books, to give you an instant high-school education. With laser-like intensity, its 600 pages focus on one thought and one thought only: "What can we do to help you get the highest possible score, whether you actually possess the skills you are being tested on or not?"

The book's entire approach is unique. For example, since between 20 and 40 percent of GED questions are based on visuals of some sort (charts, graphs, etc.), after disposing of the usual "what is the GED?" and "what guessing strategies help me close in on the right answer?" questions, you get an entire chapter on how to answer graphic-based questions. But instead of using graphs such as are actually found in the GED (e.g., World Oil Reserves, Rabbit Population) author Geoff Martz spices things up by presenting you with a graph of Liz Taylor's marriages and a chart relating talk-show hosts to their relative acidity or baseness (on a pH scale, I kid you not!). For map reading, you get to compare a map of the U.S.A. before and after "The Big One," in which the entire West Coast slides into the ocean. Question: "After the Big One, which state will be the most northern state on the West Coast?"

This craziness isn't constant, popping up only to defuse tension when dealing with skills that tend to snow students. However, the book maintains an interactive, chatty tone throughout, asking you questions within the instructional sections as if it expects an answer.

No time is wasted studying skills that won't be on the test. You can be sure that every scrap of available help to make studying easier and the test less intimidating is tucked between these covers.

You don't get a diagnostic test to start with, but then, *Cracking the GED* doesn't include lots of marginal information that you'll be dying to skip. You do get separate sections on how to beat the writing skills multiple-choice test and how to beat the writing skills essay test (the key here is to have a definite "template" in mind that you plan to construct your answer around, no matter which of the various essay question types is asked). One section each also offers a brief review of what you need to know for each other subject test. Finally, you get two practice tests, which oddly only comes with answer keys, *not* with explanations of why each answer is correct or incorrect.

This is a very useful book, well worth the price. It should diminish your test-taking anxiety considerably. *Mary Pride*

The Cliffs Notes people throw their hat in the GED ring at last! Like all the rest of one-book GED test preparation volumes, Cliff's You Can Pass the GED is an oversized, thick book. Unlike the rest, it's printed in two colors, which makes it easy for you to spot important information. The highly visual design of the book—they never use just words when they can show you with a pie chart or handwriting sample—also makes it stand out from the competition.

The introduction is pretty standard fare: how to get the most out of your study time, format of the GED questions, test-taking strategies, and answers to frequently-asked questions.

Now the book goes test section by test section, explaining each question type and how to answer it. How to use the page of math formulas you will be given at the exam is also covered in this section, as are charts, graphs, maps, cartoons, and diagrams.

The next section is a complete review of skills tested on the GED. This is followed by two practice exams, with answer keys and explanations. Finally, an extremely helpful touch—glossaries of terms arranged by subject area: behavioral sciences, economics, geography, U.S. history, political science and government, American social problems, American political process, arithmetic, algebra, and geometry. If you take the time to make flashcards of the terms you don't already know, and study them, it should be a big help not only for this exam but for your general vocabulary and college comfort level.

Cliffs Notes are known for making advanced literature understandable. This book does its best to keep up the tradition by doing everything it can to help you understand and succeed at the GED. Recommended. *Mary Pride*

CHAPTER 48

College Credit for High School Via AP or CLEP

What could be nicer than starting college with credit for up to a year of courses already under your belt?

With the Mickey Mouse difficulty level of many freshman courses offered these days, homeschoolers who have applied themselves to their high-school studies may well be in position to take advantage of the two main ways for getting college credit without taking college courses:

- The Advanced Placement (AP) exams
- The College-Level Examination Program (CLEP)

The Advanced Placement Exams

Before I say any more, I'd better warn you at once that some colleges use the AP exams for purposes of granting college credit *and* more advanced course placement, while others use them *only* to grant advanced course placement and refuse to grant you any extra credits at all. This latter is terribly unfair; why should you be penalized (or at least not rewarded) for proving you have done college-level work on your own, when you would have received college credit had you taken the course? Suspicion mutters that such institutions probably are more anxious for your money than for your success. By refusing to grant credit, they force you to take the full number of courses, and naturally pay them the full amount of money.

In any case, *be sure to check* whether the colleges you are applying to grant credit for a good performance on the AP exams you plan to take. ("Good performance" usually means that you got a passing grade of 3 out of 5.)

The AP tests are not graded on a curve. If for some reason every student in the country who took a given AP exam did excellent work, every student would receive an excellent grade. There is no attempt to make the average grade correspond to a mid-level score. You are competing against a standard, not against your fellow test-takers.

AP Test Dates

2000: May 8–12 and May 15–19
Each exam is only offered *once* during the test weeks. Exams are scheduled for mornings and afternoons all ten days.

CLEP Test Dates

Test dates are selected by your local test center, and can be any day of the month. Exception: The CLEP English Composition with Essay Examination is given nationally only in January, April, June, and October.

IMPORTANT!

As a homeschooler not known personally by the AP Coordinator administering the test at your local school, you must bring a photo ID to the test. If you don't have a driver's license, you can still get a photo ID at your local Department of Motor Vehicles. They provide photo IDs for people who don't drive, but still need identification. You'll need to provide several proofs of identity to the DMV, such as a Social Security card, birth certificate, and correspondence addressed and mailed to you. Call the DMV in advance to find out their requirements. Be sure to also ask how long it will take them to get your photo ID ready.

Registering for the AP Exams

You have to register for the AP exams through a local school. You can't register through the Educational Testing Service. To find a school near you that offers these tests, call or write before March 1 of the year you intend to take the tests:

AP Services
PO Box 6671
Princeton, NJ 08541-6671
(609) 771-7300

You then must contact the school's AP Coordinator to get permission to take the test at the school and to give them the fees and the information necessary for them to register you. This may be harder than you think, especially if the school doesn't offer AP courses in the subjects you want to be tested in. I had to contact my state legislator before our local high school would allow our kids to take the AP tests they needed this year. Clearly, every state needs to pass a law *requiring* public schools to allow homeschoolers to sign up for AP testing in *any* subject they require.

AP exams are available in the following subject areas:

Languages

- **English Language and Composition.** A three-hour exam corresponding to a full year of introductory English. Please note, by the way, when describing these tests, that a "full-year course" means a full-year college (not high-school) course, and a "one-semester course" means one college semester. It differs from the Literature and Composition test below in that you analyze a variety of "regular" prose passages and write essays on a variety of topics, not just about literature.
- **English Literature and Composition.** Similar to the above, except you analyze poems and literary passages and "write critical or analytical essays on poems, prose passages, and complete novels and plays," the latter obviously not being included in the test booklet itself. In other words, you are expected to have read widely in the current public high-school literary canon (see my comments about same in the SAT II chapter).
- **French Language.** About 2½ hours on understanding written and spoken French and writing and speaking in French. How much college credit you might get for this, or any of the other foreign or classical language courses, is a mystery; the AP Bulletin doesn't even speculate on how many semesters of material these tests are supposed to cover.
- **French Literature.** Three hours with multiple-choice questions and essay questions, all in French, on presented literary passages and a text from the required reading list. Obviously it behooves you to get a copy of this list well in advance of preparing for the test.
- **German Language.** A three-hour exam corresponding to a college-level advanced German course. You have to demonstrate you read and understand German, and can write and speak it.
- **Latin Literature.** A two-hour exam on Latin sight reading. For the free-response section, you have your choice of writing about Catullus and Cicero, Catullus and Horace, or Catullus and Ovid. This is supposed to be mid-level college work.
- **Latin-Vergil.** Same as above, except instead of dear old Catullus and friends you get to expatiate on Vergil.
- **Spanish Language.** About 2½ hours of listening to, speaking, and writing Spanish, corresponding to an advanced college Spanish course.
- **Spanish Literature.** Over 3 hours of listening to, reading, and analyzing Spanish authors from the required reading list. Again, this corresponds to an advanced college Spanish course.

Sciences

- **Biology.** A 3-hour exam covering the material you'd find in a "full-year introductory college course in biology with laboratory."
- **Chemistry.** A 3-hour exam covering the material you'd find in a "full-year introductory college course in chemistry."
- **Physics B.** A three-hour exam covering a "full-year noncalculus college course on general physics." Not recommended for physical science or engineering majors. The easier one.
- **Physics C-Mechanics.** A 90-minute exam covering one introductory semester of physics with calculus. Recommended for physical science and engineering majors.
- **Physics C-Electricity and Magnetism.** A 90-minute exam covering one introductory semester of physics with calculus. Recommended for physical science and engineering majors. To get up to a full year's credit, science and engineering majors will need to take both Physics C exams.

Mathematics

- **Calculus AB.** The easier exam. Three hours covering "differential and integral calculus topics that are typically included in an introductory Calculus I college course."
- **Calculus BC.** The tougher exam. You can get up to two semesters (one full year) of credit if your target institution grants AP credit and you get an acceptable score on this three-hour exam. In addition to the topics covered in the Calculus AB exam, this one includes "advanced topics in integral calculus, sequences, and series."

History & Social Sciences

- **European History.** Slightly over 3 hours corresponding to a "full-year introductory college course on European history from approximately 1450 to the present." Sad news for those of us who spent years studying the histories of Greece, Rome, and medieval Europe, back when things were much more interesting.
- **Government & Politics—Comparative.** A 90-minute exam corresponding to material covered in a one-semester introductory course. The five nations compared include France, Great Britain, China, "Russia/the former Soviet Union" (the booklet sounds rather confused at this point, as these are not the same), and "one of the following: India, Mexico, or Nigeria." In light of what's happening in the European Economic Community, I bet Germany makes it onto this list sometime soon.
- **Government & Politics—U.S.** A 90-minute exam corresponding to material covered in a one-semester introductory course. Much emphasis on the federal level, little or none on the state and local levels.
- **Macroeconomics.** A two-hour exam corresponding to a one-semester introductory-level college course. Mainstream (e.g., "as seen in *Time*, *USA Today*, and *Newsweek*) doctrines and concepts are tested.
- **Microeconomics.** Ditto.

Other Ways to Obtain AP Information

- **Gopher site:** *gopher.ets.org.* Go to Tests & Services, then College Board Programs, then AP.
- **Web:** *www.collegeboard.org*
- **America Online:** Go *College Board* (in the Learning & Reference area)

AP Publications from the AP People

The following publications are available from
Advanced Placement Program
Dept E-22
PO Box 6670
Princeton, NJ 08541-6670
Tel: (609) 771-7300
Fax: (609) 530-0482
TTY: (609) 882-4118
Email: apexams@ets.org

A check must be included with your mail order. CA, DC, and GA residents must add sales tax; Canadians must add GST. You should allow 4–6 weeks for delivery.

Advanced Placement Bulletin for Students & Parents. This includes an up-to-date ordering form for all the items below. It also includes invaluable basic information about each test, how to register, special accommodations, fees, what you may and may not bring to each test, the score cancellation option, and other important things to know. Best of all, it includes a list by state of colleges that grant sophomore standing to students who demonstrate successful completion of a year's college work (five full-year course equivalents). If you

are an advanced high-school student capable of passing several AP tests, I would seriously suggest you save yourself a year's frustration and costs by limiting your college options to the colleges in this list. Free

Student Guides to the AP . . . English Course & Examinations, European History Course & Examination, French Courses & Examinations, Mathematics Courses & Examinations, Physics Courses & Examinations, Spanish Courses & Examinations, and U.S. History Course & Examination. $12 each

AP Course Descriptions in . . . Art, Biology, Chemistry, Computer Science, Economics, English, French, German, Government & Politics, History, Latin, Mathematics, Music Theory, Physics, Psychology, and Spanish. Here are where you find out what exactly you are supposed to know, and what books are on the "required reading lists." I advise you get the appropriate course descriptions before planning the homeschool courses you'll be taking or giving in these subjects. $10 each

AP Computer Science Directory Manager Course Study Student Manual (choice of 5¼" DOS disk, 3½" DOS disk, or 3½" Macintosh disk), $15 each.

The Princeton Review people have finally entered the AP test-prep biz. Their new **Cracking the AP** series is now available, in the 1999–2000 editions, for:

- Biology
- Calculus AB & BC
- Chemistry
- English Literature
- U.S. Government & Politics
- U.S. History
- Physics

Each book includes a full-length practice test, up to 1,000 practice questions, and review of the materials covered on the exam. More serious tone than other "cracking" series; same emphasis on test-taking strategies; much more factual instruction, all geared precisely to what the exam will test. Books are $16–$17 each and are available in bookstores or from (800) 733-3000.

- **Psychology.** Ditto.
- **U.S. History.** Slightly over 3 hours, corresponds to a full-year introductory course covering from the Age of Exploration to right now. Like the European History exam, this includes multiple-choice, essays, a lengthy "exercise on the use of historical evidence," otherwise known as the "document-based question" or DBQ.

Miscellaneous

- **Computer Science A.** The easier exam. Three hours covering programming how-tos, Pascal programming, program design, algorithms, and how you put your data together. All this is considered equivalent to a first-semester course.
- **Computer Science AB.** The tougher exam. All the above plus "more in-depth algorithm analysis (Big-O notation) and data structures involving pointers." This is equivalent material to a full-year introductory course.
- **History of Art.** Three hours covering material you'd find in a one-year introductory course.
- **Music Theory.** A 2½ hour exam covering material comparable to a "full-year introductory college course in music theory."
- **Studio Art-General Portfolio.** For this test, there is no written exam. Instead, you submit a portfolio of artwork created by you according to the specific requirements given on the Studio Art Poster (item #271562: limit of 5 free copies per person).
- **Studio Art-Drawing Portfolio.** Same as above: no written test, you submit a portfolio. Different portfolio requirement from General Portfolio.

As you can see, across the board the AP exams are usually designed to be *tougher* than the introductory college courses most students take. When they are "introductory level," typically the subject is one that few college students are willing to tackle, such as history. And the foreign-and classical-language courses require you to be working at a *mid*-level or *advanced* level (corresponding roughly to second- and third-year college courses). This does not seem quite fair, since kids who stumble along with Basic Math 101 and Algebra I end up earning (and paying for) two years of college math, while the AP Calculus AB test-taker, who has already mastered all this material, only gets one semester's credit, at most. On the other hand, the AP test-passer is starting out at a genuine college level, not warmed-over high school. He or she has the opportunity to get a real education (assuming the college in question offers a full complement of challenging courses), and not waste any time on high-school-level material.

So my advice is, "Go for it!" Try to knock a year off your college studies, impress the admissions people, and maybe even win one of the AP scholarships. If you *do* win a scholarship, drop us a note at Practical Homeschooling, PO Box 1190, Fenton MO 63026. We're interested in your success!

Help with the AP Exams

Everyone contemplating taking an AP exam should get the free *Advanced Placement Bulletin for Students and Parent* from the College Board. The contact info is on the previous page. Other publications to help you with the AP exams are also available from the College Board, and well worth the money. But the resources you can get from ETS are not enough all by themselves, in my opinion. You really need to work through a test-preparation book, including sample tests and test-taking tips, before tackling these extremely difficult tests. It may cost a bit, but remember you are potentially saving the cost of an entire year's college tuition, housing, and the rest—up to $20,000—if you can pass five AP exams. Seen in those terms, it's well worth investing $100 or so in resources from ETS and other sources that can help you achieve AP success.

"This volume can be a useful supplement to classwork and study materials." Once again, Barron's marketing department pours on the charm.

Barron's AP offerings are notably more meager than other publishers, including only the following books:

- *Biology,* 5th edition ($13.95)
- *Calculus,* 6th edition ($14.95)
- *Chemistry,* 2nd edition ($14.95)
- *English,* 6th edition ($13.95)
- *European History,* 2nd edition ($12.95)
- *French* ($24.95)
- *Physics B,* 2nd edition ($14.95)
- *Spanish,* 2nd edition (book & cassette package, $24.95)
- *Statistics,* 1st edition ($14.95)
- *United States Government and Politics,* 2nd edition ($14.95)
- *United States History,* 5th edition ($13.95)

Each of these attempts to systematically introduce the subject, bring you up to speed on the necessary study skills, introduce you to the AP exam in question, and review the skills and content covered in the exam. You also get a model AP exam, with *brief* explanatory answers. Basically personality-free, these books should be very comforting to those who are used to textbooks and who mistrust the "wilder" types of prep books. *Mary Pride*

You tell me if this sounds like the "best" way to prepare for the AP test. First, the **Best Test Preparation** book describes the test. Next, it teaches every bit of knowledge that will be tested. No practice exercises are included during the instructional part. Several practice tests are at the end of each book, (e.g., four at the end of the *Computer Science* book, three for *European History*) with answer keys and detailed explanations. If two levels of a test are available (e.g., Calculus AB and Calculus BC), there are two practice tests for each test level.

The publisher is proud of these practice tests. According to it,

Unlike most Test Preparation books that present only a few practice tests which bear little resemblance to the actual exams, REA's series presents tests which accurately depict the official exams in both degree of difficulty and types of questions. REA's practice tests are always based upon the most recently administered exams, and include every type of question that can be expected on the actual exams.

Should we be impressed? Probably not. It may have been true years ago, when REA was about the only player in the AP market, that "most Test Preparation books" weren't careful about mirroring the actual exams, but every AP series I reviewed for this book went out of its way to present every question type and have accurate tests. Many now have features REA

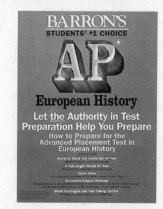

Their new REA Testware Software, which comes on separate diskettes for Macintosh and Windows, both bound into the back of the book, livens things up a bit. It includes three full-length, timed practice AP tests, with computerized scoring that reveals your strong and weak points. If you use this series, I'd definitely go for the book/software combination.

doesn't, such as diagnostic pre-tests, lots of graphics, in-depth strategy tips, and so forth.

Available AP test books in this series:

- Biology
- Calculus AB & Calculus BC
- Chemistry
- Computer Science
- English Language & Composition
- English Literature & Composition

- European History
- Government & Politics
- Physics
- Psychology
- Spanish (includes two cassettes)
- United States History

These aren't exciting books, falling mostly into the "refresher course plus practice test" category. However, for some of the AP tests, REA's offerings are about all you'll find on store shelves, so you're pretty much stuck with them. *Mary Pride*

Schlepp to the CLEP

Yet another "test instrument" from Educational Testing Service and the College Board is the College-Level Examination Program, or CLEP. This was originally developed with older adults in mind, who wanted to earn college credit for what they had learned through independent study or "on the job." Other uses for a test series that determined if an individual had mastered course content then became apparent:

- When a student transfers from a local two-year college, to help the four-year college determine which courses he took are worthy of credit
- To help determine which courses from unaccredited institutions may be accepted for credit at an accredited institution
- In government circles, to demonstrate an applicant has mastered necessary knowledge needed for a position or promotion

For homeschoolers, the main value of CLEP tests is probably

- If you're one of the many homeschoolers to take community college courses at a young age, good CLEP scores will help ensure you get proper credit when you switch to a four-year college
- If you took high school entirely at home, and the college you want to attend accepts good CLEP scores in place of introductory courses, or if you did advanced work at home, and for some reason you prefer the CLEP to the AP tests

The CLEP General Examinations Battery consists of five subject area tests, as outlined below: English Composition, Humanities, Mathematics, Natural Sciences, and Social Sciences & History. You don't have to take all five, and in fact you should only do so if your intended college will grant credit in all five areas. Each test covers the general skills and knowledge you are expected to gain as a result of taking introductory "core"-type college courses in that area. See the chart on page 474 for details.

Again, I *strongly* urge you to get a book on what the exam battery is and how to take it. In my searches, I only found one such book; it is reviewed below.

Friends and fellow pilgrims, on a journey through out local Border's bookstore, where tens of thousands of square feet are devoted to displaying just about any book you can conceivably want, turned up only *one* book written to help you succeed at the College Level Examination Program (CLEP) tests. This one.

The good news is that this book is all you probably need. Starting with the obligatory "What on earth is the CLEP" and "What will this book do for me?" chapters, **Barron's How to Prepare for the CLEP** segues quickly into five sections, one for each of the five CLEP General Examinations in English composition, humanities, mathematics, natural sciences, and social sciences/history. Each of these sections follows the same format:

- A pre-test (here called a "trial test") with answer key, scoring chart, and answer explanations
- Test description
- Study sources (books you can use to teach yourself the subject material)
- Bare-bones teaching as follows: a couple of sentences or a paragraph explaining each skill or concept followed by a couple of examples, bunches of practice questions, answers, and (sometimes) explanations
- Four practice exams in each subject, for a total of 20 practice exams in all, each with answer key, scoring chart, and explanations

The price is more than reasonable, for over 750 pages of preparation and the chance to save thousands of dollars on your college tuition costs. *Mary Pride*

Too late to review it for this edition, I just found out about **Cracking the CLEP**. This brand-new book will undoubtedly have a looser, more hip feel than the one reviewed above, considering its source. It includes one sample test for each of the five general exams; subject area reviews; and an array of Princeton Review's famous "cracking" strategies that "help you earn points even when you don't know the answer" (!). Your bookstore should have both this and the book above—check them out! *Mary Pride*

NEW!
Barron's How to Prepare for the CLEP (8th edition)
Grade 11–college. $14.95 plus $4.95 shipping.
Barron's Educational Series, Inc., 250 Wireless Blvd., Hauppauge, NY 11788. (800) 645-3476. Fax: (516) 434-3217. Web: www.barronseduc.com.

NEW!
Princeton Review Cracking the CLEP, 1999
Grade 11–college. $20 plus shipping.
Princeton Review, Random House, 400 Hahan Rd., Westminster, MD 21157. (800) 733-3000. They prefer you to order from bookstores. Web: www.randomhouse.com.

Contents of CLEP General Examinations Battery

From *How to Prepare for the CLEP*, 7th edition

(NOTE: Percentages are approximate in every instance and may vary from test to test.)

Test	Section	Content Or Item Types		Time/Number Of Questions
English Composition				
	I	35–40%	Usage	45 minutes
		35–40%	Sentence Correction	55 questions
		25–30%	Paragraph Revising	
	II	60–65%	Paragraph Revising and Analysis	45 minutes
	(All-Multiple-Choice Version)	35–40%	Construction Shift, Sentence Correction	45 questions
	II		Written Composition	45 minutes
	(Essay Version)			
Humanities				
	I & II	50%	Literature	45 minutes each section
		10%	Drama	75 questions each section
		15–20%	Poetry	
		10–15%	Fiction	
		10%	Nonfiction	
		50%	Fine Arts	
		20%	Visual Arts (painting, sculpture, etc.)	
		15%	Music	
		10%	Performing Arts (film, dance, etc.)	
		5%	Architecture	

Note: On the Humanities examination, questions from all 8 categories are mixed together.

Test	Section	Content Or Item Types		Time/Number Of Questions
Mathematics				
	I	30%	Arithmetic	30 minutes
	(Basic Skills and Concepts)	35%	Algebra	40 questions
		15–20%	Geometry	
		15–20%	Data Interpretation (graphs and charts)	
	II	10%	Sets	60 minutes
	(Content)	10%	Logic	50 questions
		30%	Real Number System	
		20%	Functions and Their Graphs	
		15%	Probability and Statistics	
		15%	Miscellaneous Topics	

Test	Section	Content Or Item Types		Time/Number Of Questions
Natural Sciences				
	I	50%	Biological Science	45 minutes
		10%	Origin and evolution of life, classification of organisms	60 questions
		10%	Cell organization, cell division, chemical nature of the gene, bioenergetics, biosynthesis	
		20%	Structure, function, and development in organisms; patterns of heredity	
		10%	Concepts of population biology with emphasis on ecology	
	II	50%	Physical Science	45 minutes
		7%	Atomic and nuclear structure and properties, elementary particles, nuclear reactions	60 questions
		10%	Chemical elements, compounds and reactions; molecular structure and bonding	
		12%	Heat, thermodynamics, and states of matter; classical mechanics; relativity	
		4%	Electricity and magnetism, waves, light and sound	
		7%	The Universe: galaxies, stars, the solar system	
		10%	The Earth: atmosphere, hydrosphere, structure, properties, surface features, geological processes, history	

Test	Section	Content Or Item Types		Time/Number Of Questions
Social Sciences and History				
	I & II	35%	History	45 minutes each section
		10–15%	United States History	60-65 questions each section
		10–15%	Western Civilization	
		5–10%	African/Asian Civilizations	
		65%	Social Science	
		25–30%	Sociology	
		15–20%	Economics	
		15–20%	Political Science	
		3–5%	Social Psychology	

Note: On the Social Sciences and History examination, questions from all 7 categories are mixed together.

PART 10

College & Alternatives

Aric Arduini graduated from Ark Academy, a private/home school in Chicago, at age 18. Aric had been taught at home since second grade. He subsequently was awarded a Harold Washington Academic Achievement Scholarship to Richard J. Daley College in Chicago. Aric went on to attend De Paul University, where he's a student in the College of Liberal Arts and Sciences. Aric is an art major with a graphic design focus.

Brandon Geist is studying at Princeton University, where he's involved in activities that include acting in the theater, writing for the college newspaper, and running programs for the radio station. His present success is no surprise, considering that as a 12th-grade homeschooled student from Schwenksville, PA, he won a Shakespeare recitation competition. Representing the Delaware Valley Homeschoolers, Brandon competed against 33 other Philadelphia-area high-school winners. He won a $500 scholarship and an expense-paid trip to New York City to attend the National Shakespeare Competition, where he faced 54 other regional winners.

CHAPTER 49

Choosing a College or Career

"What do you want to be when you grow up?"
How many times have you been asked that question?
Now you finally have to make that decision.

Why? Because picking the right career direction should come *before* picking a college or college alternative.

Today, the typical college student struggles through six or more years of college before getting a degree that may or may not lead to a job at work he may or may not enjoy. Why this clueless bumbling? Because of poor or nonexistent career planning. Picking the wrong major, then switching once or twice to new majors, is enough to rack up two extra years of college without even trying. Picking the wrong career can lead to distress, poverty, and a wasted life spent failing at a job you hate when you could be succeeding at a job you like. Worst of all, you'll miss out on your chance to change the world for the better.

Most Christian young people go off to college with no mission, no focus, no goal for their lives. What a surprise that when you have no direction, and someone else is paying the bills, you end up just wanting to have a good time and to fit in. What a surprise that when you are just trying to have a good time and fit in, you quietly lose your commitment to living a Christian life. This happens to 80 percent or more of Christian kids when they go to college.

So I have to ask it: what was your main reason for homeschooling your kids in the first place? Was it to raise them as Christians? As people who would make a difference? Then don't you owe it to your young "arrows" (Psalm 127) to help them find the right target to aim at? Finding the right career target is something that should interest *every* parent, Christian or not.

Yet most teens today have received little or no preparation for making genuine career choices.

This is an area where homeschoolers need to surpass the public schools, or all our good work may go for nothing. The consequences of choosing

Why College is Not Always the Best Choice

It is hard not to conclude that too much undergraduate education is little more than secondary school material—warmed over and reoffered at much higher expense, but not at correspondingly higher levels of effectiveness . . .

Half of those entering college full-time do not have a degree within five years.

—An American Imperative: Higher Expectations for Higher Education, Report of the Wingspread Group on Higher Education

the wrong career range from distressing to disastrous. This waste of time, hope, and money is all unnecessary. With prayer, an understanding that a vocation is a calling from God suited to your exact talents and desires (and not just a choice based on personal whims, ambition, or greed), and the help of the resources in this chapter, you can be an arrow that hits the target.

Finding Your Calling

How would you like to graduate college in four years or less, and go straight into the job ideally suited for you? Think it's going to happen automatically? Think again!

Life Pathways can just possibly save your kids from years or even a lifetime of drifting, if you're willing to invest two hours of time and around $100 (or less if you can get a group together: see sidebar on next page). As a division of Larry Burkett's organization, Christian Financial Concepts (see review elsewhere in this volume), they have available a **CareerDirect Assessment** package for high-school and college students and adults. For students, the goal is picking the right college major. For adults, it's the right career. The materials mention God and faith, but I can't see anything that should frighten a non-Christian away from using them. The approach is refreshingly straightforward and free of psychological head games.

Here's what you fill out:

- **Questionnaire**, designed to help you evaluate where you are right now and what your goals are, in which you write out sentence answers to the questions
- **Personality Inventory**, in which you rate yourself from 1 ("not like me") to 5 ("very much like me") on a list of 116 personality traits and 24 financial behaviors. Personality traits include such things as *quiet*, *precise*, and *warm-hearted*. The financial behaviors section is optional, and includes such things as "I pay my bills on time" and "I have bounced a number of checks." This is a familiar fill-in-the-ovals type of machine-scorable form.
- **Interests, Skills, & Values Inventory** is longer. In its 12 machine-scorable pages you rate how much you like or dislike 192 activities, e.g., "Interact with people from different cultures" and "Compete, using athletic skills." You then rate how much you like 18 subject clusters and 98 occupations. You rate yourself on your ability to perform 74 skills (e.g., *typing* and *illustrating*), and your values and preferences for work environment, work expectations, and life values.

A postage-paid envelope is provided for you to send all this in. And here's what you get back:

- **Personality Inventory Report** After an introduction to the personality traits profiled, you are given extensive evaluation of where you stand on the following six ranges of traits: complaint/dominant, cautious/adventurous, introverted/extroverted, detached/compassionate, unstructured/conscientious, and conventional/innovative. Your composite score for each range is shown on a bar, along with a two- to three-paragraph description of what this score means for what "work style" is best for you. In addition, you get a page each of "Typical Strengths" and "Typical Weaknesses" of people who score like you. This is all brought together in a page of "Career Implications"—specific recommendations for choosing a work environment to match your personali-

NEW!
CareerDirect Assessment Youth Exploration Survey
Grade 9–adult (CareerDirect), age 10–16 (Youth Exploration Survey). CareerDirect Assessment or Student Assessment paper version, $99 each. CD-ROM version (requires a Pentium processor with Windows 95/98, 16 MB hard disk space available, 1 MB video memory, printer, and sound card), $89. Additional administration via CD-ROM, plus Action Pack, $15. Institutional version CD-ROM, $399; 5 Action Packs, $30. Self-study training course, $195. Youth Exploration Survey, $29.95. YES Leader's Guide, $14.95. Shipping extra.
Life Pathways, division of Christian Financial Concepts, 601 Broad St., S.E., Gainesville, GA 30501-3729. (800) 722-1976. Fax: (770) 503-9447. Web: www.cfcministry.org.

ty strengths. The last page gives you a score on "Critical Life Issues": stress (where you fall on a range of low stress to high stress), indebtedness, and financial management (sound versus unsound).

- **Interests, Skills, & Values Inventory Report** The introduction explains how to use the report, and lists 20 possible career areas under five major headings: Doing, Helping, Influencing, Analyzing, and Expressing. A bar graph then shows how you scored from low to high interest, on a scale of 20 to 80, on each of the 20 areas. Next, you are given detailed information about your areas of highest interest. Your general-interest scores follow, breaking down the specific areas of highest interest *within* your general interest areas. For example, if you score high interest in consumer science, you may have more or less interest within the specific activities of *food* and *styling,* the specific occupations of *fashion* and *home economics,* and the specific subjects of *home economics* and *domesticity.* Your next set of scores covers three separate reports: Activity Factors, Occupations Factors, and Subject Factors. Each is graduated from the highest-scored activity, occupation, or school subject to the lowest-scored. Following is some helpful information on how to take advantage of knowing what your *lowest* interests are. Now we get to the skills ranking, summarized into 12 categories: artistic, clerical, musical, interpersonal, organizing, analytical/math, cross-cultural, mechanical, persuasive communication, relating to others, marketing, and athletic. Again, your top five categories are analyzed in detail. Your weakest skills are also analyzed. The final section helps you see your own priorities when it comes to choosing a congenial work environment and achieving your life goals.
- **CareerDirect Action Plan** This is a set of pointed questions for you to answer, according to what you've discovered from the other reports. You are led to analyze the results, uncovering the motivations that caused you to choose your highest interest areas, and the common skills that make up your greatest strengths. Matching your skills to your interests should now lead you to determining an optimal career path.
- **CareerDirect Job Sampler**, listing over 800 jobs by career groupings tied to the reports
- **Your choice of career planning guides**—either *The PathFinder,* a 124-page manual for workers looking to find the ideal career or the *Guide to College Majors and Career Choices,* a 180-page book for students

To test this service, my husband Bill, our three oldest children, and I all went through the evaluation process. There were some surprises! I'm way more outdoorsy than anyone realized (true, I spend days at a time in front of a computer, but that doesn't mean I *like* it!). It's too late to become a forest ranger, but at least I can be sure to plant a garden this year, instead of skipping it because other projects are "more important." Other than that, it turns out that what I'm already doing is a good fit for my skills and interests—which in turn shows that the testing process is pretty accurate. If Bill does end up pursuing a Ph.D., we now know the exact field that's a perfect fit—and we also now know why Bill, who's at the top of the chart in both "mechanical" and "technical" skills and interests, can't stop tinkering with any tech-support problem that comes his way. Son Ted, who wants to start his own business, pegged out tops in management and sales skills and interests. Maybe the kid knows what he's talking about! The other kids' results have already led to some very helpful narrowing down of college and career choices.

To help you further evaluate the results, you can purchase up to two hours of personalized consulting from a specially trained career consultant, available by phone, fax, or email, for $199. For further savings, "group coaching" and seminars are available. Contact CareerNet, PO Box 270503, Flower Mound, TX 75027-0503. Orders: (888)-478-8880. Inquiries: (972) 783-3475. Fax: (972) 539-4396. Email: careered@gte.net.

If your support group or Christian school is interested, an "institutional" CD-ROM edition of CareerDirect is available. This offers unlimited use for a year, so you can do dozens or even hundreds of assessments. To accompany this, sets of five Action Packs are available. So, if you have 40 kids who want assessments, it would work out to $10 per kid for the CD-ROM use, and $6 apiece for the Action Pack. Not a bad price!

A self-study training course, leading to certification as a Career Direction Associate, is also available. This is a relatively inexpensive way to become an "instant" guidance counselor for your support group or Christian school.

A **CD-ROM edition** is now available. This comes in a very nice binder, with all the following:

- Three audiocassettes containing the following messages: *Understanding Your God-Given Design, Principles of Career Fulfillment, How to Get the Best Results from CareerDirect, Action Plan to Your Future,* and *Special Message to Parents.*
- "Choosing a College/Technical School Major," a four-page pamphlet
- Questionnaire
- CareerDirect Action Plan
- CareerDirect Job Sampler
- *Guide to College Majors and Career Choices*

These last four items are the same as those that you get with the paper edition.

Benefits of the CD-ROM edition: instant feedback with printable reports and less initial cost. If you have a Pentium, you'll probably want this version.

The CD-ROM edition comes set up for use with one person. To use with an additional person, you have to contact CareerDirect and pay an additional $15. This also entitles you to receive an additional Action Pack, consisting of an additional copy each of the "Action Plan" booklet, "Career & Education Planning" questionnaire, and "Choosing a College Major" pamphlet.

For younger children, the **Youth Exploration Survey** (YES for short) is available. The publisher recommends it for ages 13–16, but if your preteen is a good reader and has reached the analytical stage, you could go as low as age 10. This comes with:

Leaders' Guide

- A parent's guide entitled *Unfolding Your Child*
- The *YES! Passport,* a booklet in which you record the results of "your extreme career and education journey"
- The *YES! Survey* itself, an oversized four-color book studded with colorful cartoons and complete with "Personality Trait" symbol stickers

The personality traits in question are Adventurer, Commander, Creator, Encourager, Entertainer, and Organizer. The Survey takes you through discovering your personality style, interests, abilities, and priorities, followed by a career evaluation process, defining your life purpose, and a job sampler.

The *YES! Leader's Guide* is helpful, especially when conducting the Youth Exploration Survey with a group. It was initially designed with this in mind, and is much more fun for the students done this way.

With the CareerDirect Assessment and Youth Exploration Survey, you can fine-tune your plans to avoid wasting years in the wrong college, college major, or job. That's certainly worth a hundred bucks or two, isn't it? I'm impressed, and would recommend this service to anyone facing a college or career decision. In fact, I have already recommended it to my brother, who's in film school, to help him decide which of the many careers in film production is best for him. *Mary Pride*

NEW!
Ferguson What Can I Do NOW? series
Grades 7–12. Each hardbound volume, $16.95. Set of all 8, $119.95. Shipping extra.

You know what career you want. That's good—it will save you a lot of time and money later on. But did you know you can start preparing for it as early as junior high?

That's the premise behind Ferguson Publishing's brand new **What Can I Do NOW? series**. Two-color throughout, each volume gives you full details on the career field it covers, as well as on 6–10 specific careers within that field. You find out what a radio or TV anchor (for instance) does for a living, what the job is like in the words of someone in that job, personal characteristics you need to succeed in that job, steps to take to get into that job, advancement possibilities, salary expectations, related

jobs, and fun facts, such as the top 25 markets for TV anchors. So far, not so unusual. But look at what else you get:

- Ways to get involved in that field—volunteering, internships, summer camps, summer study opportunities
- Ways to get a head start—hobbies, clubs, museum visits, summer jobs
- Books and magazines that can prepare you well for success that field, with descriptions of each—for example, the best book to prepare you for taking the police officer exam, or one about backstage intrigue in the television field
- Web sites about that field, with descriptions of each
- Scholarships in that field, with full contact information so you can apply
- Professional organizations in that field

The series has one volume each for engineering, journalism, nursing, the environment, radio and TV, sports, travel and hospitality, and public safety (this last category is about careers such as firefighting and FBI, not OSHA inspectors). Each of these books is fascinating reading, filled with facts about each career that I never knew. The books, magazines, web sites, and other resources are not only well chosen, but clearly hand-picked from a much larger list as the best available. I'm especially sensitive to this last point, because so many "resource" books are crammed with lists obviously constructed during an afternoon library trip.

If your student has an interest in a particular area, but is not sure about it or can't narrow it down to a particular career, the volume about that career area would be a good investment. The entire set would be a fitting purchase for a support group library—and with the durable library-quality bindings, it will stand a lot of use. Recommended. *Mary Pride*

Should your teens consider full-time Christian service? **Vision of Glory**, a six-lesson teaching series designed for Sunday school classes, urges young people to consider whether God is calling them to serve Him in the ministry. A videotape, student workbook, and teacher's guide help teach young people about the following min-

istries: missionary work, the preaching ministry of a pastor, the shepherding ministry of a pastor, children's ministry, youth ministry, and Christian camps. These lessons are quite in-depth. It would require two weeks to cover all of the material adequately. Even those who are not interested in a specific ministry would learn much of value.

Ferguson Publishing Company, 200 West Madison St., Suite 300, Chicago, IL 60606. (800) 306-9941. Fax: (800) 306-9942. Email: fergpub@aol.com. Web: www.fergpubco.com.

NEW!
Vision of Glory
Grades 9–12. $53.95 plus shipping. *Bob Jones University Press Customer Services, Greenville, SC 29614. Orders: (800) 845-5731. Fax: (800) 525-8398. Web: www.bjup.com.*

My husband and I enjoyed the conservative nature of the video. There was no question that only men are called to be pastors. The Word of God was emphasized as sufficient, authoritative, infallible, etc. Everyone looked so wholesome—even the class troublemaker in the youth group! This course gives a wonderful Bible-based vision for what ministry can and should be.

Support groups might consider this resource for their libraries. Church members, even well beyond the teen years, could benefit from the materials. *Rebecca Prewett*

Finding the Right College

Good colleges do exist. By "good" I mean "still dedicated to quality education rather than to trendy political and social goals." Good departments also can be found buried in less-than-perfect institutions. Here are some tools to help you find the ivy-covered campus of your dreams.

Barron's Profiles of American Colleges defines the word "hefty." At 1,600 pages and 2¾ inches thick, this one is going head-to-head with the *Peterson's Guide to Four-Year Colleges* (see review later in this chapter).

The 23rd edition contains white pages with profiles of over 1,650 schools, blue pages with lists by major of schools with that major, diskettes for both Windows and Macintosh (more about that later), and "Barron's exclusive rating system" that ranks colleges according to degree of academic competitiveness (Most Competitive, Highly Competitive, Very Competitive, Competitive, and Noncompetitive).

The book opens with an introduction to college: knowing yourself, finding the right college, scoring high on entrance exams, getting in, finding the money, and surviving the freshman year. The advice and information provided is excellent, particularly the section on identifying your college goals and how you can use this book to find colleges that fulfill those goals.

I found this book's individual entries to be more helpful than Peterson's. You find out what exactly the admissions officers are looking for (leadership? extracurricular? service? grades?), visiting procedures, and more, as well as what is covered in Peterson's. Instead of separate in-depth profiles of selected schools, as in Peterson's, all schools are covered with slightly more detail. I found the Barron's typeface much harder to look at for longer periods, though.

The included Macintosh and Windows diskettes contain computerized forms you can fill out for college applications, as well as brief profiles of all schools listed in the book. This is a lot less than you get on the Peterson's software, if that influences your decision. *Mary Pride*

Concerned about the future of your college-bound child? Not sure about what to do for college? Do not wait until the last minute. I strongly recommend that parents and children start early in researching colleges.

Choosing the Right College breaks down the top 100 colleges in an orderly fashion. Each college listed contains the school's postal and email address, total student enrollment, SAT ranges, number of applicants, application deadline, financial aid deadline, tuition, and core curriculum. This information is followed by a lengthy description about the school. Reading these descriptions was an eye-opening experience. My son is in tenth grade and we have already begun researching colleges, but in many cases all you can find about a particular college comes from sources published by the college.

This book is a brave undertaking because it definitely informs the parent about the politically-correct schools. I was amazed and embarrassed by some of the required courses at many of the top schools in our country. This book also talks about several not-so-politically-correct schools, which

NEW!
Barron's Profiles of American Colleges, 23rd (1999) edition
Grades 9–12. $25.
*Barron's Educational Series, Inc., 250 Wireless Blvd., Hauppauge, NY 11788. (800) 645-3476.
Fax: (516) 434-3217.
Web: www.barronseduc.com.*

NEW!
Choosing the Right College
Grades 9–12. $25 postpaid.
*Wm. B. Eerdmans Books for Young Readers, 255 Jefferson Ave. S.E., Grand Rapids, MI 49503. (800) 253-7521. Fax: (616) 459-6540.
Email: sales@eerdmans.com.*

was very reassuring. After homeschooling a child, whether for one year or several, you want the best for your child and you want the best education for the child that fits into their philosophy. Books like this really help.

Choosing the Right College is definitely not your run-of-the-mill college guide. It is written from a conservative slant and I appreciate the directness and information listed. During our homeschooling years money is tight and purchases must be carefully considered. I strongly recommend this book for those considering college. An excellent choice for parents who are concerned about their child's character and the quality of the child's education, instead of just the college credentials. *Michele Fitzgerald*

If you absolutely can't live without a college experience, ACT's 1999–2000 **College Planning/Search Book** is an excellent place to start. The Planning Section helps you decide what you're looking for in a college, and guides you through the application process. The Search Section displays up-to-date information about more than 3,000 colleges in several helpful ways. You can, for example, look up schools that offer Forestry, or colleges in Wisconsin, or the student profile of St. Louis U. Vital facts such as cost, religious affiliation, and composition of student body are laid out straightforwardly. *Mary Pride*

The National Review College Guide by Charles Sykes and Brad Minor actually tells the student where he should go to college—that is if he wants an education, not just a degree. The guide consists of four sections. Section 1, a preface, outlines the authors' philosophy and the three criteria by which they judged colleges. The criteria are: (1) a strong required liberal arts core, (2) a qualified and available faculty, and (3) an environment that values academic freedom and true educational experiences. Section 2 critiques 58 colleges which passed the three criteria. Some Christian schools are included. Section 3 tells why most big name schools didn't cut it, and Section 4 tells you how to get a decent education wherever you go.

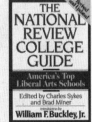

This is not a "quantitative" guide like the elephantine tomes at the high school counselor's office. The only stats for each school are its year founded, total cost (room, board, tuition, etc.), total enrollment, total applicants (including percent accepted and percent of those that graduate), SAT averages, financial aid (percent who apply and get it), and whether or not the college has a ROTC program. Addresses and enrollment schedule are of course also provided.

Aside from that, the book is made up mainly of insightful reviews of the institutions themselves: their histories, core curriculums (described in detail), religious and social atmosphere, special programs (such as student years abroad), and any current power struggles agitating the faculty and administration. The authors, university insiders, know if a liberal coup is in the offing or has just been foiled, giving you clues to the future of each institution as well as to its past.

Remember, we're talking about liberal arts colleges. Many of these colleges are strong in science and math, though, and all of them have at least some courses in those areas. Some even have arrangements with affiliated engineering colleges, so don't skip this book just because you're technically oriented.

Bible institutes are not included, although Wheaton, Baylor, and a whole group of Roman Catholic institutions made it in. The editors' definition of "sectarian" also somehow allows them to include Brigham Young University while leaving out Bob Jones University (whose graduates also have impressive records).

College Planning/Search Book

Grades 9–12. $10 postpaid.
American College Testing Program (ACT), 2727 Scott Blvd., PO Box 1008, Iowa City, IA 52243. (800) 498-6065. Fax: (319) 337-1578. Web: www.act.org.

NEW!
The National Review College Guide

Grades 9–12. $13 plus shipping.
Simon & Schuster, Att: Order Dept., 200 Old Tappan Rd., Old Tappan, NJ 07675. (800) 223-2348 ext. 6. (800) 445-6991. Web: www.simonsays.com.

The reason why "many religious schools are missing from NR's recommended list" is that "although these schools are conservative, they fail effectively to educate their students in the full spirit of academic freedom." Another reason: many Christian colleges are more strongly vocational than the liberal arts schools the guide intends to profile. Yet another reason: students who wish to attend a Christian school presumably find it easy to discover those schools, thanks to knowledgeable pastors.

The updated edition of the *National Review College Guide* not only lists over 50 schools worthy of attendance, it also lists 12 highly-esteemed schools to avoid if you're looking for an education, not just a degree.

This guide is valuable reading (or should we say "valuable browsing"?) for anyone looking for a traditional liberal-arts education. *Charles & Betty Burger and Mary Pride*

NEW!
Peterson's Guide to Four-Year Colleges, 2000 Edition

Grades 10–12. $24.95.
Peterson's, PO Box 2123, Princeton, NJ 08543-2123. (800) 338-3282. Fax: (609) 452-0966.
Email: custsvc@petersons.com.
Web: www.petersons.com.

This tome of over 3,200 pages, suitable for use as a child's booster seat, is the Big Daddy of college reference books. More than 2,000 schools are represented here.

If you're looking for "pretty," this isn't your book. Small print and a two-column format, all on paper just one step up from newsprint, give **Peterson's Guide to Four-Year Colleges** a real "phone book" feel. But if you're looking for *information*—busloads of information covering just about anywhere you could possibly think of going—this book is The One.

In the beige pages you'll find introductory advice on how colleges differ from each other, how to narrow your list (important when you have so many to choose from!), how to survive standardized tests, information on military and ROTC opportunities, a tiny bit on admissions and financial aid, and short profiles of over 2,000 colleges. In the yellow pages are an Entrance Difficulty Index, a Cost Range Index, a Majors Index, college index in alphabetical order, and geographical index of the in-depth college descriptions. The white pages include detailed two-page descriptions of over 1,000 of the colleges *written by college officials*. Oddly, some of the "top 311" colleges listed in Peterson's book by that name aren't included among these. The mystery is solved when you realize that submitting information to this guide is *voluntary*, and apparently some college officials just don't get around to it every year. Included on the companion CD-ROM is Peterson's *College Quest* software, which allows you to quickly search Peterson's web site for colleges meeting your criteria. A good first book to start with, to discover all your options before you start narrowing them down to a few schools. *Mary Pride*

Additional software on the CD-ROM: SAT and ACT prep tests with computerized scoring, a sample of Peterson's new Custom Campus video visit program, the college financial planner *Keyscape*, all the in-depth descriptions in the book, and more.

NEW!
Peterson's Guide to Christian Colleges

Grades 10–12. $14.95.
Peterson's, PO Box 2123, Princeton, NJ 08543-2123. (800) 338-3282. Fax: (609) 452-0966.
Email: custsvc@petersons.com.
Web: www.petersons.com.

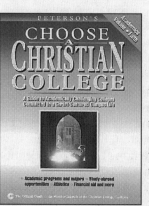

Straight up I'll tell you, if the college of your dreams isn't a member of the Christian College Coalition, it won't be in this book. This means that Bob Jones University and Pensacola Christian College (home of A Beka Books) aren't included, among many others in **Peterson's Guide to Christian Colleges**. I mention this, not because I have a "thing" for those two institutions (which I don't), but because both are prominent in homeschool circles due to their popular K–12 curricula.

What you get: Over 80 detailed college profiles, plus a map showing where all the member colleges are located, a listing by state, various indexes (by major, by athletics, by graduate majors, and by overseas study programs), reasons to choose a Christian college, and information on special programs available through these affiliated colleges, such as Oxford summer studies, Middle East studies, Los Angeles Film Study Center, and so forth. The "detailed college profiles" contain about the same information as you would find in one of the bigger Peterson's guides, plus a scattering of photos. Invaluable if you want a college that's a member of the Coalition; less useful if you want to cast your net more widely. *Mary Pride*

Why would you want to get a book that's called **The Best 311 Colleges**, instead of one of the guides that tries to review just about every college? For one thing, it's based on what 56,000 students say about their colleges. For another, you get "insider" information on how hard it *really* is to get into each college, and *all* the financial-aid options for each college. Lots of indexes: college counselors, learning-disabled programs, schools, and schools by state. An unusual 16 pages entitled "My Roommate's Feet Really Stink" with excerpts from the "wittiest, pithiest, and most outrageous free-form essays" contributed by the students interviewed for this book. The kids mostly natter about their schools, so you find out that St. John's students are called "Johnnies," and similar bits of trivia.

The bulk of the book is devoted to two-page writeups of the "best 311 colleges," with statistics in the margin. In keeping with the book's emphasis on what students think, categories such as "What's Hot" and "What's Not" are included, as well as useful information such as the *other* colleges that applicants look at and sometimes, rarely, or often prefer to *this* one. Male/female rations, financial-aid statistics, Quality of Life and Academic ratings, application dates, a short list of "most popular" majors, and much more is attractively displayed in grey sidebars, while a student's-eye view of each school's life, academics, and students takes up the rest of one page and admissions and financial-aid requirements take up the other page.

I found the writeups to be both funny and right on the button, for schools with which I and people I know have had experience. A very good book if you're in the running for a "top college" education. *Mary Pride*

Is lack of money a looming obstacle to your college plans? Then you might want to invest in **America's 100 Best College Buys**.

Keep in mind that, if your grades and extracurriculars are great enough, or you have a desired ethnic or racial background along with above-average academics, many expensive schools are willing to craft a financial-aid package that may lower the cost of attendance to your price bracket. Community colleges all cost less than the colleges profiled in this book. And military academies are free (*if* you can get in and *if* you don't mind serving your country for five years in exchange). But if you can't claim outstanding status, you don't want to attend community college, and the thought of trying for a college where room and board plus tuition can run $20,000–$30,000 a year scares you to death, this book could be just what you're looking for.

This year, 1,658 four-year colleges were considered. To be chosen one of the "100 Best Buys," a college had to be accredited, offer full residential facilities and dining services, offer need/academic/athletic-based financial aid, have an entering freshmen class in the fall of 1996 with academics *above* the national average, and have a cost of attendance in 1997–98 *below* the national average.

Each college profile is a two-page spread, including statistics, photos of the school and/or its students, and a friendly writeup of the school's personality and history. Each college's profile includes a list of the most popular majors.

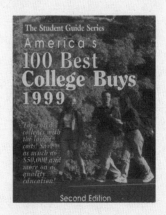

An index of colleges by major in the back makes it even easier for you to determine which colleges in this book offer the majors that interest you.

Typically, attending one of these institutions for a year costs from $6,000 (in-state cost at an included state university) to $11,000–$13,000 (out-of-state cost at a state university, or full cost at a private university). The cost includes room and board, tuition, and fees. It would be entirely possible to live at home, work for a year or two, and save the entire cost of your education at one of these institutions. Of course, that may not be necessary, since just like the more expensive schools, they offer scholarships and grants, and most students receive some form of financial aid.

Checking the profiles of the colleges with which I am somewhat familiar, the information was accurate and helpful. Clearly a book worth checking out. *Mary Pride*

I have to confess, I grabbed for **The Totally Usable Summit Ministries Guide to Choosing a College** the minute it hit our office. Summit Ministries is famed for their worldview-training seminars and courses, designed to help Christian teens survive the college maelstrom with their faith intact. With their years of experience in dealing with college fears and fallout, I was eager to see what kind of college advice Summit had to offer.

The book's outlook can best be shown by the following direct quote:

> *College professors claim to be teaching their students truth—the truth about reality, about the way things work. If no absolute truth exists, any professor's version of the truth is just as good as any other's (and so which college you choose is simply a matter of taste). But the Christian realizes that absolute truth does exist, and college may be more or less "in line" with that truth. For the Christian, truth matters. And so choosing the school that will teach you truth matters.*

Right off the bat we discover that Christian colleges are not necessarily the safe haven many parents fondly believe them to be. The 192-page book opens with one of the authors describing his bizarre experiences in a *required* class on feminism the Christian college he attended forced him to take. His experience was not all that unusual, as it turns out, since most Christian colleges and universities today have strayed some distance from their founders' original intentions.

More on this in a minute. But first, what is this book about?

The Summit Ministries Guide to Choosing a College takes you from having no clue as to which college to attend, to narrowing it down to a small list, to picking a favorite. The book provides methods for picking colleges to examine more closely, and tells you how to get the facts you need to check them out. Naturally, the pros and cons of Christian versus secular colleges are covered. So are the current wrong worldviews that are popular on campus, from deconstructionism to four varieties of Marxism, including "chameleon Marxism." (In case you're wondering, the latter is not an appeal to chameleons of the world to unite. Rather, it's a mindset bent on portraying history as a constant battle between the oppressed and the oppressor, with special attention to disregarding or distorting any evidence to the contrary.)

If you're looking for lists of specific recommendations, you'll be disappointed. The authors refer to a dozen or so politically-correct institutions by name, but vouch by name only for Hillsdale College, Bryan College, and Liberty University. That doesn't mean they're trying to track you into one of these three schools, as they themselves are quick to say. They just didn't want to get caught up in publishing 1,000 pages of warnings about individual professors, departments, and administrations—for, according to

NEW!
The Totally Usable Summit Ministries Guide to Choosing a College
Grades 10–12. $8.95
Summit Ministries, PO Box 207, Manitou Springs, CO 80829.
(719) 685-9103. Fax: (719) 685-5268.
Email: info@summit.org.
Web: www.summit.org.

them, the vast majority of Christian colleges and universities would in fact deserve to be tagged with such warnings. Scary thought. *Mary Pride*

Getting a Closer Look at the Colleges You Picked

The blurb on the cover of **Peterson's Guide to College Visits** says it all:

> *The Guide that Gets You Ready to Travel!*
> - *People to talk to*
> - *Questions to ask*
> - *Places to see*
> - *And Rand McNally software to get you there!*

A special Peterson's edition of Rand McNally's popular TripMaker software is included. The software helps you plan the quickest and best route from one destination to the rest and prints you out a map with directions. Sadly for Mac owners, the CD-ROM runs only on Windows 9.5 or Windows 4.0 NT.

The book is printed in two colors (a nice touch) and organized by state (no surprise). Each of the 487 college entries includes:

> - Who to contact and where to show up when you arrive,
> - Quick facts and general information about the college (the sort of information found in the massive *Peterson's Guide to 4-Year Colleges,* only a lot less of it)
> - Campus calendar (a paragraph of text—no handy calendar as in the *Princeton Review: Visiting College Campuses* book reviewed below)
> - "Visit Opportunities" chart that includes campus tour, information session, admission interview, classroom visit, and faculty meeting—whether appointments are recommended or required, and who may come (everyone, applicants only, applicants and parents, or whatever)
> - Campus facilities
> - Local attractions, if any, so you can combine your campus visit with some sight-seeing

None of this information will help you if you ignore the unspoken etiquette of campus visits, so the book starts with a section titled "The College Visit: An Overview." First, you are told the whats and whys: what visit options are there, what goals do colleges have for campus visits, what can you expect from a campus visit. Then you are invited to create a visiting strategy, told how to schedule visits and what questions to ask in advance, and how to manage the visit to your best advantage. Post-visit etiquette and how to make use of the data you gathered on your excursion are also covered.

Peterson's tried hard to make sure that the colleges in this book are those most visited by out-of-state students, who need the most help arranging and scheduling the visit. I was happy to see that the two St. John's "Great Books" colleges both made it into this book (they weren't in the Princeton Review book).

If you're using public transportation, or want the calendar format, you'll need the Princeton Review book below. If you're driving yourself, or taking a cab from the airport, the additional entries and trip-planning software in this Peterson's book make it a better buy. *Mary Pride*

NEW!
Princeton Review: Visiting College Campuses, 4th edition

Grades 11–12. $20 plus $4 shipping. ISBN: 0375-0886. *Princeton Review, Random House, 400 Hahan Rd., Westminster, MD 21157. (800) 733-3000. They prefer you to order from bookstores. Web: www.randomhouse.com.*

NEW!
Video Visits

Grades 11–12. Free. *VIDEC, 109 Holiday Court, Franklin, TN 37067. (800) 255-0384. Fax: (615) 790-3024. Email: orders@videc.com. Web: www.videc.com.*

Visiting College Campuses is the book for those who want to efficiently plan a number of college visits. One page per college, and one page per state for a state map and mileage chart, for 250 of the most toured campuses. In the back, mileage charts for each region (Middle Atlantic, Midwest, etc.) showing distances between major cities and reviewed colleges. The transportation focus continues, as each college entry features detailed info on available forms of public transportation you can use to get there. Taxis? Airports? Limo service (they're kidding, right?). Amtrak! Greyhound! Even instructions for those with cars, on how to arrive right at the admissions office door. Overnight accommodations are also listed, as well as local attractions. Finally, a grey sidebar in each college entry tells you when to show up for what—campus tours, on-campus interviews, class visits, or overnight dorm stays. No information about the colleges themselves—for that, you need a different kind of book. New in this edition: college calendars by month and state. For example, in Missouri you can find our for each month what's going on at St. Louis University, University of Missouri (Mizzou), and Washington University. Entries are right on top of each other, so you can glance down the "month" column and see at a glance when classes are in session and when students are taking exams. An "Additional Info" column lets you know such facts as whether any students are on campus during the summer and whether visits are discouraged during exam periods. Great for those who plan to spend a lot of time flitting from campus to campus. *Mary Pride*

Is this useful or what? Call VIDEC to request a free **Video Visit** to any one of about 50 private colleges. Request as many as four videotapes at a time! You will be asked your student's name, address, and phone number. Since the service is for prospective college students, not the merely curious, the operator will also ask whether your student is a high-school junior or not—although many of the colleges and universities will send videos to students down into the junior-high years or even lower.

Which colleges and universities offer videos? I asked and found out that Vanderbilt University, Hillsdale College, Emory University, Southern Methodist University, and Tulane University are among the more popular choices.

Tapes run anywhere from eight minutes to 40 minutes. The shorter ones mainly consist of a campus tour. Most also include interviews with faculty and students. Some also include financial information and information on majors offered.

Normal turnaround time to process your tape request is 24 hours, but it may take longer for VIDEC to ship out the tapes for some popular colleges and universities.

Your video tour comes with a prepaid mailer, in which you return the video within 15 days of receipt. If you need longer—for example, you'd like to show the video to your support group—you can call and request an extension. Be sure to fill out the questionnaire enclosed with each tape, to let the sponsoring colleges and universities know what kind of response their tapes are generating. *Mary Pride*

CHAPTER 50

What You Need to Know About College, But Probably Don't

College today is overpriced.

OK, you already knew that.

College today is overrated. The number of higher-paying jobs is decreasing, while the yearly crop of college-educated students chasing those higher-paying jobs keeps increasing. So those charts that guidance counselors love to show you, of "Lifetime Earnings with a College Degree" versus "Lifetime Earnings with No College Degree," are obsolete. By the time Junior and Janie arrive at middle age, it's an even bet that they would have done better to invest their college tuition in stocks and bonds—or at least not have wiped out their operating capital for years paying off college debts.

Bet you didn't know that!

Finally, college today is not at all like college used to be. Vast numbers of freshmen get credit for remedial English courses. I mean really stupid stuff, like "How to Write a Paragraph." The core curriculum has practically vanished, as have courses that require prerequisites. What remains is a writhing sea of

- Remedial courses. Think of this as Son of High School, or even Son of Junior High School.
- Propaganda courses in New Age, feminist, anti-European, anti-family, and other such "philosophies" and "studies"
- Whimsical courses about tiny slivers of knowledge of interest to the professor and no use to anyone else.
- Outrageous courses. In the Sixties, such courses typically featured nude teachers. Today, the class watches X-rated videos or learns the ins and outs of homosexual practices instead.

Where Have All the Marxists Gone?

According to *U.S. News & World Report* of January 25, 1982, there were more than 10,000 Marxists at that time teaching in American college campuses. Are they all still there? Probably, except for those who have died or gone on sabbatical. Thanks to what Arnold Beichman calls "the magic of the tenure system" they can't be removed, and thanks to the way new professors are hired, we can expect to keep getting a lot of whatever worldview fad is already entrenched in a given department.

The Last Stronghold

When American students return to U.S. colleges and universities, they will make an extraordinary voyage—from a summer where the whole world was denouncing and renouncing Marxism to just about the only place where self-righteous Marxists still exist and thrive.

—*Journalist Georgie Anne Geyer, writing in 1989 after the fall of the Berlin Wall.*

The four faces of Marxism, according to Summit Ministries, and all propagated in college

- **Classic Marxism/Leninism** ("the only interpretation of Marx that is actually a complete worldview")
- **Social-democratic Marxism** ("many social-democratic Marxist in Great Britain and the United States prefer to be known simply as socialists"). Identifiable by their "belief that an economic system should be planned and controlled rather than driven by the free market."
- **Neo-Marxism** (identifies four forms of worker alienation, blames them all on capitalism, ignores the fact that workers in Socialist and Marxist Paradises also experience alienation)
- **Chameleon Marxism** ("bent on obliterating the past from our memory and on rewriting history")

- Entertainment courses. "The Films of Jerry Lewis." Frisbee. Surfing. Etc.
- Vocational courses. These teach you the skills you need to get your degree and a job. In fields such as engineering and science, these courses can be very good. In fields such as education and humanities, see "remedial," "propaganda," and "whimsical" above.

This is not sour grapes: I have two college degrees, as does my mother. My father is a college professor, and my husband taught for two years in a community college. The problem is that almost immediately after I graduated (with, thank God, two engineering degrees), college tuition went through the roof and college faculties fell under the spell of Political Correctness. To quote from Brad Miner and Charles Sykes, two guys who edited the *National Review College Guide* and who know a lot about life on campus:

American higher education is in crisis: admissions standards have been lowered, curricula debased, and courses trivialized. Many professors have put aside teaching in favor of research and writing, leaving their students in the hands of graduate teaching assistants (T.A.s), who have little more education than undergraduates and no classroom experience (let alone tested skill); and restrictions on free speech have been imposed on students in the name of diversity, with the result that the educational environment has become highly politicized. Universities that were once bastions of Western civilization are today centers of deconstruction and despair.

If you are a high school student who has yet to visit a college, or a parent whose last days on campus were twenty years ago, you may be shocked to discover how far the intellectual environment at some schools has deteriorated, how politicized things are. Feminism (including its lesbian subspecies) and feminist studies, black studies and affirmative action, gay rights and "sensitivity" rules—these are few of the enthusiasms that now parade in academia under the banner of diversity. . . . [Some] professors and administrators have taken to using the classroom—almost no matter what subject is supposed to be taught—as a propaganda cell.

One might be able to live with that if students were being well educated, but in many cases they are not. As the Gallup Organization recently reported, 25 percent of America's college seniors could not tell the difference between the words of Stalin and Churchill; could not distinguish the language of Das Kapital [Karl Marx's communist opus] from the U.S. Constitution; could not even recall that Christopher Columbus first reached the New World before 1500. . . . The Gallup report concluded: "Using the standard 'A' to 'F' scale . . . 55 percent of the students would have received a grade of 'F' and another 20 percent a 'D.'"

Meanwhile, *Reader's Digest* runs articles with titles like "Who Says College Campuses are Safe?," in which we discover that

Despite the idyllic images college brochures present, violence is a fact of life on the nation's campuses. Last year colleges reported to the FBI a total of 1,990 violent crimes—robbery, aggravated assault, rape, and murder. This is a startling number, considering the fact that about 90 percent of U.S. colleges do not report crime statistics. [In other words, the real number of violent crimes was at least 19,900, and since the colleges who don't report are likely to be those with the greatest crime rates, it may be a whole lot higher than that.—MP] The incidence of property crime was even greater—more than 107,000 cases of burglary, larceny, arson, and motor-vehicle theft at reporting schools alone. [Again, you need to multiply by 10 or more to get the true number of property crimes—a startling 1,000,000-plus.—MP] Shockingly, 78 percent of the violent crimes were committed by students, according to the Center for the Study and Prevention of Campus Violence.

Well, I'm not all that shocked, because human nature being what it is, once people get the idea that they can commit crime with impunity, it's natural for them to do so. When I went to college, kids knew that you could do almost anything on campus and get away with it, from smoking pot to stealing food from dorm refrigerators. Even rape and assault aren't handled the same way on campus as they are in the real world.

Since the downfall of *locus parentis* rules, when colleges took responsibility for acting as students' parents and monitoring their behavior, colleges have gone to the other extreme of avoiding all responsibility for keeping students in line. The new solutions to the crime problem on campus still do not include holding the culprits personally responsible; that would mean up to a million kids expelled from college per year, according to the crime statistics.

Think I'm being too hard on our institutions of higher learning? Here are some well-researched books that take you behind the scenes to unveil the very real problems in colleges and universities today.

Books That Take You Behind the Scenes

Do you want an extensive idea of what is wrong with our system of higher education here in America? What part do government and big business play in the unraveling of true academics in our colleges and universities? **The Academy in Crisis** covers the many aspects of government and business influences on the decisions that affect the future of American colleges.

This 328-page book explores many common myths regarding student aid programs and federally subsidized research, and the control that these programs give to the government. It touches upon the hidden agendas of those in control, and offers solutions to the many problems that are decaying higher education in our country.

Don't think of this as pleasure reading, but as a book that will cause you to reflect about the assumptions we make regarding what is necessary for the success of higher education and how our government determines those assumptions. *Maryann Turner*

Most of you reading this are aware of the P.C. movement and its effort to push "tolerance" to its highest limits while in fact tolerating everything but traditional monotheistic religions and family values.

While I didn't read author David Thibodeaux's first book, *Political Correctness: The Cloning of the American Mind,* I don't think I missed much. The phrase, "As I stated in my previous book on this subject" is repeated *ad nauseam* throughout **Beyond Political Correctness**. In fact I'm not clear exactly why this

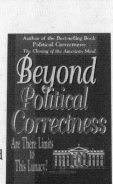

How to Spot a Marxist Prof

When a professor shows a real disregard for historical facts, when he portrays all of history as a battle between oppressed and oppressors, when he portrays America as the primary source of evil in the world, or when he suppresses all opinions that don't mesh with his version of reality, it would be reasonable to assume that he is a Marxist. At the very least, these warning signs will make you aware that the professor is a radical with little regard for the truth.

—Dr. Ronald Nash and Jeff Baldwin, The Totally Usable Summit Ministries Guide to Choosing a College

---

NEW!
The Academy in Crisis
Parents. $34.95 hardback, $19.95 paperback.
The Independent Institute, 100 Swan Way, Oakland, CA 94621. Orders: (900)927-8733. Inquiries: (510)568-6047. Fax: (510)568-6040. Email: orders@liberty-tree.org. Web: www.liberty-tree.org.

NEW!
Beyond Political Correctness
Parents. $10.99 plus shipping.
Huntington House Publishers, P.O . Box 53788, Lafayette, LA 70505. (800) 749-4009. Fax: (318) 237-7060.

book was written. Why not just update the first one? More anecdotes, more quotes, and more instances of out-of-control academia at its worst. Genderism, multiculturalism, Afrocentrism, and more are thoroughly explored in these 221 pages.

The author insists that he does not want to disparage the value of a college education. In fact, he succeeds in disproving that very point. You end up feeling that anyone who continues to support good ol' State U and fund this P.C. humbug deserves everything he gets. *Renee Mathis*

NEW!
College Bound

Grades 11–12 and parents. $6.99 plus shipping.
Concordia Publishing House, 3558 S. Jefferson Avenue, St. Louis, MO 63118-3968. (800) 325-3040. Fax: (314) 268-1329.

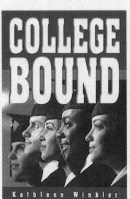

The realities of college life can be overwhelming to new freshmen on campus for the first time. It's pretty overwhelming for parents too! All of these realities are addressed in this book. **College Bound** covers subjects ranging from adjusting to college life to drugs, alcohol and promiscuity. Staying healthy, relationships, academics, faith, political correctness, returning home and a chapter for your parents are also included in this modern-day assessment of the college scene.

The format makes this 159-page paperback book easy to read. Although the book is written from a Christian perspective, the topics are addressed in a somewhat less conservative fashion than you might feel comfortable with. Everything is presented in a straightforward manner and includes stories of real-life experiences of college students. It includes advice from other students and warnings about the common pitfalls of college life. The chapters on promiscuity, relationships, drugs and alcohol are frank discussions about what happens on college campuses. They include sound advice about avoiding the destructive behaviors, but also include reminders about not drinking to excess in the event you choose to drink. Dating, date rape, and suicide are three more topics that are discussed frankly in the book.

This book has possibilities as a discussion starter between parents and teens about the hazards of college life, as long as the the teens' Christian faith is firmly planted and the parents are readily available to reinforce their values on the various topics. *Maryann Turner*

NEW!
Countdown to College

Grades 11–12 and parents. $14.99 plus $3 shipping.
Blue Bird Publishing, 1916 W Baseline #16, Mesa, AZ 85202. Orders: (888) 672-2275. Inquiries: (602) 831-6063. Fax: (602) 831-6728. Email: bluebird@bluebird1.com. Web: www.bluebird1.com.

Countdown to College is addressed to the parents of high schoolers in order to help the parents prepare their children for life in college and beyond, though a mature teen would find it enormously helpful to read on his own. The 184-page paperback speaks about virtually all aspects of college life, and is packed with helpful information.

Countdown to College is intended to quell the anxieties of "every parent who is worried about sending his or her student to college," so there is frank discussion of some of the more potentially disturbing aspects of college such as co-ed dorms, the fraternity/sorority system, and drinking/partying. The majority of the book, however, focuses on subjects that will concern every family and student — the family's adjustment to "losing" a family member, choosing a major and career, adjusting to the academic load of college, and coping with roommates, money, and emergencies.

While other books may help you pick the right college, this book will equip your teen with the right tools for college life. You and your teen will not be disappointed in the sound advice given here, if you take the time to think through these issues before you face them. *Kristin Hernberg*

The Crisis of Western Education by Christopher Dawson, first issued in 1961 and now reprinted, is a prescription for what ails the modern Catholic (and secular) university. If the patient was sick in 1961, it is near death now. Dr. Dawson's medicine then was a heaping dose of the study of Christian culture—today we need at least a double dose.

Dr. Dawson first describes the development of Western education from its Christian and classical roots through the Middle Ages to today's technological society. Then, in part 2, he unabashedly offers the study of Christian culture as a substitute for the combined utilitarianism and specialization of today's higher education. In part 3 he points out that nothing else will provide a rein to bring the modern Frankenstein of technology dominated by self-interest and the mass cult of power under control. Only when we have begun again to graduate persons who have been taught what their inheritance is, who it came from and how it was lost, will we have people equipped to deal with the problems of our age.

This book is thoroughly Catholic. Protestants (while disagreeing strongly with parts such as his views on the Reformation) can profit from Dawson's portrayal of the Christian church that in the past conquered the entire Western world and, though suffering severe setbacks these days, cannot ultimately be defeated. *Charles & Betty Burger*

Richard Mitchell, a professor of English at Glassboro State College and publisher of *The Underground Grammarian*, carves up the educrats and serves them for supper. Mitchell exposes the problems in public education, not by telling horror stories, but by quoting the illiterate rascals who perpetrate them. As, for example, in this delightful vignette, titled "The Missouri Compromise":

You will not be astonished to learn that there are some people in Missouri who cannot manage commas, cannot avoid sentence fragments, cannot regularly make verbs agree with subjects and pronouns with antecedents, and cannot help sounding like literal translations from Bulgarian. If you are a regular reader of this column, you'll also be unastonished to hear that those pitiable illiterates are members of the Missouri Association of Colleges of Teacher Education.

These poor saps have finally noticed that lots of irate citizens "have indicated concern of [yes, of] the decreasing standardized test scores of students." They even know that a "sensitivity has become quite manifest in the development in state wide [yes, two words] assessment systems." But they don't seem too worried. They've cleared up the whole mess in a "position statement" called Assessment of Basic Skills Competencies of Potential Teachers . . .

"The teacher," they say, "must have a high degree of proficiency in the basic skills. They are expect to transmit to their students through precept and example."

Yeah. And here are some of the precepts and examples through which these Missouri Teacher-training Turkeys transmit: . . .

"There is a question of the relationship of secondary and co-secondary schools in terms of relationships. The authors [!] of this position paper agreed that such an assessment process can have a significant impact [they never discuss insignificant or mere impacts] on secondary school curriculum in turning to an assessment instrument to which the public schools might be inclined to reach toward."

NEW!
The Crisis of Western Education
$12.95 plus $4 shipping.
Franciscan University Press, 1235 University Blvd., Steubenville, OH 43952. (740) 283-6357. Fax: (740) 283-5454. Web: www.franuniv.edu.

The Graves of Academe
Parents. $14.95.
Time Warner Trade Publishing, % Order Entry, 3 Center Plaza, Boston, MA 02108. (800) 759-0190. Fax: (800) 286-9471. Email: cust.service@littlebrown.com. Web: www.littlebrown.com.

Fragmented Smorgasbord

The failure to cultivate our students is evident in a 1992 analysis of college transcripts by the U.S. Department of Education, which reveals that 26.2 of recent bachelor's degree recipient earned not a single undergraduate credit in history; 30.8 percent did not study mathematics of any kind; 39.6 earned no credits in either English or American literature; and 58.4 percent left college without any exposure to a foreign language. Much too frequently, American higher education now offers a smorgasbord of fanciful courses in a fragmented curriculum that accords as much credit for "Introduction to Tennis" and for courses in pop culture as it does for "Principles of English Composition," history, or physics, thereby trivializing education—indeed, misleading students by implying that they are receiving the education they need for life when they are not.

An American Imperative:
Higher Expectations for Higher
Education, Report of the
Wingspread Group on Higher
Education

NEW!
The Hollow Men

$19.95 plus $3 shipping. ISBN: 089-526-5397
Regnery Gateway, c/o National Book Network, PO Box 190, Blue Ridge Summit, PA 17214-0190. (800) 462-6420. Fax: (800) 338-4550. Web: www.nbnbooks.com.

Why do the good people of Missouri suffer such humbug without turning to some blunt instrument to which they might be inclined to reach toward? We can tell you why. It's because these ugly crimes against nature are committed in private among consenting Turkeys. How many "authors," do you suppose, conspired to write, rewrite, edit, and finally to approve all that gibberish? . . .

We have some advice for the good people of Missouri. Turn those rascals out. Pension them off for life at full pay, requiring only that they never again set foot on a campus. Don't worry about the cost. In fifty years or so, there won't be any cost. As it is, you're planning to pay more and more of them for ever and ever. . . .

We have forgotten that the storekeepers used to pay miscreants to stay away. It worked. We've gotten it backwards. We pay them to hang around and smash the windows. Let's be realistic and pay the miscreants to do that one thing that we most need them to do—nothing, nothing at all.

Mitchell has focused on the real root of our public education problems—the teacher-training colleges through which all potential public-school teachers must pass. *The Graves of Academe* pins the rap for the rise of an incompetent elite, jealous of real scholars and real learning, on two prominent, although unintentional, villains: the Wundterkinder (a nineteenth-century school of psychologists named after Wilhelm Max Wundt), and the 1913 NEA Commission on the Reorganization of Secondary Education. The Wundterkinder "viewed education as a science: teaching was a stimulus, learning a response thereto. Wundterkind educators have turned out generations of teachers who don't teach, but instead try to modify behavior." The NEA Commission followed up this disaster by insisting that the true purpose of education was to produce "good citizens" rather than to teach anyone anything. This Commission was the first to introduce Worthy Home-membership, Worthy Use of Leisure (see Barbara Morris's *Great American Con Game*) and other nonacademic goals *in place of* the traditional curriculum.

Recently many citizens in my state went to a great deal of effort to oppose an omnibus Education Act that threw millions more dollars at the public school establishment. The opponents, however, had no positive program of their own. If they had read this book, they would have known what to ask for: removal of the certification requirement for public-school teachers and disbanding of the publicly-funded teacher training colleges.
Mary Pride

The Hollow Men: Politics and Corruption in Higher Education by Charles Sykes is a book about what a college can and should be. In it Mr. Sykes chronicles the history of Dartmouth College as a microcosm of what has happened at other colleges and universities across America.

Sykes first introduces us to the Dartmouth that existed under President Hopkins (1916–1945): a true college characterized by a strong core curriculum, an emphasis on teaching, a concern for educating the student as a whole person, and genuine academic freedom. He chronicles the school's descent from that high point in its history to its present intolerant state as a P.C. propaganda house, including detailed, graphic examples which are not fun reading.

While Mr. Sykes does not write from a Christian point of view, his work raises questions for the Christian community about the traditional liberal arts and especially academic freedom. What is the value to the Christian of the age-old dialog between "Athens and Jerusalem" (or reason and faith)?

How should a Christian view academic freedom? How far should the privilege of free speech go? There are issues here that the Christian community needs to address. *The Hollow Men* gives a lot of food for thought. *Charles & Betty Burger*

If you don't know what all the fuss is about over Political Correctness (P.C.), but plan on sending your children off to college, you should read **Political Correctness: The Cloning of the American Mind**. Upon completion, you'll know the origins of P.C., understand its theoretical basis (i.e. deconstructionism), how to spot it, how it affects university administration and teaching, and much more. Written by "insider" David Thibodaux, English professor at the University of Southwestern Louisiana, it is concise, scholarly (many quotes from professional journals), and easily understood by the layman. You get all you need to know in only 173 pages of medium-size print. An additional 33 pages at the end contain interviews with other university professors—interesting, but not necessary reading.

Unlike some other books on the topic, this one isn't packed with shocking examples of university life. Oh yes, some examples are given—such as the dormitory run by militant lesbians and sensitivity workshops to rid students of their Christian principles—but only enough to make the point. Much of the content is more practical: the author evaluates curricula, defines terms, and exposes the motives and methods of the leftist establishment, such as how euphemisms and labels are used to suppress free speech. *Charles & Betty Burger*

NEW!
Political Correctness
$10.99 plus $3.50 shipping.
Huntington House, PO Box 53788, Lafayette, LA 70505.
Orders: (800) 749-4009.
Inquiries: (318) 237-7049.
Fax: (318) 237-7060.

College Does Not Always Equal Knowledge

There is further disturbing evidence that [college] graduates are unprepared for the requirements of daily life. According to the 1993 National Adult Literacy Survey (NALS), surprisingly large numbers of two- and four-year college graduates are unable, in everyday situations, to use basic skills involving reading, writing, computation, and elementary problem solving.

Results of the NALS survey, conducted by the Educational Testing Service of the U.S. Department of Education, were released in September 1993. The largest effort of its type ever attempted, the survey offers a comprehensive analysis of the competence of American adults (both college- and non-college-educated) based on face-to-face interviews with 26,000 people. We note with concern that the 1993 survey findings reflect a statistically significant decline from those of an earlier survey conducted in 1985.

The NALS tasks required participants to do three things: read and interpret prose, such as newspaper articles, work with documents like bus schedules and tables and charts, and use elementary arithmetic to solve problems involving, for example, the costs of restaurant meals or mortgages. The NALS findings were presented on a scale from low (Level 1) to high (Level 5) in each of the three areas. The performance of college graduates on these scales is distressing:

- In working with documents, only eight percent of all four-year college graduates reach the highest level.
- In terms of their ability to work with prose, only 10 percent of four-year graduates are found in Level 5.
- With respect to quantitative skills, only 12 percent of four-year graduates reach the highest level.

In fact, only about one-half of four-year graduates are able to demonstrate intermediate levels of competence in each of the three areas. In the area of quantitative skills, for example, 56.3 percent of American-born, four-year college graduates are unable consistently to perform simple tasks, such as calculating the change from $3 after buying a 60 cent bowl of soup and a $1.95 sandwich. Tasks such as these should not be insuperable for people with 16 years of education.

An American Imperative: Higher Expectations for Higher Education, Report of the Wingspread Group on Higher Education

Profscam

Parents. $10.95 plus $4 shipping.
Publisher's Book and Audio, PO Box 070059, Staten Island, NY 10307. (800)288-2131. Fax: (800)818-9907. Email: pba@email.com. Web: www.publishersbook-audio.com.

The Ultimate Academic Success Manual

Grade 9–college. $9.95 plus $3 shipping.
American Vision, PO Box 724088, Atlanta, GA 31139-9690. (800) 628-9460. Fax: (770) 952-2587. Email: avision1@aol.com. Web: www.avision1.com.

Another book you shouldn't miss is **Profscam**, in which author Charles J. Sykes, who like me is the child of a college professor, proves beyond a shadow of a doubt that the direct and ultimate reason for the collapse of higher education in the USA—which has led directly to the collapse of K–12 education as well—is "the selfish, wayward, and corrupt American university professor." Harsh words, yes? But Sykes (a former editor of *Milwaukee* magazine) proves, in a very readable and not at all hysterical style, that what used to be Higher Education has become Hire Education. Thanks to tenure, professional peer review, and above all the university professor's built-in financial incentive to prefer research to teaching, the concept of Christian civilization that used to underpin university education has given way to trendier-than-thou civilization-bashing.

College kids, Sykes proves, are not, in most cases, receiving the education their parents have sacrificed to provide. Instead, they are being "educated" in mass classes and by graduate students, many unable to speak English fluently, who themselves are controlled by what amounts to an academic Thought Police.

This all has tremendous implications for the Christian parents, and particularly the homeschooling parents, who persist in setting a college education as their children's highest academic goal.

There are still some good colleges out there, but you are not likely to find or recognize them until you read this book. *Profscam* shows you how to tell the turkeys from the winners. *Mary Pride*

This new book by Gary DeMar has essentially the same material as part 1 of his now out-of-print book *Surviving College Successfully*. Your kids, Gary says, are going to face real battles in college. That kindly college professor may (and probably will) try to destroy their religious faith. Those great guys at the frat house may (and probably will) apply pressure to sleep around, swear, get drunk, and other ungood things. (Can we call this "beer pressure"?) Get wise, kid, before they get you.

The Ultimate Academic Success Manual is a very clear and helpful explanation of what young Junior from Oshkosh will find lurking in the halls of Harvard or even good ol' State U. Gary not only tells you that your Christian worldview will be challenged; he goes beyond that and explains *what those other worldviews are* and *why they matter*. This information is better and more useful than what Junior is likely to get in his philosophy courses. Gary also includes a section on how to keep the faith even though Junior is submerged in (and subsidizing) the anti-Christian collegiate culture.

The main effect of this book on parents should be to make us question the dubious value of four or more years at $5,000–$10,000 or more per year with the Thought Police thundering away at our offspring's head. Gary doesn't even tell the worst of it, either. Such as the feminist profs who persecute students who even *ask questions* in class. Or the proposed (and installed, in some places) courses in "sensitivity" that require you to *affirm* (not just study about) a non-Christian belief in the equal goodness of, say, homosexuality and Christian marriage. Not to mention the courses in witchcraft, porn films, and so on funded with your and my tax dollars.

The one question this book never answers, and that I hope Gary will address in the future is: What can Christians do to change the university? And if we *can't* change the university, why should we subsidize it? Questions that demand a verdict, to paraphrase Josh McDowell (who, by the way, has been barred from many college campuses because his message is "too Christian"). *Mary Pride*

CHAPTER 51

How to Apply to College

You are here!

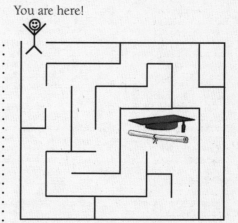

When it's time to apply to college, you have five things to keep in mind:

(1) Courses you've completed
(2) Activities worth mentioning
(3) Tests
(4) Paperwork
(5) Interviews

Courses You've Completed

You will need to present the colleges of your choice with a high-school transcript. Since you did not attend a "regular" school, the paperwork you give them may include

- A "home" transcript, listing courses you completed solely at home
- Transcripts from any correspondence schools, online academies, or other academically acceptable work you did under the auspices of people outside your home environment
- Certificates of completion from seminars and other short-term academic experiences

The home transcript is a little tricky, so let's describe one way you could do this. You start by creating a syllabus for each high-school course given at home. This lists the books and other major material used, the course content, and the work required. Here's an example:

English 101. *A one-semester course, three credits. Texts: Zinsser's On Writing Well, E.B. White et. al Elements of Style, Princeton Review's WriteSmart, and a variety of readings from authors with distinctive styles (Dickens, Jane Austen, Sir Walter Scott, P.G. Wodehouse, Andre Norton, etc.) Review of grammar, followed by instruction in basic writing competencies, and analysis of writers in order to analyze and imitate their styles. 10 short 2-page papers, a final 15-page paper, midterm, and final. Grade: A-.*

313 Colleges Which Have Accepted Homeschoolers

Adrian College, MI
Allegheny College, PA
American River Community Junior College, CA
American University, Washington, DC
Amherst College, MA
Anderson University, IN
Antelope Valley College, CA
Antioch College, OH
Appalachian Bible College, WV
Arkansas State University, AR
Asbury College, KY
Austin College, TX
Azusa Pacific, CA
Baptist Bible College, PA
Barber College,, OH
Baylor College, TX
Belhaven College, MS
Belmont College, TN
Bennington College, VT
Bethany College of Missions, MN
Bethany Lutheran College, MN
Bethel College, IN
Biola University, CA
Birmingham-Southern College, AL
Blackburn College, IL
Bob Jones University, SC
Boston University, MA
Brigham Young University, UT
Broome Community College, NY
Brown University, RI
Bryan College, TN
Buffalo State, NY
California Polytechnic University, San Luis Obiospo, CA
Calvin College, MI
Carleton College, MN
Carnegie Mellon University, PA
Casper College, WY
Cedarville College, OH
Central Piedmont Comm. College, NC
Centre College, KY
Christendom College, VA
Christian Brothers University, TN
Christian Heritage College, CA
Christian Liberty College, VA
Chowan College, NC
Cincinnati Bible College, OH
Circleville Bible College, OH
The Citadel, SC
Clearwater Christian College, FL
College of Lake County, IL
College of Southern Idaho, ID
College of William and Mary, VA
College of Wooster, OH
Colorado Baptist, CO
Colorado Christian University, CO
Columbus College, GA
Concordia College, MN
Cooke County College, TX
Cornell University, NY
Corning Community College, NY
Covenant College, TN
Crichton College, TN
Criswell College, TX
Cumberland County College, NJ
Dallas Christian College, TX
Dartmouth College, NH
David Lipscomb University, TN
Davidson College, NC
DeKalb Community College, GA
Delta State University, MI
De Paul University, IL
Diablo Valley College, CA
Dickenson State University, ND
Dordt College, IA
Drake University, IA
East Central College, MO
East Texas Baptist University, TX
Eastern Hillsdale College, MI
Eastern New Mexico University, NM
Elon College, NC
Emmaus Bible College, IA
Emory University, GA

Empire State Baptist Seminary, NY
Enterprise State Junior College, AL
Evangel College, MO
Evansville University, IN
Evergreen State College, WA
Evergreen Valley Comm. College, CA
Faith Baptist Bible College, IA
Fitchburg State College, MA
Freed-Hardeman University, TN
Fresno Pacific College, CA
Garden City College, KS
Geneva College, PA
George Fox College, OR
George Mason University, VA
Georgetown College, KY
G.M.I. School of Engineering, MI
Goddard College of Plainfield, VT
Gonzaga University, WA
Gordan College, MA
Goucher College, MD
Grand Rapids Baptist College, MI
Grand Valley State University, MI
Grove City College, PA
Hagerstown Junior College, PA
Hampshire College, MA
Harding University, AR
Harrisburg Area Community College, PA
Harvard University, MA
Haverford College, PA
Hendrix College, AR
Heritage Baptist University, IN
Hillsdale College, MI
Hope College, MI
Houghton College, NY
Houston Baptist University, TX
Huntington College, IN
Indiana University, IN
Joliet Junior College, IL
John Brown University, TX
Johnson & Wales University, RI
Kalamazoo Valley Comm. College, MI
Kansas State University, KS
Kent State University, OH
Kenyon College, OH
Keystone Community College, PA
King College, TN
Kings College, NY
Lake County College, IL
Lancaster Bible College, PA
Lansing Community College, MI
Lawrence Technological Univ., MI
Lee College, TN
LeTourneau College, TX
Lewis and Clark College, OR
Liberty University, VA
Lipscomb University, TN
Louisiana State University, LA
Loyola College, MD
Lubbock Christian University, TX
Lutheran Bible Institute, WA
Magdalen College, NH
Maranatha Baptist Bible College, WI
Maryland Bible College and Seminary, MD
Massachusetts Institute of Technology, MA
The Master's College, CA
Memphis State University, TN
Messiah College, PA
Michigan Institute of Technology, MI
Middlebury College, VT
Mid-Plains Community College, NE
Milligan College, TN
Millsaps College, MS
Mississippi State University, MS
Mississippi College, MS
Modesto Junior College, CA
Montana Wilderness School of the Bible, MT
Montreat Anderson, NC
Moody Bible Institute, IL
Morrisville College, NY
Mt. Vernon Nazarene College, OH
Nazareth College, NY
Nebraska School of Tech. Agriculture, NE
New Mexico State University, NM
New River Community College, VA

New York University, NY
Niagra University, NY
Northampton Community College, PA
Northeast Missouri State University, MO
Northern Michigan University, Marquette, MI
Northland Baptist Bible College, WI
Northwest Christian College, OR
Northwest College, WA
Nyack College, NY
Oakland University, MI
Oberlin College, OH
Ohio State University, Agricultural Technical Institute, OH
Oklahoma Baptist University, OK
Oklahoma City Comm. College, OK
Oklahoma State University, OK
Oklahoma University of Science & Arts, OK
Old Dominion University, VA
Onondago Community College, NY
Oral Roberts University, OK
Owens Technical College, OH
Oxford University, England
Pennsylvania State University, McKeesport, PA
Pennsylvania State University, York, PA
Pensacola Christian College, FL
Pepperdine University, CA
Purdue University, IN
Prince Georges Community College, MD
Princeton University, NH
Redlands College, OK
Redwoods Junior College, CA
Reed College, OR
Rensselaer Polytechnic Institute, NY
Rice University, TX
Ricks College, ID
Roberts Wesleyan College, NY
Rose-Hulman Institute of Technology, IN
St. Johns College, MD
St. Joseph's College, ME
St. Joseph's School of Nursing, NY
St. Joseph's University, PA
St. Louis Christian College, MO
St. Louis University, MO
St. Phillips College, TX
St. Vincent College, PA
Salem College, WV
Samford University, AL
Sam Houston State, TX
Shelton State Junior College, AL
Shimer College, IL
Simpson College, CA
Smith College, MA
Stanislaus State University, CA
State University of New York, Buffalo, NY
Stephens College, MO
Stockton State College, NJ
Southern Arkansas University, AR
Southern Illinois University, Carbondale, IL
Southern Nazarene University, OK
Southwest Baptist University, MO
Southwest Texas State University
Southwestern Oklahoma State University, OK
Sul Ross State Univeristy, TX
Swarthmore College, PA
Taylor University, IN
Tennessee Temple University, TN
Texas A&M, TX
Texas Christian University, TX
Texas Tech University, TX
Texas Woman's University
Thomas Aquinas College, CA
Thomas More Institute, NH
Tidewater Community College, VA
Towson State University, MD
Trinity College, VT
Tyler Junior College, TX
Union University, TN
United States Air Force Academy, CO
United States Naval Academy, Annapolis, MD
University of Akron, OH
University of Alabama in Huntsville, AL
University of Alaska, Fairbanks, AK
University of Arizona, AZ
University of Arts, PA

University of California, Berkley, CA
University of California, Los Angeles, CA
University of California, Sacramento, CA
University of California, Santa Cruz, CA
University of Chicago, IL
University of Colorado, Colorado Springs, CO
University of Dallas, TX
University of Delaware, DE
University of Denver, CO
University of Evansville, IN
University of Florida, FL
University of Hawaii, HA
University of Houston, TX
University of Idaho, ID
University of Iowa, IA
University of Kansas, KS
University of Maine/Orono, ME
University of Maryland, MD
University of Mary Hardin Baylor, Belton, TX
University of Massachusetts, Amherst, MA
University of Michigan, MI
University of Minnesota, MN
University of Mississippi, MS
University of Missouri-Rolla, MO
University of Montana, MT
University of Nebraska-Lincoln, NE
University of New Hampshire, NH
University of New York, NY
University of North Carolina, Chapel Hill, NC
University of North Dakota, ND
University of North Texas, TX
University of Oklahoma, OK
University of Pennsylvania, PA
University of St. Thomas at Houston, TX
University of South Carolina, SC
University of Southern Indiana, IN
University of Steubenville, OH
University of the South, TN
University of Stubenville, OH
University of Tennessee, TN
University of Texas, Austin, TX
University of Texas, El Paso, TX
University of Toledo, OH
University of North Texas. TX
University of Virginia, Charlottesville, VA
University of Washington, WA
University of Wisconsin, Madison, WI
University of Wyoming, WY
Vanderbilt University, TX
Victoria College, TX
Virginia Military Institute, VA
Virginia Polytechnic Institute & State University, VA
Virginia Wesleyan, VA
Walsh University, OH
Washington Bible College, DC
Washington and Lee University, VA
Washington Univ. Medical Center, MO
Wayne State College, NE
Western Texas College, TX
Western Baptist College, OR
Western Michigan University, MI
Western Washington University, WA
Westmont College, CA
West Point Military Academy, NY
Wharton County Junior College, TX
Wheaton College, IL
Whitman College, WA
Whitworth College, WA
Williams College, MA
Wisconsin Lutheran College, WI
Word of Life Institute, NY
Yale University, CT
York College of Pennsylvania, PA

List compiled September, 1996, by Home School Legal Defense Association. Used by permission

To summarize the entire at-home experience in an easy-to-read fashion, create a master transcript with each grade divided into two semesters, and each course listed with its letter grade.

You may prefer to list AP, SAT II, and CLEP grades next to the courses they correspond to, or make test grades into a separate sheet. Be sure to include an explanation of your grading system, e.g., "The 'A' grade is for a total score of 93 percent and up."

It's easier to do this one semester at a time, than in one final marathon session just before college applications are due, so start putting these records together the first semester of ninth grade, if you can.

Activities Worth Mentioning

The *Princeton Review Student Access Guide to College Admissions* describes the ideal college applicant thusly:

> *When college admissions officers, high school guidance counselors, and how-to-get-into-college books describe the perfect college applicant, they all describe more or less the same person. The ideal candidate, they say, has good grades, high scores, solid extracurricular activities (editor of the newspaper and captain of the football team), a fascinating after-school job (teaching English to immigrant children), terrific hobbies (managing a food relief program in Africa, playing medieval instruments), and a shelf filled with awards for everything from writing poetry to playing tennis. This candidate also lives on a farm, conducts unusual physics experiments, holds an elected political office in his town, restores old houses, coaches a Little League baseball team, and never once mentions SAT scores during an interview.*

Notice that "good grades" and "high scores" form only a small percentage of this description. This comes as a rude shock to those of us who always automatically associated "college" with "academics."

Assuming you have the mental horsepower to get those good grades and high scores, what do colleges really want from you?

According to the same book,

> *Colleges are most interested in students who do interesting things, stick with them, and rise to positions of leadership in them. Beyond this, they are most interested in activities that show you have the respect of your peers. You should be careful about putting too much emphasis on activities that don't bring you into contact with other people.*

Volunteering at the YMCA or library (you practically live there anyway) would be a good extracurricular activity. So would being the captain of your local homeschool basketball team. Any contests you have entered and done well in are worth mentioning, such as the Scripps-Howard Spelling Bee, the National Geography Bee, and the Math Olympiad. Many homeschool support groups field teams for these events—be sure to ask what team contests your group enters. There are also many "individual" contests for schoolkids each year: writing contests, art contests, music contests . . . . Get a book on contests of this nature and enter a few. These are just a few suggestions; you have four years to do *something* notable, after all!

Tests

You already know all about the PSAT, SAT I, ACT, SAT II, AP, GED, and CLEP. If you don't, go back and read those chapters. The main thing to remember here is, "Sign up in time and work through at least one practice book first!"

Paperwork

This can get pretty ugly. While there's a "standard" college application form which *in theory* is accepted by hundreds of colleges, *in practice* they usually prefer you fill out *their* form. And send in the fee. And send your transcripts and syllabi. And arrange for any transcripts from "outside" courses to be sent directly to them. And fill out their financial aid forms. And include letters of recommendation from adults who know you well (Mom and Dad don't count). And maybe write an essay just for them. Leave plenty of time for all this, and maybe you'll survive.

Interviews

You visit the campus. You wear conservative, clean clothes. You talk to the admissions officer. You *don't* mention your SAT scores (they have the scores on file). You figure out if you like the college, and they figure out if they like you.

That's all there is to it! Sounds easy, right? No? Then by all means buy one or two or three or more of these "get-ready-for-college" helps below. At $15,000 to $100,000 for a college degree, now is not the time to get cheap. Get all the help you need, and get it *now*.

Help for Applying to College

NEW!
And What About College?
Grades 9–12 and parents. $18.95 plus shipping.
Holt Associates, Inc., 2269 Massachusetts Ave., Cambridge, MA 02140. (617) 864-3100. Fax:(617) 864-9235. Email: holtgws@aol.com. Web: www.holtgws.com.

And What About College? is the first book on this subject every homeschooler should buy. Written by homeschooler Cafi Cohen, whose children have been accepted into the U.S. Air Force Academy and Agnes Scott College, this book answers the questions homeschoolers must face—and that mass-market college books don't answer. This is not off-the-cuff advice, but detailed instructions in how to put together a transcript, make up a scope and sequence, handle college requirements and testing, and much, much more. All major kinds of homeschools are covered: traditional, unit studies, unschooling, and eclectic. She even helps you pick out the best college for your child and walks you through the entire application process, from the cover letter to every other item your application should include. Eleven excellent appendices add even more details, from web addresses of sites for families homeschooling teenagers, to suggestions for how to get into a military academy. Don't try to leave home without it! Highly recommended. *Mary Pride*

NEW!
From Homeschool to College and Work
Grades 7–12. $11.95 plus shipping.
Bittersweet House, PO Box 5211, Madison, WI 53705-5211. (608) 238-3302. Email: amckee@mailbag.com.

How can you translate your flexible, creative homeschool years into a portfolio that will get you into the college or job of your choice? **From Homeschool to College and Work** answers this question. Based on the experience of the McKee family, whose "highly praised and successful" college portfolio got their son accepted at all six schools he applied to, and including samples from their son's college and work portfolios, this book shows how to do it yourself. Using a question-and-answer format, it shows how to document your academic work, a list of activities you might consider keeping records for, and how to put it together. It addresses such common questions and concerns as high school diplomas, the GED test, credits, transcripts, grades, class standings, standardized achievement tests,

and teacher and counselor recommendations. Most of the books and resources in the bibliography can be found in *The Big Book,* but you'll also
find a handy list of web sites for college-bound homeschoolers.

If you haven't followed the correspondence-school path—or even if you
have, but just want to know how to claim credit for everything you learned
outside of your structured classes—you should buy this book.
Recommended. *Mary Pride*

The second chapter of **Guide for the College Bound** is alone enough to
sway your opinion toward a Christian college! This book is labeled "A
Christian Guide to Choosing the School That's Right for You" on the back
cover, and this particular subtitle would definitely fit. *Guide for the College
Bound* guides you through the key differences between secular schools and
Christian colleges. It offers insight into life on secular campuses in the
nineties. For the uninformed the insights alone are enough to make you
shudder! To be fair, it also points out some of the shortcomings of Christian
campuses across our country, and offers suggestions about making your secular college experience a spiritually healthy, Christian experience.

Topics covered in the book are:

- Choosing a college
- Comparing secular colleges to Christian colleges
- Affording college
- Using the Internet to help choose a college
- 12 questions to ask the college recruiter
- Visiting the college campus
- How to know a Christian college when you see one
- How to live out your faith in any setting
- The meaning of college accreditation
- The first 6 weeks of college
- Advice for parents of new college students
- How to solve college problems
- How to transfer to another college
- Distance learning
- Educational choices for adults who want degrees

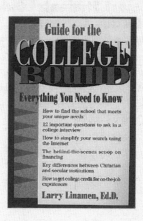

This 202-page, paperback book helps you clarify the options in the college market that best meets your needs. It arms you with the ammunition
to carry on your Christian faith in the setting where you choose to further
your educational pursuits. *Maryann Turner*

The "Form-U-La" in **Senior High: A Home-Designed Form-U-La** is a
set of reproducible record-keeping tools designed to help you figure out
how to quantify real life activities into high-school credits. There are plenty
of charts and forms included to help you plan your high-schooler's course
of study, hours needed, credits per subject, and more. Detailed instructions
are given for producing an official looking transcript.

What about college? If you are not among the college-bound, this book
will certainly help assemble a good-looking set of high-school records.
While Mrs. Shelton doesn't rule out the option of college, the focus of this
book is more "life prep" than "college prep." If that appeals to you, then
you have found a kindred spirit. If not, then this book will probably help
in filling in your transcript with an elective or two. (Warning: the correspondence school she recommends as a source for "accredited" transcripts
is rather poorly regarded in *Walston's Guide to Earning Religious Degrees Non-
Traditionally.* We would definitely *not* recommend pursuing that option.)

Mrs. Shelton offers a hefty dose of her "real world" (non-textbook)
teaching philosophy and includes sample fill-in sheets to help you get

This book is not easy to read. Mrs. Shelton spends a few pages telling us that all her friends and book testers love this book so much, and that the Lord God Himself inspired it. Surely that space would have been better spent on giving us actual information—after all, the reader has already bought the book and doesn't need to be "sold" on it! (Not to mention the questionable practice of using God as a testimonial for your product.)

NEW!
The Smart Students' Guide to Selective College Admissions

Grades 10–12. $25.
Academic Coaching Services, Inc., 3540 W. Sahara, #129, Las Vegas, NV 89102-5816. (702)876-3000. Fax: 702-693-4554. Email: Academic@lvdi.net. Web: www.lvdi.net.

NEW!
The Winning Way College and Career Guide

Grades 9–12 and parents. $24.95 plus shipping.
American Academic Services, PO Box 208, Westminster, MD 21157. (800) 868-5543. Email: billcs@erols.com. Web: www.winningway.com.

started: book reports, museum reports, play critiques, Bible studies, and menu planners to name a few. Hunting trips, baseball games, and listening to pre-recorded health tapes from a local hospital are all fair game for "school." This approach, however, seems taken to an extreme. When organizing your purse counts for high-school credit, why bother keeping track of credits at all? You may not need to turn every Jell-O-making session into a home ec class.

Along with the conversational writing style, the ever-changing type style and size can be tiresome. I was frustrated by the absence of clarity and conciseness, as with some lack of organization. Recommended only for those who enjoy a "chatty" style of writing, or can make use of the transcript tools. Personal teaching philosophy, PMS jokes, scripture devotions, and a preponderance of parentheses will either endear you to this author or have you wringing your hands in frustration. *Renee Mathis*

If the college application process seems overwhelming to you, **The Smart Student's Guide to Selective College Admissions** is the book for you. This spiral-bound, 68-page guide is chock-full of information that will help your child be accepted to the college of your choice. It not only explains the difference between selective and less selective colleges, it guides you through the entire application and admission process. It helps you decide if a selective school is, in fact, for you. Then it explains what colleges are looking for in their applicants. There are also chapters that help you develop recommendations, improve your essays and personal statements, and write your resume. The chapter on mastering the college interview is extremely helpful, offering insight into what the interviewer is searching for during the interview.

The guide includes a timeline that suggests courses needed for each year from eighth grade through your senior year. It ends with questions and answers about the application process. *Maryann Turner*

The Winning Way College and Career Guide by William Sarangoulis is intended to guide high-school students and their parents from high school into the college and/or career of their choice in a traditional school setting. This 200-page spiral-bound manual is designed to be used as the text of a course taught by high-school guidance counselors to high-school juniors and seniors, or used at home by motivated families

The Winning Way takes you from finding colleges and a major that will suit you, through SAT, ACT, and AP testing, recommended high-school courses, college applications, and financial aid. Chapters include an Overview, What You Need to Know Now, Getting Organized, College Testing, Majors: the Core Decision, How to Select the Best College, The College Visit, The College Interview, Applications I & II, Financial Aid, Scholarships and other Sources of Aid, The Financial Aid Officer—Closing the Deal, Special Consideration for Athletes, Career and Technology Alternatives to Four-Year Colleges, Great Careers for the Year 200 and Beyond, Information for Home Schooled Students, and a reference section.

Although *The Winning Way* is intended for those who come from a traditional school background, almost all of the advice applies to homeschoolers, and a new chapter includes extra information that will be especially helpful to homeschooling families. The book is written in an engaging way which explains the entire process clearly for everyone involved. The author exhorts both parents and students to be open-minded and not reject each others' ideas. Because this book is intended for families as well as schools, it allows homeschoolers to see that they can replace the traditional guidance counselor. *Kristin Hernberg*

CHAPTER 52

Paying for College

I hate to break your heart, but I have to be honest. So here goes: Doing your taxes is lots easier than applying for college financial aid. What's more, tax forms make much more sense than the way colleges compute financial aid.

Here's how it works:

- **Colleges give "grants" and "loans."** The "total package" of grants and loans is usually computed so the final up-front cost will be similar between expensive, elite schools and less-expensive schools.
- **But a loan is not a gift.** So even if your "total package" looks good, remember which parts of it you'll have to pay back.
- **When computing the amount of your grant,** any scholarship money you have earned from other sources is applied *against* the grant. So if you have a $6,000 grant and a $2,000 National Merit Scholarship, the college only gives you $4,000, and you still wind up with $6,000.
- **When figuring your financial need,** colleges count on grabbing the vast majority of any money the student has earned. So the more you earn, the more of your money they'll take. If you make above a certain amount, it will also reduce your eligibility to get any help at all. On the other hand, if you're a lazy slacker who never earned a cent, you probably will get a higher grant.
- **Colleges also figure your parents have worked and slaved for years** for nothing more than the privilege of giving up their total savings and taking out a second mortgage in order to finance your college education. They also figure your parents have nothing better to do than provide full financial data in humiliating detail—more than the IRS ever asks for. On the other hand, if your parents never owned a house or saved any money, and their current annual income is low, you might get an all-expenses paid vacation to the land of kegs and parties.

Applying for a Private-Sector Scholarship

Don't think you can't apply because you make too much money: 80 percent of the private sector does not require a financial statement or proof of need.

Don't think that application deadlines occur only in the fall: private-sector deadlines are passing daily because often they are set to coincide with the tax year or organizational meeting date.

Don't believe that grades are the only consideration for an award: many application questions deal with personal, occupational, and educational background, organizational affiliations, talent, or ethnic origins; 90 percent are not concerned with grades.

—*The Scholarship Book 2000*

So I suggest the following strategies:

- **Pick an inexpensive school.** Or at least *start* with one. Community colleges and state colleges (of the state you reside in) are usually affordable enough that you can pay the total tuition out of earnings from a reasonable one- or two-year job, or a succession of well-paid summer jobs, *without* any need for the financial-aid dance. Military academies are *free!*
- **Win enough scholarship money** to pay the majority of your college expenses.
- **Don't even *consider* saddling yourself with huge student loans.** Bankers will tell you to "protect your capital with low-interest loans" and that "you'll make it all back easily when you get your first job." If you think filling out financial aid forms is fun, just wait until you're trying to support a family and pay back college loans at the same time.
- **Read the following books** on how to pay for college *before* making any financial moves. Preferably read these books years before college is even an issue.
- **Vote** for people who will change the whole rotten system back to one that rewards merit instead of poverty and laziness. Poor kids can have merit, but meritorious kids aren't always poor.

Books that Can Help You Save Big Bucks

From the Finaid Pocket Calendar just inside the front cover to the handy index in the back of the book, **College Financial Aid for Dummies** does a bang-up job of leading you through the perils and pitfalls of the biggest financial decisions you may ever make. Sections cover:

- Who qualifies for financial aid, and how does it work?
- How to find the aid you need (from the college, from the government, merit scholarships, and more)
- Long-term planning and ways to avoid paying for college altogether
- How to fill out the complicated forms, and what forms you have to fill out
- How to handle paying back your student loans . . . or maybe not (ways to get them fully or partially forgiven)
- The "Part of 10s": ten ways to improve your chances of getting a big financial aid bundle, ten strategies for cutting college costs, the facts finaid counselors don't tell you, ten common goofs that can cost you money, ten tips on using a computerized scholarship search service, ten ways to avoid fakes and frauds
- A 40-page scholarship resource guide, with full contact information for each scholarship, divided into categories such as "Academic/Merit/Leadership," "Agriculture," and "Minorities/Heritage/Disabilities"—18 categories in all
- A 10-page glossary of finaid terms
- Forms: a copy of the "FAFSA" form (the basic finaid application everyone uses) and a College Board scholarship search service application

NEW!
College Financial Aid for Dummies
Grades 9–12 and parents. $19.99. *IDG Books Worldwide Inc., an International Data Group Company, 919 E. Hillsdale Blvd., Suite 400, Foster City, CA 94404. All IDG materials are sold in bookstores. Consumer Customer Service: (800) 762-2974. Web: www.dummies.com.*

Like all "Dummies" books, this one has cartoons introducing each section, a lively reading style, handy sidebars and icons. You'll also find web links where helpful (e.g., to valid online scholarship search services).

College Financial Aid for Dummies manages to simplify this complicated subject, while also being thorough in what it covers. Whatever other finaid books you buy, this one should definitely end up on your shelf. Recommended. *Mary Pride*

Go to college . . . and struggle with debt from student loans for the next 10 to 30 years. Sound good to you? If not, you'll probably want to get a copy of **Debt Free College**, the only book I've run across totally dedicated to the subject of graduating with no money problems hanging over your head.

Author Gordon Wadsworth, a frequent writer for Larry Burkett's Christian Financial Concepts ministry, has put together more detailed information on debt avoidance than you can find in other financial-aid books. Other books note the problems associated with student loans, but still try to sell them as a necessary evil. *Debt Free College* works hard to help you avoid student loans completely. The last chapter, entitled "The Last Resort," reveals the real cost of the most popular student loan programs, and stresses again and again that it's worth making major efforts to avoid such loans entirely.

Written both for students and parents, Mr. Wadsworth's book makes no assumptions about the financial savvy of the reader. Students are warned against the easy overuse of credit cards and taught how to balance a checkbook and make up a monthly budget. He even includes planning sheets and checklists! Parents are given financial-planning tools to help them start saving for a college fund. So far, this is just common sense. But the book also includes:

- Basic instructions on how to apply for financial aid, including a sample FAFSA form
- Suggestions on how to choose a college, get accepted, and win scholarships
- Chapters with detailed information including addresses and phone numbers for grants and scholarships, service cancelable programs, alternative funding programs such as co-op and prepaid tuition plans, and military options
- The latest tax provisions and how they affect student savings, loans, and grants
- A Scholarship Search Form you can send in with a $20 processing fee to a national scholarship search organization
- A free computer analysis by mail of your Estimated Family Contribution and which major grants you might qualify for

My advice? Read *Debt Free College* first, *then* read your other finaid books. Make sure you get the big picture—graduation without financial enslavement—in focus *before* you get involved in the details of financial aid. *Mary Pride*

NEW!
Debt Free College
Grades 9–12 and parents. $16.95 plus $3 shipping.
Gordon Wadsworth, 5830 Haterleigh, Suite 130, Alpharetta, GA 30005. (770) 656-1635. Fax: (770) 495-7993. Email: fais@flash.net.

The **Princeton Review Student Advantage Guide to Paying for College Without Going Broke** is a really complete book that tells you everything you need to know about how the unfair, degrading, and time-consuming game of financial aid is played nowadays. At 288 over-sized pages, this is all the information and worksheets you'll probably be able to stand. With line-by-line instructions for how to fill out the standard financial aid application form, as well as "insider" advice on all stages of financial preparation and how the financial-aid process

NEW!
Princeton Review Student Advantage Guide to Paying for College Without Going Broke, 1999 edition
High school. $18. ISBN: 0-375-752-110. *Princeton Review, Random House, 400 Hahan Rd., Westminster, MD 21157. (800) 733-3000. They prefer you to order from bookstores. Web: www.randomhouse.com.*

works, going right back to why you should *not* set up a trust for your new-born, it's hard to see how the authors could possibly have left anything out. Highly recommended. *Mary Pride*

Over 100,000 free money opportunities! Does this sound enticing? With the cost of higher education escalating faster than the number of new phonics programs for our kindergartners, many of us face the overwhelming task of financing our children's college education. This book offers a variety of ideas and practical information for attaining college funds for you or your children.

Not only does **Scholarships, Grants, Fellowships, & Endowments** lists colleges and financing resources, it is a wonderful guide for preparing your high-school students for planning their academic futures. It walks you through the process of preparing and submitting the proper paperwork to apply to various colleges. In turn, it also supplies you with an up-to-date list of funding, grants, scholarships, and endowments available, as well as telephone numbers and addresses to contact for more information.

In addition to the wealth of information about available financing for your college bound student, it suggests ways to cut college expenses and even supplies a "money saving worksheet" to help plan ahead for college. A glossary of college terms is included that will come in handy when you are delving into the mountain of paperwork necessary to apply to the colleges of your choice. With all the ideas and information in this 355-page, large paperback book, the opportunities to save money on college grows by leaps and bounds. *Maryann Turner*

The Scholarship Book 2000 lists 4,000 private scholarship sources, totaling 400,000 awards worth over $2 billion. One-third of the awards are new in this edition.

OK, this much you could have found out from the cover. How does the book work?

1. You look in the Quick Find Index in the front of the book.
2. Find the categories for which you qualify.
3. Look up the entries, listed by their code numbers. You may well find that you do *not* qualify after all, because there are multiple requirements for the award you're interested in, and you don't meet all of them.
4. Repeat steps 2 and 3 for the Field of Study Index (this lists majors from Business Administration to Vocational Education)
5. If you haven't got a clue about your intended major, check out the resources for choosing a major in Chapter 49.

The Quick Find Index includes these categories: Armed Forces, City/County of Intended Study, Companies, Continent of Intended Study, Country of Intended Study (only includes Canada, Mexico, and USA), Country of Residence, Current Grade Point Average, Current School Program (e.g., grade in school, including high-school dropout, transfer student, and a few other unusual options), Degrees Received, Ethnic Background (African American, American Indian/Eskimo, Arab, Asian, Hispanic, and Minority Affiliation), Extracurricular Activities, Family Ancestries from African to Welsh, Foreign Languages Spoken, Honors/Awards/Contests, Legal City of Residence, Legal Continent of Citizenship, Legal Country of Citizenship, Legal County of Residence, Legal State/Province of Residence, Marital Status, Occupational Goals, Occupations, Organizations (that you belong to), Physical Handicaps,

NEW!
Scholarships, Grants, Fellowships, & Endowments

Grades 11–12 and parents. $29.95 plus $5 shipping.
LoKee Publishing Company, 2630 Fountainview, Suite 300, Houston, TX 77057. Orders: (800) 830-1417. Fax: (713)783-1097. Web: www.lokee.com.

NEW!
The Scholarship Book 2000

Grades 11–12. $25.
Prentice Hall, Order Processing Center, PO Box 11071, Des Moines, IA 50336. (800) 947-7700. Fax: (515) 284-6719. Email: simon@neadata.com. Web: www.phdirect.com.

Present/Current/Future Schools, Religious Affiliation, Sex (male or female), State/Province of Intended Study, Unions (to which you or a family member belong), and Unusual Characteristics (such as Descendant of Declaration of Independence Signer).

The remaining 521 pages are the Scholarship and Awards Listings, followed by an alphabetical listing of the scholarships.

Individual listings include the name of the scholarship or award: address, phone, fax, email, and web contact information, where available; the award amount; deadlines for applying; fields of study to which the award applies; and a description of who qualifies for the award, how to apply for it, and what the award hopes to achieve.

There are a fair number of kooky awards out there. The odds you qualify for one of these are slight. But if you come from a union family, or have minority or "old-time immigrant" ethnic status (Italian is good), or belong to one of the organizations or companies who likes to dole out awards, you might find some money here. Bear in mind that any such award will be deducted from whatever aid package your college of choice might award you, which isn't fair at all, but that's the way the system currently works. However, if the aid they offer is heavy on the loans, it would be nice to replace some of that with outright scholarship grants, wouldn't it?
Mary Pride

> The awards are not listed alphabetically; they are listed by college majors. This can result in multiple listings for the same scholarship. For example, under "Unusual Characteristics" I found the listing "Homeschooled," followed by 11 code numbers. Excitedly, I look them up. Each and every one of the code numbers turned out to refer to the exact same scholarship from Rose Hill College. But because the scholarship is available to students in any of 11 majors, it got listed 11 times.

Wondering About Those College Scholarship Services? DON'T!

by Susan Richman
©1999 Home Life, Inc.
Originally published in
Practical Homeschooling

'Tis the season for . . . wondering how in the world you might pay for your homeschooled kid to go to college. I'm doing a lot of that right now, with two boys in college and Molly going into her senior year of homeschooling. Some of you might be in the same boat.

Heard those terrific ads that sound too good to be true about millions of dollars of scholarship aid going unclaimed every year—and if you just use this college scholarship service, you'll find out about thousands of dollars that your student is qualified to receive?

Be wary—these scholarship search services, while usually not totally bogus, at least are not worth the $75 to $175 you will pay the company who will do the search. I know—I myself, who should have known much better, almost fell for one of these a while back.

It started innocently enough. I got a postcard in the mail as the parent of Jesse Richman, who was then in his freshman year at college. It was recognized that my son had been specifically chosen, because of his strong academic record, to be eligible for this "national" organization's scholarship opportunity. At least $1,000 was guaranteed to him in non-loan scholarships. I called the 800 phone number listed, just to get more information. The nice counselor I reached made it appear that they gave

scholarships themselves ("We work very closely with a number of major corporations who offer non-loan scholarships to students just like your son . . ."), and that for the small fee of $175 Jesse would indeed be guaranteed to get at least $1,000 for college expenses—or my money would be returned in full. With Jesse planning to go on the round-the-world Semester at Sea program, which would cost more than his scholarship at the University of Pittsburgh provided, we could use some extra funds.

Fool that I was, I grabbed at this. My husband Howard was out of town on one of his homeschooling evaluation trips so I didn't have his leveler head to put a stop to the nonsense—he can even refuse a Kirby vacuum cleaner saleslady who's just shampooed our rug in the middle of a snowstorm . . . After giving my credit card number to cover that $175 right over the phone, they then sent me out an application form. But as I later read through the questions, I began realizing that indeed this outfit was simply a computer college scholarship search company. They gave no scholarships themselves. They would only get the data from me that would let them print out a list (hopefully for them a very long list) of possible scholarships that Jesse could apply for himself, from all sorts of private corporations or organizations.

Reading the fine print further, I realized that my $175 would only be refunded if we could prove, through rejection letters from *every* scholarship opportunity they had provided us with, that Jesse had been formally turned down from each and every one (and I didn't even remember then that most scholarships or contests only notify winners, not losers). I realized that many of these scholarship applications would involve long essays, making posters, sending in formal transcripts, getting recommendations, and more and more—in short, it would be very time-consuming for Jesse to follow up on even a selected few, let along all of them. I realized pretty quickly that Jesse would be furious with me if he found out that I'd gotten him into this mess.

At this point I came to my senses, and with a stern letter to the company, was able to get my money back promptly. If I'd actually sent in the application form filled out, I would have had no recourse. Luckily I realized this in time. I'm wiser now. I hope you will be too.

So what can you do if you want to find out about those private scholarships that really may be out there? Don't pay anyone to do a computer search. Do your own, using the Internet. The site to look up (and go to your library if you don't have a computer hooked up on line yourself, or visit at a friend who does) is *www.finaid.org.* This site is an independent site created by Mark Kantrowitz, author of *The Prentice Hall Guide to Scholarships and Fellowships in Math and Science,* and it's consistently recommended by college financial aid administrators as a site to trust. You'll find full info on *all* aspects of paying for college here. It's truly a virtual guidance counselor, something all homeschoolers can use!

This site will let you do a complete scholarship search right online, and you can choose from several scholarship search options. You simply key in answers to a series of questions (many of them trying to see if you fit any odd target groups, like "left-handed Polish Americans who live in Pittsburgh who are interested in forestry careers"). Within minutes you'll get a full listing of scholarships your student is probably eligible to apply for. You then write off for applications, apply if you want to, and that's it. There is even a feature that updates your scholarship possibilities every month or so, as the site finds out about new scholarships that are out there. They have loads of info on all the scholarship scams to avoid, and how to spot them. I'm sure I recognized the group that sent me the nice postcard. There was even a story about a student who had started his "own" scholarship—publicized it somehow (probably on the Internet), had an application form readied, collected about $15 from each person's "application fee," and then declared himself the winner. All those $15 fees added up to a good "scholarship" for this young scam artist.

Most of us won't find the scholarships that will really help us pay for college through these types of searches, though. Often your place of business, the colleges you are seriously considering, and even the local newspaper are just as good in finding out about scholarships that

The Virtual Guidance Counselor . . .

Do your own scholarship search online! Learn all you need to know about applying for financial aid for college, and get prepared for doing well on admissions testing. Homeschoolers are no longer at any disadvantage because they don't have guidance counselors at high schools—all the info is now readily available right online. Here are some great websites to get you started:

- *www.finaid.com* This huge site has everything, answering almost every imaginable question on money and college admissions—and much more. Links to hundreds of related sites also. Scholarship search engine links right there enable you to do a search for free.
- *www.collegeboard.org* Go to the College Board site for quality info on test preparation (doing well on tests is often crucial to getting an academic scholarship), financial aid, Advanced Placement exams, National Merit Scholarships, and so much more. There is even a wonderful section specifically aimed to homeschool students, addressing the unique concerns homeschoolers may have. The site also has its own free scholarship search engine. It's often recommended to try several different computer searches, as their databases may be somewhat different.
- *www.testprep.com* A nifty site from Stanford Testing System with a free online SAT prep course that is very comprehensive. This course is also available on CD-ROM for home use, and the site also sells a number of good books on scholarship opportunities.
- *www.ed.gov/pubs/Prepare/* This site from the US Department of Education is the online version of a helpful book called *Preparing Your Child for College.* Also check out *www.ed.gov/studentaid* for full info on applying for federal student aid—you can even apply electronically!

might be good possibilities for your kids. In fact, many of us choose which colleges our kids will apply to based on whether or not the institution offers any sorts of merit scholarships. No Ivy League school offers merit scholarships, and many schools that wish they were Ivy League don't either. The next tier of schools does, as they are working very hard to attract bright students to their programs. Offering scholarships based on merit is their best way of doing this.

Still, doing an online scholarship search is entertaining, costs nothing, and may net you some good leads. Try it out. All the other financial aid info is really worthwhile and helpful too.

Just ditch any little postcards you get in the mail about the wonderful opportunities available to your son or daughter if you just call this 800 number.

Howard and Susan Richman have four always-homeschooled children, two in college, and have written several books about homeschooling, including Three R's at Home. *You can visit their web site at www.pahomeschoolers.com.*

CHAPTER 53

College At Home

If you read the chapter on "What You Need to Know About College but Probably Don't," you now realize that today's colleges need a good stiff dose of competition. Unfortunately, starting a new campus-based college isn't the answer, because of all the gazillion federal and state regulations forcing any new college to hire people whose philosophies and lifestyles toe the line of orthodox liberalism. Between federal and state requirements and accreditation-committee requirements, hardly any higher-education institution can call its soul its own.

Accreditation and Diplomas v. Education

Historically, accreditation only became an issue after the G.I. Bill was passed. This provided federal funds for World War II veterans to attend the college of their choice—provided it was accredited. All this was done with the best intentions. The unintended result was to enslave higher education to the ever-wackier demands of the elite who pull the accreditation committees' strings.

I became acutely aware of this while locating resources for the very first edition of the *Big Book*. I found plenty of great, inexpensive resources for preschool through grade 12. But when I got to grade 13—freshman year in college—suddenly the list shrank to "college courses from accredited institutions."

In the past few years, people have come up with all sorts of innovative programs to teach K–12 subjects. But the minute you hit college level, the unit studies and history timelines disappear.

Because homeschoolers tend to study advanced subjects at younger ages than schoolkids, I began to see that there was considerable overlap between the subject matter for junior high, high school, and college. A workbook that could teach Greek to junior-high students could also teach Greek to 19-year-olds. But the innovative Greek workbook, although designed by a college professor, was not *accredited*. Only institution-based classes are accredited; resources aren't. Therefore, college students could only use it if their classroom professor decided to assign that particular Greek workbook for use in his class.

Dumbed-Down Diplomas

Accreditation matters, because all of college life is structured around the quest for a *diploma*. But what is a diploma? Some institution's statement that you completed X number of required courses plus Y number of electives. This used to make sense, back when institutions taught that a core curriculum was central to a well-rounded education. But today, it's simply phony.

As a recent National Association of Scholars report revealed, the number of required courses in core areas in 1914 was 9.9. Today it's only 2.5. Furthermore, the kinds of courses that you can get in college have changed. As the *American Information Newsletter* of May 1996 said, summarizing the NAS report:

> *Increasingly, fields of study in mathematics, history, science, and literature, which lead to deeper and more sophisticated understandings, are being dropped in favor of invented or artificial one-time courses, like "Homosexual Film Makers." In 1914, the universities offered an average of only 23 courses per college which did not require a prerequisite course. This indicated that most courses were building upon past knowledge and thus were teaching an authentic corpus of knowledge. By 1964 the number of courses without prerequisites— "invented knowledge"—reached 127. Today it averages 582. In 1914, colleges universally required the teaching of writing skills. Today, only 36 percent require it. In 1914, 86 percent required math. Today, only 34 percent have a mathematics requirement. In 1914, 90 percent required some history. Today that has fallen to 2 percent. In 1914, 75 percent required literature courses. That dropped to 50 percent in 1964. Today not one of the "elite" institutions require literature. The number of courses in the contemporary college has increased by a factor of five over the number given in 1914. The majority of these additional courses are of two types. Either they are remedial courses designed to teach basic high-school skills or they are "narrow and idiosyncratic subjects of interest to the professors but almost worthless to the students."*

Who needs an "accredited" college if all it offers is recycled high-school and "college" courses that offer no more than you could get by reading a trendy book or watching a few TV shows? Who needs a "diploma" that certifies you took high school over again and added an assortment of unrelated "courses" that did not build on each other to provide any advanced knowledge?

We Need an Alternative

I submit to you that the entire diplomas-and-accreditation concept is

- hypocritical
- outdated
- monopolistic and anti-innovative
- ineffective in providing good education
- and dangerous.

It's *hypocritical*, because as we saw, accredited institutions are abandoning the traditional core curriculum in order to offer scores of remedial and wacko courses.

Diplomas are *outdated*, because we're living in a world of lifelong learning, not one in which you can get a degree and plan on never taking a course again.

Accreditation is *monopolistic and anti-innovative,* because it prevents talented individuals and groups of individuals from providing college courses, unless they have millions of dollars to spend on campus facilities, and unless they are willing to follow the latest social fads in order to meet accreditation requirements.

It's *ineffective in providing good education,* because Mickey Mouse courses are proliferating, rather than vanishing, as the NAS report quoted above demonstrates.

Finally, the combination of college accreditation with the concept that "only the degree matters" is downright *dangerous,* as I will now explain.

Dangerous Tests of Political Correctness

Christians are familiar with this Bible verse that predicts the terrifying totalitarian regime of the Anti-Christ: "None could buy or sell unless he had the mark of the beast, or the number of his name." This verse connects tyranny with control over who can earn money and who can spend it.

There are three ways to control who can earn money:

1. Tell colleges who they can and can't admit.
2. Tell colleges who they can and can't allow to graduate.
3. Tell businesses who they can and can't hire.

The Soviets chose Option 1. They used to keep Christians from achieving any influence in their society by denying them college entrance. This worked just great for over 70 years. However, it was a pretty obvious and heavy-handed method.

Any ill-intentioned Western government could accomplish the same thing, with far less effort, by simply implementing Options 2 and/or 3. As a student approaches graduation, with all the years and money invested in college so far, it's easy to get him to submit to pressure to do this or say that, if he is threatened with not being allowed to graduate unless he complies. Better yet, tests of political and religious orthodoxy can be disguised as courses required for graduation. Thus, students can be required to affirm homosexuality, or goddess worship, or anything the administration wants, in order to continue on the path to graduation.

If you think I'm kidding, or being paranoid, I'm not. Universities everywhere are installing freshman courses in "sensitivity and tolerance." While none of these are so blatant as to say straight out, "Yo! Christian and Jewish and Muslim kids! Are you willing to deny your religion's most basic teachings in order to continue in this institution?" what they are teaching *in practice* comes mighty close to this. Already simply sharing information about what your religion teaches about certain behaviors qualifies as a campus "hate crime" in many places.

College the Homeschool Way

Combine this with recent Congressional efforts to establish a national workforce policy, and you see that we have serious reasons for worry. That is, *unless* large numbers of us start applying the Homeschool Way to college and workforce training right now.

What is the Homeschool Way? Well, when applied to the lower grades, homeschoolers have learned that

Other books lead you into the world of distance education. **How to Get a College Degree Via the Internet** focuses in one one type of distance education—online education. This is the book you need if you're wondering

- Is distance education right for me?
- What equipment and skills will I need?
- How can I choose a school?
- How do I apply?
- How can I finance an online degree?

The first part of the book includes online educational resources, special information for international students, and even information about how to find a job online.

All this advice is very practical and helpful, as you'd expect when the author is Director of Online Education at Vatterott College and an active member of the United States Distance Learning Association.

The rest of the book is mostly made up of full-page listings of over 70 university online programs. These have good contact information and general detail about the schools and courses. Price information is more spotty. This is too bad, as price is one of the main concerns when choosing an online program. An appendix of nationally recognized accrediting agencies and associations is also included, as are a glossary and index. *Mary Pride*

- credentials don't create better educators
- good resources (from whatever source) beat bad, state-approved resources
- interesting teaching methods work better than boring lectures
- well-designed software can teach you more than a textbook can
- you can learn a lot from library books
- you can stitch together the courses and resources of your choice into an impressive transcript
- you can prove what you have learned by assembling a portfolio of finished projects and assignments
- when you stick to your convictions, you can create a whole new educational system

I would urge everyone reading this book to reexamine what you truly hope to get out of college. If you're hoping for "a good job," then why not apply for an internship program or apprenticeship at the company of your dreams? If "a good education" is the main objective, then consider seriously the value of taking some *un*-accredited courses.

I could provide each of you, right now, with a quality college education that costs one-fifth to one-tenth what a "regular" college education costs, if I knew you were willing to pay serious money for good education that did not require campus-based accreditation or a final diploma. There are literally tens of thousands of retired college professors, and qualified people who would like to teach college courses but can't get a university position, plus people who wouldn't want a full-time college professorship but who know advanced subjects inside and out.

What is stopping all these people from inventing and providing great college courses and resources?

Nothing, except a public that unjustifiably expects all "real" college courses to be provided by accredited campus-based institutions and to culminate in a degree.

If we, as parents, students, and business owners, can get it through our heads that "accreditation" and "diploma" have nothing to do with education, this will open the way for a flood of great resources, just as the original homeschool movement opened the doors for people to invent mountains of great educational materials. It will also make it possible for *existing* institutions to improve.

If students demanded the right to take courses *"à la carte,"* then courses whose primary purpose is indoctrination into the professor's religious or political worldview would wither and die. If business owners wanted to see what students have actually *done,* and what courses they have actually taken, instead of just asking if you have a degree, then Mickey Mouse and "fringe" courses would have no financial value whatsoever, and we can hope most of them would disappear.

College at Home on the Internet

Remember that "good stiff dose of competition" I said today's colleges need? This may be on the horizon, thanks to the surging popularity of the Internet. While campus-based institutions require huge endowments and have been stationary targets for government regulators, setting up a college on the Internet basically means buying a couple of computers, leasing a fast phone line (T-1 or T-3), hiring professors (who don't have to live anywhere near each other or even in the same country as the college), getting software to keep track of grades and transcripts, and finding a techie to keep the equipment running. No parklike campuses or million-dollar buildings required. Even library size requirements, traditionally the bane of small institutions seeking college accreditation, may become a problem of the past, thanks to the thousands of books being "ported" to electronic (and therefore downloadable) form every week.

Campus-based institutions are not blind to the advantages of college at home via the Internet. Quite a few are dipping their toe into these waters with selected courses now offered via email or the World Wide Web. However, their courses are usually priced quite high, in line with their outrageously high campus tuition. And what they offer *on* campus isn't always that great, these days.

So I'm going to make a bold prediction:

College at home will be a major option for many homeschoolers in the near future.

Especially for those who read this book!

Here's another one:

Unless college lobbyists persuade Congress to make this so difficult it's illegal for all practical purposes, the majority of tomorrow's Internet college courses will *not* be offered by today's "major universities," just as the majority of educational software was not designed by IBM.

If you're involved with one of these startups, send me your press kit. Paul Allen should stop fooling around with A.P. courses (although more online A.P. courses *are* needed). Online *college* is the huge growth opportunity here.

And just to make sure you get your money's worth, here's one more:

Soon your fellow homeschoolers will be putting together their own colleges.

I wrote these three predictions in 1996, for the first draft of this book. Already the third one is coming true, as Home School Legal Defense Association is launching Patrick Henry College.

Plenty of homeschool parents have college degrees, even advanced degrees. Lots of us would love a job that allows us to work at home, and heaven knows we've had enough teaching experience. Just about all of us already own computers. It wouldn't be that hard for those of us with experience in college administration or who have already worked in a college environment to put together some excellent college courses.

In fact, it's already being done. The only problem is that none of the institutions doing it have college accreditation . . . yet. Scholars Online Academy (reviewed in Volume 1) has high-school courses that are more advanced than most college-level courses today, for example. They plan to seek accreditation at the college level in the near future. We'll be reporting on this, and other developments in online courses for homeschoolers, in my magazine *Practical Homeschooling*.

In the meantime, plenty of correspondence-school options exist. There are ways and means of getting a college degree without ever setting foot on campus . . . or at most spending a couple of weeks a year on campus. And you can take quite a few courses online, although you might not yet be able to cobble an online degree together in your chosen major.

The books in this chapter show you how to find courses right now that you can take at home. Not all college education has to occur at home—but trying a few online courses, or correspondence courses, even from (gasp!) accredited institutions can revolutionize your thinking about college. Before you commit to spending umpteen thousand dollars, and up to six or more years of your life, away from home in an overpriced hot tub of political correctness, why not try the Homeschool Way first?

Two Plus Two Equals Half of Four

Students working toward a bachelor's degree can avoid a lot of expenses and debt by staying home the first two years and attending a local community college.

In a society in which parents go into debt to finance their children's higher education, it is alarming to learn that the average tuition at American colleges and universities continues to rise each year.

Throughout the 1980's, tuition costs rose at a rate much higher than the general rate of inflation in the economy.

By academic year 1990–91, there were 255 private colleges where tuition alone was $10,000 per year or more. (Sowell, 1992.)

An annual survey by the College Board showed that college costs for the 1995–96 academic year averaged $19,762 at private colleges and $9,285 at state-run universities. Among the costs represented by these figures are room and board, fees, tuition, books and transportation.

Such costs represent a serious problem to most American families. Today, many of them turn to financial aid packages offered by institutions as a way to finance education.

Many families feel that the college degree will at least ensure a middle-class standard of living, and the sacrifice of making hefty loan payments after graduation would be worth it.

The rationale is, after all, many students graduate from colleges with loans to repay. The president of MIT noted that financial aid applicants at that institution are "distributed almost uniformly across the spectrum of family income." (Sowell, 1992.)

The reality is that many colleges are responding to complaints about high tuition costs with the offer of financial aid packages. However, a good student financial aid package may not be necessary to pay for all four years of college with a little planning on the part of the student

What if you could save almost half the cost of a college education? Suppose you choose to begin your college education at a two-year community college? A student could complete the first years of a four-year degree at a fraction of the cost of a four-year school, then after two years, the student could transfer to a four-year college or university.

Currently, the average tuition costs at a public, two-year school are approximately $1,300 per year. This is substantially lower than most four-year schools.

Choosing a two-year community college for the first two years of the college education is definitely a cost-effective decision. The savings are obvious when compared with the tuition at the four-year schools (public or private).

Research also shows that the two-year college student does not necessarily sacrifice educational advantages. A federally funded study of what education refers to as "outcomes" (what a student is supposed to learn in a course or discipline area), or how college affects students, reported that "the cognitive impacts of two-year colleges may be indistinguishable from four-year institutions that enroll similar students." (Schrof, 1995.)

Professor Earnest Pascarella of the University of Illinois at Chicago, who heads the research project, said that "a student who chooses to attend a community college does not necessarily sacrifice intellectual gains. The myth that more selective schools must offer a superior education just doesn't hold up under scrutiny. My bet is that there's a relatively flat curve in the quality of education schools offer until you get to the 15 or 20 most selective liberal arts colleges." (Schrof, 1995.)

Other research studies comparing the achievement of two-year college students with four-year colleges/universities have found similar results.

A study in Arizona found that the more courses students take at the community college level, the better they do once they are in a four-year school.

In a study in Michigan, students who transferred from two-year colleges consistently achieved higher grades than those who began their education as freshmen at four-year schools. (Schrof, 1995.)

A study in Georgia from 1989 to 1996 of two-year community college graduates at one public institution found that two-year college graduates were satisfied with their education at the two-year level and would recommend their two-year school highly.

These same students were surveyed again one year after graduation and were asked to rate their satisfaction with the two-year institution after they had experienced one year of study at a four-year school. The students were asked to rate their overall preparedness for upper-level course work. Once again, the students consistently rated the two-year school high on preparation for continuing their education at a four-year college or university.

Overall, students in the study felt well-prepared for upper-level college course work, and they would continue to recommend the two-year school to their friends.

In addition to academic preparedness, students in the Georgia study continued to cite cost and convenience as top reasons for choosing to attend a two-year community college. Other reasons cited were small class sizes and individual attention from the instructors in their classes.

As families face the time to make college decisions, they should think long and hard before they accept a loan, borrow on the equity of their home, or disturb their retirement savings.

It is probably not necessary for the first two years. The payoff on those debts is very far away and may jeopardize future financial security years.

After two years of study at the community college, the bachelor's degree can then be pursued at a four-year college or university.

In the end, the bachelor's degree (which was the goal) comes from the "school of choice" without the high tuition costs for all four years.

References:

Schrof, J.M. (1995). "A cheaper path to a college degree." *U.S. News & World Report*, 119 (12), 88-89.

Sowell, T. (1992). "The scandal of college tuition." *Commentary*, 94 (2), 23-26.

This article reprinted from Christian Financial Concepts Money Matters newsletter. Used by permission.

The author of this article, Dr. Rhonda Morgan, is an associate professor of business administration at Gordon College, a two-year unit of the University System of Georgia, Barnesville, GA.

Four-Year College Degree at Home from Penn State and University of Iowa

Penn State University announced at their high school-at-home workshop that they have reached a co-operative agreement with the University of Iowa so that you can get a liberal arts diploma entirely by correspondence by beginning at Penn State and finishing at Iowa. This new homeschooling option should appeal to homeschool graduates, eight percent of whom are currently homeschooling for college, according to our surveys.

Those interested could pursue an Associate in Liberal Arts from Penn State for their first 68 credits (about 23 courses), and then transfer to the University of Iowa for their remaining 56 credits (about 19 courses). They would then graduate with a Bachelor of Liberal Studies degree from the University of Iowa. Cost is $102 per credit (plus book fees) from Penn State and $77 per credit from Iowa plus a $15 application fee —a total of less than $12,000 for a college degree!

Both the Penn State and Iowa programs have been around a long time. The Penn State program was originally designed to let people do the first two years at home before coming to Penn State main campus for their junior and senior years. The Iowa program was originally designed to help adults finish up their college degrees. Now, with the two programs working together, you can go all the way through at home. The Iowa program has found that 83% of their graduates who apply get into their graduate school of choice.

Each Penn State course has a textbook and study guide and some also have videos and audio tapes. Written assignments are mailed to the instructors and two or three exams (per course) are taken at a local Penn State campus. Each course is normally completed in a half year, though students can proceed at their own pace and take up to a full year if necessary. Final grades go on standard Penn State transcripts without any indication that they are correspondence courses, and credits can be transferred to any college that accepts Penn State credits.

Unfortunately, for most of these courses, students will have little contact with their instructors except for instructor's brief responses to their written assignments. Both Penn State and Iowa are currently taking steps to permit communication with instructors and/or between students by e-mail and some instructors are already available to students by phone or e-mail.

If current high-school students want to get started on college-level work before they graduate, they can do so. They could later transfer their credits to any college that accepts Penn State credits. They would need to show Penn State they are ready for college work.

To apply, homeschooling high school students should:

1. Fill out a request and send it without payment.
2. Attach letters of recommendation from their parent and/or from their evaluators indicating that the student has the ability to do college-level work.
3. Send in a copy of their current home education transcript and evaluations, and copies of any available SAT or PSAT scores, AP scores, etc.
4. Meet specific course pre-requisites, such as passing grades on Penn State's placement tests or on AP tests.

For more information about distance education at Penn State:
Department of Distance Education
Pennsylvania State University
207 Mitchell Building
University Park, PA 16802-3601
Tel: 1-800-252-3592
Email: psude@cde.psu.edu

This article by Howard Richman originally appeared in the Pennsylvania Homeschoolers newsletter #56, under the title "New Option for College at Home at Penn State." Copyright ©1996 Pennsylvania Homeschoolers. Used by permission.

Guides to College at Home

Barron's Guide to Distance Learning is *the* book to reference to find the exact distance learning schools that offer the degree you want to earn. The strengths of this 537-page oversized book lie in its huge up-to-date listings of colleges and its indexes that tell which colleges offer what degree. Our oldest son, who for medical reasons can't attend college away from home, used this book to find the college and program that was best for him. (The B.A. in Business Administration program from Texas Tech University, in his case. Tuition is inexpensive and Texas Tech has an excellent reputation.)

Barron's Guide starts with 88 pages of discussions of what distance learning is, whether it is right for you, accreditation, earning and transferring credits, financing the cost, and how to get started. This is OK, but not as in-depth and helpful as the information on these topics in the *How to Earn a Degree* books reviewed elsewhere in this chapter.

The bulk of the book—378 pages—consists of profiles of the various schools. Each profile gives information on where each school is and how it can be reached by mail, phone, fax, and email; what degree programs it has; class titles; teaching methods; whether they grant credits for life experience, portfolio, etc.; admission requirements; on-campus requirements; tuition and fees; financial aid; accreditation; and a fairly lengthy description.

The indexes list the colleges by state and province, on-campus requirements, undergraduate fields of study, graduate fields of study, doctorate fields of study, certificate and diploma programs, and individual classes. You can look up whatever you want in any of these categories and find a list of the college programs that meet your needs.

Barron's Guide is an invaluable tool for anyone who wants to discover the options available without having to travel to a college campus, and for narrowing your search down to the distance learning program in which you will actually enroll. *Bill Pride*

Don't commit to any college option until you've checked out the latest edition of **Bear's Guide**. This oversized, 416-page book gives you an education in what non-traditional education is all about, what accreditation is all about, ways to earn credit even in a traditional institution without darkening its doors (through exams/life experience/learning contracts/etc), the lowdown on honorary doctorates (one of the least painful ways of getting a Ph.D.), how to tell the difference between a legitimate non-traditional school and a diploma mill, and so much more.

Why do you care? Because, even if you decide to attend a traditional campus-based institution, you can save thousands of dollars with the advice in this book. And if you decide that a more nontraditional approach is for you, you can save tens of thousands of dollars!

The heart of the book is about 250 pages of detailed school listings—over 2,000 in all. These include accredited schools with nonresident programs, accredited schools with short residency programs, accredited schools with nontraditional residential programs, unaccredited schools with nonresident programs, unaccredited schools with short residency programs, unaccredited schools with nontraditional residency programs, high-school diplomas and associate's degrees, law schools, and medical and other health-related schools. Full contact information is provided for all of these, as well as descriptions of what each school offers and its relative cost. There's even a listing of known diploma mills. Addresses for these "mills" are *not* provided, as Dr. Bear does not want to encourage anyone to patronize them.

NEW!
Barron's Guide to Distance Learning

Grade 11–college. $18.95 plus shipping. ISBN: 0-7641-0725-9.
Barron's Educational Series, Inc., 250 Wireless Blvd., Hauppauge, NY 11788. (800) 645-3476. Fax: (516) 434-3217. Web: www.barronseduc.com.

NEW!
Bears' Guide to Earning College Degrees Nontraditionally, 13th edition

Grade 10–adult. $29.95 plus $3 shipping.
Home Life, Inc., PO Box 1190, Fenton, MO 63026. Orders: (800) 346-6322. Inquiries: (636) 343-7750. Fax: (636) 343-7203. Email: orders@home-school.com. Web: www.home-school.com.

What can I say about this book? It's a classic. I could do without the smidgin of salty language that has crept into this edition, but not without the book itself. With the typical nontraditional degree program costing thousands less each year than a campus-based program, while allowing you to stay where you are and keep working for at least most of the year, it's an option any college-bound student should definitely consider. *Mary Pride*

Discover Dr. Bear's choice of the 100 best fully-accredited schools that offer Bachelor's, Master's, doctorates, and law degrees by home study. He devotes an entire page to each school, giving a full description, address, phone, fax number, email and or web site information, key person to contact, cost, programs offered, accreditation status, and a personal evaluation.

In all, you get much more info—on fewer schools—than in *Bear's Guide* (reviewed above). This book focuses solely on college degrees from accredited institutions, and forgoes the lengthy instruction in what distance-learning is all about.

Unlike so many resource books, **College Degrees by Mail** is delightful to read. Bear's descriptions of the colleges and universities are lively as well as informative. Dr. Bear also includes information on getting personalized counseling and assistance, equivalency and entrance exams; and advice for people in prison who want to earn college degrees.

Bear gets his information both from extensive questionnaires and phone calls, and from the letters readers write telling him about their educational experiences. You can't find a better guide. Someone you know could save thousands of dollars by reading this book. *Mary Pride*

Though the most recent editions of these books were first published in 1994, **How to Earn a College Degree Without Going to College** and **How to Earn an Advanced Degree Without Going to Graduate School** are still excellent sources of advice on how to pursue a college degree without physically attending classes on a college campus. Think of these books as your personal guidance counselor. They will inform you about what distance education is all about and where to look for information.

Some of the topics discussed in *How to Earn a College Degree* are:

- What a college degree is, who decides who can grant them, and who accredits the institutions giving them
- What alternative education is and whether it is for you
- Advice for how to successfully study at home, learning contracts and degree plans
- Selecting a program, financing a program, and banking your credits
- Directory of external degree programs.

How to Earn an Advanced Degree starts with a discussion of accreditation very similar to the one in the other book, but goes on to discuss topics unique to getting a graduate school degree. Some of the topics unique to this book are:

- Graduate schools and how to enroll in them
- The Graduate Record Exam (GRE), required for entrance into most advanced degree programs
- Sources other than colleges for graduate level credits: directory of correspondence schools, life experience credits, building a portfolio

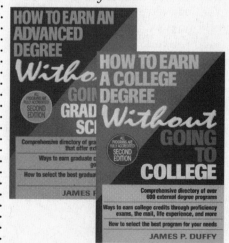

- Directory of external masters degree programs
- Directory of external doctorate degree programs.

The college listings in these books were created five years ago, so they they may leave out programs that have started more recently. Unless one of the programs included in these books strikes you as the perfect college program for you, you should check the *Barrons Guide* or *Bear's Guide* for more up-to-date and complete listings.

On the other hand, the advice that makes up the bulk of these books is sound and still applies to the current college situation. These books are well worth their price. *Bill Pride*

Here are two books that show you how to carry "homeschooling" right into college and graduate school. For those of you unfamiliar with the concept of distance learning, **Virtual College** gives the answers to "why and how," while **Peterson's Distance Learning** delves into the "what and where."

A two-hour read, *Virtual College* brings you up to speed quickly on the essentials: what it's like to be a student in a virtual classroom, types of courses available, the equipment needed, and how long it will take and how much it will cost to complete a course or earn a certificate or degree. It also directs you to where you can find out about courses, costs, financial aid, when and how to apply, and more.

With this background, you can tackle the much larger and quite definitive *Peterson's Distance Learning*. This huge 504-page tome provides detailed information on over 1,200 degrees and certificate programs available from more than 750 accredited public and private two- and four-year colleges and graduate institutions in all 50 states and Canada. To give you an idea how quickly distance education is growing, the first edition of this book listed less than 100 institutions providing distance courses—and 96 percent of the distance education program directors surveyed in this edition indicate they plan to expand the number of programs they will offer in the next three years.

The book takes its mission as "the only complete sourcebook of accredited college and university programs available through television, computer, videocassette, and audiocassette" seriously. It begins with essays providing a basic understanding of distance learning, and includes a glossary of distance-learning terms. Next comes the bulk of the book: individual institution profiles. These include information about the institution itself, who may take the courses, the media used, how to apply, typical costs, and degree or certificate programs and individual courses offered. Media used may include television or satellite transmission, videocassette or audiocassette, one- or two- way videoconferencing or audioconferencing, synchronous (real-time) or asynchronous (not in real time, as in the case of ongoing email discussions or message boards) Internet class discussions, etc. Courses may be credit or non-credit, and apply to a certificate, associate's degree, bachelor's degree, master's degree, or doctoral degree. Expanded two-page descriptions follow for a number of institutions, as does a listing of distance-education consortiums (groups of institutions that have banded together to increase the distance-learning opportunities they can offer). To wrap up, you'll find indexes to degrees and certificate programs offered, individual courses offered, and geographical location, and a list of institutions participating in the PBS "Going the Distance" program. *Mary Pride*

NEW!
Peterson's Distance Learning Books

Grade 10–adult. Peterson's Guide to Distance Learning Programs, $26.95. Virtual College, $9.95. *Peterson's, 202 Carnegie Center, PO Box 2123, Princeton, NJ 08543-2123. (800) 338-3282. Outside U.S. and Canada: (609) 243-9111. Fax: (609) 452-0966. Web: www.petersons.com.*

Even if you plan to attend a traditional college campus, you need to know about these books. You may not be able to complete your campus experience, due to family or health problems. Your college may not offer a needed course when you need it. You may have a child and find that on-campus attendance is no longer easy. You may discover that it's more sensible to stay where your job is and let the school "come to you." Homeschool parents who want to pursue further college education, but who need to keep food on the table at the same time, and advanced homeschool graduates who are too young to leave home safely, should definitely consider these books. Recommended.

CHAPTER 54

Learning the Ropes

Most young adults have no idea what the business world is really like. According to TV shows and cartoon strips all bosses are evil and nothing is funnier than smarting off to the person who signs your paychecks. What bosses expect and want from you . . . how to properly relate to co-workers and superiors . . . how to handle office politics . . . how to present a grievance . . . none of this is automatic. You have to *learn* the ropes. And here's help with just that!

Books to Help You Learn the Ropes

The **9–5 Series** are small books with easy-reading vocabulary and short sentences. Each is the story of a young man or woman with a summer job who has to solve a mystery concerning his job. The books are intended to teach preteens and teens how to solve problems that might arise in applying for and keeping their first blue-collar job. Some of the problems—like learning to not "talk silly" around the boss—are part of everyday life, and others—like trying to catch the person who is poisoning food at the supermarket—are thrown in to make the books more interesting. The main characters model good character traits like diligence and honesty.

In *Box Girl*, Patty Walker learns to overcome her impetuousness while working as a supermarket box girl. Troy Martin learns he likes nursery work in *A New Leaf*, but are those really mushrooms Pete is growing in his greenhouse with the windows painted black? In *A Nugget of Gold*, Lucy goes to work at the animal shelter, where the dog she likes the best is "adopted" under suspicious circumstances. Jake gets his friend Lee a job at City Auto in *The Set-Up*, only to wonder if Lee is the person ripping cars off from the lot. In my personal favorite, *The Secret Solution*, Jim gets accused of robbing the houses his crew has been painting.

Like the other High Noon books, these are absorbing reading. Kids can painlessly discover which work attitudes lead to rewards and which will get you fired by reading these books. *Mary Pride*

9–5 Series

Grades 5–12 (3rd grade readability). $17 for all five books. Shipping $3. *High Noon Books, 20 Commercial Boulevard, Novato, CA 94949-6191. (415) 883-3314. Fax: (415) 883-3720. Email: atpub@aol.com. Web: www.atp.com.*

NEW!
BJUP Manners at Work

Grade 8–adult. $19.95 plus $4.95 shipping.
Bob Jones University Press Customer Service, Greenville, South Carolina 29614-0062. (800) 845-5731. Fax: (800) 525-8398. Web: www.bju.edu/press/

Ever wonder how you could possibly remember all the manners necessary to succeed in the business world *and* teach them to your children? Just pop this video tape, **Manners at Work: A Guide to Professional Etiquette**, into the VCR and let Janiece Robinson do the job for you. Janeice Robinson is a wonderful host. She never assumes you know something and she is never condescending.

"Many topics vital to today's business person, including appropriate dress, proper introductions, gender equality, desk etiquette, and business dining" are dealt with in this tape. She does not become preachy in her role as host. She guides you through the proper steps and points out mistakes not to make. For example, in our daily lives, we expect men to hold open doors for women—but in the business world, they are equals, so women can just as easily open those doors for men. She also points out obvious items which we take for granted: if in doubt, take your cue from your boss. If the boss dresses up even on casual Friday, so should you; do not wear your favorite jeans, just because some of the others do. Take your cue from the boss!

I expected amateurish results, but the tape is very professionally done, thanks to the director, Daniel Boone and the cameraman, Jim Jordan.

Janeice Robinson lectures on professional etiquette and has taught communication and speech classes. So who better to communicate professional etiquette to the future business leaders of the world? This is a must-view video for anyone in the public's eye. *Barbara Buchanan*

NEW!
Everything I Needed to Know About Business I Learned in the Barnyard

Grade 7–adult. $9.95 plus $3 shipping.
Home Life, Inc., PO Box 1190, Fenton, MO 63026. Orders: (800) 346-6322. Inquiries: (636) 343-7750. Fax: (636) 343-7203. Email: orders@home-school.com. Web: www.home-school.com.

Even if you didn't grow up on a farm, you'll enjoy these object lessons from the animal world. Frustrated with higher education's tendency to make even the simple unnecessarily complicated (can't we relate to that!), Don Aslett decided it was time for some down-home illustrations. In **Everything I Needed to Know About Business I Learned in the Barnyard**, life's lessons are presented here for the benefit of all. Cows ("If you feed the stock, they stay in the corral"), pigs ("Pedigree is no guarantee"), and chickens ("Roost high!") all have something to contribute. The bottom line? Work hard, stay honest, don't go for the quick buck, and treat others the way you want to be treated. You already knew that, of course, but it's a lot of fun to read anyway! *Renee Mathis*

NEW!
Ferguson Career Skills Library

Grades 7–12. Each volume, $13.95. Set of all 8, $99.95, includes teacher's guide. Shipping extra.
Ferguson Publishing Company, 200 West Madison St., Suite 300, Chicago, IL 60606. (800) 306-9941. Fax: (800) 306-9942.

How do you learn the skills they don't teach in school? I'm talking about persuasive and clear communication, on-the-spot problem-solving and decision-making, and getting people to want to work with you instead of against you. These skills are critical when it comes to landing a job, keeping it, and moving ahead, but they don't fall under traditional academic headings.

Up to this point, books on these subjects have all been written for adult business people. Some of these books are quite lively and easy to read, but it's still clear they weren't written for teens.

That's why Ferguson Publishing Company, known for their extensive catalog of books on career preparation, has come out with the new **Career Skills Library**.

Eight skill areas are covered, one in each 128-page library-bound volume. The four volumes most useful for homeschoolers are:

- **Learning the Ropes** (what the world of work is really like, what bosses and coworkers expect of you, your legal rights and responsibilities, how to avoid office politics, and a lot more)
- **Communications Skills** (a terrific condensed course: business writing with all sorts of practical examples, public speaking, learning to listen, and working in teams)
- **Teamwork Skills** (an excellent how-the-world-really-works book that makes its points in clever ways, such as giving names to personality types such as "Carl Choleric" and describing how you can work with someone like Carl)
- **Leadership Skills** (more nitty-gritty business info—what leadership is, why it matters, how to work with others to get things done, ways professionals organize a project such as Gantt charts and other scheduling devices, completing a project, and learning to lead)

Somewhat less useful are the following four volumes:

- **Self-Development Skills** (not as good as the others—this one is about improving the business-friendly parts of your character, such as dependability/professionalism/niceness/being organized, but unfortunately takes a "figure out your own personal ethics approach," and even appears to condone lying in some cases)
- **Problem-Solving Skills** (all about what logic is and how to use it to solve problems—not needed by most homeschooled students, who are up to seven years ahead of public-school students in thinking skills, on average)
- **Information Management Skills** (how to research, keep track of, and use information—an O.K. summary, but there are curriculum products that teach this better and in more depth)
- **Organizational Skills** (pretty basic advice)

Each volume includes interviews with young people who explain how the particular skill covered in that volume has been essential to their on-the-job performance. They also include quotes from famous people, cartoons, and thought-provoking lists of all sorts. A rather piddly glossary and complete index are at the back of each book.

The 29-page teacher's guide has the following for each book: a vocabulary-matching exercise, creative writing assignments, role-playing activities, discussion starters, art projects, and research projects. An answer key is in the back of the guide.

I would definitely recommend the first four listed volumes to any homeschool family or support group. *Mary Pride*

How many times have you stood at the counter of Bargain Mart or Hamburger Haven wondering whatever happened to the notion of customer service? If society's workforce only had a copy of this **How to be #1 with your Boss**! Everyone can use these training ideas. If you have employees, they need to know how to conduct themselves. If you are self-employed, you need to know how to serve your customers. If you are a

NEW!
How to be #1 with your Boss

Grade 7–adult. $5.95 plus $3 shipping.
Home Life, Inc., PO Box 1190, Fenton, MO 63026. Orders: (800) 346-6322.

Inquiries: (636) 343-7750.
Fax: (636) 343-7203.
Email: orders@home-school.com.
Web: www.home-school.com.

teenager entering the working world, you can use this book to help you sail far above the competition. And if you are a mom at home (the most valuable management position of all—read what Mary Pride has to say in chapter 11 of *All the Way Home*) then you can really use this book. The next time the kids balk at chores, try training them using some of the principles in this book. Sometimes a new approach works wonders!

Don Aslett provides you with plenty of examples from his own experience as head of a large company: what bosses look for, how to deal with a difficult boss, a day in the life of a boss, and your place in the work place. All top-notch info, presently humorously and humorously illustrated, from someone who knows. *Renee Mathis*

CHAPTER 55

Careers Without College

Adult education has come a long way. Only 20 years ago, adult education meant rows of high-school dropouts bent over dog-eared textbooks under the fluorescent lights of an after-hours high-school classroom. For many people, adult education still means pursuing a diploma, but in your home, not a classroom. Nor are high-school diplomas the only credentials available to after-hours scholars. You can get a college degree, a Master's, or even a legitimate Ph.D. at home!

Academic degrees are not the whole story, either. You can learn hundreds of marketable skills at home, from accident investigation to zookeeping. Upgrade your present job, or change jobs, *without* wearing yourself to a frazzle with late-night classes!

And then there's the sheer joy of learning. Dazzle your friends with your wok cookery! Learn how to make new slipcovers! Design your own clothes! Immerse yourself in history! Develop a gorgeous calligraphic handwriting style! Study French and read Blaise Pascal in the original, or Russian and grapple with Dostoyevski and Solzhenitsyn.

I'm not saying you should try to "reach your potential." You can *never* reach your potential! If you lived a thousand years, you could still be learning new things in your tenth century. And wouldn't it be *fun!*

How to Find a Career Without College

Do you have a year and a half free after high school? Are you a Christian young man with a desire for practical training that will enable you to help in a wide range of service and disaster scenarios? Are you an alumnus of Bill Gothard's Institute in Basic Life Principles "Basic" and "Advanced" seminars?

Since its inception, IBLP's homeschool program, called Advanced Training Institute International (ATI), has stressed the value of real-world apprenticeships. The **ALERT** program, which as of 1998 has been in operation for four years and has graduated over 400 young men, is an example of this apprenticeship approach for high-school graduates.

You do not have to have graduated from the ATI program to apply, although you do have to have attended and agree to the basic principles taught in IBLP's seminars, as I mentioned above. Starting in January 1999, ATI graduates get a price break on the tuition; this is because ATI is partially funding the ALERT program.

Home education is much more than college degrees. It's vocational training, and hobbies, and religious instruction. It's courses on writing and art and fashion design. Where can you go to not only find academic degree programs, but also vocational programs and self-improvement courses?

It's true that not every reputable home study course is accredited by the Distance Education Training Council (formerly that National Home Study Council). But the DETC's *voluntary* accreditation program can increase a shopper's confidence.

To receive the free DETC *1999–2000 Directory of Accredited Home Study Schools* brochure, just write to the Distance Education Training Council office at 1601 18th St., N.W., Washington, DC 20009.

NEW!
Air Land Emergency Resource Team (ALERT)

High school graduates, age 17 or older, medically and physically qualified, who have attended IBLP's Basic and Advanced Seminar. M-Team tuition, 5 weeks tuition plus $575 non-refundable ALERT uniform fee. ALERT Phase One, 8 weeks tuition plus $575 non-refundable uniform fee. Phase Two: 16 weeks tuition plus $800 required equipment and textbooks;

Intermediate High Angle Rescue option, $155; Advanced High Angle Rescue option, $85. Phrase Three: 44 weeks tuition plus required program fee for one of the following: aircraft maintenance, $130; aquatics, $1,900; auto mechanics, $45; construction, $50; EMT, $315; paramedic, $500; leadership, $200; technical rescue, $1,500; aviation—solo, $500—private pilot license, $2,200—instrument license, $3,000–$4,500. Tuition is $115/week for ATI students, $145/week for non-ATI students. Distribution of weeks between Phase Two and Three can vary, based on deployments. Non-uniform gear, tools for some options purchased separately. Application packet, $10.
ALERT Headquarters, E21800 Wolf Lake Rd., Watersmeet, MI 49969. (906) 358-4500. Fax: (906) 358-4517. Email: alert@nwcc.iblp.org.

This 68-week program is divided into three phases:
Phase One, "Basic Training," is a military-style "boot camp" that features discipline and fitness, without the weapons training common to military programs. Training is provided in:

- Leadership by example
- First aid, with wilderness applications
- Physical training in strength and endurance development. This training is intense. I've been told that after the ALERT program, Marine basic training didn't seem all that hard!
- Rope work, with an emphasis on knots and river crossing
- Outdoor survival, including making fire, shelter construction, and orienteering
- Rapelling, i.e., using ropes to make your way down steep surfaces, useful in high-angle rescue
- Character training in quick, cheerful obedience to authority
- Personal discipline

Phase Two, "Crisis Response," is medical and rescue training that equips young men to help in a variety of crisis and service settings. Trainees will learn all the following, which they will practice in teams:

- High-angle rescue (e.g., on mountainsides, in crevasses, and other locations where reaching the victim is itself a hazardous undertaking)
- Medical MFR training with state certification
- Response diving with underwater search patterns
- Short-term work projects and disaster relief
- Ham radio VHF licensing and basic operating skills
- Fire fighting in structures and wildnerness
- Counseling in IBLP's principles
- Land search-and-rescue techniques
- Evangelism

Phase Three, "Ministry Support," provides advanced training in a specialty of choice. Students can choose *one* of the following:

- Emergency medicine, including EMT and paramedic state and national certification
- Auto mechanics
- National Academy of Police Diving certification
- Construction, including classes and experience in various construction trades
- Aircraft maintenance
- Advanced rescue skills
- Aviation, with FAA-certified ground school and flight instruction
- Leadership—learning to be the guy who coordinates a team's efforts in ministry or rescue

Phase Four, "Eagle Response Unit" (ERU), is actual deployment in ministry and service assignments, or service with ALERT's headquarters. This is full-time work. Graduates who are not able or willing to handle a full-time commitment are considered on "reserve" status, which makes them eligible for ongoing service and training opportunities as feasible.

All phases run concurrently. This means you don't have to wait a year if you miss the next starting date. For example, if you miss the June start of

Basic Training, you can start in September. As a rule, phases start three months apart, except that there is no Basic Training starting in January, because the facility is in the Michigan northwoods, and it can get down to 42 degrees below zero up there in the middle of winter!

ALERT's services are free, but must be requested by a local government official. (If *you* are a local government official, you might want to put their num-

ber in your Rolodex!) So far they have helped clean up after the Oklahoma City bombing incident; after tornadoes in Arkansas, Alabama, Tennessee, Wisconsin, and Kentucky; after floods in Ohio, Oregon, and Kentucky; and during snow emergencies in upper Michigan and Wisconsin. ALERT has also repaired hurricane-damaged roads in Oaxuaca, Mexico; repaired a Moscow orphanage; and provided their construction and repair services to a poverty-stricken Indian community in Chiapas, Mexico. This is *not* glamorous work, unless being hip-deep in mud under someone's mobile home appeals to you. ALERT's search-and-rescue work, which has included diving for drowning victims and searching for lost hunters, seems more glamorous, but also involves long, weary hours in all kinds of weather. You're training hard to work hard.

Since the training is so demanding, ALERT now offers a preparatory program, called Mighty Men Team (M-Team). The objective of this five-week course is to prepare young men for success in ALERT's Basic Training. Spiritual training, including memorizing Scripture passages, and character development are emphasized. Scripture passages studied include those required for Basic Training, giving M-Team grads a head start. "Emotional maturation and crossing fear boundaries" is handled more gently than in Basic Training. M-Team trainees are eased into the experiences of hiking in swamps, camping in the wildnerness and climbing heights, rather than faced immediately with abrupt challenges as in Basic Training. Finally, physical training is brought up to the level needed to enter Basic Training.

You might be interested in what those Basic Training physical fitness entrance levels are. As a requirement for acceptance, a father or other like authority must time and sign off on the following:

- Running a minimum of 20 continuous minutes without stopping to rest or walk. In Basic Training, you will work up to runs of 40 minutes or longer
- 32 full pushups in two minutes without bending your back or resting your body or knees on the ground
- 42 bent-knee sit-ups, with hands behind the head and feet held down, touching elbows to knee cap, in two minutes without lying your head down or grabbing on your legs to sit up
- 40 left-right flutter-kicks (feet and head about six inches off ground, hands under buttocks, fists clenched to support lower back, move one leg at a time up to a 45 degree angle)

You'll also have to fill out a questionnaire that deeply probes into your outward and inward godliness, according to IBLP standards. What movies

ALERT program instructors, of whom there are presently 20, have impressive combined experience and backgrounds. The list includes

- medical doctor
- West Point Military Academy instructor
- retired Lt. Colonel with 20 years of U.S. Army experience in leadership, operations, and training
- pilot with 21 years of Air Force experience in flying and instructing, including FAA certification as a flight instructor in multi- and single-engine and instrument airplanes
- police diver who has logged over 4,000 law-enforcement dives, who has trained federal, state, local, and foreign police and fire personnel, as well as U.S. Air Force and Navy divers
- licensed airframe and power plant mechanic, with pilot ASEL and sea, commercial, and instrument ratings, who has served as a missionary pilot and mechanic in Indonesia for seven years
- experienced construction tradesmen
- music instructor/choir director with over 50 years experience
- firefighters, including one with specialty ratings in confined space rescue and hazardous materials
- Grade A master electrical technician
- Evangelism Explosion teacher trainer
- paramedics
- police officers

Among the certifications held by the instructors are

- National Association of Search and Rescue
- National Registry Emergency Medical Technicians
- National Academy of Scuba Educators
- National Academy of Police Diving

Program facilities include an aircraft hanger, a 5000-foot FAA-approved runway, an 80-acre lake, and 2,000 acres of wooded terrain, as well as a large lodge and other buildings.

and TV you watch . . . what temptations you struggle with . . . how much time you spend playing video games . . . whether you subscribe to IBLP's standards of "godly music" (no rock beat) or not . . . your family relationships . . . your sexual innocence or lack thereof . . . and much more . . . is all questioned in detail. Fathers also have to fill out a questionnaire describing their spiritual position in the family and beliefs in several areas, as well as essay questions such as, "Is your son out from under authority in any area?" and "What change would you like to see take place in his life?"

Finally, there's the matter of tuition, uniforms, and other necessary gear. Backpacks and other necessary clothing and camping items, except ALERT uniforms, are not included in the tuition and fees, and must be purchased separately. Detailed lists of tools you must purchase separately if you choose one of the Construction, Auto Mechanic & Auto Body, and Aircraft Maintenance Technician options are also provided. My guess is that the tools (each and every one of which must be engraved with your name, for obvious reasons) won't run you more than $100 or $200 at the most, if you have to buy them all new, and the clothes and camping items could set you back about $500.

Although families only pay about two-thirds of the actual ALERT training expenses, it's still not a negligible sum. If you add up all the fees, a non-ATI student will end up paying between $11,275 (for the Auto Mechanics option) and $18,435 (if he chooses the most expensive specialty of Aviation and gets every licensing option available), extra clothing and tools not included. ATI students save about $1,300. For the price, you learn a lot more than you will in a year and a half of college, you are prepared for future work or training in a wide variety of useful industry and government jobs, you're in the best physical and spiritual shape of your life, and you've already done some good in the world.

I've read a number of newspaper articles from communities served by the ALERT teams, and they are uniformly lavish in their phrase for the young men's service and attitudes.

This is a high-powered program with a lot behind it, that should definitely interest fit young Christian men with a yen for active service. *Mary Pride*

"What do I do after high school?" Before you buy entirely into the "straight from high school into a typical college program" mindset, isn't it good to know all your options? If you'd like a full range of choices to consider, **Choices for the High School Graduate** just may be your book! In its handy-sized 180 pages, you'll learn all about:

- apprenticeships
- deferred admissions ("stopping" out for a year instead of "dropping" out)
- early admissions (special live-away-from-home college programs for bright kids aged 14–16 years old, with full contact information for each)
- exchange programs
- internships
- job search
- military service, possibly followed by college with financial help as a result of your service
- overseas study
- part-time work
- ROTC
- short-term missions work
- special academic programs

NEW!
Ferguson Choices for the High School Graduate
Grades 9–12. $9.95 plus $4 shipping.
Ferguson Publishing Company, 200 West Madison St., Suite 300, Chicago, IL 60606. (800) 306-9941. Fax: (800) 306-9942. Email: fergpub@aol.com. Web: www.fergpubco.com.

- travel
- volunteer work with organizations such as Americorps (which will earn you government money for college) and Habitat for Humanity

Choices is loaded with real-life stories of teens who took a chance and got off the "straight from high school to college" highway. Sometimes it worked out great, other times not so great. Getting fired, feelings of loneliness, and tight cash awaited some of those who went right to work after high school. Volunteer work, military enlistments, and internships had their up and down sides, too. On the other hand, even negative experiences often helped kids make up their own minds to attack future education diligently or pick different career paths. And lots of kids had positive experiences. In the section about early admissions, every single kid said they loved it!

The most surprising thing I learned reading this book is that most college admissions officers feel positive towards delayed college entry. So taking a year or two after high school to work, travel, or volunteer can actually work in your favor when applying to college. Many colleges will even hold your scholarship package open for a year to let you take time off.

Teens who benefit from taking time off, diving into college early, or skipping college entirely have a variety of reasons for making their choices—but they all share a quality of independent-mindedness. The more strongly you feel that you want to try something else, and the more planning you are willing to do, the greater the chance that it will turn out to be the right choice. Even the "wrong" choice is seldom irreversible, as many of the real-life stories show!

That's fine for them, but what about you? A lengthy self-assessment form is provided, to help you decide how ready you are to take "the road not traveled."

Every page of this book rings true. What better way to check out your options than to learn from other people's experiences? Packed with details about programs and opportunities you might never run across otherwise, I would recommend this book to every independent-minded homeschooled teen (in other words, all of you!) *Mary Pride*

Want to find out more about careers that interest you, without spending much more than postage? Does the title **Free and Inexpensive Career Materials** appeal to you?

Each listing gives the career materials provider's name, address, phone number, and an annotated list of materials available through them. Some listings also include fax numbers and web addresses.

Here some examples of the type of materials available:

- *Consider a Career in Cytotechnology* and *Accredited Programs in Cytotechnology.* Two free brochures from the American Society of Cytopathology (evaluation of cells by microscope) that give you the skinny on a career I bet you didn't even know existed.
- *College Guide: 39 Places to Expand Your Mind,* a free 47-page booklet from the United Negro College Fund describing the 39 historically black colleges and universities.
- *Your Pipeline to Hot Careers and Cold Cash,* a $5.25 purchase that includes a nine-minute video and 16-page booklet for those interested in the plumbing, heating, and cooling industry.
- *Working Abroad,* a free 14-page brochure that describes how to go about obtaining a job in several work programs and *au pair* programs offered in Europe.

NEW!
Ferguson Free and Inexpensive Career Materials, 1998 edition
Grades 9–12. $19.95 plus $4 shipping.
Ferguson Publishing Company, 200 West Madison St.,Suite 300, Chicago, IL 60606. (800) 306-9941.
Fax: (800) 306-9942.
Email: fergpub@aol.com.
Web: www.fergpubco.com.

As you can see, this is an eclectic mix. Materials providers include academic societies, college departments, commercial publishers, foundations, government agencies, and professional associations. Keep in mind that in general these groups want to make the careers and opportunities they offer sound attractive; for a more unbiased look at careers, you should consult some of the other books in this section. With that said, your support group could put together a nice little library of career brochures if you bought the book and one of you volunteered to write away for the free resources! *Mary Pride*

From High School to Work: 150 Great Tech Prep Careers is a bit misleading in its title. The best jobs it covers often turn out to require "some postsecondary training" or "bachelor's degree." I don't know if that's because the requirements for some of these jobs have been inflated since the editors first started writing the book, or what. I certainly can't figure out why aerobics instructors must have a bachelor's degree, let alone courses in chemistry and physics—from what I've seen, the main requirements seem to be big hair and strong lungs!

In any case, if you don't think of this as just "jobs you can get with only a high-school diploma," but rather "jobs well suited for kids who don't want to pursue typical college degrees," the book makes much more sense.

You'll be relieved to know there are indeed still quite a few jobs that you can get with only a high-school diploma. Do you dream of being a bodyguard? An animal breeder or caretaker? A locksmith? A police officer? A pet detective? (Sorry, that last one wasn't actually in the book!) These are just a few of the more glamorous opportunities available at the drop of a GED. Less glamorous, but readily available, jobs such as telemarketer, typist, and title examiner are also covered.

Each of the 150 listings in this 634-page oversized paperback provides detailed information on what the job requires, what kind of work you can expect to do, background and skills necessary for that career, ways to get into that line of work, advancement prospects, and more, including sources for additional information about that job. A sidebar at the beginning of each listing also reveals with school subjects are most important for obtaining that job, which personal interests may indicate an interest in that job, what kind of work environment and salary range you can expect, minimal educational level required to land the job, whether certification or licensing is necessary, the employment outlook, and the number of that job category in three standard resources used by guidance counselors. Overall, you get quite a clear picture of what each career is like.

If your student is the hands-on type who can't see spending his or her life behind a desk, or if they really enjoy helping people, or if college prices just don't seem worth it to them, *From High School to Work* may open some doors. An excellent support-group purchase as well. *Mary Pride*

Fergusons Guide to Apprenticeship Programs is an example of the kind of books homeschool support groups should be buying for their career and guidance libraries. This huge resource—over 1,000 pages in its two library-bound volumes—is the most comprehensive information you can buy. More than 7,500 programs in 52 job categories are listed and described.

Each job category listing begins with a list of related sections, a synopsis of what these guys do for a living, who employs them, apprenticeship salaries, post-apprenticeship salaries, job outlook, national programs available, a personal profile of someone who walked that particular apprenticeship road, and a list by state of actual apprenticeship programs available in that job category.

Section 1, "Apprenticeships by Career Field," is just that—listings from Agriculture to Welders. Section 2, "Apprenticeships by Eligibility," covers Goodwill Industries, Job Corps, and Job Training Partnership Act programs. Section 3, "Schools, Job Centers, and Administrative Offices," gives you all the contact info you need if you are seeking this kind of training and placement, including the Bureau of Apprenticeship and Training Offices in each state. Further appendices include on-line employment services, career resources on the Internet, Dictionary of Occupational Titles index, a Job Title index, and a State index. *Mary Pride*

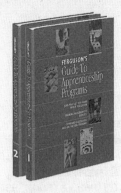

The *Health Career Starter* is one of a growing series of **Career Starters** published by **Learning Express** (no relation to the chain of teacher's stores). After a short introduction on why you want to have a career in the health care field, the book jumps right into telling you what health care careers are all about. Chapters are as follows:

- Hottest healthcare jobs and how to get them—lists the entry-level jobs with a couple of encouraging quotes, then, for each job, gives a description of typical duties, typical salaries, hiring trends, personal abilities and personality traits needed, and advancement opportunities. After that this chapter outlines the process by which you can become a health care worker, from evaluating yourself to filling out your job application.
- Training programs—outlines the types of training programs that are available and gives partial lists of the courses needed for each of the entry-level jobs; gives advice on choosing a program and tips on how to succeed.
- Directory of training programs by state with addresses and phone numbers
- How to finance your training—how to gather your financial records and apply for financial aid; what types of aid are available
- How to land your first job—conducting a job search, networking, how to write a cover letter, how to make a resume, and the ins and outs of interviewing
- How to succeed once you've landed the job—personal relationships, time management, dealing with your boss, dealing with pressure, finding a mentor, promotions,
- List of professional associations
- Additional resources

This book is full of interviews and quotes from successful people in the field. For example, the chapter on healthcare jobs and how to get them starts with three quotes: one from a recruiter who says that healthcare jobs abound anywhere you want to work, the second from a man who moved up to being a heart surgeon from a start as a surgical technologist, and the third from someone who was content to remain a surgical technician. Each chapter ends with a "The Inside Track" article about someone who has been a success in the medical field. The "insider" gives advice based on his experience, then lets us know his plans for the future.

This is a great survey of the field. It got *me* considering if I should consider switching to a health care career; not that far-fetched with a brother and brother-in-law who both are doctors!

Other Career Starters in this series (same price and format) are *Administrative Assistant, Civil Service, Computer Technologist, EMT, Firefighter,*

NEW!
Learning Express Test Preparation series
Grade 10–adult. Prices are in table.
Learning Express, 20 Academy Street, Norwalk, CT 06850. (800) 295-9556. (212) 995-2566. Fax: (212) 995-5512. Web: www.learnx.com.

Law Enforcement, Paralegal, Teacher, and *Webmaster.* If you know what you want to be when you grow up, and it's on this list, the book is well worth the money. *Bill Pride*

In addition to the Career Starter series reviewed earlier in this chapter, Learning Express publishes dozens of **Test Preparation guides** for various careers you typically enter via an exam rather than through college graduation. Many are custom designed for the exact exams given by a particular state or locality. Information on hiring procedures, interview preparation, sample applications, job hunting tips, job requirements, and more are often included in these oversized, thick books. See the table below for what tests are available and their prices.

Test Name	National Test Price	States/Regions/Cities/ Tests	Price Range for State/ Regions/ Cities	Exam for certification?
ASVAB (Armed Services Vocational Aptitude Battery)	$14.95			No
Bus Operator	$12.95	NYC		No
Corrections Officer		CA, FL, NJ, NY, TX	$35	No
Cosmetology	$20			No
EMT Basic	$20			Yes
Federal Clerical	$15			No
Federal Law Enforcement: Border Patrol	$19.95			No
Federal Law Enforcement: Treasury Enforcement Agent	$18.95			No
Firefighter		CA, NJ, NY, TX, MidW, S, NYC	$25–$35	No
Home Health Aide	$20			Yes
Nursing Assistant	$20			Yes
Paramedic Licensing	$20			Yes
Police Officer		CA, FL, MA, NJ, TX, MidW, S, Chi, NYC/Nassau Cnty, Suffolk Cty	$25–$35	No
Postal Worker	$12.95	CA, FL, NJ, NY, TX	$30	No
Real Estate		AMP, ASI, CA, PSI, TX	$30–$35	Yes
Sanitation Worker	$12.95	NYC	$25	No
State Police		CA, MA, NJ, NY, TX	$30–$35	No

Test preparation guides are also available for the following careers and degree programs that necessarily involve college attendance. The *Allied Health* guide has practice tests based on actual entrance exams for two- and four-year Allied Health degree programs. It includes extensive drills in important biology and chemistry concepts, information on Allied Health certification requirements and requirements by state, and the same type of job information found in the guides above. *College Entrance* guides prepare you for the tests offered by the state university systems in New York or Texas. The *Teacher* guide prepares you for the tests indicated.

Test Name	National Test Price	States/Regions/Cities/Tests	Price Range for State/Regions/ Cities
Allied Health	$20	CA, FL, IL, MA, NJ, NY, TX	$25–$32.50
College Entrance		NY, TX	$15.95–$18.95
Teacher		CBEST, PPST	$18.95

My feeling is that if you are interested in one of these careers, you would be nuts to take the exam without first buying the guide. Why go in blind? *Bill Pride*

Have you ever wanted to sail around the world on a yacht? How about living at a ski resort with unlimited free skiing? Or getting a great tan in the Australian Outback?

If you are a flexible single person or enjoy an especially flexible family life, all this is possible. **Work Your Way Around the World** gives you all you need to find fascinating work overseas or at home, including ways to scrounge free transportation to and fro. Some of the more memorable sections:

- "Working a Passage" includes how to get work on freighters, inland boating, and the invaluable "How To Win Friends & Influence Captains," plus salty details on crewing in waters around the world (beware of Caribbean pirates!).
- "Travel Ways and Means" covers every continent and provides tips for border-passing.
- "Enterprise" presents local entrepreneurship possibilities, some shady (gambling), most not.
- "Work Your Way" lays out the possibilities in Tourism, Picking (fruit), Farming, Teaching English, Domestic Work, Business and Industry, and Voluntary Work.

Plus over 170 pages on how to work your way in Europe, country by country, and another 110 pages on how to work your way worldwide, continent by continent. Fascinating personal stories from those who have done it intermingle with practical tips on how to do it.

New Careers Center has more than a dozen books on dream employment opportunities from many different publishers. I listed titles and prices for a few above.

They also sell subscriptions to **International Employment Hotline**, a unique newsletter that devotes about 75 percent of its space to current international job openings.

On top of *that*, they also carry hundreds of the best books on how to make career changes, how to start your own business, how to get hired or moonlight, and lots more! *Mary Pride*

Irreverent but mostly practical advice aimed mostly at college graduates. **How to Survive Wothout Your Parents' Money** goes beyond irreverent to brash in spots, for example using the "F" word on page 14 and dissing parents in general on page 6. If this does not deter you, here's what you get:

- Advice on job-seeking while you're still on campus
- How to get noticed via resumé, a "Great Letter," and "new technologies" (like gee whiz, *email!* Wowsers!)
- Connections and networking
- Employment agencies, career counselors, and headhunters
- Advertising for a job

- Interviewing
- Surviving while you're looking for the job (options include living in squalor and babysitting, among other helpful hints)
- Solo survival skills, such as doing your own taxes, getting insurance, paying your student loans, applying for credit cards, finding an apartment, the pros and cons of roommates, and selecting clothes suitable for your office
- A whole chapter on what it really means to have a "career in the arts," i.e., how to survive when your dream job pays squat
- Other options besides jobs (bumming, traveling, more school, Peace Corps . . .)
- Deciding whether to accept a job offer
- Basic office survival skills (Dilbert is better on this subject)
- Resource lists

Books for adults on how to get or change jobs are mostly better than this. However, you may find it useful for the "advice to the clueless" directed at students. I don't mean this sarcastically; heaven knows I was clueless about a lot of things myself when I graduated. *Mary Pride*

What Color Is Your Parachute? is the best-selling job-hunting book in the world, just as its cover proclaims, having gone through 29 editions, with over 6 million copies in print in 10 languages. Revised and updated annually, the 1999 edition now features a section about job-hunting on the Internet. The phrase "golden parachute" was coined from this book's title.

In short, everyone else already knows about this book . . . except you. And now *you* are going to find out why it's so enduringly popular.

Committee-written? Not a chance. This prodigious (350 pages long), bi-color (headings and other important stuff is in red) tome is one man's labor of love. Richard Nelson Bolles, now 71 years old, has for over a quarter of a century been sharing his iconoclastic, avuncular advice with the goal of helping his readers find, not just any old job, but the *right* job.

You're making a mistake if you wait to read *What Color Is Your Parachute?* until you're looking for a job. The book's advice about how to find the right field, and the right job in that field, and how to prepare for getting that job, can save you years of expensively educating yourself with the wrong college degree. You'll learn to avoid the trap of preparing for "hot fields" that vanish or get clogged with too many applicants chasing too few jobs. You'll learn to "walk through" a job before you waste *any* time on preparing for it. You'll learn to change your whole way of looking at work. Some hints: *All* jobs are temporary. *All* jobs are learning experiences you can use to prepare for the next job. There are *always* plenty of jobs available, despite the misleading picture given by government statistics. Most importantly, you can dare to look for work you love.

A totally unexpected extra is the section on "How to Find Your Mission in Life." Since the author has been an ordained Episcopalian minister for the last 43 years, this is written from a Christian point of view, complete with Scripture quotes.

In my opinion, all high-school juniors would benefit from reading the entire book and working through the workbook exercises. It sure would have saved *me* a lot of heartache and wasted time (and it was even in print back then, too!). *Mary Pride*

NEW!
The 1999 What Color Is Your Parachute?

Grade 10–adult. $16.95.
Ten Speed Press, PO Box 7123, Berkeley, CA 94707. (800) 841-2665. Fax: (510) 524-1052. Email: order@tenspeed.com. Web: www.tenspeed.com.

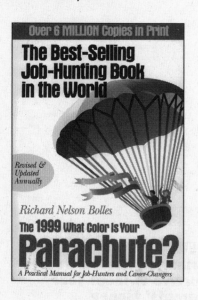

Appendixes

The Myth of the Teenager

W hat is a teenager? Are teenagers necessarily rebellious? Aren't the teen years a time when children need to break their ties with their parents and begin focusing more on peers?

We printed an article once in *Practical Homeschooling* that answered these questions. It immediately became our most popular reprint request. Literally dozens of newsletters, church groups, homeschool organizations, and mission groups have printed thousands of copies of this article (after asking and receiving our permission, of course!).

Why was—and is—this article so popular?

Because for several decades now parents have been trained to fear and submit to The Teenager, as a necessary evolutionary phase in their child's growth. Yet most of us still find it hard to live with the thought that disdain and discourtesy should be our natural portion, after years of sacrifice and love on our part. So read on and find out why Dr. Michael Platt believes that "teenagers" are a marketing fiction—and what a difference this makes in the education we should provide them.

Dr. Michael Platt

The Myth of the Teenager

by Dr. Michael Platt

"We have two teenagers," I sometimes hear parents say. "Oh, I'm so sorry," I sometimes reply. Although I say it with a smile, the truth is sad.

While the growing-up process is inevitable, natural, and God-given, the process of children turning into Teenagers is not. The Teenager was invented, fashioned, permitted—let loose you might say—by the generation of our parents and grandparents. Discovering that may help us to raise our children differently.

The Teenager is a Modern Invention

There were no "teenagers" before World War II. Ask those still living who raised their children before then. Or spend a rainy Saturday in the basement of your library, comparing old *Life* magazines from before the War and after.[1]

Instead of Teenagers, there were Youths. Youths were young people who wanted to become adults. However confused, wayward, or silly they acted, however many mistakes they made, they looked to the future. They knew

[1] Cf. the issues for 6/6/38, 6/14/43, 6/11/45, 12/20/48, and 4/2/56.

that adult life was different than a child's life. They planned to grow up, leave childhood behind, and become adults. They were aware that life is more than youth.

The Teenager has no such horizon. Beyond the "Teeny" world there is no adult life, no past with heroes, no future with goals.

Naming the Teenager

A new word was needed to describe these never-grown-up Peter Pans. Previously human beings between childhood and adulthood were called *kids, boys* and *girls, young people, adolescents,* and *youths.* These young human beings were addressed as "Young man" and "Young woman." Looking at them, their parents thought, "My growing son," and "My growing daughter," and they addressed them as "Daughter" and "Son." Sometimes others addressed them as "Master" and "Miss." Even the words "gentleman" and "lady" were sometimes heard. To name a kind or aspect of youth, *lass* and *lad, stripling* and *maiden, whipper snapper* and *squirt, sport* and *shaver, minor* and *juvenile* were employed, and the latter, *juvenile,* did not yet invariably go with *delinquent.* Words such as *upstart, brat, tough, rogue,* and *slut* described deviations from the general good of "youth," not its characteristic features. The word "teenager" did not exist. **Compare the entries in Webster's Second (1934) and Third (1961) editions; only after the war does the adjective "teen-age" become the noun, "teenager."**[2]

When parents today say "We have two teenagers," the reason why I can reply "I'm so sorry" is that they say this with a sigh. Indeed, there is a world of difference between having youths in your home and teenagers. Consider Tolstoy's *Childhood, Boyhood, and Youth.* Author Tolstoy is honest to a fault; youth Tolstoy was a bag of vices, poses, and miseries. However, youth Tolstoy was never a Teenager, for in the midst of his confusion, he was always striving to become a man. The world of grown-ups was there around and above him, not shut out.

Youths associated with other youths, sometimes dressed alike, talked alike, but never separated entirely from their teachers and parents. When you saw youths with their parents, they were not pretending to be unrelated to the family. After all, they wanted one day to become like their parents, or like their grandparents, or like their teachers.

Youths chose presidents, inventors, scientists, explorers, warriors, saints, teachers, and parents for their heroes. In American history they looked to the likes of Washington and Jefferson, Boone and Crockett, Lincoln, Lee, and Grant, Frederick Douglass and Booker T. Washington, and Clara Barton. In literature they looked to the likes of the Virginian, Robinson Crusoe, Hamlet, Odysseus, and Leather-stocking. The cowboy and the saint filled their imagination. Above these they looked to Abraham, Moses, Paul and Christ.

The Teenager has no such heroes; he may be miserable, he may not like himself, but his heroes are no more happy or worthy than himself. **The highest desire of a Teenager is to become a more perfect Teenager,** a rock or movie star, certainly not a man or a woman.

What a Youth Wants and a Teenager Does Not

A youth wants to be trusted, given responsibility, and the opportunity to deserve esteem. Youths make more mistakes than adults. Usually their mistakes lead to lighter consequences, but they suffer more from them than adults; they like their mistakes less; they feel more shame. Shame is the other side of the respect they have for the virtues they see in adults.

[2] In the nineteenth century, the words "boy" and "girl" extended up to adulthood; for example, college students were called college boys. And they were called this despite the fact that more was expected of them, in the way of diligent study, moral conduct, and good manners than is now. Even in the late 1930s, F. Scott Fitzgerald, writing to his daughter at Vassar and expecting a lot, speaks of once being a Princeton boy. In the sixteenth century Ascham speaks the same way, and also calls those from seven to seventeen "young gentlemen." "This day I go out of my teens" wrote Queen Victoria in her diary upon her twentieth birthday, not "This day I am no longer a teenager." (*Oxford Book of Ages*, ed. A. & S. Sampson, s. v.) The word "teenager," as we now use it, was first noted in the third edition of *Webster's Dictionary* (1961); it was not in the second (1934); there it is noted only as the adjective "teenage."

Being immature, youths will always be tempted by pleasures, by flattery, and by illusions, but with an adult world around them, they will be able to make comparisons and judgments. Candy is candy, candy is sweet, candy can be given to you, but nothing in the world can substitute for knowing how to ride your bike. No one can give that to you. No one can do that for you.

Youths tend, then, to know the difference between the things that are really your own—the virtues—and the things that come from others, such as wealth, or come easy, such as the pleasures. **Good youths like good tests.** They want to enjoy adult pleasures *after* they have earned them by performing adult duties. Thus during World War II many of them served their country, as young husbands on the front and as young wives at home, before they could enjoy the mature "blessings of liberty." Like many others, Audie Murphy was a hero before he could vote.

What a Teenager most fears is a child of his own. His second greatest fear is death. And his third greatest fear is solitude. The thoughts "I can beget a child," or "I can bear a child," "I will die," and "I am alone," have often been the beginning of wisdom. The Teenager flees them. The Teenager cannot stand to be alone. For such a human being the natural mode of association is the gang. And how does one picture a gang of Teenagers, if not in a car speeding down the road, listening to rock music, and on drugs? Or at the rock-concert in a gang of gangs? Or at the orgy?

These pleasures are powerful, absorbing, and "quickie." The Teenager craves a melody that will rock him around the clock forever, seeks an experience so intense that he will forget what time it is, and so absorbing that it will blot out all eternity.

Never does one see a smile on the faces of those enjoying these pleasures. The Teenager is the most free and the least happy of beings. Thoreau said most people lead lives of "quiet desperation." The desperation of the Teenager is not quiet. With the Rolling Stones, they shout, "I can't get no satisfaction." A being less acquainted with joy there has never been. A being more dangerous, it is hard to imagine. "Paint it black."

So far as I know, there have never been such youths on earth before. The Teenager is a novelty not only in the history of twentieth-century America, but in the history of the human race.

Teenagers are Youths Orphaned by Their Own Parents

The day the Teenager was created was a sad day for every youth in America. Imagine yourself young again, unsure of yourself, swayed by strong passions, by turns ashamed and proud, sometimes shy, sometimes assertive, always awkward, filled with new desires and hard on yourself for having them, drawn toward cliques, tempted by clique cruelty, by affectation, by enslaving pleasures, and by premature bonds, but fighting on, knowing that you want to become something better, someone capable of good work, deserving your own respect, and maybe one day becoming a good parent — imagine such struggling youths hearing their own parents say, "Relax, take it easy, enjoy yourself, adulthood will happen, don't sweat, this is the time of your life."

We see this parental neglect in the films of James Dean, especially in *Rebel Without A Cause*, where "Jimmy" must face his trials alone, hindered by a contumacious mother and a helpless father. An even less justified self-pity was inculcated by the effete Salinger in *Catcher in the Rye*, when he taught young readers to "trust no one over 14." In *On the Road*, Jack Kerouac taught that pleasure never disappoints. Waiting in the wings were other dubious adults: the porn merchants Henry Miller and Hugh Hefner. A new music, Rock, through whose dances the couple was annihilated, contributed mightily to the destruction of courtship. The pill divorced *eros* from responsibility. Owning a car provided a hideout from home. Dope became a way of life. And TV brought soft versions of all this corruption right into the home. Behind these intermediary causes was the deepest one—the altered relation of man to eternity. The substitution of daily newspapers for daily prayers is the briefest indication of it. All these things went into the "creation" of the Teenager, but no one was more responsible than the parents.

These parents said, "The kids have to work things out on their own," felt guilty, and gave them discretionary money. The junk, record, porn, and dope merchants said, "Let us at 'em." And the statesmen watched; Ike grinned and Jack joined in. In other words, the most vulnerable were exposed to the most predatory by those most naturally interested in their welfare, their own parents. Absolutely astonishing! **What Plato thought no parents would ever do, turn over their own children to others to be reeducated, the parents of America did after World War II.** Before then there were no TVs, a few disk jockeys, and some movie stars, but they were seldom allowed in the home, and certainly not allowed to educate the children. Suddenly after the War, into the American home came hordes of them. Few parents would have invited these persons in as guests and yet they turned over the souls of their own children to them to be educated.

In raising Teenagers these parents were committing a crime against their own children. No one complained. In raising Teenagers these parents also committed a crime against society, but although society noticed the crimes of the children, as "juvenile delinquency," it did not point to who was responsible, the parents. It is true that nearly every piece of social or court legislation since then has weakened the family, but alas equally true that the voters, that is the parents of the nation, have either supported the legislation or acquiesced to the legislators.

I'm a Teenager, You're a Teenager

We are now into the third generation of Teenagers. This means most people have had considerable experience of things that made the Teenager. **In truth, many parents today are not much different from Teenagers.** To disapprove of the Teenager, then, they would have to disapprove of much in their past and much that still exists in their lives.

The truth is that modern parents are often mixed beings; our experiences have not always been good, our deeds virtuous, our hearts true, our minds clear. Parents who want to do better than this by their children have to face up to and repudiate their own past and present Teenage sins. I doubt that anyone is really O.K. who is still justifying their past and present Teenage behavior. Such people cannot think clearly, live well, or help others. When they form a group large enough to determine the social policies and mores of a nation, that entire nation takes on the characteristics of a Teenager. The Prodigal Daughter is a portrait of America at the present time, free but not brave enough to be virtuous, discontented but not enough to free herself from bondage.

All the Excuses

The most potent impediment to modern parents acknowledging their negligence is the doctrine of choice. "Yes, we see rock music is bad; we don't like it ourselves. Yes, we see TV is shallow. Yes, we see that loose money is not good for our children. They have so much more than we had. Yes, they are not better off for it. But what can you do? The kids have to have some responsibility. You have to give them some choice." Thus runs the pro-choice excuse for negligence.

Its plausibility derives from two sources. In our political life, it is often good to tolerate deeds we would not commit and listen to opinions we do not hold. Of course, there are limits to this tolerance. Still, in a republic many points of view deserve toleration and consent is one principle of good government..

However, what is right for a federal republic is not right for a family. A family run on "democratic lines" with all members, children as well as adults, considered equal would be unnatural, for it would deny the difference between adults and children. Such a family cannot educate its younger members. **"One child, one vote," is a formula for the end of the family**. Parents who encourage their children to call them by their first names should not be surprised when they do not respect, seldom will obey, and do not often learn from them. To forgo the high titles Mother and Father is not benevolent; it is negligent; and it does not win friends; it loses children. **Not to be able to call someone "Mother" and "Father" is to be an orphan.**

The second plausible excuse for negligence is that it is good for young persons to take responsibility for their deeds. An example often supplied is how desirable it is to have an allowance, to own your own bike, to save up for it, and be responsible for its upkeep. Well and good, provided the chores contributed to family life are greater than the allowance. When older children keep all the money they make at a summer or after-school job, something has gone wrong. What could be more irresponsible than to get your room, board, laundry, and education fees from your working parents, and have all your paycheck for discretionary purchases?

We know how welfare recipients often lose their spirit, unlearn responsibility, and fall into dependency. **As a class Teenagers are less deserving of welfare and are just as debilitated by it.** The parents who set up a "pro-choice" version of welfare are as unlikely to exhort their children, discuss responsibility with them, give them maxims, or give them examples of responsibility, fiscal or otherwise as the current Federal Government is. And even if the parents do exhort their children, by setting them up with discretionary money they are showing them the way to avoid such discussions.

Few such parents will exhort their children anyway. The advantage of welfare for them is that you don't have to exhort your children. You don't risk a stormy argument. You can just forget the children and get on with your own life. To justify this negligence parents who "welfare" their children say, "We are tired." Recognize a "right to be tired" and you can justify anything.

Growing Up

Fortunately, third generation Teenagers are not the only parents in America now. Having experienced the emptiness of the material advantages their negligent parents gave them, many parents have resolved to give their children something truly good, an education in the virtues.

Nothing should make us more happy about our children today and more confident about our future public life than the number of parents who have chosen to educate their own children at home. In order to teach you must know and in order to know you must learn. Thus both generations grow up at once. Parents leave their own Teenage behind and become true adults. Children never have to become Teenagers at all.

The benefits last unto the third generation and beyond. A generation of parents whose good children could declare, "You set us on the good path you first trod" would constitute a mighty nation, might reconstitute this once almost chosen one, and would surely please God.

Dr. Michael Platt studied at Harvard, Oxford, and Yale. Here in the States, at Dartmouth and the University of Dallas, and abroad, at Heidelberg, he has taught philosophy, theology, political philosophy, statesmanship, American government, Texas government, biomedical ethics, Rembrandt, and lots of literature. In these fields, especially on Shakespeare, Plato, and Nietzsche, he has published widely.

At Dartmouth he proposed a Liberal Arts Program, which continues to this day at Queens College; at the University of Dallas, he taught its undergraduate core curriculum and directed the Literature part of its integrated Ph.D. program. Of his classes, John Randall, Esq. once wrote, "We all felt that we were a part of something extraordinary. No experience has matched those classes in scope or lasting effect upon myself as a student of the world."

He and his wife Patricia are raising four youngsters—never to grow into Teenagers—in their home school in Vermont. His newest book, Seven Wonders of Shakespeare, *is published by Rowman. Copies of the much longer essay from which this is taken, entitled "The Teenager and the West," can be purchased from the author for $10. Send to: Friends of the Republic, Sugar Hill, East Wallingford, VT 05742.*

Suggested Course of Study for Junior and Senior High School

First things first. Has your teen student mastered the tools of learning and the basic content areas? If not, you might want to pick up a copy of volume 2 of *The Big Book of Home Learning* and check out the Suggested Course of Study for the Elementary grades outlined in that volume. Remember, we are going to be talking about an *ideal* course of study for the teen years—at least, one as ideal as I can think of at the present time—and this assumes an excellent educational background for grades 1–6.

Keeping that in mind, my suggestions for the teen years boil down to the following:

(1) Spend enough time with important subjects to make sure the student learns *and remembers* the material he invested the time to study.

(2) Condense sequential material (such as math) as much as possible, and introduce serious math earlier, thus opening up access to serious science and engineering courses earlier.

(3) Skip all trendy, irrelevant, and faddish subjects.

(4) Explore unit studies in areas of special interest.

(5) Take advantage of hands-on and real-world learning wherever possible

(6) Recognize that the dividing line between high school and college isn't always obvious. Don't be afraid to tackle "college" material (which in yesterday's world would have been high-school material anyway) during the teen years.

In contrast to these suggestions, I believe the present typical course of study followed in the schools (both public and private) doesn't do a good job of equipping students with the tools of learning or of presenting them with useful knowledge. The typical high-school curriculum wastes hours, days, and weeks on political propaganda about women's role in society, ethnic and racial "studies," peace education, sex education, nuclear education, and other cause-oriented trendy stuff. This leaves little time for the serious intellectual work students of this age are capable of doing.

Most fundamentally, the very reasons for studying the subjects required are outdated. Example: *all* high school students now must take science courses, because American leaders of the 1950s were frightened by the Russians beating us into space. This makes as much sense as forcing *all* students to take three years of gymnastics, because Eastern Bloc nations wipe the floor with us in international gymnastics competitions!

Subject Checklist

Who should decide, after all, the relative importance of sports, science, math, practical life skills, literature, history, and so on for every single student in the country? I believe that *families* should decide these issues, not educational bureaucrats. So here's a handy checklist to help you determine which subjects make the most sense for you to study.

Ask yourself the following questions:

(1) Will it prepare me for my future work?

(2) Will it prepare me for my future ministry (unpaid service to others)?

(3) Will it prepare me for leadership in the business world or my community?

(4) Will it prepare me for my future home life?

(5) Will it enrich my life?

Any subject that flunks all five of these tests has obviously little reason for taking up your time. Unhappily, such subjects often are the very ones required by states and colleges.

Let's walk through an example. You are, let's say, a people person with a decided artistic flair. Math has always bored you. So has science: you studied it in grade school, but you have no intention of going into a technical career of any sort. The value of a series of high-school science courses is obviously small in your case, let alone both biology *and* chemistry with their associated lab work. However, most colleges require just such a science sequence as an entrance requirement.

It's true that sometimes you have very little initial interest in an area, but yet that area would be extremely valuable for you later on. It's fair to say, for example, that few high-school students are wild about history. Yet a knowledge of history is indispensable for wise leadership. Those who don't learn from the mistakes of the past are doomed to repeat them, as it has been said, and those who are responsible for the welfare of others shouldn't make more mistakes than they can help. (This explains something about our current congressfolks, few of whom have any significant knowledge of even American history.) However, studying history from the angle of "what did these people do wrong?" and "what did this other bunch do right?" is a whole different approach from typical school history courses, which either skip such issues entirely or fail to present an absolute moral base by which to judge past leaders and movements.

Whether you can follow your own ideal course of study or not, though, it's worthwhile going through the exercise of determining what it would be if you had the choice. You can then sculpt the actual graduation requirements to fit your particular needs and abilities. If you're technically oriented, you might want to take math and science to the max while taking it easier on your literature studies. If, on the other hand, you foresee more use for the liberal arts in your future, you might be content to satisfy the minimum science requirements with some all-purpose science courses.

Graduation Requirements

Before we get too excited about the educational possibilities of the teen years, let's look first at the standard graduation requirements set up by the various states.

Junior high still can be very much what you make it in most places, but by high school things start to get serious.

In general, states require three or four years of English, two years of math (can be consumer or survival math), two years of science (can be basic science with no lab work), a year of U.S. history, a year of world history, one semester of government (citizenship), one year of either foreign language or fine arts (art appreciation, music, drama, etc.), and two years of physical education. These are *minimum* graduation requirements. Most students also take driver's education. The smart ones take typing class.

For college entrance, somewhat more is required. Generally colleges require four full years of English, three years of math (including at least algebra and geometry), biology and chemistry plus lab work, and a year of fine arts. Some colleges also require two years of the same foreign language. Driver's education and keyboarding are virtual necessities for the college-bound. On top of *this,* Christian families will try to include Bible education as well.

For more details on graduation requirements, see Appendix 5.

English

Are we having fun yet? No? Then let's get into a better way of doing things!

Studying **grammar** in high school is boring. Thus, suggestion #1 is to teach it *before* high school. Failing that, give your student a *condensed* one-book grammar course instead of spinning out grammar instruction into 12th grade.

The tools of learning needed in high school are **note-taking, outlining, and research skills.** (We assume your student is already an excellent reader; if not, see the Suggested Course of Study for grades 1–6 in Volume 2.) Teaching these skills can be picked up in less than a month.

Now's also the time to teach **keyboarding**. **Word processing** is even better. Either of these will make your high school and college work much speedier and neater.

Handwriting: develop an attractive hand, if you haven't by now.

Creative writing: now we're really starting to have fun! Here's a menu of creative-writing assignments to complete before graduation:

- Poems—traditional, blank verse, limericks, haiku, epic, ballads

- Essays—persuasive, how-to, factual, humorous
- Short stories—tragic, humorous, adventure, first-person, third-person, historic, mystery, fantasy/science fiction (if desired)
- Drama—one-act plays
- Journalism—articles, reviews, editorials

All writing assignments should be edited for spelling and grammatical correctness, as that is exactly what happens to authors in real life!

For extra fun, have your student write assignments in the styles of the authors you are studying in Literature class!

Oral presentation skills: the Middle Ages curriculum emphasized what was called "rhetoric," the art of persuasive speaking. Although I have provided you in this volume with resources to develop this skill (see Chapter 11), this skill is more readily caught than taught. However, you can provide opportunities for public speaking, from helping out in a Sunday school class to emceeing a neighborhood talent show.

Now, **Literature** with a capital *L*. High-school literature typically includes American Literature, and British/European/World literature: one year each. This just isn't enough time. I suggest you start your serious literature studies in grade 7 and take *two* years per course. This will give you enough time to thoroughly enjoy the reading selections *and* to branch out into unit studies on the authors that particularly interest you.

It just makes no sense to "study" Shakespeare for two weeks (if that long) and then rush on to someone else. How much better to read the biographical information about Shakespeare in a good literature textbook (or encyclopedia or library book) and then read several of his plays and poems aloud as a family! The same goes for any other major author. You can't really *know* a writer by gobbling 10 pages of his writings, so let's take the time and do it right!

Basically, what I'm suggesting is that you give your teen a college literature course. The only difference is that the college prides itself on assigning 100 pages to read per night, which guarantees your child won't remember most of it, and that the college forces him to write umpteen reports and papers on what he read, which guarantees he won't enjoy it. I'm suggesting that you let him read the same amount *at his own pace*, and that you discuss what he read (with perhaps an *occasional* writing assignment thrown in) rather than overdoing the writing.

If the student in question is one of the strong, silent types who is much happier tinkering with a machine, there's no need to beat him over the head with Shakespeare. Looking back at our five-point checklist, such a student is not likely to use advanced literary knowledge in his lifework, ministry, or home life. Although being able to quote the notables does add points to your leadership quotient, generally such people are *not* the glib, crowd-pleasing orators who could make maximum use of a wide literary background. You would accomplish more in such a case by giving him just a good taste of the classics than by making him hate them forever by pushing him too far beyond his interest level.

Mathematics

Every child in this country except those with major physical brain damage could know algebra by ninth grade. Math is a totally sequential subject; A leads to B leads to C leads to D. When it's taught properly, that is!

Math class is *not* the time for units on careers, hands-on experiments with thermometers, lectures on behavior, and so on. The more you interrupt math with measuring, experimenting, graphing, and other scientific studies, the less obvious its sequential nature becomes. Ditto for non-math-related topics of all sorts.

If math is taken at a reasonable speed, your student will have finished at least **a year of real algebra by the end of eighth grade.** He then has plenty of time for trigonometry, geometry, advanced math topics, and calculus, if desired.

The reason it's good to speed up math instruction is that you then will be able to have a really excellent six-year course of science instruction. See below!

Science

What's true of high-school and college literature goes double for high-school and college science. Typically, science teachers don't even expect to finish the textbook by the end of the course. They move rapidly through the material—rapidly enough to leave a lot of their students scratching their heads—but it doesn't help, because there's just too much material in the typical text to be covered in the hours of the typical course.

Here's how to change all that. Instead of twiddling with basic science/physical science/life science for three years in junior high, **take two years each for biology, chemistry, and physics in grades 7–12.** That will give you enough time to digest all the material, enjoy all the experiments, add some unit studies on areas of special interest, and finish the textbook!

Of course, you need basic algebra to do the work in a good chemistry course—which is why it's good to speed up the math studies to the level expected of average Japanese kids, as per my suggestions in the Math section above.

Christians will want to introduce some serious **creation science** in these grades. This is easy, thanks to the excellent videos, books, and seminars now available. We also should make a serious effort to apply biblical thinking to these areas rather than just regurgitating the man-manipulates-objects point of view of secular science texts, or the man-is-a-destroyer view of New Age and ecology texts, or even the no-growth man-is-a-steward view of the Christian ecology popularizers. (For the record's sake, you and I are supposed to build and be fruitful, not keep things in some supposedly utopian static state. The Creation is *fallen,* just like the rest of us, and keeps needing to be brought back into order.)

Remember, again, there is no transcendent reason why teens must take all these science courses in the first place, other than arbitrary college-entrance and high-school graduation requirements. However, if we're going to do it at all, why not do it *right*?

Social Studies

You may have noticed that **geography** isn't even on the list of high-school graduation requirements. That's because it's presumably being taught right along with the history—which, once again, is zipped through too rapidly for the students to digest.

Yes, I know kids have been taking U.S. history over and over and over again since kindergarten. I also know they haven't learned it, because at each level the schools throw more material at them than they can retain. We, however, can do it right. How? By, once again, **taking two years each for U.S. and world history,** ideally starting in grade 7, instead of the one year each in the high school curriculum. That leaves one year each for **economics** and **citizenship**—which are excellent introductions to philosophy, if tackled right.

Fine Art and Foreign Languages

No problem. You just move to France and do your school lessons on a bench in the Louvre art museum!

Impractical, you say? Well, learning to draw or learning to play a musical instrument are two fun ways to fulfill a fine-arts requirement. Seriously, I don't expect home schoolers, who accumulate more arts 'n music 'n crafts goodies than anyone else, to have any problems in this area.

If you plan to go to Bible college, Biblical Greek might be a good language choice. Latin is also a good choice, as it helps with many other school disciplines (vocabulary, science, grammar, etc.). Or go wherever your fancy leads!

Practical Life Skills

Beryl Singer, a reader of my now-defunct *HELP* newsletter, had the brilliant idea of making a checklist of household management skills for teens. (Of course, some of these skills could be learned much earlier!) Here's Beryl's list:

For specific instructions on how to clean all these items as efficiently and inexpensively as a professional, check out the Don Aslett books in Chapter 40.

Cleaning Kitchen
- ❑ set table
- ❑ clear table
- ❑ dry dishes
- ❑ wash dishes
- ❑ wipe off table
- ❑ clean sink area
- ❑ clean stove top
- ❑ clean oven
- ❑ clean microwave
- ❑ clean burner drip pans
- ❑ clean refrigerator, outside
- ❑ clean refrigerator, inside
- ❑ clean refrigerator drip pan
- ❑ defrost freezer

Bathroom
- ❑ clean sink
- ❑ clean toilet
- ❑ clean bathtub
- ❑ clean shower walls
- ❑ clean tile walls
- ❑ wash shower curtain
- ❑ clean brushes and combs
- ❑ clean mirrors

Living Room
- ❑ clean upholstery
- ❑ clean fireplace doors
- ❑ clean fireplace brick
- ❑ remove ashes
- ❑ build a fire in fireplace

Floors
- ❑ mop vinyl floor
- ❑ strip and wax vinyl floor
- ❑ vacuum carpets

- ❑ clean throw rugs
- ❑ clean door mats
- ❑ change vacuum cleaner bags
- ❑ shampoo carpets
- ❑ remove carpet stains
- ❑ dust mop wood floor
- ❑ strip and wax wood floors

Windows
- ❑ wash windows
- ❑ wash window frames
- ❑ wash curtains or blinds
- ❑ lubricate sliding parts
- ❑ wash exterior windows

Other
- ❑ dust furniture
- ❑ dust high places
- ❑ make beds
- ❑ change bed linens
- ❑ empty wastebaskets
- ❑ clean wastebaskets
- ❑ clean telephones
- ❑ clean doorknobs
- ❑ clean light fixtures
- ❑ clean walls
- ❑ paint walls

Housecleaning
- ❑ houseclean bedroom
- ❑ houseclean bathroom
- ❑ houseclean living room
- ❑ houseclean kitchen
- ❑ Plan and execute one week cleaning schedule, including delegation and follow-up.

Wash

- ❑ put away clothes
- ❑ fold clothes
- ❑ sort clothes to wash
- ❑ load and set washing machine
- ❑ clean lint trap—washer
- ❑ load and set dryer
- ❑ clean lint trap—dryer
- ❑ mend straight seams
- ❑ sew on a button
- ❑ patch a hole
- ❑ wash hand washables
- ❑ hang wash on clothesline
- ❑ Handle the family wash for one week.

Food Preparation

- ❑ read recipe and follow directions
- ❑ measure ingredients
- ❑ set oven temperature & timer
- ❑ operate crockpot
- ❑ operate microwave

Menu Planning

- ❑ plan week's menus
- ❑ write up shopping list
- ❑ shop for groceries
- ❑ Plan one week's menus, plan shopping list within regular food budget, shop for groceries, and do the cooking for the week.

Organizing Skills

- ❑ sort belongings—things to keep and things to discard
- ❑ sort belongings—store like things together
- ❑ sort belongings by frequency of use
- ❑ store belongings by frequency of use (most used belongings in most accessible places)
- ❑ know and use the four storage alternatives (on a shelf, in a drawer, on the floor, on the wall)
- ❑ sort the mail

Baby Care

- ❑ change a diaper
- ❑ dress baby
- ❑ wash diapers
- ❑ bathe baby
- ❑ feed baby
- ❑ keep choking and suffocating hazards away from baby
- ❑ handle baby safely

Simple Repairs

- ❑ change light bulb
- ❑ turn off main water supply
- ❑ oil squeaky door
- ❑ use fire extinguisher
- ❑ reset digital clock
- ❑ unstop clogged drain
- ❑ unstop clogged toilet
- ❑ check circuit breakers
- ❑ shut off main power
- ❑ install curtain rods
- ❑ find studs
- ❑ hang picture
- ❑ replace faucet washer

Telephone

- ❑ know phone number
- ❑ know address
- ❑ place local calls
- ❑ make emergency calls—fire, 911, etc.
- ❑ take phone messages
- ❑ handle telephone solicitation
- ❑ place long distance calls
- ❑ place collect calls
- ❑ use calling card

Financial

- ❑ write a check
- ❑ fill out mail order
- ❑ pay bills
- ❑ read bank statement
- ❑ read electric meter
- ❑ balance checkbook
- ❑ plan budget
- ❑ open a checking or savings account

Breakfast

- ❑ cold cereal
- ❑ toast
- ❑ granola
- ❑ scrambled eggs
- ❑ pancakes
- ❑ french toast

Lunch

- ❑ peanut butter and jelly sandwiches
- ❑ lunchmeat and cheese sandwiches

See Chapter 40 for resources that help teach many of these skills.

Supper	**Other**
❑ hot dogs	❑ instant pudding
❑ hamburgers	❑ hard boiled eggs
❑ meat loaf	❑ tea
❑ barbecued chicken	❑ biscuits
❑ chili	❑ bread
❑ baked beans	❑ cookies
❑ mashed potatoes	
❑ rice	
❑ corn	
❑ green beans	

This list is only a beginning—but a very good one! Add to it any skills particularly applicable to your household. One hundred percent hands-on learning!

Bible

We will assume that your teen is thoroughly familiar with the Bible's contents. If he or she isn't, go back to Volume 2 and read the Suggested Course of Study for grades 1–6!

Once basic Bible knowledge is under control, it's time for the **Bible study tools.** Learning the Greek and Hebrew alphabets only takes a few weeks. Learning to use Bible dictionaries, concordances, interlinear translations, and other helps can take up to a year of relaxed study. The goal is to have your student able to find things for himself and answer his own questions straight from the Book.

Now is also the time for a serious study of **church history,** a topic on which virtually all Christians are ignorant. It's also time to start learning how to teach others: how to lead a Bible study, how to teach a flannel lesson, how to lead family worship, how to evangelize, and so on.

(You're not a Christian. You're sitting here gritting your teeth, totally disgusted at the thought of all those hundreds of thousands of home-schooled Christian students who are going to be out there teaching other people about the Bible. Well, look at it this way. Who would you rather meet in a dark alley: a teenager with a Bible in his hand who wants to tell you about the Ten Commandments, or a teenager with a knife in his hand who wants to break them?)

Non-College-Bound Students

The course I've outlined above may seem overwhelming to someone who doesn't plan to go on to college in the first place. That's a *lot* of writing and reading and science and math!

Fair enough. The beauty of home school is that you don't have to do what other people think you "ought" to do. I'm all for the traditional core curriculum that people used to study back in the good old days—but if God made you to be a carpenter, or a juggler, or a farmer, who am I to dictate to you?

Those who already have a calling firmly in mind should feel free to cut and paste my suggestions above to fit the demands of their callings. After all, they *are* just suggestions, and they *are* rather strongly tilted toward higher education. If you're going to play in a symphony orchestra, I agree that you need music and foreign language studies more than you need calculus. (Orchestras travel a lot.) If you're going to farm, soil chemistry would be more helpful than abstract studies of covalence and oxidation-reduction. If you absolutely can't stand Shakespeare and Chaucer—if they don't enrich your life at all—then read someone who does. (You can't go wrong with P. G. Wodehouse.)

Don't sweat it. You can always pick up anything you missed later on—maybe when you're teaching your own children! In the meantime, if you can read and write and find Japan on an unlabeled world map, you're better off than a large minority of high school graduates.

Real-World Learning

Now's the time to talk about *emphasis*—what gets the most attention and what gets the least.

If you're mainly concerned about graduation and college-entrance requirements, the course of studies outlined above ought to satisfy these while providing a superior academic education.

However, if you are also concerned about bringing a Christian world-view to your educational program, and are not convinced that academics are the entire heart and soul of an education, then it's time to bring up a few more points.

The literature-science-history-etc. content of the better high school programs (note that we are *not* talking about fad programs and Mickey Mouse courses) tends to virtually exclude the real world. In biology class, students handle only dead plants and creatures, or creatures so small you can only see them through a microscope. In chemistry class, they deal with purified materials and specialized equipment. History is learned through textbooks rather than through discussions with older people who lived through the times in question, or lectures by historians, or visits to historic sites. Literary excerpts are read in isolation from the cultural history of the times. During the entire process, students live in a specialized world of their own, cut off from the daily life of the community.

I don't think that this obsession with lab science and with manipulating regulated objects is balanced. You could make a pretty strong biblical case for teaching all teens the hands-on principles of gardening, farming, and animal husbandry, for example, rather than abstract biology from a textbook. According to the Bible, the human race's original assignment *was* gardening and animal husbandry! This would be an entirely different approach, focusing on nurturing plants and animals and helping the good ones be fruitful rather than on observing and manipulating dead plants and animals. Yes, you would end up studying microscopy, but from the viewpoint of analyzing and controlling plant and animal diseases and parasites rather than as a sheer abstraction.

Nurturing, as opposed to theorizing, is a hands-on process. Taking care of a baby is quite different from filling out workbook pages on child development. Building a toolshed is quite different from theorizing about architecture or physics. The real world, including the local community, is different from the classroom.

Biblically, the church and the home are supposed to prepare teens for independent life in the community. One way we can do this is to give teens opportunities for genuine community involvement, from helping out at the State Fair, to passing out political flyers at voting places, to starting a business.

Teens need a variety of non-institutional experiences with people *not* their own age, from the very young to the very old. This is more difficult because of our segregated society in which the old live in nursing homes or retirement communities and the babies are warehoused in daycare centers.

The family and the church, however, both provide natural age-integrated environments, as does the business world to a lesser degree.

Teens also need real-world experiences: weeding a garden, baking a cake, sawing wood, sewing a dress. Ancient societies used to emphasize these real-world skills almost exclusively. Ours ignores them, relegating them to a small section of the revised Home Economics syllabus. We reward people for memorizing other people's theories, not for knowing how to make things work themselves.

I sometimes wonder: if all our expensive economic infrastructure were removed, how many of us could even survive? How many could find water, grow food, make their own clothes and shelter, raise our own children? How many could survive in a situation where we were suddenly cut off from police and fire protection? Surely such basic human wisdom counts as the *real* survival skills.

Final Thoughts

Homeschooled students have a great advantage over classroom-based students when it comes to following these suggestions. At the present time, it's doubtful that many of these ideas even could be implemented in traditional classrooms. Group education, especially age-segregated group education, is a whole different process from individual instruction and self-study.

But, on the other hand, if you've got it, why not flaunt it? I firmly believe that home-based instruction has potential to provide the *best* possible education for our children—if, that is, we have the courage to look at *all* our options, and not just keep treading on the same old tired K–12 treadmill! Let's all start thinking seriously about what we really *want* to learn and *want* to teach. Then go out, give it your best shot, and share your experiences with the rest of us!

Suggested Classical Reading List

Book suggestions are by Fritz Hinrichs. Notes in parentheses are added by Mary Pride, whose children have been taking Fritz's Great Books tutorial via the Internet and enjoying it very much! Please note that many other books could be added to this list, but life being short, here is plenty to start with.

Fritz also would like to point out that ALL the books on this list, and 3400 others, are now available on the World's Greatest Classical Books CD-ROM from I. Hoffman & Associates (this product was formerly sold by Corel Corporation), which sells for around $30. (No, that is not a typo!) You can add your own annotations, which are saved to your hard disk, you can search for particular words and phrases, and there's a built-in dictionary to look up the meanings of difficult words. If you prefer not to sit in front of a computer, you can print out the books you want, and they come out "nicely formatted," says Fritz. Considering that the books alone would cost hundreds of dollars, this is just another reason why buying a multimedia-equipped computer can SAVE you money!

Many of these books can also be found on AbleSoft's Library of the Future CD-ROM. Where to find these CD-ROMs? Turn the page!

Fritz Hinrichs is a graduate of St. John's College in Annapolis, MD which is based on the classical model, and of Westminster Seminary, in Escondido, CA. He is presently the owner of Escondido Tutorial Service and has been conducting tutorials for homeschoolers for the past four years. He can be reached at his email address *gbt@gbt.org* or through his Web page *www.gbt.org*. He resides in Escondido and is the proud uncle of five nephews and four nieces.

AESCHYLUS—*Agamemnon, Libation Bearers, Eumenides* (Ancient Greek writer whose works explore many human dilemmas)

ANSELM—*Proslogium, Monologium, Cur Deus Homo* (11th century founder of Scholasticism, a movement which used logic to prove Christian doctrines and to ferret out the answers to theological and other questions)

AQUINAS—*Summa Theologica* (Masterpiece of the most influential medieval Catholic writer. This multi-volume work is so long that you may prefer to read the condensed *Summa of the Summa*, available at discount from Conservative Book Club)

ARISTOTLE—*De Anima, Metaphysics, Nicomachean Ethics, Physics, Poetics* (One of the three fathers of Greek philosophy, and arguably the man who, besides the biblical writers, most influenced Western thought)

ATHANASIUS—*On the Incarnation* (Church Father who successfully squelched the Arian controversy almost single-handed, leading to the phrase "Athanasius contra mundum," or "Athanasius against the world.")

AUGUSTINE—*Confessions* (Prodigal youth who converted to Christianity in the 4th century and became a major force in Church theology)

AUSTEN—*Emma, Pride and Prejudice* (Flawless novels of 19th century British manners by one of the first women novelists)

Where to Get It

World's Greatest Classical Books CD-ROM

$29.99 plus shipping.
I. Hoffman & Associates, 34 Ross Street, Toronto Ontario, CANADA M5T 1Z9. (416) 977-6732. Email: orders@h-plus-a.com. Web: www.h-plus-a.com.

Library of the Future

$39.95 plus shipping.
AbleSoft, 8550E Remington Ave., Pennsauken, NJ 08110. Orders: (800) 545-9009. Phone: (609) 488-8200. Web: www.ablesoft-inc.com

- **BACH**—*St. Matthew Passion* (Great church music from the greatest church musician)
- **BACON**—*Novum Organon* (17th century work that introduces the modern scientific method)
- **CALVIN**—*Institutes of the Christian Religion* (An appeal to the king of France to stop persecuting Protestants, and incidentally an organized description of the entire Protestant theological system)
- **CERVANTES**—*Don Quixote* (The famed "tilter at windmills," demonstrating the dilemma of the modern man who may yearn for heroic deeds but who lives in an increasingly petty and nonheroic age)
- **CHAUCER**—*Canterbury Tales* (From the father of English literature)
- **CLEMENT**—*Exhortation to the Greeks* (Another influential Church Father, considered the founder of Alexandrian theology)
- **DANTE**—*Divine Comedy* (Italian Dante's concept of heaven and hell has greatly influenced Western literature)
- **DESCARTES**—*Discourse on Method* ("I think, therefore I am")
- **DOSTOYEVSKI**—*The Brothers Karamazov* (Analysis in novel form of the moody, ultimately penitent, soul in novel form from this moody, penitent Russian)
- **FREUD**—*The Interpretation of Dreams, A Case of Obsessional Neurosis, The Ego and the Id* (Freud's underlying theory is terribly wrong, and may in fact have been prompted by his need to justify his own sexual sins and other misdeeds, but the religion of psychoanalysis which he founded, in which denial of guilt is substituted for forgiveness of guilt, has arguably become the civil religion of the entire modern Western world)
- **HEGEL**—*Phenomenology of Spirit* (Another German thinker with a major influence on the modern world, Hegel believed that a "thesis"—a particular worldview—and its "antithesis"—an opposing worldview—would always ultimately meld into a new "synthesis," which in turn would eventually meld with its own antithesis, and so on. For one example, Communism (a thesis) and capitalism (an antithesis) meld into the "managed state," in which Big Business and Big Government cooperate. Such cooperation is largely made possible by the mindset Hegel introduced.)
- **HERODOTUS**—*The Persian Wars* (Ancient Greek history from the "first historian" outside the biblical writers, otherwise known as "the father of history")
- **HOMER**—*Iliad, Odyssey* (The greatest poet of the ancient world. His tales of Odysseus trying to make his way home in the face of constant interference from gods and goddesses must be read in order to understand much of Western literature.)
- **HUME**—*Treatise on Human Nature* (18th century British thinker who argued that all human knowledge comes from what we experience through our senses, as opposed to the Christian view that God can and has revealed facts outside our sensory experiences)
- **HUSSERL**—*Phenomenology and the Crisis of Philosophy* (Founder of 20th century philosophical movement by that name)
- **KANT**—*Prolegomena, Foundations of a Metaphysic of Morals* (Major thinker behind the abandonment of classical Christian thinking in favor of a "leap of faith")
- **KIERKEGAARD**—*Fear and Trembling* ("Christian" existentialist who promoted the search for a "religious experience" in place of religious truth. Very influential, moved many from "Is it true?" to "Does it work for me?")
- **LEWIS**—*God in the Dock, Essays* (Excellent defense of the Christian religion, from the author of the *Screwtape Letters,* the Narnia books, and dozens of other fiction and nonfiction masterpieces)
- **LINCOLN**—*Speeches* (As in "President Abraham Lincoln")

LOCKE—*Second Treatise on Government* (Political philosopher who influenced the Founding Fathers)

LUCRETIUS—*On the Nature of Things* (Major Roman philosopher)

LUTHER—*Commentary on Galatians* (John Wesley became "born again" as a result of reading this book of Luther's. A powerful exposition of the teaching that we are saved by "faith alone," from one of the major fathers of the Protestant Reformation.)

MACHIAVELLI—*The Prince* (From this discussion of the duties and strategies of rulers, we get the word "Machiavellian," meaning "amoral and sneaky." Naturally, rulers and the elite have studied this treatise for hundreds of years.)

MARX—*Das Capital* (The work ultimately responsible for hundreds of millions of deaths, from the father of Communism. Marx, the great "friend of the working man" who paid his housemaid slave wages and made her his mistress as well, believed that capitalism would die on its own, but Lenin and his followers decided to help it along with any means necessary, including terrorizing the people, lying to them, and denying the system's failure even when that failure became evident.)

MILTON—*Paradise Lost* (Famous poem that deals with Heaven and Hell, including Milton's own psychoanalysis of Satan and others)

MONTAIGNE—*Essays* (Famous 16th century French author whose prose style set the standard)

NIETZSCHE—*Beyond Good and Evil* (German book that introduced the idea of the "superman," not a flying being who wears Spandex, but a noble soul who, by virtue of his superior qualities and strength, is above all human laws. The Nazis loved this book.)

PASCAL—*Pensées* (Literally, "thoughts." The great French Christian author handles eternal questions in a cool, elegant manner.)

PLATO—*Apology, Crito, Euthyphro, Gorgias, Meno, Phaedo, Republic, Theatetus* (The second great father of Greek philosophy. He taught Aristotle, who ended up disagreeing violently with many of Plato's conclusions. Plato believed in the existence of eternal realities of which earthly objects are only "shadows." In the *Republic*, written over 2,000 years ago, he also designed a system of socialist government run by "philosopher kings" who control everything from childbearing to military service (for both sexes!) which eerily resembles what Hillary and her friends are trying to introduce today.)

PLUTARCH—*Greek Lives, Roman Lives* (All the dirt on many famous figures of the ancient world. Parts are not suitable for reading by children—for them, obtain an expurgated edition.)

ROUSSEAU—*Discourse on the Origins of Inequality, Social Contract* (The Frenchman who believed people should be "forced to be free" if they didn't want to accept the "freedom" of a system based on rebellion against God's laws and worship of Nature and Reason. This later culminated in many clients for Madame Guillotine during the French Revolution, where Rousseau's theories were enthusiastically enforced. All from the man who deposited his own babies at the nearest orphanage door, while exhorting French mothers to nurse their babies and extolling natural affection.)

SHAKESPEARE—*Coriolanus, Hamlet, King Lear, Macbeth, The Tempest, Troilus and Cressida* (Actually, *anything* by Shakespeare is famous, and *everything* should be read in order to understand the countless literary allusions to his work that pop up everywhere from classical novels to *Star Trek*.)

SMITH—*Wealth of Nations* (Proponent of an "invisible hand," e.g., the hand of God, which caused supply and demand to balance in an economy if government didn't step in to muck up the waters. The father of "laissez faire" capitalism, vastly influential in an earlier America, ignored by economists today who *love* the thought of government tinkering with the economy.)

- **SOPHOCLES**—*Oedipus Rex, Oedipus at Colonus, Antigone* (Ancient Greeks agonizing over awful dilemmas, thus revealing their character in these plays.)
- **SPENSER**—*The Faerie Queene* (Very long 16th century poem that influenced the later Romantic movement)
- **SWIFT**—*Gulliver's Travels* (The original "angry young man," Dean Jonathan Swift acerbically trashed what he hated about 19th century England in this series of allegorical stories.)
- **TACITUS**—*Annals* (First century Roman public official whose histories cover much of the period of the early Emperors)
- **THUCYDIDES**—*Peloponessian War* (Another early Greek historian, chronicling the devastating war between Athens and Sparta.)
- **TOCQUEVILLE**—*Democracy in America* (Insightful commentary on what made America great, and how we could lose that greatness, written by a French count who visited us several centuries ago.)
- **TOLSTOY**—*War and Peace* (The original "empire" book. Someone has said that the only two ways to write a great novel are to either chronicle the entire history of a nation or to chronicle a single day in one man's life. Solzhenitsyn did the latter, with *A Day in the Life of Ivan Denisovitch*. A century earlier, the pacifist Russian Tolstoy did the former, with his epic *War and Peace*. You will have to master the intricacies of Russian nicknames to understand this monumental book, which in turn inspired an eight-hour movie.)
- **TWAIN**—*Huckleberry Finn* (Insight into the American soul from the quintessential American writer, through the eyes of a young boy having adventures)
- **VIRGIL**—*Aeneid* (Monumentally famous Roman work: the "Odyssey" of Rome, telling the story of Aeneas and his wanderings after Troy fell, and incidentally promoting the idea that Emperor Augustus was descended from the goddess Aphrodite, ostensible mother of Aeneas)

GED Requirements by State & Province

For more information on taking the GED in your area contact, American Council on Education GED Testing Service, One Dupont Circle NW, Washington, DC 20036-1163. Phone: (202) 939-9490. Fax: (202) 775-8578. Web: www.acenet.edu/programs/CALEC/GED/home.html.

Requirements for Issuance of Certificate/Diploma

Location	Minimum Test Score	Minimum Age for Credential	Residency Requirement	Minimum Age for Testing	Testing Fee per Battery	Title of Credential
UNITED STATES						
Alabama	35 min & 45 avg	18[1]	30 days	18[1]	$20[2]	High School Equivalency Certificate
Alaska	40 min & 45 avg	16[1]	resident	16[1]	maximum $25	High School Diploma
Arizona	40 min & 45 avg	18[1]	none	18[1]	$10[2]	High School Equivalency Diploma
Arkansas	40 min & 45 avg	16	resident	16[1]	no charge	High School Diploma
California	40 min & 45 avg	18[1]	resident	17[1]	$12	High School Equivalency Certificate
Colorado	40 min & 45 avg	17	resident[1]	17	varies	High School Equivalency Diploma
Connecticut	40 min & 45 avg	17[1]	resident	17[1]	over 21, $13 otherwise free	High School Diploma
Delaware	40 min & 45 avg	18	resident	18[1]	$20	State Board of Education Endorsement
DC	40 min & 45 avg	18[1]	resident[1]	18[1]	$20[2]	High School Equivalency
Florida	40 min & 45 avg	18	resident	18[1]	$25[2]	High School Diploma
Georgia	40 min & 45 avg	18[1]	none	18[1]	$35[2]	High School Equivalency
Hawaii	40 min & 45 avg	17	resident[1]	17[1]	$10[2]	Department of Education High School Diploma
Idaho	40 min & 45 avg	16[1]	resident	16[1]	$30[2]	High School Equivalency Certificate
Illinois	40 min & 45 avg	18[1]	30 days	18[1]	$25	High School Equivalency Certificate
Indiana	40 min & 45 avg	17[1]	30 days	17	maximum $25	General Education Diploma
Iowa	40 min & 45 avg	18[1]	none	17[1]	$20[2]	High School Equivalency Diploma
Kansas	40 min & 45 avg	18[1]	resident[1]	16[1]	$30	High School Diploma
Kentucky	40 min & 45 avg	16	resident	16[1]	$25	High School Equivalency Diploma
Louisiana	40 min & 45 avg	17[1]	resident[1]	17[1]	maximum $20[2]	High School Equivalency Diploma[1]
Maine	40 min & 45 avg	17[1]	none	17[1]	none[1]	High School Equivalency Diploma
Maryland	40 min & 45 avg	16[1]	3 months	16[1]	$25[2]	High School Diploma
Massachusetts	40 min & 45 avg	16[1]	resident	16[1]	$50[2]	High School Equivalency Diploma
Michigan	40 min & 45 avg	18[1]	30 days	17[1]	varies	High School Equivalency Certificate
Minnesota	40 min & 45 avg	19[1]	resident	19[1]	$20–$45[2]	General Education Diploma
Mississippi	40 min or 45 avg	17	30 days[1]	17[1]	$20	High School Equivalency Diploma
Missouri	40 min & 45 avg	16[1]	resident[1]	16[1]	$18[2]	Certificate of High School Equivalence
Montana	40 min & 45 avg	16[1]	resident[1]	16[1]	$24	High School Equivalency Diploma
Nebraska	40 min or 45 avg	18	30 days[1]	18[1]	$20–$35	Department of Education High School Diploma

Location	Minimum Test Score	Minimum Age for Credential	Residency Requirement	Minimum Age for Testing	Testing Fee per Battery	Title of Credential
Nevada	40 min & 45 avg	17	resident	17	$25	Certificate of High School Equivalency
New Hampshire	40 min & 45 avg	16[1]	resident	16[1]	$40[2]	Certificate of High School Equivalency
New Jersey	see requirement	16[1]	none	16[1]	$25	High School Diploma
New Mexico	40 min & 45 avg	18	resident	17[1]	varies	High School Diploma
New York	40 min & 45 avg	17[1]	1 month	16[1]	no charge	High School Equivalency Diploma
North Carolina	40 min & 45 avg	18[1]	resident[1]	18[1]	$7.50[2]	High School Diploma Equivalency
North Dakota	40 min & 45 avg	18[1]	30 days[1]	18[1]	varies	GED High School Diploma
Ohio	40 min & 45 avg	19[1]	resident	19[1]	$42[1,2]	High School Equivalency Diploma
Oklahoma	40 min & 45 avg	18[1]	resident	18[1]	maximum $30	Certificate of High School Equivalency
Oregon	40 min & 45 avg	18[1]	resident[1]	18[1]	varies	Certificate of General Educational Development
Pennsylvania	40 min & 45 avg	18[1]	resident[1]	18[1]	varies	Commonwealth Secondary School Diploma
Rhode Island	40 min & 45 avg	18[1]	resident[1]	18[1]	$15	High School Equivalency Diploma
South Carolina	40 min & 45 avg	17	resident[1]	17[1]	$30[2]	High School Equivalency Diploma
South Dakota	40 min & 45 avg	18[1]	resident[1]	18[1]	$7	High School Equivalency Certificate
Tennessee	40 min & 45 avg	18	resident	18[1]	varies	Equivalency High School Diploma
Texas	40 min or 45 avg	18[1]	resident[1]	18[1]	varies[2]	Certificate of High School Equivalency
Utah	40 min & 45 avg	18[1]	resident[1]	18[1]	varies[2]	Certificate of General Educational Development
Vermont	40 min & 45 avg	16	resident	16[1]	$25–$30	Secondary School Equivalence Certificate
Virginia	40 min & 45 avg	18[1]	resident	18[1]	$35[2]	Commonwealth General Educational Development Certificate
Washington	40 min & 45 avg	19[1]	resident	19[1]	$25	Certificate of Educational Competence
West Virginia	40 min & 45 avg	18[1]	30 days	18[1]	varies	High School Equivalent Diploma
Wisconsin	40 min & 50 avg	18.5	resident	18[1]	varies	High School Equivalency Diploma
Wyoming	40 min & 45 avg	18	resident[1]	see state requirement	maximum $20	High School Equivalency Certificate

CANADA—PROVINCES & TERRITORIES

Location	Minimum Test Score	Minimum Age for Credential	Residency Requirement	Minimum Age for Testing	Testing Fee per Battery	Title of Credential
Alberta	45 each test	18[1]	resident	18	$50	High School Equivalency Diploma
British Columbia	45 each test	19[1]	resident	19	$25	Secondary School Equivalency Certificate
Manitoba	45 each test	19[1]	resident	19	$22	High School Equivalency Diploma
New Brunswick	45 each test	19	3 months	19	$10	12th Year High School Equivalency Diploma
Newfoundland	40 min & 45 avg	19[1]	3 months	19	$20	High School Equivalency Diploma
NW Territories	40 min & 45 avg	18[1]	6 months	18[1]	$5	High School Equivalency Certificate
Nova Scotia	45 each test	19[1]	none	19	$20	High School Equivalency Diploma
Prince Edwd Island	45 each test	19[1]	resident	19[1]	$20	High School Equivalency Certificate
Saskatchewan	45 each test[1]	19	resident	19[1]	$25	High School Equivalency Certificate
Yukon	45 each test	19[1]	resident	19[1]	$25	Secondary School Equivalency Certificate

U.S. TERRITORIES

Location	Minimum Test Score	Minimum Age for Credential	Residency Requirement	Minimum Age for Testing	Testing Fee per Battery	Title of Credential
American Samoa	40 each test	18	resident	18[1]	$10	High School Diploma of Equivalency
Canal Zone	40 min & 45 avg	17	resident[1]	17	$35	Certificate of High School Equivalency
Guam	35 min & 45 avg	18	resident	18[1]	$10	High School Equivalency Diploma
Kwajalein	35 min & 45 avg	18		18	$22.25	Certificate of Equivalency
Mariana Islands	40 min or 45 avg	18	30 days	18[1]	$5	High School Equivalency Diploma
Marshall Islands	40 min or 45 avg	18	30 days	18[1]	$7.50[2]	High School Equivalency Certificate
Palau	40 min & 45 avg	16		16[1]	$10	Certificate of Equivalency
Puerto Rico	35 min & 45 avg	18	resident	18	no charge	High School Equivalency Diploma
Virgin Islands	35 min & 45 avg	18	3 months	17	$20	Certificate of Equivalency

[1]See jurisdiction requirements for exceptions and limitations
[2]See jurisdictional requirements for credential and other fees

APPENDIX 5

Graduation Requirements

Graduation Requirements			
Subject	Credit Hours	Carnegie Units	Equivalent # of Single-Semester Courses
Language Arts	**40**	**4 units**	**8 courses**
Option 1:			
• English **and**	30	3 units	6 courses
another language	10	1 unit	2 courses
Option 2:			
• English	40	4 units	8 courses
Social Studies	**30**	**3 units**	**6 courses**
Including:	Including:	Including:	Including:
• American History	10	1 unit	2 courses
• American Gov't	5	½ unit	1 course
• Social Studies	15	1½ units	3 courses
(courses of student's choice)			
Mathematics	**20**	**2 units**	**4 courses**
Science	**20**	**2 units**	**4 courses**
Multicultural Studies	**5**	**½ unit**	**1 course**
Financial Skills	**5**	**½ unit**	**1 course**
Career Planning	**5**	**½ unit**	**1 course**
Electives	**75**	**7½ units**	**15 courses**

The charts in this appendix are excerpted and edited versions of those found in the 1999–2000 catalog of University of Nebraska-Lincoln's Department of Independent Study. The original charts are ©1999 UN-L, used by permission.

5 credit hours = one-semester course
10 credit hours = two-semester course
Two semesters per school year

One Carnegie unit = a full year course = 10 credit hours (e.g., a class meeting 1 hour a day, 5 days a week, all school year long.) The "Carnegie" unit is named after the Carnegie Commission on Secondary Education, whose mission was and is to standardize high-school education in the USA. Homeschoolers oppose the idea of nationally-enforced standards on principle; however, the Carnegie unit is a handy way of recording your courses, one that colleges will recognize.

Electives may be taken from any area of study. Once the requirements have been met in the above areas, any additional courses taken within those areas are applied to elective credit. Diploma students must earn **a minimum of 200 credits (or 20 units of Carnegie credit).**

* Starred items have been added to the UN-L Curriculum in the last few years, at the command of the Nebraska Legislature.

You do not have to rigorously follow this course sequence. Consider it as a guide, and feel free to substitute studies of your own choice, as long as they clearly relate to the subject area shown. (e.g., General Science for Health Science, or Computer Use 101 for Intro to Technology)

This is the course sequence for high-school diploma students. You, as a parent, can issue a diploma when your students complete these courses. If you have strong objections to this curriculum outline, then study what you wish, and wait until you are old enough to take the GED. But be aware that business and the military give less consideration to a GED certificate than to a high-school diploma. Irrational, yes—you don't *have* to know *anything* to graduate from a public high-school, whereas the GED requires you to have a good bit of knowledge—but true.

Course Sequencing for Diploma Students

General

The following program is suggested for students whose immediate after-graduation plans include vocational or technical school, a job, or other non-college situations

Ninth Grade

Subject	First Semester	Second Semester
English	Effective Reading Skills or Reading Comprehension	Basic Expository Writing or Beginning Composition
Mathematics	Basic Math I (arithmetic)	Basic Math II (arithmetic)
Science	Health Science I	Health Science II
	(lifestyle, sex ed, drug ed, exercise, nutrition, disease)	
Social Studies	Civics	
Elective	Study Skills	Beginning Typing

Tenth Grade

Subject	First Semester	Second Semester
English	Multicultural Literature*	The Short Story
Mathematics	General Math I (fractions, decimals, percents)	General Math II (other pre-algebra/ pre-geometry math)
Science	Physical Science I	Physical Science II
Social Studies	Sociology or Psychology	
Elective	Intro to Technology	10 credit hours

Eleventh Grade

Subject	First Semester	Second Semester
English	General Literature	Advanced Typing
Mathematics	Business & Consumer Math I	Business & Consumer Math II
Science	Biology I	Biology II
Career Planning	Career Planning*	
Social Studies	American History I	American History II
Elective	5 credit hours	

Twelfth Grade

Subject	First Semester	Second Semester
English	General Literature	5 credit hours
Social Studies	Ethnic Studies*	American Government
Mathematics	Beginning Algebra I	Beginning Algebra II
Financial Skills	Consumer Ed or Personal Finance	
Elective	Career Protocol: Business & International Etiquette	Personal Adjustment and Family Living

Course Sequencing for Diploma Students

College Prep

The following program is suggested for students preparing for college. These recommendations reflect most colleges' entrance requirements.

Ninth Grade

Subject	First Semester	Second Semester
English	Ninth Grade English I (grammar, literature and composition)	Ninth Grade English II (grammar, literature and composition)
Mathematics	Beginning Algebra I	Beginning Algebra II
Science	Physical Science I	Physical Science II
Social Studies	5 credit hours	5 credit hours
Language	5 credit hours	5 credit hours

Tenth Grade

Subject	First Semester	Second Semester
English	Tenth Grade English I (grammar, lit & comp)	Tenth Grade English II (grammar, lit & comp)
Mathematics	Geometry I	Geometry II
Science	Biology I	Biology II
Social Studies	5 credit hours	5 credit hours
Language	5 credit hours	5 credit hours

Eleventh Grade

Subject	First Semester	Second Semester
English	American Literature I	American Literature II
Mathematics	Advanced Algebra I	Advanced Algebra II
Science	Chemistry I	Chemistry II
Career Planning	Career Planning*	
Social Studies	American History I	American History II
Elective	5 credit hours	

Twelfth Grade

Subject	First Semester	Second Semester
English	British Literature I	English Literature II
Mathematics	Precalculus I (Calculus w/Analytical Geometry)	Precalculus II (Trigonometry)
Science	Physics I	Physics II
Social Studies	Ethnic Studies*	American Government
Financial Skills	Personal Finance or Economics	
Elective	5 credit hours	

---

* Starred items have been added to the UN-L Curriculum in the last few years, at the command of the Nebraska Legislature.

You pretty much have to rigorously follow this course sequence in order to have your college appplication taken seriously, but can use some creativity in course *content*. E.g., writing and directing your own play, and receiving feedback from a professional dramatist, could be a semester of 10th grade English.

If you want to enter a selective college, science courses must be *lab* courses. See Chapter 27 for information about how to do lab science at home.

High School Guidance Overview

The wisely planned high school experience will prepare teens for life and give them every advantage for their future development. God has called each Christian teen to a life of influence for His glory. God calls some to Church work. The calling of most will lead them to godly impact in the broader society through education, law, public policy, medicine, technology, management, entrepreneurism, the arts, various trades and so on. Use this High School Guidance Overview and Calendar as a checklist to procure the advantages of wise preparation.

High School Guidance Overview

Discover how God designed you for life and work. Seek to discover your calling

- Pray and study the Word of God
- Utilize a godly career assessment from a biblical worldview
- Observe or intern in your fields of highest interest
- Discuss this with parents, teachers and your pastor
- Write a brief mission statement for your life

Academics

- Choose the right courses
- Determine to achieve great grades
- Learn how to take college preparation exams
- Learn biblical principles of managing money

Extracurricular Activities

- Participate in church, community, and service activities
- Engage in sports if appropriate
- Seek a part-time job to learn skills

This article is by Rodney Marshall. Rodney Marshall, M.Div. is Education Marketing Manager for Larry Burkett's Christian Financial Concepts/Life Pathways providing career and educational guidance and money management products and services with a biblical worldview. He can be reached at (972) 539-1574 or rjmarsh@sprynet.com.

Colleges, Technical Schools, and Apprenticeships

- Select a school or apprenticeship opportunity
- Navigate the application process
- Plan to finance your education

High School Calendar
Freshman Year

Fall
- Take a life and career survey now to find out how God designed you for life and work. Begin to find direction for your future.
- Draft a four-year schedule of courses that meets the requirements for graduation and college/school admission
- Draft a four-year schedule of athletic and extracurricular activities you'd like to become involved in
- Commit yourself to learn Biblical principles of managing money during high school
- Build a schedule that allows for these things

Spring
- Set a goal to get higher grades in the key subject areas (English, math, science, history, foreign language)
- Begin a vocabulary building program
- Look into work, study, or sports summer programs

Summer
- Volunteer some time in a good cause
- Pursue extracurricular and athletic interests
- Read at least four books
- Consider a part-time job

Sophomore Year

Fall
- Update your four-year class schedule. Seek to complete most of the minimum requirements for college/school admission by the end of your junior year.
- Update your four-year athletic and extracurricular calendar
- Register for the PSAT/NMSQT
- Take the PSAT (given only once in October)
- If your are pursuing a sport seriously, research NCAA requirements

Spring/Summer
- Continue to set and achieve higher grade averages in key subject areas
- Sharpen math and vocabulary skills
- Read at least four books
- Involve yourself in at least one organized work, athletic, or study program in the summer

Junior Year

Gear up for the college/school application process.

Fall
- Register and take the PSAT/NMSQT in October (This time it counts)

- Use a sophisticated career assessment which considers your entire unique pattern of personality, vocational interests, skills, and values now or in the spring semester, and choose a college major field of study or vocational direction.
- Begin the college search process. Narrow a list to no more than 20 schools. Write for admissions information. Write to college coaches if college sports are a goal.
- Attend local college fairs and begin visiting colleges/schools
- Compare academic requirements to your course schedule and adjust as necessary
- Identify SAT I, ACT and SAT II test requirements for your target schools. Match these with your PSAT scores (multiply PSAT by 10 to compare with SAT)
- Begin preparing for the SAT I or the ACT
- Estimate college costs
- Begin searching for scholarships

Spring
- Complete study for the SAT I or ACT
- Take the SAT I in March, or in May if you need extra time to prepare, or take the ACT
- Take the SAT IIs in the courses and key areas in which your have completed the last course for high school study and have scored a B+ or better, and have an interest
- Take the Advanced Placement test for those AP or college level courses your will complete this spring
- Plan for the summer

Summer
- Begin visiting college/school campuses
- Prepare drafts of your essays for your target schools
- Become involved in at least one organized study, athletic, or work activity. Seek experience in your chosen field of post secondary pursuits
- Read at least four books
- Prepare to retake the SAT I or ACT if you need higher test scores

Senior Year

Time to get serious about applying for colleges, technical school and apprenticeships. Stay organized as you approach numerous deadlines

Fall
- Narrow your target college/school list.
- Retake the SAT I or ACT if you need higher test scores and have prepared over the summer to improve them
- If pursuing collegiate athletics, make telephone contact with coaches. Update your athletic resume. Find out Letter of Intent date for your sport from the NCAA.
- Send for college/school applications, and financial aid materials. Complete and submit materials.
- Send for scholarship and grant program application materials. Complete and submit materials.
- Visit your target college/school campuses
- Select two teachers and two extracurricular advisors to write glowing recommendations about you
- Obtain a copy of the Free Application of Federal Student Aid (FAFSA)

Spring

- Complete the FAFSA by March 1 to qualify for most financial aid
- Review your Student Aid Report (SAR) for accuracy and completeness
- Decide the college, university or technical school you will attend and notify them of your decision to matriculate
- Take SAT II exams if high scores will allow you to place out of academic requirements
- Estimate college/school costs and sources for the two to four or more year college/school period. If in a deficit, investigate minimum loan sources.
- Take the Advanced Placement exams for appropriate courses
- Begin evaluating housing options for the fall
- Consider summer employment to earn money for college expenses
- Confirm biblical principles of managing money and establish a budget for post secondary life
- Get ready for a great time training to fulfill your calling

Resources

- For a catalog of career assessments and money management tools, contact Christian Financial Concepts/Life Pathways education office at 972-539-1574, rjmarsh@sprynet.com, *www.findafuture.com*
- For career and college how tos, see the Career Corner: *www.cfcministry.org/library/career*
- For PSAT, SAT contact Educational Testing Service at 609-771-7600
- College Board Online *www.collegeboard.org/features/home/html/intro.html*
- For ACT, contact American College Testing Board at 319-337-1827
- Free Application of Federal Student Aid (FAFSA), 800-433-3243, *www.ed.gov/offices/OPE/express.html*
- Student Guide to Financial Aid, *www.ed.gov/prog_info/SFA/*
- Free financial aid assistance SallieMae, at 888-888-3460 or *www.salliemae.com*
- Free scholarship search engine at *www.fastweb.com*
- Free information about Christian colleges: *www.christianconnector.com*

FIND IT FAST

Index

Find It Fast

Index

100 Greatest Books Ever Written, 91
25 Questions on the U.S. Constitution, 254
30 Second Mysteries, 344
300 in One Electronics Lab, 244
313 colleges which have accepted homeschoolers, 498
5 Minutes a Day to Perfect Spelling, 103
9-5 Series, 519

A

A Beka Bible Studies, 24
A Beka Biology, 192
A Beka Chemistry, 213
A Beka *Consumer Mathematics*, 141
A Beka Economics: Work and Prosperity, 274
A Beka French I and II, 122
A Beka General Science series, 181
A Beka *Heritage of Freedom*, 298
A Beka Literature Curriculum, 81
A Beka *Basic Mathematics I*, 138
A Beka Physics, 228
A Beka *Pre-Algebra*, 138
A Beka Spanish I and II, 122
A Beka Vocabulary, Spelling and Poetry series, 102
A Beka World Geography, 282
A Beka *World History & Cultures*, 320
A Beka's Handbook of Grammar and Composition, 58
Abrams, Daniel, 383
Academy in Crisis, 491
ACT American College Testing Program, 448
Activity Based Supplies, 247
Adams, Scott, 276
Adams-Gordon, Beverly, 105

Adler, Mortimer, 90
Advanced Algebra Through Data Exploration, 150
Advanced Placement Bulletin for Students and Parents, 469, 470
Advanced Winston Grammar, 72
Adventurous World of College Algebra videos, 159
Air Land Emergency Resource Team, 523
ALERT, 523
Algebra the Easy Way, 152
Algebra: An Introductory Course, 150
All About Language series (foreign languages), 125
All About Language series (English), 130
Allied Aircraft Piston Engines of World War II, 241
Almond, Mark, 386
Alpha Omega American History LIFEPACs, 298
Alpha Omega Art LIFEPACs, 368
Alpha Omega Biology LIFEPACs, 193
Alpha Omega Chemistry LIFEPACs, 215
Alpha Omega Civics Elective LIFEPACs, 259
Alpha Omega Consumer Mathematics LIFEPACs, 141
Alpha Omega Geography Elective LIFEPACs, 282
Alpha Omega Greek LIFEPACs, 113
Alpha Omega Language Arts LIFEPACs, 49, 82
Alpha Omega Physics LIFEPACs, 229
Alpha Omega Science LIFEPACs, 182
Alpha Omega Spanish LIFEPACs, 122

Alpha Omega Western History LIFEPACs, 320
America's Best 100 College Buys, 485
America's British Culture, 295
America's Christian History: The Untold Story, 295
America: Roots of Our Nation, 304
America: The First 350 Years, 298
American Classical League, 116
American Family Album series, 309
American Heroes 1735-1900, 305
American History for Christian Schools, 301
American History on the Screen, 314
American Information Newsletter, 510
American Institute of Music accredited music courses, 382
American Reference Library 1 CD-ROM, 306
American Science & Surplus catalog, 247
An American Imperative: Higher Expectations for Higher Education, Report of the Wingspread Group on Higher Education, 477, 494, 495
Analogies series, 105, 440
Ancient City: Life in Classical Athens and Rome, 336
Ancient Philosophy, 345
Ancient Rome: How It Affects You Today, 258, 276
Ancient World magazine, 330
And What About College?, 500
André Previn Guide to Music Kit, 389
Annotated Mona Lisa, 375
Answers in Genesis catalog, 202
AP Course Descriptions series, 469
ARCO SAT SuperCourse, 438
ARCO Sat II SuperCourse, 454

Are You Liberal, Conservative or Confused?, 258, 276
Art Masters, 377
Artist's and Graphic Designer's Market, 67
Artists from A to Z series, 376
Aslett, Don, 98, 408, 414, 520, 521
ATI Sentence Analysis course, 73
Audio-Forum foreign language courses, 122
Automobile Design, 241

B

Back to Genesis video series, 203
Backgrounds to World Literature, 81
Baldwin, Jeff, 93, 293
Barfield, Rhonda, 412
Barna Research Group, 41
Barron's Guide to Distance Learning, 516
Barron's How to Prepare for the ACT, 449
Barron's How to Prepare for the AP Examination series, 479
Barron's How to Prepare for the GED, 462
Barron's How to Prepare for the SAT I, 439
Barron's How to Prepare for the SAT II, 455
Barron's How to Prepare for the CLEP, 473
Barron's How to Prepare for the PSAT/ NMSQT, 434
Barron's Profiles of American Colleges, 482
Basic Chemistry for Christian Schools, 216
Basic Digital Electronics, 244
Basic Electronics, 244
Basic Economics, 275
Basic Greek in 30 Minutes a Day, 113
Basic History of the United States series, 302
Basic Physics: A Self-Teaching Guide, 234
Basic Science for Christian Schools series, 188
Basics of Systematic Grammar, 74
Basketball Championships, 422
BBC English Courses, 129
BBC Learning Kits, 129
Beach House, 39
Bear, Dr. John, 516, 517
Bears' Guide to Earning College Degrees Nontraditionally, 516
Beautiful Feet Books, 300
Bedrick Inside Story series, 240
Bedrick Timelink series, 335
Beechick, Ruth, 26

Beginner's Dictionary of Prayerbook Hebrew, 112
Behrman House Hebrew courses, 111
Berlitz Foreign Language Courses, 123
Best 311 Colleges, 485
Best Little Stories series, 308
Best Test Preparation for the Advanced Placement Examination series, 471
Beyond Political Correctness, 491
Bible Discovery series, 25
Bible Foundations series, 25
Bible in Verse, 31
Bible Quest series, 25
BibleQuizmania, 32
Big Ideas/Small Budget, 413
Biology for Christian Schools, 194
Biology: God's Living Creation, 192
Biology the Easy Way, 193
BJUP *American Government*, 260
BJUP American History for Christian Schools series, 301
BJUP *Basic Chemistry for Christian Schools*, 216
BJUP *Basic Science for Christian Schools*, 188
BJUP *Basics of Systematic Grammar*, 74
BJUP Bible Curriculum, 24
BJUP *Biology for Christian Schools*, 194
BJUP *Consumer Mathematics*, 141
BJUP *Earth Science for Christian Schools*, 186
BJUP *Economics for Christian Schools*, 275
BJUP *French, German and Spanish*, 123
BJUP *Geography for Christian Schools*, 282
BJUP *Life Science for Christian Schools*, 184
BJUP Literature for Christian Schools series, 83
BJUP *Manners at Work*, 520
BJUP Math for Christian Schools series, 138
BJUP *Physics for Christian Schools*, 230
BJUP Vocabulary for Christian Schools series, 106
BJUP *World History for Christian Schools*, 320
BJUP *World Studies for Christian Schools*, 320
Blackstone Audiobooks, 93
Blakey, Barbara, 51
Bloom, Alan, 40
Bluestocking Guide to Economics, 279
Bolchazy-Carducci Greek Readers, 114
Bolchazy-Carducci Latin Readers, 116
Bolles, Richard Nelson, 532

Bond, Jill, 411
Book of Many Colors, 369
Bornstein, Arthur, 104
Bornstein, Scott, 108
Bramson, Morris, 150
Builder Boards, 407
Building Believable Characters, 58
Buongiorno Italia! series, 124
Burkett, Larry, 413, 478
Burritt, Amy, 289
Buskin, Richard, 322
But What If?, 34

C

Calculus the Easy Way, 175
Calculus Tutoring Book, 177
Calculus: Concepts and Applications, 173
Calliope magazine, 330
Calvert Spelling and Vocabulary CD-ROMs, 102
Cambridge Latin Courses, 117
Canon Press Latin Grammar, 117
Canon Press introductory Logic, 339
Cardulla, Frank, 224
Career Skills Library, 520
Career Starter series, 529
CareerDirect Assessment, 478
Carolina Biological catalog, 247
Carrel, Annette, 264
Carson, Clarence, 275, 302
Cartoon Guide to Physics, 235
Cartoon History of the Universe, 330
Case of Red Herrings series, 340
Castle Heights *Experiences in Biology*, 194
Castle Heights *Experiences in Chemistry*, 217
Chalk Dust Algebra Videos, 157
Chalk Dust Basic Math, 143
Chalk Dust Calculus, 177
Chalk Dust Geometry, 168
Chalk Dust Precalculus, 172
Chalk Dust SAT Math Review Videos, 439
Chalk Dust Trigonometry, 171
Challenge of Godly Government, 260
Challenge of Godly Justice, 260
Changing Gears, 241
Charteris, Leslie, 253
Cheaney, Janie B., 65
Chem City chemistry course, 220
Chem Lab Supplies catalog, 247
Chemistry Made Simple, 221
Chemistry the Easy Way, 221
Chemistry: Precision and Design, 213
Chemy Named Al, 225
Children's Classics Library, 94
Children's Writer's & Illustrator's Market, 66

Choices for the High School Graduate, 526

Choosing the Right College, 482

Choosing Your Way Through America's Past series, 315

Christian Camping Today, 423

Christian Financial Concepts, 413, 561

Christian History of the American Revolution, 296

Christian History of the Constitution, 296

Christian Leadership, 41

Christian Liberty *Masterpieces in Art,* 377

Christian Liberty Streams of Civilization series, 321

Christian Light Biology, 195

Christian Light Chemistry, 218

Christian Light General Science, 183

Christian Light *God's World—His Story,* 322

Christian Light Literature series, 84

Christian Light *Math at Work,* 139

Christian Light Physics, 231

Christian School Band Method, 387

Christian Writers' Market Guide, 59

Chronicles magazine, 44, 357

CHRONOGRAF magazine, 315

Church History, 324

Civil War Songs on cassette, 309

Clare, John, 335

Clark, Dr. Gordon, 342, 345

Classic Critiques series, 86

Classical Music for Dummies, 391

Classical Music for Everybody, 391

Cleaning Encyclopedia, 408

Clear and Lively Writing, 59

Cliffs Notes on Greek Classics, 86

Cliffs Notes on Literature series, 85

Cliffs Notes on Mythology, 85

Cliffs Notes on Roman Classics, 86

Cliffs Quick Review: Algebra I, 152

Cliffs Quick Review: American Government, 260

Cliffs Quick Review: Calculus, 176

Cliffs Quick Review: Chemistry, 221

Cliffs Quick Review: Geometry, 165

Cliffs Quick Review: Linear Algebra, 153

Cliffs Quick Review: Microbiology, 195

Cliffs Quick Review: Physics, 235

Cliffs Quick Review: Trigonometry, 170

Clipper Ship Strategy, 276

Clutter Free!, 414

Cobblestone magazine, 316

Cohen, Cafi, 500

Cohen, David Bennett, 384

College Bound, 492

College Degrees by Mail and Modem, 517

College Financial Aid for Dummies, 504

College Planning/Search Book, 483

College scholarship services, 507

Commas Are Our Friends, 74

Community Service for Teens series, 425

Compete with Confidence, 97

Complete Idiot's Guide to American History, 302

Complete Idiot's Guide to Baking, 410

Complete Idiot's Guide to British Royalty, 322

Complete Idiot's Guide to Cooking Basics, 409

Complete Works of Francis Schaeffer, 360

Complete Yes Minister, 258

Connolly, Peter, 336

Conscience game, 42

Constitutional Law for Christian Students, 261

Contemporary's GED Essay, 462

Contemporary's GED Math Problem Solver, 463

Contemporary's GED Satellite series, 463

Contemporary's GED: The Complete Book, 462

Contemporary's Pre-GED Satellite series, 464

Contents of CLEP chart, 474

Converse All Star series, 416

Cook, Robin, 79

Cooking for Dummies, 410

Copan, Paul, 345

Countdown to College, 490

Country magazine, 209

Country Extra magazine, 209

Country Woman magazine, 209

Covenant Home Curriculum, 86, 108, 377

Crabtree Lands, People and Cultures series, 284

Cracking the ACT, 450

Cracking the AP, 470

Cracking the CLEP, 475

Cracking the GED, 465

Cracking the SAT and PSAT, 443

Cracking the SAT II series, 456

Crafts Supply Source Book, 368

Cranfill, Shelby, 327

Create a Culture, 350

Creation magazine, 202

Creation ex Nihilo Technical Journal, 202

Creative Problem Solving Activities, 340

Creative Writing and the Essay for the Beginner, 60

Credenda/Agenda, 358

Creepy, Crawly World of Calculus videos, 178

Crisis of Western Education, 493

Critical Thinking in United States History series, 303

Cuisenaire math & science catalog, 247

D

Dangerous World of Pre-Calculus videos, 178

Dateline: Troy, 331

David Bennett Cohen Teaches Blues Piano course, 384

Davidson Music courses, 382

Davidson, Diane, 98

Dawson, Christopher, 493

Debt Free College, 505

Deep Fried World of Organic Chemistry videos, 224

Defeating Darwinism by Opening Minds, 203

Deitschmann, Craig, 264

Dell Logic Puzzles, 341

Delta Education, 247

DeMar, Gary, 295, 496

Desserts for Dummies, 411

Dilbert Principle, 276

Dinner's in the Freezer, 411

Directory of American Youth Organizations, 426

Discovering Geometry, 165

Dissected World of Biology, 197

Dobbins, Durell C., 183

Dobson, Dr. James, 32

Don Aslett Cleaning Center, 409

Downing, Dr. Douglas, 152, 169

Dr. Paul Zaps the ACT, 449

Drive Right, 401, 403

Duffy, Matthew, 15

Dufner, J. Mark, 103

Dykema, Dale, 377

E

Ear Training, 385

Earth Science for Christian Schools, 186

Easy Adult Piano course, 383

Eat Well for $50 a Week, 412

Ecce Romani Latin course, 118, 120

Economics for Christian Schools, 275

Economics in One Lesson, 277

Economics of Liberty, 278

Editor In Chief series, 60

Edmund Scientific's catalog, 248

Edward de Bono's Super Mind Pack, 341

Eidsmoe, John, 263

Elementary Catechism on the Constitution of the United States, 262

ElementO game, 225

Elements of Literature, 83

Elliot, Kathy, 412
Elvis in Latin, 117
Emery, Carla, 406
Emmaus Correspondence Course Series, 25
Encyclopedia of Country Living, 406
English as a Second Language, 130
English Vocabulary Quick Reference, 106
Enough About Grammar, 75
Epstein, L. C., 236
Escondido Tutorial Service, 551
España Viva course, 124
Essay Handbook, 61
Evaluating Books, 87, 276
Everyday Math for Dummies, 142
Everything I Needed to Know About Business I Learned in the Barnyard, 520
Exciting World of Creative Writing, 62
Excursions in Literature, 83
Experiences in Biology, 194
Experiences in Chemistry, 217
Explorations in Literature, 83
Exploratorium Science Snackbook series, 231
Explorer's Bible Study Curriculum for the Young Scholar, 25
Expository Writing Book, 61

F

Fabulae Gracae, 118
Fabulae Romanae: Stories of Famous Romans, 118
Facts not Fear, 210
Faith Lessons video series, 32
Faith of Our Fathers, 262
Families that Play Together Stay Together, 417
Family Classics Library, 94
Family Reading Guide series, 87
Farm & Ranch Living magazine, 209
Farris, Christy, 95
Farris, Michael, 261
Fascinating Facts from American History, 311
Ferguson *Choices for the High School Graduate,* 526
Ferguson Career Skills Library, 520
Ferguson *Free and Inexpensive Career Materials,* 527
Ferguson *From High School to Work,* 528
Ferguson's Guide to Apprenticeship Programs, 528
Ferguson What Can I Do Now series, 480
Fields, Suzanne, 319
Fills and Runs by Ear, 383
Firebaugh Algebra on Videotape series, 158

Firebaugh, Leonard, 158
First Hebrew Primer, 112
First Hebrew Primer for Adults, 112
Fitness at Home, 418
Flansburg, Scott, 146
Flax models, 368
Fleischman, Paul, 331
Floren, Joe, 75
Foerster, Paul, 173
Foltzer, Monica, 55
For Dummies classical music series, 392
For the Layman: A Survey of the Old Testament course, 27
Foreign Languages and Your Career, 131
Forgotten Calculus, 175
Format Writing, 62
Found, Jim, 113
Foundation for Economic Education, 279
Free and Inexpensive Career Materials, 527
Freedom Philosophy, 263
Freeman magazine, 280
Freistat, Mitchell, 421
Friendly Chemistry: A Guide to Learning Basic Chemistry course, 226
From High School to Work, 528
From Homeschool to College and Work, 500
From Sea to Shining Sea, 304
Fun Physical Fitness for the Home, 418
Fundamentals of Literature, 83

G

G. A. Henty series, 332
Gaining Favor with God and Man, 43
Gardner, Debbie, 422
Gebra Named Al, 225
GED Essay: Writing Skills to Pass the Test, 462
GED Math Problem Solver, 463
GED Satellite series, 463
GED: The Complete Book, 462
Geisler, Dr. Norman, 265
General Punctuation, 75
Genesis: Finding Our Roots, 26
Genevieve Foster "World" books, 301
Geography for Christian Schools, 282
Geometric Playthings, 167
Geometry the Easy Way, 165
Getting into the ACT, 450
Geyer, Anne, 490
Giants of Philosophy series, 346
Giants of Political Thought series, 264
Gish/Doolittle Debate, 204

Glaser, Matt, 385
God and Government series, 263
God's Law for Modern Man, 33
God's Revelation, 27
God's World—His Story, 322
Gonick, Larry, 235, 330
Good Heavens game, 187
Gordon, John, 373
Gordon School of Art, 373
Gourmet Cooking for Dummies, 410
Grammar Free Fall, 76
Grant, George, 44
Graphing calculators, 151
Graves of Academe, 493
Great American Statesmen and Heroes, 309
Great Authors of the Western Literary Tradition series, 88
Great Books Guides, 89
Great Christian Revolution, 325
Great Cities of the Ancient World videos, 332
Great Economic Thinkers series, 280
Great Explorations in Editing, 63
Great Minds of the Western Intellectual Tradition series, 347
Great Race to Nome, 350
Greeenburg, Robert, 394
Greene, Lorne, 257
Greenlee, Carolyn Wing, 34
Gruber's Complete Preparation for the New SAT, 440
Gruber, Gary, 440
Guide for the College Bound, 501
Guide to Literary Agents, 66
Guyot, Arnold, 282

H

Hackes, Peter, 283
Hail to the Chief game, 253
Harcourt Brace Living History series, 335
HarperCollins College Outline Introduction to Calculus, 176
Harris, Sono Sato, 418
Harvard Classics series, 91
Harvey's Elementary Grammar and Composition, 76
Harvey's Revised English Grammar, 76
Hatcher, Carolyn, 329
Hazlitt, Henry, 277
Heathkit Electronics Courses, 242
Hebrew in the Church, 111
Hechler, Ellen, 142
Heinlein, Robert, 40, 274
Helminiak, Marilyn Moevs, 388
Help! I Want to Drive!, 400
Help! My Teenager Wants to Drive!, 400
Heritage of Freedom, 298

Heston, Charlton, 346
Hinrichs, Fritz, 551
Histomap of World History, 333
Historical Albums series, 317
History of Everyday Things series, 334
Hollow Men: Politics and Corruption in Higher Education, 494
Home Music Lessons, 383
Home School Family Fitness, 419
Home Training Tools catalog, 245
Homeschool Greek course, 114
Homespun Piano Courses, 383
Homespun Songwriter's Workshop, 385
Homespun Tapes Learn to Play Irish Tinwhistle, 384
Homespun Tapes Understanding the Language of Music, 393
Homespun Tapes video courses, 385
Hoobler, Dorothy and Thomas, 309
Horton, Bobby, 185, 308, 309
Hothouse Transplants, 15
Hottelet, Richard C., 283
How Great Thou Art course, 369
How Should We Then Live? video series, 360
How to Accompany, 383
How to be #1 with your Boss, 521
How to Earn a College Degree Without Going to College, 517
How to Earn an Advanced Degree Without Going to Graduate School, 517
How to Get a College Degree Via the Internet, 512
How to Have a 48-Hour Day, 414
How to Manage Your Money, 414
How to Play Intros & Endings, 383
How to Play Gospel Music, 383
How to Prepare for the ACT, 449
How to Prepare for the Advanced Placement Examination series, 471
How to Prepare for the CLEP, 475
How to Prepare for the GED High School Equivalency Examination, 462
How to Prepare for the PSAT/NMSQT, 434
How to Prepare for the SAT I, 439
How to Read a Book, 90
How to Say No and Keep Your Friends, 45
How to Survive Without Your Parents' Money, 531
How to Write, 63
How We Live: Economics Wisdom Simplified, 279
Huff, William, 262
Huffman, Art, 235
Hymnplayer series, 387

I

Improve Your Typing, 70
In God They Trusted, 304
In Search of the Holy Temple, 34
In the Beginning, 204
In the Light of the Cross series, 317
Indiana University Driver's Education, 401
Ingles en Tres Meses course, 129
Ingles Esencial course, 130
Ingles Para Emergencias course, 129
Inheritance Publications, 325, 328
Inside the SAT, 441
Instant Physics, 236
Institute on the Constitution, 263
Interactive Mathematics Program, 161
International Employment Hotline, 531
Into Their Skin, Both Now & Then, 34
Introduction to Argumentation and Debate, 95
Introduction to English Literature, 82
Introductory Logic for Christian Schools, 339
Is There Life After Housework, 408
Isdell, Wendy, 225
Issues in American History, 296
It's Greek to Me!, 115
It's the Law! A Young Person's Guide to our Legal System, 264
Italic Letters: Calligraphy & Handwriting, 69
Ivrit Alfon: A Hebrew Primer for Adults, 111

J

Janice VanCleave's A+ Projects for Young Adults series, 187
Janice VanCleave's A+ Projects in Biology, 196
Janice VanCleave's A+ Projects in Chemistry, 218
Janice VanCleave's A+ Projects in Earth Science, 187
Jenny's Latin series, 118
Jensen's Grammar series, 77
Jensen, Frode, 75, 77, 108
Johnson, Phillip, 203
Johnstone, Patrick, 284
Jones, Bob, 378
Josephus: The Essential Writings, 326
Juggling Step-by-Step, 419
Julicher, Kathleen, 217
Julius, Edward H., 147

K

K'NEX Construction Kits, 242
KNHS Driver Education, 401

Kaegi's Greek Grammar, 115
Kaplan SAT Books 1999-2000, 441
Kaplan SAT II series, 455
Kavanaugh, Patrick, 394
Keizer, Rev. P.K., 324
Key to Algebra series, 153
Key to Geometry, 164
Keystone National High School Driver Education, 401
Kidd, David, 418
Kids' Art Pack, 378
Kids' Volunteering Book, 427
Kielburger, Craig, 427
Kilpatrick, William, 40
Kingdom Come, 24
Kingsley, Ben, 346
Kirk, Russell, 274, 295
Knapp, Dr. Brian, 212
Knight, Joan, 55
KONOS Electing America's Leaders, 256
Koontz, Dean, 80
Kornegay, Chris, 138
Kuhn, K. F., 234
Kurz, Rich, 315

L

Lander und Sitten course, 124
Lapide, Pinchas, 111
Larson, Ron, 157, 168, 171, 177
Latin Easy Readers, 119
Latin Grammar for Christian Private and Home Schools, 117
Latin Made Simple, 119
Latin Stories, 116
Launch to Discovery, 35
Laurita, Raymond, 427, 428
Leaders in Action series, 44
Learn Chords for Piano, Organ, and Electronic Keyboard, 383
Learn to Play Irish Tinwhistle, 384
Learn to Write the Novel Way, 64
Learning English with the Bible, 73
Learning Express Career Starter series, 529
Learning Express Test Preparation series, 530
Learning Games History series, 312
Learning Grammar through Writing, 77
Learning to Read Music, 386
Learning to Write Spencerian Script, 68
Legislating Morality, 265
Lénart Sphere Math, 167
Let the Authors Speak, 329
Let's Talk, 97
Letters from Steven, 288
Levy, Ken, 27
Library of the Future, 551, 552
Life Science for Christian Schools, 184
Lifetime Conversation Guide, 96
Light and the Glory, 304

Lightbearer's Christian Worldview Curriculum, 350
Literature of England, 82
Literature for Christian Schools, 83
Living History series, 335
Living Language series, 129
Living Sea game, 285
Lockhart Level IV Adult Intensive Phonics Program, 54
Lockman, Vic, 28, 33, 37
Logic, 342
Lyrical Life Science series, 185

M

Macaulay, David, 240
Maier, Paul L., 326
Mainspring of Human Progress, 266
Major Punctuation, 77
Manners at Work, 520
Mapping the World by Heart course, 285
Market Guide for Young Writers, 66
Marks, Dave, 67
Marshall, Peter, 304
Marshall, Rodney, 561
Master Your Keyboard, 70
Mastering Algebra—An Introduction, 154
Masterpieces from World Literature, 82
Masterpieces in Art, 377
Masters of Art series, 376
Math Anxiety Reduction, 137
Math at Work, 139
Math for Christian Schools series, 138
Math Magic, 146
Math Shortcuts to Ace the SAT, 442
Math Smart, 139
Mathematics Made Simple, 139
Mattson, Lloyd, 423
Maybury, Richard J., 258, 275, 279
McCloud, Scott, 379
McCullough, L. E., 384
McDaniel, Ruth E., 62
McDowell, Josh, 41
McKee, Jack, 407
McKee family, 500
Memory Techniques for Spelling, 104
Mental Math in Junior High, 147
Mentes, Sherilyn, 363
Metrics at Work, 142
Millard, Catherine, 309
Millbrook Arts series, 370
Miller, Bryan, 411
Milliken History series, 323
Mind Benders series, 342
Mindbend, 79
Minor, Brad, 483, 490
MIT Periodic Table Accessories, 226
Mitchell, Richard, 493
Money Mystery, 276
Moneychanger newsletter, 358

Moore, Douglas, 125
More Music Maps of the Masters, 393
More Quizzles, 343
More Rapid Math Tips & Tricks, 147
Morgan, Dr. Rhonda, 515
Morris, Dr. John D., 206
Mosely, Dana, 143, 168, 171, 439
Mr. Murder, 80
Mulligan, David, 113
Murphy, Dr. Dwight D., 296
Music & Memories of the Civil War video, 308
Music Invaders, 387
Music Maps of the Masters, 393
Music of the Great Composers, 394
My American Adventure, 289
Mystery Writer's Sourcebook, 67

N

NASCO science catalog, 247
Nash, Dr. Ronald, 93, 293
Nation Adrift, 312
National Geographic Society, 286
National Review College Guide, 483
New Revised Cambridge GED Program, 464
New Way Things Work, 240
Newman, Steven, 288
Newport Classics Libraries, 94
Noggle, Jim, 168
Noonan, Peggy, 96
Norton Anthologies, 92
Not One Jot, 113
Novel & Short Story Writer's Market, 66
Nugent, S. Georgia, 88
Number Sense series, 140

O

Odyssey Atlasphere, 287
Of People, 81
Of Places, 81
Official Guide to the SAT II Subject Tests, 456
On Speaking Well, 96
One Man's Vision, 241
Opera for Dummies, 391
Operation World, 284
Original Logic Problems magazine, 342
Oryx International Government and Politics series, 267
Oxford Latin Course, 120
Oxford School Shakespeare series, 90

P

Partow, Donna and Cameron, 417
Patrick Henry College, 513
Paul Silhan's political parodies, 257

Paul, Dr. Douglas J., 441, 449
Peer Pressure Reversal, 45
Penny Marketing Logic Puzzles magazines, 342
Penmanship Instruction Kit, 68
Pennsylvania State University, 515
Perfect Model mannequins and hands, 368
Perspectiva : World News Monthly in Intermediate Spanish, 131
Perspective Without Pain, 370
Perspectives of Life in Literature, 84
Perspectives of Truth in Literature, 84
Perspectives on the World Christian Movement, 352
Petersen, Dennis, 205
Peterson's Guide to Christian Colleges, 484
Peterson's Guide to College Visits, 487
Peterson's Guide to Distance Learning Programs, 518
Peterson's Guide to Four-Year Colleges, 484
Peterson's PSAT/NMSQT Flash, 434
Peterson's SAT Success, 442
Phenomenon of Language, 120
Phonics Game, 54
Photographer's Market, 67
Physical Geography, 282
Physics for Christian Schools, 230
Piano for Quitters, 386
Pimsleur Method, 127
Platt, Dr., Michael, 545, 540
Play Equipment for Kids, 407
Play Your Favorite Piano Classics, 383
Play Gospel Songs by Ear, 382
Playing in Church, 383
Playing in Church by Ear, 383
Poet's Market, 67
Portland State University Self-Study Italic Materials, 69
Political Correctness: Cloning of the American Mind, 495
Positive Peer Groups, 45
Practice Techniques for All Musicians, 384
Praise Hymn Band Method, 387
Prayerbook Hebrew the Easy Way, 112
Pre-GED Satellite series, 464
Price, Randall, 35
Princeton Review: Cracking the ACT, 450
Princeton Review: Cracking the AP, 470
Princeton Review: Cracking the CLEP, 475
Princeton Review: Cracking the GED, 465
Princeton Review: Cracking the SAT and PSAT, 443
Princeton Review: Cracking the SAT II series, 456
Principles from Patterns: Algebra I, 154
Profscam, 496

Programmed learning, 74
Progressive Gospel Piano, 387
Pronunciation and Reading of Ancient Greek course, 114
Pronunciation and Reading Guide to Classical Latin course, 116
Propaganda, 257
Proverbs: Lessons for the Growing Years, 28
Put Your Hands on the Piano and Play, 383

Q

Questions That Matter, 347
Quick Calculus, 176
Quizzles series, 343

R

Radio France Internationale, 130
Radio Shack Electronic Kits and Books, 243
Rainbow Science curriculum, 183
Rand, Ayn, 39
Rapid Math in 10 Days, 147
Rapid Math Tricks and Tips, 147
REA Testware software, 472
Reader's Digest, 490
Reading and Understanding the Bible, 28
Reading Course in Homeric Greek, 115
Ready-to-Use American History Activities for Grades 5-12, 313
Real-Life Experiences Using Classified Ads, 142
Reasoner, Harry, 283
Reformation Overview, 326
Reitz, Victoria W., 143
Religion, Scriptures & Spirituality series, 346
Religious Apartheid, 361
Remembering God's Awesome Acts, 29
Reminisce magazine, 209
Reminisce Extra magazine, 209
Richman, Howard, 515
Richman, Susan, 507
Right from Wrong, 41
Robbins, Dorothy E., 60
Robinson, Janice, 520
Rod & Staff *Applying Numbers,* 142
Rod & Staff's Truth for Life series, 29
Romans Speak for Themselves, 120
Ross Alex, 23, 24
Rothman, Tony, 256
Rudiments of America's Christian History and Government, 296
Rukseyer, Louis, 280
Runkle Geography, 283
Runkle, Brenda Brewer, 283
Ruvolo, Carol J., 30

S

Saint Abroad, 253
Sam the Dectective, 111
Sally Stuart's Guide to Getting Published, 59
Sarangoulis, William, 502
Sarris, George, 38
SAT & College Preparation Course for the Christian Student, 443
Saxon Advanced Mathematics, 170
Saxon Algebra series, 155
Saxon Calculus, 174
Saxon Physics, 232
Saxon's Algebra on Video Tape series, 159
Say It by Signing video, 129
Schaeffer, Dr. Francis, 360
Schaner, Frank, 245
Schaum's Outline Series: Beginning Chemistry, 222
Schaum's Outlines Series: Biology, 196
Schaum's Solved Problems Series: Biology, 196
Scholarship Book, 503, 506
Scholarships, Grants, Fellowships & Endowments, 506
School of Tomorrow Biology, 197
School of Tomorrow Biology videos, 200
School of Tomorrow Chemistry, 219
School of Tomorrow Chemistry Videos, 223
School of Tomorrow Missions Curriculum, 353
School of Tomorrow Physical Science, 188
School of Tomorrow Physics, 233
School of Tomorrow Physics Videos, 234
Schumacher, Mike, 113
Science Fiction Writer's Marketplace, 67
Science Labs-in-a-Box series, 248
Science: Matter and Motion, 182
Science of the Physical Creation, 182
Science: Order and Reality, 182
Scientific Creationism, 204
Scott, Otto, 325
Scott, Sharon, 45
Scripture Search, 29
Scripture Search Junior, 29
Sealfon, Rebecca, 101
Searching for Treasure, 30
Secrets of Learning a Foreign Language, 121
Senior High: A Home-Designed Form-U-La, 501
Serra, Michael, 165
Sethna, Dhun H., 391
Severance, W. Murray, 36

Shakespeare for Young People series, 97
Shakespeare on Stage series, 98
Shanker, Albert, 57
Shelton, Barb, 501
Short Latin Stories, 117
Short Guide to Classical Mythology, 91
Showforth Art Videos, 378
Shultz, Leroy, 387
Silhan, Paul, 257
Silver, James F., 313
Singer, Beryl, 546
Sivnksty, Jerry, 36
Sky & Telescope magazine, 187
Smart Student's Guide to Selective College Admissions, 502
Smith, David, 285
Society of Automotive Engineers, 241
Songwriter's Market, 67
Sound Track to Reading, 55
Spanish for Business course, 124
Speak Out!, 97
Speak Up, 98
Speechphone English courses, 129
Spelling Newsletter, 428
Spelling Power, 105
Spencer, Platt Rogers, 68
Spencerian Handwriting books, 70
Spencerian Script Copybook, 69
Spiral learning, 26
Spirit of Freedom, 267
Spirit of Seventy-Six, 310
Spiritual Lives of the Great Composers, 394
Sport Rules Book, 420
Standard Bible Atlas, 35
Standard Bible Maps and Charts series, 35
Standard Deviants Basic Math video, 145
Standard Deviants Biology videos, 197
Standard Deviants Calculus videos, 178
Standard Deviants Chemistry videos, 223
Standard Deviants College Algebra videos, 159
Standard Deviants Physics video, 234
Standard Deviants Pre-Calculus videos, 178
Standard Deviants Spanish videos, 126
Standard Deviants Trigonometry video, 172
Standpunkt: World News in Intermediate German, 131
Stansbury, Arthur, 262
Starship Troopers, 40, 274
Starting Over, 55
Stine, R.L., 39
Stones Cry Out, The, 35
Story Behind the Scenery series, 313

Story of America's Liberty, 298
Story of Law, 267
Straightforward Math: Algebra, 156
Straightforward Math: Calculus AB, 177
Straightforward Math: Geometry, 164
Straightforward Math: Pre-Calculus, 170
Straightforward Math: Trigonometry, 171
Streams of Civilization series, 321
Street French series, 131
Street German, 131
Street Spanish, 131
Strickland, Carol, 375
Strong's Math Dictionary & Solution Guide, 138
Stuart, Sally, 59
Student Advantage Guide to Paying for College, 505
Student Guide Series: America's Best 100 College Buys, 485
Student Guides to the AP exams, 469
Sugrue, Michael, 88
Sull, Michael, 68
Summit Ministries, 350, 354, 490
Super-Charged World of Chemistry, 224
Super Sitters course, 406
SuperStar Teachers Algebra, 160
SuperStar Teachers Basic Math, 146
SuperStar Teachers Chemistry, 224
SuperStar Teachers Early American History, 304
SuperStar Teachers Geometry, 168
SuperStar Teachers Great Minds of the Western Intellectual Tradition, 347
SuperStar Teachers Great World Religions, 362
SuperStar Teachers How to Understand and Listen to Great Music, 394
SuperStar Teachers World History, 324
Surf's Up! Website Workbook series, 132
Survival English course, 129
Sybervision Language Courses, 127
Sykes, Charles, 483, 490, 494, 496

T

Talent searches, 436
Tall Tales Told and Retold in Biblical Hebrew, 112
Taylor, Charles Lamont, 400
Teach Yourself Calculus, 176
Teach Yourself to Read Hebrew, 112
Teaching American History Through the Novel, 292

Teaching and Learning America's Christian History, 296
Term Paper Book, 61
That for Which Our Fathers Fought, 311
That of Which Our Fathers Spoke, 311
That's Easy for You to Say, 36
Thaxton, Carole, 64
Themes in Literature, 81
They Came From Babel, 327
Thibodeaux, David, 491, 495
Think-A-Grams series, 343
Thinking Physics, 236
Thompson, Lin, 304, 324
Tobin's Lab catalog, 248
Tools for Musicianship, 384
Total Language Plus curriculum, 51
Totally Christian Karate, 421
Totally Usable Summit Ministries Guide to Choosing a College, 93, 293, 486
Traditional Logic, 343
Treasures of Peru video, 363
Trigonometry the Easy Way, 169
TripMaker software, 487
Trotter, Charlie, 410
Trudeau, Kevin, 103
True for You, But Not for Me, 345
Truth for Life series, 29
Turek, Frank, 265
Turning on the Light, 30
Twisted World of Trigonometry video, 172
Two-Edged Sword Memory Program, 36

U

Ultimate Academic Success Manual, 496
Understanding Comics, 379
Understanding the New Testament Without Attending Seminary, 28
Uncle Eric, 87, 258, 268, 275
Uncle Eric books, 275
Understanding the Language of Music, 393
Understanding the Times, 354
United States Map Skills, 286
University of Iowa, 515
University of Nebraska-Lincoln Biology, 198
University of Nebraska-Lincoln catalog, 557
University of Nebraska-Lincoln Chemistry, 219
University of Nebraska-Lincoln Driver's Education, 402
University of Nebraska-Lincoln Physical Science, 189
University of Nebraska-Lincoln Physics, 233

Unlocking the Mysteries of Creation book and videos, 205
Up Your Score, 445
U.S. News & World Report, 489
Usborne Acting & Theatre, 99
Usborne Athletics, 421
Usborne Beginner's Dictionaries, 133
Usborne Book of Europe, 336
Usborne Calligraphy, 70
Usborne Calligraphy: From Beginner to Expert, 370
Usborne Dictionary of Biology, 199
Usborne Dictionary of Physics, 237
Usborne Ecology, 210
Usborne Essential Guides (foreign languages), 199
Usborne Essential Guides (sciences), 133
Usborne Guide to Drawing, 371
Usborne Guide to Painting, 371
Usborne How Machines Work, 241
Usborne How Things Began, 241
Usborne Illustrated World History series, 333
Usborne Introduction to Biology, 198
Usborne Introduction to Chemistry, 222
Usborne Introduction to Physics, 237
Usborne Introduction to... series, 241
Usborne Learn French, Spanish and German, 133
Usborne Photography, 371
Usborne Physical Education books, 422
Usborne Protecting Our World series, 210
Usborne Real Tales series, 337
Usborne The Twentieth Century, 338
Usborne Understanding Geography series, 211
Usborne Understanding Modern Art, 380
Usborne Understanding Science series, 190
Usborne World of Ballet, 421
Usborne World of Dance, 421
Usborne Young Cartoonist, 371
Usborne Young Naturalist, 212
Using Verbs series, 130

V

Van Doren, Charles, 90
VanCleave, Janice, 187
Vander Laan, Ray, 32
Video Tutor Algebra I series, 160
Video Tutor Real Life Math series, 146
Video Visits service, 488
Virtual College, 518
Vis-Ed American history flashcards, 314

Vis-Ed classical languages flashcards, 120
Vis-Ed foreign language flashcards, 134
Vis-Ed SAT Prep Set, 446
Vis-Ed Think English/French/ German/Spanish/Russian, 128
Vision of Glory, 481
Vision Video Biographies of Famous Christians, 327
Visual Bible video series, 37
Visual Manna art courses, 372
Visual Vocabulary, 107
Vocabulary for Christian Schools series, 106
Vocabulary from Classical Roots series, 107
Vocabulary Mastery Study Course, 108
Vocabulary: Greek I, 108
Vocabulary: Latin I & II, 108
VocabuLearn, 125
Vocal Advantage, 99
Voice of the Martyrs ministry, 359
Voyage of the Democritus chemistry course, 220

W

Waid, Mark, 23
Weather Book, 188
Weaver, Henry Grady, 266
Weinstein, Arnold, 89
Wesolowski, Pat, 413
Westminster Shorter Catechism, 37
Wetzel family, 104

What Can I Do NOW? series, 480
What Color Is Your Parachute?, 532
What Do We Know About Grasslands, 212
What's for Dinner?, 412
Whatever Happened to Justice?, 268, 276
Whatever Happened to Penny Candy?, 276, 279
Whatever Happened to the Human Race? video series, 364
When to Say Yes and Make More Friends, 45
Where's That Found? New Testament Memory Cards, 38
Whitehead, John, 361
Why Don't You Play LOUD?, 388
Why Johnny Can't Tell Right from Wrong, 40
Wilkins, Steve, 44, 298
William and Mary Trilogy, 328
Williamson, Chilton, 44
Winitz, Harris, 125
Winning Way College and Career Guide, 502
Winning: Race to Independent Reading Ability course, 55
Winston Grammar series, 72
Wizard magazine, 24
Woods, Madonna, 382
Word Smart, 109
Words that Sell, 65
Wordsmith, 65
Wordsmith Craftsman, 65
Work Your Way Around the World, 531
World & I magazine, 360

World Geography in Christian Perspective, 282
World History & Cultures in Christian Perspective, 320
World History for Christian Schools, 320
World History and Literature: A Simultaneous Look, 329
World Studies for Christian Schools, 320
World's 50 Greatest Composers Audiocassette Collection, 395
World's Greatest Classical Books on CD-ROM, 551, 552
World's Greatest Stories series, 38
World's Political Hot Spots series, 283
Write Now, 69
Writer's Digest Books, 66
Writer's Market, 67
Writing Smart, 67
Writing Strands: Creating Fiction, 67

X,Y,Z

Yes Prime Minister, 258
Yes You Can! Surviving a Personal Attack video, 422
You Can Pass the GED, 465
Young Earth, 206
Young Masters Art Program, 373
Your Checking Account: Lessons in Personal Banking, 143
Youth Exploration Survey, 480
Zany World of Basic Math video, 145

Yes, I want to keep up with the latest in homeschooling!
Sign me up for:

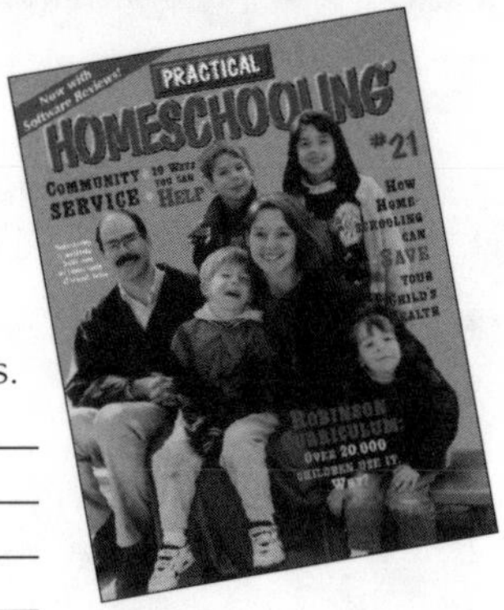

- ☐ Three years of Practical Homeschooling, $45
- ☐ Two years of Practical Homeschooling, $35
- ☐ One year of Practical Homeschooling, $19.95
- ☐ Trial subscription (3 issues), $10

Foreign and Canadian subscribers, add $10 per year.
MO residents, add 5.975% tax. Please pay in U.S. funds.

Name ______________________________
Address ______________________________
City, State, Zip ______________________________
Country ______________________________
Phone (in case we need to check on your order): ______________________________

I'm paying by ☐ check made out to Home Life, Inc. ☐ credit card (MC, Visa, AmX, Disc)
Card #: ______________________________ Exp: _____ / _____
Signature: ______________________________

Return with payment to Home Life, PO Box 1190, Fenton MO 63026
Or call **1-800-346-6322** for fastest service

____
____
____

AFFIX
POSTAGE
HERE

New!
from Mary Pride!

Alpha Omega Publications
300 North McKemy Avenue
Chandler, AZ 85226-2618

Your Name ______________________________
Address ______________________________
City ______________ State ______ Zip __________
Phone (________) __________ - ______________

NO POSTAGE
NECESSARY
IF MAILED
IN THE
UNITED STATES

BUSINESS REPLY MAIL
FIRST CLASS MAIL PERMIT NO. 21 CHANDLER, ARIZONA

POSTAGE WILL BE PAID BY ADDRESSEE

ALPHA OMEGA PUBLICATIONS
300 N MCKEMY AVE
CHANDLER AZ 85226-9912